D1269218

Below: *Janus* as completed. (Swan Hunter)

Below: *Casque* in August 1942. Note AA guns added on the quarter deck, No. 2 gun and the after superstructure. (M. Bar)

DESTROYERS OF WORLD WAR TWO

An International Encyclopedia

M. J. Whitley

NAVAL INSTITUTE PRESS

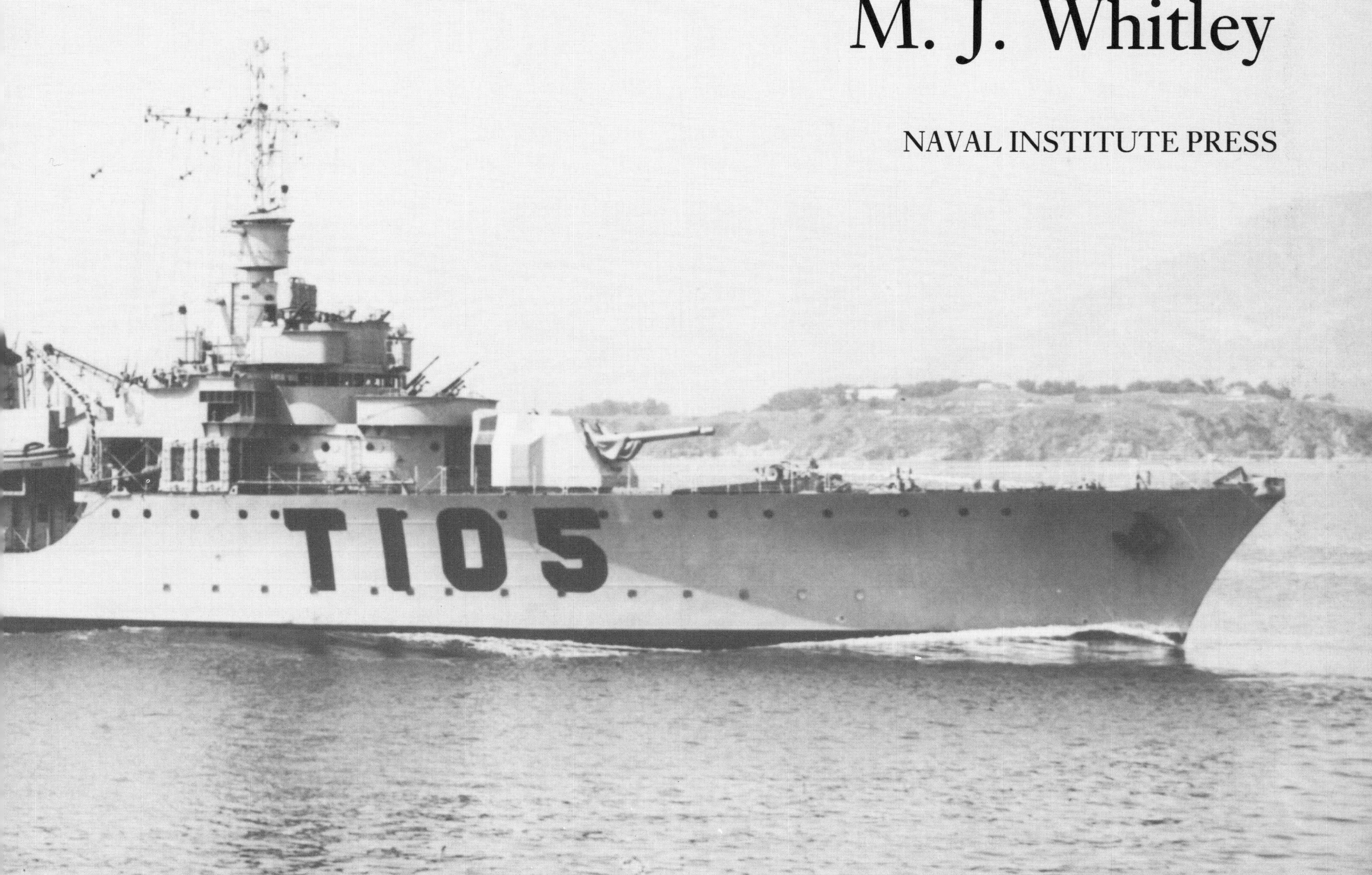

To my parents, Herbert and Marguerite Whitley, for their continual interest and encouragement.

Published and distributed in the United States of America by the Naval Institute Press, Annapolis, Maryland 21402.

Library of Congress Catalog Card No. 87-63596

ISBN 0-87021-326-1

This edition is authorized for sale only in the United States and its territories and possessions.

Jacket illustration: The *Gearing* class USS *Chevalier* (DD805) (USN). Colour simulation by Robert W. Phasey.

Line illustrations were drawn by the author.

The photographs in this book have been collected from many sources and vary in quality owing to the variety of circumstances under which they were taken and preserved. As a result, certain of the illustrations are not of the standard to be expected from the best of today's equipment, materials and techniques. They are nevertheless included for their inherent information value, to provide an authentic visual coverage of the subject.

Designed and edited by DAG Publications Ltd.
Designed by David Gibbons; edited by Michael Boxall; layout by Anthony A. Evans; typeset by Typesetters (Birmingham) Ltd., camerawork by M&E Graphics, North Fambridge, Essex; printed and bound in Great Britain by Adlard & Sons Ltd, Letchworth, Herts.

Contents

Preface

This book attempts to record all destroyers extant, completed or laid down during the period 1939–45 by the world's naval powers, combattant and neutral. The exact definition of a destroyer and hence which ships to include and which to exclude has been rather difficult. A seemingly obvious definition is: 'A warship designed to act offensively against an enemy by means of torpedoes.' But this definition, if strictly applied, would exclude those destroyer types which were not equipped with torpedoes, i.e., some of the British *Hunt* class and the American destroyer-escort types. This would surely lead to criticism because other *Hunt*s and DEs, equipped with torpedoes, *would* be included and coverage would be unbalanced. Similarly, if the term destroyer is taken to mean 'Fleet' vessel, this would also exclude all *Hunt*s, DEs and many of the smaller torpedo-boat designs, particularly those of France, Italy and Germany which in actual fact played a considerable role in the war at sea during the years 1939–45. If the torpedo-boat were to be included, however, down to what size vessels should this book include. Some torpedo-boats were less than 200 tons and of relatively little fighting value compared to say, a *Fletcher, Tribal* or *Kagero*. In the end, the net was cast fairly widely and all destroyers, torpedo-boats and destroyer-escorts down to 300 tons displacement were included, to give as comprehensive a coverage as possible. This has led to a huge number of individual ships being included for which I have attempted to list complete building dates – something never done before. Here it should be noted that while full building dates for major warships are usually readily available, this is not the case for the smaller, more obscure vessels of minor and some not so minor nations. While much effort has been expended in locating full building dates for as many ships as possible, there are still many gaps and the author would be pleased to hear from anyone who might be able to fill these.

Each class has been dealt with under three headings, Design, Modifications and Service. Space restraints have restricted consideration of the modification and service details to the 1939–45 period only, but some inconsistencies may be noted in the way the service histories are examined. The main casualty here has been the United States Navy, where the sheer number of destroyers constructed to the *Benson, Gleaves, Fletcher, Sumner* and *Gearing* designs has allowed only a cursory coverage of their service careers, despite their importance. On the other hand, some of the minor navies have received relatively more detailed treatment, merely because of their fewer numbers. For this, I must crave the reader's indulgence, and in no way is this intended as a slight on the USN's huge contribution to the war at sea. Details of final disposals too have to be limited to date only because of space limitations. So far as the Soviet Union is concerned, the usual difficulties have been experienced, in that the obsessive secrecy still, after forty years, makes the obtaining of any data or photographic material almost impossible. Approaches to the Soviet Embasy, Naval Attaché and Naval Museum have met with a conspicuous silence. Even a direct appeal to President Gorbachev had no effect!

No one can claim to be an expert in such a wide field as this book covers, and I am indebted to many individuals, government departments, navies and companies throughout the world, who have given me help in many directions in the compilation of this book. Especially I should like to mention and thank the following individuals: the late Ricardo Azuero, Bogota, Colombia; Dott. Guido Alfano, Italy; Frank Abelsen, Norway; Michael Bullen; D. K. Brown, RCNC; Captain A. de Medeiros Cabral, the Brazilian Naval Attaché, London; A. D. Baker III, USA, for much valuable assistance with photographs; S. Breyer, Germany; Ammiraglio di Divisione Carlo Gottardi, Museo Storico Navale, Venice; R. M. Coppock, MOD, NHB; Contre Ammiral Chatelle, Etat Major Service Historique, France; Captain Droguett, Chilean Embassy; Anne Davies, Vickers Shipbuilding; A. J. English; K. A. Ford, Vosper Thornycroft; Jean Guiglini and Captain C. Huan, for much assistance on French building dates; Pierre Hervieux, France; Christian de Saint-Hubert, Kenya; Mrs K. W. Harrison, Isle of Wight County Council; Dr Dieter Jung and Norbert Kelling of Archiv Gröner; Commander K. Erkal, Turkish Embassy; Major Kure of the Norwegian Embassy and the staff of the Marinemuseet, Horten; Paul Kemp, IWM; Lieutenant-Colonel Longden of the British Embassy, Bucharest; W. C. McMillan of Yarrow's, for much invaluable assistance with their trials books; Mrs H. Mitchell, Cammell Laird; P. R. Melton, MOD, NHB; Nicolae Petrescu, Romanian Naval Museum; Commander Passiopoulos, and Commander G. Cremos, Royal Hellenic Navy; G. J. A. Raven, Netherlands Ministerie van Defensie; I. Rae, Swan Hunter; George Ransome, both for his allowing me to copy his destroyer records so long ago, and his recent assistance; Erwin F. Sieche; Captain Sompong Sirihong, Royal Thai Navy; Commander B. Steed, British Embassy, Bangkok; D. J. Lyon, R. G. Todd, K. M. McLennan and J. Falconer of the National Maritime Museum; Rinya Takayama, Japan; Lieutenant-Commander Turner, British Embassy, Moscow; H. A. Vadnais of the US Naval Historical Center; Doctor Richard Osborne; Captain G. M. Watkins, Chilean Navy; Premyslav Budzabon; Björn Westburg, Göteborg; Rene Greger, Dip.Ing, Prague; Gerd Garms, Kiel; J. Meister, Australia; Erwin Sieche. I hope that I have not missed anyone from this list, but if I have, my humble apologies! Finally, my thanks to Norman Thomas for comments upon the draft manuscript and last, but far from least, to my wife Rita, for the vast amount of typing involved.

Introduction

The Birth of the Torpedo-boat

The destroyer, as it emerged from the Second World War, owed its existence to the Industrial Revolution, whose impetus had led to the introduction of new technology into the navies of the great powers of the day, some sixty years earlier. Naval warfare and tactical thinking had changed little over the previous two centuries but the invention of the steam engine, locomotive torpedo and steel-making very quickly revolutionised both ship-building and tactics. Suddenly, the venerable 'wooden walls' were rendered obsolete as the potential of the new inventions was realized, a factor not quite to the liking of the then premier sea power, Great Britain, whose fleets had ruled the world's oceans for two hundred years or so. Other nations, however, saw in the new technology a means to challenge economically the long-held supremacy of the Royal Navy by constructing large numbers of fast torpedo craft and later, submarines, with which to threaten an enemy's battle fleets. In fact, it was not quite so simple or as straightforward as this, for the introduction of the new technology raised its own problems, not least in its acceptability to more conservative officers who tended to comprise the higher echelons of naval command. Thus the exploitation of the steam engine, for example, got off to a slow start because, among other things, it made decks and sails dirty! Another factor of importance was the capability of actually employing the new technology. Great Britain was at this time undoubtedly the leader in the industrialization race, with France and Germany close behind. In consequence, it would have been difficult, for example, for Russia to build large numbers of torpedo-boats without the assistance of these industrialized nations. It is true to say also that the reliability of the early products of the technological age was open to doubt, and in action it was vital that men be able to rely upon their weapons. Nevertheless, the combination of steam engine and torpedo gave rise to the practicability of building small, fast craft, packing a powerful enough punch to give an enemy battle fleet serious tactical problems.

The term 'torpedo' had been used in the nineteenth century to describe any underwater weapon, including the mine as we know it today, but the forerunner of the torpedo as used by the destroyers of the twentieth century was the spar torpedo. This was quite simply, an explosive charge attached to a long spar secured to the bows of a suitable launch or primitive submarine, which was rammed into the target by the carrying vessel. Obviously this was a risky undertaking for the attacker, who was just as liable to be destroyed as was the target. Spar torpedoes achieved some success in the American Civil War and were later used by a number of lesser powers in the numerous small wars of the nineteenth century. One of the earliest European users of this weapon were the Russians who employed them with some effect against the Turks in 1877. Several years later, the French torpedo-boats *45* and *46* were in action at Foochow in Indo-China during 1884 when ships were sunk by the same weapon. By this time, however, its day was over and the Whitehead self-propelled torpedo had appeared on the scene and had obviously much more potential as an effective weapon.

The British Admiralty, impressed by the performance of the Whitehead torpedo, had purchased the rights to the invention in 1870, but it was not until 1874 that a ship (*Vesuvius*) was available to actually fire these weapons and another three years were to pass before a ship *designed* to carry torpedoes was put into commission. At this time, three names were at the forefront of fast steam launch construction in England, names still known today: John I. Thornycroft, Alfred Yarrow and Samuel White, although the latter now no longer exists. These men had constructed spar torpedo-boats for a variety of second-rate and coast defence navies, and were quick to realize the potential of the Whitehead torpedo. At first, the Royal Navy, geared to 'blue water' operations, saw little use for the new weapon, but faced with its increased adoption abroad, was forced somewhat reluctantly to enter into its construction, and placed an order with J. I. Thornycroft in 1877. This was purely and simply a modified steam launch, fitted with a single torpedo tube at the bows, and two more sided amidships in dropping gear. Named *Lightning*, she measured 84 feet overall and could attain a speed of about eighteen knots when fully armed.

Across the Channel, the French *Commission des défenses sous-marins* was considering the same subject, and in July 1875 ordered a torpedo-boat from Claparede & Cie of Saint-Denis. Unlike *Lightning*, this boat was considerably larger at 101.4 tons and carried two 356mm torpedo tubes on the centre-line submerged, one each at bow and stern. She received the appellation *Torpilleur No. 1* and began a long line of 370 torpedo-boats which were to form the basis of the *Défense Mobile* for the next twenty years. Her size was dictated by the intended theatre of operations, which included the North Sea and Baltic, thus she was envisaged as a *sea-going* torpedo-boat. To this end several features, advanced for her time, were included in the design. Among these was a provision for the ship's company to move from forward to aft below decks – vital in a vessel with such low freeboard. On trials in March 1877, she attained a maximum speed of 15.42 knots and, despite her contract speed being not less than 15.7 knots, the Directeur des Constructions navales authorized acceptance on the grounds that she was, even so, an effective warship. In service she was considered superior in some respects to later boats but her manoeuvrability was poor, and stability insufficient. In 1883 she was named *Isard* and was finally discarded in 1889.

Despite the potential of the larger hull, this trend was not perpetuated by the French, and *Torpilleur No. 2* displaced only 32 tons. She and her subsequent sisters were, therefore, to all intents and purposes, useful for coast or port defence only. Displacements rose slowly with new batches, but by 1907 had only risen to about 100 tons (*Torpilleur No. 369*). The

Royal Navy, too, continued construction of torpedo-boats (now also numbered only) with a series of eleven in 1878–79, very similar to *Lightning*, until 1908 when 130 had been completed, by which time their displacement had risen to about 260 tons, and they were armed with three 18-inch torpedo tubes and two 12pdr guns. The increasing size of British and German torpedo-boats towards the turn of the century forced the French to reconsider their 'small torpedo-boat' policy and there was an obvious requirement for a larger vessel able to escort the fleet at sea. Thus despite the protests of the 'Jeune Ecole'* a series of nine larger boats called *torpilleurs-éclaireurs* were ordered to a Normand (Le Havre) design and known as the *Balay* class. These boats, displacing 50–60 tons, were later re-rated *torpilleurs de haute mer* or high-seas torpedo-boats, and began a coexistent line with the small torpedo-boats which was to continue in continental navies until the close of the Second World War, nearly fifty years later.

Counter-Measures. The Advent of the Torpedo-boat Destroyer

Towards the turn of the century, it had become a matter of necessity for capital ships to possess some form of defence against these fast vessels. Battleships' main armament guns, slow in both rate of fire and training, were useless for the purpose and the ships themselves were too slow and un-handy to out-manoeuvre the nimble torpedo-boats. Torpedo nets attached to battleships like great crinolines were only of use when at anchor; some other counter-measure was obviously necessary. Quick-firing guns were the initial self-defence weapon given to battleships, which, as their name implied, allowed rapid fire against the attacking craft. Searchlights too were fitted to counter night attacks by the black-painted torpedo-boats. In parallel with this development, the British Admiralty decided that the best defence was probably a somewhat more powerful vessel as fast as or – better still – faster than, the torpedo-boat as it then existed. The first attempt in this direction was the 'torpedo ram' which was armed with guns and torpedoes, a reinforced bow and sufficient speed to catch the little torpedo-boats. *Polyphemus*, as she was named, proved a hopeless failure, being unable even to catch the torpedo-boats let alone sink them. The solution turned out to be a private venture vessel built by Samuel White and taken into service as *Torpedo-boat No. 81*. Very manoeuvrable, although not quite so fast as the smaller torpedo-boats, her armament of six 47mm guns made her a potent threat to them. Unfortunately, the Admiralty-designed follow-ups proved once again hopeless failures, mainly due to the inadequacies of the power plants of the day. Speeds of the battlefleets had been increasing steadily and the torpedo-boats were now hard pressed to catch them, especially in any sort of a seaway. Attempts to produce an even faster small vessel to catch the torpedo-boats therefore presented a considerable challenge to the shipbuilders and engineers of the late 1890s.

Quite apart from France, by 1892 Russia had 152 torpedo-boats, Germany 143 and Italy 129. Russia in particular, with her long island-studded Baltic coastline (Finland was at this period part of Russia) saw much potential in these craft for coastal defence. Lurking behind small islands to dash out and surprise an enemy squadron was an obvious role for these small craft. They were, however, very small, poor sea-boats and mechanically unreliable. Known as '*Minonoski*' large numbers were built at the Baltic works (St. Petersburg), Kronstadt, Kreighton (Ako) and other Russian yards, mainly to Yarrow designs but also to those of Schichau and Vulkan. Early boats were equipped with spar torpedoes and on several occasions accidental detonation resulted in damage and loss of life as in 1878 during an inspection by Rear-Admiral Schmidt aboard *Ugor* when an order was misinterpreted. This resulted in the firing mechanism being pulled, causing casualties.

In the Black Sea that same year Lieutenant S. O. Makarov equipped some launches with Whitehead torpedoes and managed to sink the 2,000-ton Turkish steamer *Intibah* off Batum, one of the first successes of its type. This able and energetic officer was later promoted to Admiral and might have altered the course of the Russo-Japanese war had his flagship *Petropavlovsk* not been mined off Port Arthur in April 1904.

The previous year, the renegade Peruvian monitor *Huascar* had been engaged by the British *Shah* both using Whitehead torpedoes without success, but in 1891 during the Chilean Civil War, the cruiser *Blanco Encalada* fell victim to a 14-inch torpedo from torpedo-boats. Three years later, in April 1894, the first capital ship was sunk by the weapon. This was the Brazilian *Aquidaban* wearing the flag of Admiral Mellow, which had rebelled against the Government. Caught by the torpedo gunboat *Sampis* and three Schichau-built 130-ton torpedo-boats, (*Silvado, Pedro-Iro* and *Pedro-Alfonso*) in St. Catharine Bay, she was hit by a single torpedo in the bows, sending her to the bottom after a brief action. Also in 1894 Chinese and Japanese torpedo-boats used their weapons in anger at Wei-Hai-Wei during another Sino-Japanese squabble. The torpedo-boat had proved itself, and was here to stay.

German-designed boats were generally larger and speeds of more than 27 knots were being attained by Schichau-built designs. These fast and seaworthy ships were an obvious source of concern to Great Britain in the face of increasing German naval might; they included a number of torpedo-boats of larger size known as 'Division Boats'. Although their function is described by their name they can legitimately be regarded as the forerunner of the torpedo-boat destroyer and as such pre-date the entry by Great Britain into this category. These boats, a series of ten of which the last, *D10*, was the most effective, displaced up to 250 tons. *D10* of 310 tons carried five 4pdr guns and three torpedo tubes at a speed of 27.5 knots, a fact of which Britain was well aware since she was built by Thornycroft's!

The numbers and capabilities of these foreign torpedo-boats were like a red rag to a bull to the fiery Admiral John fisher who had become Third Sea Lord and Controller of the Navy in February 1892 and, as a result of the dismal performance of the so-called torpedoboat catchers, he asked Alfred Yarrow to investigate a suitable counter-measure. Yarrow's final recommendations were, 27 knots minimum speed, and a powerful gun armament. The final design displaced 240–260 tons and was armed with one 12pdr, three 6pdr and three 18-inch torpedo tubes (one submerged bow, two in single centre-line trainable tubes). Four boats were ordered, two each from Yarrow and Thornycroft, the former equipped with triple expansion engines and the latter with three-stage compound machinery for a contract speed of 27 knots. The names

*A group of forward thinking younger officers of the French Navy whose figurehead was Admiral Aube. Their belief, unusual before the turn of the century, stated that the French Navy should rely on 'number, speed, invulnerability and specialization'. The torpedo-boat fitted these ideas very well.

allocated were *Havock, Hornet* (Yarrow), *Daring, Decoy* (Thornycroft) and the orders were placed on 27 June 1892. *Havock*, the first to complete (28 October 1893) achieved 26¼ knots on trials and was accepted by the navy on 15 January 1894, thus becoming the first TBD in a very long line of such vessels in the Royal Navy.

The Formative Years: 1900–14

Construction of the '27 knotters' as they were known, continued until the completion of *Fervent* in May 1900, a total of 42 ships followed by 75 '30 knotters' the last of which, the private speculation boats *Albacore* and *Bonetta*, commissioned in March 1907. Within this period, many important advances had been made, including experiments with oil-firing (*Speedy* and *Surly*, 1898) and the introduction of turbine propulsion in *Albacore* and *Bonetta*. These two ships made 26.8 knots and 26.75 knots respectively on trials. The turbine was a timely invention, the existing reciprocating engines having reached the limit of their development. In comparison, the turbine offered much less vibration and greater potential.

Events abroad were still of very much concern to the Admiralty; the French Torpilleur de Haute-Mer *Forban*, built by their premier torpedo-boat constructor Normand and laid down in April 1893, had achieved 31.029 knots on a displacement of 145 tons in the course of trials during September and October 1895. This result, and the power development of her machinery, shook the Admiralty as did the later report of Schichau boats achieving 35.1 knots with 6,000ihp on 280 tons. Germany had introduced turbines in *V161*, completed on 17 September 1908 from which time all their boats were so equipped as were British destroyers, commencing with the *Tribal* class of 1908–10. French designs, on the other hand, did not adopt turbines until *Chasseur*, accepted into service in November 1909. Oil-firing became standard with the British *Tribal* class (although the later *Basilisk* class made a brief return to coal-firing), but German ships adopted only partial oil-firing with *V162*, a sensible decision in view of Germany's lack of oil resources, and did not switch to full oil bunkerage until *V25* completed in June 1914. France experimented with oil-firing in *Fantassin* of 1911 and switched fully with the *Bouclier* class of 1911–13.

During the years from 1900 to 1914, the majority of the lesser powers purchased their torpedo-boats and torpedo-boat destroyers from the most experienced shipyards in the field, i.e., White, Yarrow and Thornycroft in Great Britain, Normand in France and Krupp or Schichau in Germany. Thus their flotillas mirrored the advances of the major powers and, in some instances, outstripped them. The reason for this was that the major powers had to look for numbers and have smaller size for cost reasons, while the minor powers, looking for powerful units for prestige and local tactical reasons, could afford one or two 'supertorpedo-boats' in the knowledge that only small numbers were required. Thus for example Argentina, having shopped around from 1900 until 1914, chopping and changing requirements in her desire to obtain the best, ended up with a powerful Krupp design which outclassed contemporary German and British types, only to have the four destroyers commandeered by Germany in 1914! Japan, assisted mainly by Britain, and Russia assisted by every leading designer, eventually developed their own TBD construction and design abilities, while across the Atlantic the USA, newly appreciating the importance of seapower following the Spanish-American War (which had highlighted the deficiencies of torpedo-boats), was going its own way in isolation.

One of the original builders of torpedo craft in the United States was the Herreshoff Manufacturing Co. of Bristol, Rhode Island, who had built spar torpedo-boats as early as 1878, one of which, *Yard No. 44*, was in fact purchased by the Royal Navy. On arrival in England she was taken into service as the second-class *Torpedoboat No. 63* and was eventually expended as a target in 1888. Further boats had been built for Peru and Russia, but the first true torpedo-boat built for the US Navy equipped with Whitehead-type torpedoes was the *Cushing*, Torpedo-boat No. 1 (TB-1), armed with three 1pdr Hotchkiss guns and three torpedo tubes. Pre-dating her entry into service had been *Stiletto*, purchased by the US Navy in 1887 and equipped with a single above-water torpedo tube. She was used as a trials vessel. Herreshoff built a number of the early torpedo-boats of the US Navy until disagreements with them over the construction of *Duport* and *Porter* in 1896 led to their refusal to tender for further navy orders. By 1900, the Bath Iron Works had arrived upon the scene, building the last of the US torpedo-boats, the *Barney* class (175 tons, three 3pdrs, three 18-inch TT, 28.5 knots). Also in 1900 came the first American destroyers, the 400-ton *Lawrence* class. By 1900, destroyers were being built by most of the later well-known yards such as Cramp, Newport News, Fore River, among others. Turbines were introduced in the *Flusser* class, well-armed vessels with five 3-inch guns and three torpedo tubes. These boats were the last of the US coal-burners.

Destroyers of all nations grew in size as they developed, because better armaments, faster speeds and improved endurances were continually demanded. Thus by the outbreak of the First World War, displacements had reached 1,000 tons and gun calibre 4 inches. A comparison of individual classes is of interest at this time.

	'L'	*'V-25'*	*Bisson*	*Alwyn*
Nationality	British	German	French	American
Displacement	965 / 1072	812 / 975	850 / 880	1020
HP	22,500 / 24,500	23,500 / 25,000	14,300	16,000
Speed	29 / 31 knots	33 / 36 knots	31 knots	30 knots
Guns	3×4in, 1×2pdr	3×3.5in	2×4in, 4× 9pdr	4×4in
Torpedoes	4×21in (2×2)	6×19.7in (2×1, 2×2)	4×18in (2×2)	8×18in (4×2)

The Impetus of War

The declaration of war in August 1914 soon saw destroyers in action in the Atlantic, North Sea, Mediterranean and Baltic. The British *Lance* and *Landrail* fired the opening shots against the German minelayer *Königen Luise* on 5 August and from that time onwards destroyers of all the combatants were in great demand by their various flag officers for a multitude of tasks, including anti-submarine patrol, escort and minelaying duties as well as the traditional torpedo attack role. Due to the situation in the land war, the French Navy's resources were quickly turned over to supply the needs of their hard-pressed armies, and destroyer construction (as well as most other categories) lapsed. Britain and Germany, however, continued construction at full pace although the latter eventually tailed off construction in favour of U-boats. Under wartime conditions it was necessary to standardize and simplify in order to put the maximum numbers into service so classes became much larger, the Admiralty *M* class, for example, numbering over one hundred units. Although this number was eventually far exceeded by later US classes, it was very large for the time. Design advances were not great during hostilities (reliability being the keynote).

Semi-geared turbines had been introduced in *Beagle*, completed 24 October 1910, and *Beaver*, completed in November 1912. The advent of gearing allowed optimization of turbine and propeller performance since it enabled high turbine revolutions (at which it was most efficient) to be coupled with lower (more efficient) propeller speeds. *Leonidas* and *Lucifer*, completing in August 1914, introduced the first all geared turbines, but despite their success partially geared machinery was reverted to in the *M* class upon the outbreak of war due to the shortage of gear hobbing machinery. By 1915, however, the Admiralty were sufficiently confident to install single reduction fully geared sets in destroyers ordered that year, the *R* class.

The armament of British destroyers (except for specials and ex-foreign ships) generally remained at three guns and four torpedo tubes in pairs. German destroyers too adopted the geared turbine and carried a heavier torpedo armament (but of lighter calibre) than their British opponents. Their gun outfit was increased to 4.1-inch calibre with *V47* in 1915 which became standard for the remainder of the war with the exception of the *S113* and *V116* classes which were to mount four 5.9-inch guns. Only two of these had been completed by the end of the war, however, and the usefulness of such a heavy gun on a small platform such as a destroyer proved questionable, as had been found with *Swift* by the Royal Navy when armed with one 6-inch gun. The Italian Navy experienced similar problems with their *Aquila* and *Carlo Mirabello* classes.

An innovation on the British side was the introduction of a smaller destroyer not intended for fleet work, but to be used in the patrol and escort field in the North Sea. This design, the *S* class, displaced 1,075 tons and carried the standard three-gun, four-tube outfit with an additional pair of single 14-inch torpedo tubes at the break of the forecastle. Large numbers of these ships were built, many of which were not completed until after hostilities. A second and major step forward in destroyer design, were the British *V & W* class which introduced the superfiring gun on the centre-line, and in the *W* ships triple torpedo tube mountings. The other important feature to go to sea was the 4.7-inch gun, initially aboard the larger leaders of the *Shakespeare* class. This gun was to remain the standard British destroyer gun until superseded by the 4.5-inch in the *Z* class of 1944. The rising menace of the U-boat also caused alterations including the carrying of depth-charges and the fitting of hydrophone gear. In fact, destroyer action against capital ships proved a rare occurrence (Jutland was the exception) and more often engagements were with other destroyers or U-boats. In this respect, the entry of the USA into the war on 6 April 1917 was of the greatest importance to the war in the Atlantic, as much-needed reinforcements to the anti-submarine strength were supplied by the US Navy. A few days after the American declaration of war, the destroyers *Wadsworth, Conyngham, Porter, McDougal, Davis* and *Wainwright* were ordered to New York to fit out for 'distant service'. These six destroyers, some of the newest of the US Navy, slipped from Boston on 24 April under the command of Captain Taussig and arrived in Queenstown, Ireland, on 4 May 1917. These ships, and many more which followed (there were 37 at Queenstown in the summer of 1917) gave great service in the Western Approaches until the end of the war.

In the Mediterranean, and the narrow waters of the Adriatic, destroyers of the Royal, Australian, French and Italian navies faced the threat of German and Austro-Hungarian U-boats as well as the surface fleet of the latter navy. Later, Japanese destroyers joined in on the Allied side too. Italian destroyer construction had been influenced by early designs built to Thornycroft, Schichau and Yarrow plans. They had adopted the 4.7-inch gun before the British, but generally only carried one such gun, on the forecastle and some flotilla leaders carried a 6-in gun. Their torpedo armament too was weak, with only two 18-inch tubes. The Austro-Hungarian fleet was small but fairly well equipped, and could boast a strength of 67 destroyers and torpedo-boats with a further 25 under construction. Of these, however, six were large destroyers and a further twelve smaller destroyers. The remainder were small or old torpedo-boats. The most powerful units were the six *Tatra*-class ships, of 1,000 tonnes (deep), armed with two 3.9-inch guns and six 12pdrs as well as four torpedo tubes. Supporting them were the older and slower *Huszar* class with six 12pdrs and two torpedo tubes. Four modified *Tatra* ships joined the fleet late in 1917/early 1918. During the war, all of the *Huszar* class and the torpedo-boats were engaged upon convoy escort duties for the Albanian front or on coastal patrol duty. They were also used for escorting both Austrian and German U-boats to and from patrol. This left only the *Tatra* class for offensive duties, but as *Lika* and *Triglav* were both mined off Durazzo on 29 December 1915 and the first modified unit was not taken into service until 27 July 1917, the Austro-Hungarian destroyer force actually comprised only four ships for much of the time.

The focal point of naval activity in the central Mediterranean was the Straits of Otranto across which Narrows the Allied destroyers and drifters patrolled to prevent or hinder the breakout of Austrian or German U-boats into the open Mediterranean. Sorties by the cruisers and destroyers of the Austro-Hungarian fleet were in consequence aimed at this patrol line. During the course of one such raid in April 1918, five of the Austrian destroyers attacked *Jackal* and *Hornet*, severely damaging them both before being driven off by Australian destroyers. When Austria-Hungary surrendered in November 1918, the surviving destroyers were ceded to Italy and France with whom they remained in service until the 1930s.

The war in the Adriatic, land-locked as it was, bore some similarities to that in the Baltic, where the Kaisermarine faced the Imperial Russian fleet. The German torpedo-boat flotillas were, as has already been indicated, comprised of fast, well-armed craft with well-trained crews. The Russians, with a long experience in torpedo warfare, as has been recounted, had on their strength the 'super destroyer' *Novik*, arguably the most powerful of its day, and a number of sister ships in service or under construction. However the Baltic theatre was very much a secondary one as far as naval activities were concerned and, as in the Second World War, became mainly a submarine and mine warfare battleground.

The major theatre of the naval war, as opposed to the commerce war, was without doubt the North Sea, across which Britain and Germany had faced each other with increasing tension from 1900. After the actions in the Heligoland Bight in August 1914, the destroyers of both sides settled into a routine of patrol and screening duties with their respective battle fleets. On the British side, 207 destroyers were available, but more than half were fit only for coastal duties. With the Grand Fleet were the Second and Fourth Flotillas comprised of about forty ships of the *H* and *K* classes, while the new *L* class joined the Third Flotilla at Harwich, an obvious focal point for light forces operations. Here too were the *I* class boats of the First Flotilla. The older boats of the *A* to *E* classes and the *Tribal*s formed the patrol flotillas stationed at Dover, and in the Humber, Tyne and Forth, with the Fifth Flotilla (*G* class) in the Mediterranean. A number of *River*s or *E* class were in China and several older boats were attached to depots.

Some reinforcements were obtained by the requisitioning of ships under construction for foreign powers, and among these were four powerful ex-Chilean destroyers, four building for Greece and four stock boats* from Hawthorn Leslie. These joined the Fleet from August 1914, *Falknor* (ex-Chilean) to May 1916 *Turbulent* (stock boat). The origins of the stock boats is rather obscure, it being believed, and quoted in many sources, that they were ordered originally by Turkey. Two further stock boats of the *L* class laid down by Beardmore, received Admiralty orders and were completed in October and December 1915 as *Lassoo* and *Lochinvar* respectively.

At the outbreak of hostilities, Germany had 133 destroyers (or *torpedoboote* as they were still referred to by the Kaisermarine) available for service. Like Britain, Germany also pre-empted boats building to foreign orders, for example, four boats originally laid down for Argentina. She also built a few more using turbines originally ordered in Germany for destroyers under construction in Russian yards for the Imperial Russian Navy. Despite Germany's shipbuilding industry being far below that of Britain in terms of capacity, her yards nevertheless managed to match British destroyer construction until September 1915, by which time each had completed 32 more destroyers. By the end of 1916, however, German construction had only reached a total of 78 new boats whereas the Royal Navy had taken delivery of nearly twice that number, 142. After 1916, the U-boat took precedence and from January 1917 to November 1918 only a further nineteen boats were commissioned to Britain's 133 new boats in the same period. The German constructional effort up to 1916 was negated by their heavier losses, twenty to the British eight, but after Jutland their loss rate declined whereas that of the British, more offensively employed, rose (chiefly due to mine and torpedo attacks). The final score was sixty-three British losses to six-six German.

German Naval forces were stationed in Wilhelmshaven, the base for the High Seas Fleet, and on the Flanders coast. Action in the classic destroyer style upon an opponent's battle line was limited to the engagement at Jutland and, like the Royal Navy's destroyer, German counterparts were mainly employed as 'maids of all work'. Although the capital ships seldom went to sea, the destroyers made numerous sorties against the Dover Patrol from Flanders bases and sorties against shipping in the North Sea.

At the close of hostilities, the destroyer as a ship type had been perceived to be one of the most useful in the fleet. They had acquired some degree of anti-submarine ability although, despite popular opinion, they were not as well equipped for this task as the sloops designed for AS work. Also, in view of the great advances made in aviation, it was recognized that some form of anti-aircraft defence would be necessary in the future. Gun calibre had increased to 4.7-inch and director-firing introduced for the main armament which was now all axially-mounted as well as including superfiring guns. Torpedo calibre was now 21-inch in general with triple tubes becoming standard. Sheer size had increased considerably, necessitating sizeable increases in propulsive power, from 24,500shp in *Acasta* of 1912 to 40,000shp in *Stuart* of 1918. There were at this time only four nations building destroyers: Great Britain, the United States, Japan and Italy; France had other problems. Russia was in a state of Revolution and obviously Germany had been defeated. Of these nations, the United States had put in hand a huge programme of new construction before they entered the war and by 1917 were laying down the first of the famous four-funnelled flush-deckers. These ships displaced about 1,000 tons and were armed with four 4-inch guns and twelve 21-inch torpedo tubes. The calibre of their guns was weak compared to British and Japanese destroyers (now beginning to ship 4.7-inch guns) nor were the guns well sited, having two guns on the beam. Likewise the torpedo outfit, in four triple mounts, was sided and therefore capable of only a six-tube broadside. The existence of these ships, outmoded even by 1918 standards, coupled with a natural post-war parsimony, meant their retention in service for longer than their design warranted. Nevertheless the Royal Navy was grateful for them in 1940.

1919–39: Inter-War Economics

The initial heady years of peace, having fought the 'War to end Wars', resulted in great reluctance to spend on armaments. The wartime fleets, expanded far beyond the needs of peace, were quickly reduced, initially by paying off surplus ships, and releasing large numbers of men into a civilian world ill-equipped to receive them. Meanwhile, the Kaiser's fleet, interned in Scapa Flow, had scuttled itself (including fifty destroyers) and the Allied powers were somewhat reluctantly engaged in a war with Soviet Russia in the White, Baltic and Black Seas. Despite a handful of losses, however, including the modern ships *Vittoria* and *Verulam*, there would quite obviously be no requirement for most of the paid-off ships. The older boats of the '30 knotter' *River* and *Tribal* classes were well over-age, outdated and worn out from the rigours of war service, while the newer boats of the *M* class, many of which had been built under wartime conditions, were also worn out. From 1919, the great execution began; in the next three years, almost 300 British destroyers went to the breakers' yards and a small number transferred to Dominion navies. In addition, contracts were cancelled for another 45 units, mostly *W*-class ships, a number of which had been laid down and a few launched, while construction was slowed down on the remaining contracts. Some incomplete and suspended hulls were taken from their builders' yards and, probably for political reasons, completed in very leisurely fashion by the Royal Dockyards, namely, *Witch* by Devonport in March 1924, *Whitehall* by Chatham in July 1924 and *Rooke* (re-named *Broke*) as late as April 1925 at Portsmouth.

At the beginning of the 1920s, the *V & W*-class destroyers formed the back-bone of the Royal Navy's flotillas with the remaining Admiralty *R*

*Speculative building by shipyards either in the hope of orders, or to prevent laying-off of skilled men.

and *S* types. The latter, however, embodied an outdated concept and were soon being discarded, 31 of the *R* class going for scrapping from 1926 to 1928, while wholesale disposal of the *S* class began in 1931 with 35 ships disappearing from the Navy List by 1936.

The United States, too, began a programme of disposal, which affected all the pre 'flush-decker' designs with but few exceptions. Having completed six prototypes of the *Caldwell* class under the 1915 programme, huge orders for the 'flush-deckers' followed, and by Armistice Day, 172 had been laid down of which 37 had been completed. Orders for 96 more quickly followed with only five being cancelled, so that by 1922 there were 268 in commission. Obsolescent as they were, their recent completion dates prevented any attempts at building more modern designs with the result that the US Navy were saddled with them for many years.

The French Navy was in extremely poor condition by 1918, having completed only a handful of small warships since 1913. All its ships were hopelessly obsolete, not least the destroyer-force, and only two new destroyers had been completed in home yards during hostilities, while a third, *Enseigne Gabolde*, was not commissioned until 1925. War losses had amounted to seven large and five small destroyers. Such was the position of the French Navy that it was forced to retain these pre-war *reciprocating*-engined destroyers until the mid-1920s and some as late as 1933! A few, used for instructional purposes, lasted even longer. Their fleet had also been reinforced by twelve destroyers built in Japan to an order placed on 12 November 1916. These ships, based upon the Japanese *Kaba*, were delivered into French hands at Port Said in September and October 1917, and remained in service until 1933/36. They too were of obsolete reciprocating-engine design.

Japan, having fought on the Allied side, finished the war with a strong fleet and had just begun construction of the *Minekaze* class of 1st Class destroyers and was about to lay down the 2nd Class boats of the *Momi* class. The *Minekaze* ships were powerful vessels of Germanic appearance due to the retention of the well, forward of the bridge, in which were mounted torpedo tubes. Displacing about 1,200 tons, they had adopted 4.7-inch guns but not superfiring, although four mountings were fitted. The majority of these ships served during the Second World War.

With the close of the First World War, the torpedo-boat destroyer or 'destroyer' as it was now almost universally called, had come of age. The various designs adopted by the major powers had been arrived at through a protracted period of development lasting until about 1914, while the years of conflict had forged the new weapon into an effective and useful class of warship. Such was the demand for these vessels that every commander or flag officer was wont to declaim that there 'were never enough destroyers'. After nineteen all too brief years of peace, the complaint was to be heard time and again in the second conflict which would embrace all the world's oceans from Arctic to Pacific.

Destroyers in the Second World War

During the last decade prior to the outbreak of the Second World War, the most significant factor affecting the world's navies was aviation. Aircraft, both land-based and carrierborne, had become significantly more potent and the development of dive-bombing techniques measurably increased accuracy and effectiveness. While British naval aviation lagged behind both contemporary naval and land-based aircraft performance, it would be these contemporary forces, notably those of Germany, Italy and Japan, against which British and Allied destroyers would be ranged. Destroyers were a legitimate target for enemy aircraft just as any other naval unit, but suffered the disadvantage of size, or lack of it, wherewith to ship the augmented light AA outfits. On the other hand their manoeuvrability was an asset. However, none of the major naval powers seemed able to develop an effective light AA weapon pre-war, and few had an effective high-angle control system for any sort of weapon. Only Japan and the USA had produced effective dual-purpose guns for destroyer use (and the latter, as good a control system as well), probably as a result of their appreciation of any future Pacific conflict in which their respective carrier forces, the best equipped in the world, would play a major role. Great Britain, Germany, Italy and France, on the other hand, had no DP capability to speak of. As far as light weapons were concerned, it was two neutral nations, Sweden and Switzerland, who laid the basis for new weapons in this category and their designs were taken up and produced in huge quantities by the combatants once the experiences of the early days of war had been digested.

Low-angle gunnery had not advanced greatly and, although control methods had improved, radar had still not arrived, even for search purposes, as far as destroyers were concerned. The main weapon of destroyers remained the torpedo, of which up to sixteen tubes were carried by some US ships, reflecting their major design role – surface attack on capital units.

Destroyers, therefore, were conceived and designed to perform similar functions to those of their forebears of 1914–18, i.e., (1) defence of their own battle fleet and conversely (2) the attack of the enemy battle fleet plus (3) anti-submarine screen duties for the fleet.

In 1939, of course, there were still battleships to be screened and even later there were the carrier task groups which required similar services. The call to attack an enemy battle fleet came but rarely in 1939–45; apart from a few skirmishes in the Mediterranean, the only opportunities in this direction were in the Pacific War. Aircraft on the other hand were an enemy to be found everywhere from the Norwegian fjords of 1940 to the *Kamikaze* of 1945 and, given the poor standards of light AA outfits, destroyers suffered accordingly. In fact the major development of destroyer design throughout the war years was a recognition of this. Low-angle main armaments were replaced or given DP capability where possible, and light AA was augmented by large numbers of additional guns, usually between 20 and 40mm calibre, often at the expense of main guns or torpedoes. Which was given up depended upon the theatre and nation concerned, but was not always logical. German torpedo-craft, for instance, rarely sacrificed torpedoes, but then they were seldom deployed where they could use them. These measures were a tacit admission that the age of the battle fleet had passed and that for every day a low-angle gun was needed there were probably twenty when a 20mm was vital.

Submarines remained a menace to shipping and as the war progressed also affected destroyer design and operation. In contrast to popular opinion, destroyers were not ideal A/S craft; their speed was of little use, except for positioning, at least until the advent of the Types XXI and XXIII U-boats, and their endurance was limited. Any A/S armament was always at the expense of their other functions, but because of the seriousness of the U-boat menace, particularly to Great Britain, Royal Navy destroyers of older types received extensive modification for A/S duties and were thereafter suitable only for escort work. In the Royal and French Navies, recognition of the limitations of the fleet destroyer for A/S work led even before the war to specialized A/S vessels such as sloops whose speed was sufficient for the job and no more, but which were well armed for A/S duties. It also led to the development of fast escort vessels such as the *Hunt* class of the Royal Navy and, eventually, the vast DE programme of the United States. Japan disdained A/S development until very late in the war when forced by catastrophic losses at the hands of US submarines to initiate a crash programme of escort destroyers. Neither Germany nor Italy modified their destroyers for A/S work to any great extent, the former relying on huge numbers of requisitioned trawlers while the latter had a large programme of torpedo-boat and corvette construction which was actually to become a very effective A/S force.

The other major combatant, the Soviet Union, played a very minor role in the war at sea, mainly due to the low standard of efficiency of the Red Navy and the huge territorial losses on the Eastern Front which resulted in the battle fleet being trapped in Leningrad for about three years. Only in the Black Sea did Soviet destroyers see much service and even that was restricted by the loss of all the major pre-war bases. In consequence little development took place in destroyer designs although some interesting classes were emerging towards the end of hostilities.

Thus by the middle war years there were several parallel lines of development, not all of which were pursued farther:

- Pure fleet destroyers (all nations)
- Purpose-built A/S escort destroyers (Great Britain, USA)
- AA destroyers (Japan, Great Britain*)
- Small destroyers or torpedo-boats (Germany, Italy)
- Extra large destroyers/light cruisers (France).

The actions in which destroyers participated are too numerous to detail individually here, but the text of each class described later gives a good idea of the wide variety of service seen by this type of warship. Certain actions can however be cited as classic destroyer engagements, for example, the Battle of Narvik in April 1940, in which German and British destroyers took part; the attacks upon *Bismarck* in 1941; Italian destroyers and torpedo-boats fought hard to protect the North African supply routes in 1940–41; the Battle of the Java Sea in 1942 when British, Dutch and US destroyers fought their Japanese counterparts in a large-scale cruiser action; US and Japanese destroyers clashed frequently in and around the Solomon Islands, Guadalcanal, Vella Gulf, the Komandorski Islands and many other places in 1942–43; while the battle for Leyte Gulf saw US destroyers in action against Japanese capital units.

For all these highlights, however, there were many, many more days when a destroyer's role was one of quiet, boring routine, escorting an Atlantic convoy or shepherding a US troop ship across the vast Pacific basin when the most dangerous enemy might be the weather – ice, fog or hurricanes. On occasion the close-quarter manoeuvring necessary in convoy work or fleet screening led to losses when diminutive destroyers were run down in darkness by larger vessels, and there was always the chance of accidental loss by grounding when operating poorly charted waters.

The following pages illustrate the heavy losses sustained by destroyers in the period September 1939 to August 1945 as well as the huge building programmes put in hand by Great Britain, but more particularly the United States. These far outstripped losses with the result that at the end of hostilities many hundreds were immediately surplus to requirements. Pre-1939 ships were generally scrapped quickly, sometimes even before hostilities ended. Many more war-built ships, constructed to somewhat lower standards than peacetime, were just worn out and, with the increase in speeds of submarines, many destroyers were converted to frigates as the older corvettes, sloops and war-built frigates were now too slow for the anti-submarine role. Even so, in the United States large numbers remained. Outdated but too young to discard, and impossible to replace on financial grounds in the same numbers, these ageing ships had considerable effect on post-war US construction plans. Many, of course, were sold or given to Allied western nations where they are still serving today.

The role of the destroyer as envisaged in 1939 was gone by 1945. Surface torpedo attack had become a thing of the past, to be replaced by, initially, air-to-sea missiles and later sea-to-sea missiles which in turn rendered the gun of less importance. Submarines and aircraft assumed even greater menace with the effect that destroyers still remained maids of all work, but assumed the general role of 'escort' and in doing so came to be regarded more as defensive units than offensive ones.

*But note, almost all US Navy destroyers had good DP outfits although not classified as AA destroyers.

Argentina

One of the most powerful nations of South America, Argentina has suffered continually from the scourge of that subcontinent, turbulent politics. This in turn has affected the size and composition of the Argentine Fleet together with a continuing desire always to have the best of what was available. As Argentina possessed no industry capable of building ships of destroyer size, the navy turned to the most famous names in Europe for their torpedo-boats and destroyers and an unfortunate sense of timing allied to the choice of British, French and German yards led, upon the outbreak of war in 1914, to the loss of all their new construction when they were requisitioned by the nations building them. Argentina remained neutral throughout the First World War, and economic considerations post-war delayed any re-equipment until the late 1920s. In consequence, the navy possessed only four, 1912-vintage, destroyers of British and German design until the purchase of two Spanish destroyers in 1927. This began a period of reconstruction for the Argentine Navy which was halted by war once more in 1939. This time no ships were caught building abroad, but five more units of the *Buenos Aires* class, reportedly projected in 1939, never materialized. Again, Argentina remained neutral during the Second World War and in consequence received no material benefits from the Allies in terms of Lease-Lend or 'free transfer' warships. Post-war policy was to obtain ex-US warships now cheaply available surplus to requirements.

MENDOZA CLASS

Ship	Builder	Launched	Commissioned	Fate
E4 *La Rioja*	S. White (Cowes)	2 Feb 29	23 July 29*	Discarded 30 April 62
E3 *Mendoza*	S. White (Cowes)	18 July 28	24 Jan 29*	Discarded 30 April 62
E5 *Yucuman*	S. White (Cowes)	16 Oct 28	3 May 29*	Discarded 30 April 62

*Trials

Displacement: 1,570tons/1,595tonnes (standard); 2,120tons/2,154tonnes (full load).
Length: 335ft/102.11m (oa); 332ft 3in/101.2m (wl).
Beam: 31ft 9in/9.68m.
Draught: 12ft 6in/3.81m (mean).
Machinery: four 3-drum boilers; 2-shaft Parsons geared turbines.
Performance: 42,000shp; 36kts.
Bunkerage: 540 tons/549 tonnes.
Range: 4,500nm at 14kts.
Guns: five 4.7in (5×1); one 3in AA; two 2pdr.
Torpedoes: six 21in (2×3).
Complement: 160.

Design Part of the pre-war modernization programme of the Argentine Navy, this class carried the names originally intended for destroyers building in France (*La Rioja* and *Mendoza*) and Germany (*Tucuman*), but appropriated by those countries on the outbreak of war in 1914. The contract was placed with Samuel White in 1927 at a time when shipbuilding work was at a low ebb and in consequence it was a very welcome boost to Cowes. On trials, the ships proved faster than their contract speed with *Mendoza* and *Tucuman* reaching 38 knots and *La Rioja* nearly 39 knots. All three ships sailed together for Argentina, arriving in November, *Tucuman* and *La Rioja* having steamed the 5,800 miles from Lisbon to Puerto Belgrana without intermediate ports of call. By all accounts, they were successful and popular ships, certainly the head of the Argentine Naval Commission in Europe, Admiral Galindez, thought so, and said as much to White's when enclosing the cheque!

Modifications All three were converted to anti-submarine escorts from 1958.

Below: *Mendoza*.

Service Like so many ships of Latin American powers, economic restraints ensured their being kept in service for many years and they were not stricken until 30 April 1962 after the arrival of three *Fletcher*-class destroyers second-hand from the USA.

Note. Also in existence during the Second World War were the even older ships of the *La Plata* and *Jujuy* classes, four ships altogether. These had been built before the First World War and were armed with three 4-inch guns and four 21-inch (2 × 2) torpedo tubes.

Above: *La Rioja* in 1955. She still retains her 1920s appearance but has received 40mm bofors guns. (A. D. Baker)

CERVANTES CLASS

Ship	Builder	Launched	Commissioned	Fate
E1 *Cervantes*	La Carraca (Cartagena)	26 June 25	3 Sept 27	Stricken 24 June 61
E2 *Juan de Garray*	La Carraca (Cartegena)	2 Nov 25	3 Sept 27	Stricken 25 Mar 60

Below: *Corrientes.* Note the director tower and tripod mainmast. (Vickers Ltd)

Displacement: 1,522tons/1,546tonnes (standard); 2,087tons/2,120tonnes (full load).
Length: 318ft 3in/97m (oa).
Beam: 31ft 6in/9.6m.
Draught: 10ft 6in/3.2m (mean).
Machinery: four boilers; 2-shaft Parsons geared turbines.
Performance: 42,000shp; 36kts.
Bunkerage: 540tons/548tonnes.
Range: 4,500nm at 14kts.
Guns: five 4.7in (5×1); one 3in AA; four MG.
Torpedoes: six 21in (3×2).
Complement: 175.

Design These two destroyers were purchased from Spain on 10 June 1926 where they were under construction as *Churruca* and *Alcalá Galiano* respectively. A development of the British *Scott*-class flotilla leaders, eighteen of this class were built in Spain (q.v.) of which these were two of the earliest laid down. *Cervantes* reached 39.76 knots on trials, but without armament.

Modifications The midships 4.7-inch gun was landed post-war and replaced by two twin 40mm and a further twin 40mm eventually displaced the 3-inch gun.

Service Reclassified as *torpederos* in the 1950s, these two ships lasted a little longer than many of their former Spanish compatriots and were not stricken until 24 June 61 (*Cervantes*) and 25 Mar 60 (*Juan de Garray*).

BUENOS AIRES CLASS

Ship	Builder	Laid Down	Launched	Commissioned	Fate
E6 *Buenos Aires*	V.A. (Barrow)	1936	21 Sept 37	4 April 38	Stricken 1971
E8 *Corrientes*	V.A. (Barrow)	1936	21 Sept 37	1 July 38	Collision 3 Oct 41
E7 *Entre Rios*	V.A. (Barrow)	1936	21 Sept 37	15 May 38	Stricken 1973
E11 *Misiones*	Cammell Laird		23 Sept 37	5 Sept 38	Stricken 3 May 71
E9 *San Juan*	John Brown		24 June 37	23 Mar 38	Stricken 1973
E10 *San Luis*	John Brown		23 Aug 37	23 Mar 38	Stricken 3 May 71
E12 *Santa Cruz*	Cammell Laird		3 Nov 37	26 Sept 38	Stricken 73

Displacement: 1,375tons/1,397tonnes (standard); 2,010tons/2,042tonnes (full load).
Length: 323ft/98.45m (oa).
Beam: 34ft 8in/10.58m.
Draught: 10ft 6in/3.2m (mean).
Machinery: three 3-drum boilers; 2-shaft Parsons geared turbines.
Performance: 34,000shp; 35kts.
Bunkerage: 450tons/457tonnes.
Range: 4,100nm at 14kts.
Guns: four 4.7in (4×1); eight .5in MG.
Torpedoes: eight 21in (2×4).
Complement: 130.

Design One of several classes of destroyer built in British yards to standard British designs of the 1920s and 1930s, these ships served the Argentine navy for more than thirty years. Basically of the same type as the British *Glowworm*, but with some modifications to suit Argentine requirements, they were originally classified as 'exploradores' and gave the Argentine fleet a robust, modern destroyer force, which together with the *Veinticinco De Mayo*-class cruisers, *La Argentina* and the five older destroyers, constituted a powerful force in South America.

Modifications After the Second World War, the .5 MG were replaced on the platform between the funnels by two single 40mm and in 1956, the after torpedo tubes were landed and the former searchlight platform was extended to accommodate two twin 40mm mountings. Radar was also added.

Service *Corrientes* sank on 3 October 1941, after a collision with *Almirante Brown* during exercises, but the remainder of the class survived into the early 1970s, although reclassified as *torpederos* in 1952 and 'destructores' in 1957. *Buenos Aires, Misiones* and *San Luis* were discarded on 3 May 1971; *Entre Rios, San Juan* and *Santa Cruz* in 1973.

Below: *Entre Rios.* (Vickers Ltd)

Australia

The various States which made up the continent of Australia had made some attempt at naval defence by the acquisition of a few gunboats and torpedo-boats during the late nineteenth century, but it was not until 1908 that an established strength was laid down for an Australian Squadron. This was to comprise one battlecruiser, three light cruisers, six destroyers and three submarines and it is greatly to the credit of the Australian government that, by 1914, this strength, with the exception of one submarine, had been reached. The six destroyers, named after rivers, were built half in Great Britain and half in Australia so that at an early stage Australia gained experience in the construction of these complex vessels. *Yarra* was the first to complete in September 1910, with the last *Swan* in August 1916. These destroyers operated in the Bismarck Archipelago in the course of the occupation of New Guinea and New Britain, then after a spell on the Australian coast, were sent to the South China Sea. In 1917 they were ordered to the Mediterranean and operated from Malta, on the Adriatic Patrol and, after the surrender of Turkey, went to the Black Sea. In 1919 they steamed to England and finally arrived back in Australia in April 1919. They were discarded in 1929–1930 except for *Huon* and *Torrens* which were sunk as targets in 1930, the latter by the heavy cruiser *Canberra*.

Being worn out as well as outdated, the six destroyers were replaced in the active fleet by five new *S*-class destroyers transferred from the Royal Navy in June 1919. These ships, *Stalwart, Success, Swordsman, Tasmania* and *Tattoo* had been completed only a few months earlier. They were armed with three 4-inch guns and four 21-inch torpedo tubes. Their careers with the Royal Australian Navy lasted until they were placed on the sales list in June 1937, by which time they had themselves been superseded by *V&W*-class ships, also from the Royal Navy.

During the Second World War, as in the First, the Royal Australian Navy had, despite the age of its ships, an enviable fighting record, sending them to fight in the Mediterranean before the Japanese onslaught forced their return to Pacific Waters in 1942. Here, fighting alongside their American allies, they acquitted themselves well despite their small numbers.

SCOTT CLASS

Ship	Builder	Laid Down	Launched	Commissioned	Fate
D00 *Stuart*	Hawthorn Leslie	18 Oct 17	22 Aug 18	21 Dec 18	Sold 21 Feb 47

Displacement: 1,580tons/1,605tonnes (standard); 2,050tons/2,083tonnes (full load).
Length: 332ft 6in/101.3m (oa); 320ft/97.5m (pp).
Beam: 31ft 9in/9.7m.
Draught: 12ft 6in/3.8m (mean).
Machinery: four Yarrow boilers; 2-shaft Brown-Curtis geared turbines.
Performance: 40,000shp; 36.5kts.
Bunkerage: 500tons/508tonnes.
Range: 5,000nm at 15kts.
Guns: five 4.7in (5×1); one 3in AA; two 2pdr.
Torpedoes: six 21in (2×3).
Complement: 188.

Design One of a class of enlarged leaders which were ordered for the Royal Navy in late 1916, of which two were cancelled. Five sister ships were still extant in the Royal Navy at the outbreak of the Second World War (Admiralty Leaders, see page 86). *Stuart* was transferred to the RAN in October 1933. On trials when first completed, she attained 34.66 knots on a displacement of 1,935 tons with 43,890shp, but it is doubtful if her effective speed was more than 30 knots by the time of the Second World War.

Modifications 'Q' and 'Y' guns were landed in 1941, each being replaced by a pair of single 20mm. A fifth 20mm was also added, as well as a captured

Left: *Stuart* as she appeared in 1939. (RAN)

Italian Breda gun. Two throwers and two depth-charge racks formed the A/S outfit. By 1942, her armament had been further altered for escort duties when 'A' gun was replaced by a hedgehog AHW. Two 2pdr were fitted between the funnels and two 20mm single guns moved into the bridge wings. Aft, only a single 20mm now occupied the site of 'Y' gun. Both banks of tubes were landed and radar 271 added atop the bridge. Finally, in her role as a fast transport, to which she was converted early in 1945, her armament was reduced to one 4-inch HA, three single 2pdr and five, later seven, 20mm (1×2, 3–5×1). She retained her hedgehog and depth-charges. The light AA was disposed as follows: 20mm single – bridge wings, amidships on the iron deck abreast the position of the original 3-inch gun and three on the after shelter deck. 2pdr – two single in place of the after tubes and one on the position of 'Y' gun.

Service After the outbreak of war, *Stuart* operated in the Indian Ocean and East Indies and was then sent to the Mediterranean, together with the other Australian destroyers of the 10th Flotilla, under the command of Captain J. W. A. Walker, RAN (who later commanded HMAS *Perth* during the Java Sea battles) where, assisted by *Diamond* she sank the submarine *Gondar* in September 1940. In March 1941 she was present at the Battle of Matapan where, in company with HMS *Havock, Stuart* took part in the sinking of the Italian destroyers *Alfieri* and *Carducci*. She later played a part in operations in the eastern Mediterranean, the evacuation of Crete and the Tobruk supply convoys, until sailing home for Australia on 22 August 1941, badly in need of a refit. From late 1942, *Stuart* operated with other Australian units under US command in the New Guinea theatre, but her age was beginning to tell and by 1944 she was being employed mainly in the fast transport role. The end of the war in the Far East saw her immediate reduction to reserve for disposal, being sold out on 21 February 1947 and broken up at Sydney.

VAMPIRE (ADMIRALTY V & W) CLASS

Ship	Builder	Laid Down	Launched	Commissioned	Fate
D68 *Vampire*	S. White (Cowes)	10 Oct 16	21 May 17	11 Sept 17	Lost 9 April 42
D69 *Vendetta*	Fairfield	1916	3 Sept 17	4 Oct 17	Scuttled 2 July 48
D31 *Voyager*	A. Stephens	17 May 17	8 May 18	8 June 18	Lost 23 Sept 42
D22 *Waterhen*	Palmer	July 17	26 Mar 18	19 July 18	Lost 29 June 41

(Pendant changed to I 1940)

Displacement: 1,188tons/1,207tonnes (standard); 1,490tons/1,513tonnes (full load).
Length: 312ft/95m (oa); 309ft/94.1m (wl); 300ft/91.4m (pp).
Beam: 29ft 6in/8.99m.
Draught: 10ft 9in/3.27m (mean).
Machinery: three Yarrow boilers (White-Foster in *Vampire*); 2-shaft geared turbines (Brown-Curtis in all except *Waterhen*, Parsons).
Performance: 27,000shp; 34kts.
Bunkerage: 367tons/373tonnes.
Range: 2,600nm at 15kts.
Guns: four 4in (4×1); one 3in AA; two 2pdr (2×1).
Torpedoes: six 21in (2×3).
Complement: 134.

Design See Great Britain, *V* & *W* class.

Modifications Initially a quadruple .5 MG mounting supplanted the after tubes, but this was soon replaced by a 12pdr except for *Vampire* which received two 2pdr single guns instead. All except *Waterhen* were given a quadruple .5 MG in the bridge wings and another quadruple mounting was fitted aft of the second funnel in all four, on the original 2pdr platform. Only the survivor, *Vendetta*, was altered further, when as an escort she was armed with two 4-inch HA, two 2pdr (2×1), four 20mm and eight machine-guns as well as 50 depth-charges.

Service These veteran destroyers were transferred to the Royal Australian Navy in October 1933 and commissioned on 11 October. All four were sent to the Mediterranean in 1939, arriving before Christmas, *Vendetta* being the first. En route, they operated against surface raiders in the East Indies and Indian Ocean. As the 10th Flotilla, known for obvious reasons as the 'Scrap Iron Flotilla' they participated in the Greece and Crete campaigns, as well as the Tobruk run, ferrying supplies to that beleaguered garrison. *Waterhen* became the first loss when near misses during a bombing attack off Sollum flooded the engine room on 29 June 1941 and she sank the following day. *Vampire* had already left the Mediterranean by this time (in fact in May) and *Voyager* followed her in July. *Vendetta* was the last to sail for Australian waters in October 1941 as the Japanese threat became more serious. When war did actually break out in the Far East that December, *Vendetta* was under refit at Singapore, but *Vampire* was able to sail with *Prince of Wales* and *Repulse* on their fateful last sortie. She escaped on that occasion and returned to Australia, but was finally lost to air attack in the Bay of Bengal on 9 April 1942. *Vendetta*, her refit incomplete, was towed out of Singapore in a hurry, to be finished in Australia. *Voyager* was damaged in a bombing attack off the south coast of Timor on 23 September and put ashore as a total loss, leaving *Vendetta* the only survivor. After completion of her refit she spent 1943–45 active in the south-west Pacific and New Guinea areas and was present at the Japanese surrender at Rabaul on 6 September 1945. Paid off at the war's end, *Vendetta* was scuttled off Sydney on 2 July 1948.

Below: *Vendetta* about 1941. Note after tubes landed and twin machine-guns in bridge wings. (RAN)

Right: *Vendetta* modified for escort duties, re-armed with two 4in HA ('B' and 'X' turrets), hedgehog forward, radar and 20mm guns. (RAN)

Right: *Vendetta* about 1942, 'Y' gun landed, 12pdr fitted in lieu of quad. 5 machine-gun (moved aft), 20mm added and depth-charge outfit increased. (RAN)

TRIBAL CLASS

Ship	Builder	Laid Down	Launched	Commissioned	Fate
I30 *Arunta* D5	Cockatoo Dkyd.	15 Nov 39	30 Nov 40	3 Mar 42	Foundered 13 Feb 69
I91 *Bataan* (ex-*Kurnai*) D9	Cockatoo Dkyd.	18 Feb 42	15 Jan 44	25 May 45	Sold out 1958
I44 *Warramunga* D18	Cockatoo Dkyd.	10 Feb 40	6 Feb 42	23 Nov 42	Sold out 19 Jan 63

(D Pendant for service with US Pacific Fleet 1945)

Displacement: 1,927tons/1,958tonnes (standard); 2,745tons/2,788tonnes (full load).
Length: 377ft/114.9m (oa); 364ft 8in/111.1m (wl); 355ft 6in/108.35m (pp).
Beam: 36ft 6in/11.13m.
Draught: 13ft/3.96m (mean).
Machinery: three Admiralty 3-drum boilers; 2-shaft Parsons geared turbines.
Performance: 44,000shp; 36.25kts.
Bunkerage: 505tons/513tonnes.
Range: 5,700nm at 17kts.
Guns: eight 4.7in (4×2); four 2pdr (1×4); eight .5in MG (2×4).
Torpedoes: four 21in (1×4).
Complement: 190.

Design Australia decided to order the British *Tribal* design (q.v.) into production for her navy in 1939 and to build them in Australia at the Cockatoo Island dockyard in Sydney. This was a major step forward for the Australian shipbuilding industry as its previous largest vessel had been the seaplane tender *Albatross*. Although this ship was larger, the building of such complex fast vessels as destroyers required a much higher degree of technology. Assistance was provided by Britain and the machinery was built in the UK. *Arunta* and *Warramunga* were ordered in January 1939 and four more in May that year, but only *Kurnai* (re-named *Bataan* in 1944 in honour of General MacArthur) was in fact laid down. The Australian *Tribal*s were able to benefit from the Royal Navy's early war experience and incorporated several changes from the outset. 'X' 4.7-inch gun being replaced by a twin 4-inch and the after funnel being cut down. Construction was naturally extended by the need to send out equipment from the UK, and inexperience in building this type of vessel no doubt also contributed to the fact that the first ship did not enter service until spring 1942.

Modifications Initially six 20mm Oerlikon guns were added as they became available. They were replaced later by 40mm Bofors, but the 2pdr was retained. Surface and air warning as well as gunnery radars were added and the tripod mast was replaced by a lattice mast in about 1944. Post-war, *Arunta* and *Warramunga* were refitted and modernized to extend their ASW capabilities. 'Y' gun was landed and the after deck-house was extended to increase accommodation and serve as a squid handling room, the mortar itself being fitted on the quarter-deck. The AA outfit was increased to eight 40mm by the addition of a twin mounting on the after shelter deck, and the radar outfit was updated.

Service *Arunta* and *Warramunga* saw extensive action in the SW Pacific, operating between New Guinea and the Philippines under US command. An early success was the sinking of the Japanese submarine *Ro33* off New Guinea in August 1942 by *Arunta*. In 1944, the same ship took part in destroyer attacks on the *Yamashiro*, but in January 1945 she suffered damage from Kamikaze attack in the Philippines and in consequence was not able to be present in Japan with her sisters on VJ-Day. *Warramunga* lasted until the 1960s in her A/S role, but was finally sold out in January 1963 for breaking up in Japan. *Arunta* herself foundered in tow en route to the breakers in Taiwan, 60m east of Broken Bay on 13 February 1969, having been previously sold to the China Steel Corporation. *Bataan*, the newest ship, surprisingly was not converted; declared for disposal in 1957, she was sold to Messrs T. Carr & Co. of Sydney for breaking up.

TRANSFERRED UNITS

Napier, Nizam, Norman, Nepal, Nestor

Design These five destroyers, part of a class of eight, were allocated to the RAN while under construction and commissioned with Australian crews on completion. (See Great Britain for full design data.)

Modifications Operating in the eastern Mediterranean they received the standard treatment to increase AA defences by the addition of a 4-inch HA gun in lieu of the after torpedo tubes, and the addition of Oerlikon guns to replace the useless .5 MG. Final armament included four twin Oerlikon guns, on the signal deck and searchlight platform.

Service The five ships served with the 7th Destroyer Flotilla from completion, initially with the Home Fleet (*Napier, Nestor, Nizam* and *Norman*) before joining the Mediterranean Fleet in March 1941 (*Napier* and *Nizam*), *Nestor* too joined the Mediterranean Fleet in July 1941. *Nepal* and *Norman*, however, went instead to the Eastern Fleet in January 1942. In Mediterranean waters, both *Napier* and *Nizam* received damage from near misses by bombs during the evacuation of Crete in May 1941. In August 1941, *Nestor* was damaged by premature depth-charge explosions and was sent home to Devonport to repair after which she was transferred to the Eastern Fleet. On passage to her new station *Nestor* sank *U127* off Cape St. Vincent in December 1941. From January 1942 the whole flotilla served with the Eastern Fleet, but in May all except *Nepal* (in South African waters) were detached to the Mediterranean once more for Malta convoy work. Here on 15 June, in the course of Operation 'Vigorous', *Nestor* was severely shaken by near misses from an Italian bomber. The bombs exploded under 'A' boiler room fracturing steam lines. Without power, *Nestor* was taken in tow by *Javelin* but in the face of further air attacks she was abandoned and sunk by *Javelin*. *Nepal* remained in South Africa until March 1943, joined by *Nizam* from September to December 1942, but the latter was lent to South African command from May to August 1943, as was *Norman*.

By late 1943 all had returned to the Eastern Fleet, going to Australia to refit at various times and in 1944 saw action in the various sorties against the Malayan coast. *Napier, Nepal, Nizam* and *Norman* moved to the Pacific with the British Pacific Fleet in April 1945, remaining in the Pacific until the Japanese surrender. *Napier, Nepal* and *Nizam* were in Japanese waters at or after the surrender, before returning to Australia. On 11 November, *Napier* and *Norman* sailed for the UK followed later that month by *Nepal* and *Nizam*. After their return to Britain they paid off to reserve, except *Nepal* which was disarmed and used as a trials ship until November 1950. She was broken up in 1956.

Below: *Arunta* on trials. (RAN)

Brazil

Brazil had only declared itself independent from Portugal in 1822, 322 years after Pedro Alvares Cabral had chanced to land there in 1500. War against Argentina, newly independent from Spain, followed in 1851–52 and then against Paraguay in 1864 to 1870, this time allied with Argentina and Uruguay. During this period the naval forces available to Brazil were minimal apart from the odd gunboat and riverine craft, and it was not until the late 1890s that a major effort was directed at the building up of a navy to patrol the 4,000-mile coastline of Brazil. Torpedo-craft had an obvious place in this navy, and torpedo-boats bought from Yarrow and Schichau as well as torpedo gunboats from Krupps and Elswick. In fact these vessels were some of the earliest to use torpedoes in action – see page 8. By the outbreak of the First World War, the Brazilian Navy had achieved a respectable size with two dreadnoughts and two relatively modern cruisers on its strength, as well as ten new destroyers. These ships, the *Para* class, had been built in England to the 1904 *River*-class design by Yarrow, and were completed between 1908 and 1910. They had a long service career with six still on strength in 1939 although by this time they were fit only for subsidiary duties. One other old destroyer was also in service, *Maranhão* formerly the British *Porpoise* completed in January 1914 thus only marginally younger than the *Paras*. She had been sold to Thornycroft in February 1920 for refit and transfer to Brazil, being finally discarded in 1945 followed in 1946 by the last of the *Paras*, *Matto Grosso*. During the war she served with the Southern Naval Force on convoy escort duties between Rio and Recife as well as carrying out fourteen ocean patrols.

American influence was strong in Brazil in the post-1918 period, which led in 1937 to an American attempt to lease six destroyers to the Brazilian Navy, but because of objections from Argentina, the idea was dropped and instead the destroyers were ordered from British yards. The outbreak of the Second World War prevented their delivery.

A belligerent partner in the Second World War as in the First, Brazilian ships took part in convoy duties in the South Atlantic as well as in the African and Italian campaigns.

JURUA CLASS

Ship	Builder	Laid Down	
Jurua	V.A. (Tyne)	3 June 38	All purchased by Gt. Britain 4 Sept 1939
Javary	S. White (Cowes)	30 Mar 38	
Jutahy	S. White (Cowes)	31 May 38	
Juruena	Thornycroft	6 July 38	
Jaguaribe	Thornycroft	28 Sept 38	
Japarua	V.A. (Tyne)	30 June 38	

Displacement: 1,340tons/1,361tonnes (standard); 1,859tons/1,889tonnes (full load).
Length: 323ft/98.4m (oa); 320ft/97.5m (wl); 312ft/95.1m (pp).
Beam: 33ft/10.06m.
Draught: 12ft 9in/3.89m (mean).
Machinery: three Admiralty 3-drum boilers; 2-shaft Parsons geared turbines.
Performance: 34,000shp; 36kts.
Bunkerage: 443tons/450tonnes.
Range: 5,530nm at 15kts.
Guns: four 4.7in (4×1); eight .5in MG (2×4).
Torpedoes: eight 21in (2×4).
Complement: 145.

Design and Service All were sold before launching. Half the class were lost while serving with the Royal Navy where they were mainly employed on escort duties. The survivors were not re-acquired by Brazil because replacements had been put in hand in Brazilian yards during the war years.

M CLASS

Ship	Builder	Laid Down	Launched	Commissioned	Fate
M3 *Greenhalgh*	Ilha das Cobras, Rio de Janeiro	1937	8 July 41	29 Nov 43	Stricken 1966
M1 *Marcilio Dias*	Ilha das Cobras, Rio de Janeiro	8 May 37	20 July 40	29 Nov 43	Stricken 1966
M2 *Mariz e Barros*	Ilha das Cobras, Rio de Janeiro	1937	28 Dec 40	29 Nov 43	Stricken 1972

Displacement: 1,500tons/1,524tonnes (standard); 2,200tons/2,235tonnes (full load).
Length: 357ft/108.81m (oa); 341ft/103.94m (pp).
Beam: 34ft 10in/10.61m.
Draught: 10ft/3.04m (mean).
Machinery: four Babcock & Wilcox Express boilers; 2-shaft GEC geared turbines.
Performance: 42,800shp; 36.5kts.
Bunkerage: 550tons/559tonnes.
Range: 6,000nm at 15kts.
Guns: five 5in (4×1); four 40mm; four 20mm.
Torpedoes: eight 21in (2×4).
Complement: 190.

Design The first ships of any size to be constructed in Brazilian yards, this class naturally relied heavily upon outside assistance, particularly from the USA, and the design itself was basically the same as the US Navy's *Mahan* class. The turbines were supplied by the General Electric Co., boilers by Babcock & Wilcox with guns from Bethlehem. Fire control and sonar equipment was also of US origin. Brazil's entry into the Second World War on 22 August 1942 was of great benefit to the armed forces, as her status as one of the Allies gave access to almost unlimited American aid but even so, the construction of these destroyers was slow and it was not until the end of 1943 that they entered service.

Modifications While under completion, one 5-inch gun was deleted as was one of the quadruple banks of torpedo tubes. The 20mm guns were increased to eight. The 5-inch guns were not fitted with shields, except for No. 1 mounting, which also had zareba protection. Two depth-charge racks, four throwers and sonar completed the ASW outfit.

Service All three destroyers served with 'Naval Forces North-East' and were mainly occupied upon ocean patrol work in the South Atlantic to intercept Axis blockade runners. These patrols were usually of fourteen days' duration. *Marcilio Dias* participated in nine such patrols from March 1944 until April 1945, sometimes as part of a mixed US-Brazilian force with the escort carriers *Wake Island* and *Mission Bay*. They were also occasionally employed on convoy work between Rio, Recife and Trinidad. In July 1944 all three were used to escort the five convoys which transported the Brazilian Expeditionary Force to Italy. After the end of the war, they continued in service and were later modified. *Greenhalgh* and *Marcilio Dias* were stricken in 1966. *Mariz e Barros* which in the meantime had received a Seacat missile system, was not discarded until 1973.

ACRE CLASS

Ship	Builder	Laid Down	Launched	Commissioned	Fate
A4 *Acre*	Ilha das Cobras, Rio de Janeiro	28 Dec 40	30 May 45	10 Dec 51	Stricken 1974
A3 *Ajuricaba*		28 Dec 40	30 May 45	Dec 51	Stricken 1964
A1 *Amazonas*		20 July 40	29 Nov 43	10 Nov 49	Stricken 1973
A6 *Apa*		28 Dec 40	30 May 45	Dec 51	Stricken 1964
A2 *Araguary*		28 Dec 40	14 July 46	23 June 51	Stricken 1974
A5 *Araguaya*		20 July 40	24 Nov 43	3 Sept 49	Stricken 1974

Displacement: 1,340tons/1,361tonnes (standard); 1,800tons/1,829tonnes (full load).
Length: 323ft/98.45m (oa).
Beam: 35ft/10.67m.
Draught: 8ft 6in/2.59m (mean).
Machinery: three 3-drum boilers; 2-shaft geared turbines.
Performance: 34,000shp; 35.5kts.
Bunkerage: 450tons/457tonnes.
Guns: four 5in (4×1); two 40mm (1×2); four 20mm (4×1).
Torpedoes: six 21in (2×3).
Complement: 150.

Design The sale to Great Britain of the six destroyers of the *Jurua* class in 1939, left the Brazilian Navy with only one destroyer, the over-aged former British *Porpoise*-class ship, *Maranhão*. Three *Marcilio Dias* class were under construction, but these were obviously insufficient to provide escort screening for the two battleships (*Minas Gerais* and *São Paulo*) and two cruisers (*Bahia* and *Rio Grande do Sul*). To fill the gap left by the *Jurua* class, six replacement vessels were ordered from the Ilha das Cobras yard in 1940, to a design broadly similar to the cancelled ships, but with Great Britain at war, much technical assistance had to be sought from the still neutral USA. In consequence, the design had to be modified to incorporate US equipment and, as completed, these destroyers more closely resembled in outward appearance the *Craven* class (DD380–408) than the original British *H*-class design, mainly due to the trunking of the boiler uptakes into a single funnel. Completion was greatly extended and the first unit did not enter service unti well after the war, when the design was quite obsolete. Like many US destroyer designs, only No. 1 gun received a shield and the torpedo tubes were sited amidships. US-pattern radar was fitted at the foremost truck.

Modifications Despite their obsolescence, these ships formed a valuable part of the Brazilian destroyer force and were not in fact at a disadvantage as compared with their South American counterparts. In the 1960s, they received major refits, when No. 2 gun was landed and replaced by a twin 40mm mounting and a tripod mast stepped similar to that fitted to *Mariz e Barros*. The radar outfit was considerably enhanced.

Service It is probable that this refit did not extend to *Ajuricaba* and *Apa*, as they were discarded in 1964, but the remaining four served until 1974 (except *Amazonas* 1973).

Below: *Araguari*. Note sided torpedo tubes. (A. D. Baker)

Left: *Greenhalgh*. Note shield only to No. 1 gun. (Brazilian Navy)

Right: *Acre* in 1961. (A. D. Baker)

B CLASS

Ship	Builder	Laid Down	Launched	Commissioned	Fate
B1 *Bertioga* (ex-*Pennewill*)	Federal (Newark)	26 April 43	8 Aug 43	1 Aug 44	Stricken 1964
B2 *Beberibe* (ex-*Herzog*)	Federal (Newark)	17 May 43	5 Sept 43	1 Aug 44	Stricken 1968
B3 *Bracuí* (ex-*Reybolt*)	Federal (Newark)	3 May 43	22 Aug 43	15 Aug 44	Stricken 1974
B4 *Bauru* (ex-*McAnn*)	Federal (Newark)	17 May 43	5 Sept 43	15 Aug 44	Stricken 1975
B5 *Baependi* (ex-*Cannon*)	Dravo (Wilmington)	14 Nov 42	25 May 43	19 Dec 44	Stricken 1974
B6 *Benevente* (ex-*Christopher*)	Dravo (Wilmington)	7 Dec 42	19 June 43	19 Dec 44	Stricken 1975
B7 *Babitonga* (ex-*Alger*)	Dravo (Wilmington)	2 Jan 43	8 July 43	10 Mar 45	Stricken 1964
B8 *Bocaina* (ex-*Marts*)	Federal (Newark)	26 April 43	8 Aug 43	20 May 45	Stricken 1975

Displacement: 1,253tons/1,273 tonnes (standard); 1,602tons/1,627 tonnes (full load).
Length: 306ft/93.27m (oa); 300ft/91.44m (wl).
Beam: 36ft 7in/11.15m.
Draught: 10ft 5in/3.2m (mean).
Machinery: 2-shaft General Motors diesels.
Performance: 6,000bhp; 21kts.
Bunkerage: 300tons/305 tonnes.
Range: 10,800nm at 12kts.
Guns: three 3in (3×1); two 40mm (1×2); eight 20mm (8×1).
Torpedoes: three 21in (1×3).
Complement: 200.

Design US-designed destroyer-escorts transferred after serving in the US Navy, following successful Brazilian operation of sixteen smaller SC and PC type vessels from December 1942.

Modifications Probably none during hostilities.

Service Transferred at Natal by the United States to enable Brazil to take over greater responsibilities in the South and Central Atlantic, these modern ships represented a great advance for the Brazilian Navy and at the same time tacit recognition of its training and ability. All eight units eventually served with the North-eastern Command employed on convoy escort duties. At the beginning of October 1944, Brazil began to assume exclusive responsibility for the Trinidad convoys with Escort Group 46.8 which included *Bertioga* (leader) and *Beberibe* as well as four '*G*'-class submarine-chasers. This convoy (JT46) sailed from Recife on the 8th, but the first use of these new escorts had been on 21 August 1944, when *Bertioga* sailed from Recife with JT41 for Trinidad. *Beberibe* escorted JT42 and both *Bracul* and *Bauru* JT43 in August and September respectively. These convoys had a passage time of ten days. However, a second, exclusively Brazilian, convoy operation, JT54, did not sail until 23 December 1944. *Baependi* escorted her first convoy (JT58) on 12 January 1945 and *Benevente* (JT68) on 2 March 1945. By the end of March 1945 when the escorts ceased, ten outward and eight inward convoys had had all-Brazilian escorts. These ships were also occasionally employed on ocean A/S patrols as far out as the south of the Cape Verde islands. *Beberibe* and *Bracui* participated in two such operations, *Benevente* and *Baependi* one each. In March 1945, Task Force 46.8 comprised of *Babitonga, Bertioga* and two '*G*'-class sub-chasers were also so used. The collapse of Germany in May 1945 was essentially the end of hostilities for Brazil because Japan had never operated in the South Atlantic while an Axis partner, and by mid-1945 had too many problems in the Pacific to bother with the area after Germany's collapse.

Below: 'B' class destroyer escort post-war. (A. D. Baker)

Canada

Canada, unlike its Dominion sister, Australia, appeared to consider naval matters of little importance despite her two long and separated coastlines. In 1914 the only vessels of any size were the ancient protected cruiser *Niobe* and the only slightly younger *Rainbow*, both transferred from Great Britain. During the First World War, Canada's war effort was predominantly military and the Navy suffered accordingly. By 1924 the only large ship, the cruiser *Aurora*, completed in 1914 and presented to Canada in 1920, was already hulked and useless. It was the era of American isolationism and there was a strong body of similar opinion in Canada. The first sign of an interest in naval defence was the transfer of two Thornycroft-built *S*-class destroyers in March 1928 followed by the first Canadian order for destroyers to the design of the British *A* class.

In total, 27 destroyers were transferred to or built for the RCN between 1928 and 1944, but the main contribution of the Canadians was in the Battle of the Atlantic where the RCN manned large numbers of corvettes, frigates and minesweepers. Their destroyers too were mainly employed on this task and, with the exception of the invasion of France in 1944, did not take part in many true destroyer operations.

Destroyer construction was undertaken in home yards towards the end of the war, but not to indigenous designs. Nevertheless the British-designed ships being built were considerably modified to Canadian ideas and standards, and this wartime shipbuilding activity laid the basis for the post-war Canadian ship design expertise.

TOWN CLASS

Ship	Builder	Laid Down	Launched	Commissioned USN	Commissioned RCN	Fate
I04 *Annapolis* (ex-*MacKenzie*)[1]	Union Iron Works	4 July 18	29 Sept 18	25 July 19	24 Sept 40	For disposal 21 June 45
I49 *Columbia* (ex-*Haraden*)[1]	Seattle D.D.	30 Mar 18	4 July 18	7 June 19	24 Sept 40	For disposal 7 Aug 45
I24 *Hamilton* (ex-*Kalk*)[1]	Fore River	17 Aug 18	21 Dec 18	29 Mar 19	6 June 41*	For disposal 2 Aug 45
I57 *Niagara* (ex-*Thatcher*)[1]	Fore River	8 June 18	31 Aug 18	14 Jan 19	24 Sept 40	For disposal 13 Jan 46
I65 *St. Clair* (ex-*Williams*)[1]	Union Iron Works	25 Mar 18	4 July 18	1 Mar 19	24 Sept 40	For disposal 5 Mar 46
I81 *St. Croix* (ex-*McCook*)[2]	Bethlehem, Quincy	11 Sept 18	31 Jan 19	30 April 19	24 Sept 40	Torpedoed 20 Sept 43
I93 *St. Francis* (ex-*Bancroft*)[2]	Bethlehem, Quincy	4 Nov 18	21 Mar 19	30 June 19	24 Sept 40	For disposal 2 Aug 45

*Originally commissioned for R.N. 23 Sept 40

For technical details see Great Britain:
(1) *Town* Class *Bath* group
(2) *Town* Class *Belmont* group

Design These ships formed part of the fifty old destroyers transferred from the USN in 1940 to Great Britain (q.v.).

Modifications Basically along the lines of the RN ships of this type. Radar was generally SW1C at the masthead in lieu of the British Type 286M.

Service Used, like their RN counterparts, on Atlantic escort duties, these ships were not highly regarded by the RCN, only *St. Croix* being regarded as an effective unit. *Columbia* avoided two torpedo attacks (by *U553* and *U522*) while escorting convoys, and *Niagara* was involved in the bringing in of the captured *U570*. *St. Croix* served successively with Escort Groups *C1*, *C2* and *C4* as well as the 9th Support Group, when she sank *U90* and assisted in the sinking of *U87*. As more and more Canadian-built escort vessels were completed, these old destroyers were relegated to the training role in Canadian waters. *Annapolis* was reduced to a training hulk in April 1944 and finally paid off on 4 June 1945 and *Columbia* ran aground suffering severe damage on 25 February 1944 being paid off on 17 March after which she was employed as a fuel and ammunition hulk at Liverpool, Nova Scotia. *Hamilton* was not originally intended for the RCN, but was badly damaged in collision with *Georgetown* shortly after transfer to the Royal Navy. After completion of repairs, she ran aground while undocking, suffering further damage, and was promptly reduced to care and maintenance with a Canadian skeleton crew. After re-commissioning in the RCN in 1941, she was eventually reduced to a training tender on 8 November 1943 and finally paid off on 8 June 1949. *Niagara* too was reduced to a torpedo training tender on 2 March 1944 and paid off on 15 September 1945. *St. Clair* became a submarine depot ship before being hulked as a training ship on 23 August 1944. She eventually sank in tow to the breakers on 6 October 1946. *St. Francis* was a training ship by 1944, paid off on 11 June 1945 and she too sank off Rhode Island en route for breaking up on 14 July 1945.

Below: *Annapolis* in September 1944. (PAC)

SAGUENAY CLASS

Ship	Builder	Laid Down	Launched	Commissioned	Fate
D79 *Saguenay*	Thornycroft	27 Sept 29	11 July 30	22 May 31	For disposal 30 June 45
D59 *Skeena*	Thornycroft	14 Oct 29	10 Oct 30	10 June 31	Lost 25 Oct 44
(D Pendant changed to I 1940)					

Displacement: 1,337tons/1,358tonnes (standard).
Length: 320ft/97.53m (oa); 309ft/94.18m (pp).
Beam: 32ft 6in/9.91m.
Draught: 10ft 6in/3.2m (mean).
Machinery: three Thornycroft boilers; 2-shaft Parsons geared turbines.
Performance: 32,000shp; 35kts.
Bunkerage: 380tons/386tonnes.
Range: 4,800nm at 15kts.
Guns: four 4.7in (4×1); two 2pdr (2×1).
Torpedoes: eight 21in.
Complement: 138.

Design The first new destroyers ordered by the RCN, these ships were modifications of the contemporary British *A* class (q.v.). Two earlier destroyers operated by the RCN were the *Champlain* and *Vancouver* (ex-*Torbay* and *Toreador* respectively) which had been transferred from Great Britain on 1 March 1928. These two were of First World War vintage having been completed in 1919, and were finally paid off at the end of November 1936 having been used to train crews for the new ships. These new destroyers introduced a number of new features, including the Mk IX 4.7-inch gun (30° Mounting) and quadruple torpedo tubes, as well as full-depth gun shields. Torpedoes were initially Mk IV, but were later replaced by the Mk IX version. Bearing in mind their intended theatre of operations, the hulls were strengthened for ice navigation, an ironic feature in view of their fates! Like their British counterparts, they were woefully weak in anti-aircraft defence, but were otherwise robust and well-armed vessels with good seagoing properties.

Modifications The after torpedo tubes were landed and replaced by a 3-inch AA gun. *Saguenay* landed 'X' gun and shipped a 12pdr in lieu. Single Oerlikon guns were added when available as was Type 286 radar. Guns were later reduced to two, 4.7in ('A' & 'X') and Oerlikons increased to six singles. Hedgehog and four dct with 141 depth-charges added.

Service At the beginning of the war, both ships escorted Halifax convoys and then spent the years 1940 to 1943 on Atlantic convoy duties as part of Escort Group C3, but *Saguenay* was torpedoed and damaged by the Italian submarine *Argo* while escorting Convoy HG47. By 1944, *Skeena* had been returned to offensive duties as part of the 12th Support Group operating in the English Channel, off the Normandy beaches and in the Brest area where she saw action against German light forces. Transferring to the 11th Support Group she then returned to Atlantic convoy duties until she was wrecked on Videy Island near Reykyavik. The wreck was sold to Arsaell Jonasson for scrap in June 1945. *Saguenay* was repaired and returned to convoy duties only to be heavily damaged in collision with SS *Azara* off Newfoundland on 15 December 1942. Much of the damage was caused by the explosion of her depth-charges, and after being brought back to port she was laid up, used only as a training ship, until paid off on 30 July 1945. Handed over to the War Assets Corporation on 18 April 1946, *Saguenay* was finally sold for scrapping on 17 July 1948.

Left: *Skeena* prior to 1939. (Real Photos)
Below: *Saguenay* as yet unaltered, in October 1940. (Public Archives, Canada)

FRASER CLASS

Ship	Builder	Laid Down	Launched	Commissioned	Fate
H48 *Fraser*	V.A. (Barrow)*	1 Dec 30	29 Aug 31	17 Feb 37	Lost 28 June 40
H83 *St. Laurent*	V.A. (Barrow)	1 Dec 30	29 Aug 31	17 Feb 37	For disposal 9 Nov 45
H00 *Restigouche*	Portsmouth Dkyd.	12 Sept 30	30 Aug 31	15 June 32	For disposal 9 Nov 45
H60 *Ottawa*	Portsmouth Dkyd.	12 Sept 30	30 Aug 31	6 April 38	Lost 14 Sept 42

*Completed at Chatham Dkyd.

Displacement: 1,375tons/1,397tonnes (standard); 1,865tons/1,895tonnes (full load).
Length: 329ft/100.28m (oa); 326ft/98.45m (wl); 317ft 9in/96.85m (pp).
Beam: 33ft/10.06m.
Draught: 12ft 6in/3.78m (mean).
Machinery: three Admiralty 3-drum boilers; 2-shaft Parson geared turbines.
Performance: 36,000shp; 36kts.
Bunkerage: 473tons/480tonnes.
Range: 5,500nm at 15kts.
Guns: four 4.7in (4×1); one 3in AA; two 2pdr (2×1); .5in MG.
Torpedoes: eight 21in (2×4).
Complement: 145.

Design Built originally for the Royal Navy as *Crescent* (commissioned 21 April 32), *Cygnet* (5 April 32), *Comet* (2 June 32) and *Crusader* (2 May 32) respectively, these ships were transferred to Canada because a four ship class did not fit into RN destroyer flotilla organization (the class having been reduced from the usual eight as a disarmament gesture by the current Labour government). The first pair were transferred on 17 February 1937 and the second pair on 15 June 1938. On completion, *Comet* (later *Restigouche*) reached 36.79 knots with 36,057shp on a displacement of 1,575 tons. The two built by the Royal dockyards were the first to be built by these yards and their inexperience led to delays in their construction. Hawthorn Leslie supplied the machinery of the two units. Director towers were introduced in this class and the bridge was 'split'. Like the *Saguenay* class, these destroyers were of the standard British fleet design and had no particularly outstanding merits but were perfectly adequate for their role.

Modifications Probably limited to the usual addition of Oerlikon guns and radar. 'A' and 'X' guns were removed to increase ASW outfits and by 1943 at least *Ottawa* had landed all torpedo tubes. *Fraser* landed the after TT and received a 4-inch gun in 1940.

Service Just prior to the outbreak of war, all the class were based on the Canadian west coast, but on 31 August 1939, they were transferred east via the Panama Canal to Halifax where they operated as escorts on the Halifax-Bermuda convoy routes until 24 May 1940 when ordered to the UK for Western Approaches Command. After taking part in the evacuation of France in June–July 1940, when *Fraser* was rammed and sunk in poor visibility by *Calcutta* in the Gironde estuary with the loss of 66 men, Atlantic convoy duties followed for the survivors. Operating from Halifax, Greenock and Londonderry as part of the 10th, C1 and C4 Escort Groups from 1940 until 1944, during which period *St. Laurent* assisted in the sinking of *U356* and *U845*. However, *Ottawa* was torpedoed and sunk by *U91* in the Gulf of St. Lawrence on 14 September 1942, while escorting convoy ON127. *Restigouche* took part in operations off the west coast of France in July and August 1944 as part of the 12th Support Group when several German minesweepers and coastal craft were sunk. Both surviving ships were declared for disposal on 9 November 1945, having been paid off on 6 (*Restigouche*) and 10 October 1945.

KEMPENFELT CLASS

Ship	Builder	Laid Down	Launched	Commissioned	Fate
D18 *Assiniboine*	S. White (Cowes)	1 Oct 30	29 Oct 31	30 May 32 (RN) 18 Oct 39 (RCN)	Lost 10 Nov 45

(Later I18)

Displacement: 1,390tons/1,412tonnes (standard); 1,901tons/1,931tonnes (full load).
Length: 329ft/100.28m (oa); 326ft/99.36m (wl); 317ft 9in/96.85m (pp).
Beam: 33ft/10.06m.
Draught: 12ft 6in/3.78m (mean).
Machinery: three Yarrow boilers; 2-shaft Parsons geared turbines.
Performance: 36,000shp; 36kts.
Bunkerage: 473tons/480tonnes.
Range: 5,500nm at 15kts.
Guns: four 4.7in (4×1); one 3in AA; two 2pdr; .5in MG.
Torpedoes: eight 21in (2×4).
Complement: 175.

Design The *C*-class leader followed the design of her destroyers as far as armament and dimensions were concerned, but displaced a little more at 1,390 tons (standard). She was fitted with Yarrow boilers and achieved 36.39 knots on 1,516 tons displacement during 6-hour full-power trials.

Modifications After completion, a prototype 5.1-inch gun on a single mounting CP XIV was shipped on No. 2 position for sea trials, but as these were not successful it was removed. No further modifications were made until the war. In July 1941, two single Oerlikons were added and one set of torpedo tubes had been landed. Radar 286 was fitted at the masthead. Later her radar outfit included Types 271Q and 291 plus HF/DF. 'Y' gun was landed and Oerlikons increased to six. Only two torpedoes were now carried and two Mk 10 depth-charges. The remainder of the A/S outfit consisted of four Mk IV dct and a split Mk II hedgehog with 132 depth-charges.

Service *Assiniboine* spent the first seven years of her service in the Royal Navy and had been built as the flotilla leader for the *C*-class destroyers which were subsequently transferred to Canada. During her Royal Navy service, she took part in patrols off Spain during the Civil War and, in company with *Boreas*, rescued some 400 men following the loss of the Spanish heavy cruiser *Baleareas* in March 1938. On the outbreak of war in 1939, *Kempenfelt* was transferred to the RCN and re-named *Assiniboine* assisting, with the cruiser *Dunedin*, in the capture of the German blockade-runner *Hannover* off San Domingo in the West Indies, during February 1940. This was an important seizure, not particularly in the capture of the cargo but more for the ship herself. She was to become the first of the escort carriers and provided an incalculable boost to ocean convoy defences. *Assiniboine* then participated in Atlantic escort duties and by mid-1941, had been fitted with two Oerlikon guns, MF/DF, Type 286 radar and increased depth-charge stowage. On 6 August 1942, while escorting convoy SC94, *Assiniboine* rammed and sank *U210* after a gun duel, but was seriously damaged in doing so. After repairs, she returned to convoy duty but collided with another U-boat on 2 March 1943. As she was still in dockyard hands, repairing the damage on 30 June 1943, it was decided to convert her to an escort-destroyer. In 1944, she formed part of the RCN's contribution to the Operation 'Overlord' naval forces. Off the coast of Brittany, in company with her Canadian sisters, she took part in several sweeps and engagements with German surface forces in the autumn of 1944. Returning to home waters at the end of the war, she was paid off on 8 August 1945 but was wrecked on Prince Edward Island, 10 November 1945. The hull was sold for scrapping to Guard Salvage Co. (Halifax) on 17 July 1952.

Left: *Fraser* as completed. (Public Archives, Canada)

Below left: *Ottawa*, September 1940, with only rifle-calibre AA guns added. (Public Archives, Canada)

Right: *Assiniboine* in March 1942 with early war alterations. A 12pdr has replaced the after tubes, splinter matting added to the bridge and radar 286 fitted. (Public Archives, Canada)

TRIBAL CLASS

Ship	Builder	Laid Down	Launched	Commissioned	Fate
G07 *Athabaskan* (i) (ex-*Iroquois*)	V.A. (Tyne)		18 Nov 41	3 Feb 43	Lost 29 April 44
R79 *Athabaskan* (ii)*	Halifax Shp. Yd.	15 May 44	4 May 46	20 Feb 48	Broken up 1969
R04 *Cayuga**	Halifax Shp. Yd.	7 Oct 43	28 July 45	20 Oct 47	Sold out 1964
G63 *Haida*	V.A. (Tyne)	29 Sept 41	25 Aug 42	18 Sept 43	Museum Ship 1964
G24 *Huron*	V.A. (Tyne)	15 July 41	25 June 42	28 July 43	Broken up 1965
G89 *Iroquois* (ex-*Athabaskan*)	V.A. (Tyne)	9 Sept 40	23 Sept 41	10 Dec 42	Broken up 1966
R10 *Micmac**	Halifax Shp. Yd.	20 May 42	18 Sept 43	14 Sept 45	Sold out 1964
R96 *Nootka**	Halifax Shp. Yd.	20 May 42	26 April 44	9 Aug 46	Sold out 1964

Displacement: 1,927tons/1,958tonnes (standard); 2,519tons/2,559tonnes (full load).
Length: 377ft/114.9m (oa); 364ft 8in/111.1m (wl); 355ft 6in/108.35m (pp).
Beam: 36ft 6in/11.13m.
Draught: 13ft/3.96m (mean).
Machinery: three Admiralty 3-drum boilers; 2-shaft Parsons geared turbines.
Performance: 44,000shp; 36.25kts.
Bunkerage: 505tons/513tonnes.
Range: 5,700nm at 17kts.
Guns: six 4.7in (3×2); two 4in (1×2); four 2pdr (1×4); six 20mm except * eight 4in (4×2); four 40mm; 4 20mm.
Torpedoes: four 21in (1×4).
Complement: 240.

Design After a good deal of discussion and consideration, Canada decided to order destroyers to the British *Tribal* design in 1940, but unlike the Australians, eventually placed orders with Vickers-Armstrong and not with Canadian yards. The reasons for this were basically the shortage of skilled workers in the Canadian yards and the difficulty of obtaining British assistance under wartime conditions. The order for the first pair was placed early in 1940 and that for the second pair later the same year. As they were not laid down until late 1940 at the earliest, all of the modifications made to British *Tribals* in the light of costly war experiences could be incorporated in the Canadian ships. These involved the suppression of 'X' 4.7-inch mounting and its replacement by a twin 4-inch AA, substitution of .5in MG by 20mm guns and the reduced height of the after funnel. In addition, the positions of the searchlight and 2pdr pom-pom were reversed allowing the latter a much improved field of fire. *Iroquois* was the first to complete with *Athabaskan* (i) following two months later. Their radar outfit comprised Type 285 on the range-finder, with 291 and 242 on the foremast. *Athabaskan* reportedly completed with ten 20mm, having twins in the bridge wings and on the after shelter deck. The second pair, *Haida* and *Huron*, completed with all 20mm twins in power-operated mountings. A combined rangefinder/director tower replaced the two separate stands. In June 1941, two more units were ordered in Canada from the Halifax shipyard with machinery being supplied from J. Inglis & Co. Ltd. A final pair was ordered from the same yard in 1943. None of these four completed in time to see active service during the Second World War.

Service *Iroquois* and *Athabaskan* began their operational careers with offensive patrols into the Bay of Biscay, operating down to the Straits of Gibraltar in June 1943. At this time, much effort was being expended in trying to prevent U-boats from breaking out into the Atlantic by means of stationing destroyers and sloops in the Bay across their exit routes. It was dangerous work because the Luftwaffe was far from idle and, in fact, on 28 June 1943, Hs293 glider bombs, air-launched from Do 217 bombers, were used against the 1st Support Group of which *Athabaskan* formed part. She was hit and badly damaged while the sloop *Egret* was sunk. Repaired, *Athabaskan* joined her sisters once more and by December 1943 was engaged upon Russian convoy duties, but with the imminent launch of Operation 'Overlord' they were once more moved south, to the English Channel, where their task was to eliminate the few remaining Kriegsmarine destroyers and torpedo-boats. On 25 April, *Haida* and *Huron* accompanied by *Black Panther* and *Athabaskan*, engaged three torpedo-boats (*T29, T24* and *T27*) north-west of Les Sept Iles, sinking *T29* and damaging the other two. A few days later on the 27th, *T24* and *T27* were again engaged, this time by *Haida* and *Athabaskan*. After a hot action, *Athabaskan* was torpedoed by *T24*, exploding the forward magazines and sinking the ship. *Haida* then drove *T27* ashore. In the course of 'Overlord' the Canadian *Tribals* were allocated to the 10th Destroyer Flotilla with orders to cover the western entrance to the English Channel. Here on 9 June, in company with British and Polish destroyers, *Haida* and *Huron* fought an action with the German 8th Destroyer Flotilla during which, the German *ZH1* and *Z32* were sunk at the cost of some damage to one British destroyer. Later, on 24 June, *Haida* and *Eskimo* sank *U971* and then fought a series of actions against minesweepers, patrol vessels and escorts throughout the summer of 1944, usually assisted by a British light cruiser. 1945 saw the Canadian *Tribals* back on Arctic convoy duty before *Iroquois* moved to Copenhagen at the German surrender, while her two sisters took part in the liberation of Norway.

Huron, Haida and *Iroquois* arrived back in Canadian waters on 10 June 1945, to begin refits for operation in the Pacific against Japan, but the war in the Far East was over before completion of the refit. The outbreak of war in Korea in June 1950 saw *Athabaskan, Cayuga* and *Sioux* in action with the UN forces, the first named steamed 60,000 miles by the time of her return to Canada in the summer of 1951.

The appearance of the three surviving Group I ships had not altered greatly by the end of the war except for the fitting of a tall lattice mast, with which the Group II ships were so completed. The final four to complete, *Athabaskan* (ii), *Cayuga, Micmac* and *Nootka*, shipped a uniform HA armament of four twin 4-inch AA augmented by a twin 40mm in lieu of the pom-pom and two singles between the funnels. Two twin power-operated 20mm were carried in the bridge wings. Fire control was provided by a single Mk VI director with parabolic radar dishes Type 275.

Light AA outfits varied somewhat during the immediate post-war period, but in 1953–54 all except *Athabaskan* and *Nootka* were modernized and uniform armament was fitted. The latter two units were refitted in 1954–55. All were now equipped with four 4-inch (2×2), two 3-inch (1×2) and four 40mm. The after deck-house was extended to form a squid handling room and the mortars (2) were fitted on the quarter deck. A squat lattice mast with increased and updated radar, together with funnel caps, completed the change of appearance. Rated now as Destroyer Escorts (DDE), they continued running until the early 1960s by which time they were hopelessly out-dated, some being almost twenty years old. The elder sister, *Iroquois*, was in fact paid off to reserve on 24 October 1962, followed by *Huron* on 30 April 1963 and *Haida* on 11 October 1963, all three being declared for disposal in 1964. In 1964, *Nootka* paid off on 6 February, *Cayuga* on 27 February (she had been extensively damaged by fire at Halifax S.Y. 14 March 1961) and *Micmac* on 31 March, leaving only *Athabaskan* (which had had a further refit in 1958) still in service). In 1964, *Cayuga, Micmac* and *Nootka* were sold to Marine Salvage Inc. of Port Colbourne, Ontario and subsequently resold to Shipbreaking Industries Ltd. (Faslane), the former two arriving in the UK on 14 October 1964 and the third on 6 October 1964. *Haida* was sold to 'HAIDA Inc' for use as a museum and handed over at Sorrel on 21 August 1964 arriving in Toronto on 24 August. *Huron* arrived in La Spezia for breaking up on 20 August 1965 and *Iroquois* at Bilbao in September 1966. *Athabascan* was paid off on 21 April 1966.

Above: *Huron*, also in 1944, armed as *Haida*, but note absence of searchlight. (Public Archives, Canada)
Below: *Haida* in the summer of 1944. She has six twin 20mm, radars 271 and 291, with HF/DF at the mainmast truck. (Public Archives, Canada)

Below: *Nootka* in September 1948. She has 40mm Bofors on a new platform aft. (Public Archives, Canada)

Below: *Sioux* on 17 December 1945. She has single boffin 40mm guns aft of the funnel and 20mm twin in the bridge wings. (Public Archives, Canada)

War-Time Transfers All these destroyers were transferred to the RCN by Great Britain, with the exception of the old 'flush deckers' received from the USA.

Margaree (ex-*Diana*) Transferred to RCN 6 September 1940 to replace *Fraser*. She was sunk in collision with SS *Port Fairy* in the North Atlantic on 22 October 1940 when 142 of her crew were lost.

Kootenay (ex-*Decoy*) Transferred to the RCN on 12 April 1943. Operated with Escort Group C5 and the 11th Escort Group in the North Atlantic, moving to the English Channel and western France in 1944. Sank *U678* in the Channel with *Ottawa* and *Statice* on 6 July, *U621* (with *Chaudière* and *Ottawa*) near La Rochelle on 18 August 1944 and later *U984* west of Brest with the same ships. On 28 January 1946 she was sold for scrapping at Sydney, NS.

Gatineau (ex-*Express*) Transferred to the RCN on 3 June 1943, operating with Escort Group C2, assisting in the sinking of *U744* on 6 March 1944. Later she served with the 11th Escort Group. Sold to D. Mainwaring in 1956 and hull used as a breakwater in Oyster Bay, Puget Sound.

Saskatchewan (ex-*Fortune*) Transferred to the RCN on 31 May 1943, serving on North Atlantic convoys with the 11th, 12th and C3 Escort Groups until invasion duties in June 1944. Finished the war on Atlantic convoys. Paid off for disposal on 28 January 1946.

Ottawa (ii) (ex-*Griffin*) Transferred to the RCN on 22 March 1943. Leader, Escort Group C5 then served with the 11th Escort Group. In company with *Kootenay* and *Statice* sank *U678* off Beachy Head on 6 July 1944 and later assisted in sinking *U621* and *U984* (see *Kootenay*). For disposal at Sydney NS 28 January 1944.

Chaudière (ex-*Hero*) Transferred to the RCN on 15 November 1943. In company with *Gatineau* at the sinking of *U744* and also assisted the sinking of *U621* and *U984*.

Qu'Appelle (ex-*Foxhound*) Transferred to the RCN on 8 February 1944, serving with the 12th and 11th Escort Groups. Sold out post-war and scrapped by German & Milive Inc. in 1948.

Sioux (ex-*Vixen*) Transferred to the RCN on 5 May 1944. Limited conversion to A/S frigate in 1950 by removal of after torpedo tubes and after 4.7-inch guns. After deck-house extended to accommodate two 'squid' depth-bomb mortars. A distinctive funnel cap was also added. Paid off into operational reserve 30 October 1963. Sailed in tow for scrapping at La Spezia. Arrived 20 August 1963.

Algonquin (ex-*Valentine*) Transferred to RCN on 28 February 1944, on completion. Fully converted to Type 15 A/S frigate by Esquimalt Dockyard in 1954. Re-armed with two 4-inch aft (twin mounting) and a US-pattern twin 3-inch mounting forward. Two 40mm were retained and two squid added. Sold to Jacques Pierot and left Victoria for Taiwanese shipbreakers on 21 April 1971.

Chile

Like several of her Latin-American neighbours, Chile possessed an extremely long coastline to defend and one which stretched from the tropics to the Antarctic. Her naval forces had been in action as early as 1879 when the war with Peru began, which lasted until 1882. In this war the Chilean Navy was instrumental in achieving victory and it was also extremely active during the Civil War of 1891 when some of the first torpedo successes were achieved as recounted in the Introduction. Towards the turn of the century, the Chilean Navy comprised in the main a number of cruisers of Elswick design and a couple of torpedo gunboats not dissimilar to those of the Royal Navy. Torpedo-craft included about ten old Yarrow-type boats and seven British-built destroyers of the '30 knotter' type, but in 1912 Chile had ordered a class of six big destroyers from J. S. White. These were a major advance upon existing Chilean destroyers and were much more powerful even than contemporary British destroyers. Only two had been delivered by August 1914 and the remainder were purchased for the Royal Navy. Between the wars there were no additions to the fleet until the purchase of the *Serrano*-class destroyers in the 1920s. Chile remained neutral during the Second World War and her fleet remained unchanged as far as destroyers were concerned until well after the war.

ALMIRANTE LYNCH CLASS

Ship	Builder	Laid Down	Launched	Commissioned	Fate
L *Almirante Lynch*	S. White (Cowes)	9 Nov 11	28 Sept 12	1913	Stricken 19 Dec 45
C *Almirante Condell*	S. White (Cowes)	11 Dec 11	27 Jan 13	Jan 1914	Stricken 19 Dec 45

Displacement: 1,430tons/1,453tonnes (standard); 1,850tons/1,880tonnes (full load).
Length: 330ft 10in/100.8m (oa); 320ft/97.5m (pp).
Beam: 32ft 6in/9.9m.
Draught: 11ft/3.35m (mean).
Machinery: six White-Foster boilers; 3-shaft Parsons direct drive turbines.
Performance: 30,000shp; 31kts.
Bunkerage: 433tons/440tonnes (coal); 83 tons/ 84tonnes (oil).
Range: 4,205nm at 15kts.
Guns: six 4in (6×1); four MG.
Torpedoes: six 21in (3×2).
Complement: 160.

Design and Service These two venerable ships were the survivors of a class of six powerful destroyers ordered from Samuel White in 1911. Four were caught incomplete in the yard in August 1914, (*Almirante Williams Rebolero, Almirante Goni, Almirante Simpson* and *Almirante Riveros*) and later commissioned into the Royal Navy after having been purchased by Great Britain. Although three of these did survive the First World War, and were re-purchased by Chile in May 1920, strenuous war service had taken its toll, with the result that by the late 1930s they were worn out; they were broken up from 1933 to 1937. At the time of their laying down, these destroyers represented a considerable advance on what was being constructed for the Royal Navy and were the largest of their type in the world. Their armament was twice as heavy as that of the contemporary British *L* class and habitability was much superior as the extremes of climate along the Chilean coast necessitated catering for both tropical and antarctic conditions. Both ships sailed from Southampton on 7 February 1914 bound for Chile and arrived at Valparaiso on 22 April. Chile remained neutral throughout the Second World War and the ships had no opportunity to see action, but both were kept on hand until the war's end. *Almirante Condell*, however, suffered a serious boiler explosion on 26 October 1944 and was paid off. Both were stricken in 1945, but *Condell* lasted until 1955 used as a pontoon, before being broken up.

Above: *Lynch.* (Chilean Navy)

Left: *Condell.* (Chilean Navy)

Top right: *Aldea.* (Chilean Navy)

Right: *Vidella*, post-war with 20mm guns and radar. (Chilean Navy)

SERRANO CLASS

Ship	Builder	Laid Down	Launched	Commissioned	Fate
A *Aldea*	J. Thornycroft (Southampton)	8 Mar 28	24 Nov 28	26 July 29	Stricken 12 Feb 58
H *Hyatt*	J. Thornycroft (Southampton)	23 Sept 27	21 July 28	15 April 29	Stricken 30 Jan 63
O *Orella*	J. Thornycroft (Southampton)	21 June 27	8 Mar 28	18 Dec 28	Stricken 29 Sept 66
R *Riquelme*	J. Thornycroft (Southampton)	18 July 27	21 May 28	15 April 29	Stricken 30 Jan 63
S *Serrano*	J. Thornycroft (Southampton)	21 June 27	25 Jan 28	18 Dec 28	Stricken 29 Sept 66
V *Videla*	J. Thornycroft (Southampton)	25 Jan 28	16 Oct 28	26 July 29	Stricken 12 Feb 58

Displacement: 1,090tons/1,107tonnes (standard); 1,430tons/1,452tonnes (full load).
Length: 300ft/91.44m (oa); 288ft 3in/87.86m (pp).
Beam: 29ft/8.84m.
Draught: 12ft 9in/3.86m (mean).
Machinery: three Thornycroft boilers; 2-shaft Parsons geared turbines.
Performance: 28,000shp; 35kts.
Bunkerage: 320tons/325tonnes.
Guns: three 4.7in (3×1); one 3in AA; three MG.
Torpedoes: six 21in (2×3).
Complement: 130.

Design Thornycroft secured the contract to build six new destroyers for the Chilean Navy against fierce international competition, but there was no doubt that British destroyer designs were extremely well regarded during the inter-war period. The design adopted the standard layout of British destroyers of the period both internally and externally, on dimensions rather less than those of their British contemporaries. One notable feature was the relatively low power of the installed machinery, being only 28,000shp, i.e., similar to that of the First World War *V & W* design, whereas *Acheron*, laid down at Thornycroft in October 1928 shipped 34,000shp machinery. Nevertheless, these destroyers all exceeded their contract speed by 1 to 1½ knots. Sensibly, and with operations south of Cape Horn in mind, no doubt, the Chileans did not overgun their ships and only specified three 4.7in guns, mounted in half height shields which were retained to the end of their careers. The absence of the quarter-deck gun allowed three ships (*Serrano, Orella* and *Hyatt*) to be equipped for minelaying, while the remainder were fitted for minesweeping. In service, their light construction proved inadequate for operations off the southern coast of Chile and in consequence, the older *Lynch* and *Condell* had to be used to screen the battleships when they operated in this region.

Modifications For the first 25 years (!) or so of their careers, little outward change was made in the appearance of the ships with the exception of the removal of the mainmast and the addition of two single 20mm guns, but in the mid 1950s, four, *Hyatt, Orella, Riquelme* and *Serrano*, were taken in hand for conversion to destroyer escorts. When *Orella* recomissioned in 1956, however, the only evidence of this refit was the fitting of modern pattern US radar at the truck of the new tripod foremast. Internally, bunkerage was increased and sonar installed, while the light AA outfit was increased to four single 20mm guns.

Service These ships had long if peaceful careers in the Chilean fleet. *Aldea* and *Videla* were both paid off on 21 June 1957, *Hyatt* and *Riquelme* on 31 August 1962 and the other pair on 18 December 1962.

Colombia

A relatively poor South American republic with a large hinterland but only a small coastline, split between the Pacific Ocean and the Caribbean Sea, Colombia had never maintained much of a naval force. Her neighbours, Equador to the south and Venezuela to the east, also had negligible navies, and thus presented little threat at sea. Strangely, it took a quarrel with Peru over boundaries in the interior, to the east of the Andes, before Colombia expanded her navy beyond a handful of elderly gunboats, in the early 1930s.

At the turn of the century, Colombia possessed only a couple of armed yachts and a small gunboat originally built in Italy for Morocco. Armed with two 4.7in guns and four 4in, she was typical of the period and could steam at 16 knots. After the First World War, some further acquisitions were made including a former German minesweeper and four LM-type motor boats, these latter vessels being the country's first experience with torpedo craft. In the mid-1920s, a small construction programme was begun when three coastguard vessels were ordered in France. Some five years later, three river gunboats were contracted to British yards for use on the upper reaches of the river border with Equador and Peru. The purchase of the two large, modern destroyers from Portugal therefore represented a huge step for the tiny navy; it is doubtful if they could have been made fully operational by the Colombians without considerable assistance from the vendors.

ANTIOQUIA CLASS

Ship	Builder	Laid Down	Launched	Commissioned	Fate
Antioquia	Yarrow		10 May 33	24 Feb 34	Discarded 1961
Caldas	Yarrow		18 Nov 33	16 May 34	Discarded 1961

Displacement: 1,219tons/1,238tonnes (standard); 1,563tons/1,588tonnes (full load).
Length: 323ft/98.45m (oa); 307ft/93.6m (pp).
Beam: 31ft/9.44m.
Draught: 8ft 11in/2.74m (mean).
Machinery: three Yarrow boilers; 2-shaft Curtis/Parsons geared turbines.
Performance: 33,000shp; 36kts.
Bunkerage: 292tons/297tonnes.
Range: 5,400nm at 15kts.
Guns: four 4.7in (4×1); three 40mm.
Torpedoes: eight 21in (2×4).
Mines: 20.
Complement: 147.

Design These two ships were originally ordered by Portugal on 12 June 1931, as *Tejo* and *Douro* respectively (not the other way round as is commonly quoted). However, as a result of political tensions with Peru, Colombia found herself without any real navy to defend her long coastlines in the Caribbean and Pacific, and turned to Portugal for assistance. The result was the purchase of these two destroyers before their completion to counter the two former Estonian units obtained by Peru in 1933. In fact, the dispute was short-lived and neither fleet had any opportunity for action, perhaps fortunately, for both sides in view of their unfamiliarity with these foreign-bought ships.

Modifications Both destroyers remained in service for many years with little change in their appearance. Two single 20mm guns were added amidships during or just after the Second World War. *Antioquia* was re-fitted and modernized at Cartagena in 1952 and the following year went to the USA for re-arming. She emerged from this refit with only two main guns, in 'A' and 'Y' positions, now single, fully automatic US pattern 5-inch with Mk 52 fire control. Light armament was increased to six 40mm guns and a 'hedgehog' was fitted. *Caldas* underwent a similar refit 1945–55.

Service Colombia being neutral during the war and having only a tiny navy, these two ships saw no real action during hostilities, but some patrol work was undertaken in local waters where, on 29/30 March 1944, *Caldas* took part in sweeps for *U154* which was then attacking shipping in the Caribbean. They served into the early 1960s, being discarded in 1960. Both were ordered to be stripped for sale on 25 October 1960, then sold for scrapping to International Technical Services of Barranquilla. *Caldas* was broken up at Cartagena in 1961 and her sister arrived at Barranquilla in November of that year.

Below: *Antioquia*, with 20mm and 2pdr guns. (A. D. Baker)

Denmark

Denmark, like Norway, had paid little attention to naval defence between the wars, having remained neutral during the First World War. Even the possession of overseas territories such as Greenland and the Faroes, distant as they were, did not motivate the Danes to provide for their defence, apart from a few fishery protection vessels. A small amount of new construction was put in hand between the wars, including a Coast Defence ship (*Niels-Juel*), six torpedo-boats and a like number of submarines of which only the four *H*-class submarines were of equivalent fighting power to foreign contemporaries. Two small destroyers were the final new construction ordered prior to the outbreak of war.

Denmark's armed forces offered no resistance to the German invasion force in April 1940 and in consequence, suffered no losses. From 1940 to 1943, various ships were requisitioned by Germany, but the major event was the scuttling of the Fleet in August 1943 as the Germans attempted to seize it.

DRAGEN CLASS

Ship	Builder	Laid Down	Launched	Commissioned	Fate
T1 *Dragen*	Copenhagen N Yd.		8 Nov 29	July 1930	Lost 14 May 45
T2 *Hvalen*	Copenhagen N Yd.		13 June 30	July 1931	C.T.L. 14 June 45
T3 *Laxen*	Copenhagen N Yd.		28 Nov 30	July 1931	C.T.L. 14 June 45
T4 *Glenten*	Copenhagen N Yd.		6 Jan 33	July 1934	C.T.L. 14 June 45
T5 *Högen*	Copenhagen N Yd.		20 Oct 33	July 1935	C.T.L. 14 June 45
T6 *Ornen*	Copenhagen N Yd.		19 Oct 34	July 1935	C.T.L. 14 June 45

Above: *Glenten*. (RDN) **Below:** *Dragen*. (RDN)

Displacement: 290tons/294tonnes (standard); 335tons/340tonnes (full load).
Length: 200ft 2in/61m (oa).
Beam: 19ft 8in/6m.
Draught: 7ft 6in/2.3m (mean).
Machinery: two Thornycroft boilers; 2-shaft Atlas geared turbines (*Dragen* and *Hvalen* Brown-Boveri).
Performance: 6,000shp; 27.5kts.
Bunkerage: 40tons/40.6tonnes.
Guns: two 3in (75mm) in first three, two 3.4in (87mm) in rest; two 20mm.
Torpedoes: eight 18in (2×1, 2×3).
Complement: 51.

Design Built in two groups of three, which differed only in their main armament, these torpedo-boats carried a heavy torpedo battery for their size, disposed in unusual fashion, having two single tubes in the forecastle as well as two triple banks abaft the funnels. By comparison with foreign torpedo-craft they were slow but no doubt had their uses in the island-studded Danish coastal area.

Modifications In German hands, they were disarmed except for a single 20mm, and fitted for torpedo recovery duties.

Service Captured intact and immobilized after the German invasion in April 1940, all six ships were leased to the Kriegsmarine in a disarmed condition on 5 February 1941. There after they were employed as torpedo recovery vessels and target ships for the 26th U-Boat Flotilla, a training formation based in the eastern Baltic. In 1942 they were renamed *TFA3, 5, 6, 1, 4* and *2* respectively. *TFA3* was mined and sunk in Geltinger Bay at the end of the war, but the others survived only to be irreparably damaged by the blowing up of the depot ship *Donau* alongside which they were berthed. *TFA4* (*Glenten*), foundered in July, but the remainder were broken up from 1949 to 1952.

NAJADEN CLASS

Ship	Builder	Laid Down	Launched	Commissioned	Fate
Najaden	Copenhagen N Yd.	3 July 42	17 Mar 43	30 June 47	Sold for breaking up 27 May 66
Nymfen	Copenhagen N Yd.	3 July 42	22 June 43	31 July 47	Sold for breaking up 27 May 66

Displacement: 782tons/794tonnes (standard); 892tons/906tonnes (full load).
Length: 283ft/86.2m (oa); 279ft/85m (pp).
Beam: 27ft 4in/8.32m.
Draught: 11ft 6in/3.5m (mean).
Machinery: 2-shaft Atlas geared turbines.
Performance: 24,000shp; 35kts.
Bunkerage: 100tons/101tonnes.
Guns: two 4.1in (2×1); two 40mm (2×1); six 20mm.
Torpedoes: six 18in (2×3).
Mines: 60.
Complement: 92.

Below: *Willemoes* (ex-*Najaden*)

Design The first modern torpedo-craft to be built for the Royal Danish Navy, these were small destroyers or torpedo-boats, rather larger and better armed than their Scandinavian cousins of the *Sleipner* class under construction in Norway. Although the orders were placed in 1939, the German invasion in 1940 delayed their laying down until 1942. They were handsome, flush-decked ships, well armed for their size. One gun was carried on the forecastle and one aft, with the 40mm guns superfiring on them. As completed, the 20mm guns were carried two on the forecastle and two between the tubes. Construction proceeded only slowly during the war years and they were not completed until long after hostilities ceased. Before completion *Najaden* was renamed *Willemoes* and *Nymfen*, *Huitfeld*.

Modifications They were completed with 21-inch torpedo tubes in lieu of the 18-inch planned. Two 20mm between the tubes were replaced by a third 40mm in the 1950s and later all 20mm guns were landed.

Service Not completed until after 1945, both ships had long peacetime careers, being re-classified as Coastal Destroyers in 1951 and Patrol Vessels in 1958.

France

The French destroyer force in 1919 comprised a motley collection of over-aged French-built ships, ceeded German and Austrian ships and twelve relatively new Japanese-built destroyers. Having been in the forefront of torpedo-boat design during its formative years, war and politics had, by the close of the First World War, reduced the French fleet to a pitiful state.

At one stage, an offer by the British yard, Thornycroft, to complete two of their launched but uncompleted *W*-class hulls for the French Navy was seriously debated. These were some of the many *W*-class destroyers cancelled by the Royal Navy in 1918 and in all probability, the vessels were *Wishart* and *Witch*, both later completed for the Royal Navy. In the final event, the French had no finance available for the project.

After much cajolery, the French eventually managed to obtain a number of ex-German and Austrian warships with which to begin the rebuilding of their post-war fleet. These consisted of the large destroyer *S133* placed in service in May 1922 as *Amiral Sénès*, which displaced 1,525 tons (standard), armed with five 6inch (150mm) guns and four (600mm) torpedo tubes, as well as *Buino* (ex-*V130*), *Vesco* (ex-*S134*), *Deligny* (ex-*S139*), *Delage* (ex-*H147*), *Chastang* (ex-*S133*), *Mazaré* (ex-*S135*), *Rageot De La Touche* (ex-*H146*) and *Pierre Durand* (ex-*V79*). With the exception of *V79*, which had been completed in July 1916, these boats represented the final German destroyers to be put into production and in fact *H147* did not complete under the Kaiserlischesmarine ensign. The French Navy was considerably impressed by many of the qualities found in these ex-German vessels, in particular, their reliable machinery, excellent gunnery outfit and good fire-control equipment. In general, their seakeeping properties were also admired, even the heavily loaded *Amiral Sénès*, with the exception of the low freeboard common to most German destroyers. However, habitability was not up to French standards and, in the later war-built ships, the shortage of copper and brass resulted in the use of steel for much of the sea-water piping systems which led to early corrosion problems in service. Nevertheless, the French crews were pleased with the ships; they had not been used to single gun calibre armaments with robust and efficient breech mechanisms for instance, and these destroyers gave good service for many years.

Considerable discussion now took place as to the desirable composition of the post-war fleet, in particular, the requirements of destroyer designs. Three main roles were identified, i.e.: (i) reconnaissance, (ii) fleet screening and (iii) offensive duty against the enemy line. These tasks all required speed, endurance and good armament, and for the first two tasks implied a speed and armament in excess of the likely enemy destroyer, which in turn required a larger tonnage than an ordinary destroyer. For the third task, it was envisaged that torpedo attacks would be launched from longer range (particularly during daylight) at which the percentage of hits would be small. In consequence, a large torpedo broadside was believed necessary in order to achieve success. Unlike the Japanese, the French discarded the idea of reloading as being impracticable on such a small vessel in a sea-way and opted instead for a larger number of tubes. For night work, it was reasoned that ramming would be a distinct possibility in a confused mêlée, hence hull strength was of great importance. Finally, torpedo attack would in all probability be required at short notice and therefore it was important to be able to raise steam quickly. These ideas led to two distinct types of torpedo-craft, the *contre-torpilleur* and the *torpilleur* of 2,400 tonnes and 1,500 tonnes respectively.

Left: The French destroyer *Guépard* in November 1931. (M. Bar)

As early as April 1920, the Ministry of Marine had decided to order two *contre-torpilleurs* of a displacement between the two figures given above, armed with five 3.9-inch (100mm) guns, two forward and aft superfiring with the fifth gun between the funnels. This vessel was to be powered by twin shaft single reduction geared turbines with 42,500shp (max), with a speed of 32 knots on a displacement of 1,780 tonnes. There was, however, a good deal of opposition to this project, particularly from *Conseil Supérieur de la Marine*, it being pointed out that this gun calibre had long been superseded by foreign navies, notably the Italians who had gone over to 120mm (4.7-inch). Construction of these two units was grudgingly agreed, but only on condition that no more than these two ships were to be so armed. Future construction was to be designed for a new calibre then under development. This was the 5.1-inch (130mm) Model 1919 which would equip the ships built under the 1922 programme.

In fact, the French Parliament refused to vote the necessary funds for these two *contre-torpilleurs* and the idea of their construction was therefore abandoned. The first torpedo-craft to be built for the post-war French Navy were therefore the *contre-torpilleurs* of the *Jaguar* class and the *torpilleurs* of the *Simoun* class authorized under the 1922 programme.

French flotilla craft generally operated in divisions of three, and most classes were therefore of multiples of this number. The fortunes of war did not favour the *Marine Militaire*, however; having built up a respectable modern fleet by 1939, unlike the position in 1914, the fall of France in 1940 led to the division of that fleet into two parts. The smaller component operated under the Free French Colours with the Royal Navy, while the bulk of the fleet remained either in Metropolitan France (Toulon) or in the French African colonies such as at Oran and Dakar. These ships served Vichy France. The fear that this latter powerful fleet might fall into the hands of the Germans, led to British operations against those units based at Oran and Dakar in July 1940, to the lasting detriment of Anglo-French relations. Four *contre-torpilleurs* (*Bison*,

Chacal, Jaguar and *Maillé Brézé*) as well as seven *torpilleurs* (*Bourrasque, Cyclone, Orage, Sirocco, L'Adroit, Foudroyant* and *La Railleuse*) had already been lost fighting alongside the Royal Navy prior to the French collapse. Then the invasion in May 1940 severely disrupted the completion programme of the *Le Hardi* class, while the Dakar operation resulted in severe damage to *L'Audacieux*. *Chevalier Paul* was another loss at the hands of the British, this time off Syria. The major losses to the Vichy ships, however, were caused indirectly by the Anglo-US invasion of North Africa in November 1942, which itself resulted in several losses, but this invasion led directly to the German occupation of the formerly unoccupied Vichy France. Admiral Darlan maintained his pledge of preventing his fleet from falling into German hands, then ordered its scuttling. Thus, in North Africa itself, three *contre-torpilleurs* and seven *torpilleurs* were sunk resisting the Allied invasion, while in Toulon no less than eighteen *contre-torpilleurs* and eleven *torpilleurs* were scuttled.

Such Free French flotilla craft as remained operational, notably five *contre-torpilleurs* and seven *torpilleurs* served mainly in the Mediterranean and Indian Ocean theatres, while one of the major tasks of the Vichy ships had been to escort the supply convoys from North Africa to France. From 1943 onwards, several of the survivors were sent to the USA for much needed refit and modernization, but the state of the French fleet at the end of the Second World War in many ways resembled that at the end of the First World War and similar acrimony was to arise once again over the distribution of captured destroyers.

2100 TONNES CLASS

Ship	Builder	Laid Down	Launched	Commissioned*	Fate
Chacal	At. & Ch. de St-Nazaire–Penhoët	16 Aug 23	27 Sept 24	12 June 26	Lost 24 May 40
Jaguar	Ars. de Lorient	22 Aug 22	7 Nov 23	24 July 26	Lost 23 May 40
Léopard	At. & Ch. de la Loire (St-Nazaire)	Aug 1923	29 Sept 24	10 Oct 27	Wrecked 27 May 43
Lynx	At. & Ch. de la Loire (St-Nazaire)	14 Jan 23	25 Feb 24	10 Oct 27	Scuttled 27 Nov 42
Panthère	Ars. de Lorient	23 Dec 22	27 Oct 24	10 Oct 26	Scuttled 27 Nov 42
Tigre	At. & Ch. de Bretagne (Nantes)	15 Sept 23	2 Aug 24	1 Feb 26	Scuttled 27 Nov 42

*Clôture d'armament = Final completion after trials.

Displacement: 2,126tons/2,160tonnes (standard); 3,050tons/3,098tonnes (full load).
Length: 416ft/119.7m (oa); 392ft 9in/126.8m (pp).
Beam: 37ft 3in/11.2m.
Draught: 13ft 6in/3.65m (mean).
Machinery: five du Temple boilers; two sets Rateau single reduction geared turbines. (Bretagne in *Léopard* and *Lynx*).
Performance: 50,000shp; 35kts.
Range: 2,900nm at 16kts.
Guns: five 5.1in (130mm); two 75mm AA.
Torpedoes: six 21.7in (550mm) (2×3).
Complement: 8+187.

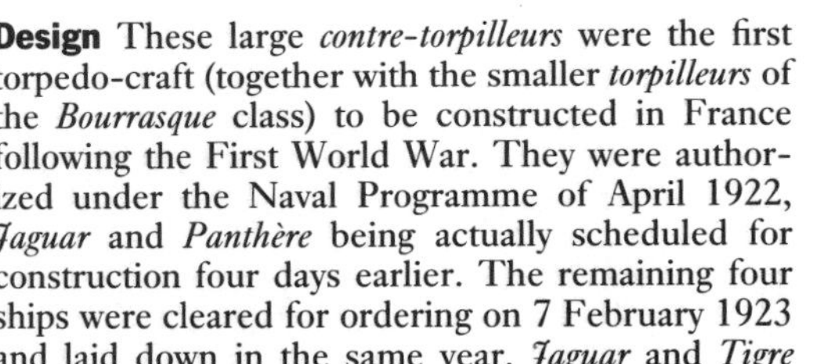
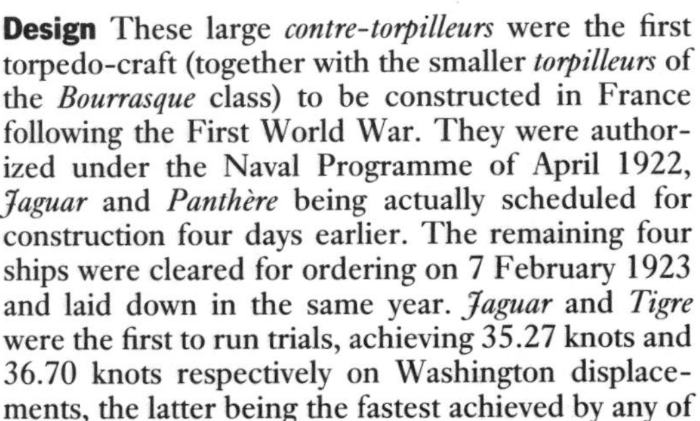

Design These large *contre-torpilleurs* were the first torpedo-craft (together with the smaller *torpilleurs* of the *Bourrasque* class) to be constructed in France following the First World War. They were authorized under the Naval Programme of April 1922, *Jaguar* and *Panthère* being actually scheduled for construction four days earlier. The remaining four ships were cleared for ordering on 7 February 1923 and laid down in the same year. *Jaguar* and *Tigre* were the first to run trials, achieving 35.27 knots and 36.70 knots respectively on Washington displacements, the latter being the fastest achieved by any of the class. On 3 October 1925, *Tigre* maintained 35.93 knots on a displacement of 2,540 tonnes for eight hours with 55,200shp. A ninth hour at 2,237 tonnes gave 36.7 knots with 57,200shp. None of the other ships reached 36 knots, but the class was fast, the slowest being *Jaguar* (35.27 knots).

The main armament, disposed forward and aft, was superfiring for the first time in French destroyers, with the fifth gun abaft the third funnel. This 5.1-inch gun, conceived during the First World War as being more powerful than that of contemporary foreign destroyers, finally emerged as the Model 1919 firing a 70.4lb (32kg) projectile. Its range of 20,226 yards (18,500m) was good, with the ability to pierce 80mm armour at 11,000 yards (10,000m), but this range was only achieved at the expense of excessive trunnion height and its superiority was more theoretical than real, the rate of fire being only 4 or 5 rounds per minute. This was a serious drawback because the *raison d'être* of these vessels was to raid and engage targets of opportunity when the ability to discharge maximum offensive power in the shortest possible time was vital. In addition the fire-control equipment was at best rudimentary. On paper, in fact, these *contre-torpilleurs* were not a good investment, for the *torpilleurs* of the same programme carried only one 5.1-inch and one 75mm gun less on only 1,500 tonnes!

By 1939, their age was beginning to tell, with growths of about 200 tonnes helping to reduce speeds to about 31 knots maximum. It had been realized some five years after completion, that the anti-aircraft armament was inadequate with the result that in February 1932 it was decided to land the long-range, but slow-firing 75mm AA and replace them by eight Hotchkiss 13.2mm machine-guns in twin mountings. Two were fitted on the bridge wings, and No. 3 gun was landed to provide space for the second pair. Although some improvement, the range and stopping-power of such a light gun was poor, and plans were made in the spring of 1939 to re-construct *Jaguar* as an AA destroyer (along the lines of that already done by the Royal Navy) armed with 3.9-inch (100mm) AA guns.

Left: *Chacal* in 1936. (Wright & Logan)

Above: *Léopard* after major war alterations in British hands. The forward boiler room and funnel have been removed. No. 3 gun has been replaced by a 20mm gun and the after tubes by 2pdr pom-poms. (IWM)

Outbreak of war in September, however, frustrated these plans.

Modifications Due to the fortunes of war, only *Léopard* and *Tigre* underwent much in the way of modifications. *Léopard*, in Portsmouth at the time of the French armistice, was seized by the Royal Navy on 3 July 1940 and transferred to the Free French forces on 31 August 1940 for their use. Her anti-aircraft armament was augmented by the addition of a 4-inch (102mm) gun on No. 3 position, a 2pdr pompom and six machine-guns. Extra depth-charges were carried, increased now to 52, and the mainmast was removed to reduce top-weight. Based on the Clyde, *Léopard* escorted North Atlantic convoys during the winter of 1940/41, but, not having been designed for such work, her radius of action was far too poor, necessitating frequent detachment to Iceland to re-fuel. By mid-1941, her boilers were in dire need of attention and opportunity was taken to rectify matters. During the course of a long refit, the forward boiler and its funnel were removed, the space being used to increase bunkerage and accommodation. Bunkerage now totalled 780 tonnes, giving a radius of action of 4,200 nautical miles at 13 knots. Her AA armament reportedly now comprised ten 37mm (5×2), seven 20mm (7×1) and two 13.2mm MGs as well as four single 8mm guns. Radar was added and 100 tonnes of interior ballast added for stability. After trials, when 31.5 knots was reached, *Léopard* resumed escort duties once more. Photographs, however, show a CRA of three single 2pdr, four single 20mm and at least one machine-gun.

Tigre, after her return by the Italians, also had her forward boiler removed at the same time as being repaired after bomb damage in April 1944. Her bunkerage was increased to 745 tonnes, giving 4,000 nautical miles at 13 knots. Light AA was altered to two 40mm Bofors and ten 20mm, but one triple torpedo tube bank was removed.

Service Looking to Italy as her major future enemy, at least at sea, the bulk of the French fleet was stationed in the Mediterranean. Of the *contre-torpilleurs*, all except three were stationed in that theatre. These were *Léopard, Jaguar* and *Chacal*, which moved from the Bay of Biscay into the English Channel in the early months of the war. When the German offensive was launched in the west, the effectiveness of the French ship's anti-aircraft defence was, like that of the Royal Navy, exposed as being totally inadequate. Not only that, but the general unhandiness of these large ships in the confined waters of the English Channel proved problematic in the face of strong Luftwaffe and *S*-boat attacks. *Jaguar* was the first to be lost, torpedoed during the night of 23 May 1940 by *S21* and *S23*, followed only twelve hours later by *Chacal* to Luftwaffe Stuka bombs. On the fall of France, *Léopard*, as recounted, was taken over by the Royal Navy, while the remaining three were disarmed at Toulon in September 1940.

Lynx, Panthère and *Tigre* remained at Toulon until the scuttling of the French fleet in November 1942. At this time, all three were moored in the Petite Rade at piers along the Appontements de Milhaud, *Lynx* and *Panthére* alongside each other with *Tigre* on the opposite jetty. The former pair were successfully scuttled although not irreparably damaged, but the small care and maintenance crew aboard *Tigre* were overwhelmed before they could sabotage their charge. The Italian Navy lost little time in securing the rights to many of the scuttled ships from the Germans and took over *Panthère* (as *FR22*) and *Tigre* (as *FR23*). *Panthère* was raised on 23 March 1943 and towed to La Spezia for refitting, but work had not been completed by the time of the Italian collapse and she was finally scuttled on 9 September 1943. *Tigre* on the other hand being almost intact, was commissioned into the R.It.N. for use as a troop transport. Restituted to France on 28 October 1943, *Tigre* received a refit at Casablanca when radar was added and the AA outfit modified before re-entering service in March 1944. Used initially on convoy escorts to Corsica, she suffered badly from shock damage as a result of air attacks after which she was employed on transport duties. Shaft vibration, however, forced her into dockyard hands as described earlier. On her return to service she saw action off the French/Italian Riviera before the end of the war. *Léopard* was eventually wrecked on the coast of Libya.

Post-war, *Tigre* served in a training role in the Mediterranean until condemned for disposal in November 1954.

2400 TONNES CLASS

Ship	Builder	Laid Down	Launched	Commissioned*	Fate
Bison	Ars. de Lorient	14 Mar 27	29 Oct 28	10 Oct 30	Lost 3 May 40
Guépard	Ars. de Lorient	14 Mar 27	19 April 28	13 Aug 29	Scuttled 27 Nov 42
Lion	At. & Ch. de France (Dunkirk)	6 Aug 26	5 Aug 29	21 Jan 31	Scuttled 27 Nov 42
Valmy	At. & Ch. de St-Nazaire–Penhoët	5 May 27	19 May 28	1 Jan 30	Scuttled 27 Nov 42
Verdun	At. & Ch. de la Loire (St-Nazaire)	10 Aug 27	4 July 28	1 April 30	Scuttled 27 Nov 42
Vauban	At. & Ch. de France (Dunkirk)	22 May 27	1 Feb 30	9 Jan 31	Scuttled 27 Nov 42

**Clôture d'armament.*

Displacement: 2,436tons/2,474tonnes (standard); 3,200tons/3,251tonnes (full load).
Length: 427ft/130.2m (oa); 403ft 9in/123.1m (pp).
Beam: 38ft/11.76m.
Draught: 13ft 3in/4.03m (mean).
Machinery: four small-tube vertical Penhoët boilers; two sets single reduction geared turbines (Zoelly in *Lion* and *Vauban*; Parsons in remainder).
Performance: 64,000shp; 35.5kts.
Bunkerage: 572tons/581tonnes.
Range: 3,450nm at 14.5kts.
Guns: five 5.5in (138.6mm); four 37mm; four 13.2mm; four DCT; two DC racks.
Torpedoes: six 21.7in (550mm) (2×3).
Complement: 10+220.

Design Designed by *Ingénieur-Général* Antoine, who had become chief of the minor warships section of the *Service Technique des Constructions et Armes Navales* in 1923, this new class of *contre-torpilleurs* represented a 300-tonne increase on their predecessors and began a series which was to reach eighteen units by 1934. The major military difference compared to the *Jaguar* type, was the adoption of a heavier gun, the 1923 Model 5.5-inch (138.6mm), while their external appearance was distinctive in that four funnels in pairs made them the only modern vessels to have so many funnels. The 5.5-inch gun (40cal) fired an 89lb (40.4kg) projectile with a maximum range of 20,000 yards (19,000m). Its muzzle velocity was on the low side and, moreover, gunnery control facilities were limited initially to a single 3m rangefinder. The guns were capable of 35° elevation with a rate of fire of about 5–6 rounds per minute at best, 140 rounds per gun being the rate book allowance. Four 1925 Model 37mm guns in single mountings disposed abreast No. 3 funnel comprised the main AA armament, but it would appear that the 13.2mm guns allowed for in the design were not shipped until some time after completion. The torpedo tubes were disposed on the centre-line, similar to those of *Jaguar*, and used the 1923 Model D torpedo with a 189lb (415kg) warhead. This torpedo had a performance of 14,200 yards (13,000m) at 35 knots or 9,840 yards (9000m) at 40 knots.

The machinery installation showed an advance on *Jaguar* in that only four boilers were installed, reflecting an increase in individual boiler power. Like most other nations, France was not ready for high-pressure steam concepts, and boiler pressures were of the order of 285psi (20kg/cm). The turbines comprised HP, LP and cruising stages on each of the two shafts. On trials all exceeded their designed speeds by some margin, only *Guépard* and *Valmy* falling below 40 knots. Eight-hour trial results varied from 35.47 knots (*Bison*) to 37.07 knots (*Valmy*).

Like all French torpedo-craft, which operated in divisions of three, these ships were authorized three in 1925 and three in 1926.

Modifications *Guépard* was unusual in that on entry into service, her 5.5-inch guns were fitted with shields similar to those of the 1,500-ton *Adroit* class, but in 1931, these were replaced with shields similar to the remainder of the class. Within the six ships, there were minor appearance differences particularly in the bridge and gunnery control platforms. Pre-war, a number of modifications were carried out, one of which was the installation in 1933 of two 1m rangefinders for each group of 37mm guns. In 1935, a second rangefinder (4m) was added aft and in 1937, a 5m stereoscopic rangefinder on the bridge. At about this time, the four 13.2mm Hotchkiss guns were added. Initially, *Guépard, Valmy* and *Verdun* received them on the main deck abaft the 37mm weapons, and the others around the bridge deck, but by the outbreak of the Second World War, their position had been standardized on two small platforms on the ammunition handling room abaft No. 2 gun. Finally, the depth-charge throwers, which had been landed in 1932, were re-shipped 1939–40.

The major modifications undertaken were to augment the ASW and AA outfits, both of which were handicapped by poor control or volume. As the major tasks of these ships did not include ASW duties, no detection set had been included, indeed none was available from French sources. Only 24 depth-charges were carried, dropped from rails below the quarter deck. To rectify matters, Asdic sets were ordered from Britain, Type 128 for the *Jaguar* class and a further order for the same type to equip sixteen of the eighteen 2,400 tonnes *contre-torpilleurs*. Before the French armistice, *Bison* and *Vautour* were fitted from the first order and *Kersaint* and *Gerfaut* in April and May 1940. Of the remainder, *Vauquelin, Tartu, Cassard* and *Albatros* were fitted after the Armistice, but *Chevalier Paul*, for example, was never so fitted.

The inadequacy of the AA outfit had long been recognized, plans being laid as early as 1938 to improve matters. However, the means were not available and, like British ships, the French also suffered cruelly at the hands of the Luftwaffe, 1939–40. However, plans to replace the 1925 Model 37mm guns by 1933-pattern guns did not include the six *Guépard* and *Valmy* ships. Not until June 1940 was it envisaged that these earlier ships would receive these newer weapons (three twin mountings), but the armistice prevented this being carried out. Such modifications as were made after

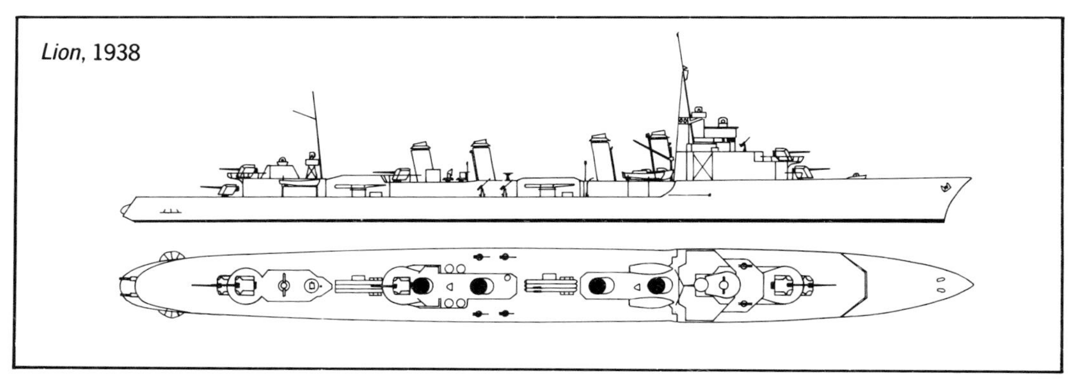
Lion, 1938

Below: *Verdun* in July 1941, showing augmented AA armament. (M. Bar)

the armistice were dependent on the means at hand in Toulon, Bizerte and Oran as and when the ships were present.

Lion and *Vauban* appear to have received little or no modifications by November 1942, but *Guépard* received considerable attention, including the removal of mainmast, forward torpedo tubes, 1925 Model 37mm guns and forward searchlight. A 1933-Model twin 37mm mounting was added aft, the 13.2mm Hotchkiss guns moved aft and two 13.2mm Brownings fitted in their original position. *Valmy* was similarly treated except that it was the after tubes which were removed, while *Verdun* retained both hers.

Service Before the outbreak of war, *Bison* was rammed by the light cruiser *Georges Leygues* on the night of 7/8 February 1939, losing everything forward of the bridge face. Six months' repairs were necessary at L'Orient. *Bison* was actually the only unit to serve in the Atlantic, as part of the 4th Division prior to the war, but joined the 11th Division based in Greenock, Scotland by April 1940. The early months of the war were limited to patrol and convoy escort duties in the Atlantic, but once again, the 'short legs' of these fast ships proved an embarrassment. No success was achieved against U-boats. When the Norway Campaign began, the French Navy played an important part with the cruiser *Emile Bertin*, the 5th Division (*Tartu, Chevalier Paul* and *Maillé Brézé*) and the 11th Division (*Bison, Epervier* and *Milan*) being sent to the North Sea for duties in Norway. Here, *Bison* paid the price of poor AA defence when, during the evacuation of Namsos, Stukas of *1/St.G.I.* bombed and sank her.

In the Mediterranean, *Vauban* and *Lion* as part of the 1st Division, and the 3rd Division (*Guépard, Valmy* and *Verdun*) together with cruisers and other *contre-torpilleurs* took part in a bombardment of Genoa in June 1940, but at the armistice retired to Toulon or North Africa, where they remained largely inactive. However, *Guépard* and *Valmy* moved to Syria in 1941 and, based on Beirut, intervened in the British attack on the French colony. The two French ships bombarded Australian troops before meeting the British destroyer *Janus* and heavily damaging her. After then hitting *Jackal*, the French destroyers withdrew. Following the Armistice of St-Jeanne d'Arc, both escaped back to Toulon with *Vauquelin* which had been sent out in mid-June.

At the time of the scuttling of the fleet, in November 1942, all five survivors were present in Toulon and scuttled on the 27th. Only two, *Lion* and *Valmy* were judged fit for salvage being renamed *FR21* and *FR24* respectively. Both were towed to Italy but neither entered service under the Italian ensign, the latter being hit and badly damaged by RAF fighter-bombers on 20 January 1944 while lying at Savonna.

2400 TONNES CLASS

Ship	Builder	Laid Down	Launched	Commissioned*	Fate
Aigle	At. & Ch. de France (Dunkirk)	8 Oct 28	19 Feb 31	10 Oct 32	Scuttled 27 Nov 42
Vautour	F. & Ch. de la Méditerranée (Le Harvre)	30 Jan 29	26 Aug 30	2 May 32	Scuttled 27 Nov 42
Albatros	At. & Ch. de la Loire (Nantes)	21 Feb 29	27 June 30	25 Dec 31	Scrapped 9 Sept 59
Gerfaut	At. & Ch. de Bretagne (Nantes)	13 May 29	14 June 30	30 Jan 32	Scuttled 27 Nov 42
Milan	Ars. de Lorient	1 Dec 30	13 Oct 31	20 April 34	Beached 8 Nov 42
Epervier	Ars. de Lorient	18 Aug 30	14 Aug 31	1 April 34	Beached 9 Nov 42

**Clôture d'armament.*

Displacement: 2,441tons/2,480tonnes (standard); 3,140tons/3,190tonnes (full load).
Length: 421ft 6in/128.5m (oa); 401ft 6in/122.4m (pp).
Beam: 39ft/11.84m.
Draught: 13ft 9in/4.23m (mean).
Machinery: As *Bison* class, except *Milan* and *Epervier*. *Milan* and *Epervier* superheated boilers, 384psi (27kg/cm^2) Rateau turbines in *Gerfaut* and *Epervier*; Zoelly in *Aigle*; Parsons in remainder.
Performance: 64,000shp (68,000shp last two); 36 knots.
Bunkerage: 562–575tons/572–585tonnes.
Range: 3,650nm at 18kts.
Guns: As *Bison* except 5.5in guns of semi-automatic 1927 pattern.
Torpedoes: As *Bison* except last two seven 21.7in (1×3, 2×2).
Complement: 10+220.

Below: *Aigle* in October 1932. (M. Bar)

Design This group of six was authorized under the 1927 programme and orders were placed on 3 October 1928. They differed little externally from the *Bison* group, except for a slight variation in the shape of the stern. The major difference was in their effective fighting power, for these ships were given the 1927 Model 5.5-inch gun. This had been developed from the 6-inch guns of German pattern aboard *Amiral Sénès*, the former *S113*, taken over after the First World War. It was fitted with a horizontal sliding wedge breech, semi-automatic in operation, with power for elevation and training. Rate of fire was double that of the earlier model, due mainly to the breech design and lower trunnion height which, however, limited elevation to 28° with a consequent reduction in range to 18,260 yards (16,700m). Nothing, however, was done to improve rate of ammunition supply or ammunition capacity.

Advances in the field of marine engineering began to make themselves felt in all the maritime nations and while even with the standard boilers, trial speeds of between 38.66 knots (*Aigle*) and 41.20 knots (*Gerfaut*) were obtained, it was decided that, in view of the success of the superheated type of boilers fitted in the seaplane tender *Commandant Teste*, these boilers should be tried in *contre-torpilleurs*. The last two ships, *Milan* and *Epervier* were chosen as the trials ships and received different types of boiler for evaluation, F. et Ch. Méditerranée and Yarrow-Loire in *Milan*, Thornycroft-Penhoêt and du Temple in *Epervier*. The turbine design (Parsons in *Milan*) comprised HP, IP and LP stages in addition to cruising turbines. On trials, both proved fast, with *Milan* fastest of all the 2,400 tonnes ships at 41.94 knots. Fuel economy and hence radius were noticeably improved with this

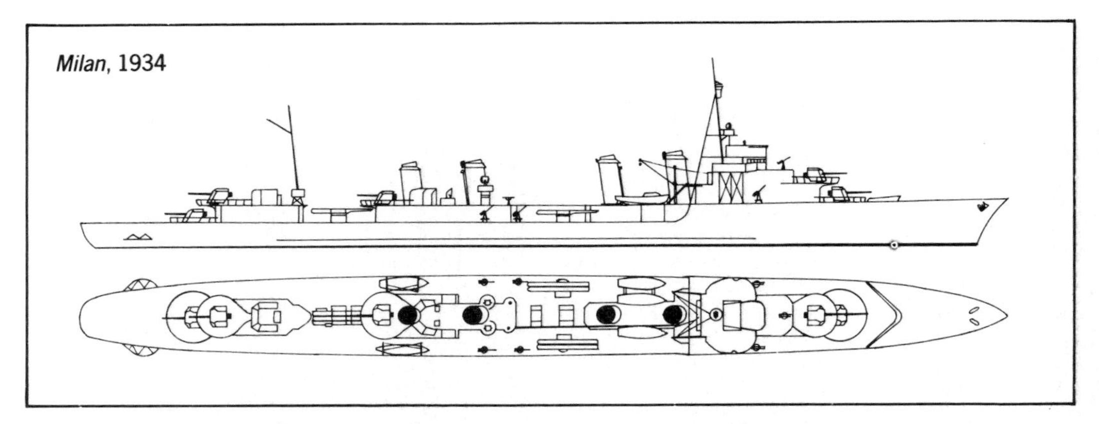

new machinery, but their laying down was seriously delayed by this decision.

Modifications Better fire-control equipment, a stereoscopic 5m base unit forward and a 4m unit aft, was fitted from 1936, while improvements were also made to the ammunition slides fitted around the gun positions. As with the earlier ships, the obsolete 75mm AA gun was also landed. Other modifications also conformed to those carried out in the *Bison* type, but *Gerfaut* carried an experimental director aft from 1935 to 1937 which was later fitted as standard to the two 'specials' as well as the final 2,400-tonnes series ships. The 'specials' were characterized by a new shape of stern, rounded bridges and regrouped searchlights as well as a new arrangement of torpedo tubes, the two twin banks being sided between Nos. 2 and 3 funnels. These two units also received a depth-charge thrower port and starboard abreast the after funnel, on the main deck.

Pre-war improvements planned for the AA outfit have already been outlined for the *Bison* type and basically applied to this group as well. Post-June 1940 improvements provided for the installation of a twin 37mm 1933 Model mounting on the centreline aft for *Milan, Epervier, Vautour* and *Albatros* as well as two extra Browning guns. The four 'standard' ships of the group retained all their torpedo tubes and also two of the four Model 1925 guns in the waist, but *Aigle* never received either the 1933 Model 37mm nor the Browning guns. *Milan* and *Epervier* received refits in 1941 at Oran and Casablanca respectively, losing their mainmasts and gaining a twin 37mm aft. In the case of *Epervier* two of the original Model 1925 37mm guns were relocated on the after shelter deck, while *Milan* retained hers on the main deck. These two ships also received protective shields to the side torpedo tubes.

Service Serving with the 11th Division, *Epervier* and *Milan* took part in the Norwegian operations and in May, *Milan* made a sweep into the Skagerrak with *Chevalier Paul, Tartu* and the British *Sikh* and *Tartar*. On 22 May she received damage from bombs. The remaining four were based in the Mediterranean with the 1st Division (*Aigle*) and 7th Division (*Vautour, Albatros* and *Gerfaut*) taking part in operations against Italy in June 1940 when *Albatros* received a hit in the after boiler room causing casualties. All six ships returned to the Mediterranean after the French armistice, the 11th Division being based in North Africa thus bearing the brunt of the Anglo-US invasion in November 1942. Faced with the overwhelming might of the American and British task forces, the French *contre-torpilleurs* attacked with great gallantry. The result was inevitable. At Casablanca, *Milan* and *Albatros* were driven ashore badly damaged by US Task Force 34 while at Oran, *Epervier* in company with three 1,500-tonnes *torpilleurs* attacked the British cruisers *Aurora* and *Jamaica* and destroyers *Boadicea* and *Calpe* with disastrous results. *Epervier* was heavily hit and beached while of her smaller escorts, *Tornade* was sunk and *Tramontane* wrecked. *Typhon* escaped. Trapped in an impossible situation, the French ships could not have achieved any success without good luck and that was not with them that day.

The units in Toulon, *Aigle, Gerfaut* and *Vautour* all scuttled themselves. They were salvaged in 1943, but never restored to operational condition. The hulk of *Aigle* was sunk by Allied bombs on 24 November 1943 and that of *Gerfaut* on 7 March 1944. Likewise, *Vautour* on 4 February 1944. In North Africa, *Epervier* was salvaged on 16 October 1946 and scrapped, as was *Milan*, but *Albatros*, salvaged in December 1942, was towed to Toulon after the war and placed in Special Reserve on 31 July 1944. At first used for cannibalization purposes, it was decided in 1945 to refit her for training use. Many delays and lack of funds extended the date for her re-entry into service until September 1948. During this time, the forward boilers and forward funnel pair were removed and various armament combinations were fitted throughout her service period as a trials ship until placed in reserve on 10 September 1956. She was finally condemned on 9 September 1959, after a service life of almost 30 years.

Below: *Vautour* in November 1940. (M. Bar)

2400 TONNES CLASS

Ship	Builder	Laid Down	Launched	Commissioned*	Fate
Cassard	At. & Ch. de Bretagne (Nantes)	12 Nov 30	8 Nov 31	10 Sept 33	Scuttled 27 Nov 42
Chevalier Paul	F. & Ch. de la Méditerranée (La Seyne)	28 Feb 31	21 Mar 32	20 July 34	Torpedoed 16 April 41
Kersaint	At. & Ch. de la Loire (St-Nazaire)	19 Sept 30	14 Nov 31	31 Dec 33	Scuttled 27 Nov 42
Maillé Brézé	At. & Ch. de St-Nazaire–Penhoët	9 Oct 30	9 Nov 31	6 April 33	Blew up 30 April 40
Tartu	At. & Ch. de la Loire (St-Nazaire)	14 Sept 30	7 Dec 31	31 Dec 32	Scuttled 27 Nov 42
Vauquelin	At. & Ch. de France (Dunkirk)	13 Mar 30	29 Mar 31	3 Nov 33	Scuttled 27 Nov 42

**Cloture d'armament.*

Displacement: 2,441tons/2,480tonnes (standard); 3,140tons/3,190tonnes (full load).
Length: 424ft 2in/129.3m (oa); 401ft 6in/122.4m (pp).
Beam: 39ft/11.84m.
Draught: 14ft 5in/4.39m (mean); 16ft 4in/4.97m (max).
Machinery: four small-tube vertical Penhoët boilers; two sets single reduction Parsons geared turbines (Rateau in *Cassard* and *Kersaint*).
Performance: 64,000shp; 36kts.
Bunkerage: 562–575tons/572–585tonnes.
Range: 3,650nm at 18kts.
Guns: five 5.5in (138.6mm); four 37mm; four 13.2mm; two DCT.
Torpedoes: seven 21.7in (550mm) (1×3, 2×2).
Mines: 50.
Complement: 10+220.

Design These six ships formed the fifth and last group of the 2,400-tonnes *contre-torpilleurs* design. They differed little from the earlier groups in terms of size and offensive power and did not incorporate the uprated machinery given to *Milan* and *Epervier*, but they did feature the new stern shape.

Modifications By early 1941, *Chevalier Paul* had received considerable alteration, mainly with the intention of augmenting the AA armament. The mainmast was removed to improve arcs of fire and the W/T aerials re-located to the after funnel. On the after shelter deck, around the after director were mounted a Mk 1933 twin 37mm on the centre-line and two single Mk 1925 37mm guns abreast the director which was raised by about a metre. The 37mm on the main deck were removed, as were the after triple torpedo tube bank. Finally, two 13.2mm Browning guns were fitted in place of the AA range-finders just forward of No. 3 funnel. Later, the other four survivors received similar treatment except that as a result of complaints from the Fleet, the after director was landed in lieu of the triple torpedo tubes. It had been intended that this after position would be equipped with three twin 37mm but this was never realized. *Tartu* and *Cassard* were fitted as *Chevalier Paul*, while *Vauquelin* had one twin on the centre-line, one in the port tub and a single Mk 1925 37mm in the starboard tub. *Kersaint* on a temporary basis from June 1941, had only three 25mm single Hotchkiss aft, with her original four single Mk 1925 37mm guns on the main deck. She also originally had her Browning guns on the after deck-house, but this proved unsatisfactory and they were later re-sited on the forward ammunition handling room as in the remainder of the class.

One ship, *Kersaint*, received a British asdic set in April 1940. *Vauquelin* received hers after the armistice in December 1940, *Tartu* in August 1941 and *Cassard* at the end of that year. *Chevalier Paul* was never fitted. Two depth-charge throwers were fitted, abreast No. 4 funnel and it was intended to fit two more as well as hydrophone equipment, but this was never done. One other modification was the fitting of protective shields to the torpedo control positions of the twin torpedo tube banks.

Service The 5th Division comprising *Tartu*, *Chevalier Paul* and *Maillé Brézé* took part in the Norwegian campaign, based upon Greenock where, on 30 April 1940, *Maillé Brézé* was destroyed by the explosion of one of her torpedoes. This division, now with *Cassard* replacing the lost ship, moved south to the Mediterranean where on 14 June 1940, they participated in the French fleet's bombardment of Genoa. Six days later, however, all offensive action had to cease on the signing of the armistice. As a result of British actions in Syria in the summer of 1941, *Chevalier Paul* was dispatched to the Levant from Toulon, carrying ammunition. She was sighted

Below: *Chevalier Paul* in 1939. (M. Bar)

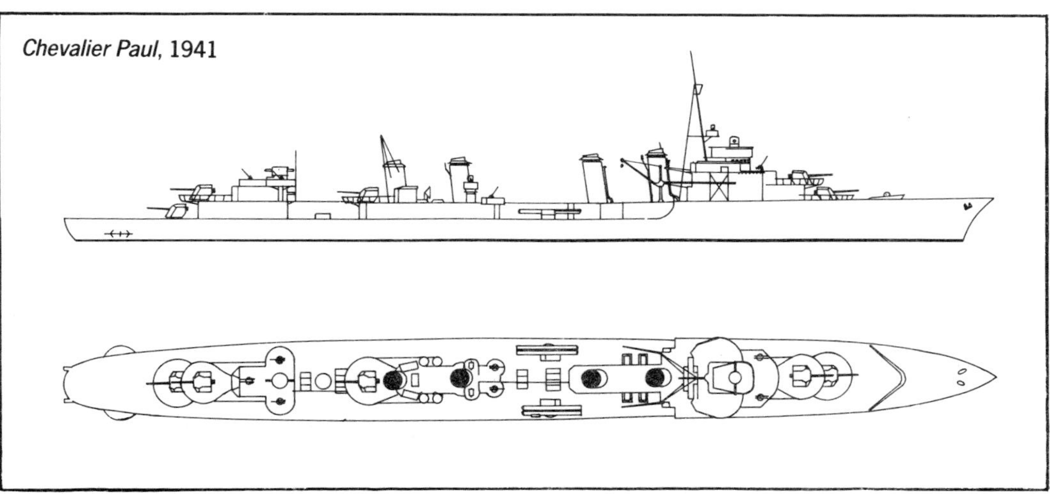

by British aircraft on 15 June off Castellorizo and attacked in the early hours of the following day by five Swordfish of 815 Squadron Fleet Air Arm. One of the aircraft managed to torpedo the destroyer in a boiler room, bringing her to a stop and in a sinking condition. One of the attackers was shot down, both her crew and that of the destroyer being rescued by *Guépard* and *Valmy*. *Vauquelin* too made an ammunition run suffering only slight damage, then in mid-July she and *Guépard* were ordered back to Toulon. All four surviving ships were therefore in Toulon when the fleet was scuttled, none being fit for salvage.

Right: *Tartu* with augmented AA outfit in October 1941. (M. Bar)

2610 TONNES CLASS

Ship	Builder	Laid Down	Launched	Commissioned*	Fate
L'Audacieux	Ars. de Lorient	16 Nov 31	15 Mar 34	27 Nov 35	Lost 7 May 43
Le Fantasque	Ars. de Lorient	15 Nov 31	15 Mar 34	10 Mar 35	Stricken 2 May 57
L'Indomptable	F. & Ch. de la Méditerranée (La Seyne)	25 Jan 32	7 Dec 33	10 Feb 35	Scuttled 27 Nov 42
Le Malin	F. & Ch. de la Méditerranée (La Seyne)	16 Nov 31	17 Aug 33	1 May 36	Stricken Feb 1964
Le Terrible	Ch. Nav. Français (Caen)	8 Dec 31	30 Nov 33	1 Oct 35	Stricken June 1962
Le Triomphant	At. & Ch. de France (Dunkirk)	28 Aug 31	16 April 34	25 May 36	Stricken Dec 1954

**Clôture d'armament.*

Displacement: 2,569tons/2,610tonnes (standard); 3,400tons/3,454tonnes (full load).
Length: 434ft 6in/132.4m (oa); 411ft 6in/125.4m (pp).
Beam: 40ft 6in/12.25m.
Draught: 16ft 6in/5.01m (mean).
Machinery: four Penhoët small-tube vertical boilers (Yarrow-Loire in *Le Terrible*); 2-shaft Parsons geared turbines (Rateau in *L'Audacieux, Le Fantasque* and *Le Terrible*).
Performance: 74,000shp; 37kts.
Bunkerage: 580tons/589tonnes.
Range: 4,000nm at 15kts.
Guns: five 5.5in (5×1); four 37mm (4×1).
Torpedoes: nine 21.7in (3×3).
Mines: 50.
Complement: 210.

Design This design represented a further advance upon the previous class, both in terms of size and power. The rise in nominal displacement of some 200 tonnes was accompanied by an increase of 8 per cent in the installed engine power. In addition, these ships were to receive a new model 5.5-inch gun, (Model 1929) which had elevation increased to 30° and were of longer (45) calibre. For the first time power was provided for laying and training and the maximum range of the gun was 21,800 yards (20,000m). More advanced machinery practice had been adopted in the earlier *Milan* and *Epervier* and without awaiting service experience with these two ships, it was decided to go ahead with similar machinery for the new class.

The result was a very successful design which, given more favourable circumstances, might have had a magnificent war record. Even so, the design proved itself in an all too brief war career.

Orders were placed on 7 May 1931 for *Le Triomphant*, that for *Le Terrible* the following day and for *Le Malin* and *L'Indomptable* on 13 May, all these ships being constructed in private yards. *Le Triomphant* was the first to run trials, in July 1934 achieving 43.24 knots on Washington displacement, but the fastest was *Le Terrible* with 45.02 knots under similar conditions. This record still stands. On eight-hour trials, speeds varied between 42.9 knots (86,443shp) and 41.4 knots (93,802shp). Even with these high speeds, fuel consumption did not exceed the stipulated 32.5 tonnes per hour on the eight-hour trials, with *L'Indomptable* returning the best results of 30.76tonnes/hour. The turbines of the Rateau type, fitted to half the class, were found to be more robust than those of Parsons design and in fact *Le Triomphant* suffered turbine trouble during full-power trials, which delayed her entry into service. *Le Fantasque* was also delayed, but this was due to her touching bottom on trials.

This class presented a very pleasing and modern appearance after the somewhat old-fashioned looking four-funnelled designs already in service. The main armament, in single mountings, was disposed two forward and two aft with the fifth gun at the forward end of the after shelter deck. A noticeable feature of the gun positions was the very close spacing between Numbers 1 and 2 and 4 and 5 guns, which drew favourable comment from British

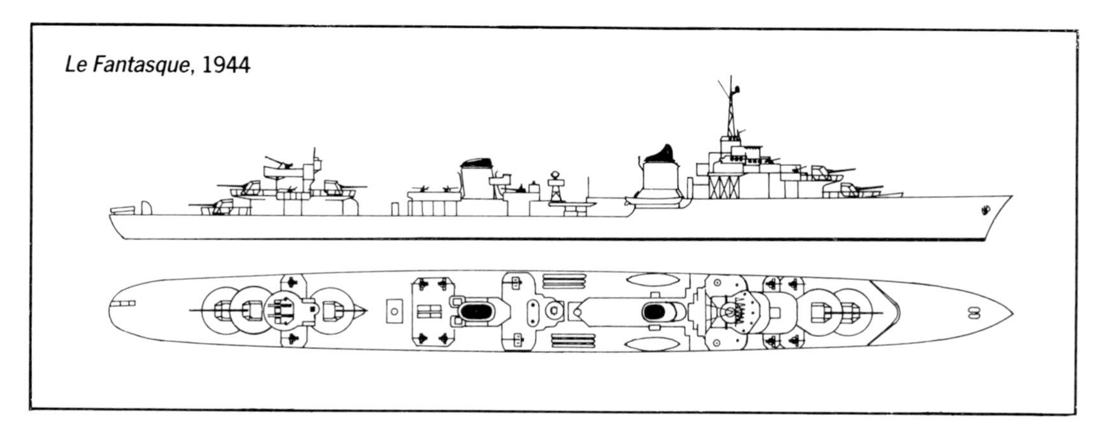

constructors at the time. Internally, the machinery was arranged on the unit principle, boiler rooms alternating with turbine rooms. Like previous designs, the torpedo armament was partially disposed upon the beam, with one axial and two sided mountings. All however, were triple, giving an increase to nine torpedoes.

In common with all warships of the inter-war period, the anti-aircraft armament was poor, the more so in this case, considering the size of the ships.

Modifications During the three years or so before the outbreak of the Second World War, few modifications were made to the class. It was not until the fall of France, which left *Le Triomphant* in British hands at Plymouth and the remainder either at Algiers or Mers-el-Kebir, that differences and modifications began to appear. At this time, it was mainly *Le Triomphant* which was the subject of modifications because of her unfamiliar equipment and lack of spares available to the British. On joining the Free French Naval Forces, No. 4 5.5-inch gun was landed and replaced by a single 4-inch HA, the heavy AA augmented by two single 2-pounders in the bridge wings and ten (1×4, 2×2, 2×1) machine-guns added. She also received an asdic set and a British radar. Much of her career was spent in the wilderness of the South-West Pacific and it was not until April 1944 that she started the major refit in the USA which her sisters had received in 1943. Nevertheless, while in Pacific waters, she received at least seven single 20mm guns disposed on the after end of the forecastle, midships structure, between No. 4 gun and the 4-inch (replacing the quad .5in MG) and on the quarter deck. During the course of her US refit, No. 4 gun was re-embarked, the after director tower suppressed and the anti-aircraft outfit further enhanced. Forward of the after funnel, deck-houses were added port and starboard, each carrying a twin 40mm Mk 1, Mod. 1 Bofors mounting and director with a third on the deck-house between Nos. 3 and 4 guns. Ten 20mm completed the outfit, and the axial torpedo tubes were removed.

Following the Allied invasion of North Africa, *Le Fantasque* and *Le Terrible* both went to the USA for refit and modernization, arriving in New York on 14 February 1943. After completing makeshift repairs to damage caused by a 16-inch shell from USS *Massachusetts, Le Malin* finally reached Boston (Ma) on 26 June 1943, the day after *Fantasque* had sailed for Casablanca and two days before *Le Terrible* sailed for Guadaloupe, both having completed their refits. All axial torpedo tubes and existing AA guns were landed, being replaced by two twin Mk 1, Mod. 640mm Bofors forward of the second funnel and one Mk 2 Mod. 13 quadruple 40mm Bofors between Nos. 3 and 4 guns plus eight 20mm guns (*Le Malin* received ten). US-pattern radar for air warning and navigation was also added. All these three ships received a light lattice foremast. Both *Le Fantasque* and *Le Terrible* reached 40 knots on post-refit trials, despite a displacement growth of 500 tonnes.

L'Audacieux and *L'Indomptable* the two war losses, received no major modifications, but the latter was given at least three extra 37mm twin mountings. These were fitted between Nos. 3 and 4 guns and on platforms abreast the deck-house to port and starboard.

Service These ships, when first commissioned, formed the 8th (*Indomptable, Malin* and *Triomphant*) and 10th (*Fantasque, Audacieux* and *Terrible*) divisions of *contre-torpilleurs* ('DCT'). Both divisions served with the Atlantic Fleet prior to the outbreak of war. Based upon Brest, and later Dakar, the ships took part in many of the Fleet operations during 1939–40, mainly in connection with attempts to track down German raiders such as *Admiral Graf Spee*. In the course of one such patrol, *Le Terrible* stopped the German merchantman *Halle* which scuttled herself and later the *Santa Fé* was captured by *Le Fantasque*. Early in 1940, the ships of the 8th DCT were sent to the North Sea for the Norway Campaign, where they operated into the Skagerrak but the threat of Italy entering the war forced the French Admiralty to withdraw them to the Mediterranean. At the time of the armistice, all except *Le Triomphant* were in the Mediterranean but this ship, at Plymouth, was seized by the British and turned over to the Free French Naval Forces.

Terrible, at Mers-el-Kebir at the time of the British attack on 3 July 1940, managed to escape with other *torpilleurs* and *contre-torpilleurs*, escorting *Strasbourg* safely into Toulon. Early in September, the 10th DCT (now comprising *Malin, Fantasque* and *Audacieux*) sailed to Dakar with the 4th Cruiser Squadron and were thus in this base when the Royal Navy and Free French Forces attempted to seize the port on 23 September. In the course of this action, *Audacieux* while probing for landing forces, ran into the heavy cruiser *Australia* which promptly shelled and very badly damaged the French ship. *Audacieux*,

Left: *Le Malin* in 1938. (M. Bar)

Right: *Le Malin* in December 1943 following refit in the USA. Note removal of the after tubes and the addition of 20mm and 40mm guns. US-pattern radars have been fitted to a new lattice mast. (USN)

Above: *Le Triomphant* in May 1943. Note 4-inch gun in No. 4 position, 2pdrs in the bridge wings and at least six 20mm added. (USN)

burning fiercely, was beached and abandoned. Her two division mates fought off air attacks and protected the cruisers until the attacking forces withdrew. *Audacieux* was eventually towed to Bizerta for repairs, but these were far from complete when she was again badly damaged by Allied air attacks. As has already been recounted, *Fantasque* and *Terrible* went to the USA for refit in January 1943, *Malin* following in June. In the meantime, *Triomphant* had been sent out to the Pacific, partly for political reasons, and used as an escort for which duty she had not been designed and did not have the endurance. For her, much of 1942 was spent under refit at Sydney, Australia. *Indomptable*, in Toulon with her division at the time of the German occupation of Vichy, was scuttled at the coaling pier on 27 November 1942.

By August 1943, *Fantasque* and *Terrible* were back in the Mediterranean taking part in the Salerno landings, the re-occupation of Corsica and sweeps into the Aegean Sea in November. December saw operations in the eastern Atlantic to prevent German blockade-runners from reaching Western France[1] and in January 1944 both ships were engaged in diversionary bombardments for the Anzio landings. *Malin* re-joined the division in January and returned to the Mediterranean following which all three ships took part in Adriatic offensive sweeps. In the course of these, five[2] ships were sunk.

Moving to the eastern Mediterranean, further sweeps were conducted in the Aegean in April before once more returning to the Adriatic. The division took part in the invasion of the South of France in August, seeing a good deal of action, but later in the year, in December, *Malin* collided with *Terrible* when both were badly damaged.

Triomphant, after her US refit, passed out to the British Eastern fleet and by July 1944, was based at Trincomalee operating in the Indian Ocean. In September, after taking part in the re-occupation of Singapore, *Triomphant* with *Richelieu* escorted troop-ships to re-occupy Indo-China, arriving in Saigon on 3 October. On 27 October, *Fantasque* reached Saigon, meeting her sister two days later for the first time since 1940. Both ships saw continual action against the Viet Minh until March 1946, before returning home in the summer and autumn of that year. Thereafter, until their deletion from the active list, all four survivors served in a training role in French Mediterranean waters except that *Malin* went out to Indo-China with the aircraft carrier *Arromanches* in 1951–52. *Malin* was deleted from the active list in 1955, as was *Fantasque*. *Triomphant*, condemned a year earlier, was still afloat as a hulk four years later in Malaga, while *Terrible* served as a cadets' training tender until 1961, being scrapped the following year.

1. *Nicoline Maersk* was intercepted by *Fantasque* and beached on 24 December 1943.
2. *Kapitän Diederichsen* (by *Terrible*), *UJ201* (*Le Malin*), *SF273* and *SF274* (*Terrible* and *Fantasque*) and *Giuliana* (*Terrible* and *Fantasque*).

2930 TONNES CLASS

Ship	Builder	Laid Down	Launched	Commissioned*	Fate
Mogador	Ars. de Lorient	28 Dec 34	9 June 37	8 April 39	Scuttled 27 Nov 42
Volta	At. & Ch. de Bretagne (Nantes)	24 Dec 34	26 Nov 36	6 Mar 39	Scuttled 27 Nov 42
Kléber	At. & Ch. de France (Dunkirk)	Not laid down			
Desaix	At. & Ch. de France (Dunkirk)	Not laid down			
Marceau	At. & Ch. de Bretagne (Nantes)	Not laid down			
Hoche	At. & Ch. de Bretagne (Nantes)	Not laid down			

**Clotûre d'armament.*

Displacement: 2,884tons/2,930tonnes (standard); 3,954tons/4,018tonnes (full load).
Length: 451ft 3in/137.5m (oa); 429ft 9in/131m (pp).
Beam: 41ft 6in/12.67m.
Draught: 15ft/4.57m (mean).
Machinery: four Indret small-tube vertical boilers; 2-shaft Rateau-Bretagne single reduction geared turbines.
Performance: 92,000shp; 39kts.
Bunkerage: 721tons/710tonnes.
Range: 4,000nm at 18kts.
Guns: eight 5.5in (4×2); four 37mm (2×2); four 13.2mm.*
Torpedoes: ten 21.7in (2×3, 2×2).*
Mines: 40.
Complement: 264.

*See text for *Kléber* sub-type data.

Design This class represented the peak of development of the French *contre-torpilleurs*, but like all the French Navy's ships, had little opportunity to demonstrate its merits. It was a significant advance, both in terms of size and fire power over the preceding *Malin* design, displacing something like 17 per cent more and carrying eight guns instead of five. The torpedo outfit was also increased and, overall, this design moved very close to the cruiser category. Their only real contemporaries were the US destroyers of the *Porter* and *Somers* classes, which were physically smaller but carried approximately the same fighting power. In European waters, however, they had no opposition below light cruiser level.

The major external difference as compared with *Le Malin*, apart from a longer hull, was the adoption of twin mountings for the main armament, disposed in typical cruiser fashion, two forward and two aft. The guns themselves, though of a similar calibre, 138.6mm (5.5in) to those of *Le Malin*, were a new mark, 1934 shipped in weatherproof gun-houses, which offered obvious operational advantages over open mountings. Fire-control arrangements were also improved, comprising two 5m and one 4m stereoscopic rangefinders. One 5m unit was placed aft, the other two coaxially in the upper bridge. A change was also made in the disposition of the torpedo tubes, the after set being replaced by two twin mountings on the beam giving a total of two twin and two triple banks. The anti-aircraft outfit was not improved upon.

The main machinery remained a twin-shaft single reduction Rateau geared turbine installation, but in view of the increased displacement, the designed power had to be increased to 92,000shp for a speed of 39 knots. A notable advance however, was the increased steam pressures adopted for this design. While nowhere near approaching contemporary German practice in this respect, it was in advance of current British practice. The boilers were designed to secure rapid raising of steam so that an increase in speed from 14 knots to 35 knots took only a few minutes instead of the twenty or so required by earlier designs. The cruising turbines gave 15 knots with only 2,760shp and were fairly flexible in that 27 knots could be achieved in the cruising mode before it was necessary to switch to the main turbines. Altogether the machinery installation was considered by the navy to be very satisfactory.

One ship was authorized under the 1932 programme (*Mogador*) and a second (*Volta*) under the 1934 programme, but neither was laid down until the end of 1934. Both entered service at the close of 1938. On trials, *Mogador* achieved 41.274 knots with 104,925shp over eight hours, and her sister 42.09 knots although her power output is not recorded. The maximum speeds obtained were 43.45 knots and 43.78 knots, on displacement of approximately 3,050 tons, respectively. These high speeds were, however, only of use in the restricted theatres of the North Sea and Mediterranean and it is a fact that the endurance of these ships was as poor as that of their predecessors. The other problem encountered by *Mogador* and her sister was potentially more serious. This concerned the main armament where considerable problems were experienced with the ammunition supply to the guns. The shell hoists suffered from a lack of robustness, and frequent defects reduced the rate of fire to six rounds per minute, a great handicap for a ship designed to fight short, sharp engagements. Additionally, the ammunition outfit was sufficient for only about twenty minutes' action. The faults in the shell hoists were not rectified until March 1940.

Above: *Volta* in August 1939. (M. Bar)

Below: *Mogador* in November 1940, minus her stern after the action at Mers-el-Kebir. (M. Bar)

Modifications Following repairs to her action damage received at Mers-el-Kebir in July 1940, 'X' turret was removed from *Mogador* and replaced by two Mk 1933 twin 37mm mountings with two further mountings replacing the original 1927 Model 37mm guns. *Volta*, on the other hand, retained her full main armament but received in addition, in 1941, two single Mk 1933 37mm aft, two single 25mm in the bridge wings and eight Browning or Hotchkiss machine-guns, two on the bridge, two on 'X' turret and two on the deck.

Service These two *contre-torpilleurs* formed the 6th DCT and, together with the 8th and 10th DCTs, constituted the 2nd Light squadron attached to the *Force de Raid* based at Brest in 1939. They operated in the Atlantic against German raiders during the winter of 1939–40 but in July 1940, following the armistice, both were at Mers-el-Kebir on the day of the British attack. In the course of engaging a destroyer of Admiral Somerville's squadron, *Mogador* received a hit by a 15-inch shell aft which exploded the depth-charges on the quarter deck and destroyed almost everything from the after shelter deck to the stern. Wreathed in smoke and flames, with many casualties, the unfortunate ship luckily remained afloat. After many hours, the fires were extinguished and she was towed back into port. *Volta*, next in line astern, avoided her crippled sister, dodged the British shellfire and managed to close *Strasbourg* with other *contre-torpilleurs* and escorted her safely into Toulon. *Mogador*, after temporary repairs, was later towed to Toulon for repairs, which had hardly been completed when, on 27 November 1942, she and her sister were scuttled together with the rest of the fleet. *Mogador* was raised on 5 April 1943 and *Volta* on 20 May 1943, but neither was repaired for further service.

***Improved Mogador* design** The 1938 programme did not originally envisage the construction of further *contre-torpilleurs*, but in April 1939 it was decided that three would be built at the expense of other vessels in the programme. Then, because of the three-ship division organization, a fourth was authorized in April 1940, to form two divisions together with *Mogador* and *Volta*. Six further units were projected. The decision to build further ships of the *Mogador* type had, in fact, been taken well before any official authorization was forthcoming! These new ships were not to be exact replicas of *Mogador*, however, and there was much discussion as to their design, particularly in respect of the main armament. This was due to the problems then being experienced with the 5.5-inch turrets aboard *Mogador* and also to the desire for an increase in the anti-aircraft capability of the ships. An initial suggestion to replace two wing torpedo tube banks and the 37mm mountings by four single 3.9-inch (100mm) mountings, as carried by *Algérie*, did not find favour as it would have allowed only two guns on each beam, while at the same time it displaced the sole effective close-range guns. Instead, it was proposed that the troublesome 5.5-inch turrets be replaced by twin 5.1-inch DP mountings of a type then under consideration for an improved *Le Hardi* type. However, despite the known problems with the twin 5.5-inch guns, the decision was taken to proceed with the original idea of the same main armament as *Mogador* because of doubts as to the availability and time-scale of the new gun.

At the outbreak of war, the four ships ordered had not yet been laid down and were suspended in view of other pressing priorities. Then as a result of another re-assessment of the performance of the twin 5.5-inch guns, under wartime conditions, the twin 5.1-inch gun was once again re-considered. This time the new armament was specified as four twin 5.1-inch, one twin 37mm, two twin 13.2mm and ten torpedo tubes. Suspension of construction was lifted in February 1940, for completion dates from September 1942 (*Marceau*) to December 1943 (*Hoche*). Modifications were made to the design in the light of early war experience, including a stronger hull, reduction in tactical diameter and an alteration to the turbines to allow faster acceleration. Bunkerage was increased to 850 tonnes, giving a useful increase in endurance. Main armament was to be that fixed in December 1939, i.e., eight 5.1-inch DP. However, magazine space presented a problem in that there was insufficient room to stow a useful outfit for both low- and high-angle use! In April 1940, the light AA was modified to four 37mm by the addition of two single guns and the 13.2mm (or 25mm) to three twin mountings, but the torpedo outfit was reduced to six tubes.

It seemed that everything was now finally agreed, but at the last minute before the French capitulation, the gunnery branch succeeded in arguing that the 5.1-inch gun might not be ready in time and therefore on 1 June 1940, the main armament was altered back to eight 5.5-inch (with 35° elevation in lieu of *Mogador*'s 30°), four 3.9-inch AA and eight 13.2mm machine-guns! This was the last change to be made, for the armistice effectively stopped all further construction.

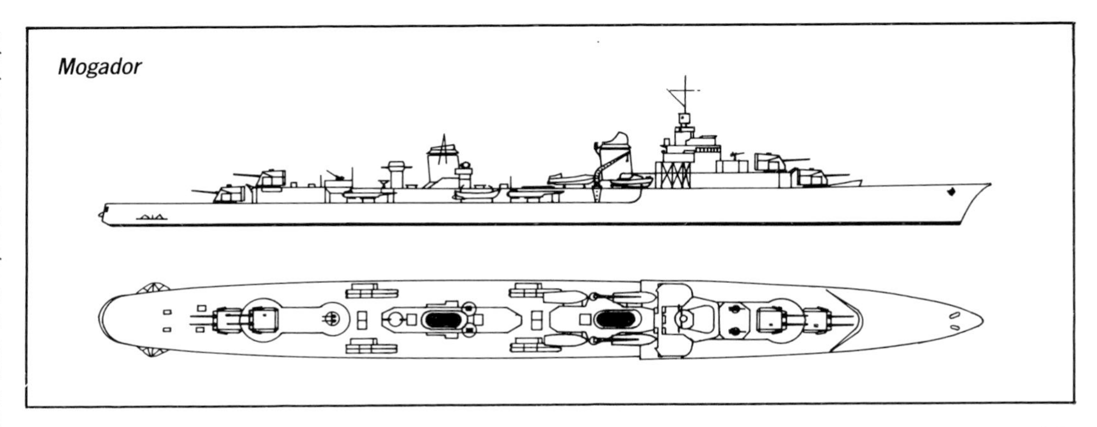

Below: *Volta* in August 1941. (M. Bar)

1500 TONNES CLASS (1922 Programme)

Ship	Builder	Laid Down	Launched	Commissioned*	Fate
Bourrasque[1]	At. & Ch. de France (Dunkirk)	12 Nov 23	5 Aug 25	23 Sept 26	Lost 30 May 40
Cyclone[1]	F. & Ch. de la Méditerranée (Le Havre)	29 Sept 23	24 Jan 25	1 June 28	Lost 30 May 40
Mistral[1]	F. & Ch. de la Méditerranée (Le Havre)	28 Nov 23	6 June 25	1 June 27	Stricken 17 Feb 50
Orage[3]	Ch. Nav. Français (Caen)	20 Aug 23	30 Aug 24	1 Dec 26	Lost 23 May 40
Ouragan[2]	Ch. Nav. Français (Caen)	3 April 23	6 Dec 24	19 Jan 27	Stricken 7 April 49
Simoun[1]	At. & Ch. de St-Nazaire–Penhoët	8 Aug 23	3 June 24	29 April 26	Stricken 17 Feb 50
Sirocco[1]	At. & Ch. de St-Nazaire–Penhoët	Mar 1924	3 Oct 25	1 July 27	Lost 31 May 40
Tempête[1]	Anciens Ch. Dubigeon (Nantes)	3 Dec 23	21 Feb 25	28 Sept 26	Stricken Feb 1950
Tornade[2]	Ch. Dyle & Bacalan (Bordeaux)	25 April 23	12 Mar 25	10 May 28	Lost 8 Nov 42
Tramontane[2]	F. & Ch. de la Gironde (Bordeaux)	June 1923	29 Nov 24	15 Oct 27	Lost 8 Nov 42
Trombe[2]	F. & Ch. de la Gironde (Bordeaux)	5 Mar 24	29 Dec 25	27 Oct 27	Stricken Feb 1950
Typhon[2]	F. & Ch. de la Gironde (Bordeaux)	Sept 1923	22 May 24	27 June 28	Scuttled 9 Nov 42

*All *Clôture d'armament.*

Displacement: 1,298tons/1,319tonnes (standard); 1,968tons/2,000tonnes (full load).
Length: 347ft/105.77m (oa); 326ft/99.33m (pp).
Beam: 31ft 7in/9.64m.
Draught: 14ft/4.3m (mean).
Machinery: three du Temple small-tube boilers; 2-shaft single reduction geared turbines ([1]Parsons, [2]Zoelly, [3]Rateau).
Performance: 33,000shp; 33kts.
Bunkerage: 335tons/340tonnes.
Range: 2,150nm at 14kts.
Guns: four 5.1in (4×1); two 37mm (2×1); two 13.2mm (2×1).
Torpedoes: six 21.7in (2×3).
Complement: 138.

Design The parameters of this class were originally proposed in April 1920 and were based on a displacement of 1,350 tonnes (normal), armed with four 3.9-inch guns, with a speed of 33 knots. However, foreign designs had already adopted the 4.7-inch gun and in consequence the main armament calibre was reconsidered. The choice lay between a new gun of 4.7-inch calibre or the existing 5.1-inch gun already chosen for the new *contre-torpilleurs* and, quite sensibly, the decision was made in favour of the latter. This was the 1919 Model with a 32kg projectile. Thus the new *torpilleurs* would carry the heaviest calibre guns to be mounted in contemporary torpedo-craft. Otherwise the design was unremarkable and even anachronistic given the three-funnelled appearance.

Twelve ships were authorized under the 1922 programme, all being ordered from private yards. On trials they achieved around 34.5 knots maximum, but an average figure was more like 33.5 knots. *Orage*, for example, could only reach 32.57 knots on eight-hours' trial and just 32.80 knots on a ninth hour. Under normal service conditions, 30 knots represented a realistic figure for most of the class.

As completed, the anti-aircraft armament comprised one Mk 1927 75mm gun and two 8mm machine-guns. In the anti-submarine role, twenty 200kg depth-charges could be dropped from twin racks on the quarter-deck and two throwers for 100kg depth-charges were also fitted. The main armament had a maximum elevation of 36°, for a maximum range of 20,000 yards, achieved at the cost of excessively high trunnion height. This led in turn to a rather low rate of fire – only about four or five rounds per minute – and it would doubtless have been better to sacrifice some range for an increased rate for fire. With this new class, the torpedo calibre was also increased, to 21.7 inches, giving a welcome increase in hitting power and range, because the 1919 Model torpedo carried a charge of only 522lb, whereas the 1923 Model nearly doubled that to 913lb and had a range of 15,300 yards at 25 knots.

Modifications In April 1931, approval was given to replace the 75mm gun with two 37mm single mountings which, while not having the range of the heavier gun, had a much greater rate of fire. Before the war, the only other modification had been the cutting down of the funnel height. Sea-worthiness remained somewhat of a problem and in the first weeks of the war, sea experience led to the decision, in December 1939, to land two torpedoes and at the end of January 1940, a similar decision was taken in respect of No. 3 gun (those units outside the Mediterranean). This latter decision was, however, unpopular with the Fleet and brought forth strong demands for its reinstatement. The fall of France intervened, but after June 1940, those ships in British hands, *Mistral* and *Ouragan*, were given modified armaments because of a general shortage of spares and ammunition for the French weapons, receiving four 4.7-inch BL Mk I, two forward two aft, one 12pdr and three 20mm guns, while losing one bank of torpedo tubes. Units which remained in French hands received only limited augmentation of their AA outfits, due to lack of means. *Tornade, Tramontane* and *Typhon*, based in North Africa, received one 25mm gun and two twin 13.2mm machine-guns but while the first mentioned ship retained all its torpedo tubes, *Tramontane* retained only one triple bank and *Typhon* had only a twin mount. All however, retained four guns. After the Allied invasion of North Africa in November 1942, *Simoun* and *Tempête* rejoined the Allied forces and, in 1943, received better AA outfits, namely one 40mm and six or eight 20mm at the cost of No. 3

Below: *Mistral* in British service, re-armed with 4.7-inch guns, a 12pdr and 20mm guns. (IWM)

gun and one bank of tubes (where not already landed). *Simoun*, however, lost all tubes but carried extra depth-charges. *Trombe*, taken over by Italy in November 1942 at Toulon, was finally returned to French colours in October 1943 and in all probability received similar treatment.

Service Operating in the Channel during the early days of the war, *Sirocco* claimed a U-boat sunk, but in fact, the boat in question, *U49*, managed to regain her base, although badly damaged. On the other hand, *Simoun* carried out another attack in February 1940 but without result.

In the spring of 1940, as the German Army pressed into France, the units in the Channel became embroiled with German light forces and aircraft. During the run-up to the Dunkirk evacuations and during them, losses were particularly heavy. *Orage* was the first loss, when, as part of a force of French destroyers, she provided fire support off Boulogne during the evacuation of that port on 23 May. Caught by the Luftwaffe, she was bombed and sunk. Her sister, *Bourrasque*, sank on 30 May off Nieuport on the third day of Operation 'Dynamo', when she hit a mine while evacuating troops and that same day, *Cyclone* lost her bows to a torpedo from *S.24*. The following day, *Sirocco* was sunk by torpedoes from *S23* and *S26* while off Dunkirk. *Cyclone* moved to Brest for repairs and was in dry dock at the time that port was evacuated. On 18 June 1940, she was destroyed to prevent her capture.

At the time of the Allied invasion of North Africa, *Tornade*, *Tramontane* and *Typhon* were based upon Oran, forming the 7th Division of *Torpilleurs*. Here *Typhon* sank the British cutter *Hartland* in the early hours of 8 November as she and *Walney* attempted to put troops ashore, but later that day, her two division mates sortied to attack the British forces off the port, with disastrous results. Outside the harbour, the cruiser *Aurora*, in company with destroyers, engaged the French flotilla, sinking *Tornade* and damaging *Tramontane* so badly that she was driven ashore. *Typhon* remained in port, being scuttled as a blockship the following day.

Two weeks later, *Trombe* lying in care and maintenance at Toulon, was captured before her small crew could effectively sabotage her and was later turned over to the Italian Navy as *FR23*.

There were now only four of the original twelve units left afloat: *Mistral* (in use as a gunnery training tender by the Royal Navy), *Ouragan* (used initially by the Polish Navy, but later returned to the Free French Forces), *Tempête* and *Simoun*. They were later re-joined by *Trombe* when she was given up by the Italians on their surrender in 1943. With the exception of *Mistral* and *Ouragan*, the survivors served in Mediterranean waters for the remainder of the war, *Trombe* being torpedoed and badly damaged by an S-boat off San Remo on 17 April 1945. This was to be the last mishap to be suffered by the class before the end of hostilities, but with the coming of peace, the usefulness of these old ships was at an end. All were stricken from the Navy List by 1950.

1500 TONNES CLASS (1924, 1925 & 1926 Programmes)

Ship	Builder	Laid Down	Launched	Commissioned*	Fate
L'Adroit[1]	At. & Ch. de France (Dunkirk)	26 May 25	1 April 27	1 July 29	Bombed 25 May 40
L'Alcyon[1]	F. & Ch. de la Gironde (Bordeaux)	Feb 1925	26 June 26	15 July 29	Stricken 10 Nov 52
Le Fortuné	Ch. Nav. Français (Caen)	11 Sept 25	15 Nov 26	1 July 28	Stricken 31 Aug 50
Le Mars	Ch. Nav. Français (Caen)	8 July 25	28 Aug 26	20 Jan 28	Scuttled 27 Nov 42
La Palme	Anciens Ch. Dubigeon (Nantes)	16 May 25	30 June 26	6 Feb 28	Scuttled 27 Nov 42
La Railleuse	Anciens Ch. Dubigeon (Nantes)	30 July 25	9 Sept 26	15 Mar 28	Blew Up 24 Mar 40
Basque	At. & Ch. de la Seine-Maritime	18 Sept 26	25 May 29	5 Mar 31	Stricken 10 Dec 52
Bordelais	F. & Ch. de la Gironde (Bordeaux)	19 Nov 26	23 May 28	8 April 30	Scuttled 27 Nov 42
Boulonnais	Ch. Nav. Français (Caen)	4 May 26	1 June 27	25 June 28	Sunk 8 Nov 42
Brestois	Ch. Dyle & Bacalan (Bordeaux)	17 May 26	18 May 27	15 June 28	Sunk 8 Nov 42
Forbin	F. & Ch. de la Méditerranée (Le Havre)	29 June 27	17 July 28	1 May 30	Stricken 10 Nov 52
Foudroyant	Ch. Dyle & Bacalan (Bordeaux)	28 July 27	24 April 29	10 Oct 30	Bombed 1 June 40
Fougueux[2]	At. & Ch. de Bretagne (Nantes)	21 Sept 27	4 Aug 28	15 June 30	Sunk 8 Nov 42
Frondeur[1]	Ch. Nav. Français (Caen)	9 Nov 27	29 June 29	28 Oct 31	Sunk 8 Nov 42

**Clôture d'armament.*

Displacement: 1,356tons/1,378tonnes (standard); 1.968tons/2,000tonnes (full load).
Length: 351ft 9in/107.2m (oa); 331ft/100.9m (pp).
Beam: 32ft 3in/9.84m.
Draught: 14ft/4.3m (mean).
Machinery: three du Temple small-tube boilers; 2-shaft single reduction Parsons (except [1]Zoelly and [2]Rateau) geared turbines.
Performance: 34,000shp; 33kts.
Bunkerage: 335tons/340tonnes
Range: 2,150nm at 14kts.
Guns: four 5.1in (4×1); two 37mm (2×1); two 13mm (2×1).
Torpedoes: six 21.7in (2×3).
Complement: 138.

Design Outwardly virtually identical with the 1922 programme ships, this later series differed a little in their basic dimensions and in consequence came out slightly heavier. However, the main operational difference was the adoption of a new model gun, the 5.1-inch Mk 1924, which was of auto-frettage construction. The French Navy had little experience of turbine drives before the construction of the 1922 series and as a result, had tried three different designs of turbine in that series. For the new ships, it had been decided that the Parsons' design was superior and thus all but four ships received this type. Like many contemporary French ships, unfortunately, the endurance was below expectations. It had been assumed that their main role would have been short-range operations between Metropolitan France and North Africa, but when war came their services were needed in a number of different theatres and roles. It was very quckly found that their endurance under service conditions was greatly different from the theoretical figures. The latter were in any case somewhat below contemporary foreign figures and the additional requirements of being on a war footing made fuel a constant problem for the ships' captains.

Modifications Like the earlier series, the later ships received 37mm guns in lieu of their 75mm gun prior to the outbreak of war. Similarly, one 5.1-inch gun was to be landed for stability reasons early in 1940 which was usually No. 3 gun but sometimes No. 4 (e.g., *La Fortuné*). Only four ships survived the fatal year of 1942, (*L'Alcyon, Basque, Forbin* and *Le Fortuné*) and these landed one bank of tubes as well as one 5.1-inch gun to augment the AA guns by one 40mm and four to six 20mm. Asdic and Radar were also installed. After the war, *L'Alcyon* received an ex-German 4.1-inch twin mounting in No. 4 position while engaged on trials.

Service Together with the twelve earlier units, these ships formed the backbone of the French *Divisions de Torpilleurs* during the late 1920s and up to the beginning of the Second World War. From the outbreak of war, patrol and escort duty were the order of the day, which, as has been mentioned, highlighted differences in endurance. An early loss was *La Railleuse*, destroyed by a torpedo warhead explosion while lying at Casablanca in March 1940. In April 1940, the 5th Division (*Boulonnais, Brestois* and *Foudroyant*) were ordered to Norway for the abortive Anglo-French landings, and later many units took part in covering the evacuations from the Belgian and French Channel ports. *L'Adroit* and *Foudroyant* both fell victims to the Luftwaffe off Dunkirk in May and June 1940 respectively. The latter was on her third evacuation trip. *Fougueux* and *Frondeur* were both damaged but managed to reach harbour safely.

With the armistice in June, the survivors retired to French Mediterranean and North African ports where they remained until the end of 1942. At this time, just prior to Operation 'Torch', *Boulonnais, Brestois, Fougueux, L'Alcyon* and *Frondeur* lay at Casablanca; *Le Mars, La Palme* and *Bordelais* at Toulon with *Le Fortuné, Basque* and *Forbin* at Alexandria. The last three had been disarmed with Admiral Godfrey's squadron since June 1940. On 8 November 1942, the American Task Force 34 opened fire on the French ships at Casablanca and the *torpilleurs* sortied to counter-attack. In another unequal battle, *Fougueux* was destroyed by gunfire from *Massachusetts* and *Tuscaloosa*, while *Boulonnais* was sunk by *Brooklyn*. *Brestois*, hit by at least six

Right: *Boulonnais* in 1933. (M. Bar)

Below: *Le Mars* in June 1939. (M. Bar)

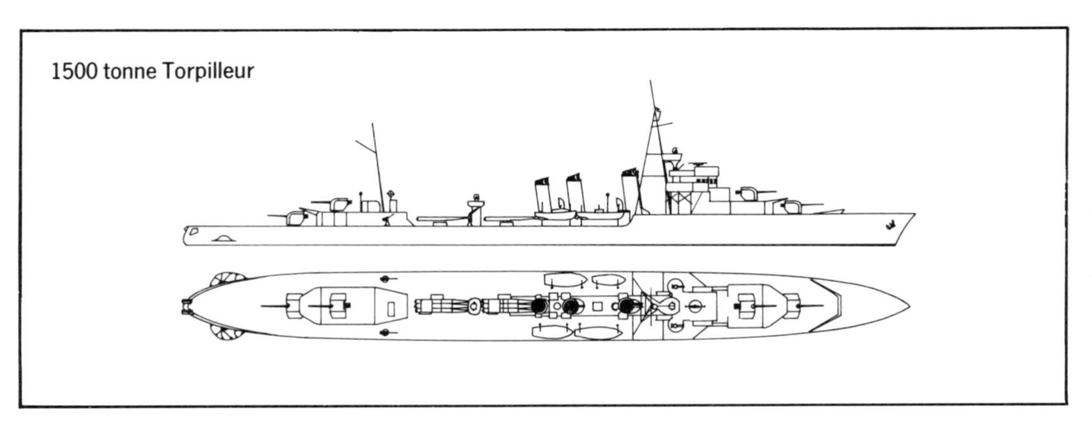

8-inch shells and *Frondeur* with four compartments flooded, including the machinery spaces, succeeded in returning to harbour but continued to make water and capsized the following night. *L'Alcyon* although also badly hit, managed to remain afloat and in action.

Le Mars, La Palme and *Bordelais* were all scuttled with the Fleet at Toulon on 27 November 1942. The survivors, *Le Fortuné, Basque, Forbin* and *L'Alcyon* joined the Allied Forces and from the summer of 1943 served in the Mediterranean, later against pockets of German resistance on the French Atlantic coast. After the end of the war, these ships served for a further period until discarded from 1950 to 1952.

LE HARDI CLASS

Ship	Builder	Laid Down	Launched	Commissioned	Fate
Le Hardi	At. & Ch. de la Loire (Nantes)†	20 May 36	4 May 38		Scuttled 27 Nov 42
Fleuret	F. & Ch. de la Méditerranée (La Seyne)	18 Aug 36	28 July 38		Scuttled 27 Nov 42
Epée	F. & Ch. de la Gironde (Bordeaux)	15 Oct 36	26 Oct 38		Scuttled 27 Nov 42
Mameluk	At. & Ch. de la Loire (Nantes)†	1 Jan 37	18 Feb 39		Scuttled 27 Nov 42
Casque	F. & Ch. de la Méditerranée (La Seyne)†	30 Nov 36	2 Nov 38		Scuttled 27 Nov 42
Lansquenet	F. & Ch. de la Gironde (Bordeaux)	17 Dec 36	20 May 39		Scuttled 27 Nov 42
Le Corsaire	F. & Ch. de la Méditerranée (La Seyne)†	31 Mar 38	14 Nov 39		Scuttled 27 Nov 42
Le Flibustier	F. & Ch. de la Méditerranée (La Seyne)	11 Mar 38	14 Dec 39		Scuttled 27 Nov 42
*L'Intrépide**	F. & Ch. de la Méditerranée (La Seyne)†	16 Aug 39	26 June 41		Bombed 11 Mar 44
*Le Téméraire**	F. & Ch. de la Méditerranée (La Seyne)†	28 Aug 39	7 Nov 41		Bombed Aug 1944
*L'Opiniâtre**	F. & Ch. de la Gironde (Bordeaux)	1 Aug 39	–		Scrapped incomplete
*L'Aventurier**	F. & Ch. de la Gironde (Bordeaux)	4 Aug 39	20 April 47		Discarded 19 May 50
*L'Eveillé**, *L'Alerte**, *L'Inconstant**, *L'Espiègle**	Not ordered				

Displacement: 1,772 (*2,180)tons/1,797 (*2,215)tonnes (standard); 2,536 (*2,882)tons/ 2,577 (*2,929)tonnes (full load).
Length: 384ft 6in/117.2m (oa); 366ft 3in (*398ft 3in)/111.6m (*118.6m) (pp).
Beam: 36ft 6in (*39ft 6in)/11.1m (*11.8m).
Draught: 13ft 9in/4.2m (mean).
Machinery: four Sural-Penhoët boilers; 2-shaft single reduction Rateau geared turbines (Parsons in †).
Performance: 58,000 (*60,000)shp; 37 (*35)kts.
Bunkerage: 462tons/470tonnes.
Range: 2,760nm at 20kts.
Guns: six 5.1in (DP only in *); two 37mm; four 13.2mm MG (eight in *); four 3.9in *L'Opiniâtre* only.
Torpedoes: seven 21.7in (1×3, 2×2); six (2×3) *L'Optiniâtre* only.
Complement: 187.

Design The necessity of providing a screen force for the new battleships *Dunkerque* and *Strasbourg* as well as the fast light cruisers of the *Georges Leygues* class led to the decision in 1932 to build a new class of *torpilleurs* because the older ships of the 1,500-tonnes type did not have sufficient speed. The 1,500-type had in fact been criticized on numerous grounds; their 5.1-inch guns were complicated and had a slow rate of fire, loading was difficult at elevations greater than 15° and the gun disposition was disliked because the superimposed guns forward led to an over-high bridge structure. Finally, the AA outfit was regarded as very poor.

In consequence, a staff requirement outlining desirable qualities to be incorporated in the design was issued in June 1932. These were in the main: (a) speed of 34–35 knots at normal displacement; (b) low silhouette; (c) good stability; (d) reinforced stem; (e) good bridge accommodation; (f) special attention to torpedo requirements; (g) re-arranged fuel bunkers as compared with the 1,500-tonnes type.

By late 1932, it was envisaged that the new design would displace 1,300/1,400 tonnes, armed with four 5.1-inch guns in two twin turrets. However, difficulties with the necessary speed requirements and the desire to have the ships at least as well armed as their foreign contemporaries (i.e., the Italian *Navigatori* class) led to increased dimensions. Thus, in August 1934 when the design was finalized, the parameters had grown to 1,772 tonnes and six 5.1 inch guns.

The new design incorporated some advance in machinery in that steam pressures were increased by comparison with the earlier 1,500-tonnes type and only two designs of turbine utilized, Zoelly-pattern types being discontinued. The design improvements, particularly in the boiler plant, allowed a reduction in machinery weights, so that power to weight ratio was 18.26kg/hp as compared to 28.92kg/hp for the last of the 1,500-tonnes type. An important improvement was the increase in bunker capacity by more than 30 per cent. This, and the inclusion of a separate cruising turbine drum gave a useful increase in radius of action.

The main armament, 5.1-inch Mk 1930, was the same gun as that carried by *Dunkerque* and was semi-automatic. Following the example of *Mogador*,

Right: *Le Hardi* in April 1941. Note extra AA guns on No. 2 gun. (M. Bar)

twin mountings were adopted for the first time in French *torpilleurs*, in weatherproof gun-houses. In line with the requirement for a low silhouette, hence low bridge, the gun-houses were to be disposed one forward and two aft. The Mk 1930 gun had a rate of fire of 14 to 15 rounds per minute and an elevation of 30°, being for low-angle use only. Two 5m stereoscopic rangefinders were provided which could also be used for torpedo purposes. Two Mk 1925 37mm guns and four 13.2mm Hotchkiss machine-guns comprised the AA outfit. The torpedo armament was increased by one tube by the usual expedient of replacing the after bank by two twin sets on the beam. However, this also reduced the broadside by one tube from 6 to 5.

Despite the commencement of design studies as early as 1932, the design was not finalized until 10 August 1934, and another 23 months were to pass before the name ship was laid down. This loss in time was never made up and had a disastrous effect on the *torpilleur* forces when war broke out. Ordering proceeded only slowly, two further units being authorized in 1935, three in 1936, two in 1937 and three in 1938. Finally the 1938 *bis* programme authorized a further five units of which four were later deleted in favour of more units of the *Mogador* class.

By the outbreak of war, only six had been launched and none had yet been completed. *Le Hardi*, the lead ship, did not commence preliminary trials until 21 July 1939 and due to the war situation, was the only one to run full peace time trials. On her eight-hour full-power trials in November 1939, she achieved 39.09 knots. (The only other recorded result was *Fleuret* with 40.2 knots). The armistice on 18 June 1940 found eight of the class afloat, fitting out or on trials. Of these, *Epée, Mameluk* and *Lansquenet* were in French Atlantic shipyards and therefore in some danger from the occupying German forces. The former two were considerably further advanced than *Lansquenet* and were able to escape south without too much trouble, but *Lansquenet* had only been put afloat on 20 May 1939. She was in dry dock with her machinery installed but no armament yet aboard. She was quickly put afloat and that same afternoon hurriedly shipped her 5.1-inch guns and gun-houses before being towed to Pauillac for fuel. Two of her four boilers were complete but had never been steamed, and her engines had never been turned. Nevertheless, she got under way and despite an engagement with German shore batteries at the mouth of the Gironde, arrived safely in Casablanca on 27 June.

Four ships remained incomplete at the armistice, two in the Mediterranean (*L'Intrépide* and *Le Téméraire*) and two in the Gironde (*L'Opiniâtre* and *L'Aventurier*), none of which had been launched. This second group were to have been somewhat different from the first group because the lessons of the Spanish Civil War had highlighted the dangers of air power. During the latter half of 1938, consideration was given to the re-arming of the *Le Hardi* design with dual-purpose 5.1-inch mountings of the same type as carried by *Dunkerque*. While in theory this meant the use of an already proven mounting, it proved impossible to fit it to the first eight units and it was decided that only the second group would be adapted for it. But, because of the three-ship divisional organization, one of the second group (*L'Opiniâtre*) was scheduled to receive the earlier low-angle mounting in order that nine ships would be so equipped. Her extra displacement was, however, to be utilized to fit two twin 3.9-inch AA mountings and an ASW outfit. Other armament variations for the second group were also considered, including four 5.1-inch LA (two twin) or alternatively eight 3.9-inch guns in four twin mountings. Finally, despite the requirement for better AA defence, another suggestion was for eight 5.1-inch LA guns in four mountings!

At the beginning of 1939, the question of providing a certain amount of protective plating against machine-gun fire was raised, with the proviso that the displacement would not be increased. To compensate, the torpedo outfit would be reduced to six tubes, and the 37mm and 13.2mm guns replaced by three or four twin 23mm guns, a new calibre under consideration.

Modifications The circumstances of their entry into service rather precipitately in June 1940 meant that in some cases, final completion had to be carried out far from the builder's yard and it is likely that some units were not completed as designed. During the period 1941–42, some modifications were made to the AA outfit. *Le Hardi* was fitted with a twin 37mm Mk 1933 in lieu of her 1925 Model, two single 25mm in the bridge wings, four twin 13.2mm (fitted on the quarter deck, after deck-house and bridge wings) as well as five 8mm guns fitted to the torpedo tube mountings. Other units were probably so fitted.

The two units in the Gironde fell incomplete into German hands and lay unattended for more than two years. The Kriegsmarine, always short of destroyers, inspected the French ships in October 1942, by which time, the elements had had some effect on the unprotected hulls and many plates required replacement. The guns and mountings were not available as they were in unoccupied France, but the Kriegsmarine decided to try to complete *L'Opiniâtre*, then only some 16 per cent complete and allocated the name *ZF2*. *L'Aventurier* was not proceeded with. Flag Officer (Destroyers) Admiral Bey, decided that if the French turrets could not be obtained, an alternative armament of either three twin 12cm Dutch-pattern guns or four German 5-inch (12.7cm) guns would be used. In the end, the 5-inch German gun was selected, together with four 37mm, ten 20mm and two quadruple banks of torpedo tubes. However, further work was delayed under every pretext and the ship was never launched, construction being abandoned in July 1943.

Service After the armistice, based in Casablanca, *L'Epée*, *Le Hardi* and *Fleuret* formed the 10th *Division de Torpilleurs*. Following the British attack on Dakar, *L'Epée* and *Fleuret* took part in a reprisal raid against Gibraltar on 24/25 September, in company with two units of the 2nd Flotilla (*Fougueux* and *Frondeur*). In conjunction with Vichy air raids on the Rock during 24/25 September, the French destroyers had a brief and halfhearted engagement with a British destroyer, during which *L'Epée* fired only fourteen rounds before all her 5.1-inch guns developed defects. *Fleuret* did not even fire a shot, as her fire-control equipment refused to follow the target. The two older ships only fired six rounds between them and it was fortunate for them that the British destroyers did not pursue the engagement. The other ship of the flotilla, *Le Hardi*, was in Dakar at the time of the British attack. She screened the incomplete *Richelieu* with smoke and replied to British gunfire but without inflicting or receiving damage.

Casque and *Le Corsaire* escaped from Toulon to Mers-el-Kebir on 20 and 22 June 1940 respectively, but took no part in the action on 6 July because *Casque* had only her AA outfit operational and *Le Corsaire* had left France before shipping her 5.1-inch guns!

After Dakar, the units of the 10th Division returned to Toulon where they were joined by *Fleuret* and *Lansquenet* in November 1940 after the latter pair had escorted *Provence* back to Metropolitan France. *Casque* and *Le Corsaire* also later returned to Toulon, the former replacing *Le Hardi* in the 10th Division (1 May 1942), which by now comprised *Casque, L'Epée* and *Mameluk*.

On 1 April 1941, *Fleuret, L'Epée, Le Corsaire* and *Le Flibustier* were re-named to commemorate earlier war losses, becoming *Foudroyant, L'Adroit, Sirocco* and *Bison* respectively. Only this division was kept in active service, the remainder of the ships being reduced to care and maintenance. Thus all eight ships were present and were scuttled when the Fleet destroyed itself in November 1942. Because a number of the ships did not have full complements aboard, their destruction was not as complete as those ships that had been in commission, and in consequence were in a salvageable condition. Somewhat surprisingly, the Germans left the bulk of this task to the Royal Italian Navy, presumably as they themselves lacked the necessary salvage equipment. The Italians seized the chance of using these modern destroyers to replace some of their heavy destroyer losses and ear-marked six for salvage. These were re-named: *FR32* (*Sirocco*), *FR33* (*L'Adroit*), *FR34* (*Lansquenet*), *FR35* (*Bison*), *FR36* (*Foudroyant*) and *FR37* (*Le Hardi*). *Bison* was only 75 per cent complete when she was scuttled and the remaining pair *Mameluk* and *Casque* were judged irreparable.

FR32 (*Sirocco*) was raised and then towed to Genoa on 10 June 1943 where she was being refitted and having her armament altered when Italy surrendered. Later she was scuttled as a blockship in Genoa on 28 October 1943. *FR33* (*L'Adroit*) was raised on 20 April 1943, then seized by the Germans in September 1943 and finally given back to the French in 1944 in an irreparable condition. She was later sold for scrapping. *FR34* (*Lansquenet*) was towed to Italy on 31 August 1943 after her salvage and en route to Genoa, was taken by the Germans at Imperia on 9 September. She was scuttled once more on 24 April 1945, re-floated post-war and towed back to Toulon on 19 March 1946 for repairs. In the event, repairs were never started and the ship was stricken for disposal in 1946. *FR35* (*Bison*) like *FR33*, was seized in September 1943 after salvage but before she was towed to Italy. Used as a smoke-generator hulk by the Germans, she was first damaged by Allied bombers in the spring of 1944 and eventually torpedoed as a blockship on 25 June by a German submarine. *FR35* (*Foudroyant*) was raised on 20 May 1943, captured by the Germans, then finally scuttled again as a blockship by them in August 1944. *FR37* (*Le Hardi*) was captured by the Germans in the port of Savona in Italy en route to Genoa for refit, having left Toulon on 7 September 1943. She was finally scuttled un-repaired at Genoa on 24 April 1945.

Of the remaining ships, *L'Intrépide* and *Le Téméraire* were only about 20 per cent complete when captured in November 1942 and lay untouched until the end of the war when they were broken up. *L'Opiniâtre* too was broken up on the slip, but her sister, *L'Aventurier*, was launched post-war in order to clear the slipway and later towed to Brest for experimental purposes. Her hull remained in existence as a mooring hulk until recent years. She was put up for sale on 21 April 1971.

600 TONNES CLASS

Ship	Builder	Laid Down	Launched	Commissioned*	Fate
*La Melpomène***	At. & Ch. de Bretagne (Nantes)	13 Dec 33	24 Jan 35	20 Nov 36	Stricken 15 May 50
*La Flore***	At. & Ch. de Bretagne (Nantes)	26 Mar 34	5 Mar 35	25 Nov 36	Stricken 31 Aug 50
La Pomone	At. & Ch. de la Loire (Nantes)	22 Nov 33	25 Jan 35	1 Dec 36	Scuttled 27 Sept 43
L'Iphigénie	At. & Ch. de la Loire (Nantes)	14 Dec 33	18 April 35	1 Nov 36	Sunk 10 Sept 43
La Bayonnaise	Ch. Maritime du S-O (Bordeaux)	18 Oct 34	28 Jan 36	1 April 38	Scuttled 25 Aug 44
*La Cordelière***	Ch. Augustin-Normand (Le Havre)	16 Aug 34	9 Sept 36	1 Dec 37	Stricken 17 Feb 50
*L'Incomprise***	At. & Ch. de la Seine-Maritime	20 Oct 34	14 April 36	16 Mar 38	Stricken 31 Aug 50
La Poursuivante	At. & Ch. de France (Dunkirk)	13 Aug 34	4 Aug 36	5 Nov 37	Scuttled 27 Nov 42
*Bombarde***	At. & Ch. de la Loire (Nantes)	18 Feb 35	23 Mar 36	16 Aug 37†	Sunk 23 Aug 44
Branlebas	Ch. Augustin-Normand (Le Havre)	27 Aug 34	12 April 37	16 Mar 38	Foundered 14 Dec 40
Bouclier	At. & Ch. de la Seine-Maritime	18 Oct 34	9 Aug 37	6 Aug 38	Stricken 31 Aug 50
*Baliste***	At. & Ch. de France (Dunkirk)	20 Sept 34	17 Mar 37	24 May 38	Sunk 24 Nov 43

**Clôture d'armament.* †Date of admission to active service.

Displacement: 669tons/680tonnes (standard); 911tons/926tonnes (full load).
Length: 264ft 9in/80.7m (oa); 249ft 3in/76m (pp).
Beam: 26ft 3in/7.96m.
Draught: 10ft/3.07m (mean).
Machinery: two Indret boilers; 2-shaft single reduction Parsons (**Rateau) geared turbines.
Performance: 22,000shp; 34.5kts.
Bunkerage: 167tons/170tonnes.
Range: 1,000nm at 20kts.
Guns: two 3.9in; four 13.2mm MG.
Torpedoes: two 21.7in (1×2).
Complement: 5+100.

Design Conceived under the provisions of the 1930 London Naval Treaty, which placed no limit on the numbers of ships permitted under 600 tons, this class was originally rated as 'escorts' and authorized under the 'Coast defence' section of the Estimate. As escorts, the required speed was fixed at 34.5 knots, armament two 75mm guns and four 400mm torpedo tubes. This design received an unfavourable reception, particularly in respect of its armament and it was re-worked, finally resulting in 3.9-inch guns being shipped and larger calibre but fewer torpedoes. The original intention of having single tubes placed so as to bear fire on the bow was dropped, leaving only a paired bank on the centre-line.

Two single 3.9-inch Mk 1930 guns, with 34° elevation fired separate ammunition with a 33lb (15kg) projectile and had an effective range of 17,274 yards (15,800m). The torpedoes carried were the 1923 pattern with a weight of 2,100kg.

The ship's hull was modelled upon that of the 2,400-tonnes *contre-torpilleurs* of the *Albatros* class and it was hoped that these small *torpilleurs* would have better sea properties than their larger sisters.

Four units were authorized under the estimates of 31 March 1931, four under that of 10 July 1931 and four more under the following year's estimate on 31 March 1932. All were constructed in private shipyards.

Modifications In French hands, few modifications, if any, were carried out due to circumstances and it was in fact, the British and Germans who were to alter the armament after the vessels fell into their hands. *Branlebas* became an early loss and her armament in British service is uncertain, but it is probable that she received a couple of single 2pdr guns to bolster her weak AA outfit. By early 1942 *La Melpomène* had landed her after 3.9-inch gun and had its adjacent deck-house removed. Two 2pdr single guns were fitted in lieu as well as two single 20mm guns. Her torpedo tubes were retained and she is also reported as having a single 2pdr gun fitted on the quarter deck. The other units in British hands, *Bouclier, La Cordelière, La Flore* and *L'Incomprise* were employed on subsidiary duties and any alterations to their armament was probably on the lines of *La Melpomène.*

Those ships which ended up in German hands, *Bombarde* (*TA9*), *La Pomone* (*TA10*), *L'Iphigénie* (*TA11*), *Baliste* (*TA12*) and *La Bayonnaise* (*TA13*) were altered according to Kriegsmarine requirements. The torpedo tubes were removed and the AA outfit augmented by the addition of a 20mm quadruple gun on the handling room just forward of the after 3.9-inch gun, two single 37mm on the maindeck in the waist and a number of single 20mm guns making a total of about twenty. Radar was added on the foremast, which was converted to a tripod to carry the weight.

Service At the beginning of the war, six of these ships were in the Channel theatre based at Dunkirk, and six in the Mediterranean. The divisions in the North were the 11th *Division de Torpilleurs* (*La Cordelière, Branlebas* and *L'Incomprise*) and the 14th

Above: *Bombarde* in June 1939. (M. Bar)

Right: *La Melpomène* with British wartime alterations. (IWM)

(*Bouclier, La Melpomène* and *La Flore*), while in the Mediterranean were the 12th (*La Pomone, Bombarde* and *L'Iphigeénie*) and 13th *Divisions* (*Baliste, La Bayonnaise* and *La Poursuivante*). The 11th and 14th Divisions took part in support operations during the German advance to the west when their maneouvrability and small size stood them in good stead. However, the weakness of their AA outfit was painfully exposed by massed Luftwaffe attacks. *La Cordelière, Branlebas* and *L'Incomprise* were all damaged to varying degrees.

In June 1940 four (*Branlebas, Bouclier, L'Incomprise* and *La Flore*) took part in the Dunkirk evacuation when *Bouclier* was badly damaged in a collision. Then, in mid June, *La Flore, La Melpomène, Branlebas* and *L'Incomprise* moved west to support the French Army in the Cotentin peninsula. When France collapsed, all six ships put into British ports where, on 4 July they were seized by the Royal Navy.

On 14 December 1940, *Branlebas*, in service with the Royal Navy, was lost in a storm 25 miles SSW of the Eddystone light, highlighting one of the major deficiencies of this design. The French Navy had already criticized poor stability due to top weight caused in part by the height of the boilers which in turn required a deep hull. In a sea-way, the boats worked badly and their main machinery was somewhat fragile. In short, they were poor escorts and poor torpedo-boats. The forward gun was frequently washed out as were the machine-guns. Finally, their radius of action proved to be much less than their theoretical design figure.

In view of these shortcomings, the loss of *Branlebas* and a shortage of Free French crews, it is hardly surprising that the Royal Navy made little use of the five left in their hands. *Bouclier* was first Polish- then Dutch-manned before becoming a training ship and *La Melpomène* served at the Nore until 1942. Both then joined the rest of the class laid up at Hartlepool where they remained until the end of the war.

The three ships of the 12th Division, stationed at Bizerta, were captured intact in a surprise attack by German Army units on 8 December 1942 and turned over to the Italian Navy as *FR41* (*Bombarde*), *FR42* (*La Pomone*) and *FR43* (*L'Iphigénie*). However, as a result of an agreement with Germany, Italy transferred all three to the Kriegsmarine on 5 April 1943 when they were re-named once more (*TA9, TA10* and *TA11* respectively).

All three units of the 13th Division were scuttled at Toulon on 27 November 1942, after which, two (*La Bayonnaise* and *Baliste*) were taken over by the Royal Italian Navy as *FR44* and *FR45* respectively. After the Italian capitulation, both were seized by the Kriegsmarine as *TA13* and *TA12*.

1010 TONNES CLASS

Ship	Builder	Laid Down	Launched	Fate
*Le Fier**	At. & Ch. de Bretagne (Nantes)	17 Jan 39	12 Mar 40	Scuttled 11 Aug 44
*L'Agile**	At. & Ch. de Bretagne (Nantes)	26 April 39	23 May 40	Scuttled 11 Aug 44
L'Entreprenant	At. & Ch. de la Loire (Nantes)	26 Jan 39	25 May 40	Bombed 16 Sept 43
Le Farouche	At. & Ch. de la Loire (Nantes)	11 April 39	19 Oct 40	Scuttled 11 Aug 44
*L'Alsacien**	At. & Ch. de Bretagne (Nantes)	11 April 39	1942	Scrapped incomplete
*Le Breton**	At. & Ch. de Bretagne (Nantes)	Jan 1940	–	Construction abandoned
Le Corse	At. & Ch. de la Loire (Nantes)	Jan 1940	4 April 42	Scuttled 11 Aug 44
Le Tunisien	At. & Ch. de la Loire (Nantes)	Not laid down		Cancelled
Le Normand	At. & Ch. de la Loire (Nantes)	Not laid down		Cancelled
Le Parisien	At. & Ch. de la Loire (Nantes)	Not laid down		Cancelled
Le Provençal	At. & Ch. de la Loire (Nantes)	Not laid down		Cancelled
*Le Saintongeais**	At. & Ch. de Bretagne (Nantes)	Not laid down		Cancelled
Le Niçois	F. & Ch. de la Médeterranée (La Seyne)	Not laid down		Cancelled
Le Savoyard	F. & Ch. de la Médeterranée (La Seyne)	Not laid down		Cancelled

Displacement: 994tons/1,010tonnes (standard); 1,354tons/1,376tonnes (full load).
Length: 311ft 9in/95m (oa); 259ft 3in/90m (pp).
Beam: 30ft 9in/9.4m.
Draught: 10ft 9in/3.25m (mean).
Machinery: three Indret boilers; 2-shaft Parsons single reduction geared turbines (except *Rateau turbines).
Performance: 30,800shp; 35kts.
Bunkerage: 285tons/290tonnes.
Range: 2,000nm at 19kts.
Guns: four 3.9in (2×2); eight 13.2mm MG (4×2).
Torpedoes: four 21.7in (2×2).
Complement: 7+129.

Design Yet another promising French design which came too late to see service. The previous small torpedo-boats of the 600-tonnes type had been severely criticized on numerous counts, the sum total of which being that too much had been attempted on too small a displacement and in consequence, the French Navy resolved to construct two new types of torpedo-craft. One was the *Le Hardi* design already discussed, the second a 1,010-tonnes design which was intended to be much more than an extrapolated 600-tonnes design. The design characteristics envisaged by the *Comité Technique* in December 1936, showed a simple but robust *torpilleur* of an enlarged escort type. To rectify the deficiencies of the 600-tonnes design, it was necessary to increase displacement and hull weight considerably. This increased displacement was also needed for the higher design speed, 34 knots and a heavier armament of four 3.9-inch guns.

The machinery comprised a twin shaft single reduction geared turbine installation, (Rateau-Bretagne in the *Chantiers de Bretagne* boats, Parsons in the rest) with three boilers in two boiler rooms, arranged on the unit principle. The actual arrangement of the boilers was somewhat unusual in that the forward boiler room housed two boilers athwarships but the after room, restricted by the starboard shaft, housed only one, which was slightly offset to port. This after boiler, the only one normally in use under cruising conditions, was more than twice as powerful as the two in the forward room. The contract speed was 33 knots for eight hours, but none ever reached the trials stage.

The original armament proposed was to comprise two twin 3.9-inch Model 1930, eight 13.2mm machine-guns in four twin mountings and four 21.7-inch torpedo tubes (two twin), together with the usual depth-charge throwers and tracks. The armament was therefore fully dual purpose for the first time and disposed in two distinct groups. On the forward shelter deck and bridge wings were grouped the machine-guns, while both 3.9-inch mountings were aft. Another innovation was the incorporation of protective plating to the gun shields, bridge, upper deck above the machinery spaces and over the tiller flat at a cost of some 30 tonnes extra weight.

The first two units, *Le Fier* and *L'Agile* were ordered on 25 May 1938, having been authorized with two more in 1937. Three more were provided for in 1938, five under the 1938 *bis* programme of 2 May 1938 and three more under the 1938 *c* programme of 12 April 1939. By the time of the armistice, however, only seven units had been laid down and the remainder were cancelled.

Modifications As none of the ships entered service, there were of course no modifications in French service but the Kriegsmarine had intended completing some of the ships with a modified armament. In the absence of the French twin 3.9-inch guns, three single 4.1-inch (10.5cm SKC/32) mountings were to be shipped aft, disposed as typical of German destroyers. Two single 37mm guns were to replace the twin 13.2mm machine-guns forward of the bridge and nine 20mm guns added (one quadruple, five single). Two triple banks of 21-inch torpedo tubes were to replace the French 21.7-inch twins.

Service Although none of these ships saw service in the commissioned sense, their subsequent history is of interest. The three earliest ships were naturally the farthest advanced, with *Le Fier* being about 60 per cent complete. Just prior to the arrival of the German spearheads in Nantes, attempts were made to tow out these three ships to a port in unoccupied France or Morocco, but air attacks forced the beaching of *Le Fier* on the Ile d'Oleron and the attempt was abandoned. The hulls, however, were little damaged and after they had been towed back to Nantes, the Kriegsmarine decided to continue construction of all but *Le Breton*. Re-named *TA1* (*Le Fier*), *TA2* (*L'Agile*), *TA3* (*L'Alsacien*), *TA4* (*L'Entreprenant*), *TA5* (*Le Farouche*) and *TA6* (*Le Corse*), work proceeded slowly, but the three unlaunched hulls were finally put afloat between late 1940 and 1942.

Like other new construction being attempted by the Germans in French yards, these ships too were subject to continual delay and sabotage. Allied air raids damaged *TA2* and *TA4*, the latter severely, on 16 September 1943, although both were subsequently re-floated. It would appear that *TA1* and *TA5* were the farthest advanced, for by April 1944 the Kriegsmarine was considering the problem of their manning. A special 'building Party' was established that month to press their completion but further delays arose due to the need to remove French cabling in order to fit German electrical equipment. By the time that the Germans themselves were forced to evacuate Nantes, *TA1, TA3, TA4* and *TA5* were fitting out afloat with all boilers and machinery aboard. The boilers and engines for *TA2* and *TA6* were completed but still on shore. All were scuttled still incomplete on 11 August 1944. Post-war, the French considered the resumption of certain units but the idea was abandoned and the hulls were later broken up.

TRANSFERRED UNIT

La Combattante (ex-*Haldon*)

This Type III *Hunt*-class destroyer (q.v.) was transferred to the Free French Navy on 15 December 1942. Being a single unit only (the transfer of two more did not materialize), *La Combattante* served with British *Hunt* flotillas in the North Sea and Channel. She was active in the latter theatre from April 1944, operating against S-boats. In that month she sank *S147* and the following month *S141* but unfortunately also sank the British *MTB 732* in error. *La Combattante* took part in the Invasion of Normandy and spent June, July and August 1944 operating with MTB groups against German light surface forces retreating east. She finally fell victim to the German *Seehund* midget submarine *Ku330* off the Humber on 23 February 1945.

ALGERIEN CLASS

Ship	Builder	Laid Down	Launched	Commissioned	Fate
T52 *Algérien* (ex-*Cronin*)	Dravo (Wilmington)	13 May 43	27 Nov 43	23 Jan 44	Ret. USN May 1964
T51 *Hova* (ex-DE110)	Dravo (Wilmington)	5 Sept 43	22 Jan 44	18 Mar 44	Ret. USN May 1964
T21 *Marocain* (ex-*DE109*)	Dravo (Wilmington)	7 Sept 43	1 Jan 44	29 Feb 44	Ret. USN May 1964
T22 *Sénégalais* (ex-*DE106*)	Dravo (Wilmington)	24 April 43	11 Nov 43	2 Jan 44	Ret. USN May 1964
T53 *Somali* (ex-*DE111*)	Dravo (Wilmington)	23 Oct 43	12 Feb 44	9 April 44	Trials vessel 1956
T23 *Tunisien* (ex-*Crosley*)	Dravo (Wilmington)	23 June 43	17 Dec 43	11 Feb 44	Ret. USN May 1964

Below: *Somali.* (A. D. Baker)

Displacement: 1,300tons (standard); 1,750tons (full load).
Length: 305ft/93m (oa); 300ft 3in/91.5m (pp).
Beam: 36ft 6in/11.17m.
Draught: 10ft 9in/3.25m (mean).
Machinery: four GEC diesels; two electric motors; 2 shafts.
Performance: 6,000bhp; 19kts.
Bunkerage: 300tons.
Range: 11,500nm at 11kts.
Guns: three 3in (3×1); three 40mm (3×1); ten 20mm (10×1).
Complement: 185.

Service These units of the US *Cannon* class of destroyer escorts (ex-*DE107, DE110, DE109, DE106, DE111* and *DE108*) were transferred to the French Navy on 2 January 1944, prior to completion. They entered service from January to April 1944, then sailed east for the Mediterranean where they served for most of the remainder of the war. *Sénégalais*, with British escort vessels and aircraft, took part in a 2-hour A/S hunt at the beginning of May, which culminated in the scuttling of *U371*, but not before she had torpedoed and damged *Sénégalais*. While she was repairing, the remainder of the class covered the Invasion of southern France in August 1944. *Hova* was in action against German enclaves in the Bay of Biscay in April 1944 and both *Sénégalais* and *Somali* moved to Indo-China at the end of the war. All except *Somali*, retained for experimental purposes, were returned to the USA in May 1964.

Germany

Consequent upon the surrender in 1918 and the signing of the Treaty of Versailles in 1919, the Kaiserlische Marine ceased to exist in name and, with the scuttling of the fleet at Scapa Flow, in material as well. After the allocation of such modern units as still existed, to the victorious Allied powers, there was little left to form the strength of the coastal defence force which was all that was to be allowed to the defeated Germany. Under the provisions of the Treaty, she was to retain only sixteen destroyers and a like number of torpedo-boats, all of which were of pre-1914 vintage. Moreover, only twelve of each could be kept in active service at any one time. The destroyers and torpedo-boats retained were *T139, T141, T143/4, T146, T148/9, T151–158, T168, T175, T185, T190, T196, V1–V3, V5, V6, G7, G8, G10, G11, S18, S19* and *S23*, the newest of which, *S23* had been completed in November 1913. With these venerable craft, the Reichsmarine, as the navy was now known, had to make do until the late 1920s.

The entry into service of the new *Type 23* and *24* torpedo-boats, beginning with *Möwe* in October 1926, allowed the Reichsmarine to start taking the elderly pre-war boats out of service, with *T175* being the first to go in late September 1926. Two, *T139* and *T141*, were converted to target control vessels and re-named *Pfeil* and *Blitz* respectively, while the years 1927 to 1928 saw eight others discarded. By 1932, when all the new torpedo-boats had been commissioned, eight of the older ships remained in active service with the 1st Half Flotilla (*G7, G8, G10* and *G11*) and the 2nd Half Flotilla (*T151, T153, T156* and *T158*). *T158* had replaced the older *T141* and was likewise re-named *Blitz* in 1932, when both *T139* and *T141* were discarded. In 1937–38, *T153* and *T190* were converted to experimental vessels, being re-named *Eduard Jungmann* and *Claus von Bevern*. The four *G* boats alone remained in the active torpedo-boat flotillas by 1935, but *T196* was being employed as Senior Officer (Minesweepers) ship, while the remainder were employed on subsidiary duties mostly at Kiel. All the surviving ships served during the Second World War, usually as torpedo recovery vessels, attached to the submarine flotillas. *T157* fell victim to a mine off Danzig in October 1943, but the rest survived until the last days of the war, when they were either scuttled or handed over to the Allies.

The first replacement vessels to be built were the *Type 23* torpedo-boats referred to above, which were based upon wartime designs and could not compare with contemporary ships. The six *Type 24* ships were basically repeats and it was not until the advent of National Socialism provided the impetus, that construction programmes became more adventurous. The restrictions of the Treaty were by this time severely hampering design staffs, for in the ten years or so since 1920, most categories of warship had advanced considerably in terms of size and armament. Thus any design which adhered to the Treaty restrictions would be outclassed by those of the Allied navies – which was precisely what the Treaty's drafters had intended. It became a matter of necessity therefore for Germany's designers to ignore the restrictions of the Treaty, at first covertly; later, after its denouncement by Hitler, it was routine to understate the tonnages of all classes of ship.

The first new destroyer design was finalized in 1934 and began the construction of a series of large and well-armed ships intended initially to contain contemporary French and Polish destroyers. Later, it was necessary to bring Great Britain into the arena as a probable future enemy. Unfortunately for Germany, their shipyard capacity was woefully inadequate to cater for the grandiose designs of the Admirals, and in consequence there was a tendency to make a design superior in fighting power to compensate for lack of numbers. This led in turn to several weaknesses which negated the intentions of the designers. Thus the adoption of high-pressure steam propulsion, while theoretically advantageous, proved in practice to be a serious handicap, bearing in mind the small numbers of destroyers available. Likewise, the increase in gun calibre to 5.9-inch (15cm) gave a valuable increase in hitting-

power, but at the expense of seakeeping properties, with the result that lighter armed but more seaworthy British destroyers were able to take on these large ships with some success. Even the heavier guns were of little use when faced with similarly armed light cruisers, for the cruiser had far better facilities for using and controlling her guns than did the destroyers. Eventually this was realized, after a series of fifteen 5.9-inch gunned destroyers had been built, but the reversion to 5-inch guns came too late to be of use.

Germany, like France and Italy, perpetuated the distinction between destroyers and torpedo-boats, and built 21 torpedo-boats of a nominal 600 tonnes. These, armed effectively only with torpedoes, proved just as much an embarrassment as those of the French Navy and were superseded by fourteen better gunned ships which gave useful service in the Channel and Biscay theatres. In fact, the torpedo-boats probably saw more sea service than the destroyers because the latter were operating with a largely inactive fleet nucleus.

In the final analysis, the Kriegsmarine never had enough destroyers to allow them to consider them as the expendable assets they were. As a result, opportunities were not pressed home and when the oil shortage became crippling, training suffered and efficiency fell sharply. Nevertheless, the destroyer and torpedo-boat flotillas remained active to the end and played a considerable part in the evacuation of millions of refugees up until the last day of the war.

Above: *Möwe*, note quadruple 20mm gun. (W. B. Bilddienst)

Below: *Tiger* pre-war. (Drüppel)

TORPEDOBOOTE TYPE 23 CLASS

Ship	Builder	Laid Down	Launched	Commissioned	Fate
Albatros	Wilhelmshaven Dkyd.	5 Oct 25	15 July 26	15 May 28	Wrecked 10 April 40
Falke	Wilhelmshaven Dkyd.	17 Nov 25	29 Sept 26	15 July 28	Bombed 14 June 44
Grief	Wilhelmshaven Dkyd.	5 Oct 25	15 July 26	15 July 27	Torpedoed 24 May 44
Kondor	Wilhelmshaven Dkyd.	17 Nov 25	22 Sept 26	15 July 28	Paid Off 28 June 44
Möwe	Wilhelmshaven Dkyd.	2 Mar 25	24 Mar 26	1 Oct 26	Bombed 14 June 44
Seeadler	Wilhelmshaven Dkyd.	5 Oct 25	15 July 26	15 Mar 27	Torpedoed 14 May 42

Displacement: 923tons/938tonnes (standard); 1,290tons/1,310tonnes (full load).
Length: 287ft 8in/87.7m (oa); 281ft 3in/85.73m (wl).
Beam: 27ft/8.25m.
Draught: 12ft/3.65m (mean).
Machinery: three Marine boilers; 2-shaft geared turbines.
Performance: 23,000shp; 33kts.
Bunkerage: 316tons/321tonnes.
Range: 1,800nm at 17kts.
Guns: three 4.1in (3×1); two 20mm (2×1).
Torpedoes: six 21.7in (2×3).
Mines: 30.
Complement: 120.
Note. Möwe differed slightly, see text.

Design As the first new torpedo-boats designed since the First World War, this design relied heavily upon earlier techniques and technology, betraying its origins by its appearance. There was little option in fact, for it was necessary to replace the pre-war boats as quickly as possible and there was also the Treaty of Versailles to consider. The ship's armament did not differ greatly from that of their wartime predecessors except that the torpedo outfit was carried in two triple banks for the first time. The torpedo calibre was 19.6-inch (50cm) as designed, and the guns were the well-proven 1916 Pattern 4.1-inch. Geared turbines had never reached service during the war and it was deemed necessary to experiment with various different designs. Thus *Möwe* had Blohm & Voss; *Greif* and *Falke*, Vulcan; *Albatros* and *Kondor*, Schichau; and *Seeadler*, Germania turbines. *Möwe* in fact as the leading ship differed slightly in that she was about 1ft 6in shorter on overall length and 3ft 3in shorter at the waterline. Her machinery, too, was less powerful at only 22,100shp giving a speed of 32 knots.

Modifications The torpedo calibre was altered to 21.7-inch after 1931, when this heavier calibre was adopted throughout the fleet. During the war years, the main modifications were to the anti-aircraft outfit. Initially, extra 20mm single MG C/30 guns were fitted just forward of No. 2 gun and replaced later in 1942 by a quadruple Vierling. The after rangefinder was also landed and replaced by a single

20mm gun. Passive radar detection aerials ('Sumatra') were fitted on the foremast in the course of 1943, and by 1944 radar had been installed with aerials on the fore and main masts. Bridge and mast heights were reduced to cut down top-weight and like all ships, numerous life-rafts were fitted in all available places.

Service At the outbreak of hostilities, all six of these boats constituted the 5th Torpedo-boat Flotilla and were initially employed on minelaying and escort duties in the North Sea, laying out the 'West Wall' barrage defence. They also covered cruiser sorties when the Reconnaissance Forces were employed to escort destroyers home after offensive minelaying sorties off the east coast of England. During 'Weserübung', the invasion of Norway in April 1940, all except *Falke* (completing refit at Stettin) took part, when *Albatros* was lost by grounding after actions with the shore batteries in Oslofjord. On 8 May 1940, *Möwe* was torpedoed and badly damaged by HMS/M *Taku* off south-west Norway, not being operational again until spring 1943. Much of the operational service of this class was in the Channel and on the French Atlantic coast where they were used for convoy and U-boat escort, defensive and offensive minelaying sorties. Their service in western France commenced in September 1940 and continued until the spring of 1941, when all underwent refits in Rotterdam, followed by further service in the Baltic and Skagerrak. All took part in Operation 'Cerberus' in February 1942, but in May 1942, *Seeadler* was sunk by MTB torpedoes off Cape Gris Nez while escorting the raider *Steir* which was attempting passage of the Channel. *Falke* and *Kondor* went to France for a second deployment in October and November 1942, joined by *Greif* and *Möwe* in May 1943. None of the class returned to Germany. *Kondor* was badly damaged by mines on 23 May 1944, being paid off after further bomb damage at Le Havre on 1 August 1944. *Greif* fell victim to air attack in the Seine Bay and the last two, *Falke* and *Möwe*, were sunk by bombing while at Le Havre on 14 June 1944 after numerous sorties against the Allied Invasion Fleet off Normandy. The destroyer *Svenner* was a victim of these attacks.

TORPEDOBOOTE TYPE 24 CLASS

Ship	Builder	Laid Down	Launched	Commissioned	Fate
Wolf	Wilhelmshaven Dkyd.	8 Mar 27	12 Oct 27	15 Nov 28	Mined 8 Jan 41
Iltis	Wilhelmshaven Dkyd.	8 Mar 27	12 Oct 27	1 Oct 28	Torpedoed 14 May 42
Jaguar	Wilhelmshaven Dkyd.	4 May 27	15 Mar 28	15 Aug 29	Bombed 14 June 44
Leopard	Wilhelmshaven Dkyd.	4 May 27	15 Mar 28	1 June 29	Collision 30 April 40
Luchs	Wilhelmshaven Dkyd.	2 April 27	15 Mar 28	15 April 29	Torpedoed 26 July 40
Tiger	Wilhelmshaven Dkyd.	2 April 27	15 Mar 28	15 Jan 29	Collision 25 Sept 39

Displacement: 932tons/948tonnes (standard); 1,298tons/1,319tonnes (full load).
Length: 303ft 9in/92.6m (oa); 292ft/89m (wl).
Beam: 28ft 4in/8.65m.
Draught: 11ft 6in/3.52m (mean).
Machinery: three Marine boilers; 2-shaft geared turbines.
Performance: 23,000shp; 34kts.
Bunkerage: 322tons/327tonnes.
Range: 1,997nm at 17kts.
Guns: three 4.1in (3×1); two 20mm (2×1).
Torpedoes: six 21.7in (2×3).
Mines: 30.
Complement: 129.

Design Virtually a repeat of the earlier Type 23 design, this class incorporated a small increase in length and beam and, in consequence, displacement. The main machinery was similar, but the boilers were slightly different, being of greater steam generating capacity. Only one turbo-generator was shipped, with two diesel sets, a reversal of the Type 23. *Wolf* and *Leopard* shipped Brown-Boveri turbines, *Iltis* and *Tiger*, Vulcan and *Jaguar* and *Luchs*, Schichau. A new mark of gun, the 10.5cm (4.1-inch) SKC/28 was adopted after opposition from the Allied powers had prevented the intended use of 5-inch (12.7cm) guns, but otherwise the armament was identical with the earlier class.

Modifications In 1934, *Leopard* and *Luchs* were fitted with three single 5-inch guns in lieu of their 4.1-inch for sea trials preparatory to the shipping of this gun aboard the new Type 34 destroyers. Otherwise modifications were similar to those of the Type 23 design.

Service Forming the 6th Torpedo-boat Flotilla at the outbreak of war, all except *Leopard* were employed on minelaying and mercantile warfare duties until spring 1940. *Tiger* was sunk by collision with *Max Schultz* north-east of Bornholm while on exercise just prior to the declaration of war. *Leopard* and *Wolf* were allocated to Group 5 (Bergen) and *Luchs* to Group 4 (Kristiansand) during the Invasion of Norway in April 1940. *Leopard* sank following a collision with the minelayer *Preussen* in the Skagerrak after 'Weserübung' and *Luchs* was torpedoed by HMS/M *Thames* while escorting the cruiser *Nürnberg* home from Norway in July 1940. The three survivors went to the Channel in the autumn of 1940, where *Wolf* was lost on a mine off Dunkirk at the beginning of 1941. With this loss, the 6th Flotilla was disbanded in February 1941, *Iltis* and *Jaguar* being transferred to the 5th Flotilla. *Iltis* was then sunk some fifteen months later at the same time as *Seeadler* by British MTBs, with very heavy loss of life. This left only *Jaguar* which, after a short period in Norway in April 1941, then spent until early 1942 operating in the Skagerrak or Baltic. She took part in Operation 'Cerberus' before returning to the Baltic once more where she remained until March 1943. Then, after escorting *Scharnhorst* to Norway, *Jaguar* moved to western France where she operated until bombed and sunk at Le Havre during the Invasion of Europe.

Below: Early wartime shot of a *Type 24/25* torpedo-boat. (Bundesarchiv)

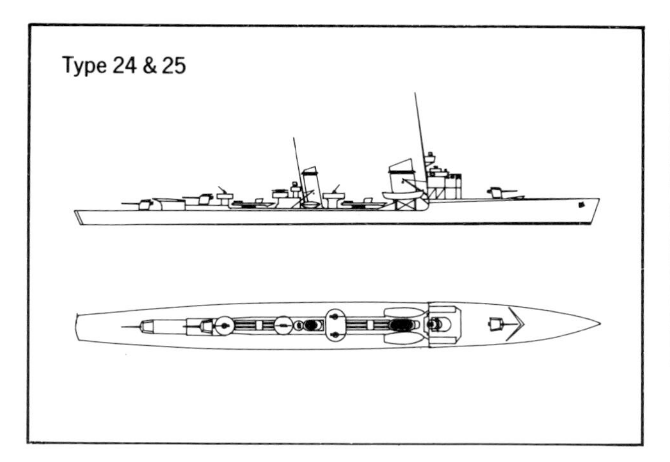

Right: Another *Type 24/25* torpedo-boat. Note depth-charges, minesweeping gear and gun arrangements aft. (Bundesarchiv)

TYPE 34 & 34A CLASS

Ship	Builder	Laid Down	Launched	Commissioned	Fate
Z1 *Leberecht Maass*	Deutsche Werke (Kiel)	10 Oct 34	18 Aug 35	14 Jan 37	Bombed 22 Feb 40
Z2 *Georg Thiele*	Deutsche Werke (Kiel)	25 Oct 34	18 Aug 35	27 Feb 37	Scuttled 13 April 40
Z3 *Max Schultz*	Deutsche Werke (Kiel)	2 Jan 35	30 Nov 35	8 April 37	Bombed 22 Feb 40
Z4 *Richard Beitzen*	Deutsche Werke (Kiel)	7 Jan 35	30 Nov 35	13 May 37	To UK 1946
Z5 *Paul Jacobi*	Deschimag (Bremen)	15 July 35	24 Mar 36	29 June 37	To UK 1946
Z6 *Theodor Riedel*	Deschimag (Bremen)	18 July 35	22 April 36	2 July 37	To UK 1946
Z7 *Hermann Schoemann*	Deschimag (Bremen)	7 Sept 35	16 July 36	9 Sept 37	Sunk 2 May 42
Z8 *Bruno Heinemann*	Deschimag (Bremen)	14 Jan 36	15 Sept 36	8 Jan 38	Mined 25 Jan 42
Z9 *Wolfgang Zenker*	Germaniawerft (Kiel)	22 Mar 35	27 Mar 36	2 July 38	Scuttled 13 April 40
Z10 *Hans Lody*	Germaniawerft (Kiel)	1 April 35	14 May 36	13 Sept 38	To UK 1946
Z11 *Bernd von Arnim*	Germaniawerft (Kiel)	26 April 35	8 July 36	6 Dec 38	Scuttled 13 April 40
Z12 *Erich Giese*	Germaniawerft (Kiel)	3 May 35	12 Mar 37	4 Mar 39	Sunk 13 April 40
Z13 *Erich Koellner*	Germaniawerft (Kiel)	12 Oct 35	18 Mar 37	28 Aug 39	Sunk 13 April 40
Z14 *Friedrich Ihn*	Blohm & Voss (Hamburg)	30 May 35	15 Nov 36	6 April 38	To USSR 1946
Z15 *Erich Steinbrinck*	Blohm & Voss (Hamburg)	30 May 35	24 Sept 36	31 May 38	To USSR 1946
Z16 *Friedrich Eckoldt*	Blohm & Voss (Hamburg)	4 Nov 35	21 Mar 37	28 July 38	Sunk 31 Dec 42

(Carried numbers Z1 to Z16, but generally referred to by names)

Displacement: 2,171–2,239tons/2,205–2,275tonnes (standard); 3,110–3.190tons/3,160–3,241tonnes (full load).*
Length: (Z1–Z8) 390ft 5in/119m (oa); 347ft/114m (pp). (Z9–Z16) 397ft/121m (oa); 380ft 7in/116m (pp).
Beam: 37ft/11.3m.
Draught: 12ft 6in/3.8m (mean).
Machinery: 6 Wagner (Z9–Z16 Benson†) boilers; 2-shaft geared turbines.
Performance: 70,000shp; 38kts.
Bunkerage: 758 (†660)tons/770 (†670)tonnes.
Range: 1900 (†1,530)nm at 19kts.
Guns: five 5in (5×1); four 37mm (2×2); six 20mm (6×1).
Torpedoes: eight 21.7in (2×4).
Mines: 60,
Complement: 325.
*Displacements varied between these figures for the whole class.

Design These destroyers were the first true destroyer-type vessels to be built by Germany after the First World War, the earlier Type 23 and 24 torpedo-boats having been handicapped by the Treaty of Versailles restrictions. Actually, this new design was conceived at a time when Germany was beginning to throw off the fetters of the much disliked Treaty. The principal adversaries envisaged by Germany were France and Poland, of which the former possessed numbers of large, well-armed *torpilleurs* and *contre-torpilleurs*. In reply to the French designs, which carried four or five 5.1-inch or five 5.5-inch guns, a calibre of 5-inch was chosen, of which four were to be carried on a 1,500-ton hull. Admiral Raeder soon increased this to five guns, ordered quadruple torpedo tubes in lieu of triples and raised the standard displacement to 1,800 tons. The guns were to be carried in a similar disposition to the French ships, with Numbers 2 and 4 guns superfiring on Nos. 1 and 5, and No. 3 gun placed on the shelter deck just forward of No. 4 gun. This was the first use of superfiring guns forward and aft in German torpedo-craft. Considerable thought was given to the anti-aircraft armament and it was decided to adopt the newly developed 37mm gun in a twin gyro-stabilized mounting (3.7cm

SKC/30). Two of these sided asymmetrically amidships gave good fields of fire, complemented by six 20mm guns, two on each side of the forecastle and two on the after shelter deck.

It was below decks, however, that this design was most unusual, for it adopted the new high-pressure steam concept. Whereas contemporary foreign practice had not much exceeded 300psi, Germany had pursued the development of several types of boiler utilizing pressures as high as 1,616psi, in order to economise on weight and space requirements. In 1935 the Norddeutscher Lloyd company had put into service for their eastern service, three steamers equipped with high-pressure boilers of the Benson (*Potsdam*) and Wagner (*Scharnhorst* and *Gneisenau*) types, which operated at 1,325psi and 737psi respectively. Further trials were conducted with 850psi Wagner boilers in *Tannenburg* and, in May 1935, the *Aviso Grille* entered service with the Kriegsmarine. This ship, the first warship with the new boilers, was fitted with the Benson type while the Wagner design entered Naval service with *Brummer* in February 1936.

The concept was a sound one, but the system was far from 'service ready' when the first ship commissioned in January 1937, with the result that numerous technical problems remained to be sorted out. Even after a satisfactory operating routine had been worked out (and that was not until the early war years), the system remained very fragile, with valves, joints, seals and packings being constant sources of weakness, while tube failures were legion. The Benson ships, with their higher pressures, were particularly susceptible to steam failures. The turbines were of Deschimag design in the first eight units and Blohm & Voss in the remainder. The first four ships were fitted with cruising turbines, which were not successful and were omitted from the remainder of the Wagner ships. In the Benson ships, the turbines proved troublesome and by January 1941, the OKM had decided to order new HP turbines from Germania (order placed 30 July 1941). In the meantime, modifications had to be made which reduced their output by 3,000hp.

Modifications Wetness forward resulted in the early raising of the forecastle by increasing the sheer in the first four units, which also had the original half-round upper bridge altered to square form to give more working space. As a result of trials experience with these four ships, certain alterations were made to the remainder while under construction, to reduce spray and wetness. In addition, the hulls had to be strengthened to prevent cracking problems.

Bruno Heinemann completed with a temporary armament of four 5.9-inch (15cm) guns in Nos. 1, 2, 3 and 5 positions, to assess the suitability of this gun for future destroyer construction. Unfortunately, the trials were conducted at very slow speeds and in

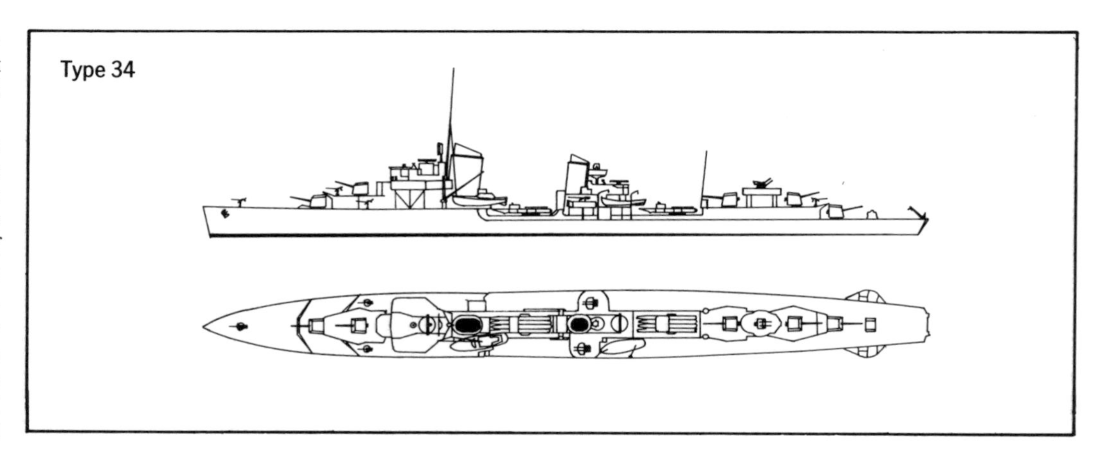

Above: *Type 34* destroyers in Cuxhaven in April 1940. (Bundesarchiv) **Below:** *Herman Schoemann* in February 1942, with tripod mast and radar. (Bundesarchiv)

good weather, when totally misleading results were obtained! By the outbreak of war, her designed armament had been reinstated.

Almost half the class were early war losses and received nothing in the way of modifications. Tripod foremasts were fitted in 1940 but little real alteration in appearance was made until 1942, when the six survivors had the funnels cut down to reduce top weight. *Jacobi, Steinbrinck* and *Lody* received major refits in 1944 when the former was given clipper bows and all were fitted with a 'goalpost' foremast to allow full rotation of the radar aerial. This refit was in fact associated with a major up-grading of the anti-aircraft outfits, which hitherto had only been augmented by a quadruple 20mm Vierling on the after shelter deck and the repositioning of the displaced 20mm singles on to the forecastle and quarter deck. Some units were also fitted with 20mm singles under the barrels of Numbers 2 and 4 guns, on the shelter deck.

Radar had been fitted to all units surviving after April 1940, but it was not until late 1944 that better radar was fitted and a second (*Hohentweil*) set was shipped abaft the after funnel. Even this was badly outdated by this time and was of little use for either air warning or AA gun control purposes. Reliance for air detection was, in fact, largely based upon a wide range of passive detector sets which picked up signals from an aircraft's onboard radars.

The ever-increasing Allied air superiority forced Germany to greatly augment the AA outfits. This was intended to be standardized for the Type 34 destroyers as follows: six, twin 37mm M42 mountings (two each before bridge, amidships and in lieu of No. 3 gun); nine 20mm (single bow chaser, two LM44 twin in bridge wings and quadruple aft); 8.6cm *Raketten Abschuss Gerate* rocket-launchers were also to be fitted. War circumstances prevented this plan from being fully realized and in the event, ships varied:

Jacobi: ten 37mm (4×2, 2×1); fifteen 20cm (1×1, 5×2, 1×4)
Steinbrinck: fourteen 37mm (7×2); ten 20mm (3×2, 1×4) and *Lody*
Ihn: four 37mm (2×2); eighteen 20mm (7×2, 1×4)
Riedel: four 37mm (2×2); fourteen 20mm (6×1, 2×2, 1×4)
Beitzen: little or no alteration.

Service At the start of operations against Poland on 1 September 1939, the 1st (*Beitzen, Thiele*), 3rd (*Ihn, Steinbrinck, Eckoldt*), 6th (*Zenker, Heinemann, Arnim*) and 9th (*Lody*) Destroyer Division together with *Maass* were stationed in the eastern Baltic off the Gulf of Danzig. On 3 September, *Maass* and *Zenker* engaged Polish warships in Gdynia when shore batteries hit the former. Operations in the North Sea quickly followed, where in the course of eleven sorties from October 1939 until February 1940, large numbers of mines were laid in British east coast coastal waters, claiming many merchantmen and warships. *Eckoldt* took part in four, *Beitzen* and *Ihn*, three; *Schultz, Heinemann, Zenker, Lody, Kollner* and *Steinbrinck*, two; and *Arnim* and *Giese* one operation each. In this period too, on 7 December 1939, *Giese* torpedoed and severely damaged the British *Jersey*.

In February 1940, an accident led to the loss of *Maass* and *Schultz* when they were bombed in error by the Luftwaffe and mined in a new and unsuspected British field while attempting avoiding action. *Thiele, Arnim, Giese, Koellner* and *Zenker* formed part of the invasion group assigned to capture Narvik where all were lost during the second engagement on 13 April 1940. Four others, *Jacobi, Riedel, Heinemann* and *Eckoldt*, were assigned to the Trondheim force and suffered no losses. After Narvik, the ships were formed into two flotillas, the 5th and 6th, but they were only loose formations and rarely, if ever, were all ships of a flotilla together. With the fall of France, the centre of operations moved into the Channel and French Atlantic coasts in late 1940–41, when another British destroyer, this time *Javelin*, was badly damaged by *Lody* and *Beitzen* in company with *Galster*.

When Germany declared war on Russia, the 6th Flotilla moved into Arctic Norway in June 1941, operating in the Barents Sea until withdrawn home for refits by the end of October. The 5th Flotilla (*Beitzen, Schoemann, Heinemann* and *Jacobi*) moved to France in January 1942 to escort the battle-

Above: *Paul Jacobi*, also in February 1942. (Bundesarchiv) **Below:** *Hans Lody* in 1946, showing final war configuration. (WSS)

cruisers home from Brest (Operation 'Cerberus'). *Heinemann*, however, struck a mine off Cap Gris Nez and sank on 25 January. After 'Cerberus', the flotilla moved to Norway where *Schoemann* was sunk by HMS *Edinburgh* while she, *Z24* and *Z25* were attempting to attack Convoy PQ14. During the remainder of 1942, the 5th and 6th Flotillas operated with the heavy units in northern Norway and the Barents Sea where, in the course of an attempted attack on Convoy JW51B, *Eckoldt* was sunk by HMS *Sheffield* with the loss of all her crew. All the remaining operational units of the class continued to serve in northern Norwegian waters in 1943, *Steinbrinck, Riedel* and *Lody* taking part in the Spitzbergen operation early in September 1943, but in November all the Type 34 ships were ordered south as their action radius was considered insufficient for northern operations. Towards the end of 1943, and into 1944, the main theatre of operations were the Skagerrak, escorting convoys of ships to and from Oslo and escorting minelayers as well as patrolling to prevent Allied merchantmen from breaking out from Swedish ports.

Jacobi was badly damaged at Kiel in December 1943 during an air raid, as was *Steinbrinck* at Hamburg in June the following year. At the close of 1944, only *Beitzen, Ihn* and *Riedel* were operational, based at Horten, but in March 1945 the former was badly damaged in a night air attack, while escorting a convoy in the Skagerrak. In the last days of the war, *Lody, Riedel, Jacobi* and *Ihn* took part in the evacuation operation from East Prussia in the face of the Soviet advance. After the surrender, *Riedel* became the French *Kléber* (condemned 3 April 1957); *Jacobi* the *Dessaix* (discarded 17 February 1954) and *Steinbrinck* probably became the Soviet *Pylkii. Ihn* was also transferred to the USSR, both she and *Pylkii* being discarded in the late 1950s. *Beitzen* and *Lody* were retained by Great Britain but sent for scrapping on 10 January 1949 and 17 July 1949 respectively.

TYPE 36 CLASS

Ship	Builder	Laid Down	Launched	Commissioned	Fate
Z17 Diether von Roeder	Deschimag (Bremen)	9 Sept 36	19 Aug 37	29 Aug 38	Scuttled 13 April 40
Z18 Hans Lüdemann	Deschimag (Bremen)	9 Sept 36	1 Dec 37	8 Oct 38	Scuttled 13 April 40
Z19 Hermann Künne	Deschimag (Bremen)	5 Oct 36	22 Dec 37	12 Jan 39	Scuttled 13 April 40
Z20 Karl Galster	Deschimag (Bremen)	14 Sept 37	15 June 38	21 Mar 39	To USSR 1946
Z21 Wilhelm Heidkamp	Deschimag (Bremen)	15 Dec 37	20 Aug 38	20 June 39	Torpedoed 10 April 40
Z22 Anton Schmitt	Deschimag (Bremen)	3 Jan 38	20 Sept 38	24 Sept 39	Torpedoed 10 April 40

Displacement: 2,411tons/2,449tonnes (standard); 3,415tons/3,469tonnes (full load).
Length: 410ft 1in/125m (403ft 6in/123m Z17–Z19) (oa); 394ft 6in/120m (pp).
Beam: 38ft 8in/11.8m.
Draught: 12ft 6in/3.8m (mean).
Machinery: six Wagner boilers; 2-shaft Deschimag geared turbines.
Performance: 70,000shp; 38kts.
Bunkerage: 774tons/787tonnes.
Range: 2,020nm at 19kts.
Guns: five 5in (5×1); four 37mm (2×2); seven 20mm (7×1).
Torpedoes: eight 21.7in (2×4).
Mines: 60.
Complement: 323.

Design The Type 36 destroyer design improved on its predecessor in that top weight was reduced by cutting down funnel height and lowering the midships superstructure. Taken together with a marginal increase in beam and a longer hull, the result was a much more seaworthy ship, especially the last three which also incorporated clipper bows. The underwater form was improved, particularly aft where a reduction in the deadwood reduced the turning circle. Inboard, the main machinery, while being basically similar to the earlier *Z1* to *Z8*, was more refined and gave somewhat less trouble despite the continued use of Wagner High-Pressure boilers. The turbines were considered by Deschimag engineers to be one of the best designs that they had produced. Electrical generating capacity was increased by installing larger diesel generators, and bunkerage was also increased to give better range. All six ships were ordered from Deschimag on 6 January 1936 as yard numbers *W919* to *W924*.

Modifications Only *Galster* survived after April 1940, when she was fitted with a tripod foremast and degaussing coils. In 1941–42, radar was fitted on the bridge which was altered to accommodate a radar hut. On the ammunition handling room, between Nos. 3 and 4 guns, a Vierling 20mm gun displaced the mainmast, which was re-positioned on the blast screen of No. 3 gun. By 1944, the two single 20mm guns on the midships platform had been replaced by two single 37mm guns, twin 20mm added in the bridge wings and on the forecastle deck abreast No. 2 gun. Single 20mm guns were added at the bows and on the forward and after shelter decks. In January 1945, *Ihn* shipped new 37mm M42 automatic guns to Norway for *Galster*. However, she never received her intended 'Barbara' refit which was to have comprised fourteen 37mm (6×2, 2×1); nine 20mm (1×1, 2×2, 1×4). *RAG* equipment was also to have been fitted.

Service The first four destroyers took part in the 'West Wall' mine barrage operations in the North Sea during early September 1939. *Heidkamp* relieved *Maass* as Commodore (D)'s ship on 10 September 1939, after which, she, *Künne* and *Galster* completed four offensive minelaying sorties off the east coast of Britain. *Lüdemann* completed two, *Roeder* and *Schmitt* one each before the operations were suspended in February 1940. *Galster* was under refit at the time of the invasion of Norway in April 1940, but her sisters were allocated to the Narvik force where all were sunk. *Heidkamp* and *Schmitt* were both torpedoed at the start of the first action on the 10th, while *Roeder* was badly damaged. In the course of the second action on the 13th, *Künne* was beached in Herjangsfjord, after expending all her ammunition and torpedoes. *Lüdemann*, after expending her torpedoes and being hit aft by gunfire, retired up Rombaksfjord and beached herself. On 16 April, her stern section, still afloat

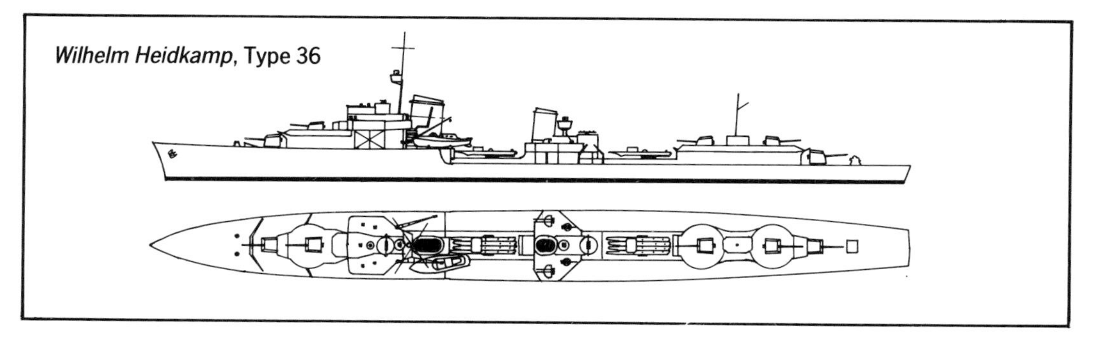
Wilhelm Heidkamp, Type 36

was sunk by a torpedo from *Hero*. Finally, *Roeder* was destroyed by scuttling charges just as *Foxhound* was about to put a boarding party on to her.

The sole survivor now was *Galster* which took part in Operation 'Juno' in June 1940, returning to Germany late in July. After minelaying operations in the south-west North Sea, she moved to western France in September 1940, remaining in French waters until her recall to Germany early in December. It was June 1941 before she was operational once more, due to problems with her turbines, but later that month she sailed for Norway as leader of the 6th Flotilla, where she operated in Arctic waters until her arrival back in Kiel in November 1941. A major dockyard refit followed until May 1942. She returned to Norway in June 1942 as leader of the 8th Flotilla, but ran aground and damaged herself during an operation against Convoy QP13 in July with the result that a home dockyard repair became necessary. After repairs she was retained in the Baltic until December 1942 when she returned to Norway, but her stay was brief, being transferred to the Skagerrak in January 1943. By the spring of that year *Galster* was back in the north once more, forming part of the Battle Group's destroyer screen at Altenfjord. She took part in the sortie to Spitzbergen in September 1943 before being recalled to Germany in November. After a refit at Deschimag in Bremen, she was based at Horten for duties in the Skagerrak from May 1944 until the end of the war, taking part in some of the evacuation convoys from East Prussia in about March 1945. Under the terms of the Potsdam Agreement, *Galster* was allocated to the USSR and renamed *Prochnyi*, surviving until the early 1960s before being scrapped.

Above: *Diether von Roeder* just before the war. (W. B. Bilddienst) **Below:** *Wilhelm Heidkamp*. Note clipper bows. (Drüppel)

TYPE 36A CLASS

Ship	Builder	Laid Down	Launched	Commissioned	Fate
Z23	Deschimag (Bremen)	15 Nov 38	15 Dec 39	14 Sept 40	Paid off 20 Aug 44
Z24	Deschimag (Bremen)	2 Jan 39	7 Mar 40	23 Oct 40	Sunk 25 Aug 44
Z25	Deschimag (Bremen)	15 Feb 39	16 Mar 40	30 Nov 40	To France 1946
Z26	Deschimag (Bremen)	1 April 39	2 April 40	11 Jan 41	Sunk 29 Mar 42
Z27	Deschimag (Bremen)	27 Dec 39	1 Aug 40	26 Feb 41	Sunk 28 Dec 43
Z29	Deschimag (Bremen)	21 Mar 40	15 Oct 40	9 July 41	To USA 1946
Z30	Deschimag (Bremen)	15 April 40	8 Dec 40	15 Nov 41	To UK 1946

Displacement: 2,603–3,079tons/2,645–3,128tonnes (standard); 3,543–3,605tons/3,599–3,660tonnes (full load).
Length: 416ft 8in/127m (oa); 400ft/121.9m (pp).
Beam: 39ft 4in/12m.
Draught: 12ft 10in/3.91m (mean).
Machinery: six Wagner boilers; 2-shaft Wagner-Deschimag geared turbines.
Performance: 70,000shp; 36–38.5kts.
Bunkerage: 788–812tons/801–825tonnes.
Range: 2,174–2,239nm at 19kts.
Guns: five 5.9in (1×2, 3×1); four 37mm (2×2); five 20mm (5×1).
Torpedoes: eight 21.7in (2×4).
Mines: 60.
Complement: 332.

Design Because of problems reconciling conflicting design requirements from various quarters of a destroyer for use in an Atlantic environment, (the Type 37), it was decided by Admiral Raeder in the interim to expand the existing Type 36 design in order to maintain continuity of destroyer production. Thus it was proposed to construct eight ships on a modified Type 36 hull, but armed with 5.9-inch guns. (One of these, *Z28*, was later modified as a leader with extra accommodation and is considered later). Discussions on the abortive Type 37 design had led to the serious consideration of twin turrets for destroyers and it was resolved to fit a lightweight twin turret forward in this design. This, it was hoped, would be lighter than two single guns with their associated shelter deck and go some way towards reducing wetness and plunging of the bows, to which earlier types were prone.

Unfortunately, the hull dimensions of the earlier Type 36 were only marginally improved upon (6 feet on length and only 8 inches in beam), nowhere near sufficient as it turned out. Quite apart from this, the very fine lines of the hull forward were perpetuated in the *36A* design and since the new LC/38 twin turret finally came out at over 60 tons, it was obvious that problems would be encountered. Considerable trouble was experienced with this twin turret, for production delays led to the realization as early as autumn of 1938, that the ships would be ready

Above: *Z24*, now fitted with the twin turret and quadruple 20mm. (Bundesarchiv) **Below:** *Z24*, summer 1941. (Bundesarchiv)

Below: *Z25* in May 1942, fitted with radar but only a single 5.9-inch gun forward. (Bundesarchiv)

before the turrets were available. (*Z23* did not receive the first until early 1942). Then, when it did enter service, it was quickly found that waterproofing was inadequate and the electrics were frequently swamped and shorted out. More seriously, the fine hull form at the fore-ends was unsuitable for the heavy weights imposed by the turret itself, with the result that the ships were extremely wet forward. In the absence of the twin turret, a single 5.9-inch gun in an open shield was mounted in its place.

Otherwise the armament remained the same as in the Type 36, but an enlarged midships AA deck allowed the siting of two single 20mm guns just abaft the twin 37mm guns. Like all German destroyers, four reload torpedoes were accommodated in lockers at the side of the half deck amidships.

The main machinery and steam plant remained similar to the Type 36, but the gearing was modified at the insistence of the OKM and resulted in a less efficient design. Bunkerage was increased, giving better theoretical radius and the stowage plan improved to help stability.

All seven ships were ordered from Deschimag in Bremen on 23 April 1938 and were given numbers in the traditional manner of German torpedo-craft, the Type 34 and 36 designs being unusual in that they were allocated names.

Modifications In view of the delays in their completion, this class completed with radar, tripod mast and degaussing cables. All completed with the extemporized armament of four 5.9-inch guns, with *Z23* receiving her turret in February 1942, *Z24* late in 1942 and *Z25* in the latter half of 1942. *Z26* and *Z27* were both lost prior to receipt of a turret and *Z29* was only fitted early in 1945, while *Z30* never received hers.

AA outfits were augmented initially by the addition of a quadruple 20mm on the forward ammunition handling lobby in about 1942 with a second being fitted on the after ammunition lobby between Nos. 2 and 3 guns, when the mainmast was repositioned. Extra 20mm guns were fitted on the forecastle and on the after shelter deck under the barrel of No. 3 gun. *Z24* fitted two quadruple 20mm amidships, at Brest in June 1944.

When the general upgrading of the AA outfits of the Fleet (code-name 'Barbara') was considered in 1944, the Type 36A design was to be considerably modified as follows: fourteen 37mm (6×2, 2×1); ten 20mm (3×2, 1×4); four 8.6cm RAG. The twin 37mm were to be fitted before the bridge, midships and in lieu of No. 2 gun, with the two singles amidships. The 20mm twins were positioned as a bow chaser and in the bridge wings, with the quadruple 20mm aft as before. By this time of course, only *Z25*, *Z29* and *Z30* remained afloat and *Z29* (still without her twin turret) was to retain No. 2 gun but added two twin 20mm aft. When the war ended, *Z25* had ten 27mm (4×2, 2×1) and twenty 20mm

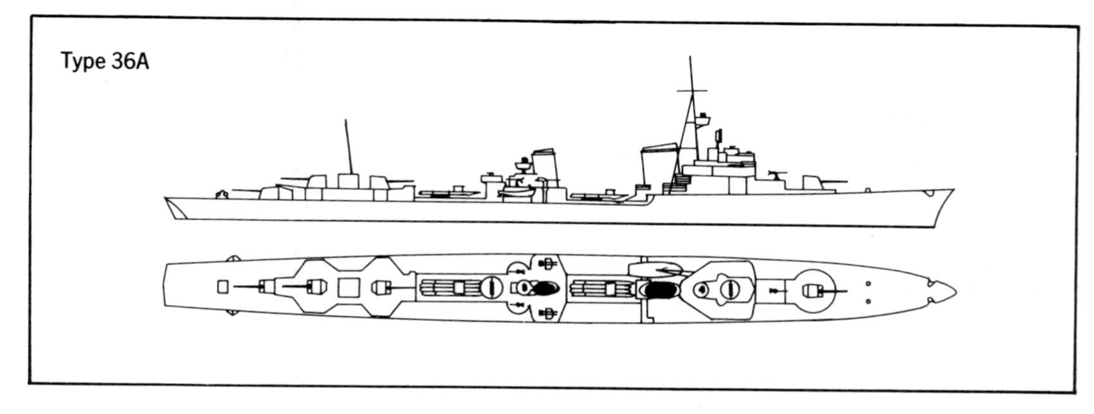

Above: *Z26*, still with only a single 5.9-inch gun. (Bundesarchiv) **Below:** *Z29* in 1945 with almost completed 'Barbara' refit. (USN)

(6×2, 2×4) while *Z29* had seven 37mm (2×2, 3×1) and twenty 20mm (3×4, 4×2). She may possibly also have received the mountings for two single 55mm guns amidships, but photographic evidence is not clear on this point. The refits were not started until November/December 1944 and in the case of *Z29*, were never finished. *Z30* never started hers for she was mined and very badly damaged in the Skagerrak off Oslofjord on 20 October 1944. She was not fully repaired before the end of the war and remained in Norway.

The original FuM021 radar outfit on the bridge was replaced by the larger FuM025 in surviving units from the summer of 1943, then from the summer of 1944, a 'Hohentweil' set was fitted just aft of the second funnel. The usual array of passive radar detectors was also fitted.

Service These ships constituted the 8th Destroyer Flotilla, known as the *8 (Narvik) Zerstörerflotilla* to commemorate the ships lost in April 1940. Only the first three units were sufficiently worked up by March 1941 to undertake the escorting of *Admiral Hipper* to Norway when bad weather showed up the deficiencies of the design, even without the turret aboard. *Z23* and *Z24* were ordered to France in June 1941, operating with the 6th Flotilla, but returned to their own flotilla in Germany in October. By the end of the year, *Z23–Z27* were in Arctic Norway, based in Kirkenes where they operated sorties along the Murmansk coast with only slight success. The flotilla was withdrawn home at the end of January 1942. After taking part in 'Cerberus' (*Z25* and *Z29*), *Z24*, *Z25* and *Z26* returned to the Arctic at the end of March 1942 forming 'Destroyer Group Arctic'. All three made a sortie against Convoy *PQ13* in the course of which they encountered the cruiser *Trinidad* which stopped and sank *Z26* having hit her in the engine room and knocked out several of her guns. *Z26* sank after her crew had been taken off by her consorts, but *Trinidad*, attempting to finish off *Z26*, managed to torpedo herself and was forced to break off the action. In April, *Z24* and *Z25* with the Type 34 *Schoemann* engaged *Edinburgh* losing the latter, but either *Z24* or *Z25* managed to torpedo the cruiser, crippling her so badly that she had to be sunk.

By mid 1942, *Z24*, *Z27*, *Z29* and *Z30* were based at Narvik, moving into the Barents Sea in September for minelaying sorties (*Z23*, *Z25*, *Z27*, *Z29* and *Z30*). *Z29* and *Z30* took part in the abortive Operation 'Regenbogen' in December 1942. *Z23*, *Z24* and *Z25* moved to western France in March 1943, tasked with escorting blockade-runners and U-boats in the Bay of Biscay. *Z27* joined them in November 1943, but the following month was sunk in action with the cruisers *Glasgow* and *Enterprise* while attempting to find an expected inward bound blockade-runner. In June 1944, *Z24* was badly damaged by British, Canadian and Polish destroyers (*Tartar*, *Ashanti*, *Huron Haida*, *Blyskawica*, *Eskimo*,

Piorum and *Javelin*) while attempting to interdict the Invasion area and was subsequently sunk by RAF strikes in the Gironde on 24 August 1944. *Z23* was damaged by bombs at La Pallice on 12 August then paid off on 20 August 1944.

There remained now only *Z25*, *Z29* and *Z30*, the last pair having been serving in the Arctic, where they had taken part in the Spitzbergen raid and escorted *Scharnhorst* on her final sortie in 1943. *Z25* operated in the Baltic and Gulf of Riga for the remainder of the war while *Z30* was based in the Skagerrak from May 1944 until mined in October that year. *Z29* came home to refit in January 1945 and took no further part in the war. After the war, *Z25* served as the French *Hoche* until 1958, *Z29* taken over by the USA, was scuttled in the Skagerrak in December 1946. *Z30*, in a non-operational condition, was broken up in the UK from September 1948.

TYPE 36A CLASS

Ship	Builder	Laid Down	Launched	Commissioned	Fate
Z28	Deschimag (Bremen)	30 Nov 39	20 Aug 40	9 Aug 41	Sunk 6 Mar 45

Displacement: 2,596tons/2,637tonnes (standard); 3,519tons/3,575tonnes (full load).
Length: 416ft 8in/127m (oa); 400ft/121.9m (pp).
Beam: 39ft 4in/12m.
Draught: 12ft 10in/3.9m (mean).
Machinery: six Wagner boilers; 2-shaft Deschimag geared turbines.
Performance: 70,000shp; 36kts.
Bunkerage: 757tons/769tonnes.
Range: 2,087nm at 19kts.
Guns: four 5.9in (4×1); four 37mm (2×2); six 20mm (6×1).
Torpedoes: eight 21.7in (2×4).
Mines: 60.
Complement: 315.

Design This ship was originally intended to be one of the eight units of the Type 36A design and was ordered as such from Deschimag on 23 April 1938, yard number W962. However, it was decided to modify her while under construction for employment as the personal vessel of Flag Officer (Torpedo boats); later the title was altered to Flag Officer (Destroyers). To enable her to function in this role, it was necessary to increase office accommodation by suppressing No. 2 gun and adding an extra deck-house on the after shelter deck. This deck-house extended forward to the after end of the after tubes. The displaced gun was then moved forward to an extended shelter deck below the bridge where it was made superfiring on No. 1 gun as in the previous Type 36 design. This was a sensible arrangement and gave *Z28* a better reputation as regards her sea-worthiness than her sisters. In all other respects except bunkerage, she was identical with the other Type 36A ships.

Modifications Few modifications were made, except that in about 1942 the main mast was moved from the after to forward end of the 'office block' in order to ship a quadruple 20mm. A square-form spray strake was fitted to the bows and plexiglass shields to the torpedo tube control positions in about 1943. Under the 'Barbara' refit programme in 1944, she was to have received a new AA outfit consisting of fourteen 37mm and ten 20mm guns or, alternatively, the same number of 37mm but only six 20mm guns depending upon whether single or twin 37mm were fitted. The proposed outfit was: one twin 20mm on folding bandstand in the bows; two twin 37mm forward of the bridge; two twin 20mm in the bridge wings; four twin 37mm amidships; plus one twin 37mm and two twin 20mm after the deck-house. In the alternative plan, two single 37mm and two twin 37mm were to be fitted amidships, the twin 20mm aft omitted and replaced by two single 37mm. Four RAG outfits were also included. Quite how closely this target was achieved is not known for certain, but she was badly damaged in late October 1944, necessitating dockyard repairs until early February 1945, during which time, it is probable that some extra armament was fitted. In January 1945, it was noted that *Z28* was to receive only three new automatic twin 37mm, replacing the old 1930-pattern guns amidships and the quadruple 20mm aft, so that it would appear that as yet, little augmentation had been carried out.

Service Although intended as a sea-going command ship for Flag Officer (Destroyers) (FdZ), *Z28* only rarely operated in that role. Her early service was in the Skagerrak, Kattegat and Baltic before sailing for Norway in April 1942. Here she did operate with FdZ for a month or two, taking part in the abortive PQ17 sortie and in September mine-laying operations in the Barents Sea. In November 1942, turbine problems required docking at Wesermünde when a machinery overhaul was carried out. After a planned deployment to France was cancelled, *Z28* returned to Norway with *Scharnhorst* in March 1943. In July, she received near miss bomb damage while at Trondheim for refit when, because of damage to the dockyard, she was brought home in

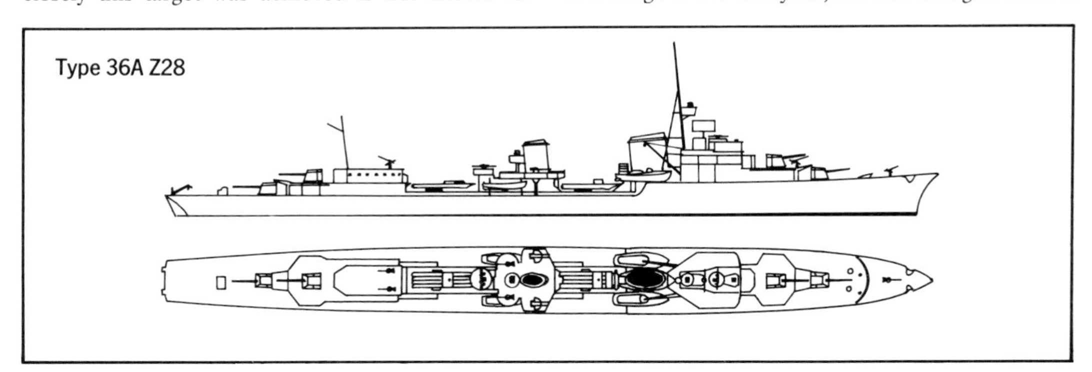
Type 36A Z28

Below: *Z28* in 1941, showing the long 'office block' aft. (Gröner)

August. Under refit until the end of 1943, *Z28* then joined the 6th Flotilla, operating in the Skagerrak until the flotilla was transferred to the eastern Baltic in February 1944. *Z28* was based upon Reval and Baltischport running minelaying and shore bombardment sorties into the Gulf of Finland until July when, after a brief visit to Turku she was transferred to the Gulf of Riga to support the army. Back in Reval in September, she operated with the 2nd Task Force off Memel in early October. On 24 October 1944 she was hit by eight bombs while off the Sworbe, but only one exploded, the rest being either duds or broke up. Nevertheless, the charthouse and radar hut were destroyed, bridge, boiler rooms and funnels damaged with several casualties. After repairs, she returned to service in February 1945, but while anchored in Sassnitz Bay on the night of 6/7 March, was hit by three bombs in all three boiler rooms, breaking the ship in two. The stern sank quickly but the bows not until mid-morning the following day.

Above: *Z28* in 1942/43 with spray strake, quadruple 20mm and plexiglass shields to the torpedo tubes. (Gröner)

TYPE 36A (MoB) CLASS

Ship	Builder	Laid Down	Launched	Commissioned	Fate
Z31	Deschimag (Bremen)	1 Sept 40	15 May 41	11 April 42	To France 1946
Z32	Deschimag (Bremen)	1 Nov 40	15 Aug 41	15 Sept 42	Beached 9 June 44
Z33	Deschimag (Bremen)	22 Dec 40	15 Sept 41	6 Feb 43	To USSR 1946
Z34	Deschimag (Bremen)	15 Jan 41	5 May 42	5 June 43	Scuttled 26 Mar 46
Z37	Germania (Kiel)	1940	24 Feb 41	16 July 42	Burned out Aug 1944
Z38	Germania (Kiel)	1940	5 Aug 41	20 Mar 43	To UK 1946
Z39	Germania (Kiel)	1940	2 Dec 41	21 Aug 43	To USA 1946

Details as Type 36A.
Differences limited to internal features and some visual details.

Design Ordered after the outbreak of war, on 19 September 1939, this group originally numbered ten, but *Z40–Z42* were never built due to various design reshuffles. Yard numbers allocated were *W1001–W1004* for the Deschimag ships, *G627–G629* and *G642–G644* for the Germania ships. They differed from *Z23–Z30* only in certain generator arrangements and in the fitting of larger, more rounded funnel caps.

Modifications As they did not begin to join the Fleet until 1942, all completed with the quadruple 20mm aft but by 1943, a second quadruple had replaced the single 20mm gun forward of the bridge. Twin 20mm began to be fitted in the bridge wings by 1944 except in *Z31* which was fitted with Infra-Red detection gear in the wings and had no space for the guns. As they became available, new fully automatic 37mm replaced the manual 37mm, in ships still afloat in home waters. *Z32* fitted two single U-boat pattern 37mm guns in lieu of the 20mm amidships, at Brest in June 1944. The planned re-armament of the 'Barbara' refit followed that for *Z25* and *Z30* but only *Z39* received the full treatment. *Z31* had her twin turret removed in 1945 after action damage, mounting a single 4.1-inch in lieu. This allowed the fitting of four twin 37mm before the bridge, with two twin and two single amidships. No. 2 gun was retained and the after deck-house remained unaltered. *Z33* finished the war with ten 37mm, two twin before the bridge, two twin and two singles amidships. No. 2 gun was given to *Z34*, but in Soviet hands was re-shipped. *Z34* shipped a 40mm Bofors in lieu of the forward 20mm, two single 37mm automatic guns amidships in lieu of 20mm singles and was fitted with and used RAG equipment in 1945. *Z37* received little or no alterations to her armament nor was *Z38* significantly altered.

Service *Z31* moved to Norway in December 1942 in time to participate in the 'Regenbögen' operation against JW51B, followed by minelaying operations in the Barents Sea in 1943. She was joined by *Z33* in July and both took part in the Spitzbergen raid in September 1943. In the course of this action, both sustained damage and casualties. *Z31* now moved down to the Skagerrak before returning to Germany to refit in January 1944. *Z34* meanwhile had moved north to Norway in November 1943 and *Z38* the month before, so that *Z33, Z34* and *Z38* formed part of *Scharnhorst*'s screen in December when she was lost. *Z31* returned to the Arctic in May 1944 and these four ships of the 4th Flotilla were to remain in the north for the remainder of the year.

Z32 and *Z37*, attached to the 8th Flotilla, sailed for western France in March 1943 where they

Below: *Z37* in Kiel Fjord, 1942. (Gröner)

remained until lost. *Z32* was finally driven ashore by British, Canadian and Polish destroyers on 9 June 1944 while attempting to reach the Allied invasion bridgehead. *Z37* had been rammed and badly damaged by her sister *Z32* on 30 January 1944 when torpedo warheads exploded and both engine rooms were put out of action. Although she was successfully towed into port and docked at Bordeaux, the deteriorating circumstances in France prevented her repair and as a result, her guns were landed for shore defence and the ship was gutted by fire.

Z39 operated briefly in the Skagerrak before moving to the eastern Baltic early in 1944 with the 6th Flotilla. She took part in sorties in the entrance to the Gulf of Finland but on 23 June 1944 was damaged by Russian bombers while lying at anchor off Reval. Under repair at Kiel in the Deutschewerk yard, she was hit once again, further delaying completion on 24 July. Early in August she was towed to Swinemünde to complete repairs and refit, including re-arming, not re-entering service again until 16 February 1945. Despite the pressing situation in the east, she saw little or no further action until early April 1945.

The 4th Flotilla was withdrawn from the Arctic at the end of January 1945. Leaving *Z33* under repair at Narvik, *Z31, Z34* and *Z38* sailed south, being intercepted and brought to action by *Diadem* and *Mauritius* off Sognefjord on 28 January. *Z31* was very badly damaged and *Z34* was hit once, but all three managed to escape. *Z34* and *Z38* then took part in the final actions in the Baltic where *Z34* was torpedoed and badly damaged by a Soviet MTB in April 1945. Both *Z33* and the temporarily repaired *Z31* returned later to the Baltic before the surrender in May.

Post-war, *Z31* became the French *Marceau*, serving until 1958, *Z33* the Soviet *Provornyi. Z38* was re-named *Nonsuch* under the White Ensign, being scrapped in 1950, and *Z39* was allocated to the USA. The latter ship was transferred to France in 1947 and cannibalized for spares.

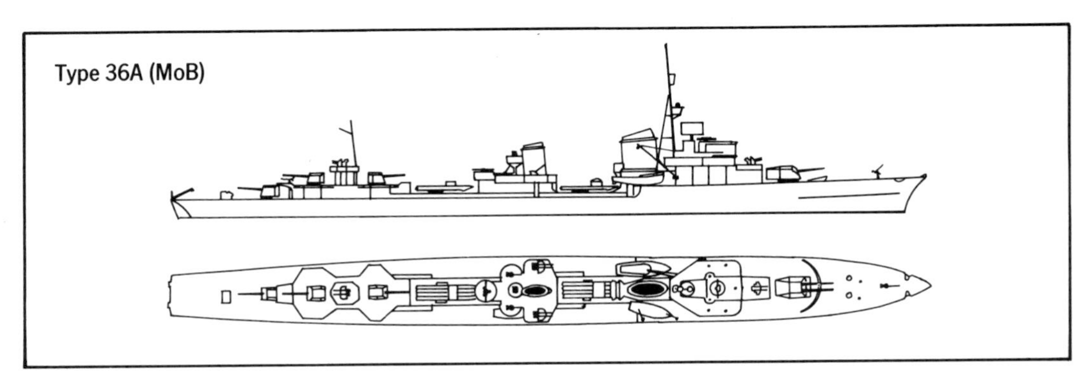

Above: *Z39* after 'Barbara' refit in 1945. (USN)

Below: *Z32*. (Real Photos)

Below: *Z37* in June 1943. (Gröner)

TYPE 36B (MoB) CLASS

Ship	Builder	Laid Down	Launched	Commissioned	Fate
Z35	Deschimag (Bremen)	6 June 41	2 Oct 42	22 Sept 43	Mined 12 Dec 44
Z36	Deschimag (Bremen)	15 Sept 41	15 May 43	19 Feb 44	Mined 12 Dec 44
Z43	Deschimag (Bremen)	1 May 42	Sept 1943	24 Mar 44	Scuttled 3 May 45
Z44	Deschimag (Bremen)	1 Aug 42	20 Dec 43	–	Sunk 29 July 44
Z45	Deschimag (Bremen)	1 Sept 43	15 April 44	–	Scuttled 20 July 46

Displacement: 2,527tons/2,567tonnes (standard); 3,507tons/3,563tonnes (full load).
Length: 416ft 8in/127m (oa); 400ft/121.9m (pp).
Beam: 39ft 4in/12m.
Draught: 11ft 7in/3.54m (mean).
Machinery: As Type 36A.
Performance: 70,000shp; 36kts.
Bunkerage: 812tons/825tonnes.
Range: 2,239nm at 19kts.
Guns: five 5in (5×1); four 37mm (2×2); fifteen 20mm (3×4, 3×1).
Torpedoes: eight 21.7in (2×4).
Mines: 76.
Complement: 321.

Design When it was realized that the increase in destroyer gun calibre to 5.9-inch had been a very qualified success, the remainder of the Type 36A series was altered to ship the proven 5-inch gun as carried by the Type 34 and 36 designs. The original hull dimensions of the 36A were retained, producing a much better sea-boat, although in fact, their merits in the Arctic or Bay of Biscay were never to be put to the test. War experience had also demonstrated the necessity for improved AA defence and this was incorporated at the time of construction. Circular gun tubs were built out over the signal deck at the after end of the bridge to accommodate two extra quadruple 20mm mountings in which position they had a very useful field of fire. In other respects, the armament was similar to the Type 36 ships.

Orders were placed on 17 February 1941 for *Z35, Z36, Z43* to *Z45*. Originally the series extended to *Z47* but later *Z46* and *Z47* were redesigned as Type 36C ships.

Modifications On completion, the 20mm single guns on the midships platform were replaced by twin mountings, but otherwise modifications were few. Their 'Barbara' refit was to have given them an AA outfit consisting of: one 20mm twin bow-chaser; two 37mm twins before the bridge; two 37mm singles in lieu of bridge quad 20mm; two 37mm twins midships; two 37mm singles midships; three 37mm twins in lieu of No. 3 gun; one 20mm quadruple; four 8.6mm RAG. As none of these ships survived the war, and both *Z35* and *Z36* were lost particularly early in their service, it is difficult to determine exactly how far this re-armament was achieved but it is very unlikely that it was completed.

Both *Z35* and *Z36* were taken in hand at Gotenhafen at the end of November 1944 to have their AA outfits improved, but in the time available it is probable that this was limited to the exchanging of the single 20mm amidships by fully automatic pattern 37mm single mountings.

Service With the increasing priority given to U-boat construction and the decree by the Führer that the surface fleet be scrapped, destroyer construction slowed down drastically. *Z35* joined the Fleet in the autumn of 1943 and was allocated to the 6th Flotilla. By March 1944, *Z36* and *Z43* had also joined the flotillas but the latter was not fully operational until about October. The flotilla operated exclusively in Baltic waters, serving in the Finnish leads at the entrance to the Gulf of Finland and in support of the army in the Gulf of Riga during 1944. *Z44*, upon which work had virtually stopped early in July 1944, was bombed and sunk in an air raid on Bremen on

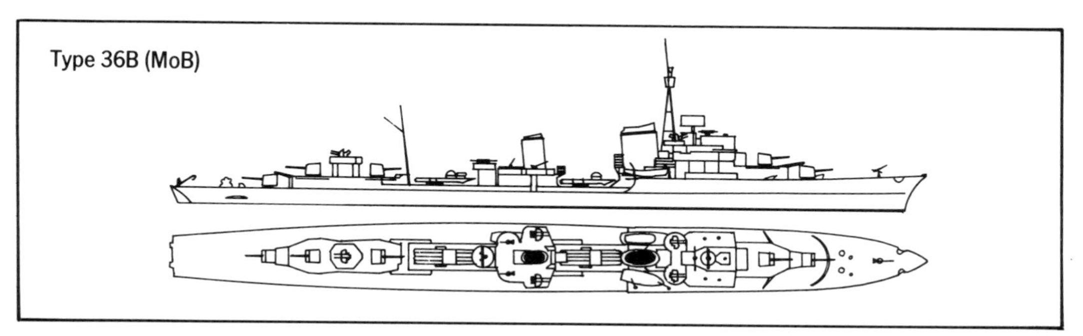

Top right: *Z43* as completed at the end of 1944. (Gröner)
Right: *Z35*. (Drüppel)

29 July, while *Z45* remained incomplete. In December 1944, *Z35*, *Z36*, *Z43*, *T23* and *T28* were ordered to lay a minefield at the entrance to the Gulf of Finland, off Reval. Because of weather conditions, constricting flotilla orders and inadequate navigation, the flotilla became set too far north and lost both *Z35* and *Z36* on a previously laid field.

Following the disaster, *Z43* escorted convoys to and from Libau throughout January until mid February 1945, when she was attached to the 2nd Task Force. She took part in shore bombardments off East Prussia in support of the army before returning to evacuation convoy duties by the end of February. March saw her escorting the *Panzerschiffe* once more, when she carried out further bombardment duties, now off Kolberg. This remained the major task throughout March and into April, but on 10 April while in the Gulf of Danzig, she was seriously damaged by a ground mine. Unable to steam, *Z43* was towed west to Rostock for repairs. She reached Kiel on 2 May 1945, then moved to Flensburg Fjord where the ship was scuttled in Geltinger Bay the following day.

TORPEDOBOOTE TYPE 35 CLASS

Ship	Builder	Laid Down	Launched	Commissioned	Fate
T1	Schichau (Elbing)	14 Nov 36	1938	1 Dec 39	Sunk 9 April 45
T2	Schichau (Elbing)	14 Nov 36	1938	2 Dec 39	Sunk 29 July 44*
T3	Schichau (Elbing)	14 Nov 36	1938	3 Feb 40	Sunk (i) 18 Sept 40* Sunk (ii) 14 Mar 45
T4	Schichau (Elbing)	29 Dec 36	1938	27 May 40	To USA 1946
T5	Deschimag (Bremen)	30 Dec 36	22 Nov 37	23 Jan 40	Sunk 14 Mar 45
T6	Deschimag (Bremen)	3 Jan 37	16 Dec 37	30 April 40	Sunk 7 Nov 40
T7	Deschimag (Bremen)	20 Aug 37	18 June 38	20 Dec 39	Sunk 29 July 44*
T8	Deschimag (Bremen)	28 Aug 37	10 Aug 38	8 Oct 39	Scuttled 3 May 45
T9	Schichau (Elbing)	24 Nov 36	1939	4 July 40	Scuttled 3 May 45
T10	Schichau (Elbing)	24 Nov 36	1939	5 Aug 40	Sunk 18 Dec 44
T11	Deschimag (Bremen)	1 July 38	1 Mar 39	24 May 40	To France 1946
T12	Deschimag (Bremen)	20 Aug 38	12 April 39	3 July 40	To USSR 1946

*Later raised.

Displacement: 845tons/859.2tonnes (standard); 1,090tons/1,108.3tonnes (full load).
Length: 276ft 7in/84.3m (oa); 269ft 6in/82.16m (wl).
Beam: 28ft 3in/8.62m.
Draught: 9ft 3in/2.83m (mean).
Machinery: four Wagner boilers; 2-shaft geared turbines.
Performance: 31,000shp; 35kts.
Bunkerage: 188tons/191tonnes.
Range: 1,200nm at 19kts.
Guns: one 4.1in; one 37mm; two 20mm (2×1). (Early units completed without the 37mm.)
Torpedoes: six 21.7in (2×3).
Mines: 30.
Complement: 119.

Design Developed from the apparent need for a more sea-worthy and larger range torpedo-craft than the *S*-boat, able to operate in the North and Baltic seas, this design made use of the '600 ton' clause of the 1930 Washington Treaty. In effect, this clause allowed any number of such craft to be built provided that they did not exceed 600 tons.

The prime weapon was to be the torpedo, the gun armament being of secondary consideration. Low silhouette and speed were two important design criteria, the latter leading to the adoption of high-pressure steam turbines to achieve the required speeds. This proved to be a considerable handicap in service, at least in the early period and similar problems were experienced to those found in the Type 34 destroyers. Actually, the problem was worse because of smaller hull dimensions which made repair and maintenance accessibility extremely difficult. The hull itself was very lightly built in a vain endeavour to keep within the 600-ton limit and was in fact rather weak. Only a single gun was shipped, on the quarter deck where it would be of maximum use in a retiring action after a silent and undetected torpedo attack.

In service, it was found that the boilers were not powerful enough to maintain the design speed because of over-optimistic calculations at the design stage, an error that was not rectified until much later. Early sea experience also showed up deficient seakeeping properties and a totally inadequate

Above: *T1* as completed. (W. B. Bilddienst) **Below:** *T10* in 1944, with radar detectors, 37mm bow-chaser, and quadruple 20mm. (Gröner)

Right: *T9* fitted with two quad 20mm and three single 20mm. (Gröner)

bridge structure. The rectification of these problems took up much valuable dockyard space and time and it was not until the end of 1940 that much operational use was had from these boats.

Modifications Those boats which participated in 'Cerberus' (the Channel Dash in 1942) landed the after torpedo tubes as a temporary measure and shipped a quadruple 20mm in lieu to bolster their very weak AA outfit, and some also carried a single 20mm bow-chaser. Main-masts were reduced in height with tripod legs and numerous square life-rafts added where space could be found. To combat wetness forward, the bows were altered to a more clipper form early in the war.

By mid 1942, the after tubes had been restituted and the quadruple 20mm moved to the after deck-house above the 4.1-inch gun in active units. Single 20mm were fitted in the bridge wings to further augment the AA outfits. In some units a single 20mm was also fitted to the midships platform between the torpedo tubes. *T1* had her searchlight removed from the foremast and transferred to a raised position on this platform, perhaps while employed non-operationally in the Baltic.

As most of the ships were employed with the Torpedo School on training duties for most of the war, little further modification was made until the closing stages of hostilities. Many had not even received radar as late as 1945 although passive radar detection antennae were fitted. The 'Barbara' programme envisaged the shipping of the following outfit: one twin 37mm (M42) or single 37mm (43M) bow-chaser; two twin 20mm in the bridge wings; two twin 20mm on the charthouse; one single 37mm (43M) on each deck-house aft. This was never fully implemented and such alterations as were made were done piecemeal. Thus *T1* and *T9* landed the after torpedo tubes in July 1944, fitting a single 37mm in lieu. *T10* had a 40mm bow-chaser added and *T8* was re-armed in July 1944. By November 1944, all active units of the 2nd Flotilla had received some increase in AA defence capability. *T11* at the end of the war, had the following AA guns: one 40mm bow-chaser; two 37mm single (one in place of after tubes); one quadruple 20mm on midships deck-house; two 20mm twin in bridge wings; two 20mm twin aft of funnel; twenty-one 8.6cm RAG rocket-launchers.

Service These ships constituted the 1st and 2nd Torpedo-boat Flotillas, but did not become fully operational until late 1940. Their early service was in the Skagerrak, followed by minelaying duties in the North Sea. Transferred to France in September 1940, *T3* was sunk by bombing in Le Havre on the night of 18 September. *T11*, of the 2nd Flotilla, was damaged the following night at Cherbourg and *T2* had been damaged on passage to France earlier. Both flotillas returned to Germany then spent a period in Norway, losing *T6* on 6 November to a British mine off the east coast of England in the only sortie of the torpedo-boats in their designed role. The 1st Flotilla was disbanded in August 1941, whereupon all boats transferred to the 2nd Flotilla. Boats of the 2nd Flotilla took part in operations during the Invasion of Russia in 1941 and later that year, moved to France on escort duties where they screened the heavy units during the 'Channel Dash' in February 1942. For the remainder of 1942, some units operated in Norway, others in France with the rest in home waters. By mid 1943, all were in the Baltic, mostly on non-operational duties with the torpedo school. At the end of that year *T3*, which had been raised and rebuilt, re-commissioned on 12 December and rejoined the flotilla. In 1944, the flotilla was engaged upon convoy escort duties in the eastern Baltic and Gulf of Finland, but *T2* and *T7* were both bombed and sunk at Bremen on 29 July 1944. The former was re-floated on 27 September, the latter on 25 October, although only *T2* was towed to Schichau for repair. *T10* was lost when the floating dock she was in at Götenhafen was hit by bombs on 18 December 1944.

In 1945, *T3* rammed and sank the Soviet submarine *S4* on 4 January, but in February both she and *T5* were lost to mines in Danzig Bay. In April, *T1* was destroyed in an air raid at Kiel and in May, *T8* and *T9* scuttled themselves in Kiel Bay.

Post-war, *T4* passed to the USA who sold her to Denmark but she did not see further service. *T11* became the French *Bir Hakeim*, but likewise was never commissioned, and *T12* was taken over by the USSR. She was re-named *Podvischny* and was finally scrapped in the 1960s.

TORPEDOBOOTE TYPE 37 CLASS

Ship	Builder	Laid Down	Launched	Commissioned	Fate
T13	Schichau (Elbing)		15 June 39	31 May 41	Sunk 10 April 45
T14	Schichau (Elbing)			14 June 41	To USA 1946
T15	Schichau (Elbing)			26 June 41	Sunk 13 Dec 43
T16	Schichau (Elbing)			24 July 41	Paid off 13 April 45
T17	Schichau (Elbing)			28 Aug 41	To USSR 1946
T18	Schichau (Elbing)			22 Nov 41	Sunk 13 Sept 44
T19	Schichau (Elbing)		20 July 40	18 Dec 41	To USA 1946
T20	Schichau (Elbing)		Oct 1941	5 June 42	To UK 1946
T21	Schichau (Elbing)		Nov 1941	11 July 42	To USA 1946

Displacement: 874tons/888tonnes (standard); 1,121tons/1,139tonnes (full load).
Length: 279ft 6in/85.2m (oa); 269ft/81.97m (wl).
Beam: 29ft/8.87m.
Draught: 9ft 2in/2.8m (mean).
Machinery: } As Type 35.
Performance: }
Bunkerage: 197tons/200tonnes.
Range: 1,600nm at 19kts.
Guns: }
Torpedoes: } As Type 35.
Mines: }
Complement: }

Design A slight modification of the Type 35 design, this class incorporated some increase in beam and a little more rake to the bows. The hull was even weaker and lighter than the earlier class (i.e., 288 tonnes *v.* 311 tonnes), but by the time of completion extra strengthening had been worked in, raising the hull weight to 301 tonnes. Bunkerage was increased by about 10 tonnes, but internally the machinery arrangements were basically identical with *T1* although 10 tonnes lighter. Externally, distinguishing features were the bow form, anchor stowage and steam pipe arrangements, as compared with the Type 35. With this new class, Deschimag was dropped from the building programme, concentrating on destroyer construction and leaving only Schichau as torpedo-boat constructors in Germany. The first six units were ordered in September 1937, the remainder the following year. Building was considerably delayed, first by mobilization on the outbreak of war and secondly by the need to make alterations in the light of experience with *T1* and her sisters. Because of this, the last ship did not complete until after the first unit of the next design.

Modifications Early alterations included the fitting of tripod legs to the foremast and fixed radar aerials of radar FuM28, angled at 45° on each beam, at the foot of the foremast. Although on 4 February 1942, the OKM ordered the landing of the after tubes in boats of the 3rd Flotilla engaged in the 'Cerberus' operation, and the shipping of a quadruple 20mm in lieu, it is not certain that this was actually done in the Type 37 ships. The designed 37mm gun was fitted to this class, unlike the Type 35, but instead of being shipped on the after deck-house as intended, it was moved forward and installed as a bow-chaser. Its position aft was then occupied by a single 20mm gun which itself was replaced by a quadruple 20mm from May 1942, the first two units *T13* and *T14* receiving theirs in the course of overhaul from May to July, and in June respectively.

This outfit remained fairly standard until about 1944 by which time a second quadruple 20mm had been fitted to many units, including *T18, T19* and *T21*, on the midships platform, where it replaced the searchlight. In September 1944, the SKL ordered the replacement once more of the after torpedo tubes in the 3rd Flotilla, this time by a fully automatic 37mm gun. (This was to apply to *T13, T17, T18, T19* and *T20*, i.e., all surviving operational boats.) However, *T18* received a 40mm gun before her loss and in November *T13* received a 40mm gun, but *T17* and *T20* still had six tubes.

The 'Barbara' programme envisaged similar treatment to that of the Type 35 design except for the extra 37mm 43M gun in place of the after tubes. Once again war circumstances prevented the full achievement of this plan. Twin 20mm replaced the singles in the bridge wings of all units, but thereafter, outfits varied. *T14* received two 37mm singles, two quadruple 20mm, two twin 20mm and 21 RAG rocket outfits. She retained only three torpedo tubes. *T19* had one 40mm and two 37mm singles (or the other way round), two quadruple 20mm, two twin 20mm and three torpedo tubes. *T20*, on the other hand, ended up with two 37mm singles, one quadruple and four twin 20mm with 21 RAG outfits. She still carried her full six torpedo tubes. *T21*, caught with a refit incomplete at the war's end, was probably not fitted with any light guns. As this flotilla was engaged in operations in the Skagerrak in 1945 when air attacks were frequent, it is likely

Above: *T19* showing late-war modifications. (Drüppel)

Below: *T17* a typical *Type 37* boat, showing the distinctive radar. (Drüppel)

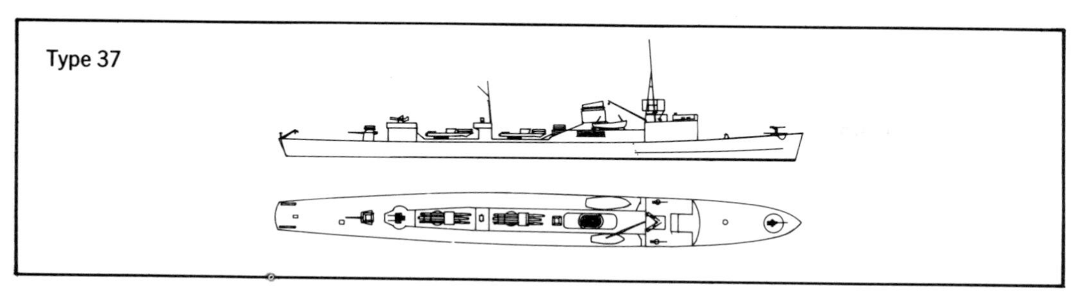

that the other units, *T13, T14, T16* and *T17* were armed similarly to *T14, T19* or *T20.*

Service All this class were nominally part of the 3rd Torpedo-boat flotilla. *T13, T15, T16* and *T17* moved down the Channel to Rotterdam at the end of January 1942 for their first operational deployment, 'Cerberus'. *T14*, however, was trapped in the ice at Flensburg. *T13* was damaged in this operation and in consequence did not move to Norway with the other three on 19 March 1942, for escort duties with *Admiral Hipper. T15* remained in Norway until July 1942, but the others returned home some time before. In July 1942, *T13* and *T14* sailed for France followed in September by *T18* and *T10* and *T17* in October. The last of these, *T14*, arrived back in Germany in November 1943. *T20* and *T21* operated in Norwegian waters until September 1943 and by the end of that year, all (less *T15*, bombed and sunk at Kiel on 13 December 1943) were either with the torpedo school or the U-boat training flotillas in the Baltic.

No operational activities took place until, with the deteriorating situation in the Baltic in late 1944, the flotilla joined the 2nd Task Force and by the end of that year, had been transferred to escort duties in the Skagerrak. *T16* had been mined and damaged off Memel on 21 February 1944, but it was not until the autumn that another ship was lost. This was *T18*, sunk off the Aaland Islands by aircraft rockets on 17 September 1944 when caught stopped and searching an Estonian refugee cutter. Unable to get under way fast enough, she could not outmanoeuvre her attacker. Finally both *T13* and *T16* were caught while escorting a convoy in the Kattegat by RAF Halifax bombers of 58 Squadron on 10 April 1945. *T13* was sunk and *T16* so badly damaged that she was paid off at Friedrichshaven on 13 April.

After the war, *T14* was briefly employed by the USN, supervising the scuttling of surplus enemy warships before being transferred to France as *Dompaire* in October 1947. She was stricken for breaking up in 1949. *T17*, transferred to the USSR as *Poriwisty* at Libau in 1946, was probably broken up in the 1950s while *T19*, which had originally been allocated to the USN, was sold to Denmark in 1947 but not put into service. She was broken up in 1950–51. *T20*, initially allocated to the RN, was eventually transferred to France as *Baccarat* but did not enter service and was stricken in 1951. *T21*, in a non-operational condition, was taken over by the USN, canibalized and then scuttled in the Skagerrak on 10 June 1946.

TORPEDOBOOTE TYPE 39 CLASS

Ship	Builder	Laid Down	Launched	Commissioned	Fate
T22	Schichau (Elbing)			28 Feb 42	Mined 18 Aug 44
T23	Schichau (Elbing)			14 June 42	To RN 1946
T24	Schichau (Elbing)			17 Oct 42	Sunk 24 Aug 44
T25	Schichau (Elbing)			12 Nov 42	Sunk 28 Dec 43
T26	Schichau (Elbing)			27 Feb 43	Sunk 28 Dec 43
T27	Schichau (Elbing)			17 April 43	Beached 29 April 44
T28	Schichau (Elbing)			19 June 43	To RN 1946
T29	Schichau (Elbing)			21 Aug 43	Beached 26 April 44
T30	Schichau (Elbing)			24 Oct 43	Mined 18 Aug 44
T31	Schichau (Elbing)			5 Feb 44	Sunk 20 June 44
T32	Schichau (Elbing)			8 May 44	Mined 18 Aug 44
T33	Schichau (Elbing)			16 June 44	To USSR 1946
T34	Schichau (Elbing)			12 Aug 44	Mined 20 Nov 44
T35	Schichau (Elbing)			7 Oct 44	To USN 1946
T36	Schichau (Elbing)			9 Dec 44	Mined 4 May 45

Displacement: 1,297tons/1,318tonnes (standard); 1,752tons/1,780tonnes (full load).
Length: 336ft 3in/102.5m (oa); 318ft 3in/97m (wl).
Beam: 32ft 9in/10m.
Draught: 10ft 8in/3.25m (mean).
Machinery: four Wagner boilers; 2-shaft geared turbines.
Performance: 32,000shp; 33.5kts.
Bunkerage: 369tons/375tonnes.
Range: 2,400nm at 19kts.
Guns: four 4.1in (4×1); four 37mm (2×2); six 20mm (6×1).
Torpedoes: six 21.7in (2×3).
Mines: 59.
Complement: 306.

Below: *T35* at the end of the war. (USN)

Design Whereas the Type 35 and 37 designs had been intended as super *S*-boats, this class was developed with fleet duties in mind as reflected by the designation *Flottentorpedoboote*. To this end, the gun armament was greatly increased although the torpedo outfit retained triple tubes. Displacement rose by 65 per cent and the ships looked heavier since there was less need to keep silhouette to the minimum. Internally, the unit principle of machinery arrangement was adopted leading to a twin funnel design, but the machinery itself was similar to the earlier designs with four boilers and two sets of turbines. With a similar designed horse power to the smaller Type 37, the extra displacement resulted in a drop in speed of some 2 knots on paper, but in service it was found that engine room auxiliaries, especially high-speed turbine-driven pumps, consumed vast amounts of steam from the auxiliary lines. Thus the steam plant was unable to generate sufficient high-pressure steam for the turbines and in practice, maximum speed dropped to 31 knots (28.5 knots continuous). A side-effect of this inefficiency in the machinery was a sharp drop in the actual endurance under service conditions viz. only 2,085nm at 19 knots and 765nm at 31 knots.

The hull retained the longitudinal framed arrangement of the earlier classes, but was not stressed as highly, representing 32 per cent of the full load displacement.

The 4.1-inch guns were of the SKC/32ns pattern in C32ge mountings, capable of 70° elevation, but no proper HA fire-control system was provided. The low-angle fire-control system was of a similar type to that of the destroyers. Radar, S Geräte and *NHG* (a navigational asdic system) were fitted. ASW capability included four depth-charge throwers and six single depth-charge cradles.

On 10 November 1939 orders were placed with Schichau at Elbing for nine ships as yard numbers *S1481* to *S1489*. At this time, it was intended to place orders for further units from Deschimag at Bremen (*T31* to *T48*) and Germania at Kiel (*T49* to *T52*). The builders of *T53* to *T60* had not been decided. In the event, only *T22* to *T30* were proceeded with and by June 1940, of these there were only firm completion dates for *T22* and *T23*. The cause of this was yard over-loading, shortage of materials and scarcity of shipyard workers. *T31* to *T36* were eventually ordered from Schichau on 20 January 1941, their hull construction being slightly simplified to ease production under wartime circumstances. The only visible evidence of this was the elimination of the knuckle at the bow.

Modifications As *T22* did not complete until February 1942, the need for increased AA defence had already been appreciated. In consequence, a quadruple 20mm was shipped aft where it had a good field of fire. *T22* was not actually so fitted at completion but received one soon afterwards. The light AA outfit now comprised, in addition to the 37mm, one quadruple and three single 20mm, two 13.2mm machine-guns and two MG34 machine-guns.

Two 'Sumatra' fixed dipole radar detection antennae were fitted on the foremast of *T22*, one facing aft just above funnel cap height and the second on the front of the radar support bracket. These were later removed and re-fitted just below the starfish yardarm with two more covering forward, aft, port and starboard. Most units had this arrangement. Some units received 'Hohentweil' radar aft, in place of the searchlight.

The 20mm single guns in the bridge wings were replaced by twin mountings in 1943–44, and *T31* onwards received quadruple 20mm on the bridge sponsons. By the time that the 'Barbara' outfits were finalized, only *T23*, *T28*, *T33*, *T35* and *T36* were still afloat and the plan was to arm them as follows: one twin 20mm port and starboard in the bows; two single 37mm *43M* in the bridge wings; two twin 37mm *M42* amidships; two twin 37mm *M42* in lieu of quadruple 20mm; two twin 20mm to port and starboard aft on mine rails. Once again, it is not known if any ship received this full outfit, but it is most unlikely. *T36* received two 2cm twin before the bridge.

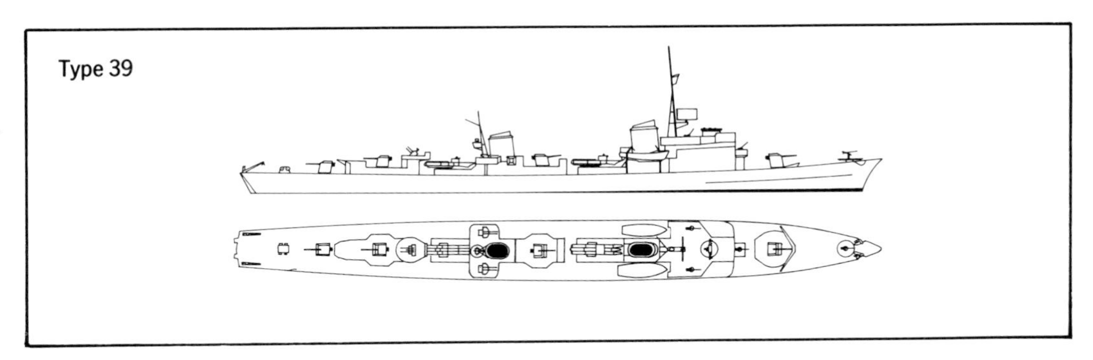

Above: *T23* in 1943, with typical class camouflage. (Author's collection)

Service The first eight boats of this class all belonged to the 4th Torpedo-boat Flotilla which was formed for them. *T22* arrived in France in October 1942, joined by *T23* in November. These two were not reinforced until the arrival of *T24* and *T25* in June 1943. Their main task was the escorting of convoys, blockade-runners and U-boats through the Bay of Biscay. At the end of August 1943, *T26* and *T27* also arrived in western France but in December both *T25* and *T26* were sunk in action with the British cruisers *Glasgow* and *Enterprise* while attempting to bring home a blockade-runner. *T28*, after a very brief deployment to Norway, arrived in France with *T29* in mid January 1944 to replace *T22* and *T23* which were due home to refit. These ships were very much in the front line at the time of the build-up to the Allied Invasion of Europe and suffered accordingly. *T29* was sunk after an action with Canadian destroyers off Brittany on 26 April, followed by *T27* on 29 April when she was driven ashore on the same coast, also by Canadian destroyers. *T24* was unable to reach the Invasion area from her base in the Bay of Biscay and was finally sunk by aircraft rockets in the Gironde on 24 August 1944. This left only *T28* which successfully fought her way back to Germany across the Invasion area at the end of July.

In the Baltic, the 5th and 6th Torpedo-boat Flotillas were reformed with the surviving ships of the 4th Flotilla and newly commissioned boats. *T31* moved to the Gulf of Finland in June 1944 for special duties but was quickly lost to a torpedo from a Soviet MTB. The remainder of the 6th Flotilla moved up to the Gulf of Finland where, on 18 August, *T22, T30* and *T32* were lost on mines in Narwa Bay. Following this disaster, all boats were reallocated to the 5th Flotilla, operating in support of the retreating land forces. *T34* fell victim to a mine off Arkona while on gunnery practise and in the last days of the war, *T36* was damaged by a mine off Swinemünde, then sunk by air attacks on 3 May 1945.

Post-war, *T23* and *T28* were allocated to the UK, but were re-transferred to France and renamed *Alsacien* and *Lorraine* respectively. They served until condemned in 1954 and 1959. *T33* was allocated to the USSR and renamed *Primernyi*, her subsequent disposal being unknown, and *T35* to the USA. *T35* was eventually given to France for cannibalization and condemned in 1952.

FLOTTENTORPEDOBOOTE 41 CLASS

Ship	Builder		Fate
T37	Schichau Elbing	Captured 97% complete	Scuttled 1946
T38	Schichau Elbing	Towed to Kiel. Captured 84% complete	Scuttled 10 May 46
T39	Schichau Elbing	Towed to Kiel. Captured 76% complete	Scuttled 10 May 46
T40	Schichau Elbing	Grounded at Brosen in tow for Kiel	Scuttled May 1945
T41–T51	Schichau Elbing	Unfinished to varying degrees at end of war	Broken up

Displacement: 1,490tons/1,514tonnes (standard); 2,155tons/2,190tonnes (full load).
Length: 347ft 8in/106m (oa); 334ft 7in/102m (wl).
Beam: 35ft 1in/10.7m.
Draught: 12ft 2in/3.72m (mean).
Machinery: four Wagner boilers; 2-shaft geared turbines.
Performance: 40,000shp; 34kts.
Bunkerage: 550tons/559tonnes.
Range: 2,800nm at 19kts.
Guns: four 4.1in (4×1); six 37mm (3×2); eight 20mm (4×2).
Torpedoes: six 21.7in (2×3).
Complement: 197.

Design The speed of the *Type 39* design having proved a disappointment, later units were to have been completed to this modified design with extra speed. Armament remained as before, but with an additional twin 37mm worked in before the bridge. Orders were placed on 25 November 1942 (*T43–T47*) and 11 January 1944 (*T48–T51*). Elbing fell into Soviet hands in 1945 and, as a result, the full progress of construction can no longer be determined, but it is believed that boats up to *T43* were launched. *T37* was very nearly complete when the war ended. Both *T38* and *T39* were towed out and scuttled by the Royal Navy in 1946, *T37* by the USN the same year.

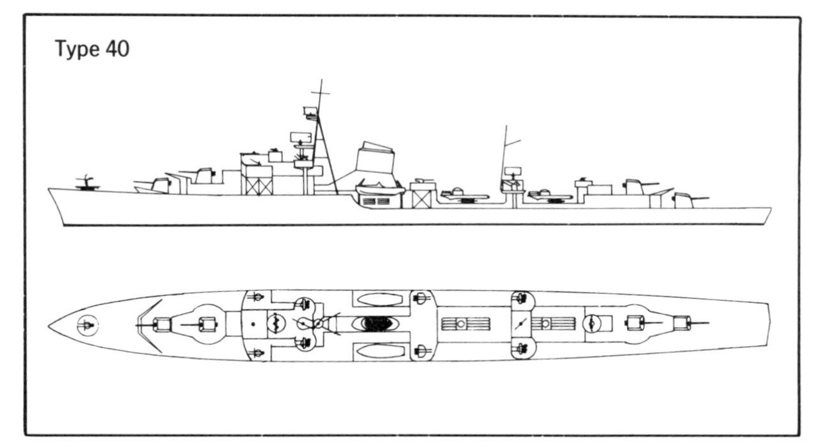
Type 40

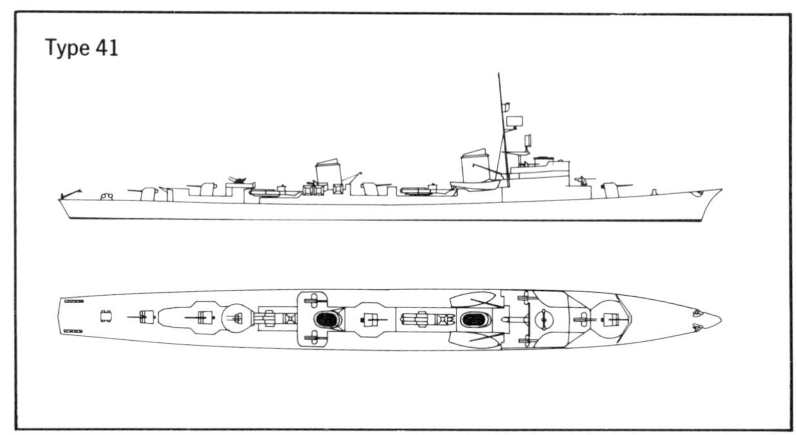
Type 41

FLOTTENTORPEDOBOOTE 40 CLASS

Ship	Builder	Laid Down	Launched	Commissioned	Fate
T61	Wilton Fjenord	1942	June 1944	–	Sunk 13 Sept 44
T63	Rotterdam Droogdok	1942	28 Oct 44	–	Scuttled 31 Dec 46
T65	De Scheldt Vlissingen	1942	8 July 44	–	Scuttled 1946

Displacement: 1,926tons/1,957tonnes (standard); 2,546tons/2,587tonnes (full load).
Length: 375ft 8in/114,5m (oa); 360ft 10in/110m (wl).
Beam: 36ft 11in/11.25m.
Draught: 11ft 2in/3.4m (mean).
Machinery: three low-pressure boilers; 2-shaft geared turbines.
Performance: 49,500shp; 35kts.
Bunkerage: 552tons/561tonnes.
Range: 2,350nm at 19kts.
Guns: four 5in (4×1); four 37mm (2×2); sixteen 20mm.
Torpedoes: eight 21.7in (2×4).
Mines: 50.
Complement: 231.

Design Built to take advantage of captured Dutch equipment and yard capacity, none of these ever completed for service. They were effectively destroyers and not torpedo-boats and had they entered service, would have given the Kriegsmarine a powerful, robust design. *T61* to *T68* were ordered from the three yards on 19 November 1940, followed by *T69–T72* on 3 May 1941. *T73* to *T84* were ordered on 27 August 1941. When the Allies landed in Normandy in June 1944, none of these ships had been launched because of shortage of raw materials and the importance of other priorities. However, with the yards threatened, it was necessary to get the three most advanced units back to Germany for completion. *T61* was sunk by a torpedo from a Beaufighter of 143 Squadron RAF off the West Friesian Islands on 13 September 1944, but the other two reached Elbing safely. In January 1945, still incomplete, they were towed to the west and captured by the Allies. *T63* was loaded with gas munitions prior to scuttling by the USN.

CAPTURED UNITS

Ship	Builder	Laid Down	Launched	Commissioned	Fate
ZH1 (ex-*Gerard Callenburg*)	R.D.M. Rotterdam	12 Oct 38	12 Oct 39	11 Oct 1942	Lost 9 June 44

Displacement: 1,604tons/1,629tonnes (standard); 2,228tons/2,263tonnes (full load).
Length: 351ft/107m (oa); 344ft 6in/105m (pp).
Beam: 34ft 9in/10.6m.
Draught: 9ft 2in/2.8m (mean).
Machinery: three Yarrow boilers; 2-shaft Werkspoor-Parsons turbines.
Performance: 45,000shp; 37.5kts.
Bunkerage: 560tons/568tonnes.
Range: 5,400nm at 19kts.
Guns: five 4.7in (2×2, 1×1); four 37mm (2×2); four 20mm.
Torpedoes: eight 21.7in (2×4).
Mines: 24.
Complement: 230.

Design Scuttled by the Dutch Navy at the fall of their country in May 1940, this incomplete destroyer was raised by the Kriegsmarine on 17 July 1940. She was repaired and construction recommenced under the supervision of Blohm & Voss, but she did not commission for service until 11 October 1942, renamed *ZH1*.

On trials after commissioning, *ZH1* reached 37.5 knots with 53,000shp. The hull and machinery was considered reliable and robust, but some trouble was experienced with the boilers whose burners were eventually changed for Blohm & Voss pattern. The guns too were generally liked, especially the fixed ammunition which facilitated their serving. On the other hand, both gun and torpedo fire-control systems were criticized and not considered up to German standard. The main battery director could only train from red 135° to green 135° through ahead despite the fact that there were three guns aft out of five. *ZH2* ex-*Tjerk Hiddes* and *ZH3* ex-*Van Galen* were not proceeded with.

Modifications Few modifications were made while the ship was being repaired, despite the obvious opportunity, because of the desire to have a ship of 'British' pattern with which to compare indigenous German destroyer designs. This was considered necessary as a result of continual criticism of German designs from the fleet. The original machinery and main armament (4.7in/45 QF Mk 8) was retained as were the Dutch gun and torpedo fire-control systems (but the torpedo tube mountings were German pattern). Light AA, however, was altered to German pattern SKC/30 37mm guns in two twin mountings, one forward, one aft and two quadruple 20mm *Vierlings* on sponsons abreast the after funnel. 'Gemma' radar was fitted while the ship was in the Baltic in the spring of 1943. Almost exactly a year later, this was removed and a 'Hohentweil' set fitted in its place when the ship was under repair at Pauillac in April 1944.

Service *ZH1* was nominally a member of the 5th Destroyer flotilla for the early part of her life and later joined the 8th Flotilla for the rest of her career, but she was considered to be essentially an experimental vessel and in consequence spent much of her brief life either on trials, in dockyard hands or working-up in Baltic waters. It was not until November 1943 that she and *Z27* sailed for operational duties with her flotilla in western France. Despite being engaged by long-range shore batteries from Dover, MTBs and fighter-bombers en route, both arrived safely in Le Verdon on 5 November. On the Atlantic coast of France she participated in blockade-runner and U-boat escort duties, but because of boiler troubles incurred on 26 December (when she had to be towed in by *T25*), she was not with her flotilla during the disastrous *Glasgow/Enterprise* action a couple of days later. When the Allies landed in Normandy on 6 June 1944, *ZH1* was ordered to interdict the Invasion Area with *Z32, Z24* and *T24* on 8 June. The following day, off the Ile de Bas, the flotilla was intercepted by four British destroyers (*Tartar, Ashanti, Eskimo* and *Javelin*), two Canadian (*Haida* and *Huron*) and the Polish *Blyscawica*. In the course of this action, *ZH1* was badly damaged in her machinery spaces after launching a torpedo salvo. Stopped and on fire, she engaged and damaged *Tartar* before a torpedo from *Ashanti* blew off her bows and she eventually sank after scuttling charges had been set off.

ZF2 (ex-*L'Opiniâtre*)

Captured on the slipway at Bordeaux in June 1940, this incomplete French destroyer was never seriously proceeded with by the Kriegsmarine. Plans were prepared to rearm the ship with German pattern 5in, 37mm and 20mm guns as well as two quadruple banks for 21-inch torpedoes. Shortages of shipyard workers, raw materials, particularly non-ferrous metals (mainly copper) and French tardiness, effectively prevented any progress towards completion once construction was abandoned in July 1943. The incomplete hull was broken up on the slipway post-war. Her sister, *L'Aventurier*, was also intended for completion but little work was ever done.

ZG3, Hermes (ex-*Vasilefs Georgis*)

Design Taken over in a damaged condition after the fall of Greece in April 1941, she was repaired under the supervision of a team of technicians from Germaniawerft and eventually recommissioned as *ZG3* for the Kriegsmarine on 21 March 1942. Germany was fortunate in that the destroyer's main armament and fire-control system was of German manufacture and, unlike that of *ZH1*, was proven and reliable.

Modifications Her light AA was altered to two single 37mm guns between the funnels and five 20mm single guns, one on the forecastle, two abaft the after funnel and two more on the forward edge of the after shelter deck. The torpedo outfit was reduced to six, one tube being removed from each quadruple bank and main rails fitted. This armament remained thus up to the time of her loss.

Service From June 1942 to April 1943, *ZG3* (renamed *Hermes* on 22 August 1942) operated in the Aegean between Piraeus, Crete and the Dardenelles, covering convoy traffic. On 16 November 1942, she detected the Greek submarine *Triton* which was later sunk by the Escort *UJ102*. In April 1943 she was transferred west for the North-Africa supply route with occasional minelaying duties. She sank the British submarine *Splendid* off Capri on 21 April 1943, but ten days later, after heavy damage from air attacks, she herself had to be towed into Tunis in a non-operational condition. As repairs were obviously impossible to complete, *Hermes* was scuttled at La Goulette on 7 May.

ZN4 (ex-?), *ZN5* (ex-?)

Design Two small torpedo-boats, enlarged versions of the *Sleipner* class, were captured at the time of the Invasion of Norway in April 1940. Both had been laid down at Horten dockyard in April 1939 and were not greatly advanced when they fell into German hands. (For details of their original design, see Norway).

Modifications The German Navy intended to replace the original Norwegian 4.7-inch guns by three 4.1-inch single weapons, and the light AA by two 37mm and six 20mm.

Service Recognizing their small size and low fighting power compared to true destroyers, the German Navy rerated this pair as 'torpedo-boats' in 1941 and they became *TA7* and *TA8*. Progress was very slow under the German regime and it was not until 1941 that *TA7* was launched and *TA8* in June 1943. *TA7* was sunk by sabotage (bomb in the turbine room) at Horten on 26 September 1944, only hours before she was to be towed to Germany and as a result it was agreed by SKL on 2 October that the hull of *TA8*, which was complete, would also be towed to Germany for completion. This was never done and *TA8* was repossessed by the Norwegians in May 1945 at Horten, but never finished.

TA1 to *TA6*

Design French *torpilleurs* of the 1,010-tonnes type, captured incomplete at the fall of France in June 1940. They were laid down as *Le Fier, L'Agile,*

L'Alsacien, L'Entreprenant, Le Farouche and *Le Corse* respectively. Construction on behalf of the Kriegsmarine was delayed on every pretext by the French and by shortages of raw materials on the German side. By April 1943, the completion of *TA1* and *TA4* was ordered and the necessary raw materials were available, but because of repairs to Sperrbrecher and Patrol Vessels in western France, construction was effectively halted. As for *TA2, TA3, TA5* and *TA6*, material shortages caused the suspension of these four, and no further work was ever done on them. The net result was that none of the six torpedo-boats were completed.

Modifications In German service, the ships were to receive three 4.1-inch guns, three 37mm and six 20mm guns.

Service None in German hands, nor after reversion to French custody.

TA7, TA8

These were the former *ZN4* and *ZN5* q.v.). It was intended that *TA7* would join the reformed 5th Torpedo-boat Flotilla.

TA9, TA10, TA11, TA12, TA13

Design *Torpilleurs* of the 600-tonnes type (q.v.) built for the French Navy before the war.

Modifications Those units which were commissioned, *TA9, TA10* and *TA11*, received a German-pattern radar set on the foremast. AA armament was strengthened by the addition of a *Vierling* 20mm on the after shelter deck and it is likely that further 20mm guns were shipped. It would seem also that the torpedo tubes were retained.

Service After transfer from the Royal Italian Navy at La Spezia in April 1943 these boats were renamed *TA9* (ex-*FR42*, ex-*Bombarde*), *TA10* (ex-*La Pomone*) and *TA11* (ex-*FR41*, ex-*L'Iphigénie*), *TA12* (ex-*FR45*, ex-*La Baliste*) and *TA13* (ex-*FR44*, ex-*La Bayonnaise*). Initially, only the first three were operable and all sailed from La Spezia for Toulon and a refit at the end of April 1943. This passage exposed the woeful material state of the boats which was, in all probability, not assisted by personnel unfamiliar with the French machinery. On reaching Toulon, they were refitted at the La Seyne yard where it was found that much of the electrical equipment was defective, the fire-control system poor and ammunition for the guns short. Even without the equipment problems, there were manning difficulties. Hitler had ordered the Kriegsmarine to take over the ships as early as 4 December 1942 and Flag Officer (Destroyers) was ordered to supply the manning. The latter was already overstretched and reluctant to do so because he felt that these boats were more suitable for escort than for torpedo-boat duties. These boats were originally suggested for the formation of a 10th Torpedo-boat Flotilla in April 1943, subordinated to the 7th *Sicherungs* (Escort) Division at La Spezia, but later operated with the 3rd and 4th Escort Divisions for their brief careers. *TA11* (*L'Iphigénie*) was the first loss, being sunk in action with Italian *MAS* boats at Pombino after being damaged by Italian tanks on the night of 9/10 September 1943 at the time of the Italian capitulation. *TA10* (ex-*La Pomone*) joined the 3rd Escort Flotilla in April 1943 and later was transferred to the 4th Flotilla, but was not operational until the end of June 1943. As a result of British activities in the Aegean, *TA10* was sent to support German forces in the Rhodes area in the autumn of 1943, where, on 23 September 1943, when some ten miles south of that island, she encountered the British destroyer *Eclipse*. After a brief and unequal engagement both *TA10*'s engines were wrecked but

Above: *ZH1*. (W. B. Bilddienst) **Below:** *ZG3*. (W. B. Bilddienst)

the British destroyer did not stay to finish her off and the German was able to reach Prassos Bay. Here, because repairs were impossible and it was unlikely that she could be brought safely to Crete, it was decided to remove her light guns and scuttle her, which was done on 27 September. *TA9* (ex-*Bombarde*) served in the Tyrrhenian Sea area until September 1943 when she was paid off at Toulon, where she was destroyed in an air raid on 23 August 1944 during the preparations for 'Avalanche'. *TA12*, contrary to other sources, never entered service with the Kriegsmarine. She was raised at Toulon on 14 May 1943 with the intention of commissioning her, but on 24 November a large force of B17s of the USAAF raided the port, one of the ships destroyed being *TA12*. *TA13* never entered service either and she was scuttled once more at Toulon on 25 August 1944, still non-operational.

TA14 (ex-*Turbine*)

Design An Italian destroyer captured at Piraeus in September 1943.
Modifications Two single 37mm Breda guns were fitted amidships between the torpedo tubes, two single 20mm on the upper bridge and two more abaft the after funnel. Other 20mm guns were fitted at the break of the forecastle.

In December 1943 a good deal of top-weight was landed for stability reasons but it is not known quite what this comprised.
Service This boat formed part of the 9th Torpedo-boat Flotilla based in the Aegean. Her first operations were in connection with the occupation of Rhodes in the autumn of 1943. This was followed by convoy escort duties in Aegean waters into 1944. On 1 February *TA14* was hit in No. 3 boiler room by aircraft rockets while escorting a merchant ship from Leros to Vathi. The merchantman, *Leda*, was sunk but *TA14* and her escorts *TA15*, *TA16* and *R*-boats made port safely. Repairs at Salamis extended until early May 1944 when she returned to escort duties. She was damaged again while in Porto Lago on 19 June by explosives, probably sabotage, when her bows were flooded. Repaired once more at Salamis, *TA14* was sunk by a USAAF air raid on 16 September before re-entering service.

TA15 (ex-*Francesco Crispi*)

Design An Italian *Sella*-class destroyer captured and pressed into service with the Kriegsmarine.
Modifications As *TA14*, but for a period up to February 1944 she lacked a forward gun. At least one quadruple 20mm was added and at the time of her loss also had 40mm weapons.
Service Commissioned for service in the Aegean with the 9th Torpedo-boat Flotilla on 30 October 1943. She took part in the Leros and Dodecanese operations and later escort duties in the Aegean Sea, but on 8 March 1944 she was hit by three rockets when under air attack off Heraklion and sank with the loss of 34 men. At this time *TA15* was suffering from engine defects and could only make 15 knots on her port machine. However, such was the pressing need for escorts that she had to be used.

TA16 (ex-*Castelfidardo*), *TA19* (ex-*Calatafimi*)

Design Both *Curtatone*-class torpedo-boats of the Royal Italian Navy.
Modifications Not known, but her light AA included 20mm and 40mm guns. Quadruple 20mm were also fitted and *TA19* at least received 37mm SKC/32 in lieu of the 40mm guns.
Service *TA16* recommissioned under the German flag on 14 November 1943 and *TA19* also late in 1943. Both were units of the 9th Torpedo-boat Flotilla, operating in the Aegean and occasionally up to the Dardenelles. On 31 May 1944 *TA16*, together with *TA14*, *TA17*, *TA19* and *UJ2101*, *UJ2110*, *UJ2105*, *R34* and *R211* sailed from Piraeus to escort an extremely important convoy to Crete, consisting of the merchantmen *Sabine*, *Tanais* and *Gertrud*. This was heavily attacked by RAF Beaufighters, Baltimores and Marauders which severely damaged *TA16* leaving her down by the bows up to her anchors. Her upper works were badly shot up and there were numerous casualties. *UJ2101* and *UJ2105* were both sunk as was *Sabine*. The damaged *Gertrud* and *TA16* reached Heraklion, but here *Gertrud* exploded and sank which in turn caused the loss of *TA16*. *TA19* on passage from Portolago to Rhodes on 19 June 1944 was attacked by aircraft and hit by four rockets, but made Heraklion in a bad way. Repaired at Skaramanga, *TA19* was operational once more on 17 July, but less than a month later she was sunk by the Greek submarine *Pipinos* off Vathi on 9 August.

TA17 (ex-*San Martino*), *TA18* (ex-*Solferino*)

Design Two Italian *Palestro*-class destroyers captured at Piraeus on 9 September 1943.
Modifications The 4in guns were reduced to two, 20mm outfit augmented and *TA18*, at least, had her twin, sided torpedo tubes replaced by a triple centre-line bank.
Service *TA17* recommissioned for the 9th Torpedo-boat Flotilla on 28 October 1943 and was employed with her flotilla in the Aegean. On 18 June 1944 she was badly damaged by sabotage or limpet mines at Porto Largo when her stern compartments were flooded. On 29 June she was able to steam slowly for Piraeus and repairs at Salamis dockyard. Damaged by air raids on 18 September (and paid off that day) and again on 12 October, *TA17* was finally scuttled without seeing further service.

TA18 was not commissioned until 25 July 1944 and then, like her sisters, was employed on Aegean convoys. She was sunk in action with the British destroyers *Termagent* and *Tuscan* south of Volos on 19 October 1944.

TA20 (ex-*Audace*)

Design A very over-aged Italian torpedo-boat captured at Venice on 12 September 1943.
Modifications Not known in German service, but in all probability the AA outfit was augmented.
Service Escort duties in the Adriatic with the 2nd Escort Flotilla until sunk in action off Pago Island in the Dalmatians on 1 November 1944, by the British destroyers *Avonvale* and *Wheatland*.

TA21 (ex-*Insidioso*)

Design Italian *Indomito*-class torpedo-boat completed before the First World War and captured at Pola on 10 September 1943.
Modifications Not known.
Service Escort duties in the Adriatic with the 11th Escort Flotilla and on the salmatian coast, after recommissioning on 8 November 1943. Damaged by air attack off Cap Salvore on 9 August 1944, *TA21* was paid off at Trieste and later sunk on 5 November 1944 by aircraft torpedo at Fiume.

TA22 (ex-*Giuseppe Missori*), *TA35* (ex-*Giuseppe Dezza*)

Design Two Italian *Abba*-class torpedo-boats captured at Durrazzo and Fiume respectively.
Modifications Not known in detail, but *TA22* had two single 20mm in lieu of the forward guns.
Service Both served with the 2nd Escort Flotilla in the Adriatic. *TA22* was badly damaged by fighter-bombers in July 1944 and paid off at Trieste on 11 August. She was scuttled on 3 May 1945 at Muggia. *TA35*, which was not commissioned until 9 June 1944, was mined and sunk only two months later off Pola on 17 August.

TA23 (ex-*Impavido*), *TA25* (ex-*Intrepido*), *TA26* (ex-*Adito*)

Design Formerly units of the Italian *Animoso* class, captured in Porto Ferraio (*TA23* and *TA26*) or under completion (*TA25*).
Modifications Not known in detail.
Service *TA23* commissioned on 9 October and *TA26* on 19 December 1943. *TA25* completed and commissioned on 16 January 1944. All served with the 3rd Escort Flotilla and later the 10th Torpedo-boat Flotilla, on the west coast of Italy. Their tasks were mainly local defence, minelaying and convoy escort duties. Both *TA23* and *TA26* carried out a bombardment of Bastia in Corsica on 22 April 1944. In the course of a minelaying sortie by *TA23*, *TA26* and *TA29*, *TA23* was mined west of Capri on 25 April, both boiler rooms being flooded. Despite being taken in tow by *TA26*, an MTB attack caused the tow to be cast off and the casualty was torpedoed by *TA29*. On 15 June, *TA26* was herself torpedoed and sunk west of La Spezia by US PT boats *PT552*, *558* and *559* and *TA25* south-west of Viareggio on 21 June by PT boats while engaged minelaying.

TA 24 CLASS

Ship	Builder	Laid Down	Launched	Commissioned	Fate
TA24 (ex-*Arturo*)	Ansaldo, Genoa	15 July 42	27 Mar 43	4 Oct 43	Lost 18 Mar 45
TA27 (ex-*Auriga*)	Ansaldo, Genoa	15 July 42	15 April 43	28 Dec 43	Lost 9 June 44
TA28 (ex-*Rigel*)	Ansaldo, Genoa	15 July 42	22 May 43	23 Jan 44	Lost 4 Sept 44
TA29 (ex-*Eridano*)	Ansaldo, Genoa	15 July 42	12 July 43	6 Mar 44	Lost 18 Mar 45
TA30 (ex-*Dragone*)	Ansaldo, Genoa	15 July 42	14 Aug 43	15 May 44	Lost 15 June 44
TA36 (ex-*Stella Polare*)	C.N. Quarnaro, Fiume	1 April 42	11 July 43	15 Jan 44	Lost 18 Mar 44
TA37 (ex-*Gladio*)	C.R.D.A., Trieste	9 Jan 43	15 June 43	8 Jan 44	Lost 7 Oct 44
TA38 (ex-*Spada*)	C.R.D.A., Trieste	9 Jan 43	1 July 43	12 Feb 44	Lost 13 Oct 44
TA39 (ex-*Daga*)	C.R.D.A., Trieste	9 Jan 43	15 July 43	27 Mar 44	Lost 16 Oct 44
TA40 (ex-*Pugnale*)	C.R.D.A., Trieste	9 Jan 43	1 Aug 43	17 Oct 44	Scuttled 4 May 45
TA41 (ex-*Lancia*)	C.R.D.A., Trieste	24 Mar 43	7 May 44	7 Sept 44	Lost 17 Feb 45
TA42 (ex-*Alabarda*)	C.R.D.A., Trieste	24 Mar 43	7 May 44	27 Sept 44	Lost 23 Jan 45
TA45 (ex-*Spica*)	C.N. Quarnaro, Fiume	14 Jan 42	1943	8 Sept 44	Lost 13 April 45
TA46 (ex-*Fionda*)	C.N. Quarnaro, Fiume	26 Aug 42	?	–	Lost 20 Feb 45
TA47 (ex-*Balestra*)	C.N. Quarnaro, Fiume	5 Sept 42	–	–	Damaged on slip

Below: *TA29* in Genoa. (W. B. Bilddienst)

Displacement: 745tons/757tonnes (standard); 1,110tons/1,127tonnes (full load).
Length: 274ft/83.5m (oa); 266ft/81.1m (pp).
Beam: 28ft 3in/8.62m.
Draught: 10ft 4in/3.15m (mean).
Machinery: two 3-drum boilers; 2-shaft turbines.
Performance: 22,000shp; 31.5kts.
Bunkerage: 210tons/213tonnes.
Range: 1,020nm at 15kts.
Guns: two 3.9in (2×1); ten 20mm.
Torpedoes: six 21.7in (2×3).
Mines: 28.
Complement: 94.

Design Former Royal Italian Navy *Ariete*-class torpedo-boats captured incomplete in the shipyards in September 1943. The possession of these modern and well-armed ships was of great importance to the Kriegsmarine forces of *Gruppe Sud* which had hitherto been able to dispose only those small units which could be brought overland from Germany. At the Italian capitulation, a large collection of motley vessels fell into German hands, but this was the only sizeable group of homogeneous units. It was intended to complete all fifteen ships, but in fact only thirteen were commissioned. All were originally intended to form the 10th Torpedo-boat Flotilla, but because of the geographical location of the shipyards and the strategic situation in the Italian theatre in late 1943, this was not possible because five units were being built on the west coast and the remainder in the Adriatic. By this time, it had become impossible for the German naval forces to move from one to the other.

Modifications Mainly limited to increased AA by the addition of 37mm and 20mm guns, the latter in single, twin and Vierling mountings. *TA37, 38* and *39* had 40mm guns in lieu of 37mm. Radar was fitted to some. Torpedo outfit varied with *TA38* and *TA39* having only one triple bank of tubes while *TA37* had one twin and one triple.

Service The five units on the west coast were allocated to the 10th Torpedo-boat Flotilla based at Genoa. Their main tasks were escort duties, minelaying and coastal defence. *TA24* and *TA28* took part in the bombardment of Bastia on 1 March 1944, and *TA29* in that on 22 April 1944. Their main adversaries were British and US coastal forces and aircraft, with whom frequent encounters occurred. These were without result in the main until June when *TA27*, after arriving at Porto Ferraio on 9 June, anchored in the harbour and was attacked by three fighter-bombers. Bombs and cannon-fire disabled the ship and knocked out part of her Flak outfit, but attempts were made to move the ship into a safer berth. However, about ninety minutes later, a further attack by eight more aircraft blew off her sternmost compartments, although *TA27* remained afloat. Without power or pumping capacity, water flooded in until she eventually capsized against the pier later that night, *TA30* taking off her crew and confidential books. *TA30* lasted only a little longer. She had completed a minelaying task south of La Spezia in the early hours of 15 June when she was hit by a torpedo aft, fired by a US PT boat. The after end broke off but the remainder stayed afloat for about ten minutes longer before capsizing. *TA26* was also lost in this encounter. The three survivors on the west coast, *TA24, TA28* and *TA29*, led an active life in the restricted area of German Naval operations until *TA28* was hit by three bombs by the USAAF while in dry dock at Genoa on 4 September 1944 and burnt out. The other pair were sunk in action with the British destroyers *Meteor* and *Lookout* in the Gulf of Genoa on 18 March 1945.

Of the ships built on the Adriatic coast, *TA37* was the first to complete, followed shortly by *TA36*. These two were immediately employed upon convoys from Pola to the Aegean and at the end of February 1944, were engaged while so doing by the French *contre-torpilleurs, Le Terrible* and *Le Malin*. The freighter being escorted and one UJ-boat were sunk and *TA37* hit by a shell and disabled. Taken in tow she reached port safely. Later *TA36*, while on a minelaying sortie, struck a mine SSW of Fiume and sank on 18 March.

In September 1944, three of the torpedo-boats, *TA37, TA38* and *TA39* were transferred to the

Aegean from 20 to 25 September to join the 9th Torpedo-boat Flotilla replacing their losses. In the Straits of Otranto, there was a brief engagement with two British *Hunt*-class destroyers, *Belvoir* and *Waddon*. *TA38* and *TA39* intercepted and sank *HDML1227* off Piraeus on 5 October. However, their service in the Aegean was brief for *TA37* was sunk together with her convoy by the destroyers *Termagent* and *Tuscan* off Kasandra-Huk, *TA38* was sunk by air attack at Volos and, finally, *TA39* was lost to a drifting mine on the west coast of the Gulf of Salonika, all in October.

In the Adriatic there remained only *TA40, TA41, TA42* and *TA45*, all completed in September 1944. These were employed on local defence and minelaying operations until early 1945, with *TA42* being bombed and sunk at Venice in January. *TA41* was damaged by bombs at Trieste in February (later wrecked in May) and *TA45* was lost in action with MTBs in April. Finally, *TA40* was scuttled at Malfalcone, having been damaged by bombing on 20 February.

TA46 was sunk, incomplete, by bombs at Fiume and *TA47* was damaged by bombing on the slipway and never launched.

TA31 (ex-*Dardo*)

Name ship of an Italian destroyer class, captured while under repair at Genoa. According to German sources this ship, whose stability was somewhat suspect, had capsized in Palermo in 1941 or 1942, but was raised and modified by the increasing of beam by 1.2 metres. The forward director and radar set were also removed. At the end of March 1944 SKL decided to commission the ship which by this time had almost completed repairs, for the 10th Torpedo-boat Flotilla. Turbine problems delayed her entry into service with the Kriegsmarine but she was eventually commissioned on 18 June 1944 at Genoa.

Modifications At the time of her entry into service as *TA31*, she was armed with twin 4.7-inch, two single 37mm Breda guns, three twin and five single 20mm Breda and one triple bank of 21-inch torpedoes. Two more 37mm and 20mm guns were added.

Service At commissioning, the ship was actually far from ready for service but circumstances were against the Kriegsmarine. She lacked radar, boats, bridge armouring and her machinery was incomplete. Like other units of the 10th Flotilla, *TA31* was employed on reconnaissance, minelaying and escort duties around Genoa and La Spezia, but had only a brief life, being paid off at La Spezia on 25 October 1944 after aircraft damage. Disarmed, the hull was later scuttled on 24 April 1945.

TA32 (ex-*Premuda*, ex-*Dubrovnik*)

Design A Yugoslav destroyer captured and put into service by the Royal Italian Navy.

Modifications At the time of the Italian capitulation, this ship was in Genoa having her armament changed when she was captured by Germany. It was originally intended to employ her as a Night Fighter Direction ship for the Luftwaffe and to this end she was altered considerably. The planned Italian 5.3-inch guns never materialized and instead, she received three 4.1-inch guns in single (Luftwaffe?) mountings and a large 'Freya' radar installation aft. Two 37mm single guns were fitted on the upper decks and the torpedoes had been removed. Then, because of changed tactical requirements, the ship was no longer required for this purpose and on 18 June 1944 was ordered to be converted to a 'TA'-boat for the 10th Torpedo-boat Flotilla to replace lost boats. To this end demands were made for alterations as follows: two twin banks of tubes to be installed amidships on the upper deck, one twin 37mm mounting (later two) fitted between the funnels to replace the singles on the upper deck, a fourth 4.1-inch gun to replace the Freya radar, fitting of mine rails and the installation of radio equipment intended for *TA25*.

TA32 eventually received four 4.1-inch guns, probably one triple bank of tubes, two quadruple 20mm on the former searchlight positions, two single (twin?) 20mm abreast the bridge, on the forecastle deck and radar atop the navigating bridge. She would also have been equipped with 37mm guns, probably in lieu of one set of tubes and between the funnels. In total, she is reported at one time to have had *seven* quadruple 20mm guns.

Service *TA32* commissioned for service on 18 August 1944 with the 10th Flotilla. She bombarded front-line positions on the river Secchio at the end of the month and in October carried out sorties in the Gulf of Genoa. In March 1945, *TA32* took part in a minelaying sortie with *TA24* and *TA29* during which she lost contact with her consorts when they were engaged and was sunk by British destroyers. *TA32* engaged briefly with guns and torpedoes without success and then returned to port. She was eventually abandoned and scuttled at Genoa on the evacuation of that port on 24/25 April 1945.

Below: *TA32*, the former Yugoslav *Dubrovnik*. (W. B. Bilddienst)

TA33 (ex-*Corsaro*, ex-*Squadrista*)

Design An Italian 2nd Series *Soldati*-class destroyer captured incomplete at Livorno on 9 September 1943. Towed to Genoa for completion, she was initially intended as a Night Fighter Direction ship similar to *Premuda* (*TA32*).

Modifications Freya radar was to be installed amidships. Three Luftwaffe quadruple 20mm were fitted on the after deck and two more on the upper deck, plus two more, positions unknown (four out of these seven were Luftwaffe equipments). For operational use as a torpedo-boat some of these were to be replaced by twin 20mm and others repositioned to allow mine rails to be fitted. Two quadruple 20mm were to be removed. The Freya radar was to be replaced by either a quadruple 20mm or a triple bank of tubes. The main armament was a 4.1-inch gun forward which was later given to *TA32* as her fourth gun.

Service *TA33* never entered service; hit by three bombs at La Spezia while carrying out steam trials on 4 September 1944, she capsized and sank.

TA34 (ex-*Carrista*)

Sister ship of *TA33* but not proceeded with.

TA43 (ex-*Sebenico*, ex-*Beograd*)

This Yugoslav destroyer was captured from the Royal Italian Navy on 11 September in Venice.

Modifications Not known with certainty.

Service Recommissioned as *TA43* on 17 October 1944 and served in the northern Adriatic with the 9th Torpedo-boat Flotilla on escort and minelaying duties. She was scuttled at Trieste on 1 May 1945.

TA44 (ex-*Antonio Pigafetta*)

Design Italian destroyer of the *Navigatori* class captured at Fiume on 10 September 1943.

Modifications Unknown.

Service Recommissioned after repairs on 14 October 1944 for service with the 9th Torpedo-boat Flotilla in the Northern Adriatic. Sunk by air attack at Trieste on 17 February 1945.

TA48 (ex-*T3*, ex-*78T*)

Design Over-aged Austro-Hungarian torpedo-boat ceded to Yugoslavia after the First World War. Captured by Italy in 1941 and by Germany at Fiume on 16 September 1943.
Modifications Not known.
Service Patrol and escort work in the northern Adriatic after commissioning on 15 August 1944, as a unit of the Croat Navy. Due to the unreliability of this formation, the boat was repossessed by the Kriegsmarine on 14 December 1944. *TA48* was sunk by bombs at Trieste on 20 February 1945.

TA49

Design *Spica*-class torpedo-boat captured from the Italian Navy when scuttled at La Spezia on 9 September 1943. She was raised by the Kriegsmarine, but while still under repair was sunk by bombs at La Spezia on 4 November 1944.

Above: *Löwe* at Gotenhafen, as a tender for U-boat training flotillas. Note No. 1 gun removed. (W. B. Bilddienst)

LOWE

Ship	Builder	Laid Down	Launched	Commissioned	Fate
Löwe (ex-*Gyller*)	Horten N Yd.		7 July 38		Returned May 1945

Displacement: 597tons/606tonnes (standard); 708tons/719tonnes (full load).
Length: 243ft 9in/74.3m (oa); 236ft 3in/72m (pp).
Beam: 25ft 7in/7.8m.
Draught: 6ft 11in/2.1m (mean).
Machinery: three Yarrow boilers; 2-shaft de Laval geared turbines.
Performance: 12,500shp; 30kts.
Bunkerage: 100tons/101tonnes.
Range: 3,500nm at 15kts.
Guns: three 4in; one 40mm.
Torpedoes: four 21.7in (2×2).
Mines: 24.
Complement: 75.

Design Formerly the Norwegian torpedo-boat *Gyller*, one of the most modern units of the Royal Norwegian Navy, captured intact at Kristiansand on 11 April 1940.
Modifications The after tubes and forward gun were removed and one single 20mm gun fitted on the forecastle. The superimposed after 4.1-inch gun was also replaced by a further single 20mm gun.
Service A unit of the 7th Torpedo-boat Flotilla until November 1940, operating in southern Norwegian waters, the Skaggerak and Kattegatt. In December 1940 the flotilla was disbanded and transferred to Flag Officer (U-Boats) for use by the 27th U-Boat Flotilla as torpedo recovery vessels. On return to Norwegian ownership she reverted to the name *Gyller* and in the early 1950s she was rebuilt as an A/S frigate. She was stricken in 1959.

PANTHER CLASS

Ship	Builder	Laid Down	Launched	Commissioned	Fate
Panther (ex-*Odin*)	Horten N Yd.		17 Jan 39		Returned May 1945
Leopard (ex-*Balder*)	Horten N Yd.		11 Oct 39	26 July 40	Returned May 1945
Tiger (ex-*Tor*)	Fredrikstad M.V.		9 Sept 39		Returned May 1945

Displacement: 632tons/642tonnes (standard).
Length: 242ft 9in/74m (pp).
Beam: 25ft 7in/7.8m.
Draught: 9ft 10in/3m (mean).
Machinery: three Yarrow boilers; 2-shaft de Laval geared turbines.
Performance: 12,500shp; 30kts.
Bunkerage: 100tons/101tonnes.
Range: 3,500nm at 15kts.
Guns: two 4.1in; one 40mm.
Torpedoes: two 21.7in (1×2).
Mines: 24.
Complement: 75.

Design Modified *Sliepner*-class torpedo-boats captured at the time of the invasion of Norway. *Leopard* and *Tiger* were completed by the Kriegsmarine.
Modifications The forward gun and torpedo tubes were removed 1941–42. Up to four 20mm guns were added.
Service As *Löwe*. Post-war after conversion to A/S frigates, all were stricken in 1959.

Below: *Panther*; note No. 2 gun landed. (W. B. Bilddienst)

Great Britain

When the First World War ended in November 1918, Great Britain had the largest number of destroyers in the world, ranging from diminutive ships built at the turn of the century to the large and powerful *V & W* types just joining the Fleet. The backbone of the wartime Fleet, the *M*, *R* and *S* classes, of which over two hundred still existed in 1919, were outmoded by the new *V & W*s and, moreover, had seen arduous war service, particularly the *M*s. In consequence, large numbers of *M*-class destroyers were sold out in 1921 and by 1923 they had all gone. The *R*s, being of slightly later construction, lasted a little longer, most being discarded in the mid 1920s, with a few lasting until the late 1930s, only one ship *Skate* surviving to see service in the Second World War. The *S* class were a reversion to a smaller type of destroyer, intended for use in the southern North Sea and English Channel which imposed special requirements on their design. They were not, therefore, ideal as fleet destroyers and in any event, the *V & W*s were far superior to them. Nevertheless, these boats remained on the Navy List, their numbers diminishing annually until by September 1939, only eleven remained.

There is little doubt that at the end of the Great War, the Royal Navy's destroyers led the world not only in numbers but more significantly in design. This proved invaluable to British shipyards for during the lean period of the 1920s and early 1930s it brought in valuable orders from foreign navies, as pages elsewhere in this volume will testify. British destroyers set the standard for future construction and layout, with the adoption of 4.7-inch guns, superfiring both fore and aft on the centre-line, triple centre-line mounted torpedo tubes and geared turbines. In fact, this basic destroyer design was to remain unaltered for the next twenty years. By that time, however, it was fast becoming outclassed by foreign designs, particularly those of potential enemy nations, especially Germany, and a reappraisal became necessary.

Two main types of destroyer were perpetuated from the First World War, the Fleet destroyer as epitomized by the 'modified V & W' design armed with four 4.7-inch guns and six torpedo tubes, and the larger leader of the *Admiralty* or *Scott* type with an extra 4.7-inch gun. These latter boats had taken over the earlier task of light cruisers and by 1918, flotilla organization was based on sixteen-boat flotillas each with a leader. Soon after the war, flotillas were reduced to a leader and eight boats, a pattern that was to continue until the *J* class in 1938.

The 4.7-inch gun was the BL Mk 1 on a 30° mounting and torpedoes Mk IV or V. AA defence had begun to be considered with either a 3-inch or a couple of 2pdr pom-poms being fitted. Derisory as this may seem, it was a significant step forward. Unfortunately, British destroyers were still equipped on a similar scale some twenty years later and the corresponding price was paid. The failure to develop an effective medium-range AA gun and an associated HA control system must rank as one of the major reasons for the heavy losses suffered in the early years of the Second World War.

Internally, a three-boiler, two-shaft single reduction geared turbine arrangement had become standardized with boiler pressures of 250psi. This layout remained basically unchanged until the *J* class of 1938 when two boilers were adopted. This class also adopted the longitudinal framing system in place of the transverse system used hitherto.

British destroyers between the wars can be summed up as robust, reliable but not outstanding. Cost and numbers were more important than size, and during the 1930s foreign designs gradually overhauled them, producing on paper at least, far more powerful ships. This eventually forced the Admiralty to reconsider their standard destroyer policy and the *Tribal*s were the result. The Second World War bought the need for a new standard design to speed construction and the *J* design was modified to suit. Although the resulting *N* to *Z* classes were not particularly outstanding and still, at least in the early years, had little in the way of AA defence, they performed all that was expected of them and gave good service for many years. It is as well to remember when comparing the ships with US war construction that British destroyers were designed for Atlantic and Mediterranean requirements and not the Pacific. Likewise, they were produced in yards under wartime conditions in a country that was under heavy bombing attack and not in an industry operating in almost peacetime conditions. Nevertheless it is probable that more could and should have been done earlier to improve AA defences, in particular an efficient dual-purpose main gun for destroyers similar to the excellent 5-inch weapon of their US counterparts.

Life in destroyers of the Royal Navy was hard, made worse by their operational theatres, particularly the commitment to the Arctic convoys. In comparison with US design policy, habitability was not overly high on the Admiralty's list of design priorities and in consequence, RN ships lagged far behind their USN contemporaries, and even German ships had better amenities. Despite arcticization, heating in mess decks was always insufficient, made worse by overcrowding due to increased war complements. Destroyers sent out to the Indian Ocean and Pacific, on the other hand, were unbearably hot and equally insanitary. Pacific requirements were never really considered by the Admiralty because this was an American sphere and they had more than enough commitments elsewhere. Certainly, the *Battle*s were *not* built with the Pacific in mind; events in the Mediterranean at the time of their planning were more relevant, and not until the *Weapon*s of 1944 was much reference made to Japan. Thus, with the defeat of Germany and Italy, all the most modern and powerful of the destroyers were sent east to fight a war for which they were not designed, but fortunately by this time, the seapower of Japan had been broken by the USN. In addition, politics prevented their employment in the most heavily engaged areas which no doubt contributed to the absence of losses. Had the war in the east continued, the arrival of large numbers of the *Battle* design would have given the Royal Navy's Pacific Fleet a much more useful and effective destroyer in an air-war environment. Even so, it is likely that further augmentation of AA outfits would have become necessary. As it turned out, the era of atomic weapons dawned and Japan collapsed resulting in the cancellation of many 1943 and 1944 design destroyers. In fact, the end of the Second World War saw also the end of true destroyer development, ending in the Royal Navy with the *Daring* class none of which saw wartime service.

ADMIRALTY R CLASS

Ship	Builder	Laid Down	Launched	Commissioned	Fate
H39 *Skate*	John Brown	12 Jan 16	11 Jan 17	Feb 1917	Sold out 4 Mar 47

Displacement: 900tons/914tonnes (standard); 1,222tons/1,241tonnes (full load).
Length: 276ft/84.12m (oa); 265ft/80.77m (pp).
Beam: 26ft 8in/8.15m.
Draught: 9ft 10in/2.99m (mean).
Machinery: three Yarrow boilers; 2-shaft Brown-Curtis single reduction geared turbines.
Performance: 27,000shp; 36kts (at completion).
Bunkerage: 296tons/300tonnes.
Range: 3,440nm at 15kts.
Guns: two 4in (2×1); one 2pdr.
Torpedoes: two 21in (1×2).
Complement: 90.

Design *Skate* was the last survivor of the *R*-class destroyers which first entered service during the First World War, and was the last three-funnelled destroyer in the Royal Navy. Long out-moded, she remained on the Navy List in 1939 by some quirk of fate, having been converted to a minelayer between the wars following mine damage in the earlier conflict.

Modifications Her conversion to a minelayer had reduced her guns from three to two and halved her torpedo outfit. As her speed was obviously now insufficient for offensive minelaying duties, in 1940 when the magnetic mine menace was at its peak, *Skate* was converted for influence minesweeping. After this conversion her AA outfit consisted of one quadruple 2pdr and two quadruple .5in machine-guns with, in all probability, the forward 4-inch gun. However, such was the shortage of escort vessels that even this venerable old ship was eventually converted to serve in the Battle of the Atlantic. In this role the armament was altered again and now comprised one 4-inch, one 12pdr in lieu of the forward tubes and four single 20mm. She no longer shipped any torpedoes, but was fitted instead with eight depth-charge throwers and two stern tracks.

Service *Skate* served on North Atlantic convoy duties in 1941–42 and in 1944 was part of the naval escort forces off Normandy. It says much for her construction that she was able to last so long, but winter conditions aboard her in the Atlantic Ocean must have been dreadful. Immediately after the war, *Skate* was sold for scrap to Cashmores and broken up at Newport.

Below: *Skate* at Liverpool in about 1943. Note the heavy depth-charge arrangements and radar fitment. (IWM)

ADMIRALTY S CLASS

Ship	Builder	Laid Down	Launched	Commissioned	Fate
H18 *Sabre*	A. Stephen	10 Sept 17	23 Sept 18	9 Nov 18‡	Scrapped 1947
H54 *Saladin*	A. Stephen	10 Sept 17	17 Feb 19	11 April 19	Sold 29 June 47
H26 *Sardonyx*	A. Stephen	25 Mar 18	27 May 19	12 July 19	Arr. for breaking up Oct 1945
H21 *Scimitar*	John Brown	30 May 17	27 Feb 18	29 April 18	Sold 29 June 47
H51 *Scout*	John Brown	25 Oct 17	27 April 18	15 June 18	Sold 11 Feb 46
D85 *Shikari*	Daxford	15 Jan 18	14 July 19	Feb 1924*	Sold 4 Nov 45
H50 *Stronghold*	Scott's	Mar 1918	6 May 19	2 July 19	Sunk 2 Mar 42
H28 *Sturdy*	Scott's	Mar 1918	25 June 19	15 Oct 19	Wrecked 30 Oct 40
H04 *Tenedos*	Hawthorn Leslie	6 Dec 17	20 Oct 18	11 June 19	Sunk 5 April 42
H29 *Thanet*	Hawthorn Leslie	13 Dec 17	5 Nov 18	30 Aug 19	Sunk 27 Jan 42
D86 *Thracian*	Hawthorn Leslie	10 Jan 18	5 Mar 20	21 April 20†	Captured Dec 1941

*Completed by Chatham Dkyd. †Completed by Sheerness Dkyd. ‡Completed by Fairfield.

Displacement: 905tons/919tonnes (standard); 1,221tons/1,240tonnes (full load).
Length: 276ft/84.12m (oa); 265ft/80.77m (pp).
Beam: 26ft 8in/8.15m.
Draught: 9ft 10in/2.99m (mean).
Machinery: three Yarrow boilers; 2-shaft Brown-Curtis single reduction geared turbines.
Performance: 27,000shp; 36kts (at completion).
Bunkerage: 301tons/306tonnes.
Guns: three 4in (3×1); one 2pdr. } as designed
Torpedoes: four 21in (2×2); two 18in (2×1). } as designed
Complement: 90.

Design The product of an earlier war, these destroyers were about twenty years old by the time a new conflict had broken out and were quite unfit for Fleet duties. Several had in any case been disarmed for subsidiary duties, *Shikari* as a control vessel for the radio-controlled target ship *Agamemnon* and later the *Centurian*; *Sabre* as a target ship and *Scimitar* which was used for training. Although their age was much about the same as the *V&W* class, their size was insufficient and the *V&W*s were always considered a better design. Their original *raison d'être* was close-quarters action in the southern North Sea and English Channel, but they were no longer capable of this task. One sister had been wrecked in 1920 and more than forty others sold out for scrapping between the wars. The majority of the survivors were in reserve by the late 1930s.

Modifications At least *Stronghold, Sturdy* and *Thracian* had been fitted for minelaying before the war, and possibly all those destined for the Far East. These ships carried two 4-inch guns. *Skate* and *Scimitar* were used for minesweeping trials during the first winter of the war and were modified accordingly. *Shikari, Sabre, Saladin, Sardonyx* and *Scimitar* were converted to ASW escorts late in 1940, equipped for 14-charge pattern DC arrange-

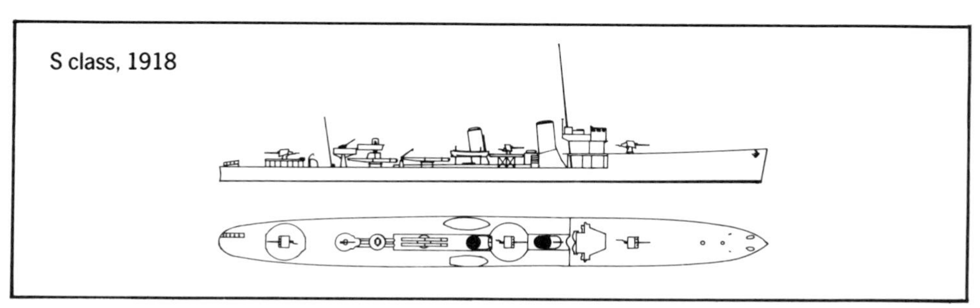

Left: *Shikari*, modified for escort duties. (IWM)
Below: *Saladin*, with radar 291, no tubes and four 20mm guns. (IWM)

ments. Both after guns and the torpedo tubes were landed, one 12pdr and two quadruple .5-inch machine-guns added. Radar Type 286 and later 291 was added, but only *Shikari* received Type 271, at the cost of the 12pdr and some of the ASW equipment. Four single 20mm mountings eventually supplanted the .5-inch equipments. Far East boats remained largely unaltered, as did *Sturdy*.

Service *Scout, Thracian, Thanet, Tenedos* and *Stronghold* sailed for the Far East in 1939 to form local defence flotillas at Hong Kong and Singapore. *Tenedos* escorted *Prince of Wales* and *Repulse* on their final sortie from Singapore in December 1941, but was detached before the Japanese attack because of her poor endurance. Despite an air attack on her as she returned to Singapore, she escaped only to be sunk the following year by Japanese aircraft off Colombo. In the meantime, *Scout* and *Thanet* had broken out of Singapore, but the latter was sunk in action with Japanese cruisers and destroyers on the night of 26/27 January 1942 while attempting to intercept an invasion convoy bound for the Malaysian coast. *Thracian* ran aground at Hong Kong on Christmas Day 1941 and was captured by the Japanese. She was salvaged by the IJN, repaired and recommissioned on 25 November 1942 as *Patrol Vessel No. 101*, then re-rated a training ship in March 1944, being attached to the torpedo school at Yokosuka. Recaptured in 1945, she was eventually broken up at Hong Kong post-war. *Stronghold* operated in the East Indies, but was eventually sunk in action with the heavy cruiser *Maya* and the destroyers *Arashi* and *Nowake* after an hour's engagement in which the cruiser alone expended more than six hundred rounds. Only *Scout* managed to escape from the East Indies, making her way to the Indian Ocean where she operated from April 1942, based at Colombo. Early in 1945 she was paid off at Trincomalee but came home post-war to be broken up at Briton Ferry. *Sturdy*, also intended for the Far East, had only reached the Mediterranean when she was detached to that Fleet. Following the fall of France she was ordered home for escort duties, but was wrecked on the island of Tiree off the west coast of Scotland after only a brief career.

The boats in home waters joined the 22nd Destroyer Flotilla operating in the Western Approaches for North Atlantic convoy duties. Their size, age and overloaded condition made things very difficult for them in the rough Atlantic. Later they were formed into the 21st Escort Group operating to Iceland, but by 1943 they had been diverted to training and trials duties in Scottish waters. *Saladin* and *Scimitar*, however, came south in 1943 for service in the Channel and off Normandy.

SHAKESPEARE CLASS

Ship	Builder	Laid Down	Launched	Commissioned	Fate
D84 *Keppel*	J. Thornycroft*	Oct 1918	23 April 20	13 Dec 24	Sold July 1945
D83 *Broke* (ex-*Rooke*)	J. Thornycroft†	Oct 1918	16 Sept 20	15 April 25	Sunk 10 Nov 42
L64 *Wallace*	J. Thornycroft	Aug 1917	20 Oct 18	29 Jan 19	Sold out 20 Mar 45

D Pendants changed later to I. *Completed at Portsmouth Dkyd. †Completed at Pembroke Dkyd.

Displacement: 1,554tons/1,579tonnes (standard); 2,009tons/2,041tonnes (full load).
Length: 329ft/100.3m (oa); 318ft 3in/97m (pp).
Beam: 31ft 6in/9.6m.
Draught: 12ft 3in/3.73m (mean).
Machinery: four Yarrow boilers; 2-shaft Brown-Curtis S.R. geared turbines.
Performance: 40,000shp; 36kts.
Bunkerage: 500tons/508tonnes.
Guns: five 4.7in (5×1); one 3in HA; one MG (*Wallace* four 4in HA (2×2); four 2pdr (1×4); eight .5in MG (2×4)).

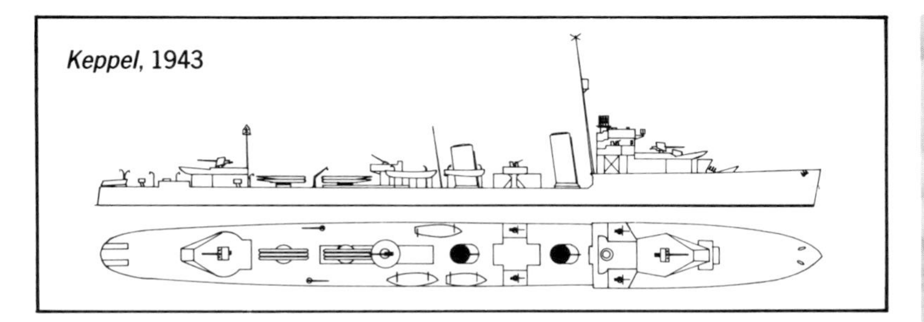

Torpedoes: six 21in (2×3) (*Wallace*, nil).
Complement: 164.

Design In 1916, Thornycroft had proposed a design for a large flotilla leader which was considered by the Admiralty and eventually amended in line with certain recommendations by the DNC. In particular, the six 4-inch guns in the Thornycroft layout were to be replaced by five 5-inch guns. However, because of the delay inherent in designing a new gun, it was decided to adopt the 4.7-inch army gun for naval use. These were to be shipped superimposed fore and aft, with the fifth gun between the funnels – a leader layout which was to be followed until the late 1930s. Stringent penalty clauses in the contract with Thornycroft covered shortfalls in speed (contract speed was 36 knots for four hours), excess draft, insufficient freeboard, low metacentric height, and the machinery was to be maintained for 12 months!

The class originally numbered seven but of these, *Saunders* and *Spragge* were cancelled in January 1919 and work stopped on *Keppel* and *Rooke*. Only *Shakespeare* and *Spencer* were completed in time to serve with the Fleet during the First World War, the former being badly damaged by a mine in June 1918. both of these ships were sold out in July 1936, going to the breakers in Jarrow and Inverkeithing respectively in September. *Rooke* was re-named *Broke* in about 1921, both she and *Keppel* being towed to and eventually completed at Royal Dockyards. *Shakespeare*, running trials under wartime conditions, reached 38.95 knots with 43,527shp on 1,605 tons displacement. *Wallace* made 38.25 knots.

Modifications Early in 1939, *Wallace* was converted to an escort destroyer more or less on the lines of the *V & W* Wair conversions. Both banks of torpedo tubes and all 4.7-inch guns were landed, the bridge rebuilt and the forward shelter deck dismantled. Two twin 4-inch Mk XIX comprised the main armament and *Wallace* was unique in having a quadruple 2pdr fitted on a bandstand aft in lieu of 'Y' gun. Quadruple .5in MG mountings were shipped in the spaces vacated by the torpedo tubes, the forward one to port, the after to starboard. Two 20mm Oerlikons in the bridge wings completed the gunnery outfit. A lattice tower over the searchlight platform supported the Type 272 radar lantern. A Type 291 radar aerial was fitted at the masthead. In late 1942, Type 285 gunnery radar was fitted to the HACS director. By mid 1944, the .5in MG mountings had been replaced by single 2pdr guns and two further single 20mm mounted in the waist.

Above: *Broke* as an escort destroyer. The censor has erased the masthead radar and HF/DF. She is fitted with 'hedgehog', but retains six TT. (IWM)

Keppel and *Broke* received little initial alterations, except for the after funnel being cut down in height. At the time of her loss in November 1942, *Broke* had been rearmed for escort duties, landing 'A', 'Q' and 'Y' guns. A 'hedgehog' replaced 'A' gun and four 20mm Oerlikons were added. Radar 272 replaced the rangefinder on the bridge. *Keppel* was converted on similar lines, No. 1 boiler room being stripped out to increase bunkerage and accommodation. Her armament was now two 4.7-inch, one 3-inch, four 20mm and six torpedo tubes.

Service *Keppel* served with the 13th Destroyer Flotilla and Force H at Gibraltar and in the Mediterranean 1940–42, but acted as escort in between to some Atlantic and Russian convoys, in particular PQ17, when she was leader of the close escort. In 1943, she was partially converted to a long-range escort and joined Escort Group B3 working Atlantic convoys. In 1944 she was predominantly employed on Arctic convoys, with the 8th Support and 20th Escort Groups, when she sank three U-boats, *U713, U360* and *U344* – the last in company with other ships. She remained on Russian convoys until 1945.

At the beginning of the war *Broke* formed part of the 29th Division, 15th Destroyer Flotilla. She served in the Western Approaches and North Atlantic until 1942 when, towards the end of the year, she moved to the Mediterranean for the North Africa landings. During the course of these, *Broke* was sunk by shore batteries while attempting to force the defences of Algiers.

Wallace, which had completed her conversion to an escort destroyer on 14 June 1939, spent a period on reserve and subsidiary duties until recommissioned on 26 August. At the outbreak of war, she served on east coast convoys between Rosyth and Sheerness until March 1945 except for a brief period in 1943 when she participated in the Invasion of Sicily. After her return to the UK in August 1943, *Wallace* reverted to east coast convoy duty, but after a collision with *Farndale* off the Humber on 16 March 1945, she was paid off into reserve unrepaired on 12 April 1945.

ADMIRALTY LEADER CLASS

Ship	Builder	Laid Down	Launched	Commissioned	Fate
D60 *Campbell*	Cammell Laird	10 Nov 17	21 Sept 18	21 Dec 18	Sold out 18 Feb 47
D70 *Mackay*	Cammell Laird	5 Mar 18	21 Dec 18	19 May 19	Sold out 18 Feb 47
D90 *Douglas*	Cammell Laird	30 June 17	8 June 18	30 Aug 18	Sold out 20 Mar 45
D19 *Malcolm*	Cammell Laird	27 Mar 18	29 May 19	14 Dec 19	Sold out 25 July 45
D01 *Montrose*	Hawthorn Leslie	4 Oct 17	10 June 18	14 Sept 18	Sold out 31 Jan 46

Pendant later changed to I.

Displacement: 1,580tons/1,605tonnes (standard); 2,053tons/2,086tonnes (full load).
Length: 332ft 6in/101.3m (oa); 320ft/97.5m (pp).
Beam: 31ft 9in/9.6m.
Draught: 10ft 6in/3.6m (mean).
Machinery: four Yarrow boilers; 2-shaft Parsons (*Montrose*, Brown-Curtis) geared turbines.
Performance: 40,000shp; 36.5kts. (*Montrose*, 43,000shp).
Bunkerage: 500tons/508tonnes.
Range: 5,000nm at 15kts.
Guns: five 4.7in (5×1); one 3in AA.

Above: *Douglas*, modified for escort duties. (IWM)

Torpedoes: six 21in (2×3).
Complement: 170.

Design Developed more or less in parallel with the Thornycroft-designed *Shakespeare* class, this design too was intended to produce a large leader with good sea-keeping properties. The armament and machinery were almost identical with the Thornycroft design and there was little difference in visual appearance. The leading ship, *Scott*, built by Cammell Laird, commissioned in January 1918 reaching 35.8 knots on trials. There was naturally a good deal of comparative evaluation between this class and the Thornycroft boats, of which the latter usually turned out the faster, at least under trial conditions. The class originally numbered ten, but *Scott* herself became a victim of the First World War when she was torpedoed off the Dutch coast on 15 August 1918 by *UC17*. *Barrington* and *Hughes*, both ordered from Cammell Laird in 1918, were cancelled in January 1919 and *Bruce*, paid off before the Second World War, was finally expended as a target and sunk by an 18-inch aircraft torpedo on 22 November 1939. *Stuart* was transferred to the Royal Australian Navy (q.v.) in 1933.

Modifications At the outbreak of the Second World War, all five surviving units remained basically unaltered from their designed layout. Early in the war, 'Q' 4.7-inch gun was landed and replaced by two single-pounders in tubs, port and starboard, and the after funnel was cut down to improve the sky arcs of the 3-inch gun. By 1941, *Campbell* and *Montrose* had landed 'X' gun, its place being taken by the 3-inch AA originally abaft the after funnel. Two 20m Oerlikons were fitted in the bridge wings, the director and rangefinder landed and in their place radar 271 fitted, with radar 290 at the masthead. Eventually, the 2pdr guns were also supplanted by 20mm Oerlikons. Both banks of torpedo tubes were retained. *Montrose*, however, by about 1943, had been fitted with a twin 6pdr at 'A' position for anti-E-boat work on the east coast. *Douglas* and *Malcolm* both employed mainly as escorts, landed 'A' and 'Y' guns, the former being replaced by a 'hedgehog'. Their radar fit was as *Campbell*, but both landed the forward torpedo tubes. 20mm Oerlikons were fitted into the bridge wings and by late 1942 had also replaced the 2pdr guns. Two twin Lewis guns were fitted on the quarter deck and depth-charge stowage increased to 70. The 3-inch remained in its original position. *Mackay* was armed similarly to *Campbell* but by 1944 had received a twin 6pdr at 'A' position as *Montrose*.

Service War service was mainly in home waters with *Campbell* operating out of the Clyde during the Norway operations in April 1940. *Douglas* had an early if inconclusive brush with a U-boat off Portugal in January 1940. The Dunkirk operations saw *Mackay, Malcolm* and *Montrose* involved when *Malcolm* received bomb damage and *Montrose* suffered damage from grounding. *Douglas* worked out of Gibraltar with Force H in 1940, but by mid 1941 had assumed escort duties in the North Atlantic with the 2nd Escort Group. The remainder of the war was with the Western Approaches Command, but she was paid off before the end of hostilities.

Campbell, Mackay and *Montrose* served mainly in the North sea and east coast convoys with the 16th and 21st Destroyer Flotillas. Both of the former two saw action against the German Brest Squadron in February 1942 during Operation 'Cerberus' but without success. All three took part in the naval side of 'Overlord', the Invasion of Europe in June 1944. *Malcolm* was in the North Atlantic in June 1941, took part in Operation 'Pedestal' in the Mediterranean in August 1942, moved north to the Arctic covering Convoy PQ18 in September 1942. She returned south to the Mediterranean in November for Operation 'Torch', the Invasion of North Africa, when she supported *Broke* in the attempt to force the defences at Algiers.

Below: *Campbell* as completed. (Abrahams)

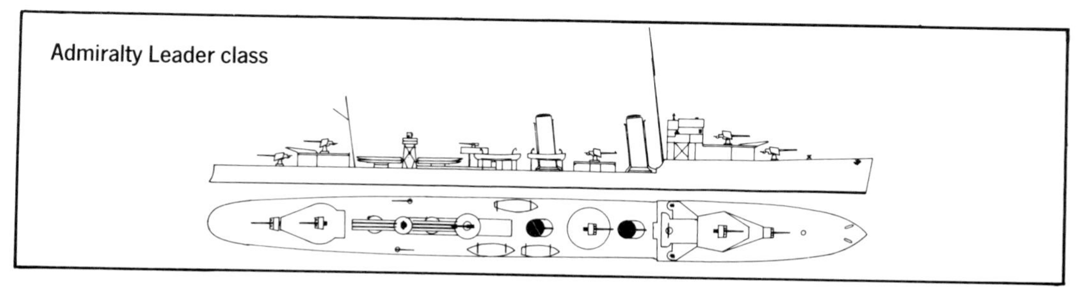

TOWN (BELMONT GROUP) CLASS

Ship	Builder	Laid Down	Launched	Commissioned USN	Commissioned RN	Fate
H46 *Belmont* (ex-USS *Satterlee*)	Newport News	10 July 18	21 Dec 18	22 Dec 19	8 Oct 40	Torpedoed 31 Jan 42
H64 *Beverley* (ex-USS *Branch*)[1]	Newport News	25 Oct 18	19 April 19	3 April 20	8 Oct 40	Torpedoed 10 April 43
H72 *Bradford* (ex-USS *Lanahan*)	Bethlehem (Squantum)	20 April 18	21 Sept 18	5 April 19	8 Oct 40	Sold out 19 April 46
H81 *Broadwater* (ex-USS *Mason*)	Newport News	10 July 18	8 Mar 19	28 Feb 20	8 Oct 40	Torpedoed 18 Oct 42
H90 *Broadway* (ex-USS *Hunt*)[1]	Newport News	20 Aug 18	14 Feb 20	8 June 20	8 Oct 40	Sold out 18 Feb 47
H82 *Burnham* (ex-USS *Aulick*)[1]	Bethlehem (Quincy)	3 Dec 18	11 April 19	26 July 19	8 Oct 40	Sold out 4 Mar 47
H94 *Burwell* (ex-USS *Lamb*)[1]	Bethlehem (Squantum)	20 April 18	25 Aug 18	17 Mar 19	8 Oct 40	Sold out 4 Mar 47
H96 *Buxton* (ex-USS *Edwards*)*[1]	Bethlehem (Squantum)	20 April 18	10 Oct 18	24 April 19	8 Oct 40	For disposal 21 Mar 46
I05 *Cameron* (ex-USS *Welles*)	Bethlehem (Quincy)	13 Nov 18	8 May 19	2 Sept 19	9 Sept 40	C.T.L. 5 Dec 40
I28 *Chesterfield*[1] (ex-USS *Welborn C. Wood*)	Newport News	24 Sept 18	6 Mar 20	25 June 20	9 Sept 40	Sold out 4 Mar 47
I45 *Churchill* (ex-USS *Herndon*)[1]	Newport News	25 Nov 18	31 May 19	17 April 20	9 Sept 40	Lost 16 Jan 45 (USSR)
I14 *Clare* (ex-USS *Abel P. Upshur*)[1]	Newport News	20 Aug 18	14 Feb 20	21 May 20	9 Sept 40	Sold out *25 Aug 45*
G60 *Ramsey* (ex-USS *Meade*)	Bethlehem (Squantum)	23 Sept 18	24 May 19	8 Sept 19	26 Nov 40	Sold out 18 Feb 47
G71 *Reading* (ex-USS *Bailey*)	Bethlehem (Squantum)	3 June 18	5 Feb 19	27 June 19	26 Nov 40	Sold out 24 July 45
G79 *Ripley* (ex-USS *Shubrick*)[1]	Bethlehem (Squantum)	3 June 18	31 Dec 18	3 July 19	26 Nov 40	Sold out 20 Mar 45
G58 *Rockingham* (ex-USS *Swasey*)[1]	Bethlehem (Squantum)	27 Aug 18	7 May 19	31 July 19	26 Nov 40	Mined 27 Sept 44
I80 *Sherwood* (ex-USS *Rodgers*)	Bethlehem (Quincy)	25 Sept 18	26 April 19	22 July 19	23 Oct 40	Scrapped 1945
I73 *Stanley* (ex-USS *McCalla*)[1]	Bethlehem (Quincy)	25 Sept 18	28 Mar 19	19 May 19	23 Oct 40	Torpedoed 18 Dec 41

*R.C.N. 1943–44.

Below: *Broadway*, typical of the ex-US destroyers. (WSS)

Displacement: 1,190tons/1,209tonnes (standard).
Length: 314ft 3in/95.7m (oa); 311ft/94.8m (wl).
Beam: 30ft 9in/9.37m.
Draught: 9ft 3in/2.8m (mean).
Machinery: four White-Foster or Yarrow boilers; 2-shaft geared turbines.
Performance: 27,000shp; 35kts.
Bunkerage: 375tons/381tonnes.
Guns: three 4in (3×1); one 3in; two MG (except[1] one 4in; one 3in; four or five 20mm).
Torpedoes: six 21in (2×3) except [1] three 21in.
Complement: 146.

Design Dating back to the 1914–18 war, these old destroyers were American contemporaries of the British *V & W* class, but, visually, they looked a decade older with their four-funnelled layout. Originally armed with four 4-inch guns and twelve 21-inch torpedo tubes, their armament looked impressive, but the four triple deck tubes, two on each beam, took up much deck space and top weight. Two of the 4-inch guns were also on the beam allowing a broadside of only three guns. Nevertheless, they were fast and numerous, serving in the USN in large numbers until 1945. Many had been laid up in reserve as newer destroyers completed in the 1930s, in which state they were to be found at the outbreak of the Second World War in September 1939. The U-boat offensive against trade to and from the United Kingdom soon had the Royal Navy's escort forces stretched to the limit in 1940, and it was against this background that in May of that year, Churchill sent a telegram to the President of the United States, Franklin D. Roosevelt, suggesting the exchange of bases for the loan of fifty old destroyers. The request was turned down but the following month, after more heavy destroyer losses to the Royal Navy, a renewed appeal fell on more responsive ears and acting without the agreement of Congress, Roosevelt agreed the exchange on 2 September 1940. Fifty of the seventy flush-deckers remaining in the US reserve fleet would be transferred to the Royal Navy in exchange for the right to establish US bases in the West Indies. No sooner had agreement been reached than the old destroyers began to move eastwards. *Aaron Ward* sailed from Boston for Halifax N.S. on 4 September to be turned over to the Royal Navy as HMS *Castleton*, quickly followed by *Hale* and *Abel P. Upshur*, renamed *Caldwell* and *Clare* respectively. All were renamed after towns with names common to both the USA and Great Britain. Seven were taken over by the Royal Canadian Navy (q.v.) being renamed after rivers rather than towns except for *Annapolis*.

The British Admiralty had some reservations about the stability of these old ships given their heavy armament, and their internal and messing arrangements were foreign to Royal Navy practice

TOWN (LEWES GROUP) CLASS

Ship	Builder	Laid Down	Launched	Commissioned USN	Commissioned RN	Fate
G68 *Lewes* (ex-USS *Conway*)	Norfolk N Yd.	20 Nov 17	29 June 18	19 Oct 18	23 Oct 40	Scuttled May 1946
G27 *Leeds* (ex-USS *Conner*)	Cramp	16 Oct 16	21 Aug 17	12 Jan 18	13 Oct 40	Sold out 4 Mar 47
G57 *Ludlow* (ex-USS *Stockton*)	Cramp	16 Oct 16	17 July 17	26 Nov 17	2 Oct 40	Sold out 5 July 45

Displacement: 1,020tons/1,036tonnes (standard).
Length: 315ft 6in/96.1m (oa); 308ft/93.8m (wl).
Beam: 30ft 9in/9.37m.
Draught: 7ft 6in/2.28m (mean).
Machinery: four White-Foster boilers (*Lewes*, Thornycroft); 3-shaft Parsons (geared in *Lewes*) turbines. (2-shaft only in *Lewes*).
Performance: 18,500shp (20,000shp *Lewes*); 30kts.
Bunkerage: 290tons/294tonnes.
Guns: two 4in; two 2pdr; four 20mm. (*Lewes* no 4in but five 20mm).
Complement: 146.

so that those who manned them received them with somewhat mixed feelings. Despite these grumbles, they were a short-term answer to an immediate problem and gave a good account of themselves in anti-submarine duties, a task for which they had not been designed.

Modifications In the role of anti-submarine escort, these destroyers were, in their original configuration, far from ideal. Like all destroyers used in this role, they had an excess of unnecessary speed and were wrongly armed. The 'flush-deckers', however, were also unhandy with an excessive turning circle and, with their fine lines, very lively in a North Atlantic sea-way. The British Admiralty, always conservative over the stability question, took immediate steps to improve this and at the same time make the armament more suitable for the task in hand, convoy escorting.

With such a large group of ships, there were obviously many different variations in outfit details, but the basic alterations included the removal of 'X' gun and two of the four triple banks of torpedo tubes. The US-pattern 3-inch at 'Y' position was removed and replaced by a British 3-inch or 12pdr in place of 'X' gun. Radar Type 271 was fitted on the bridge when it became available, as was Type 286 at the masthead. This latter was later replaced by Type 290 or 291. Depth-charge stowage was increased and asdic installed. The torpedo tubes left in were intended to give some protection against the surface raiders then (1940) at large in the oceans. Many ships later lost the beam 4-inch guns, 20mm Oerlikons being added in lieu and in these units, the torpedo outfit was usually reduced to one triple bank, repositioned on the centre-line. The *Lewis* group, however, lost 'A' gun and 'Y' gun, retaining

Below: *Clare* converted for long-range escort duties. (G. Ransome)

TOWN (CAMPBELTOWN G

Ship	Builder	Laid Do
I42 *Campbeltown* (ex-*Buchanan*)	Bath Iron Works	29 June
I20 *Caldwell* (ex-*Hale*)	Bath Iron Works	7 Oct 1
I23 *Castleton* (ex-*Aaron Ward*)(1)	Bath Iron Works	1 Aug 1
I35 *Chelsea* (ex-*Crowinshield*)(1)	Bath Iron Works	5 Nov 1
G05 *Lancaster* (ex-*Philip*)	Bath Iron Works	1 Sept
G19 *Leamington* (ex-*Twiggs*)	N.Y. Sbdg.	23 Jan 1
G42 *Lincoln* (ex-*Yarnall*)†(1)	Cramp	12 Feb
G76 *Mansfield* (ex-*Evans*)(1)	Bath Iron Works	28 Dec
G95 *Montgomery* (ex-*Wickes*)(1)	Bath Iron Works	26 June
G88 *Richmond* (ex-*Fairfax*)	Mare Island	10 July
I52 *Salisbury* (ex-*Claxton*)(1)	Mare Island	25 April
I95 *Wells* (ex-*Tillman*)(1)	Charleston	29 July

Caldwell, Chelsea, * *Leamington,* * *Montgomery, Richmond** and *Salisbury* ser RCN 1942–43. *Lincoln* (1941–43) and *Mansfield* (1940–42) served RNN Then *Mansfield* to RCN. *Lent to USSR 30 May 44. †Lent to USSR 26 Aug 44. All transferred and commissioned on same day except last three transferred 26 Nov 40.

Displacement: 1,090tons/1,107tonnes (standard).
Length: 314ft 3in/95.7m (oa); 309ft/94.2m (wl).
Beam: 30ft 6in/9.3m.
Draught: 8ft 9in/2.7m (mean).
Machinery: four Thornycroft, White-Foster or

…P) CLASS

…ched	Commissioned USN	RN	Fate
. 19	20 Jan 19	9 Sept 40	Lost 28 Mar 42
ay 19	12 June 19	9 Sept 40	Sold out 20 Mar 45
pril 19	21 April 19	9 Sept 40	Sold out 4 Mar 47
ly 19	6 Aug 19	9 Sept 40	Sold out 12 July 49
ly 18	24 Aug 18	23 Oct 40	Sold out 18 Feb 47
ept 18	28 July 19	23 Oct 40	Sold out 26 July 51
ne 18	29 Nov 18	23 Oct 40	Sold out Sept 1952
ct 18	11 Nov 18	23 Oct 40	Broken Up Canada 1944
une 18	31 July 18	23 Oct 40	Sold out 10 April 45
ec 17	6 April 18	5 Dec 40	Sold out 12 July 49
an 19	13 Sept 19	5 Dec 40	Sold in Canada 25 June 44
ly 19	30 April 21	5 Dec 40	Sold out Aug 1945

Normand boilers; 2-shaft geared turbines.
Performance: 25,200shp; 35kts. (*Leamington, Lincoln, Richmond, Salisbury* 26,000shp).
Bunkerage: 375tons/381tonnes.
Guns: three 4in (one in [(1)]); one 3in AA; four MG (three or four 20mm in[(1)]).
Torpedoes: six 21in (2×3); three 21in in [(1)].
Complement: 146.

TOWN (BATH GROUP) CLASS

Ship	Builder	Laid Down	Launched	Commissioned USN	RN	Fate
I17 *Bath* (ex-*Hopewell*)*	Newport News	19 Jan 18	8 June 18	21 Mar 19	23 Sept 40	Torpedoed 19 Aug 41
I08 *Brighton* (ex-*Cowell*)[(1)]	Bethlehem (Fore River)	15 July 18	23 Nov 18	17 Mar 19	23 Sept 40	Sold out 5 April 49
I21 *Charlestown* (ex-*Abbot*)	Newport News	5 April 18	4 July 18	18 July 19	23 Sept 40	Sold out 4 Mar 47
I40 *Georgetown* (ex-*Maddox*)[(1)]	Bethlehem (Fore River)	20 July 18	27 Oct 18	10 Mar 19	23 Sept 40	Sold out 1 Sept 52
G08 *Newark* (ex-*Ringgold*)[(1)]	Union Iron Works	20 Oct 17	14 April 18	14 Nov 18	5 Dec 40	Sold out 18 Feb 47
G47 *Newmarket* (ex-*Robinson*)[(1)]	Union Iron Works	30 Oct 17	28 Mar 18	19 Oct 18	5 Dec 40	Sold out Sept 1945
G54 *Newport* (ex-*Sigourney*)*	Bethlehem (Fore River)	25 Aug 17	16 Dec 17	14 May 18	5 Dec 40	Sold out 18 Feb 47
I07 *Roxburgh* (ex-*Foote*)[(1)]	Bethlehem (Fore River)	7 Aug 17	14 Dec 18	21 Mar 19	23 Sept 40	Sold out 5 April 49
I15 *St Albans* (ex-*Thomas*)*	Newport News	23 Mar 18	4 July 18	25 April 19	23 Sept 40	Sold out 5 April 49
I12 *St. Marys* (ex-*Doran*)	Newport News	11 May 18	19 Oct 18	26 Aug 19	23 Sept 40	Sold out 20 Mar 45

*Served RNN 1941–44 (*Newport* 1941–42). *Newark, Newmarket* and *Newport* transferred to RN 26 Nov 40. *Georgetown* RCN 1942–43. *Brighton, Georgetown, Roxburgh, St. Albans* lent to USSR 30 May 44

Displacement: 1,060tons/1,076tonnes (standard).
Length: 314ft 3in/95.7m (oa); 309ft/94.1m (wl).
Beam: 30ft 6in/9.3m.
Draught: 8ft 6in/2.59m (mean).
Machinery: four Thornycroft, Yarrow or Normand boilers; 2-shaft geared turbines.
Performance: 27,000shp; 35kts (*Bath, Charlestown, St. Albans* and *St. Marys* 25,000shp).
Bunkerage: 300tons/305tonnes.
Guns: three ([(1)] one) 4in; one 3in; seven MG ([(1)] four 20mm).
Torpedoes: six 21in (2×3) ([(1)] three 21in; *St Albans* nil).
Complement: 146.

Below left: *Lewes* with her unique armament of three 3-inch guns and two 2pdrs. (IWM)
Below: *Brighton*. She has radar 271 and 291, but has only two 20mm guns, the rest being rifle-calibre machine-guns. (IWM)

only the beam guns, but *Lewes* herself was armed only with 2pdr and 20mm guns. All torpedoes were removed from these three as well as *St. Albans*. (Note also that *Leeds* and *Ludlow* had only three funnels.) The bridge structures on many units were enlarged, canvas dodgers being replaced by light screen plating in many instances.

Bradford, Stanley and *Clare* were more extensively modified as long-range escorts, when the two foremost boilers and their funnels were removed to increase both bunkerage and accommodation. Of these, *Clare* received single 2pdrs in lieu of the beam 4-inch guns. Their bridges were considerably modified and a deck-house was built on abaft it. Hedgehog mortars were fitted to these and many others of the group and a few were also fitted with HF/DF on a mast aft. Finally, *Campbeltown* was altered to resemble a German torpedo-boat for the St-Nazaire raid in 1942. Both after funnels were removed and clinker screens were added to the forward pair.

Service All these boats served the North Atlantic convoys as soon as they had completed the necessary initial modifications, except *Cameron*, which saw little service for she was very badly damaged in an air raid while at Portsmouth on 5 December 1940. Declared a constructional total loss, she was used for shock trial purposes until scrapped in November 1944. The remainder soldiered on in the stormy North Atlantic, assisting in the sinkings of *U89, U110, U131, U187, U207, U401, U434, U587* and *U960*, plus, it must be said, the friendly Polish submarine *Jastrab* and the minesweeper *Alberic*, both by the unfortunate *St Albans*. The other side of the coin was that *Bath* was torpedoed by *U201* in the North Atlantic while under Norwegian colours as part of the 5th Escort Group, *Belmont* by *U82, Broadwater* by *U101, Churchill* (as Soviet *Deiatelnyi*) by *U956* in the Arctic, *Stanley* by *U574* and *Beverley* by *U188*. In addition, *Rockingham* was mined off Aberdeen and *Campbeltown* was expended in the St-Nazaire raid.

Only *Lewes* left home waters, going to the South Atlantic in 1943–44 before sailing for Australia, where she was used as an air target vessel for the British Pacific Fleet, based on Sydney. She never returned home and was scuttled in Australian waters on 25 May 1946. By 1943 the need for these ships had diminished with the increasing numbers of new escorts joining the convoy war and in any event, their age was beginning to tell. Some were spending a disproportionate amount of time in dockyard hands. As a result many were withdrawn from escort duties and converted to aircraft target vessels (*Brighton* as early as November 1942). In 1944, most had been reduced to reserve, but one or two remained active into 1945.

Above: *Georgetown*, fitted with radar and HF/DF for escort duties. Her AA outfit is a mix of 20mm and machine-guns. (IWM)

V & W (UNCONVERTED) CLASS

Ship	Builder	Laid Down	Launched	Commissioned	Fate
D53 *Venetia*	Fairfield	2 Feb 17	29 Oct 17	19 Dec 17	Mined 19 Oct 40
D72 *Veteran*[1]	John Brown	30 Aug 18	26 Aug 19	13 Nov 19	Torpedoed 26 Sept 42
D36 *Vivacious*	A. Yarrow	July 1916	3 Nov 17	Dec 1917	Sold out 4 Mar 47
D37 *Vortigern*	S. White	17 Jan 16	15 Oct 17	25 Jan 18	Torpedoed 15 Mar 42
H88 *Wakeful* L91	Cammell Laird	17 Jan 17	6 Oct 17	16 Nov 17	Torpedoed 29 May 40
D41 *Walpole*	Doxford	May 1917	12 Feb 18	7 Aug 18	Sold out Mar 1945
D43 *Wessex*	Hawthorn Leslie	23 May 17	12 Mar 18	11 May 18	Bombed 24 May 40
D30 *Whirlwind*	Swan Hunter	May 1917	15 Dec 17	5 Mar 18	Torpedoed 5 July 40
D77 *Whitshed*[1]	Swan Hunter	3 June 18	31 Jan 19	11 July 19	Sold out 18 Feb 47
D62 *Wild Swan*[1]	Swan Hunter	July 1918	17 May 19	4 Nov 19	Bombed 17 June 42
D42 *Windsor* L94	Scott's	April 1917	21 June 18	28 Aug 18	Sold out 4 Mar 47
D67 *Wishart*[1]	Thornycroft	18 May 18	18 July 19	June 1920	Sold out June 1946
D89 *Witch*[1]	Thornycroft	13 June 18	11 Nov 19	Mar 1924*	Sold out 12 July 1946
D66 *Wivern*[1]	S. White	19 Aug 18	16 April 19	23 Dec 19	Sold out 18 Feb 47
D78 *Wolverine*[1]	S. White	8 Oct 18	17 July 19	27 July 20	Sold out 13 Sept 45
D96 *Worcester*[1]	S. White	20 Dec 18	24 Oct 19	20 Sept 27†	Sold out Sept 1946
D88 *Wren*[1]	A. Yarrow	June 1918	11 Nov 19	27 Feb 23‡	Bombed 27 July 40
D76 *Witherington*[1]	S. White	27 Sept 18	16 April 19	10 Oct 19	Sold 20 Mar 47

[1]Modified *V&W*. *At Devonport Dkyd. †At Portsmouth Dkyd. ‡At Pembroke Dkyd.

Displacement: 1,188tons/1,207tonnes (standard); 1,490tons/1,513tonnes (full load).
Length: 312ft/95.1m (oa); 309ft/94.1m (wl); 300ft/91.4m (pp).
Beam: 29ft 6in/9m (Thornycroft boats 30ft 9in).
Draught: 10ft 8in/3.25m (mean).
Machinery: three Yarrow boilers (White-Foster in S. White boats); 2-shaft Brown-Curtis geared turbines (Swan-Hunter boats, Parsons).
Performance: 27,000shp; 34kts (30,000shp; 35kts Thornycroft boats).
Bunkerage: 367tons/373tonnes.
Range: 3,120nm at 15kts.
Guns: four 4in (4×1); ([1] four 4.7in (4×1)); one 3in HA; two 2pdr.
Torpedoes: six 21in (2×3).
Mines: 60 (originally, *Vortigen, Venetia* and *Whirlwind* only).
Complement: 134.

Design The introduction of the relatively large destroyers of the *M* class in 1915, led to the need for

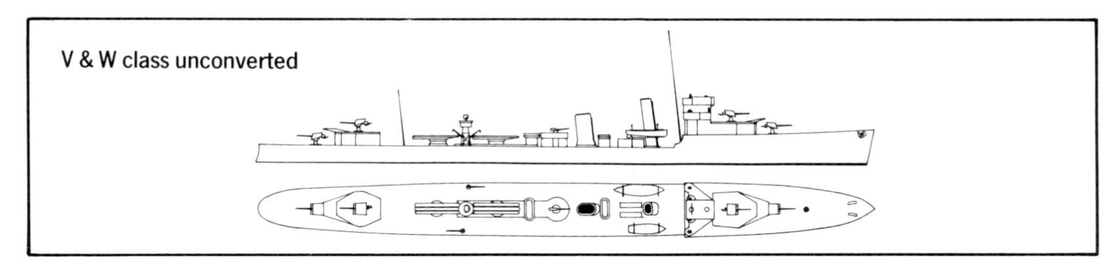

Above: *Wolverine* as a short-range escort. (IWM) **Below:** *Veteran* in about 1923. (Abrahams)

Below: *Windsor*, pre-war. (Gieves)

an even larger destroyer to act in the flotilla leader role. The design adopted for this task was known as the *V* class leader, since all their names began with that letter. Only five were built, of which two, *Valhalla* and *Valkyrie* were scrapped in 1931 and 1936 respectively. Armed with four 4-inch guns, superimposed forward and aft, they were fast, powerful and consequently well received by the fleet. Their success led to an almost identical design being adopted for the 1916–17 programme, after some discussions based on modified *R*-class designs. Twenty-five boats were built, joining the Grand Fleet from August 1917 to May 1918. *Vehement* was lost to a mine in August 1918 and *Vittoria* was torpedoed in the Gulf of Finland by the Soviet submarine *Pantera* on 1 September 1919 during the Civil War. *Verulam* too was lost on a mine in the same area on 4 September. Three others, *Vectis, Venturous* and *Violent*, were scrapped between the wars, leaving nineteen boats to serve in the Second World War.

The design was repeated for the nineteen boats ordered on 9 December 1916, with two 'specials' from Thornycroft. The names of these all began with 'W' except for *Voyager* and they differed from the earlier boats as completed by the adoption of triple torpedo tubes. All completed before the end of the First World War and only *Walrus* (which ran ashore after breaking her tow in February 1938) did not seen service in 1939–45.

In January 1918, sixteen repeat 'W' were ordered, but seven of these were cancelled at the Armistice. Thirty-eight more ordered in April were cancelled except for seven units. Of the cancelled boats, *Vimy* (1) had been laid down 16 September 1918; *Votary* 18 June 1918; *Wager* 2 August 1918; *Wake* 14 October 1918; *Welcome* 9 April 1918; *Welfare* 22 June 1918; *Wellesley* 30 August 1918; *Walton, Werewolf, Watson* and *Westphal* in 1918. *Watson* was launched in 1919 and *Werewolf* on 17 July 1919, probably to clear the slipways. These repeat *W* class were known as the *Modified W* class because reports to the effect that new German destroyers were being armed with heavier guns led the Admiralty to introduce a larger calibre gun themselves. This was the 4.7-inch BL Mk I which fired a 50lb shell 16,000 yards. In fact, the Germans were putting a 5.9-inch gun afloat but in the event, the Armistice intervened before they saw active service.

Thus, this line of development left the Admiralty with the largest and most powerful destroyers in the world at the end of 1919. The end of hostilities slowed down the rate of completion of those units not cancelled and a few were transferred to and very leisurely completed at, the Royal Dockyards. Between the wars they gave sterling service at home and abroad, but as new construction became available they were paid off to reserve, in which state most were to be found in 1939, fortunately for the Royal Navy.

Modifications With the exception of the 'Wair' conversions, the other destroyers of the *V & W* class converted to Long-Range Escorts, received interim modifications on the lines described here before their more major conversions. The eighteen unconverted units listed here did not receive major attention for these reasons: (1) they were early war losses; (2) their boiler-room arrangements did not lend themselves to LRE conversion; or (3) the Admiralty valued their 4.7-inch armament for Fleet work. The five boats lost in 1940 probably went down in their peacetime condition, with the possible exception of having exchanged the after tubes for a 3-inch gun.

The 4-inch gunned ships generally landed 'Y' gun to allow increased depth-charge stowage, fitted a 3-inch in lieu of the after tubes and, when available, radar was fitted. Two 20mm Oerlikons augmented the old 2pdr guns, usually in the bridge wings. Radar outfit generally comprised Type 271 in lieu of the rangefinder on the bridge, and a 291 aerial at the foremast truck. By 1942, many had been converted to Short-Range Escorts, which involved only the replacement of 'A' gun by a 'hedgehog' and usually the exchange of the 2pdr guns for two more Oerlikons. *Vortigern, Vivacious, Veteran, Wild Swan, Withington, Wolverine, Worcester, Wishart* and *Witch* were all serving in this status by 1942. Four ships were fitted with a twin 6pdr mounting in lieu of 'A' gun to combat E-boat attacks on east coast convoys (*Walpole, Windsor, Whitshed* and *Wivern*).

The 4.7-inch gunned ships retained all four guns until 1942 and still, in some cases, served in the fleet role. They retained their director and rangefinder and received only Type 291 radar at the masthead. As the need for such old ships in the Fleet role diminished, they were given minor modifications as described above.

Above: *Veteran*, modified for short-range escort duties. Note 'A' and 'Y' guns landed, 12pdr in lieu of after tubes, radars and machine-guns aft. (IWM)

Service Many units took part in the troop evacuations from Europe in May and June of 1940, when *Wessex* was sunk off Calais and *Wakeful* was torpedoed by *S30* on the second day of Operation 'Dynamo'. In the following days, *Worcester* and *Vivacious* were damaged among others. *Whirlwind* was sunk by *U34* south-west of Iceland and *Wren* by bombers off Aldeburgh. The final loss of 1940 was *Venetia*, mined in the Thames estuary in October. Convoy escort duties were the order of the day for most of the ships, but *Vivacious, Walpole, Whitshed* and *Worcester* of the 21st and 16th Destroyer flotillas saw action against the German ships of the Brest Squadron during their escape up the English Channel in February 1942. On this occasion, *Worcester* was very badly damaged. *Windsor* and *Walpole*, with other surface forces, were also involved in attempting to intercept the raider *Michel* in the Channel during March 1942. *Vortigern*, however, was torpedoed off Cromer by *S104* the same month. On the other hand *Whitshed* sank *U55* and *Wolverine U47*, as well as assisting in the destruction of *U76*. *Veteran*, which accounted for *U469* in September 1941, was herself sunk by *U404* in the Atlantic in 1942, and *Wild Swan*, part of a support group sent to assist Convoy HG84, was hit by bombs from Ju 88s of K.Fl.Gr 106 in the Western Approaches in July 1942.

Of the survivors, *Vivacious, Walpole, Windsor* and *Witshed* took part in Operation 'Overlord' in 1944, but their days were now almost over and they quickly left the active fleet in 1945. Their service record was superb, best illustrated by the fact that many had seen active service during the First World War and twenty-eight boats had operated in the Baltic and the Gulf of Finland in 1918–20 against Soviet forces when *Vendetta, Vortigen* and *Wakeful* captured the destroyers *Spartak* and *Gavril*, among other exploits. During the Second World War, the class was responsible for, or participated in, the sinking of 33 German and four Italian submarines. *Vanessa*, in fact, had the unique distinction of sinking *UB107* in the First World War (the only success of the class in that war) and assisting in the sinking of *U357* twenty-four years later.

V & W ('WAIR' CONVERSIONS) CLASS

Ship	Builder	Laid Down	Launched	Commissioned	Fate
D49 *Valentine* L69	Cammell Laird	7 Aug 16	24 Mar 17	27 June 17	Lost 15 May 40
L00 *Valorous* F53	Denny	25 May 16	8 May 17	21 Aug 17	Sold out 4 Mar 47
D28 *Vanity* L38, I28	W. Beardmore	28 July 18	3 May 18	21 June 18	Sold out 4 Mar 47
D52 *Vega* L41	Doxford	11 Dec 16	1 Sept 17	Dec 1917	Sold out 4 Mar 47
D93 *Verdun* L93	Hawthorn Leslie	13 Jan 17	21 Aug 17	3 Nov 17	Sold out 4 Mar 47
D23 *Vimeira* L29	Swan Hunter	Oct 1916	22 June 17	19 Oct 17	Sold out 4 Mar 47
L33 *Vivien*	A. Yarrow	July 1916	16 Feb 18	28 May 18	Lost 9 Jan 42
D91 *Viceroy* L21	Thornycroft	15 Dec 16	17 Nov 17	18 Jan 18	Sold out 18 Feb 47
D45 *Westminster* L40	Scott's	April 1917	24 Feb 18	18 April 18	Sold out 1948
L23 *Whitley*	Doxford	June 1917	13 April 18	14 Oct 18	Sold out 4 Mar 47
D56 *Wolfhound*	Fairfield	April 1917	14 Mar 18	27 April 18	Lost 19 May 40
D98 *Wolsey* L02	Thornycroft	28 Mar 17	16 Mar 18	14 May 18	Sold out 18 Feb 47
L49 *Woolston*	Thornycroft	25 April 17	27 Jan 18	26 June 18	Sold out 4 Mar 47
L55 *Winchester*	S. White	12 June 17	1 Feb 18	29 April 18	Sold out 18 Feb 47
D21 *Wryneck*	Palmer	July 1917	13 May 18	11 Nov 18	Lost 27 April 41

Displacement: 1,188tons/1,207tonnes (standard); 1,490tons/1,513tonnes (full load), (1,512tons/1,536tonnes Thornycroft boats).
Length: 312ft/95.1m (oa); 309ft/97.2m (wl); 300ft/91.4m (pp).
Beam: 29ft 6in/9m (30ft 9in/9.3m Thornycroft boats).
Draught: 10ft 8in/3.25m (mean).
Machinery: three Yarrow boilers (White-Foster *Winchster*); 2-shaft Brown-Curtis geared turbines (*Valentine, Vega, Vimeria* and *Wryneck* Parsons).
Performance: 27,000shp; 34kts (30,000shp Thornycroft boats).
Bunkerage: 367tons/373tonnes (374tons/379tonnes Thornycroft boats).
Range: 3,500nm at 15kts.
Guns: four 4in AA (2×2); eight .5in MG (2×4)

(*Woolston*, two 12pdr (2×1); eight .5in MG).
Complement: 125.

Design In 1937, recognizing the need for ships with a good long-range anti-aircraft armament, albeit rather belatedly, the Admiralty had begun construction of a series of sloops armed with high-angle twin 4-inch guns. To augment this programme, it was also decided to take in hand a number of obsolete destroyers of the *V & W* class for conversion to anti-aircraft escorts. These destroyers were now too old for Fleet duties, but had several years life still left in them. They had in fact been the trend-setters of their day, with their layout being copied abroad and, in the Royal Navy, their heirs conformed very closely to the parameters of the *V & W* design for the next thirty years. Many had seen service in the First World War and all were to give further sterling service in the new conflict.

The original Fleet destroyer design was only modified in respect of the armament – the machinery and internal layout being little altered.

Modifications All 4-inch single Mk V guns were landed and the forward shelter deck was removed. The bridge structure was enlarged and rebuilt with an HACS director replacing the former simple low-angle rangefinder. Both banks of torpedo tubes were landed, the forward set being replaced by elevated platforms carrying quadruple .5in MG mountings. A few units, including *Whitley*, *Vega* and *Woolston*, had a different arrangement with the .5in MG platforms arranged in echelon, the portside mount abreast the forward tube space. However, *Vega* later reverted to the more common disposition. The forward 4-inch gun was mounted on a bandstand protected by a Zareba, while the after gun was shipped on the after shelter deck. For some reason, *Woolston* only received two single 12pdr mountings in lieu of the 4-inch twins shipped by the remainder of the group.

Radar was fitted as soon as it became readily available, usually a Type 285 gunnery set on the HACS director and Type 286 on the foremast. Type 291 radar later replaced the 286 set and was normally fitted at the foremast truck. HF/DF was fitted to some ships including (only?) *Valorous*, but this was essentially for ocean escorts and as the 'Wairs', as they were known, were intended for coastal use, it was not widely fitted. The obsolete and useless .5in MG mountings were retained by these ships well into 1942, other classes having a higher priority for 20mm Oerlikons. When they did become available, they replaced the .5in MG with two more being fitted in the bridge wings.

Service Ten of the ships were taken in hand for conversion before the outbreak of war and the

Above: *Vanity* re-armed as an AA escort, but still with the useless .5in MGs. (IWM) **Below:** *Wallace*. Note radar outfit, new bridge, .5in machine-guns just visible below the radar tower, and 2pdr quad aft. (IWM)

Below: *Verdun* as a 'Wair'. She has radar and 20mm guns. (IWM)

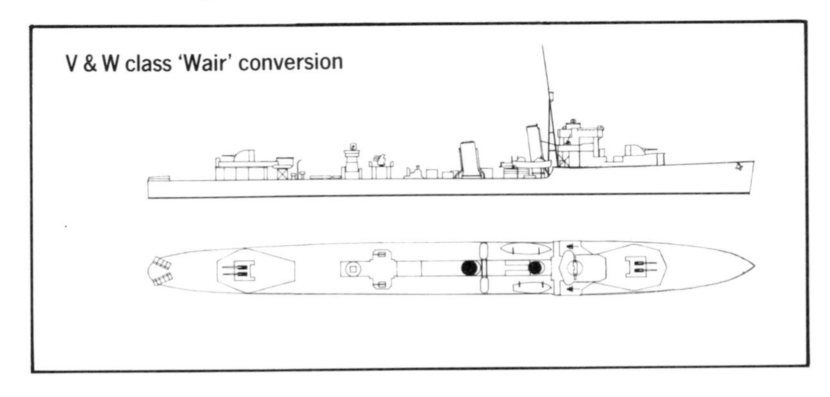

V & W class 'Wair' conversion

remaining five, *Vanity, Verdun, Wolfhound, Wryneck* and *Viceroy* on or after the commencement of hostilities. *Whitley*, the prototype, completed conversion in October 1938 and *Valorous* in June 1939, being the only two to complete before the war. *Viceroy*, not taken in hand until May 1940, did not re-enter service until January 1941.

Two ships, *Valentine* and *Whitley*, were lost to air attacks during evacuation of Dutch and Belgian ports respectively, the former after only a month's service in her new role. Most of the others that had completed conversion also took part in the 'Dynamo' operations, during which *Westminster, Winchester, Wolfhound* and *Vimeria* were damaged by aircraft, the first three seriously. East coast convoy duty was, however, their main role for the war, when their adversaries were initially aircraft and later S-boats (E-boats). *Wryneck* went to the Mediterranean and was subsequently lost when bombed by aircraft of the German VIII Fliegerkorps, south of Naupalia during the evacuation of Greece. Two others, *Viceroy* and *Woolston*, went to the Mediterranean in July 1943 for Operation 'Husky', but returned home again soon afterwards.

Back in home waters, *Vimeria* was mined in the Thames estuary in 1942, but the remainder survived the war, *Viceroy* sinking *U1274* off the east coast of Scotland on 16 April 1945. *Valorous, Viceroy, Wolfhound, Wolsey* and *Woolston* were present at the liberation of Norwegian ports in May 1945, but the war's end brought all need of these venerable ships to an end and they were soon decommissioned for scrapping.

V & W (LONG-RANGE ESCORTS) CLASS

Ship	Builder	Laid Down	Launched	Commissioned	Fate
D29 *Vanessa*	W. Beardmore	16 May 17	16 Mar 18	27 April 18	Sold out 4 Mar 47
H33 *Vanoc*	John Brown	20 Sept 16	14 June 17	15 Aug 17	Sold out 26 July 45
D54 *Vanquisher*	John Brown	27 Sept 16	18 Aug 17	2 Oct 17	Sold out 4 Mar 47
D34 *Velox*	Doxford	1 Jan 17	17 Nov 17	1 April 18	Sold out 18 Feb 47
D64 *Vansittart*[1]	W. Beardmore	1 July 18	17 April 19	5 Nov 19	Sold out 25 Feb 46
D75 *Venomous*[1]	John Brown	31 May 18*	21 Dec 18*	June 1919	Sold out 25 Feb 46
D63 *Verity*[1]	John Brown	17 May 18	14 Mar 19	17 Sept 19	Sold out 25 Feb 46
D32 *Versatile*	Hawthorn Leslie	31 Jan 17	31 Oct 17	11 Feb 18	Sold out Aug 1948
D55 *Vesper*	A. Stephen	27 Dec 16	15 Dec 17	20 Feb 18	Sold out 4 Mar 47
D48 *Vidette*	A. Stephen	1 Feb 17	28 Feb 18	27 April 18	Sold out 4 Mar 47
D33 *Vimy*	W. Beardmore	15 Mar 17†	28 Dec 17†	9 Mar 18†	Sold out 4 Mar 47
D92 *Viscount*	Thornycroft	20 Dec 16	29 Dec 17	4 Mar 18	Sold out 27 May 47
D71 *Volunteer*[1]	W. Denny	16 April 18	17 April 19	7 Nov 19	Sold out 4 Mar 47
D27 *Walker*	W. Denny	26 Mar 17	29 Nov 17	12 Feb 18	Sold out 13 Sept 45
D74 *Wanderer*[1]	Fairfield	7 Aug 18	11 May 19	18 Sept 19	Sold out 31 Jan 46
D25 *Warwick*	Hawthorn Leslie	10 Mar 17	28 Dec 17	18 Mar 18	Torpedoed 20 Feb 44
D26 *Watchman*	Cammell Laird	17 Jan 17	2 Dec 17	26 Jan 18	Sold out July 1945
D47 *Westcott*	W. Denny	30 Mar 17	14 Feb 18	12 April 18	Sold out 8 Jan 46
D94 *Whitehall*[1]	Swan Hunter	June 1918	11 Sept 19	9 July 24‡	Sold out 20 Oct 45
D46 *Winchelsea*	S. White	24 May 17	15 Dec 17	15 Mar 18	Sold out 20 Mar 45
D35, L10, I50 *Wrestler*	Swan Hunter	July 1917	25 Feb 18	15 May 18	C.T.L. 6 June 44

D Pendant changed to I. *Laid down and launched as *Venom*. †Laid down, launched and commissioned as *Vancouver*, renamed 1928. (The original *Vimy*, (ex-*Vantage*) laid down 16 Sept 18 at Beardmore, launched 1919 but cancelled 1919. ‡At Chatham Dkyd. [1]Modified *V&W*.

Displacement: 1,188tons/1,207tonnes (standard); 1,490tons/1,513tonnes (full load) (1,512tons/1,536tonnes *Viscount*).
Length: 312ft/95.1m (oa); 309ft/97.2m (wl); 300ft/91.4m (pp).
Beam: 29ft 6in/9m (30ft 9in/9.37m *Viscount*).
Draught: 10ft 8in/3.25m (mean).
Machinery: two Yarrow boilers (White-Foster *Winchelsea*); 2-shaft Brown-Curtis geared turbines (*Velox, Whitehall* and *Wrestler*, Parsons).
Performance: 18,000shp; 24.5kts (20,000shp; 25kts *Viscount*).
Guns: two 4in (three in *Vansittart*, 4.7in Modified *V&W*) (2×1); one 12pdr; two 2pdr AA (*but see* text).
Torpedoes: three 21in (1×3) (*Viscount* only).
Complement: 170 approx.

Design Although most of this group operated as normal or only slightly altered *V & W* destroyers for much of the war, it has been felt useful to catalogue Long-Range Escorts separately. It should be noted, therefore, that early war alterations conformed generally to those detailed under the unconverted *V & W* destroyer section.

Modifications The intensity of the U-boat war against trade in the Atlantic forced the Admiralty to employ any available warship, suitable or not, in the task of ocean convoy protection. By 1941, many of the older classes of destroyers had been diverted from Fleet duties to this task, including those of the *V & W* class. Destroyers, despite popular opinion, were not ideal for this employment – they had an excess of speed, lack of endurance and were overgunned, but there was no alternative until the war-ordered, purpose-designed escorts, the corvettes, frigates and sloops, became available in useful numbers. After basic alterations, which usually only included landing the after tubes for a 3-inch gun, and the removal of 'Y' gun to allow extra depth-charges to be carried, the *V & W*s operated far out into the Atlantic. Their lack of range, however, was a serious handicap but fortunately, 1942 offered the prospect of increased numbers of properly designed escort vessels joining the fleet and in anticipation of this, a design was prepared for the modification of the *V & W* destroyers to give them longer 'legs' as soon as they could be released to dockyard. At the

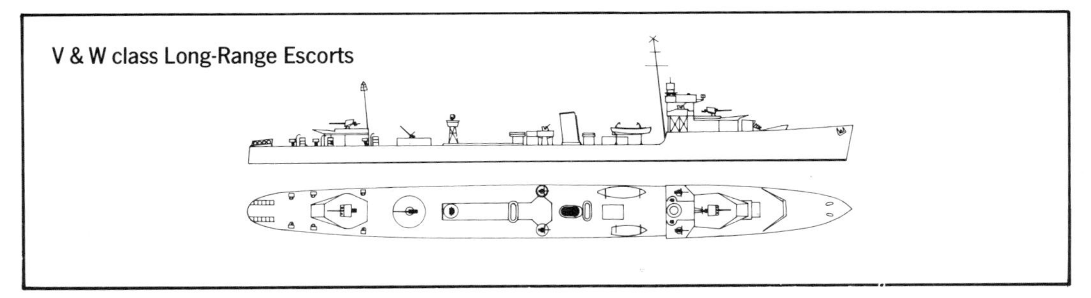

beginning of 1941, *Vimy* was taken in hand for a prototype refit, which lasted until June. This involved the removal of No. 1 boiler and its funnel, the vacated space being divided horizontally into two, the lower part for oil bunkers and the upper for extra accommodation. This latter was long overdue, for the overcrowding in these older ships was becoming a serious problem to health and morale. 'A' gun was landed and replaced by a hedgehog ASW mortar (but not in *Vansittart* which retained three 4.7-inch guns), the forward torpedo tube was removed and two 20mm Oerlikon guns fitted in the bridge wings. Initially, the single 2pdrs were retained but later they too were replaced by Oerlikon guns, to give a standard outfit of four 20mm. Individual units differed, however, as *Walker* had an extra 20mm on the quarter deck and *Verity* an extra gun amidships, making five 20mm. *Watchman* carried a 2pdr bow-chaser at one period and others may have been so fitted. The 3-inch or 12pdr gun, which was probably a feature of their initial war alterations, was retained by *Vanessa, Vansittart, Vimy, Viscount, Volunteer, Watchman, Winchelsea* and possibly *Westcott*. Of these, *Viscount* retained her forward torpedo tubes, thanks to her extra beam and greater stability margin.

Radar fitment was generally Type 271 in the distinctive lantern at the rear of the bridge for surface seach and a Type 291 air warning set at the foremast truck. HF/DF equipment was fitted to at least seven of the group, *Vanquisher, Viscount, Volunteer, Walker, Wanderer, Westcott* and *Whitehall*. After *Vimy* completed her conversion, *Viscount* and *Vaessa* were taken in hand in June and August 1941 and six more in 1942. 1943, however, saw the bulk of the conversions but the last, *Velox*, did not start her refit until the end of 1943, not completing until April 1944.

Service All except one served with the Atlantic escort groups on their return to service. The exception was *Velox* which never served operationally and was used only as a target vessel. Only two fell victim to enemy action, the first being *Warwick*, torpedoed by *U413* off the north coast of Cornwall. *Westler*, after distinguished service in the Mediterranean (prior to conversion) and the Atlantic, was eventually mined off the Normandy beach-head on 6 June 1944. Although not sunk, she was too badly damaged to be worth repair and was declared a constructional total loss. *Winchelsea* was paid off before the war's end and sold for scrap even before hostilities ceased. Her sisters paid off at or towards the end of the war and were sold for scrapping in 1946–47.

Top left: *Vidette*, pre-war. (Abrahams)
Above left: *Viscount* fitted as a long-range escort. Note mixed 20mm and 2pdr armament, radar and HF/DF. (IWM)
Left: *Verity* as an LRE, with six 20mm guns, no tubes, but fitted for 'hedgehog'. (IWM)

PROTOTYPES

Ship	Builder	Laid Down	Launched	Commissioned	Fate
D39 *Amazon*	Thornycroft	29 Jan 25	27 Jan 26	5 May 27	Sold out 25 Oct 48
D38 *Ambuscade*	A. Yarrow	8 Dec 24	15 Jan 26	15 Mar 27	Arrived for breaking up Mar 1947

D pendant changed later to I.

Displacement: 1,352tons/1,597tonnes (standard); 1,812tons/1,841tonnes (full load) *Amazon*; 1,173tons/1,192tonnes (standard); 1,585tons/1,610tonnes (full load) *Ambuscade*.
Length: 323ft/98.45m (oa); 319ft/97.23m (wl); 311ft 9in/95m (pp) *Amazon*. 322ft/98.14m (oa); 319ft/97.23m (wl); 307ft/93.57m (pp) *Ambuscade*.
Beam: 31ft 6in/9.6m (*Amazon*); 31ft/9.45m (*Ambuscade*).
Draught: 8ft 6in/2.59m (mean).
Machinery: three Yarrow boilers; 2-shaft Brown-Curtis S.R. turbines with Parsons cruising turbines.
Performance: 42,000shp; 37kts (*Amazon*); 35,500shp; 37kts (*Ambuscade*).
Bunkerage: 433tons/440tonnes (*Amazon*); 385tons/391tonnes (*Ambuscade*).
Range: 3,400nm at 15kts (*Amazon*); 3,310nm at 15kts (*Ambuscade*).
Guns: four 4.7in (4×1); two 2pdr (2×1).
Torpedoes: six 21in (2×3).
Complement: 138.

Design No new destroyer design had been prepared between 1917 and 1924 because of post-war parsimony and the existence of large numbers of still serviceable war-built ships. By the mid 1920s, however, technical advances in machinery and construction techniques needed to be exploited in a new design and in any event some thought had to be given to the replacement of now obsolescent wartime ships. In order to obtain the best consensus of thought, the Admiralty called for tenders for a prototype destroyer from five leading destroyer builders: Yarrow, Denny, Thornycroft, White and Hawthorn Leslie.

Thornycroft and Yarrow submitted the two successful tenders. The two ships differed in their design, especially internally, but were of similar external appearance. *Amazon*'s boilers were superheated 3-drum type, while her sister's were 4-drum with air pre-heating. Engines were similar, but the Thornycroft ship had a greater designed horse power. In *Amazon* the steering gear was steam as opposed to electro-hydraulic in *Ambuscade*.

The main armament was identical with the earlier *V & W* (modified) destroyers, four 4.7-inch BL Mk I on CP Mk VI** 30° mountings and six 21-inch torpedoes, but incorporated a more advanced fire-control director system. This comprised a 9ft rangefinder and a Destroyer Director Sight.

Because of their prototype nature, much interest was taken in their trial results, when *Amazon* initially reached only 34.5 knots. After modification she achieved 38.7 knots six months later. *Ambuscade* made 37.66 knots and was more economical than her sister. Endurance and performance trials in warm latitudes revealed some problems with high temperatures in the machinery spaces and it became necessary to alter the ventilation systems.

The success of these two ships led to a series of 77 similar destroyers being built from 1925 to 1937.

Modifications Early alterations included the replacement of the after torpedo tubes by a 3-inch or 12pdr HA gun to bolster the weak AA outfit. By 1942, both were becoming over-aged for Fleet duties and received conversions to escort destroyers. 'A' and 'Y' guns were landed, the former being replaced by a hedgehog and radar 286P was added at the masthead. The director and rangefinder were removed and radar 271 fitted in lieu. Two 20mm singles were fitted in the bridge wings and later two more supplanted the 2pdr. In 1943, *Amazon* landed the 3-inch gun and the forward tubes to allow the 10-pattern depth-charge outfit to be carried and also received radar 291 in lieu of the 286P set. *Ambuscade* was given a 'squid' in place of the 'hedgehog' in July 1943, necessitating the landing of all remaining tubes and the addition of 65 tons of ballast. She also lost the 3-inch gun.

Service *Amazon* was with the 18th Destroyer Flotilla at the beginning of the war and later participated in the Norway campaign of April 1940, when on the 29th, she assisted in the destruction of *U50*. After service with the 12th Destroyer Flotilla she became part of the 3rd Escort Group operating in the North Atlantic and on Russian convoys. In the course of one of the latter, QP11, she received two 5-inch shell hits when defending the convoy from an attack by German destroyers on 30 April 1942. After repair, *Amazon* served in the Mediterranean until returning home at the end of that year. In 1943 she was based on the Clyde before moving to the Western Approaches until August when she returned to Greenock. By 1944 she was in use as an aircraft target until reduced to reserve in January 1945. *Amazon* was broken up by the West of Scotland Shipbreaking Co. at Troon in 1949. *Ambuscade* was under refit at Portsmouth during 1939–40, but took part in operations off northern France in June 1940 when she received hits from a shore battery. Her subsequent service was also with the 12th Destroyer Flotilla and 3rd Escort Group before becoming a target ship for the Fleet Air Arm in 1943. After shock trials in Loch Striven in 1946, she was broken up at Troon from March 1947.

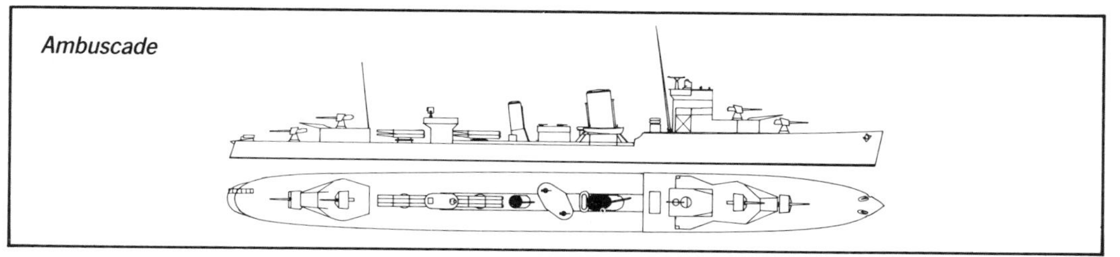

Below: *Ambuscade* in 1943 as an escort destroyer, with the prototype 'squid'. (IWM)

CODRINGTON

Ship	Builder	Laid Down	Launched	Commissioned	Fate
D65 *Codrington* I82	Swan Hunter	20 June 28	7 Aug 29	May 1930	Lost 27 July 40

Displacement: 1,540tons/1,564tonnes (standard); 2,012tons/2,044tonnes (full load).
Length: 343ft/104.54m (oa); 332ft/101.19m (pp).
Beam: 33ft 9in/10.29m.
Draught: 12ft 4in/3.76m (mean).
Machinery: three Admiralty 3-drum boilers; 2-shaft Parsons geared turbines.
Performance: 39,000shp; 35kts.
Bunkerage: 425tons/432tonnes.
Range: 4,800nm at 15kts.
Guns: five 4.7in QF Mk IX; two 2pdr.
Torpedoes: eight 21in (2×4).
Complement: 185.

Design After the First World War, the policy concerning leaders was altered in that classes of leaders were not to be built but instead each class of eight ships would have an enlarged leader built for that class. The original design proposal for the *A*-class leader was for a ship of 2,450 tons armed with five 4.7-inch guns and a speed of 37 knots. Bridge and living accommodation was increased to allow for Captain (D) and staff, but the basic requirements were similar to those for the destroyers. In the event, the design was scaled down with the hull being reduced in length by 43 feet and a corresponding reduction in displacement, although armament remained the same as the original sketch design. In this form the ship was an up-dated version of the *Campbell* class. Her 4.7-inch guns, originally QF Mk VII with 'B' gun on a 60° mounting, were finally QF Mk IX, all on 30° mountings. Two 2-pdrs remained the only AA outfit, but having been displaced by 'Q' gun between the funnels, were re-positioned abaft the after funnel. *Codrington* proved to be a fast ship, reaching 37.7 knots on a displacement of 1,674 tons with 39,257shp during 6-hour full-power trials, but her gearing was noisy and had to be re-cut before final acceptance. She was also a somewhat unhandy ship with a large turning circle, much greater than the class average, which made for difficulties when manoeuvring her flotilla.

Modifications As she was an early war loss, the only alteration made was the replacement of the after tubes by a 3-inch AA gun.

Service On completion, she assumed the duties of Captain (D), 3rd Destroyer Flotilla, in the Mediterranean, but was in home waters at the start of the war. In April 1940, she took part in the Norway operations with the Home Fleet and also escorted troop convoys. May saw her in the English Channel, having left Scapa Flow on the morning of the 10th. Two days later she evacuated the Crown Princess of the Netherlands from Ijmuiden and then, as leader 1st Destroyer Flotilla, conducted off-shore patrols during the evacuation of the BEF from France and Belgium. At the beginning of June, she evacuated troops from the beaches of Dunkirk and on the 9th, began assisting evacuating troops from Le Havre. The following month she was sunk by German bombers while lying in Dover harbour.

Below: *Codrington*, pre-war, typical of the *A* to *I* leaders. (IWM)

A CLASS

Ship	Builder	Laid Down	Launched	Commissioned	Fate
H09 *Acasta*	John Brown	13 Aug 28	7 Aug 29	11 Feb 30	Lost 8 June 40
H12 *Achates*	John Brown	11 Sept 28	4 Oct 29	27 Mar 30	Lost 31 Dec 42
H45 *Acheron*	Parsons M.S.T. Co.*	29 Oct 28	18 Mar 30	13 Oct 31	Lost 8 Dec 40
H14 *Active*	Hawthorn Leslie	10 July 28	9 July 29	9 Feb 30	Sold out 20 May 47
H36 *Antelope*	Hawthorn Leslie	11 July 28	27 July 29	20 Mar 30	Sold out 31 Jan 46
H40 *Anthony*	Scott's	30 July 28	24 April 29	14 Feb 30	Sold out 18 Aug 47
H41 *Ardent*	Scott's	30 July 28	26 June 29	14 April 30	Lost 8 June 40
H42 *Arrow*	V.A. (Barrow)	20 Aug 28	22 Aug 29	14 April 30	C.T.L. 4 Aug 43

*Hull sub-contracted to Thornycroft.

Displacement: 1,350tons/1,371tonnes (standard); 1,773tons/1,801tonnes (full load).
Length: 323ft/98.4m (oa); 320ft/97.5m (wl); 312ft/95.1m (pp).
Beam: 32ft 3in/9.83m.
Draught: 12ft 3in/3.73m (mean).
Machinery: three Admiralty 3-drum boilers (*Anthony* and *Ardent*, Yarrow; *Acheron*, Thornycroft); 2-shaft Parsons geared turbines (Brown-Curtis in John Brown boats).
Performance: 34,000shp; 35.25kts.
Bunkerage: 380tons/386tonnes.
Range: 4,800nm at 15kts.
Guns: four 4.7in QF Mk IX; two 2pdr AA.
Torpedoes: eight 21in (2×4).
Complement: 138.

Design In July 1926, requirements for the destroyers to be built under the 1927 programme were considered at length by the Admiralty. Initially, it was desired to raise endurance to 2,000nm at 16 knots plus 24 hours at ⅔ full power, as compared with the *Ambuscade* design; ship quadruple in lieu of triple torpedo tubes and give increased elevation to

Below: *Antelope* with only early alterations. (IWM)

Above: *Anthony*. 'Y' gun has been landed and the funnels shortened, but otherwise her appearance is little changed. (IWM)
Below: *Achates* in 1942, refitted for escort work. Note 'hedgehog'. (IWM)

the 4.7-inch guns, which themselves were to be of a new all steel type. However, this would have pushed displacement up to more than 2,000 tons, an unacceptable figure for destroyers in those days. As a compromise, the endurance requirement was then reduced to 1,500nm at 16 knots, with consequent reduction in displacement. On the other hand, a new requirement stated that the prime function was torpedo attack to which end it was specified that quintuple tubes were to be carried. As always, cost was a prime consideration and ways were continually being sought to bring down the unit price by reducing the number of torpedoes and the ammunition allowances.

Numerous improvements were sought, particularly with regard to habitability, but despite heating, refrigeration and sanitary facilities comparing very unfavourably with US design practice, it was only with reluctance that any change was made in this direction. One step forward was the provision of a petrol generator to supply light and power when the boilers were dead, thus eliminating the need for paraffin lamps!

The final sketch design worked out about 200 tons heavier than *Ambuscade* and it was pointed out that all that had been obtained for this were two extra torpedoes. Deep load speed had fallen to just over 31 knots and concern was expressed that more advanced machinery, particularly in respect of boiler pressures,could improve the design a good deal. Yarrow had in fact proposed a boat guaranteeing 38 knots and an endurance of 6,000nm at 13 knots. In June 1927, the Engineer-in-Chief somewhat reluctantly suggested that one or two of the class could be fitted with higher pressure boilers at 400psi (as opposed to 300psi). This resulted in *Acheron* receiving special Thornycroft boilers working at 500psi/750°F; the two Scott's boats had Yarrow boilers (275psi/600°F); and the remainder Admiralty 3-drum at 300psi. Unfortunately, the trials with *Acheron*'s boilers were badly handled and the advantages of her advanced system were not apparent.

The main armament, 4.7-inch QF Mk IX, was disposed as in *Ambuscade*, but given full length shields. All were on CP XIV mountings with 30° elevation, the 60° mounting having run into trouble and the all-steel 4.7-inch gun delayed. Anti-aircraft defence remained merely a couple of 2pdr guns, although a quadruple .5in MG mounting was in the course of development, of which great things were (erroneously) expected. Asdic was not fitted and depth-charges were limited to six, without throwers. All, on the other hand, were fitted with the 'Two Speed Destroyer Sweep' (TSDS) for minesweeping purposes.

Active was the first of the class to be laid down, commissioning on 9 February 1930, the last to complete being *Acheron* some sixteen months after the majority which completed by spring of 1930. She was probably delayed by her novel boilers. *Active* ran her full-power trials in December 1929, when she achieved a best speed of 36,73 knots. Builders' trial speeds varied from 35 knots with 34,194shp (*Achates*) to 36.3 knots with 34,415shp (*Anthony*).

Modifications The early war losses, *Acasta* and *Ardent*, probably did not receive any alterations before they were sunk and it is unlikely that *Acheron* received any modifications before her loss. In 1941, the survivors landed the TSDS, 'Y' gun, the after torpedo tubes and had the after funnel shortened by 7 feet. A 3-inch AA gun was shipped in lieu of the torpedo tubes and a 10-pattern depth-charging arrangement installed with 70 depth-charges. Four DCTs were fitted. *Achates*, however, lost 'A' gun and received instead a 'hegehog'; she also received radar 271. The others got radar 286F or 290. Two Oerlikons were fitted in the bridge wings to augment the AA outfit. By 1943, *Antelope* also had radar 271 as well as HF/DF equipment and had landed the 3-inch gun. *Active* too had further alterations in March 1943, receiving radar 291 in lieu of the 286P, two twin 20mm Mk V replaced the singles in the bridge wings, which were repositioned on the former 2pdr platforms. In 1944, *Active, Anthony* and *Antelope* received a twin 6pdr in lieu of 'B' gun.

Service On completion, the class formed the 3rd Destroyer Flotilla, operating with the Mediterranean Fleet, but by the outbreak of the Second World War, with the exception of *Active* at Gibraltar with the 13th Flotilla, all were in the Channel with the 18th Flotilla. *Antelope* scored an early success, sinking *U41* off Ireland in February 1940. *Acasta, Ardent, Acheron* and *Arrow* were attached to the Home Fleet in April 1940 for the Norway operations and *Antelope* worked out of the Clyde on escort duties. *Acasta* and *Ardent* were both sunk in action with *Scharnhorst* and *Gneisenau* while vainly attempting to protect the carrier *Glorious* during the evacuation of Norway. *Acasta*, however, managed to torpedo and badly damage *Scharnhorst* before going down. In November 1940, *Acheron* was a member of the 1st Destroyer Flotilla and a month later was mined south of St. Catherine's Point, Isle of Wight, while running trials after a refit. By early 1941, *Achates, Active, Antelope, Arrow* and *Anthony* were once again with the 3rd Destroyer Flotilla in home waters. In May 1941, *Achates, Antelope* and *Anthony* escorted *Hood* and *Prince of Wales* during the *Bismarck* operations, but in July 1941 *Achates* was badly damaged by a mine off Iceland and had to be towed back to Seidesfjord by *Anthony*. She was repaired at Swan Hunter from September 1941 to March 1942. *Anthony* and *Antelope* took part in the Spitzbergen raid in August 1941.

By early 1942, *Anthony* and *Active* were attached to Force H at Gibraltar and in March 1942, both supported the occupation of Madagascar, when *Active*, together with *Panther*, sank the French submarine *Monge*. Five months later, she was in the South Atlantic recording a second success by sinking *U179*. *Arrow* was attached to Force R in the Indian Ocean in early 1942, moving to the South Atlantic by the end of the year. 1943 saw her in the Mediterranean with the 13th Flotilla, taking part in the invasion of Sicily ('Husky'), but on 4 August 1943, she was alongside the ammunition ship *Fort La Montee* in Algiers when that vessel blew up. *Arrow* was damaged beyond repair, towed to Taranto and paid off. She remained there as late as January 1949.

Active, on her return from the South Atlantic, operated on the Sierra Leone convoy route in 1943, participating in the sinking of the Italian submarine *Leonardo Da Vinci* in May and *U340* in November. She finished the war in the Mediterranean. *Antelope* had a spell in the South Atlantic at Freetown, before taking part in Operations 'Harpoon' and 'Pedestal' in the Mediterranean in 1942. In June 1943, she assisted in the sinking of the Italian submarine *Tritone* off Bougie. By January 1945 however, she had paid off into reserve. After her services in the Indian Ocean, *Anthony* returned home and was employed on escort duties, assisting in the sinking of *U791* in February 1944. The beginning of 1945 saw her back at Portsmouth with the 1st Destroyer Flotilla. *Achates*, on her return to service after repair, served on Arctic Convoys PQ16 and PQ18, then went south for the Invasion of North Africa in November 1942. Back on Russian convoys once more that same month, *Achates* formed part of the escort for Convoy JW51B and was sunk in action with *Admiral Hipper* in the Barents Sea on 31 December 1942.

KEITH

Ship	Builder	Laid Down	Launched	Commissioned	Fate
D06 *Keith* I06	V.A. (Barrow)	Oct 1929	10 July 30	9 June 31	Lost 1 June 40

Displacement: 1,400tons/1,442tonnes (standard); 1,821tons/1,850tonnes (full load).
Length: 323ft 2in/98.5m (oa); 320ft/97.5m (wl); 312ft/95.1m (pp).
Beam: 32ft 3in/9.83m.
Draught: 12ft 3in/3.73m (mean).
Machinery: three Admiralty 3-drum boilers; 2-shaft Parsons geared turbines.
Performance: 34,000shp; 35.26kts.
Bunkerage: 390tons/395tonnes.
Range: 4,800nm at 15kts.
Guns: four 4.7in QF IX; two 2pdr.
Torpedoes: eight 21in (2×4).
Complement: 175.

Design The *B*-class leader was originally proposed in July 1928 as a modified *A* class with the after deck-house extended to provide extra accommodation, but at the cost of 'Y' gun and the TSDS gear. The bridge structure and signal deck had to be enlarged to cope with Captain D's staff and the displacement was about 8 tons greater than the *A*-class destroyers. There were three reasons for this adoption of a smaller leader, the usual one, cost – some £30,000 less than a *Codrington*, and a saving in personnel and the larger leader had not proved exactly ideal for flotilla work. However, the resultant design carried two fewer 4.7-inch guns than *Codrington*. Surprisingly, the design was adopted that October. In June 1929, after Vicker's tender had been accepted the decision was taken to mount a fourth 4.7-inch gun (but no director tower), install asdic and echo-sounder, all of which combined to increase displacement by 23 tons. *Keith* failed to make 35 knots when tried on the Skelmorlie measured mile with power excess to design requirements, but the weather was heavy and there were some doubts as to her having the correct propellers.

Modifications Probably few owing to her early loss.

Service *Keith* served in home waters from 1939. During Operation 'Dynamo' she lost her CO killed by shore gunfire while in Boulogne on 23 May 1940, then was sunk by German bombers off Dunkirk on 1 June while acting as flagship for Admiral Wake-Walker.

Below: *Keith*. Note this leader has only four 4.7-inch guns. (IWM)

B CLASS

Ship	Builder	Laid Down	Launched	Commissioned	Fate
H11 *Basilisk*	John Brown	19 Aug 29	6 Aug 30	4 Mar 31	Lost 1 June 40
H30 *Beagle*	John Brown	11 Oct 29	26 Sept 30	9 April 31	Sold out 15 Jan 46
H47 *Blanche*	Hawthorn Leslie	31 July 29	29 May 30	19 Feb 31	Lost 13 Nov 39
H65 *Boadicea*	Hawthorn Leslie	12 July 29	23 Sept 30	7 April 31	Lost 13 June 44
H77 *Boreas*	Palmer	22 July 29	18 July 30	20 Feb 31	To Greece April 1944
H80 *Brazen*	Palmer	22 July 29	25 July 30	8 April 31	Lost 21 July 40
H84 *Brilliant*	Swan Hunter	9 July 29	9 Oct 30	21 Feb 31	Sold out 18 Aug 47
H91 *Bulldog*	Swan Hunter	10 Aug 29	6 Dec 30	8 April 31	Sold out 15 Jan 46

Displacement: 1,360tons/1,381tonnes (standard); 1,790tons/1,818tonnes (full load).
Length: 323ft/98.4m (oa); 320ft/97.5m (wl); 312ft/95.1m (pp).
Beam: 32ft 3in/9.83m.
Draught: 12ft 3in/3.73m (mean).
Machinery: three Admiralty 3-drum boilers; 2-shaft Parsons geared turbines (Brown-Curtis in John Brown boats).
Performance: 34,000shp; 35.25kts.
Bunkerage: 390tons/396tonnes.
Range: 4,800nm at 15kts.
Guns: four 4.7in QF Mk IX; two 2pdr.
Torpedoes: eight 21in (2×4).
Complement: 138.

Design The destroyers projected for the 1928 programme were to be repeat *Acasta* with minor modifications, including quintuple torpedo tubes equipped for more powerful torpedoes carrying a 900lb warhead. However, the design work for the quintuple tubes was not greatly advanced and it was agreed that quadruple tubes be fitted instead. Suggestions by Yarrow for the adoption of a two-boiler design of the same power output of three standard boilers with a consequent saving in weight and space were not taken up by the Admiralty nor was the idea of eliminating No. 4 gun to allow three quadruple tubes to be carried. *Blanche* was fitted as a divisional leader. *Bulldog* received strengthened gun supports in 'B' position to take an experimental 60° 4.7-inch on a CP XIII mounting but this proved unsuccessful. TSDS was not fitted and as a result, 20 depth-charges could be accommodated with two throwers and one rail.

Modifications Early alterations comprised the usual substitution of the after torpedo tubes for a 3-inch HA gun, lowering of the after funnel and removal of the mainmast. In about 1941, *Boreas, Brilliant* and *Boadicea* landed 'Y' gun for increased depth-charge stowage and had radar 286 at the mast head. *Beagle* and *Bulldog* lost 'A' gun for a 'hedgehog', the DCT and rangefinder were replaced by radar 271 and two Oerlikon guns were fitted in the bridge wings, two in lieu of the 2pdr and two more abreast the search-light platform. 'Y' gun and the 3-inch were landed. In July 1943, it was intended to convert the survivors to long-range escorts on the lines of the *V & W* class but this was never done. *Bulldog* received a 2pdr bow-chaser in 1944.

Service *Blanche* had the dubious distinction of being the first destroyer loss of the war, when she was mined in the Thames estuary. She was one of the victims of a minefield laid by four German destroyers (*Heidkamp, Künne, Lüdemann* and *Galster*) on the night of 12/13 November 1939. *Basilisk* operated with the 19th Flotilla and saw service in the Norway campaign before taking part in the Dunkirk evacuations when she was badly damaged by aircraft off La Panne. After survivors had been picked up, the wreck was torpedoed by *Whitehall. Brazen*, too, was serving with the 19th Flotilla in the Norway campaign when, in company with *Fearless*, she sank *U49*. She was also bombed during the Dunkirk operations and sank in tow off Dover the following day. *Boreas* and *Brilliant* also took part in 'Dynamo' operations, the former receiving a direct hit on the bridge causing many casualties. After 1941, duties were mainly convoy escorting and in May 1942, both *Bulldog* and *Beagle* saw action against German destroyers in the course of Convoy QP11. In November 1942, *Boadicea* was damaged off Oran in action with French *torpilleurs* after which she returned to home waters on escort duties until torpedoed and sunk by an aircraft torpedo off Portland after D-Day. *Boreas* went to the South Atlantic in 1941 and took part in the North Africa landings in November 1942, then served with the 13th Flotilla at Gibraltar until late 1943. After a refit at Liverpool *Boreas* was transferred to Greece in April 1944 and re-named *Salamis*. (She was returned to the Royal Navy at Malta in 1951 and finally sold out for scrapping 23 November 1951.) *Brilliant* served in the South Atlantic from 1941, enjoying some success in intercepting German blockade-runners. In November 1942, she sank the French sloop *La Surprise* off Oran. By late 1944, she had returned to home waters as part of the 1st Flotilla based at Portsmouth.

Above: *Brilliant* as completed. (Author's Collection)

Below: *Beagle* with early type 286 radar. 'Y' gun has been landed and she has no 20mm guns yet. (IWM)

DUNCAN

Ship	Builder	Laid Down	Launched	Commissioned	Fate
D99 *Duncan* I99	Portsmouth Dkyd.	3 Sept 31	7 July 32	5 April 33	Sold out Sept 1945

Displacement: 1,400tons/1,422tonnes (standard); 1,942tons/1,973tonnes (full load).
Length: 329ft/100.28m (oa); 326ft/98.45m (wl); 317ft 9in/96.85m (pp).
Beam: 33ft/10.06m.
Draught: 12ft 6in/3.78m (mean).
Machinery: three Admiralty 3-drum boilers; 2-shaft Parsons geared turbines.
Performance: 36,000shp; 36kts.
Bunkerage: 390tons/396tonnes.
Range: 5,870nm at 15kts.
Guns: four 4.7in QF Mk IX; one 3in AA; two 2pdr.
Torpedoes: eight 21in (2×4).
Complement: 175.

Design The *D*-class leader was similar to *Kempenfelt* and built in dry dock by Portsmouth dockyard, the machinery being supplied by Beardmore. In this ship, the double boiler room was adjacent to the engine room, thus two large compartments could be flooded by a hit in the wrong place. On trials she reached 36½ knots with 34,595shp. After completion, she took her flotilla out to the China station.

Modifications *Duncan*, employed on escort duty by late 1942, had 'Y' gun and the after tubes removed to allow extra depth-charge stowage, the director and rangefinder replaced by radar 271 and an HF/DF mast stepped aft. Six single 20mm Oerlikon guns were added, and a split 'hedgehog'.

Service *Duncan* returned to home waters on the outbreak of war, but on 17 January 1940 was in collision with a merchant vessel off Duncansby Head and seriously damaged. Engine room and boiler rooms were both flooded and she only just remained afloat. She was at this time senior officer's ship, 12th Flotilla. Repairs took until mid 1940, after which she moved to Gibraltar and operated in the Mediterranean with Force H. In March 1942, she was involved in the occupation of Madagascar in the Indian Ocean, returning home later that year to re-equip for escort duties on North Atlantic convoys. As the leader of Escort Group B7, she saw extensive convoy service 1943–44, sinking *U381* and *U272* as well as damaging *U707*. Worn out after her arduous war service, *Duncan* was quickly sold for breaking up after the end of the war.

Below: *Duncan* in almost peacetime guise. (IWM)

D CLASS

Ship	Builder	Laid Down	Launched	Commissioned	Fate
H07 *Defender*	V.A. (Barrow)	June 1931	7 April 32	28 Oct 32	Lost 11 July 41
H22 *Diamond*	V.A. (Barrow)	Sept 1931	8 April 32	2 Nov 32	Lost 27 April 41
H16 *Daring*	Thornycroft	June 1931	7 Jan 32	24 Nov 32	Lost 18 Feb 40
H75 *Decoy*	Thornycroft	June 1931	7 June 32	4 April 33	To RCN 1943
H53 *Dainty*	Fairfield	20 April 31	3 May 32	3 Jan 33	Lost 24 Feb 41
H38 *Delight*	Fairfield	22 April 31	2 June 32	30 Jan 33	Lost 29 July 40
H49 *Diana*	Portsmouth Dkyd.	June 1931	16 June 32	20 Dec 32	To RCN 6 Sept 40
H64 *Duchess*	Portsmouth Dkyd.	June 1931	19 July 32	24 Jan 33	Lost 13 Dec 39

Displacement: 1,375tons/1,397tonnes (standard); 1,890tons/1,920tonnes (full load).
Length: 329ft/100.28m (oa); 326ft/98.45m (wl); 317ft 9in/96.85m (pp).
Beam: 33ft/10.06m.
Draught: 12ft 6in/3.78m (mean).
Machinery: three Admiralty 3-drum boilers; 2-shaft Parsons geared turbines.
Performance: 36,000shp; 36kts.
Bunkerage: 473tons/480tonnes.
Range: 5,870nm at 15kts.
Guns: four 4.7in QF Mk IX; one 3in AA; two 2pdr.
Torpedoes: eight 21in (2×4).
Complement: 145.

Design The *B*-class design had been marginally enlarged and given extra endurance by greater bunkerage in the *C* class of the 1929 programme, all of which had been transferred to Canada before the war (q.v.). The *D* class were essentially repeat *C*s with minor modifications and were not fitted with TSDS under the policy of alternately fitting for ASW and TSDS. With this class, it was intended to drop the old 2pdr AA guns and ship instead the new .5in machine-gun quadruple mountings which were belatedly coming off the production line. These guns would be carried in enlarged and strengthened bridgd wings at shelter deck level, while a 3-inch gun, as in the *C* class, would be fitted between the funnels.

Main armament remained the 4.7-inch QF Mk IX with 30° elevation despite some pressure for a calibre increase to 5.1-inch a prototype of which was under development. However, as the calibre of Japanese destroyer guns was 4.7-inch, it was felt unwise to precipitate an increase in this direction. Other reasons for not increasing calibre were the questions of power training and projectile weight (for man-handling). Actually, the Japanese had already adopted the 5-inch gun in their new destroyers of the Special (*Fubuki*) type (q.v.). The appearance of these powerful destroyers, together with the heavily armed French ships and large US destroyers, henceforth began to make the standard British design look very weak. The Destroyer Director Control tower and fire-control clock Mk I introduced in the *C* Class was continued in the *D* and later classes.

Engines and boilers were identical with those fitted in the *C* class, except that boilers in *Decoy* were fitted with air pre-heaters for greater efficiency. *Daring* and *Decoy* were fitted out as divisional leaders. Half the class did not get the .5in machine-guns, *Defender, Diamond, Daring* and *Diana* being given the old 2pdr guns. On completion all commissioned for the 1st Flotilla, Mediterranean Fleet.

Modifications Little alteration was made to the six war losses beyond the cutting down of the after funnel in some. Of the two transferred to Canada, *Diana* was lost early while *Decoy* is dealt with under Canada.

Service At the outbreak of war, the *D* class were on the China station but were ordered to the Mediterranean. *Duchess, Diana* and *Dainty* returned to home waters in 1939, escorting *Barham* and *Dunkerque* from Gibraltar to the Clyde, but on 12 December while in the North Channel off the Mull of Kintyre, *Barham* collided with *Duchess* abreast the forecastle. The destroyer capsized, blew up and sank with heavy loss of life. *Diana* was immediately transferred to the RCN (q.v.). *Daring* and *Delight* also returned to the UK for the 5th Flotilla with the Home Fleet, but Kretschmer in *U23* sank the former off the Orkney Islands in February 1940. *Delight* served with the 3rd Flotilla before being sunk by air attack off Dover in July 1940.

The other four ships served in the South Atlantic until going to the Mediterranean in May 1940. All saw a great deal of action but only one ship survived 1941. *Dainty* in company with *Decoy* and *Ilex* sank the Italian submarines *Liuzzi* and *Scebeli*, took part in the Aegean campaigns and was finally sunk by Ju 87s of 1/St.G.3 at Tobruk. *Decoy* took part in the Greek campaign, was damaged off Crete, served off Syria in 1941 and moved to the Eastern Fleet in February 1942. She was transferred to the RCN on 12 April 1943 (q.v.). *Defender* had a similar turbulent career in Mediterranean waters, and in January 1941 was one of the first ships into the newly captured Tobruk. The evacuation of Crete followed but on 11 July, while on a supply run to Tobruk, a near miss bomb exploded under her, flooding the engine rooms and a boiler room. Her back was broken and despite attempts to tow her by *Vendetta*, she had to be torpedoed by the Australian ship 7 miles north of Sidi Barani. *Diamond*'s career was even more brief; she was bombed and sunk off Greece during the evacuation in April 1941.

Below: *Dainty*. (G. Ransome)
Right: *Eclipse* with early modifications. (IWM)

E CLASS

Ship	Builder	Laid Down	Launched	Commissioned	Fate
H23 *Echo*	Denny	20 Mar 33	16 Feb 34	25 Oct 34	To Greece 5 April 44
H08 *Eclipse*	Denny	22 Mar 33	12 April 34	29 Nov 34	Lost 23 Oct 43
H27 *Electra*	Hawthorn Leslie	15 Mar 33	15 Feb 34	15 Sept 34	Lost 27 Feb 42
H10 *Encounter*	Hawthorn Leslie	15 Mar 33	29 Mar 34	2 Nov 34	Lost 1 Mar 42
H17 *Escapade*	Scott's	30 Mar 33	30 Jan 34	30 Aug 34	Sold out 1946
H66 *Escort*	Scott's	30 Mar 33	29 Mar 34	6 Nov 34	Lost 11 July 40
H15 *Esk*	Swan Hunter	23 Mar 33	19 Mar 34	26 Sept 34	Lost 1 Sept 40
H61 *Express*	Swan Hunter	23 Mar 33	29 May 34	31 Oct 34	To RCN 3 June 43

Displacement: 1,405tons/1,427tonnes (standard); 1,940tons/1,971tonnes (full load).
Displacement: 329ft/100.28m (oa); 326ft/99.3m (wl); 318ft 3in/97m (pp).
Beam: 33ft 3in/10.13m.
Draught: 12ft 6in/3.81m (mean).
Machinery: three Admiralty 3-drum boilers; 2-shaft Parsons geared turbines.
Performance: 36,000shp; 36kts.
Bunkerage: 470tons/477tonnes (480tons/488tonnes *Esk*).
Range: 6,350nm at 15kts.
Guns: four 4.7in QF Mk IX; eight .5in MG (2×4).
Torpedoes: eight 21in (2×4).
Mines: 60 (*Esk* and *Express* only).
Complement: 145.

Design This class adopted a modified hull form to that of the *C* class and were a little heavier. Internally, the boilers were in three separate spaces, but a proposal for trunking all uptakes into a single funnel was not agreed. Asdic was fitted together with two throwers, one rail and 20 depth-charges. It was originally intended to ship a 3-inch AA gun as in previous classes, but after some discussion it was agreed to omit it, if 40° elevation could be given to the 4.7-inch mountings. This was a wise decision, as its effectiveness and volume of fire was of little use and there was no effective HA control. Unfortunately, the puny .5in MG which replaced it were of even less use. It was realized as early as 1932, at least in some quarters, that Fleet defence against air attack was best carried out by the capital ships themselves, better still by fighters from the Fleet's aircraft carriers. It was therefore no task for a destroyer, but she did need to protect herself from air attack and in this area, current designs were very poorly equipped. The lack of a good AA director was realized at the beginning of the 1930s but nine years later, little had been done in that direction for small ships.

40° CP XVII mountings were adopted for all four 4.7-inch guns, fourteen inch deep wells with removable covers being employed to allow the necessary elevation while retaining a workable breech height for low-angle use. Mk IX torpedoes were adopted, as in the *D*s, which were heavier than the Mk IV. All the ships of the 1931 programme were originally intended as fast minelayers for sixty Mk XIV mines, but because new mining gear was under design, it was considered unwise to equip nine ships with new and untried gear. In consequence, only two were to be so fitted (*Esk* and *Express*). Sponsons were fitted aft to ensure a fair drop for the mines and, to compensate for the weight of the mine load, 'A' and 'Y' guns and the torpedo tubes had to be landed. This was not a very satisfactory arrangement and although the change could be made quickly, it obviously left the ship very vulnerable after laying her mines, in contrast with other nations' practice.

Modifications The usual early alterations included a 3-inch HA gun (with shield in some) in lieu of the after tubes and the cutting down of the main mast. A crow's nest was added to the foremast and a 13ft rangefinder replaced the original 10ft equipment. *Express* had a deck-house added between the funnels in 1940 but this was later removed. Two 20mm eventually replaced the .5in MG and two more fitted in the bridge wings in most units. *Escapade* was converted to an escort destroyer in 1942–43 when 'A' gun was replaced by a 'hedgehog' and 'Y' gun by four depth-charge throwers. She landed the 3-inch gun but retained the forward tubes. Six 20mm comprised the AA outfit and RDF 271 replaced the

rangefinder and director. By 1945, the hedgehog had given way to a double squid mounting and the 271 radar had been replaced by a small, modern-pattern dish-type aerial.

Service On completion, this class formed the 5th Destroyer Flotilla with the Home Fleet, but in 1939, just prior to the Second World War, all went into reserve as the new *K*-class destroyers joined the fleet for the 5th Flotilla, except for the minelayers, which formed the 20th Flotilla. *Echo* served in home waters until 1942, then went to the Mediterranean with the 8th Flotilla, taking part in the Sicily landings, Salerno and in the Aegean before being transferred to Greece as *Navarinon* on 5 April 1944. She returned to UK control in 1956. *Eclipse* was bomb damaged and abandoned in the Norway campaign, but later towed (for 5½ days) by *Escort* and saved. In March 1942 she was damaged again by German destroyers while defending Russian Convoy PQ13. A year of Home Fleet and Arctic duties followed before a spell in Western Approaches Command in spring 1943. Operating in the Mediterranean in 1943 she was present at the landings in Sicily and Salerno, then moved to the Aegean, where she struck a mine off Kalimnos. *Escort* served in the Home Fleet, off Norway and at Gibraltar but in July 1940, was hit by a torpedo from the Italian submarine *Marconi* in the forward boiler room and sank later in tow. *Encounter* went to the Mediterranean in 1940 then escorted *Repulse* to Colombo at the end of 1941 and joined the Eastern Fleet. In February 1942, she participated in the Battle of the Java Sea, together with *Electra* and on 1 March 1942, while in company with *Exeter* and the USS *Pope*, ran into a strong Japanese force in the Sunda Straits, when all three ships were lost. Prior to her loss in the Far East, *Electra* served in the Home Fleet until her arrival in Singapore on 2 December 1941. *Escapade*'s service life was mainly in home waters except for the Dakar and Mers-el-Kebir operations, until late 1942. The North Africa landings followed before she was transferred early in 1943 to ocean convoy escort duties in the North Atlantic for the remainder of the war.

Esk, operating as a minelayer with other ships in the 20th Flotilla, struck a mine 40nm NW of the Texel on the night of 31 August 1940 and sank, her flotilla mate, *Express*, being badly damaged, losing everything forward of the bridge. Repairs took more than a year. Service in the Eastern Fleet followed, *Express* being present at the sinking of *Prince of Wales* and *Repulse*. In June 1943, she was transferred to the RCN as *Gatineau* (q.v.).

Above: *Escapade* as an escort. The censor has deleted the 'hedgehog', but left in the 277 radar on the bridge and the HF/DF. (IWM)

EXMOUTH CLASS

Ship	Builder	Laid Down	Launched	Commissioned	Fate
H02 *Exmouth*	Portsmouth Dkyd.	16 May 33	7 Feb 34	3 Oct 34	Lost 21 Jan 40
H62 *Faulknor*	A. Yarrow	31 July 33	12 June 34	24 May 35	Sold out Jan 1946

Displacement: 1,495tons/1,519tonnes (standard); 2,049tons/2,082tonnes (full load).
Length: 343ft/104.5m (oa); 340ft/103.6m (wl); 332ft/101m (pp).

Left: *Faulknor* in 1935. (Vicary)

Beam: 33ft 9in/10.3m.
Draught: 12ft 6in/3.81m (mean).
Machinery: three Admiralty 3-drum boilers; 2-shaft Parsons geared turbines.
Performance: 38,000shp; 36.75kts.
Bunkerage: 470tons/477tonnes.
Range: 6,350nm at 15kts.
Guns: five 4.7in QF Mk IX; eight .5in MG (2×4).
Torpedoes: eight 21in (2×4).
Complement: 175.
Design For the flotilla leader of the 1931 programme, it was decided to revert to the enlarged leader formula with extra speed and armament on the lines of *Codrington*. Despite the marginal increase in dimensions and displacement, a three boiler room layout was adopted as a result of objections from the Controller on the valid grounds of better water-tight integrity, as compared with two boiler rooms. The original proposal for 'Q' gun to be on a 60° mounting was not proceeded with and the leader would not be fitted either with TSDS or for minelaying.

Once again, Portsmouth dockyard won the contract, with machinery being supplied by Fairfield. Like *Duncan*, *Exmouth* was also built in dry dock, No. 8.
Modifications Another of the early leader losses, *Exmouth* probably was lost in her peacetime state.
Service *Exmouth* was torpedoed and sunk with all hands off the Moray Firth by *U22* on 21 January 1940.
Design *Faulknor* was a repeat of *Exmouth*.
Modifications In January 1941, *Faulknor* received a 3-inch gun in lieu of the after tubes, and the main mast was replaced by a stump aerial for the W/T leads. In January a year later the old rangefinder platform was replaced by an H/A R/F director fitted with radar 285. The after funnel was cut down and the .5in MG were moved to new sponsons abreast the searchlight platform. HF/DF was fitted on a new pole mast on the after shelter deck. By January 1943, 'X' gun had been removed, the 3-inch HA being shifted into its place and the after tubes re-shipped. Six single 20mm were added, in the bridge wings, abreast the searchlight and at the forward corners of the after shelter deck. Radar 291 replaced the 286 set. At the beginning of 1945 the midships 4.7-inch gun was landed and replaced by a quadruple 2pdr and twin power-operated 20mm fitted in the bridge wings.
Service *Faulknor* had an extremely active career, starting the war as leader, 8th Destroyer Flotilla. In 1939, she was attached to the Home Fleet and took part in the sinking of *U39* and *U27* before the turn of the year. In March 1940, *Faulknor* and other *F*-class destroyers sank *U44*, before taking part in the Norway Campaign. On 17 June, *Faulknor* sailed for Gibraltar to begin a long period with Force H during which time, she took part in operations at Mers-el-Kebir, Dakar and in the French Cameroons, as well as escorting several sorties to fly reinforcements to beleaguered Malta. In May 1941, the *Bismarck* actions took her into the Atlantic, followed by convoy escort duties west of Gibraltar and anti-blockade runner strikes into the Bay of Biscay. Towards the end of 1941, *Faulknor* left Force H and returned home and spent the first quarter of 1942 serving on Arctic convoys. After a further brief period with the 4th Support Group in the Atlantic she returned to the Mediterranean once more for the Invasion of Sicily, the surrender of the Italian Fleet and the landings at Salerno. By October 1943 she was in the Aegean operating in the Dodecanese until November. Returning home she took part in the Normandy landings in June 1944 and saw the war out in local waters.

Above: *Exmouth* in 1938. (Vicary)

F CLASS

Ship	Builder	Laid Down	Launched	Commissioned	Fate
H78 *Fame*	Parsons M.S.T. Co.*	5 July 33	28 June 34	26 April 35	To Dominica Feb 1949
H67 *Fearless*	Cammell Laird	17 Mar 33	12 May 34	22 Dec 34	Lost 23 July 41
H79 *Firedrake*	Parsons M.S.T. Co.†	5 July 33	28 June 34	30 May 35	Lost 4 Jan 43
H74 *Forester*	S. White	15 May 33	28 June 34	29 Mar 35	Sold out 22 Jan 46
H68 *Foresight*	Cammell Laird	21 July 33	29 June 34	15 May 35	Lost 13 Aug 42
H70 *Fortune*	John Brown	25 July 33	29 Aug 34	27 April 35	To RCN 3 June 43
H69 *Foxhound*	John Brown	21 Aug 33	12 Oct 34	6 June 35	To RCN 8 Feb 44
H76 *Fury*	S. White	19 May 33	10 Sept 34	18 May 35	C.T.L. 21 June 44

*Hull subcontracted to V.A. (Barrow). †Hull subcontracted to V.A. (Tyne).

Displacement: 1,405tons/1,427tonnes (standard); 1,901tons/1,931tonnes (full load).
Length: 329ft/100.28m (oa); 326ft/99.3m (wl); 318ft 3in/97m (pp).
Beam: 33ft 3in/10.13m.
Draught: 12ft 6in/3.81m (mean).
Machinery: three Admiralty 3-drum boilers; 2-shaft Parsons geared turbines (*Fortune* and *Foxhound*, Brown-Curtis).
Performance: 36,000shp; 36kts.
Bunkerage: 470tons/477tonnes.
Range: 6,350nm at 15kts.
Guns: four 4.7in QF Mk IX; eight .5in MG.
Torpedoes: eight 21in (2×4).
Complement: 145.
Design The 1932 programme destroyers were repeat *E* class.
Modifications Few obvious modifications appear to have been made in these relatively new destroyers before the end of 1940. In about 1941, the after funnel was cut down in height, the bridge wings widened to accommodate single Oerlikons and shields were fitted to the .5in MG. A 3-inch gun replaced the after torpedo tubes and radar 291 was fitted to the mast head. Depth-charge stowage was increased and HF/DF fitted to a mast stepped at the forward end of the after shelter deck. *Fame*, following her repairs in 1941, lost her director and rangefinder, being fitted with radar 271 in lieu. 'A' and 'Y'

Above: *Firedrake* in 1936. (Wright & Logan)

guns were landed, the former being replaced by a 'hedgehog', the latter by extra depth-charge stowage. The after tubes were removed and replaced by a 3-inch gun. Radar 291 and HF/DF were added and the light AA increased by four Oerlikons. In 1943–44 'A' gun was reinstated, the 3-inch landed and the .5in MG replaced by two extra 20mm Oerlikons. *Forester* was similarly armed.

Service At completion, the *F* class formed the 6th Destroyer Flotilla, Home Fleet, being renumbered the 8th Flotilla in May 1939. *Fame* served in the North Sea and in Norway until autumn 1940, when on 17 October she (and *Ashanti*) ran aground in fog off Sunderland and was burned out. After a major operation to salvage her, repairs were made at Chatham, which included building a new stern, and extended until late 1941. On returning to service she operated with the Western Approaches command as an escort destroyer, often with Escort Group B6 and later the 14th Escort Group, during which period she sank *U353, U201* and assisted in the loss of *U767*, the last off Normandy during 'Overlord'. After the war she was sold out to Dominica and re-named *Generalisimo*, later *Sanchez. Foresight* served with Force H from June 1940, then in 1942 saw service on Arctic convoys when in the course of QP11 she was in action with, and damaged by, German destroyers, after which she had to torpedo the damaged cruiser *Edinburgh*. On her return to the Mediterranean in August 1942, she was a casualty of Operation 'Pedestal', when torpedoed by an Italian aircraft north of Bizerta. Despite being taken in tow by *Tartar* she sank the following day. *Fearless* also served with Force H, capturing a French convoy in 1941 with other destroyers. In July, whilst screening *Ark Royal* she was struck by an aircraft torpedo on the port side aft which started an oil fire. Without motive power or electric power, the damaged ship had to be sunk by *Forester* north of Bone.

Fury, Forester, Foxhound, Fortune and *Firedrake* served with the Home Fleet 1939–40 and took part in the Norway Campaign. *Forester* and *Foxhound* also participated in the second Battle of Narvik. All served with Force H from mid 1940, *Fury* and *Forester* returning to the Home Fleet for Arctic convoy duties early in 1942. The former returned to the Mediterranean in 1943, seeing action at Salerno and in the Aegean, but *Forester* transferred to North Atlantic convoy duties before rejoining her sister for the Normandy landings. *Fury* struck a mine off the Cotentin Peninsula on 21 June and was driven ashore in a gale, becoming a constructional total loss. Later salvaged, she was towed to Barrow for breaking up in September 1944. *Foxhound* and *Fortune* went to the Eastern Fleet in March 1942 before returning home in mid 1943, when *Fortune* was transferred to the RCN. *Foxhound* served in the Western Approaches until she too joined the RCN in February 1944. *Firedrake* served in the Home Fleet until August 1940 when she went to the Mediterranean for Force H. In July 1941, she was badly damaged by bombs while in the Sicilian Channel (on the same occasion as *Fearless* was lost) and was eventually brought into Gibraltar after a four-day passage partly under tow by *Eridge*. Permanent repairs were carried out at Boston USA. By April 1942, she was on the North Atlantic convoys with Escort Group B7, but in December she was torpedoed and sunk by *U211* whilst escorting Convoy ON153.

Below: *Forester*. The radar and rangefinder platform have been deleted by the censor. (IWM)

GRENVILLE CLASS

Ship	Builder	Laid Down	Launched	Commissioned	Fate
H03 *Grenville*	A. Yarrow	29 Sept 34	15 Aug 35	1 July 36	Lost 19 Jan 40
H87 *Hardy*	Cammell Laird	1935	7 April 36	Dec 1936	Lost 10 April 40

Displacement: 1,465tons/1,488tonnes (1,455/1,478 *Hardy*) (standard); 2,053tons/2,085tonnes (full load).
Length: 330ft/100.5m (337/103 *Hardy*) (oa); 327ft/99.6m (wl); 319ft/97.2m (326/99 *Hardy*) (pp).
Beam: 34ft 6in/10.5m (34/10.36 *Hardy*).
Draught: 12ft 9in/3.89m (mean).
Machinery: three Yarrow side-fired boilers (Admiralty 3-drum *Hardy*); 2-shaft Parsons geared turbines.
Performance: 38,000shp; 36kts.
Bunkerage: 470tons/477tonnes.
Range: 5,530nm at 15kts.
Guns: five 4.7in QF Mk IX; eight .5in MG.
Torpedoes: eight 21in (2×4).
Complement: 175.

Design *Grenville* was a slightly modified version of *Faulknor*, but six feet shorter on the waterline. She was unusual in that Yarrow side-fired boilers were fitted for which some internal reorganization was necessary. Armament remained the same as in the *E*-class leader, 40° elevation only being achieved by means of gun-wells.

Modifications A very early war loss, *Grenville* had no modifications carried out.

Service Pre-war service was with the 20th Flotilla in the Mediterranean. *Grenville* was mined and sunk in the Thames estuary, another victim of the clandestine German destroyer sorties, this time *Steinbrinck, Eckoldt* and *Ihn*.

Design *Hardy* was essentially a repeat *Grenville* with a tripod foremast.

Modifications None before her loss.

Service Service in the Mediterranean was interrupted by the outbreak of war when *Hardy* moved into the Central Atlantic with three of her flotilla to operate with Force K on raider interception duties. In December 1939 she took her three destroyers (*Hasty, Hostile* and *Hereward*) to the River Plate following the interception of *Admiral Graf Spee* by Commodore Harwood's squadron, but they saw no action. 1940 brought the flotilla back to home waters when *Hardy* took part in the initial stages of the Norway Campaign in April 1940. She led her flotilla against the German destroyers at Narvik on 10 April when in the course of a hot-fought action, *Hardy* was badly hit by the German *Georg Thiele*, her bridge, wheelhouse and forward guns being knocked out. Out of control, the flotilla leader drove ashore on the southern side of the fjord. Shot up later by various German destroyers, *Hardy* became a total loss.

Below: *Grenville*, as completed. (IWM)

G CLASS

Ship	Builder	Laid Down	Launched	Commissioned	Fate
H59 *Gallant*	A. Stephen	15 Sept 34	29 Sept 35	25 Feb 36	C.T.L. 20 Jan 41
H37 *Garland*	Fairfield	22 Aug 34	24 Oct 35	3 Mar 36	To Netherlands Dec 1947
H89 *Grafton*	Thornycroft	30 Aug 34	18 Sept 35	20 Mar 36	Lost 29 May 40
H05 *Greyhound*	V.A. (Barrow)	20 Sept 34	15 Aug 35	31 Jan 36	Lost 22 May 41
H63 *Gipsy*	Fairfield	5 Sept 34	7 Nov 35	22 Feb 36	Lost 21 Nov 39
H92 *Glowworm*	Thornycroft	15 Aug 34	22 July 35	22 Jan 36	Lost 8 April 40
H68 *Grenade*	A. Stephen	3 Oct 34	12 Nov 35	28 Mar 36	Lost 29 May 40
H31 *Griffin*	V.A. (Barrow)	20 Sept 34	15 Aug 35	6 June 36	To RCN 22 Mar 43

Displacement: 1,350tons/1,376tonnes (standard); 1,854tons/1,883tonnes (full load).
Length: 323ft/98.45m (oa); 320ft/97.5m (wl); 312ft/95.09m (pp).
Beam: 33ft/10.05m.
Draught: 12ft 5in/3.78m (mean).
Machinery: three Admiralty 3-drum boilers; 2-shaft Parsons geared turbines.
Performance: 34,000shp; 36kts.
Bunkerage: 470tons/477tonnes.

Range: 5,530nm at 15kts.
Guns: four 4.7in QF Mk IX; eight .5in MG (2×4).
Torpedoes: eight 21in (2×4) (*Glowworm* ten (2×5)).
Complement: 145.

Design This class differed only marginally from the *F* class, but was of slightly smaller dimensions, partly due to the omission of cruising turbines. The displacement was specified as that of the *A* class, weight being saved by the turbine alterations mentioned and improvements in boilers. Armament was to remain the same as the *F* class with 40° elevation once again being achieved only by the rather clumsy use of gun wells, but much discussion had taken place concerning massed destroyer torpedo attacks and there was a move to increase the torpedo broadside to ten tubes. This would have involved a weight penalty of some ten tons. In the event, only *Glowworm* received the prototype pentad PR Mk I tubes, the remainder quadruple Mk VIII tubes. All had torpedoes Mk IX. Fairfield proposed fitting the more advanced Johnson boiler into *Gipsy* giving advantage in weight, space and efficiency, but the Admiralty, ever-cautious and perhaps mindful of the inconclusive results from *Acheron* (q.v.) declined to take up the idea. Tripod mainmasts were fitted to all.

Modifications The early losses of *Gipsy, Glowworm, Grafton* and *Grenade* prevented any alterations being made to these units. The survivors lost the after tubes for a 3-inch gun and had the after funnel cut down and the mainmast removed. *Greyhound* and *Gallant* were probably lost in this state. *Garland* eventually lost 'Y' gun for increased depth-charge stowage and shipped two single Oerlikons in strengthened and enlarged bridge wings. A prominent bracket on the bridge front supported a D/F loop. Type 291 radar was fitted at the masthead and gunnery radar 285 on the rangefinder. Two further Oerlikons supplanted the .5in MG. HF/DF was fitted on a tall mast on the after shelter deck. By the end of the war, 'B' gun had been displaced by a hedgehog and two further 20mm fitted abreast the searchlight platform. Rocket flare projector rails were fitted on No. 1 gun and radar 271 shipped in lieu of rangefinder and director. *Griffin* received similar treatment except that a 'hedgehog' replaced 'A' gun, the 3-inch was landed and two single Oerlikons fitted in its place, making six in all. Four depth-charge throwers replaced 'Y' gun.

Service All except *Garland* and *Gipsy* were with the 1st Destroyer Flotilla in home waters on the outbreak of war. The other two were 2nd Flotilla ships, *Garland* being in the Mediterranean. *Gipsy* was the first loss, yet another victim of German destroyers, when she was mined off Harwich and subsequently beached after her crew were taken off by *Burza. Grafton* and *Gallant* were under refit at the time of the Norway Campaign, but the rest of the home-based ships took part. *Glowworm* was sunk in action with *Admiral Hipper* after ramming and damaging the heavy cruiser off the Norwegian coast. *Gallant, Grafton, Grenade* and *Greyhound* particpated in the evacuation from France and Belgium in May 1940, the former being damaged by near misses. *Grafton* was torpedoed by *U69* while returning fully loaded with troops, the explosions breaking her back and blowing off the stern. After taking off survivors, the wreck was torpedoed and sunk by *Ivanhoe. Grenade* was bombed while lying in Dunkirk, one falling down a funnel. Towed clear of the fairway, she later exploded and sank. *Greyhound* was hit by shore gunfire in the engine rooms but managed to reach Dover unaided.

After repairs, *Gallant* went to the Mediterranean with *Griffin* and *Greyhound*, the former pair sinking the Italian submarine *Lafole* on 20 October, assisted

Below: *Glowworm*, pre-war. (IWM)

Below: *Greyhound*, in a disgraceful condition! (IWM)

Below: *Hero* in 1937. Note bridge front. (Author's Collection)

by *Hotspur*. *Garland* had by this time been transferred to Poland so now only three ships remained under the White Ensign. *Greyhound* saw action at Dakar in September 1940 when, in company with *Australia* and *Fury*, the French *contre-torpilleur L'Audacieux* (q.v.) was very seriously damaged in a gun fight. She later sank the Italian submarines *Neghelli* in the central Mediterranean in January 1941, followed by *Anfitrite* off Crete on 6 March 1941. Both *Griffin* and *Greyhound* were at the action off Cape Matapan in the same month, but *Greyhound* was one of the casualties of the Crete operations when bombed and sunk in the Kithera Channel. *Griffin* also saw action off Crete, then served briefly with the Eastern Fleet, February–May 1942, before returning to the Mediterranean. By 1943 she had returned home and was transferred to the RCN on 20 March 1943. *Gallant* was mined off Malta on 10 January 1941 and towed into Malta. She was hit by bombs on 20 January and declared a constructional total loss. After being bombed again in April 1942, she was finally expended as a blockship a year later. *Garland* returned to RCN control in 1947 and was sold to the Netherlands in December that year as *Marnix*.

H CLASS

Ship	Builder	Laid Down	Launched	Commissioned	Fate
H24 *Hasty*	Denny	15 April 35	5 May 36	11 Nov 36	Lost 15 June 42
H43 *Havock*	Denny	15 May 35	7 July 36	8 Jan 37	Lost 6 April 42
H93 *Hereward*	Parsons M.S.T. Co.*	28 Feb 35	10 Mar 36	9 Dec 36	Lost 29 May 41
H99 *Hero*	Parsons M.S.T. Co.*	28 Feb 35	10 Mar 36	23 Oct 36	RCN 15 Nov 43
H55 *Hostile*	Scott's	27 Feb 35	24 Jan 36	10 Sept 36	Lost 23 Aug 40
H01 *Hotspur*	Scott's	27 Feb 35	23 Mar 36	29 Dec 36	To Dominica 23 Nov 48
H35 *Hunter*	Swan Hunter	26 Mar 35	25 Feb 36	20 Sept 36	Lost 10 April 40
H97 *Hyperion*	Swan Hunter	26 Mar 35	8 April 36	3 Dec 36	Lost 22 Dec 40

*Hulls sub-contracted to V.A. (Tyne).

Displacement: 1,340tons (standard); 1,859tons (full load).
Length: 323ft/98.45m (oa); 320ft/97.5m (wl); 312ft/95.09m (pp).
Beam: 33ft/10.05m.
Draught: 12ft 5in/3.78m (mean).
Machinery: three Admiralty 3-drum boilers (*Hyperion*, one Johnson and two Admiralty 3-drum); 2-shaft Parsons geared turbines.
Performance: 34,000shp; 36kts.
Bunkerage: 470tons/477tonnes.
Range: 5,530nm at 15kts.
Guns: four 4.7in QF Mk IX; eight .5in MG.
Torpedoes: eight 21in (2×4).
Complement: 145.

Design The 1934 programme ships were to be repeat *G* class except that a better solution had been found for achieving 40° elevation on the 4.7-inch guns. Design changes at the breech end, where the balance weight was repositioned above the loading

tray, allowed the increased elevation without the necessity for the gun wells of the previous class. This new mounting was known as CP Mk XVIII. Pentad torpedo tubes were not approved, quadruple being shipped as usual. Detail design changes and the increased use of welding in these ships produced a drop in displacement of about 50 tons compared to the *G* class. *Hero* and *Hereward* introduced a new style of bridge, the redesign being necessary because *Hereward* was intended to carry a new pattern twin 4.7-inch mounting, CP Mk XIX with 4.7-inch guns Mk XII. This new gun differed only in detail from the Mk IX, being a little heavier and fractionally longer. The mounting had a trunnion height thirteen inches greater than that of the single mounting CP XVIII and it was necessary to raise the wheelhouse to enable the helmsman to see over the gun shields. Elevation, training and ramming were hydraulic. *Hereward* received the twin mounting in 'B' position but had the requisite fittings for 'A' gun also and could receive the single Mk CP XVIII mountings when necessary. The twin mounting was in fact removed by the time war broke out. Internally, the machinery arrangements were identical with the *Gs*, except that *Hyperion* received a Johnson boiler for evaluation purposes. *Hunter* and *Hostile* were fitted with air pre-heaters to their boilers which increased their weight. All the ships of the class received the tripod mainmast and TSDS.

Modifications *Hero* and *Hereward* originally had taller funnels than the rest, but these were reduced in height before the war. *Hunter*, lost during the first Narvik action in April 1940, had no modifications. The remainder of the class underwent the usual alterations and additions, i.e., the substitution of the after tubes for a 3-inch gun, 20mm Oerlikon guns in the bridge wings and later replacing the .5in MG. *Hotspur* when converted for escort duties landed 'A' and 'Y' 4.7-inch guns and the 3-inch, but did not reship the after torpedo tubes. Instead, a 'hedgehog' was fitted forward, extra depth-charges were stowed and more throwers fitted. Radar 271 replaced the director and rangefinder, with radar 290 at the mast-head and HF/DF on a pole aft. The 20mm guns were now increased to six singles. Later, 'A' 4.7-inch gun was reinstated and the hedgehog was removed. *Hero*, as an escort with the RCN in 1943, had only two 4.7-inch ('B' and 'X'), a twin 6pdr, six Oerlikons and four torpedo tubes as well as 29 tons of depth-charges.

Service All commissioned for service with the 2nd Destroyer Fllotilla, Mediterranean Fleet, on which station they were to be found in September 1939. However, the flotilla moved immediately to the South Atlantic until ordered home early in 1940, for operations in the Norway Campaign. *Havock, Hostile, Hotspur* and *Hunter*, together with their flotilla leader, *Hardy*, took part in the First Battle of Narvik where they sank the German destroyers *Anton Schmitt* (q.v.) and *Wilhelm Heidkamp* (q.v.), but in turn lost their flotilla leader and Captain (D2) as well as *Hunter*, badly damaged by gunfire then rammed by *Hotspur*, which herself was also damaged by shell-fire. Three days later, *Hero* took part in the Second Battle of Narvik when the remaining eight German destroyers were sunk. *Hereward* was in dockyard hands at this time, as was *Hasty*.

In May 1940, the flotilla moved to the Mediterranean once more (*Hasty, Havock, Hereward, Hero, Hostile* and *Hyperion*). Here they participated in Fleet actions, Malta convoys and the evacuation of Crete. *Hostile*, however, was soon lost when mined off Cape Bon in August on a field laid a couple of days previously by the Italian destroyers *Maestrale, Grecale, Libeccio* and *Scirocco*.

Hyperion saw action in the engagement between the Australian cruiser *Sydney* and the Italian cruiser *Bartolemo Colleoni* when both she and *Ilex* finished-off the unfortunate Italian with torpedoes. However, she herself was in turn torpedoed and sunk five months later by the Italian submarine *Serpente*.

Hereward was another casualty of the evacuation of Crete when on the morning of 29 May 1941, she was hit by bombs from aircraft of 111/St.G.2 north of Plaka. *Havock* was damaged by near misses of 15-inch shells from *Littorio* during the second Battle of Sirte and was repaired at Malta, after which she sailed for Gibraltar on 5 April but ran aground at high speed on the Tunisian coast near Kelibia the following day and had to be destroyed by her crew. The Italian submarine *Aradam* later put a torpedo into the wreck. *Hasty*, taking part in Operation 'Vigorous' in June 1942, was hit by a torpedo from the German *S Boote S55* on the 14th and sunk by British forces the following day. *Hotspur* also joined her sisters in the Mediterranean after repairs to her Narvik damage. She saw extensive service until transferred to the Eastern Fleet in March 1942. *Hero* was the only other survivor of these Mediterranean days, not returning to the UK until April 1943, and was transferred to the RCN on 15 November that year (q.v.). During the operations in the Mediterranean, 1940–43, the class as a whole was responsible for or participated in the sinking of three Italian submarines (*Berillo, Niade, Lafole*) and three U-boats (*U79, U568, U559*), as well as the destroyers *Vega, Carducci* and *Alfieri*.

The last survivor in the Royal Navy, *Hotspur*, operated with the Eastern Fleet apart from a brief redeployment to the Mediterranean in June 1942 until April 1943, when she returned to the UK. Refitted for escort duties, *Hotspur* spent the remainder of the war in the Western Approaches as a unit of Escort Group C4 and the 14th Escort Group. Paid off in October 1947 she was sold out to Dominica on 23 November 1948 and renamed *Duarte*.

Below: *Hero* in 1941, with radar 286, four 20mm and a 12pdr gun. (IWM)

INGLEFIELD

Ship	Builder	Laid Down	Launched	Commissioned	Fate
D02 *Inglefield* I02	Cammell Laird	29 April 36	13 Oct 36	25 June 37	Lost 25 Feb 44

Displacement: 1,544tons/1,568tonnes (standard); 2,081tons/2,114tonnes (full load).
Length: 337ft/102m (oa); 327ft/99.6m (wl); 326ft/99m (pp).
Beam: 34ft/10.36m.
Draught: 12ft 6in/3.89m (mean).
Machinery: three Admiralty 3-drum boilers; 2-shaft Parsons geared turbines.
Performance: 38,000shp; 36kts.
Bunkerage: 470tons/477tonnes.
Range: 5,530nm at 15kts.
Guns: five 4.7in QF Mk IX; eight .5in MG.
Torpedoes: ten 21in (2×5).
Complement: 175.

Design *Inglefield* was a repeat *Hardy* but with pentad torpedo tubes.

Modifications In 1942, when *Inglefield* began Arctic convoys, the centre tube of each pentad mounting was removed, and she was carrying four Oerlikons, two of which were on the after deck-house. 'Y' gun was landed, its place being taken by the 3-inch gun formerly carried in place of the after tubes. Radar 286 and HF/DF were also fitted.

Service *Inglefield* served with the Home Fleet, assisting in the destruction of *U63* in February 1940. After service in Norway, repairs caused her to miss Dunkirk, but in August and September she moved south to participate in the Dakar operation where she was hit by shore batteries. In 1941, she took part in the *Bismarck* hunt and the raid on Petsamo. 1942 saw her engaged in the 'Wasp' aircraft transport operation to Malta before a period on Arctic convoys until early 1943. In April 1943 she served with the 4th Support Group in the North Atlantic, then went to the Mediterranean, taking part in the landings on Sicily, at Salerno and Anzio, where she was hit by a radio-controlled glider bomb and sank.

Above: *Inglefield* in November 1942. She has a 12pdr in 'X' position, four 20mm and twin machine-guns on the bridge. Radar 291 and HF/DF are fitted. (IWM)

I CLASS

Ship	Builder	Laid Down	Launched	Commissioned	Fate
D03 *Icarus*	John Brown	16 Mar 36	26 Nov 36	3 May 37	Sold out Aug 1946
D61 *Ilex*	John Brown	16 Mar 36	28 Jan 37	7 July 37	Sold out 1947
D44 *Imogen*	Hawthorn Leslie	18 Jan 36	30 Oct 36	2 June 37	lost 16 July 40
D09 *Imperial*	Hawthorn Leslie	22 Jan 36	11 Dec 36	30 June 37	Lost 29 May 41
D11 *Impulsive*	S. White	10 Mar 36	1 Mar 37	29 Jan 38	Sold out 22 Jan 46
D10 *Intrepid*	Thornycroft	13 Jan 36	17 Dec 36	29 July 37	Lost 27 Sept 43
D87 *Isis*	A. Yarrow	6 Feb 36	12 Nov 36	2 June 37	Lost 20 July 44
D16 *Ivanhoe*	A. Yarrow	6 Feb 36	11 Feb 37	24 Aug 37	Lost 1 Sept 40

(Pendant changed to I later)

Displacement: 1,370tons/1,391tonnes (standard); 1,888tons/1,918tonnes (full load).
Length: 323ft/98.45m (oa); 320ft/97.5m (wl); 312ft/95.09m (pp).
Beam: 33ft/10.05m.
Draught: 12ft 5in/3.78m (mean).
Machinery: three Admiralty 3-drum boilers; 2-shaft Parsons geared turbines.
Performance: 34,000shp; 36kts.
Bunkerage: 470tons/477tonnes.
Range: 5,530nm at 15kts.
Guns: four 4.7in QF Mk IX; eight .5in MG.
Torpedoes: ten 21in (2×5).
Mines: 60 (*Impulsive, Ivanhoe, Intrepid* and *Icarus* only).
Complement: 145.

Design These destroyers were repeat *H* class with detail alterations. Pentad tubes were adopted for all the class despite objections from the Controller, and the new bridge form tried in *Hero* was included in this class. All were to be capable of minelaying. The extra top-weight resulting from the increased torpedo outfit led to questions as to the stability of the class, which was not as good as the *H* class. To compensate somewhat the casing over the engine room was omitted, but it was still necessary to water ballast on occasion. Conversion to minelaying involved landing 'A' and 'Y' guns, all torpedoes and tubes as well as the TSDS. *Impulsive, Ivanhoe, Intrepid* and *Icarus* served as minelayers able to carry 60 mines.

Modifications Initially, a 3-inch replaced the after torpedo tubes, single Oerlikons were fitted in the bridge wings and the after funnel was reduced in height. By 1942, radar outfit was 291 at the masthead and some units had HF/DF. The .5in MG were replaced by two more Oerlikons and the centre tube of the quintuple mounting was removed to save weight. By 1944, *Icarus*, rearmed for escort duties, had exchanged 'Y' gun for extra throwers and depth-charges (110), landed the 3-inch gun and fitted two extra Oerlikons on the searchlight platform. Three units, *Isis, Ilex* and *Impulsive*, are reported to have received twin 6pdr guns in lieu of 'A' gun.

Service This flotilla was serving in the Mediterranean at the outbreak of war, but was ordered to join the Home Fleet immediately. Before the end of 1939, the flotilla had been involved in the sinkings of *U35, U42* and *U45*. Early in December 1939, the 20th Destroyer Flotilla was formed for minelaying duties, reviving a famous flotilla which performed similar duties during the First World War. *Icarus, Impulsive, Ivanhoe* and *Isis*, the minelayers, joined this flotilla and operated with the *E*-class minelayers. All the *I* class ships of the 3rd and 20th Flotillas, except *Intrepid*, saw service in the Norway Campaign but only *Icarus* took part in one of the Narvik battles, the second. During the evacuation from Belgium, Holland and France in May and June 1940, *Intrepid* and *Ivanhoe* were damaged, but *Ilex* and *Imperial* took no part, having been detached to the Mediterranean on 14 May. *Imogen*, after the

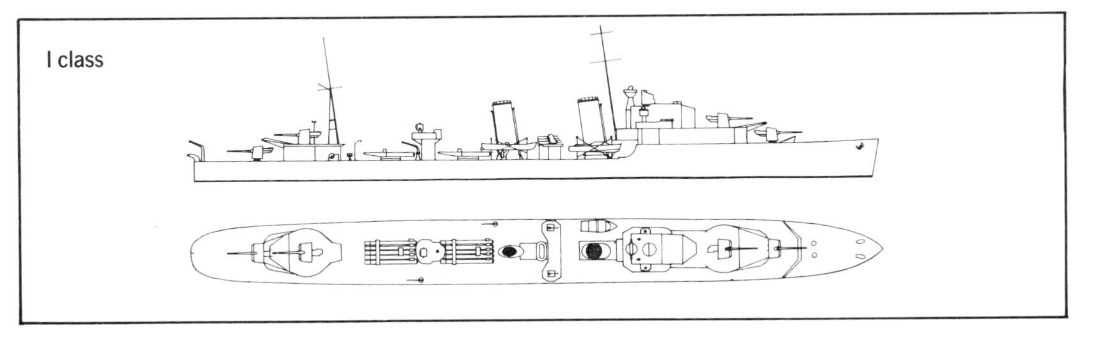

fall of France, served with the Home Fleet and on 16 July, whilst screening cruisers off the Pentland Firth in fog, collided with *Glasgow*, caught fire and had to be abandoned.

The 20th Flotilla continued its minelaying sorties, but on 1 September 1940 ran into an enemy field losing *Ivanhoe* and *Esk* sunk, with *Express* very badly damaged. *Ivanhoe* did not sink immediately and even managed to steam astern for a couple of hours, but when the shafts fractured, she was taken in tow by *Kelvin*. After about six hours, a bombing attack broke her back, whereupon *Kelvin* torpedoed her. *Icaus* and *Impulsive* remained mainly in home waters, except that the former deployed briefly to the Mediterranean for Operations 'Harpoon' and 'Pedestal' in 1942. *Impulsive* served in Arctic waters for much of her career as did *Intrepid* until mid 1943.

Ilex (with *Dainty*) sank the Italian submarines *Liuzzi* and *Scebeli* in June 1940, while serving in the Mediterranean. She also took part in the sinking of the cruiser *Bartolomeo Colleoni* and sank the MTB *MAS537* in that year. In June 1941, No. 2 boiler room was badly damaged by bombing in action off Syria, and she went to the USA to refit and repair. She returned to Mediterranean waters early in 1943, taking part in the sinking of another Italian submarine, *Nereide*, but by January 1944 had been badly damaged and declared a constructional total loss. *Imperial* also served most of her time in the Mediterranean, having moved there in May 1940, but on 11 October she was badly damaged by a deep laid mine off Malta and was under repair for more than six months. After repairs she returned to service in the eastern Mediterranean, but on 28 May 1941, was near missed by a bomb which at first appeared to have caused no damage. The next day, her steering failed and in view of the critical danger of air attack, she was abandoned and sunk by a torpedo from *Hotspur*. *Isis* took part in the evacuations of Greece and Crete in 1941, then was badly damaged by bombing off Syria (at the same time as *Ilex*). She was sent to Singapore for repairs, which were still incomplete at the time of the Japanese attack in December 1941, when she was further damaged by bombs. Just before the fall of Singapore, *Isis* was towed to Java and thence to Colombo and finally Bombay for repair. By early 1943, she was back in service in the Mediterranean where she participated in the sinking of *U562*. In 1944, *Isis* came home and took part in the Normandy landings. She was eventually sunk by *Neger* midget submarines in July 1944.

Intrepid served briefly with Western Approaches Command early in 1943, before sailing for the Mediterranean and operations off Sicily and Salerno. Service in the eastern Mediterranean followed in the Dodecanese when the Germans invased Leros. She was caught in harbour at Leros by bombers and sunk on 26/27 September 1943.

EX-BRAZILIAN H CLASS

Ship	Builder	Laid Down	Launched	Commissioned	Fate
H44 *Highlander* (ex-*Jaguaribe*)	Thornycroft	28 Sept 38	16 Oct 39	18 Mar 40	Sold out 27 May 46
H06 *Hurricane* (ex-*Japarua*)	V.A. (Barrow)	30 June 38	29 Sept 39	21 June 40	Lost 24 Dec 43
H32 *Havant* (ex-*Javary*)	S. White	30 Mar 38	17 July 39	19 Dec 39	Lost 1 June 40
H19 *Handy* (ex-*Jurua*)	V.A. (Barrow)	3 June 38	29 Sept 39	23 May 40	Lost 11 Mar 43
H57 *Hearty* (ex-*Juruena*)	Thornycroft	6 July 38	1 Aug 39	22 Jan 40	Sold out 26 Nov 46
H88 *Havelock* (ex-*Jutahy*)	S. White	31 May 38	16 Oct 39	10 Feb 40	Arrived for breaking up 31 Oct 46

Technical details as RN *H* class, except only three 4.7in.

Design These ships were purchased from Brazil on 4 September 1939 and renamed as above. However, *Handy* and *Hearty* were renamed *Harvester* and *Hesperus* respectively on 27 February 1940, i.e., after *Hearty* had been commissioned. They were similar to the RN *H* class except that 'Y' gun was deleted for extra depth-charge stowage, a combined R/F-DCT was fitted and the funnels were cut down as completed. Displacement was slightly greater than their British-ordered counterparts.

Modifications *Havant, Hesperus, Havelock* and *Highlander* were handed over with only makeshift fire-control outfits, consisting of a rangefinder tower and no director. No torpedo tubes were aboard; *Havant* being lost in this condition except that she had received her tubes. The designed combined director and rangefinder was fitted later to *Hesperus* at least, and the rangefinder tower was landed. A 3-inch gun replaced the after tubes in the usual fashion. When refitted for escort duties, 'A' gun was replaced by a hedgehog in *Hesperus, Havelock* and *Highlander* and they carried six Oerlikons. RDF 270 was fitted in the distinctive lantern on the bridge in lieu of the director tower and HF/DF on a mast aft.

Service On completion, these six ships formed the 9th Destroyer Flotilla, *Havelock, Hesperus* and *Highlander* took part in the Norwegian campaign when *Hesperus* was damaged by bombing off Mo. *Harvester, Havant, Havelock* and *Highlander* participated in the evacuation from France but *Havant* was on this occasion heavily damaged by bombs and had to be sunk by *Saltash*. *Harvester* and *Highlander* sank *U32* off Ireland in October 1940 and *Havelock* the Italian *Faa di Bruno* the following month. From 1941, the five survivors served on escort duties in the North Atlantic with various escort groups, but *Hurricane* was bombed and sunk during an air raid on Liverpool, 7/8 May 1941. Although she was raised and repaired, *Hurricane* did not return to service until January 1943. In March 1943, *Harvester* rammed and sank *U444* but in doing so was considerably damaged and thus became a sitting duck for *U432* which torpedoed her. On Christmas Eve 1943, *Hurricane* was hit and sunk by an acoustic torpedo from *U415* north-east of the Azores. *Havelock* assisted in the sinking of *U767* and *242*; *Hesperus, U357, U191, U186* and *U242*. After the war no re-sale to Brazil was forthcoming and the ships were therefore scrapped.

Left: *Intrepid* with early war modifications. (IWM)
Right: *Isis* with only initial modifications. *Duncan* is seen behind. (IWM)

EX-TURKISH I CLASS

Ship	Builder	Laid Down	Launched	Commissioned	Fate
H49 *Inconstant* (ex-*Muavenet*)	V.A. (Barrow)	24 May 39	15 Nov 41	24 Jan 42	To Turkey 1945
H06 *Ithuriel* (ex-*Gayret*)	V.A. (Barrow)	24 May 39	24 Feb 41	3 Mar 42	C.T.L. 28 Nov 42

Above: *Hurricane* in June 1940. Note director tower and lack of 'Y' gun. (MOD)

Technical details as RN *I* class, but eight 21in (2×4).

Design Two of a class of four building for Turkey at the outbreak of the Second World War. For some reason, only two were purchased by Great Britain, the other pair, built by Denny and completed in 1942 (*Sultanhisar* and *Demirhisar*) were delivered to Turkey although commissioned as HM ships for the passage to Turkey. Their design was essentially a repeat *I* class, but with eight torpedo tubes instead of ten.

Modifications When employed on escort duties in 1943, *Inconstant* had radar 270 in lieu of the director and rangefinder, with six Oerlikons fitted, including two on the after shelter deck.

Service On completion *Inconstant* served briefly in the Arctic before going to the Eastern Fleet with the 12th Flotilla. She took part in the operations at Madagascar then served in the South Atlantic until the end of 1942 when she returned to the Eastern Fleet. In 1943, *Inconstant* was ordered to the Mediterranean and took part in the Allied landings in Sicily in July, during which time she sank *U409*. In the autumn of 1943 she returned to home waters and joined the 8th Escort Group in the Western Approaches. In 1945, *Inconstant* was resold to Turkey, refitted and handed over at Istanbul on 7 March 1946. *Ithuriel* served exclusively in the Mediterranean, taking part in the Malta convoys, Operations 'Harpoon' and 'Pedestal'. In the course of the latter, *Ithuriel* rammed and sank the Italian submarine *Cobalto* sustaining moderate damage to herself. On the night of 27/28 November 1942 she was badly damaged during an air raid at Bone and the following month, her guns were landed to form a shore battery. In 1944, she was towed to Malta, then Gibraltar and finally in 1945, back to the UK for disposal.

Left: *Hesperus* in April 1942. (MOD)

TRIBAL CLASS

Ship	Builder	Laid Down	Launched	Commissioned	Fate
F07 *Afridi*	V.A. (Tyne)†	9 June 36	8 June 37	3 May 38	Lost 3 May 40
F51 *Ashanti*	Denny	23 Nov 36	5 Nov 37	21 Dec 38	Sold out 12 April 49
F67 *Bedouin*	Denny	Jan 1937	21 Dec 37	15 Mar 39	Lost 3 July 42
F03 *Cossack*	V.A. (Tyne)†	9 June 36	8 June 37	7 June 38	Lost 27 Oct 41
F75 *Eskimo*	Parsons M.S.T. Co.*	5 Aug 36	3 Sept 37	30 Dec 38	Sold out 27 June 49
F20 *Gurkha*	Fairfield	6 July 36	7 July 37	21 Oct 38	Lost 9 April 40
F24 *Maori*	Fairfield	6 July 36	2 Sept 37	2 Jan 39	Lost 12 Feb 42
F59 *Mashona*	Parsons M.S.T. Co.*	5 Aug 36	3 Sept 37	28 Mar 39	Lost 28 May 41
F26 *Matabele*	Scott's	1 Oct 36	6 Oct 37	25 Jan 39	Lost 17 Jan 42
F31 *Mohawk*	Thornycroft	16 July 36	15 Oct 37	7 Sept 38	Lost 16 April 41
F36 *Nubian*	Thornycroft	10 Aug 36	21 Dec 37	6 Dec 38	Sold out 11 June 49
F21 *Punjabi*	Scott's	1 Oct 36	18 Dec 37	29 Mar 39	Lost 1 May 42
F82 *Sikh*	A. Stephen	24 Sept 36	17 Dec 37	12 Oct 38	Lost 14 Sept 42
F33 *Somali*	Swan Hunter‡	26 Aug 36	24 Aug 37	12 Dec 39	Lost 24 Sept 42
F43 *Tartar*	Swan Hunter‡	26 Aug 36	21 Oct 37	10 Mar 39	Sold out 6 Jan 48
F18 *Zulu*	A. Stephen	10 Aug 36	23 Sept 37	7 Sept 38	Lost 14 Sept 42

(All pendants changed to G 1940). *Hulls sub-contracted to V.A. (Tyne). †Machinery by V.A. (Barrow). ‡Machinery by Wallsend Slipway.

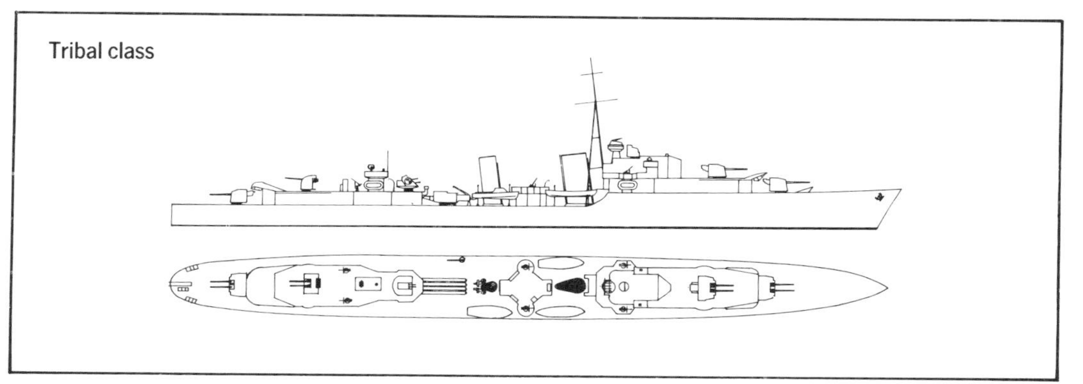

Displacement: 1,854tons/1,883tonnes (standard); 2,519tons/2,559tonnes (full load).
Length: 377ft/114.9m (oa); 364ft 8in/111.1m (wl); 355ft 6in/108.3m (pp).
Beam: 36ft 6in/11.12m.
Draught: 9ft/2.75m (mean).
Machinery: three Admiralty 3-drum boilers; 2-shaft Parsons geared turbines.
Performance: 44,000shp; 36kts.
Bunkerage: 524tons/532tonnes.
Range: 5,700nm at 15kts.
Guns: eight 4.7in QF Mk XII (4×2); four 2pdr (1×4 Mk VII); eight .5in MG (2×4).
Torpedoes: four 21in (1×4).
Complement: 190 (219 leaders).

Design By the mid 1930s it was obvious that the standard *A* to *I* class destroyers were fast becoming outclassed by certain destroyer designs built or building abroad. In particular, the Japanese *Fubuki* type with six 5-inch guns and nine torpedo tubes was especially noteworthy. Twenty-four of these destroyers had already been completed by 1932 and more were building. France too had large destroyer designs in service (*contre-torpilleurs*, q.v.) so had the USA and Italy. However, France and the USA were quite patently not considered possible future enemies, while the Italian Navy, though increasing in strength, does not seem to have entered into the Admiralty's calculations, insofar as the 1935 destroyer programme was concerned. Japan was quite a different matter, for Great Britain no longer had the Treaty links with her as she had had prior to 1914, but the British Empire still sprawled across the Far East. In the Orient, therefore, Japan had to be considered as a potential enemy and, moreover, one with a very modern and powerful fleet.

Below: *Maori* in 1939. (Author's Collection)

In view of these trends abroad there was seen a need for a large gun-armed destroyer to counter this specific threat. This was one of the few occasions when the British Admiralty purposefully developed a design to match a foreign design and like most moves in this direction, it was misplaced, in that the two types never ever met in action. However it did result in a very useful design which would serve the Royal Navy during the forthcoming conflict.

By late 1934, the new project, which was known initially as the 'V-Leader' (presumably after First World War precedents) was under active development and the staff requirements of the design can be briefly summarized as: LA armament of ten 4.7-inch; good communications facilities; 36 knots; endurance 5,500nm at 15 knots; torpedo outfit for night and low visibility; not greater than 1,850 tons. It was also hoped to use all or part of the 4.7-inch armament for long-range AA fire and to this end 40° elevation was considered desirable. In addition, the light armament requirements were for two of the new quadruple pom-poms or a mixture of pom-poms and .5in MG. The main purpose of the ship in this respect, however, was to provide AA cover for other units and not self-defence, i.e., long-range fire was needed. Unfortunately, while recognizing that effective AA fire required good control facilities, little had been done in this direction by the time that war broke out. Furthermore, 40° elevation was soon shown to be totally inadequate in wartime, particularly under dive-bomber attack.

The disposition of ten guns in five twin mountings presented some problems in a ship of destroyer size, the original suggestion being for three superimposed mountings forward of the bridge with the other pair superimposed aft. This naturally entailed an unacceptably high bridge structure which, while aiding gunnery matters, could produce tactical problems with the associated high silhouette. This arrangement was in fact employed for the 1936 programme AA cruisers of the *Dido* class.

As far as the torpedo outfit was concerned, various layouts were proposed including sided banks as in French destroyers, for example, and a novel quintuple arrangement whereby two fired one way and the other three tubes the opposite way! Actually, the torpedo outfit was almost of secondary consideration for the overall impression is that this ship was designed by and for HMS *Excellent*!

By 1935, more details of various design aspects had come to hand as development work moved from drawing-board to prototype construction. In particular, the new 4.7-inch twin mounting CP XIX came out 25 per cent over design weight, the ammunition casings for the new 4.7-inch gun Mk XII were also heavier than anticipated and Asdic installation would cost yet another nine tons. In the middle of the year, there were five main proposals being seriously considered:

(a) Five 4.7-inch twin (one between the funnels); eight .5in MG; 45,000shp=36 knots; 1,870tons (standard).

(b) & (c) As (a), but speed and displacement reduced to 35½ knots/1,850tons and 35 knots/1,812tons respectively.

(d) Four 4.7-inch twin; twelve .5in MG; 45,000shp=37 knots.

(e) As (a), but with No. 3 mounting replaced by a 2pdr pom-pom.

Yet another proposal in June saw the design with five twin guns, one set of power-operated quadruple tubes, 44,000shp, with three boilers in separate boiler rooms and the engine room divided longitudinally by a bulkhead.

There was some pressure to replace the fifth 4.7in mounting by an eight-barrelled 2pdr or two four-barrelled mountings which was a step in the right direction, but it was pointed out that the latter involved a weight of 55.7 tons as compared with 52.6 tons for an eight-barrelled mount and marginally less for the twin 4.7-inch. Nevertheless, it was soon agreed to drop the fifth 4.7-inch and replace it by a four-barrelled 2pdr, sited between the funnels. This design was approved in August 1935, but later the 2pdr between the funnels was deleted on displacement and field of fire grounds, the .5-inch machine-guns being fitted there instead.

The fire-control arrangements included separate director and rangefinder director towers, the former for low-angle use only, the latter being a rangefinder in LA use and a director R/F in HA use. There was no combined HA/LA tower available and its weight would probably have been excessive anyway. Nor was there any form of gyroscopic stable element fire control. However an AA predictor was fitted for the first time. Hydraulic power was supplied for train-

Above: *Afridi* in June 1938. (Wright & Logan) **Below:** *Nubian*. Like *Matabele* she has lost 'X' gun for a twin 4-inch. (IWM)

ing, elevation and ramming on the guns, the director and torpedo tubes also being power-worked.

Internally, the propulsion unit consisted of the by now standard three Admiralty 3-drum boilers, with a working pressure of only 300psi, there having been no serious moves to increase steam pressures since *Acheron*, at least in Royal Navy circles. The machinery arrangement was kept the same as previous classes, i.e., boiler rooms ahead of the engine room despite a discussion of the merits of the *Arethusa* (unit) arrangement. While this would have given a design with much better damage-control facilities, it would have necessitated an extra thirty or so feet on the length with a corresponding increase in displacement. As the upper limit on destroyer tonnage was 1,850 tons by Treaty definition, this course was not considered desirable.

Seven ships were ordered on 10 March 1936 and nine repeats in June of that year, by which time the design had been further modified by the adoption of a clipper bow. All except *Bedouin* were laid down before the end of the year. Like many designs, there were numerous problems and delays during construction and in particular, weight increases, some of an unforgivable magnitude, such as that for the ammunition hoists which came out at 26 tons instead of the estimated 3 tons! This pushed the displacement up to nearly 1,900 tons and reduced speed by 0.5 knots. Serious delays occurred also in the delivery of the twin mountings leading to later than anticipated completion dates.

Modifications Early on it was found necessary to stiffen the hull because of leaking problems and some difficulties were experienced with the turbine blading. The early losses, *Afridi* and *Gurkha*, had no modifications carried out, but the remainder lost 'X' gun and received a twin 4-inch Mk XIX mounting in lieu. The mainmast was cut down to a short pole and the height of the after funnel was reduced. Generally, four 20mm single Oerlikons were added, in the bridge wings and on the after shelter deck, but *Zulu* and *Sikh* initially received two single 2pdr in the bridge wings. As the war progressed, further Oerlikons replaced the .5in MGs and later, power-operated twin Oerlikons began to be fitted in the bridge wings, amidships and on the after deckhouse, although there was sometimes a mixture of power-operated twin and hand-worked singles as in *Tartar* in June 1944. All four survivors received the tall lattice mast in 1944. Radar fit was now 291 at the masthead, 293 atop the lattice mast, 285 on the rangefinder with HF/DF on a light lattice mast aft. While in the East Indies at least *Nubian* received two single 40mm Bofors amidships in lieu of the single 20mm guns, and finished the war with four power-operated 20mm twin equipments.

Service The sixteen *Tribal*s were formed into two flotillas as they commissioned, 4th and 6th, of which the former served with the Mediterranean Fleet, and the latter the Home Fleet. However, when it became clear that Italy would not be joining hostilities in September 1939, the 4th Flotilla was among those Mediterranean Fleet ships ordered to reinforce the Home Fleet. *Mohawk* was damaged by bombing in the Firth of Forth in October 1939 and out of action for nearly two months, but *Gurkha* struck an early blow when on 23 February 1940 she sank *U53* south of the Faroes. Both the 4th and 6th Flotillas participated in the Norway Campaign when *Gurkha* became the first of many losses, the victim of German bombers off Stavanger. *Bedouin, Punjabi, Eskimo* and *Cossack* took part in the Second Battle of Narvik on 13 April 1940, but *Eskimo* had her bows blown off by a torpedo from the German *Georg Thiele, Cossack* was badly hit by shellfire and *Punjabi* less seriously damaged. In addition, *Afridi* (and the French *Bison* q.v.) was sunk by Stuka dive-bombers while evacuating troops from Namsos. By June 1940, *Nubian* and *Mohawk* were serving in the eastern Mediterranean, the rest remaining with the Home Fleet. In the North Sea, *Tribal*s took part in strikes against German shipping traffic on the Norwegian coast and in the Lofoten Raid of March 1941. In May, *Somali* boarded the captured German weather-ship *München* retrieving valuable code documents and towards the end of that month, *Punjabi, Somali, Tartar, Mashona, Cossack, Sikh, Zulu* and *Maori* were all drawn into the hunt for *Bismarck* in the North Atlantic. However, only the ships of the 4th Flotilla (*Zulu, Sikh, Cossack* and *Maori*) with the Polish *Piorun* managed to get into action with the German battleship. It is doubtful if any torpedo hits were obtained in this confused night action, and air-support strikes launched by the Luftwaffe to aid the beleaguered battleship found and sank *Mashona* south-west of Ireland and badly damaged *Maori*. *Ashanti, Bedouin, Eskimo, Matabele, Punjabi* and *Somali*, all 6th Flotilla ships, served mostly in Arctic waters 1941/42, losing *Matabele*, torpedoed by *U454* in the Barents Sea with only two survivors from her company. Less than five months later, *Punjabi* was rammed and sunk by *King George V* in the Atlantic while screening the battleship in thick weather.

In Mediterranean waters, *Nubian* and *Mohawk* took part in the action off Calabria in July 1940, off Crete in August/September 1940, the Taranto Raid in November and in Aegean waters at the turn of the year. Both pariticipated in the Battle of Cape Matapan as units of the 1st Battle Squadron's screen, and in April 1941 as units of Force K destroyed an Italian convoy of five ships, escorted by three Italian destroyers. One of the Italian destroyers *Tarigo*, torpedoed and sank *Mohawk* in the early hours of 16 April. *Cossack, Sikh* and *Maori* also moved to the Mediterranean in mid 1941 after the *Bismarck* operation as did *Zulu* later. *Cossack*, however, was torpedoed by *U563* on 23/24 October

Below: *Punjabi*, with only two 20mm and radar 286 added. (IWM)

Below: *Matabele*. (IWM)

while in the Atlantic west of Gibraltar, escorting Convoy HG74. She sank later under tow on the 27th. *Maori* and *Sikh*, together with *Legion* and the Dutch *Isaac Sweers*, intercepted and sank the Italian cruisers *Da Barbiano* and *Di Giussano* off Cape Bon on 13 December without loss or damage to themselves. Two months later, *Maori*, lying in Grand Harbour, Malta, was hit by a bomb in the engine room, caught fire and blew up at her moorings. *Bedouin* was one of the Home Fleet destroyers detached to the Mediterranean for the purpose of Operation 'Harpoon'/'Vigorous', a double supply convoy to Malta in June 1942. South of Pantellaria an Italian cruiser and destroyer force led by *Eugenio* and *Montecuccoli* intercepted the convoy, but were driven off by *Bedouin, Marne, Matchless, Ithuriel* and *Patridge*, although both *Bedouin* and *Partridge* were damaged. *Bedouin* was completely disabled, but *Partridge* managed to get under way once more, towing her larger sister. When the Italian squadron later reappeared the tow was cast off as *Partridge* endeavoured to defend herself. Eventually it was an Italian aircraft which finished off *Bedouin* with a torpedo while *Partridge* escaped. The last losses in the Mediterranean were *Sikh* and *Zulu*, thrown away in a disastrous raid on Tobruk. *Sikh* was hit and disabled by shore batteries. *Zulu*, being unable to tow her to seaward, the unfortunate *Sikh* sank close inshore. *Zulu* herself was hit and sunk by bombers later that day. Only *Nubian* now remained in Mediterranean waters.

The Home Fleet ships, *Ashanti, Tartar, Somali* and *Eskimo*, continued to serve mainly in the Arctic on Russian convoy duties, with occasional detachment to the Mediterranean for important Malta convoys. Thus in August 1942, *Eskimo* and *Somali* covered 'Pedestal' then returned north for PQ18 followed by QP14 in September. On 20 September, *Somali* was hit in the engine room by a torpedo from *U703. Tartar* took her in tow but four days later in a rising gale, the torpedoed hulk folded up and sank. There were now only four survivors out of the original sixteen ships.

In 1943, *Tartar, Eskimo* and *Nubian* covered the 'Avalanche' landings at Salerno in September, but by mid 1944 all were back in home waters, *Ashanti, Tartar* and *Eskimo* forming part of the 10th Destroyer Flotilla which saw considerable action in the Channel Theatre before, during and after the Normandy landings. *Tartar* was damaged by German destroyers on one occasion during this period. With the end of the war in Europe in sight, the 10th Flotilla (*Eskimo, Nubian* and *Tartar*) were sent out to the East Indies, operating in the Indian Ocean off the coast of Malaya where they saw further action against light Japanese surface forces. These ships had, however, been fitted for Arctic service and were extremely unpleasant to live in in tropical conditions. All four were broken up soon after the end of the war.

J, K & N CLASSES

Ship	Builder	Laid Down	Launched	Commissioned	Fate
F00 *Jervis* (L)	Hawthorn Leslie	26 Aug 37	9 Sept 38	5 Aug 39	Arrived for breaking up 3 Jan 49
F22 *Jackal*	John Brown	24 Sept 37	25 Oct 38	13 April 39	Lost 12 May 42
F34 *Jaguar*	Denny	Nov 1937	22 Nov 38	12 Sept 39	Lost 26 Mar 42
F53 *Janus*	Swan Hunter	29 Sept 37	10 Nov 38	5 Aug 39	Lost 23 Jan 44
F61 *Javelin* (ex-*Kashmir*)	John Brown	11 Oct 37	21 Dec 38	10 June 39	Arrived for breaking up 17 June 49
F72 *Jersey*	S. White	28 Sept 37	26 Sept 38	28 April 39	Lost 4 May 41
F46 *Juno* (ex-*Jamaica*)	Fairfield	5 Oct 37	8 Dec 38	24 Aug 39	Lost 20 May 41
F85 *Jupiter*	Yarrow	20 Sept 37	27 Oct 38	16 June 39	Lost 27 Feb 42
– *Jubilant*	–	–	Cancelled		
F01 *Kelly* (L)	Hawthorn Leslie	26 Aug 37	25 Oct 38	23 Aug 39	Lost 23 May 41
F28 *Kandahar*	Denny	Jan 1938	21 Mar 39	10 Oct 39	Lost 20 Dec 41
F12 *Kashmir* (ex-*Javelin*)	Thornycroft	Oct 1937	4 April 39	26 Oct 39	Lost 23 May 41
F37 *Kelvin*	Fairfield	5 Oct 37	19 Jan 39	27 Nov 39	Arrived for breaking up 6 June 49
F45 *Khartoum*	Swan Hunter	27 Oct 37	6 Feb 39	6 Nov 39	C.T.L. 23 June 40
F50 *Kimberley*	Thornycroft	Jan 1938	1 June 39	21 Dec 39	Sold out 30 Mar 49
F64 *Kingston*	S. White	6 Oct 37	9 Jan 39	14 Sept 39	C.T.L. 11 April 42
F91 *Kipling*	Yarrow	20 Oct 37	19 Jan 39	12 Dec 39	Lost 11 May 42
G97 *Napier* (L) D13	Fairfield	26 July 39	22 May 40	11 Dec 40	RAN 1941
G25 *Nepal* (ex-*Norseman*)	Thornycroft	9 Sept 39	4 Dec 41	29 May 42	Arrived for breaking up 16 Jan 56
G65 *Nerissa*	John Brown	26 July 39	7 May 40	4 Nov 40	To Poland Oct 1940
G02 *Nestor*	Fairfield	26 July 39	9 July 40	12 Feb 41	Lost 15 June 42
G38 *Nizam*	John Brown	27 July 39	4 July 40	8 Jan 41	RAN 1941
G84 *Noble*	Denny	10 July 39	17 April 41	20 Feb 42	To Netherlands 11 Feb 42
G16 *Nonpareil*	Denny	22 May 40	26 May 41	30 Oct 42	To Netherlands 11 Feb 42
G49 *Norman*	Thornycroft	27 July 39	30 Oct 40	29 Sept 41	RAN 1941

(F changed to G 1940). D Pendant with US Pacific Fleet 1945.

Displacement: 1,690tons/1,717tonnes (1,965/1,996 Leaders) (standard); 2,330tons/2,367tonnes (full load).
Length: 356ft 6in/108.6m (oa); 348ft/106m (wl); 339ft 6in/103.4m (pp).
Beam: 35ft 8in/10.8m.
Draught: 9ft/2.7m (mean).
Machinery: two Admiralty 3-drum boilers; 2-shaft Parsons geared turbines.
Performance: 40,000shp; 36kts.
Bunkerage: 484tons/492tonnes.
Range: 5,500nm at 15kts.
Guns: six 4.7in Mk XII (3×2); four 2pdr (1×4, Mk VII); eight .5in MG (2×4).
Torpedoes: ten 21in (2×5).
Complement: 183 (Leaders 218).

Design The *Tribal* design had been subject to some criticism on the grounds that they were too large and overly gun-orientated. There was some feeling that a smaller ship armed with dual-purpose guns and a full outfit of torpedoes would suit tactical requirements better. However, there was disagreement over the question of dual-purpose main armament if ability to engage surface targets were thereby endangered. In fact there was no true DP gun available as the 60° 4.7-inch CP XVIII had proved unsatisfactory and the standard CP XVIII single 4.7-inch mounting allowed only 40° elevation. Due to severe problems in the manufacture and supply of the twin 4.7-inch for the *Tribal*s, there was no question of the 1935 programme ships receiving them and single had to be accepted with the possibility of their being replaced with twins later. The design would therefore ship four single mountings. Leading on from the demand for a torpedo carrier with ten torpedo tubes came the requirement for a low silhouette and a single funnel, which in turn implied a two-boiler layout if large uptake trunkings were not to clutter the upper deck space. This was entirely possible given the recent advances in boiler technology, but the Engineer-in-Chief raised objections on the grounds of boiler cleaning

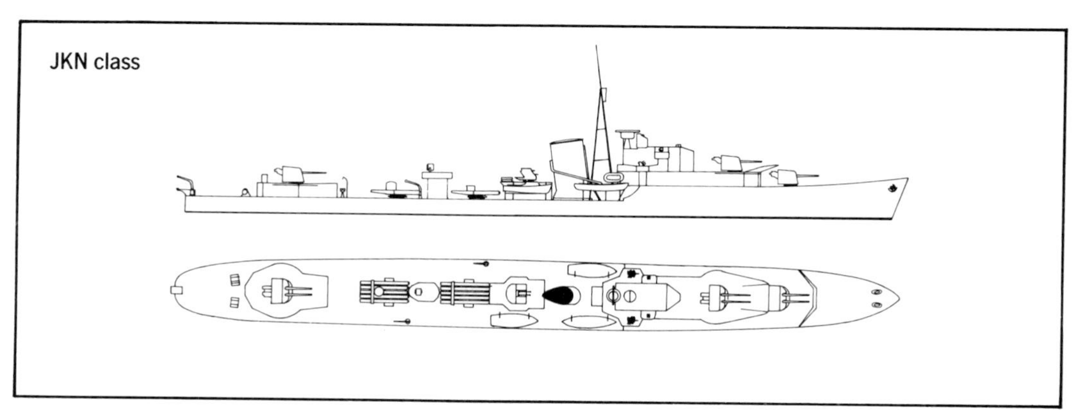

routines, which were hitherto based on three-boiler layouts. The question of power loss by a torpedo hit on the intermediate bulkhead seems to have received scant attention, possibly in line with Admiralty views that destroyers were expendable.

There were considerable doubts expressed as to the usefulness of the design as developed in the early stages (i.e., four single 4.7-inch, eight torpedo tubes), quite justifiably so in view of the lack of any extra fighting power over the *A* to *I* series, and the anti-aircraft defence was still inadequate. By mid 1936, single guns were deemed unacceptable and twin mountings substituted in lieu, two forward, one aft, allowing a shorter quarter deck. This released space for extra accommodation and in consequence, the leader could be made virtually identical in size with the destroyers. It was accepted, however, that because of the supply problem, ships were unlikely to complete with their full armament. The after gun, following a good deal of discussion, was to train through ahead and would therefore be incapable of astern fire between green 170° and red 170°. Unlike the CP XIX mountings in the *Tribal*s, which were turbo-hydraulic powered, the 1936 programme ships had electro-hydraulic power – a direct consequence of the final adoption of a two-boiler layout. To supply power in harbour and when no main steam was available, two diesel generators were fitted. The rangefinder director Mk II as fitted in the *Tribal*s for HA control was not, for some reason, given to the *J* class. They reverted to a separate director and rangefinder, the latter only supplying ranges for both LA and HA use to the former.

These destroyers were not only visually distinctive in that they had only a single funnel, but also in the basic method of their construction. For the first time since *Ardent*, built by Denny and commissioned on 21 February 1914, longitudinal framing was adopted for destroyers in lieu of the more common transverse framing. This meant that the longitudinal hull members were continuous and the transverse frames fitted over them instead of the other way round. 'D' steel was more sparingly used in these destroyers and welding only used on girders and deck plating.

The eight ships of the *J* class were ordered on 25 March 1937, *Jubilant* being cancelled because flotillas were now reduced to eight including the leader. Eight more of the *K* class were ordered in April. The *N* class were ordered in January 1940, size and cost of the *L* and *M* classes having forced a return to *J* dimensions.

Modifications In 1941, the after tubes were replaced by a single 4-inch HA Mk V and radar 286M was being fitted at the masthead, replaced later by radar 286P and, in 1942, radar 291. The original intention that the modified DCT should act as an HA director did not work out in practice and, as a result, it reverted to solely LA use. To take over the HA role, the original rangefinder had to be extensively modified turning it into a rangefinder director in its own right. Radar 285 was fitted to its roof.

Generally, about this time, four single Oerlikons were fitted, two abreast the searchlight platforms and two replacing the .5in MG, which in the meantime had been fitted with shields. As the war progressed, twin hand-worked Oerlikons replaced the singles abreast the searchlight and twin power-operated mountings in the bridge wings. The *N* class completed with 20mm guns except *Norman* which had .5in MGs. The after tubes were replaced, but often only nine torpedoes were carried as a weight-saving measure. Some units received an HF/DF aerial on a new mainmast aft, while in 1944, *Jervis* and *Javelin* were fitted with a tall lattice mast carrying radar 293 and HF/DF at the truck – the 291 radar being transferred to a new main-mast aft. The searchlight was removed. The two *N* class transferred to the Netherlands were similarly fitted.

Modifications to the *K* class followed the lines of that for the *J* class as did the *N* class. Although not a modification, it should be noted that the after 4.7-inch guns on this latter class trained through dead astern and thus had the blind sector forward. By the end of the war, *Nizam* had a single 40mm in lieu of the searchlight with twin power-operated 20mm abreast it and had landed the after tubes.

Below: *Jupiter* running trials. (Author's Collection)

Right: *Jervis* at the end of the war. Note radars, lattice mast and power-operated 20mm guns. (IWM)

Service The *J* class commissioned for service with the 7th Destroyer Flotilla and were based upon the Humber at the outbreak of war as the 5th Flotilla. *Juno* and *Jersey* were surprised by two German destroyers *Lody* and *Geise* while patrolling off Cromer on 7 December 1939 when *Jersey* was torpedoed and very badly damaged. She was under repair until the end of September 1940. The flotilla participated in the Norway Campaign of April 1940 before moving south to Plymouth on Channel patrol duties. Here their main task was to intercept and sink German destroyers which were operating minelaying sorties off the south coast. They failed to sink any German ships and instead suffered themselves when, in an action with a force of three enemy destroyers in November 1940, *Javelin* was torpedoed twice but remained afloat very seriously damaged. She was out of action for more than a year.

Italy's entry into the war in June 1940 necessitated reinforcing the weak Mediterranean Fleet to which *Jervis, Janus* and *Juno* were dispatched. *Jaguar*, repaired after bomb damage at Dunkirk, followed as did *Jersey* and *Javelin* their action damage having been repaired. The flotilla was active throughout the length and breadth of the Mediterranean, but *Jersey* was mined off the entrance to Grand Harbour, Malta in May 1941 and *Juno* lost to air attack off Crete later in the month. When *Prince of Wales* and *Repulse* were dispatched east in 1941, *Jupiter* was ordered to Colombo in November to join their screen and thus left the Mediterranean and did not return. *Jackal* was damaged by an aerial torpedo in December 1941 and *Jervis* indirectly by Italian human torpedoes at Alexandria the same month. *Janus* was badly damaged by French *contre-torpilleurs* off Sidon on 9 June 1941. *Jaguar* was torpedoed and sunk by *U652* north of Sollum in March 1942. In May, *Jervis, Jackal, Kipling* and *Lively* took part in a strike against Axis convoy routes on the North-Africa coast with disastrous results. All except *Jervis* were sunk by German bombers on the 11th, *Jackal* being finished off by *Jervis* the following day. *Jervis, Janus* and *Javelin* saw the Mediterranean campaign through to 1944 when, at Anzio, *Janus* was sunk by an aerial torpedo and *Jervis* damaged by a glider bomb. Both survivors returned to Home Waters after Anzio and took part in 'Overlord'. *Javelin*, now a unit of the 10th Flotilla too, participated in that flotilla's action against the Germans' 8th Destroyer Flotilla off Brittany on 8–9 June 1944, when *ZH1* and *Z32* were sunk.

The lone unit in the Far East, *Jupiter*, sank the Japanese submarine *I60* off Krakatoa on 17 January 1942 when she was part of the 'China Force'. *Jupiter* was present at the Java Sea battle, but on 27 February, she was mined and sank on the 28th, north of Java before the final engagement and loss of the two Dutch cruisers.

The *K* class formed the 5th Flotilla and was intended for service with the Mediterranean Fleet, but war broke out before they were commissioned and in fact the flotilla was kept in home waters with the Home Fleet in 1939. *Kelly* was damaged by a magnetic mine in the autumn of 1939, repairs taking until December. *Kashmir* and *Kingston* with *Icarus* sank *U35* in November. Several of the class took part in the Norway Campaign, but only *Kimberley* participated in the Second Battle of Narvik. In May 1940, *Kelly* was hit by a torpedo from the German *S31* which flooded both boiler rooms and almost sank the ship. *Bulldog* managed to tow her for 91 hours back to the Tyne where repairs lasted until mid December 1940.

Kandahar, Khartoum and *Kingston* were in the Red Sea by June 1940, where they engaged and sank the Italian submarine *Toriccelli*, but the latter's gunfire damaged *Khartoum*. Fires spread and after internal explosions the destroyer had to be beached near Perim as a total loss. *Kimberley* and *Kingston* also went out to the Red Sea later in 1940, seeing action during the Abbysinia Campaign. By April 1940, all seven survivors were in Mediterranean waters where *Kandahar, Kimberley* and *Kingston* took part in the evacuation of Greece in that month while the remainder operated with Force H. All were committed to the evacuation of Crete in May, where *Kelly* and *Kashmir* were lost to Stukas of I/St.G.2 and *Kelvin* was damaged. *Kandahar, Kimberley* and *Kingston* supported Allied operations in Syria in June 1941 and then operated with the Fleet, mostly in support of Malta convoys. While operating with Force K in December 1941, *Kandahar* struck a mine east of Tripoli and sank with heavy loss of life. *Kipling* sank *U75* in the same month, but in February 1942, *Kimberley* had her stern blown off by

Below: *Jupiter* with early war alterations. (Real Photos)

U77. She remained afloat but was under repair at Bombay until January 1944. In March 1942, *Kelvin, Kingston* and *Kipling* were in action at the second Battle of Sirte where *Kingston* suffered damage as a result of near misses. While in dry dock at Malta for repairs, *Kingston* was hit by bombs, rolled over and became a total loss. Next month *Kipling* was sunk by bombers as described above.

Kelvin served in the North Africa Campaign in 1943 before returning home to take part in 'Overlord' in June 1944 in which the repaired *Kimberley* also took part. The latter ship returned to the Mediterranean for the Invasion of southern France in August 1944 then went to the Adriatic before finishing the war in the Aegean. *Kelvin* also returned to the Meditteranean in December 1944 where she remained until July 1945.

Of the *N* class, *Napier, Nepal, Nestor, Nizam* and *Norman* were manned by the Royal Australian Navy (q.v.), *Nerissa* transferred to Poland and was renamed *Piorun* (q.v.) on completion, while both *Noble* and *Nonpareil* were completed as the Royal Netherlands Navy ships *Van Galen* and *Tjerk Hiddes* respectively. Thus none of the class were RN-manned until 1945 when *Napier* was exchanged for *Quality* and sailed home for the UK with *Nepal, Nizam* and *Norman*. *Piorun* returned to the White Ensign in September 1946 and was renamed *Noble*, but the two Dutch destroyers were permanently transferred.

Above: *Kimberley*. **(IWM) Below:** *Nepal*, with full radar outfit, a 4inch gun and four 20mm. (IWM)

L & M CLASSES

Ship	Builder	Laid Down	Launched	Commissioned	Fate
F99 *Laforey* (L)	Yarrow	1 Mar 39	15 Feb 41	26 Aug 41	Lost 30 Mar 44
F87 *Lance*	Yarrow	1 Mar 39	28 Nov 40	13 May 41	C.T.L. 22 Oct 42
F63 *Larne*	Cammell Laird	18 Oct 38	8 July 40	18 Feb 41	Lost 17 Jan 42
F74 *Legion*	Hawthorn Leslie	1 Nov 38	26 Dec 39	19 Dec 40	C.T.L. 25 Mar 42
F55 *Lightning*	Hawthorn Leslie	15 Nov 38	22 April 40	28 May 41	Lost 12 Mar 43
F40 *Lively*	Cammell Laird	20 Dec 38	28 Jan 41	20 July 41	Lost 11 May 42
F32 *Lookout*	Scott's	23 Nov 38	4 Nov 40	30 Jan 42	Sold out 6 Jan 48
F15 *Loyal*	Scott's	23 Nov 38	8 Oct 41	31 Oct 42	Arrived for breaking up 5 Aug 48
G14 *Milne* (L)	Scott's	24 Jan 40	30 Dec 41	6 Aug 42	To Turkey 16 Aug 57
G23 *Marksman*	Scott's	18 Aug 41	28 July 42	8 April 43	Lost 25 Feb 44
G44 *Martin*	Parsons M.S.T. Co.*	23 Oct 39	30 Oct 40	2 Dec 41	Lost 10 Nov 42
G52 *Matchless*	Stephen	14 Sept 40	4 Sept 41	26 Feb 42	To Turkey 16 Aug 57
G73 *Meteor*	Stephen	14 Sept 40	3 Nov 41	12 Aug 42	To Turkey 16 Aug 57
G86 *Musketeer*	Fairfield	7 Dec 39	2 Dec 41	18 Sept 42	Arrived for breaking up 6 Dec 55
G90 *Myrmidon*	Fairfield	7 Dec 39	2 Mar 42	5 Dec 42	To Poland 1942
G35 *Marne*	Parsons M.S.T. Co.*	23 Oct 39	30 Oct 40	2 Dec 41	To Turkey 16 Aug 57

(F changed to G 1940). *Hull sub-contracted to V.A. (Tyne).

Displacement: 1,920tons/1,950tonnes (Leaders 1,935/1,966) (standard); 2,661tons/2,703tonnes (full load).
Length: 362ft 6in/110.5m (oa); 354ft/107.9m (wl); 345ft 6in/105.3m (pp).
Beam: 37ft/11.2m.
Draught: 10ft/3.05m (mean).
Machinery: two Admiralty 3-drum boilers; 2-shaft Parsons geared turbines.
Performance: 48,000shp; 36kts.
Bunkerage: 567tons/576tonnes.
Range: 5,500nm at 15kts.
Guns: six 4.7in QF Mk XI (3×2); four 2pdr (1×4); eight .5in MG (2×4).
Torpedoes: eight 21in (2×4).
Complement: 221.

Design When the destroyers for the 1937 programme were under consideration, there was a demand for the main armament to be in weatherproof mountings. Japanese and American destroyers had already adopted such mountings and there was no doubt that efficiency was gained thereby. The *Tribals* and *J*-class destroyers both had their proponents and antagonists with the result that there was no clear way forward in design terms for the next destroyer design. Discussions ranged over a large spectrum of sketch designs from an improved *J* up to a poor man's light cruiser with six 5.25-inch guns. Cost and size, together with a poor opinion from the staff, killed the latter project and opinions were sought from the Fleet Commands. This resulted in a modified *J*-type design being suggested with a reduced torpedo outfit carrying two four-barrelled pom-poms. Ten torpedo tubes were not generally liked at sea. However, two pom-poms would increase the length unacceptably and in the end the question was resolved in favour of retaining two banks of tubes albeit quadruple.

The main armament calibre remained 4.7-inch but a new gun was adopted. This was the 4.7-inch

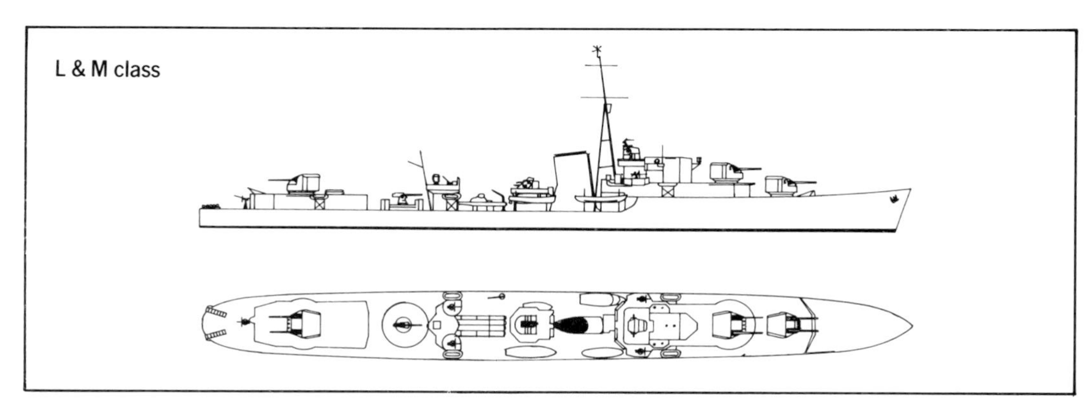

Above: *Laforey*. (Author's Collection) **Below:** *Lance*, another AA ship. Note she retains the .5in MGs. (IWM)

QF Mk XI, a 50-calibre weapon firing a 62lb shell. It had a marginally lower muzzle velocity than the Mk XII, but had a range of 21,240 yards at 45°. In its twin Mk XX mounting it had an elevation of 50° and each gun could be elevated separately. Training, ramming and shell hoists were hydraulic, but elevation was manual. Unfortunately, the mounting was complicated and took longer to manufacture than the twin Mk XIX and in consequence, there were delays in supply which led to half the class not receiving the designed armament.

A combined rangefinder LA/HA director (Mk IV TP) was fitted, a new departure for British destroyers, and provision was also made for a director for the 2pdr, although none was yet available. In fact there were also difficulties anticipated in the supply of the 2pdr quadruples themselves and it was expected that ships might have to complete without them. Not only were there production problems, but also the inevitable weight increases; the director was at least a ton over weight and the tubes 2½ tons. The gun mountings themselves increased by nearly ten tons (to 34 tons) and it was suggested that twin 4-inch HA guns be shipped in lieu, to save top-weight and improve stability. In July 1940, approval was given to arm *Lance, Larne, Lively* and *Legion* with four twin 4-inch Mk XVI, but this was a reflection of 4.7-inch supply problems rather than anything else. They also had the lighter rangefinder-director Mk V**.

The heavy gun-houses and other equipment added during and after completion resulted in a significant increase in top-weight and it was necessary to compensate for any further additions in service.

The *M* class of the 1938 programme were, after some disagreement, ordered as repeat *L* class, but all received their designed six 4.7-inch guns.

Modifications For gunnery purposes radar 285 was fitted to all atop the director while fitting out, but no other radar was fitted to *Legion* as completed. Ships completing in 1941 received radar 286M at the masthead, later replaced by radar 286PQ by December 1942. *Lookout* and some later units completed with radar 290 at the masthead, but *Marne* still had her 286 set in November 1942. The 4.7-inch gun ships generally completed with a single 4-inch gun replacing the after torpedo tubes. Early units completed with two quadruple .5in machine-guns in the bridge wings and a twin power-operated mounting on the quarter deck, but provision had been made for fitting six single 20mm as they became available, replacing the .5in MGs and being fitted also abreast the searchlight platform and on the quarter deck. By 1944, power-operated twin 20mm were being fitted in the bridge wings and abreast the searchlight platform with two singles on the quarter deck making ten in all. Tall lattice masts were fitted in some of the survivors, including *Matchless* and *Milne* upon which radar 273 was fitted, while *Musketeer* had 271 in lieu of the searchlight. By the end of the war, a 'cheese' radar aerial had been fitted in lieu of the 273 on the foremast, but 291 was still retained.

Service The greater part of the operational career of the *L*-class destroyers was spent in the Mediterranean theatre, unlike the *M* class which, being 'arcticized' spent much of their lives in northern waters. The first three to complete were *Legion, Gurkha* (*Larne* was renamed before completion) and *Lance*, all 4-inch gunned ships which served initially in home waters. *Lance* took part in the preliminary moves of the *Bismarck* hunt and *Legion* in the Lofoten raid, but by the middle of 1941, joined by *Lively*, the AA destroyers formed the 13th Destroyer Flotilla in the Mediterranean. Here they operated for much of the time with Force K from Malta, *Legion* assisting in the sinking of two Italian cruisers in December 1941. 1942, however, saw all four destroyers sunk, the first being *Gurkha*, torpedoed by *U133* north of Sollum in January. In March, *Legion* was irreparably damaged by bombing at Malta and *Lively* sunk by Ju 88s south of Crete in May. Finally, *Lance* too was wrecked by bombs at Malta in October. She was towed home in 1944 and broken up in June.

All the 4.7-inch gun units went to the Mediterranean as the 19th Destroyer Flotilla, but *Lookout* escorted Arctic Convoy PQ12 before moving south. Apart from a detachment to the Indian Ocean in April–May 1942 (*Lafforey, Lightning* and *Lookout*) service was entirely in the Mediterranean theatre. *Lightning* was torpedoed and sunk by the German *S55* off Bone in January 1943, but the other three saw action at Salerno (where *Lafforey* was hit five times by shore batteries) and Anzio. During this period, *Laforey* assisted in the sinking of the Italian submarine *Ascianghi* and *U223*, but the latter torpedoed and sank the destroyer before she herself sank. *Lookout* served in the landings in southern France, then operated in the Ligurian Sea where with *Meteor* she sank the German *TA24* and *TA29*. *Loyal* served the remainder of the war on the other coast of Italy in the Adriatic.

Of the *M* class, *Marksman* was renamed *Mahratta* and *Myrmidon* transferred to Poland before completion, being renamed *Orkan*. Their service was mainly in the Arctic on Russian convoy duties from 1942, *Matchless* having to torpedo and sink the badly damaged cruiser *Trinidad* in May 1942. *Marne* and *Matchless* both went to the Mediterranean for important Malta convoys for a couple of months in the summer of 1942 but soon returned to the Arctic. *Marne, Martin* and *Onslaught* caught and sank the minelayer *Ulm* in the Barents Sea during August. Moved temporarily south for the landings in North Africa in November 1942, *Martin* was torpedoed and sunk by *U431* north of Algiers. Two days later, *Marne* had her stern blown off by a torpedo from *U515* but remained afloat and was repaired.

Above: *Lively*, completed as an AA destroyer. (IWM) **Below:** *Mahratta*, Note power-operated 20mm and single 20mm. (IWM)

Below: *Musketeer* in October 1945. Note fire control radar and Type 271 aft. She still has the single 4-inch HA gun. (Pavia)

During 1943, *Matchless*, *Milne* and *Musketeer* operated in the Atlantic with support groups and at the close of the year were, with *Meteor* involved in the interception of *Scharnhorst* when *Matchless* and *Musketeer* got into action with the enemy ship at the close of the engagement.

In 1944, Arctic duties continued now as the 3rd Destroyer Flotilla, *Meteor* with *Whitehall* sinking *U314* in February. All remained on this task until the end of 1944 when *Meteor* and *Musketeer* went to the Mediterranean for final mopping-up operations around Italy.

Right: *Marne* fitted with a lattice mast and radar 276. (IWM)

O CLASS

Ship	Builder	Laid Down	Launched	Commissioned	Fate
G17 *Onslow* (ex-*Pakenham*) (L)	John Brown	15 Jan 40	11 Mar 41	20 Sept 41	To Pakistan 30 Sept 49
G39 *Obdurate**	Denny	25 April 40	19 Feb 42	30 Sept 42	Arrived for breaking up 30 Nov 64
G48 *Obedient**	Denny	22 May 40	30 April 42	3 Oct 42	Arrived for breaking up 19 Oct 62
G29 *Offa*	Fairfield	1 July 40	31 Mar 41	8 Oct 41	To Pakistan 3 Nov 49
G04 *Onslaught* (ex-*Pathfinder*)	Fairfield	14 Jan 41	9 Oct 41	19 June 42	To Pakistant 6 Mar 51
G80 *Opportune**	Thornycroft	28 Mar 40	21 Jan 42	14 Aug 42	Arrived for breaking up 25 Nov 55
G66 *Oribi* (ex-*Observer*)	Fairfield	15 Jan 40	14 Jan 41	5 July 41	To Turkey 1946
G98 *Orwell**	Thornycroft	16 May 40	2 April 42	7 Oct 42	Arrived for breaking up 28 June 65

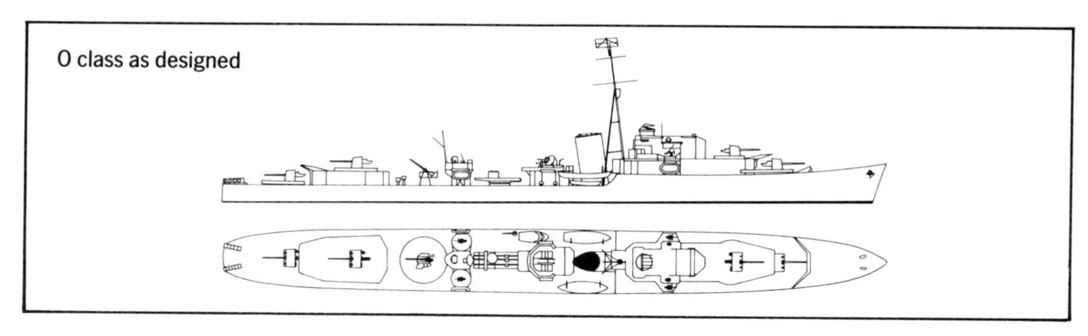

O class as designed

Left: *Offa* in 1944 with lattice mast. (MOD)

Displacement: 1,610tons/1,636tonnes (standard); 2,220tons/2,255tonnes (full load).
Length: 345ft/105m (oa); 337ft/102.7m (wl); 328ft 9in/100.2m (pp).
Beam: 35ft/10.6m.
Draught: 9ft/2.74m (mean).
Machinery: two Admiralty 3-drum boilers; 2-shaft Parsons geared turbines.
Performance: 40,000shp; 36kts.
Bunkerage: 484tons/492tonnes.
Range: 3,850nm at 20kts.
Guns: four 4.7in QF Mk IX (4×1); four 2pdr (1×4); four 20mm (4×1).
Torpedoes: eight 21in (2×4).
Mines: 60 (* only).
Complement: 175 (Leader 217, *Packenham* 228).

Design With the prospect of another war breaking out in the near future, the Admiralty in 1938 considered how best to produce the large numbers of destroyers which obviously would be needed. It was believed that sufficient destroyers were available for Fleet work, but that there was a requirement for a 'general duties' type of Intermediate destroyer between a 'Fleet' and a *Hunt*. The latter were a well-armed design, but possibly too slow to fulfil some destroyer functions. This intermediate type was to have good seaworthiness, strength and sufficient but not exaggerated speed, armed with whatever guns could be made available quickly. Anti-submarine work would form a major part of their role and a good anti-aircraft armament was required.

There was no dual-purpose main calibre gun available, no stabilized gunnery system or HA director so that the provision of an effective AA outfit was problematical from the equipment point of view. Added to this, the dangers of air attack had still not been fully appreciated by certain sections of the Naval Staff, as evidenced by such comments as 'eye-shooting weapons . . . are adequate' referring to close-range AA defence. Thus the staff opinion that a high-angle capacity for main armament was not a destroyer requirement, reflected these views, but even if it had been a requirement it could not have been fulfilled due to the lack of suitable equipment. Obviously the dangers of dive-bomber attack were yet to be fully appreciated, the main threats being considered to be high-level bombing or torpedo attack by aircraft. The former was notoriously inaccurate and it was felt that to fit a good HA capacity at the expense of LA use would be misplaced. However, the torpedo was a serious threat and it was quite possible that the dive-bomber would become so. To counter these threats, the best solution was held to be multiple pom-poms.

The initial result of all these deliberations was a design with four or five 4.7-inch in twin or single mountings with 40° elevation, i.e., a reversion to the Mk IX gun on CP XVIII mounting (giving barrage fire against torpedo planes), at least quadruple pom-pom with director, eight tubes and capable of 36 knots. This was really only an *A* to *I* design with a pom-pom, because twin mountings could not be accommodated and single mountings were available.

Internally, the *J*-class machinery layout was adopted and in fact standardized for the war period. With a displacement of 1,610 tons (standard), four 4.7-inch guns and a speed of 33 knots in the deep condition, the term 'Intermediate type' rather lost its meaning, and this layout was in fact to become the basis for the layout of all the destroyers built under the War Emergency Programme. This class was known as the '1st Emergency Flotilla', orders being placed on 3 September 1939.

By the time of the fall of France, only a few of the class had been laid down. The serious danger of the dive-bomber had by now been fully demonstrated and there was disquiet at the probability of completing the sixteen new ships of the *O* and *P* classes with only 40° elevation to their main armament. It had been intended to deploy these ships in the Western Approaches where, in 1939, there was no air threat, but the collapse of France completely altered matters. In view of this situation the possibility of their rearming with four twin 4-inch 80° mountings was mooted. Unfortunately, no twin mountings were available, most having been earmarked for the *Hunts* so that singles had to be accepted in lieu. In February 1941, approval was given for *Onslow, Onslaught* and the six *P* class to arm with five 4-inch HA Mk V and one set of tubes. Then, in order to create at least one homogeneous class, *Onslow* and *Onslaught* exchanged names with *Pakenham* and *Pathfinder*. In the end, four *O*s (*Opportune, Obedient, Obdurate* and *Orwell*) also received the 4-inch outfit and had also been converted to minelayers while under construction. These however generally retained eight torpedo tubes, while the four 4.7-inch gunned ships had a 4-inch in lieu of the after tubes.

Modifications Radar 285 was fitted to the HA director tower Mk V** and radar 286 at the masthead. The usual sequence of radar updates was carried out, with 290 and later 291, superseding the 286. *Offa* landed her searchlight to fit a trial radar 272 lantern in February 1943, and at least *Oribi* was similarly treated. Four single 20mm Oerlikon were added, in the bridge wings and abreast the searchlight platform. Power-operated twin Oerlikons were to replace the singles, but this may not have been carried out. Two single 20mm were fitted on the main deck abreast the forward end of the after shelter deck in some minelayers including *Obedient*.

Lattice masts were fitted, *Onslow* receiving the first in the fleet during April 1943 after repairs to damage received in the Barents Sea in December 1942. *Oribi* did not receive a lattice mast and was the only unit to retain the single 4-inch throughout the war. HF/DF was fitted on a pole mast aft.

Service Almost the entire war service of the *O*-class destroyers was in northern waters. *Oribi* was the first to complete and was very briefly deployed to the Mediterranean before returning home to participate in the Lofoten raid of December 1941 with her sisters *Onslow* and *Offa*. 1942 almost entirely consisted of Russian convoy work except that *Onslow* deployed to the Mediterranean to reinforce the Mediterranean Fleet for an important Malta convoy in the summer of that year. At the close of 1942, *Onslow, Obdurate, Obedient* and *Orwell* fought off an attack on their convoy in the Barents Sea by *Admiral Hipper* and *Lützow* when the first three received damage.

In the spring of 1943, the flotilla was deployed to the Atlantic forming part of the 3rd and 5th Support Groups to assist in the U-boat war then reaching its peak. *Oribi* rammed and damaged *U125* which was finished off by *Snowflake* in May 1943. *Offa* went to the Mediterranean for the Sicily and Salerno landings in the summer of 1943. *Onslow, Onslaught, Opportune* and *Orwell* were involved in the *Scharnhorst* operation of December 1943, but only *Opportune* saw action.

Service in the Arctic remained the priority into 1944 and *Onslaught* sank *U472* in March of that year. *Obdurate* was badly damaged by an acoustic torpedo while escorting JW56 early in 1944 and spent most of the remainder of the war under repair. Serving as the 17th Destroyer Flotilla, all except *Opportune* took part in the Normandy landings before returning north, finishing the war once more on Russian convoys.

Above: *Orwell*. One of the 4-inch *O*s. Note 271 radar amidships. (IWM)

P CLASS

Ship	Builder	Laid Down	Launched	Commissioned	Fate
G06 *Pakenham* (ex-*Onslow*) (L)	Hawthorn Leslie	6 Feb 40	28 Jan 41	4 Feb 42	Lost 10 April 43
G69 *Paladin*	John Brown	22 July 40	11 June 41	12 Dec 41	Arrived for breaking up 25 Oct 62
G41 *Panther*	Fairfield	15 July 40	28 May 41	12 Dec 41	Lost 9 Oct 43
G30 *Partridge*	Fairfield	3 June 40	5 Aug 41	22 Feb 42	Lost 18 Dec 42
G10 *Pathfinder*	Hawthorn Leslie	5 Mar 40	10 April 41	13 April 42	C.T.L. 11 Feb 45
G77 *Penn*	V.A. (Tyne)	26 Dec 39	12 Feb 41	10 Feb 42	Sold out 31 Jan 50
G56 *Petard*	V.A. (Tyne)	26 Dec 39	27 Mar 41	14 June 42	Scrapped 1967
G93 *Porcupine*	V.A. (Tyne)	26 Dec 39	10 June 41	31 Aug 42	C.T.L. 9 Dec 42

Technical details as *O* Class (designed)

Design These ships were repeat *O* class, armed with 4-inch guns as described previously, orders being placed on 2 October 1939. By the time they had completed, the 4-inch gun in lieu of the after tubes had been landed and the tubes reinstated, but some did retain the 4-inch. Like the *O* class, 'Y' gun had no shield except in *Paladin* and *Pakenham* aboard which No. 3 gun was the unshielded one.

Modifications Generally as *O* class. *Petard* was

refitted late in 1944 and emerged in February 1945 with a lattice mast, radar 293, radar 291 aft and two twin 4-inch Mk XIX in Nos. '2' and '3' positions. Both banks of tubes were retained.

Service The first two to complete, *Paladin* and *Panther*, went to the Eastern Fleet and were joined there in April 1942 by *Pakenham* for the Madagascar operations. In the course of this operation, *Panther*, together with *Active*, sank the Vichy French submarine *Monge*. By the summer of 1942, the flotilla had moved to the Mediterranean for Malta convoy duties, *Partridge* being badly damaged in action with Italian cruisers and destroyers in June. *Porcupine* was torpedoed by *U602* on 9 December 1942 in the western Mediterranean, being almost broken in half. She was brought into port, declared a constructional total loss, cut in half and each half shored up, then towed home to the UK. Laid up for the rest of the war, the ship was sold in May 1946 and a year later towed to Devonport and broken up. In the same month as *Porcupine* was lost, *Partridge* too was torpedoed and sunk by *U565* west of Oran.

Pathfinder and *Panther* served in the North Atlantic in 1942–43, the former sinking *U162* in the Caribbean south of Barbados in September 1942, assisted by *Quentin* and *Vimy*. In 1943, *Pathfinder* also accounted for *U203* and *U456*. *Penn* was also by this time in the North Atlantic with the 3rd Support Group. *Pakenham* and *Petard* served briefly in the Indian Ocean early in 1943, then went to the Mediterranean where *Pakenham* was almost immediately lost. She and *Paladin* engaged an Italian convoy escorted by four torpedo-boats southwest of Marsala. Two of the torpedo-boats shepherded the convoy away to safety, while *Cigno* and *Cassiopea* fought off the British destroyers. Although the former was sunk and the latter badly damaged, they had damaged *Pakenham* so severely that she had to be abandoned.

The five survivors were gathered together in the Mediterranean in July 1943 for the invasion of Sicily and *Petard* was at Salerno, then in the Aegean. *Panther*, also in the Aegean, was sunk by Stukas in the Scarpanto Channel in October that year.

1944 saw what remained of the class in the Indian Ocean with the Eastern Fleet. *Petard* sank the Japanese submarine *I27* in February and the rest of the year was taken up with the various carrier raids and strikes against the coasts of Burma and Malaya, operating as the 16th Division. On 11 February 1945, *Pathfinder* was very badly damaged off Ramree Island. After makeshift repairs she steamed home and was laid up, being finally used for bombing trials before being broken up. *Penn* served only very briefly post-war, but *Paladin* and *Petard* were converted to frigates and lasted until the early 1960s.

Top right: *Petard,* lacking all radar. (Real Photos)

Right: *Penn.* (Real Photos)

Q CLASS

Ship	Builder	Laid Down	Launched	Commissioned	Fate
G09 *Quilliam* (L)	Hawthorn Leslie	19 Aug 40	29 Nov 41	22 Oct 42	To Netherlands Nov 1945
G11 *Quadrant* D14	Hawthorn Leslie	24 Sept 40	28 Feb 42	26 Nov 42	To RAN 1945
G45 *Quail*	Hawthorn Leslie	30 Sept 41	1 June 42	7 Jan 43	Lost 18 June 44
G62 *Quality* D18	Swan Hunter*	10 Oct 40	6 Oct 41	7 Sept 42	To RAN 1945
G70 *Queenborough*	Swan Hunter*	6 Nov 40	16 Jan 42	10 Dec 42	To RAN 1945
G78 *Quentin*	S. White	25 Sept 40	5 Nov 41	15 April 42	Lost 2 Dec 42
G81 *Quiberon* D20	S. White	4 Oct 40	31 Jan 42	22 July 42	To RAN
G92 *Quickmatch* D21	S. White	6 Feb 41	11 April 42	30 Sept 42	To RAN

(D pendants when serving with US Pacific Fleet 1945). *Engined by Wallsend Slipway Co.

Displacement: 1,705tons/1,732tonnes (standard); 2,424tons/2,462tonnes (full load).
Length: 358ft 3in/109.2m (oa); 348ft/106m (wl); 339ft 6in/103.4m (pp).
Beam: 35ft 8in/10.9m.
Draught: 9ft 6in/2.89m (mean).
Machinery: two Admiralty 3-drum boilers; 2-shaft Parsons geared turbines.
Performance: 40,000shp; 36kts.
Bunkerage: 615tons/625tonnes.
Range: 4,680nm at 20kts.
Guns: four 4.7in QF Mk IX (4×1); four 2pdr (1×4); six 20mm (6×1).
Torpedoes: eight 21in (2×4).
Complement: 175 (Leader 225).

Design The *Q* class, or 3rd Emergency Flotilla, was essentially a repeat *J* class armed with four single 4.7-inch on 40° mountings, as these were easier to provide than twins. They could in fact have been later taken from earlier destroyers which landed one or two 4.7-inch guns for escort duties. For fire control a separate DCT and R/F Director Mk II(W) were fitted. Quadruple tubes were adopted and internally endurance was increased by converting one of the forward magazine spaces to an oil bunker. The final design provided for six 20mm

Above: *Queenborough.* (Swan Hunter)

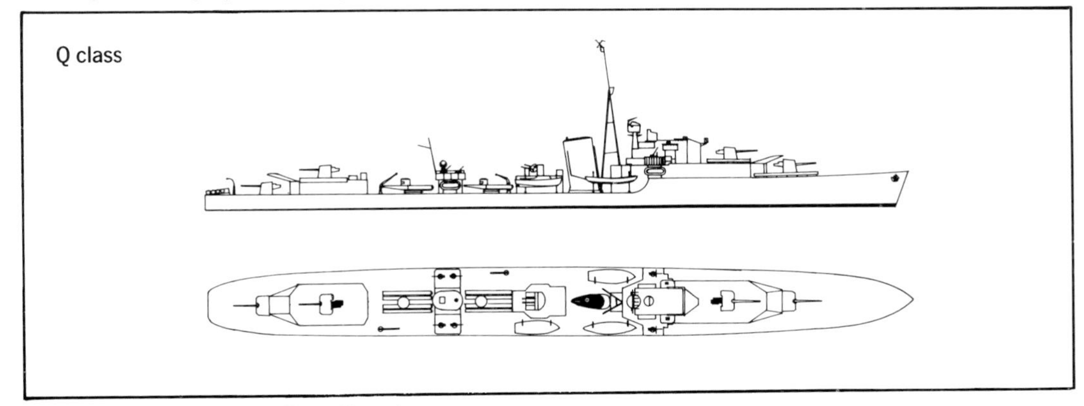

Below: *Quality,* as completed. (Swan Hunter)

Oerlikons and no .5in MG, in addition to the 2pdr quadruple pom-pom. Two of the 20mm were in the bridge wings and four around the searchlight platform. Although it was intended to substitute a 4-inch HA for the after tubes, by the time these ships were fitting out, the value of such a gun was in question and was not in fact fitted.

Eight ships were ordered in December 1939, but because of other priorities, due to losses at and before Dunkirk work was suspended in May 1940 and not resumed until September. When construction did recommence, air raid damage in the yards further delayed completion. On completion, three, *Quiberon, Quickmatch* and *Quality*, were manned by the RAN but administered by the Royal Navy.

Modifications These destroyers completed with radar 285, 290/291 and Oerlikons. Few further modifications were made, except radar 272 had been fitted amidships in lieu of the searchlight in at least *Quality* by 1944. Lattice masts were not fitted. HF/DF was added on a pole mast aft. *Quail* had received twin 20mm in the bridge wings before her loss.

Service By the time that the first ship, *Quentin*, completed in April 1942, the main theatre of British naval operations was in the Mediterranean and it was in this area that these ships saw much of their initial service. *Quentin* took part in 'Pedestal' in August 1942, but then briefly went to the Caribbean with *Pathfinder* (q.v.). Operating with *Quiberon* she then saw further Mediterranean service until, December 1942, when the two destroyers with three cruisers decimated an Italian convoy and one of its escorting destroyers (*Folgore*). While returning to base, *Quentin* was hit and sunk by a torpedo launched by an attacking aircraft north of Algiers.

Quilliam and *Quail* went to South Africa in early 1943 for the Eastern Fleet but almost immediately were recalled to the Mediterranean where they and *Queenborough* were at the landings in Sicily and Salerno as the 4th Destroyer Flotilla. In November, however, *Quail* was mined off the entrance to Bari, in the Adriatic on the 16th, blowing her stern off.

She was successfully towed into port but foundered in tow en route for Taranto some six months later.

By March 1944, the 4th Flotilla, now composed of *Quilliam, Quadrant, Quality, Queenborough, Quiberon* and *Quickmatch*, were with the Eastern Fleet in the Indian Ocean. Here they participated in the various carrier raids on Japanese-held territory, at Sabang and Soerabaya during 1944, both *Quilliam* and *Quality* being hit by shore batteries off Sabang in July. Towards the close of the year, after raids on the Nicobar Islands, the flotilla moved to Australia for duty with the British Pacific Fleet. From early 1945 until the surrender, all the ships of the flotilla saw extensive service in Pacific waters, operating with TF57 as the vast US fleet pushed closer to Japan. *Quilliam*, however, was very badly damaged in collision with *Indomitable* in May 1945. They were still in the Pacific in August 1945 when *Quadrant* was at the reoccupation of Hong Kong and *Quiberon* at Shanghai. In 1945, the three Australian-manned ships, *Quadrant, Quality* and *Queenborough*, were turned over to the RAN permanently, while the only RN survivor, *Quilliam*, went to the Netherlands as *Bankert*.

Above: *Quality* with the Easter Fleet in May 1944. Note the radar tower. (Vicary)

R CLASS

Ship	Builder	Laid Down	Launched	Commissioned	Fate
H09 *Rotherham* (L)	John Brown	10 April 41	21 Mar 42	27 Aug 42	To RIN 29 June 49
H11 *Racehorse*	John Brown	25 June 41	1 June 42	30 Oct 42	Sold out 8 Nov 49
H15 *Raider*	Cammell Laird	16 April 41	1 April 42	16 Nov 42	To RIN 4 Sept 49
H32 *Rapid*	Cammell Laird	16 June 41	16 July 42	20 Feb 43	Sunk as target 3 Sept 81
H41 *Redoubt*	John Brown	19 June 41	2 May 42	1 Oct 42	To RIN 4 June 49
H85 *Relentless*	John Brown	20 June 41	15 July 42	30 Nov 42	Arrived for breaking up 1971
H92 *Rocket*	Scott's	14 Mar 41	28 Oct 42	4 Aug 43	Arrived for breaking up Mar 1967
H95 *Roebuck*	Scott's	19 June 41	10 Dec 42	10 June 43	Arrived for breaking up 8 Aug 68

(Pendant changed to G later).

Below: *Roebuck* with single 40mm guns. (Abrahams)

Technical details as *Q* Class.

Design Essentially repeat *Q* class with altered internal arrangements, the officers berthing forward instead of aft.

Modifications These ships completed with their full designed armament, with radar 285 on the Mk II (W) rangefinder/director and radar 290 at the masthead. Radar 291 superseded the 290 set in later ships and the earlier units were altered similarly. When more up-to-date radar was fitted, *Rocket, Roebuck, Relentless* and *Rotherham* shipped radar 272 lanterns on a lattice tower which displaced the searchlight between the tubes. This was done in about 1944. *Racehorse* and *Redoubt*, however, carried theirs on a platform on the foremast. These two ships later received lattice masts to support the increased radar weight aloft. *Raider* received radar 271 amidships and also HF/DF aft, unlike her sisters.

Augmentation of the AA outfit did not take place until relatively later in the war, probably due to their use in the Indian Ocean where air attack was not a major factor. Thus *Rotherham* still had only six single Oerlikons in November 1944. In April 1945 it was approved to fit four single 40mm Bofors in lieu of the single 20mm around the former searchlight platform, this being done in at least *Raider* and *Roebuck*. Two twin power-operated 20mm replaced the singles in the bridge wings. On the other hand, *Redoubt* merely received the twin 20mm in the bridge wings and retained the singles amidships.

Service The 4th Emergency Flotilla, or *R* class were ordered in April 1940, but like the preceding group,

Above: *Raider*, very similar to *Quality*, but with HF/DF on a lattice mast. (IWM)

were delayed by the need to repair action damage to destroyers incurred during the Dunkirk operations. In February 1941, the contracts for *Redoubt* and *Relentless*, originally placed with Fairfield, were transferred to John Brown. Almost a year separated the first to complete, *Rotherham* and the last, *Rocket*.

Shortly after their completion, *Racehorse* and *Redoubt* escorted *Victorious* to the USA when the latter was en route to reinforce the USN carrier force in the Pacific. By 1943, *Rotherham, Racehorse, Redoubt* and *Relentless* were with the Eastern Fleet detached to South-African waters, while *Raider* served in the Mediterranean during the 'Husky' operations and at the surrender of the Italian Fleet. *Rocket* went to Plymouth after completion and was present during the *Charybdis* disaster off the Channel Islands in October 1943.

From 1944, the *R* class, as 11th Destroyer Flotilla, were with the Eastern Fleet in the Indian Ocean, *Rotherham, Raider* and *Redoubt* forming the 21st Division, the other four the 22nd Division. Operating against U-boat supply ships in the Indian Ocean, the flotilla scored two successes when *Relentless* caught *Charlotte Schliemann* in February and *Rocket*, the *Brake* a month later. The flotilla remained in the Indian Ocean into 1945, *Rapid* being hit by shore batteries in March when bombarding the Andaman Islands.

Racehorse was broken up not long after the war, but the four others left in the Royal Navy were converted to frigates and had a long service career. Three were sold to India and ran until the 1960s.

S CLASS

Ship	Builder	Laid Down	Launched	Commissioned	Fate
G12 *Saumarez* (L)	Hawthorn Leslie	8 Sept 41	20 Nov 42	1 July 43	Arrived for breaking up 8 Sept 50
G20 *Savage*	Hawthorn Leslie	7 Dec 41	24 Sept 42	8 June 43	Arrived for breaking up 11 April 62
G72 *Scorpion* (ex-*Sentinal*)	Cammell Laird	19 June 41	26 Aug 42	11 May 43	To Netherlands Oct 1945
G01 *Scourge*	Cammell Laird	26 June 41	8 Dec 42	14 July 43	To Netherlands Oct 1945
G94 *Serapis*	Scott's	14 Aug 41	25 April 43	23 Dec 43	To Netherlands Oct 1945
G03 *Shark*	Scott's	5 Nov 41	1 June 43	18 Mar 44	Lost 6 June 44
G26 *Success*	S. White	25 Feb 42	3 Mar 43	6 Sept 43	To Netherlands 1943
G46 *Swift*	S. White	12 June 42	15 June 43	6 Dec 43	Lost 24 June 44

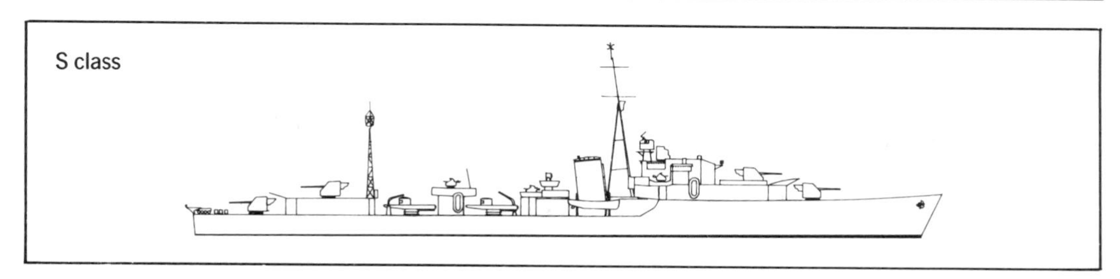

Displacement: 1,710tons/1,737tonnes (standard).
Length: 362ft 9in/110.5m (oa); 348ft/106m (wl); 339ft 6in/103.4m (pp).
Beam: 35ft 8in/10.9m.
Draught: 10ft/3m (mean).
Machinery: two Admiralty 3-drum boilers; 2-shaft Parsons geared turbines.
Performance: 40,000shp; 36kts.
Bunkerage: 615tons/625tonnes.
Range: 4,680nm at 20kts.
Guns: four 4.7in QF Mk IX (4×1); two 40mm Mk IV; four 20mm (4×1).
Torpedoes: eight 21in (2×4).
Complement: 180 (Leader 225).

Design When the requirements for the 5th Emergency Flotilla were being considered in the autumn of 1940, the chilling effectiveness of dive-bomber attack had been well and truly appreciated and in consequence there was even more pressure for destroyer main armament to be dual-purpose. To this end, 55° elevation was demanded, but against some opposition which questioned the effectiveness of such an intermediate solution and proposed instead twin 4-inch as in the *Hunt* class. The argument eventually resolved itself into the 55°

mounting but not before consideration was given to purchasing 5-inch DP mountings from the USA. For the close-range AA outfit, discussions ranged around various combinations of quadruple 2pdr, numerous Oerlikons and the new radar-directed Hazemeyer 40mm Bofors Mk IV gun. This latter had been sent to sea before the war by the Dutch Navy and was far in advance of anything developed by the Royal, US or Japanese Navies at the time. The gun had been put into production for the Royal Navy and manufacturing problems had been sufficiently overcome to be able to plan the equipment of the 5th Emergency Flotilla with it, replacing the long-serving 2pdr pom-pom. To give a better field of fire for it, the searchlight was moved forward to the funnel and the Bofors replaced it between the tubes. Four single Oerlikons were to complete the armament.

Because the *J* hull form had given rise to spray and wetness forward, *Tribal* design bows were adopted. Otherwise, the only visually distinctive features of the class were the absence of a quadruple 2pdr and the fitting of new-pattern shields to the 4.7-inch guns. The machinery and other arrangements were generally as in the *J* class.

By the time that *Scorpion* completed, there was a power-operated twin 20mm gun available, which was fitted in lieu of the four single guns, two being staggered abaft the funnel. However, the 40mm twin was not immediately available and she carried a fifth twin 20mm in lieu. She and *Saumarez* also had a lattice mast aft for an HF/DF aerial. *Scorpion, Saumarez* and *Savage* completed without lattice masts. *Savage* was unique in that she was used as a test-bed for the new 4.5-inch Mk IV twin mounting which had been developed from the BD Mk II mountings used on capital ships. This was intended for the 1942 *Battle*s described later. Then to give *Savage* a uniform main armament, the two single after guns were rebarrelled to 4.5-inch Mk V. The twin mounting was fitted in No. 1 position, leaving the spacious forward shelter deck quite bare. She was never fitted with the Mk IV Bofors and had radar 271 in lieu with two twin Oerlikons abreast it giving her a total of six twin equipments.

Modifications *Scorpion* had her fifth twin 20mm replaced by a quadruple 2pdr and never in fact received the Mk IV Bofors. Lattice masts were fitted to all except *Savage*, with radar 272 and 291 at the masthead. In 1945 radar 276 replaced the 272 set and in that year, *Saumarez* received four single 40mm Bofors on the former searchlight platform consequent upon her deployment to the Indian Ocean.

Service *Success* and *Shark* were transferred to the Royal Norwegian Navy (q.v.) before completion, being renamed *Stord* and *Svenner* respectively. All, however, served with the Home Fleet as the 23rd Destroyer Flotilla in northern and Arctic waters.

In December 1943, *Saumarez, Savage, Scorpion* and the Norwegian *Stord* were screening *Duke of York* and *Jamaica*, which had been sailed as distant cover for Convoy JW55B (of which *Scourge* formed part of the escort) in the expectation that *Scharnhorst* would attempt to attack it. The expectation turned to reality when the German battlecruiser sailed from Altenfjord on 25 December, screened by the 4th Destroyer Flotilla comprised of *Z29, Z30, Z33, Z34* and *Z38*. The following day, after engaging British cruisers screening the convoy, *Scharnhorst* retired but was eventually brought to action during the afternoon by *Duke of York* and the *S*-class destroyers. In the engagement which followed, all the destroyers got into action with gunfire and fired a total of 28 torpedoes claiming four hits. *Scharnhorst* was sunk by a combination of heavy guns of the battleship and torpedo hits from the destroyers, but she badly hit *Saumarez* in the director and range-finder and near misses caused many casualties and damage from shell-splinters.

During 1944, the flotilla took part in carrier sweeps against the Norwegian coast and in March, while escorting convoy RA57, *Swift* narrowly avoided a torpedo from *U739*. The flotilla's next task was as part of the massive naval presence at the Invasion of Normandy in June 1944. Here they took part in anti-*S*-boat sweeps and defended the Invasion area from attacks by German torpedo-boats. However, the Norwegian *Svenner* was lost and *Swift* was mined off the beach-head. After Normandy, the flotilla returned to Arctic duties involving a mixture of Russian convoys and offensive carrier sorties against the Norwegian coast. This task extended until the end of the war in Europe, except for *Saumarez* which went to the Eastern Fleet early in 1945.

Saumarez took part in the carrier raids in the Indian Ocean including the Sabang raid. Now leader of the 26th Destroyer Flotilla, she once again had the opportunity to act in the classic destroyer role when, on 16 May 1945, her flotilla (*Verulam, Virago, Vigilant* and *Venus*) torpedoed and sank the cruiser *Haguro*. *Saumarez*, however, received several shell-hits, one in her boiler room.

Only *Savage* saw much post-war service under the White Ensign for *Scorpion, Scourge* and *Serapis* were transferred to the Netherlands and renamed *Kortenaer, Evertsen* and *Piet Hien* respectively. *Saumarez*, serving in the Mediterranean in 1946, was one of the destroyers involved in the Corfu incident when she hit mines laid in international waters by Albania that October. She was badly damaged and suffered numerous casualties. Although brought home she was never repaired.

Below: *Scourge* in August 1943. She has the Hazemeyer Bofors and twin 20mm guns.

T CLASS

Ship	Builder	Laid Down	Launched	Commissioned	Fate
R00 *Troubridge* (L)	John Brown	10 Nov 41	23 Sept 42	8 Mar 43	Arrived for breaking up 5 May 70
R23 *Teazer* D45	Cammell Laird	20 Oct 41	7 Jan 43	13 Sept 43	Arrived for breaking up 7 Aug 65
R45 *Tenacious*	Cammell Laird	3 Dec 41	24 Mar 43	3 Oct 43	Arrived for breaking up 29 June 65
R89 *Termagant* D47	Denny	25 Nov 41	22 Mar 43	18 Oct 43	Arrived for breaking up 5 Nov 65
R33 *Terpsichore*	Denny	25 Nov 41	17 June 43	20 Jan 44	Arrived for breaking up 17 May 66
R11 *Tumult*	John Brown	16 Nov 41	9 Nov 42	2 April 43	Arrived for breaking up 19 Oct 65
R56 *Tuscan*	Swan Hunter*	6 Sept 41	28 May 42	11 Mar 43	Arrived for breaking up 25 Oct 65
R67 *Tyrian*	Swan Hunter*	15 Oct 41	27 July 42	8 April 43	Arrived for breaking up 9 Mar 65

(D pendant for service with U.S. Pacific Fleet 1945. *Engined by Wallsend Slipway Co. Ltd.

Technical details as *S* Class.

Design Repeat *S* class except that they were not fitted for Arctic service. Close-range armament while nominally intended to be similar to the *S* class did vary at completion due to circumstances. *Tumult* initially had tripod foremast, radar 272 amidships and no Mk IV twin Bofors. Her CRA consisted of six power-operated twin 20mm. *Terpsichore* had two twin 20mm amidships and some of the other early units only had single 20mm amidships.

Modifications All were fitted with a lattice mast (tall in *Tumult* and *Troubridge*) and radar 293 with HF/DF at the masthead and in some cases 291 on a pole aft. On the removal of her 272 set between the tubes, *Tumult* finally received her Hazemeyer Bofors. The searchlight was landed being replaced by a single 40mm Mk III and most had four 40mm Bofors singles on the other positions, either all 'boffins' (i.e., *Tuscan* and *Termagant*) or a mixture of Mk III and boffins with 'boffins' in the bridge wings (*Tumult*). On her return from the Far East, however, *Termagant* had only a single 40mm Mk III between the tubes.

Service Forming the 24th Destroyer Flotilla, these ships went to the Mediterranean on completion where *Troubridge, Tumult* and *Tyrian* took part in Operation 'Husky' (Sicily) and the landings at Salerno. Not long after her completion, *Tuscan* struck a drifting mine off Lundy Island on 14 May 1943. The explosion on the port side aft stopped the port engine and flooded the after magazines, more than 270 tons of water entering the ship. A large hole 22 feet by 18 feet was torn in the hull, distorting the hull and machinery alignment. Repairs took a considerable length of time. In 1944, the flotilla moved to the Adriatic but *Tenacious* was at Anzio in January. *U223* was sunk by *Tumult* and other destroyers in the incident in which *Laforey* was sunk, *U453* in May by *Tenacious, Termagant* and *Liddesdale and U407* by *Troubridge, Terpsichore* and *Garland* in September. All except *Tenacious* covered the landing in southern France in August 1944 before moving to the Aegean to conduct offensive sweeps against German evacuation traffic. Many small ships were sunk in numerous sweeps, including *TA37* (a former Italian torpedo-boat) on 7 October by *Termagant* and *Tuscan*, followed by *TA18*, another ex-Italian warship by the same pair on the 19th. The flotilla was subsequently transferred to the Pacific and served with the British Pacific Fleet from then on. They screened the fleet and took part in the carrier raid on Truck before the final carrier attacks on the Japanese mainland itself. Most of the flotilla was in Japanese waters for the surrender, but *Tumult, Tuscan* and *Tyrian* went to China in August to reoccupy Shanghai.

Top left: *Tuscan*, with only a single 20mm in lieu of her Bofors. (Swan Hunter)

Left: *Tyrian*, with a twin 20mm in lieu of the Bofors, and HF/DF. (Swan Hunter)

U CLASS

Ship	Builder	Laid Down	Launched	Commissioned	Fate
R97 *Grenville* (L)	Swan Hunter*	1 Nov 41	12 Oct 42	27 May 43	Arrived for breaking up 28 Feb 83
R83 *Ulster*	Swan Hunter*	12 Nov 41	9 Nov 42	30 June 43	Arrived for breaking up 29 Oct 80
R69 *Ulysses*	Cammell Laird	14 Mar 42	22 April 43	23 Dec 43	Scrapped 1970
R53 *Undaunted* D25	Cammell Laird	8 Sept 42	19 July 43	3 Mar 44	Sunk as target Nov 1978
R42 *Undine*	Thornycroft	18 Mar 42	1 June 43	23 Dec 43	Arrived for breaking up 15 Nov 65
R05 *Urania*	V.A. (Barrow)	18 June 42	19 May 43	18 Jan 44	Arrived for breaking up Mar 1971
R99 *Urchin*	V.A. (Barrow)	28 Mar 42	8 Mar 43	24 Sept 43	Arrived for breaking up 6 Aug 67
R22 *Ursa*	Thornycroft	2 May 42	22 July 43	1 Mar 44	Arrived for breaking up 23 Sept 67

(D pendant for service with US Pacific Fleet 1945). *Engined by Wallsend Slipway Co. Ltd.

Displacement: 1,777tons/1,805tonnes (standard); 2,508tons/2,548tonnes (full load).
Length: 362ft 9in/110.5m (oa); 348ft/106m (wl); 339ft 6in/103.4m (pp).
Beam: 35ft 8in/10.9m.
Draught: 10ft/3m (mean).
Machinery: two Admiralty 3-drum boilers; 2-shaft Parsons geared turbines.
Performance: 40,000shp; 36kts.
Bunkerage: 615tons/625tonnes.
Range: 4,680nm at 20kts.
Guns: four 4.7in QF Mk IX (4×1); four 2pdr (1×4); eight 20mm (4×2).
Torpedoes: eight 21in (2×4).
Complement: 180 (Leader 225).

Design Ordered on 12 June 1941, these eight destroyers were, once again, repeat *S*-class ships. They were not fitted for Arctic service. Only the leader, *Grenville*, and *Ulster* completed with tripod masts (the former without the SW radar) the remainder having the short lattice mast. *Ulysses* completed with a quadruple 2pdr and *Urchin* with two twin 20mm in lieu of the Hazemeyer Bofors.

Modifications *Grenville* and *Ulster* received tall lattice masts in lieu of their tripods. Radar 272, fitted in at least *Urchin*, *Ulster* and *Urania*, was replaced by the new 276 with the exposed cheese aerial. Radar 291 was generally moved to a stump mast at the forward end of the Hazemeyer platform. In July 1944, *Urchin* and *Ulysses* received army-pattern Bofors as they carried no Mk IV. The searchlight was landed, to be replaced by a single Bofors Mk III. Service in the Pacific Fleet led to the twin 20mm being dispensed with and replaced by single Bofors or 'boffin' mountings. *Urchin* had Hazemeyer Bofors when she arrived in the Pacific.

Service *Grenville* was the first to complete and served in the Bay of Biscay and the Channel during the latter half of 1943. *Urchin* went to the Mediterranean for Anzio in January 1944, *Ulysses* operated in the Arctic and *Ursa* took part in carrier raids against the Norwegian coast in the spring of that year. All eight ships, the 25th Destroyer Flotilla, took part in the Normandy landings in June before moving to the Adriatic and thence to the East Indies at the beginning of 1945. On 16 January, the flotilla was part of the large force transferred to the Pacific for operations with the British Pacific Fleet. Here they remained until the surrender of Japan, but *Ulster* was near-missed by a Kamikaze off Sakashima Gunto on 1 April 1945 and had to be towed to Leyte by *Gambia*. After temporary repairs by the USN, she steamed home for full repair in August. *Ulysses*, *Undine* and *Urania* were shelling the Japanese mainland by the end of July 1945. *Ursa* went to Hong Kong for its reoccupation at the end of the war.

Below: *Grenville*. (Swan Hunter)

Below: *Urania*. (Vickers)

Above: *Urchin* in late 1945. (Author's Collection)

V CLASS

Ship	Builder	Laid Down	Launched	Commissioned	Fate
R08 *Hardy* (L)	John Brown	14 May 42	18 Mar 43	14 Aug 43	Lost 30 Jan 44
R17 *Valentine* (ex-*Kempenfelt*)	John Brown	8 Oct 42	2 Sept 43	28 Feb 44	RCN 1944
R50 *Venus* (L)	Fairfield	12 Jan 42	23 Feb 43	28 Aug 43	Arrived for breaking up 20 Dec 72
R28 *Verulam*	Fairfield	26 Jan 42	22 April 43	10 Dec 43	Arrived for breaking up 23 Oct 72
R93 *Vigilant*	Swan Hunter*	31 Jan 42	22 Dec 42	10 Sept 43	Arrived for breaking up 4 June 65
R75 *Virago*	Swan Hunter*	16 Feb 42	4 Feb 43	5 Nov 43	Arrived for breaking up 4 June 65
R64 *Vixen*	S. White	31 Oct 42	14 Sept 43	28 Feb 44	RCN 1944
R41 *Volage*	S. White	31 Dec 42	15 Feb 43	26 May 44	Arrived for breaking up 1977

*Engined by Wallsend Slipway Co. Ltd.

Displacement: 1,808tons/1,837tonnes (standard); 2,530tons/2,570tonnes (full load).
Technical details as *U* class.

Design Repeat *U* class ordered on 1 September 1941 as the 8th Emergency Flotilla fitted for Arctic service. *Venus* completed with a tripod mast and *Volage* a quadruple 2pdr in lieu of the designed outfit. Some of the early units, including *Hardy* and *Vigilant*, completed with radar 272 but later units received 276 on the lattice foremast and 291 on a pole aft. HF/DF was fitted at the foremast truck.

Modifications A tall lattice mast was fitted in *Venus*. Ships with 272 radar converted to 276 later. In 1945 Arctic fittings were removed to save top-weight as was the searchlight and platform. In June 1945, *Vigilant* landed the two after twin Oerlikons and fitted two single 40mm land-pattern Bofors. Two more were fitted on the forecastle deck. *Volage* shipped four single Bofors on the deck-house abaft the funnel in 1945.

Service These ships formed the 26th Destroyer Flotilla. Two units, *Valentine* and *Vixen*, were transferred to the RCN before completion and renamed *Algonquin* and *Sioux* respectively. The six others served with the Home Fleet alternating Arctic convoy duties with screening carrier raids against the Axis shipping routes along the Norwegian coast during 1943–44. *Virago* took part in the sinking of *Scharnhorst* in December 1943 when she got into action with both guns and torpedoes. She fired seven torpedoes and claimed two hits. In the new year, a reverse occurred when *Hardy* was torpedoed by *U278* while screening JW56 and had to be sunk by *Venus*. At the end of 1944, the flotilla was transferred to the East Indies where they took part in raids against the Malayan and Burmese coasts. *Venus, Verulam, Vigilant* and *Virago* (with *Saumarez*) sank the Japanese heavy cruiser *Haguro* in May 1945. The flotilla did not go to the Pacific but returned home from the East Indies at the end of the war.

Above: *Hardy* (ii) with full designed outfit. (IWM) Below: *Virago* at completion. (Swan Hunter)

W CLASS

Ship	Builder	Laid Down	Launched	Commissioned	Fate
R03 *Kempenfelt* (ex-*Valentine*) (L)	John Brown	24 June 42	8 May 43	25 Oct 43	To Yugoslavia 1956
R98 *Wager* D30	John Brown	20 Nov 42	1 Nov 43	14 April 44	To Yugoslavia 1956
R59 *Wakeful* (ex-*Zebra*) (L)	Fairfield	3 June 42	30 June 43	17 Feb 44	Arrived for breaking up 5 July 71
R78 *Wessex* (ex-*Zenith*)	Fairfield	20 Oct 42	2 Sept 43	11 May 44	To S. Africa 29 Mar 50
R37 *Whelp* D30	Hawthorn Leslie	1 May 42	3 June 43	26 April 44	To S. Africa 1952
R87 *Whirlwind*	Hawthorn Leslie	31 July 42	30 Aug 43	20 July 44	Foundered 28/29 Oct 74
R72 *Wizard*	V.A. (Barrow)	14 Sept 42	29 Sept 43	30 Mar 44	Arrived for breaking up 7 Mar 67
R48 *Wrangler*	V.A. (Barrow)	23 Sept 42	30 Dec 43	17 July 44	To S. Africa 29 Nov 56

Displacement: 1,710tons/1,737tonnes (standard).
Length: 362ft 9in/110.5m (oa); 348ft/106m (wl); 339ft 6in/103.4m (pp).
Beam: 35ft 8in/10.9m.
Draught: 10ft/3m (mean).
Machinery: two Admiralty 3-drum boilers; 2-shaft Parsons geared turbines.
Performance: 40,000shp; 36kts.
Bunkerage: 615tons/625tonnes.
Range: 4,680nm at 20kts.
Guns: four 4.7in QF Mk IX (4×1); four 2pdr (1×4); eight 20mm (4×2).
Torpedoes: eight 21in (2×4).
Complement: 186 (Leader 222).

Design Once again repeat *U* class, the 9th Emergency Flotilla, however, adopted a new rangefinder director and dispensed with the old two-tower arrangement. The fire-control tower was the rangefinder director Mk III (w) which differed from the Mk II (w) in that it was dual-purpose, incorporating the ability to direct surface fire. Main armament remained four 4.7-inch 55° Mk XXII mountings, despite the now familiar demand for fully high-angle guns from, this time, the Captain of *Excellent*. Supplies of Hazemeyer Bofors were still inadequate and both *Whelp* and *Wessex* received quadruple 2pdrs in lieu. All completed with the tall lattice mast fitted for 276 radar except that *Kempenfelt* commissioned with 272. HF/DF was fitted at the foremast truck with radar 291 on a pole aft.

Modifications These were mainly limited to the light AA outfits. As the 20mm was found to have limited stopping power in the face of *Kamikaze* attacks, a heavier weapon was sought. Because there were not enough Bofors to go round, an interim solution in the shape of the single 2pdr in Mk XV or Mk XVI power-operated mountings was adopted. Two of these often supplanted two of the twin 20mm mountings as in *Wizard*. Other alterations included replacing the searchlight by a hand-worked Bofors and fitting 'boffins' in lieu of twin Oerlikons.

Service After working-up in home waters, the 27th Destroyer Flotilla was intended for service in the Eastern and British Pacific Fleets. However, *Kempenfelt* went to the Mediterranean for Anzio in January 1944, returning home for the Normandy landings in June. *Wakeful* and *Wizard* participated in carrier raids against the Norwegian shipping routes in May 1944, but in the following month *Wizard* was very badly damaged by the explosion of her own depth-charges and spent until the end of April 1945 under repair. *Kempenfelt* saw service on Arctic convoys in August 1944, but by November all except *Wizard* were with the Eastern Fleet in the Indian Ocean. In January 1945, the flotilla moved into the Pacific and remained there with the British Pacific Fleet until the end of hostilities. Post-war, *Kempenfelt* and *Wager* became the Yugoslav *Kotor* and *Pula* respectively, while in South-Africa hands, *Wessex*, *Whelp* and *Wrangler* became *Jan Van Riebaeck*, *Simon van der Stel* and *Vrystaat*.

Above: *Wrangler*. Note the HA/LA director. (Vikers) **Below:** *Wizard*, (IWM)

Z CLASS

Ship	Builder	Laid Down	Launched	Commissioned	Fate
R06 *Myngs* (L)	Parsons M.S.T.Co.*	27 May 42	3 Jan 43	23 June 44	To Egypt 1955
R66 *Zambesi*	Cammell Laird	12 Dec 42	21 Nov 43	18 July 44	Arrived for breaking up 12 Feb 59
R39 *Zealous*	Cammell Laird	5 May 42	28 Feb 44	9 Oct 44	To Israel 15 July 55
R81 *Zebra* (ex-*Wakeful*)	Denny	14 May 42	8 Mar 44	3 Oct 44	Arrived for breaking up 12 Feb 59
R95 *Zenith* (ex-*Wessex*)	Denny	19 May 42	5 June 44	22 Dec 44	To Egypt 1955
R19 *Zephyr* (L)	Parsons M.S.T.Co.*	13 July 42	15 July 43	6 Sept 44	Arrived for breaking up 2 July 58
R02 *Zest*	Thornycroft	21 July 42	14 Oct 43	20 July 44	Arrived for breaking up Aug 1970
R54 *Zodiac*	Thornycroft	7 Nov 42	11 Mar 44	23 Oct 44	To Israel 15 July 55

*Hull sub-contracted to V.A. (Tyne).

Displacement: 1,710tons/1,737tonnes (standard).
Length: 362ft 9in/110.5m (oa); 348ft/106m (wl); 339ft 6in/103.4m (pp).
Beam: 35ft 8in/10.9m.
Draught: 10ft/3m (mean).
Machinery: two Admiralty 3-drum boilers; 2-shaft Parsons geared turbines.
Performance: 40,000shp; 36kts.
Bunkerage: 615tons/625tonnes.
Range: 4,680nm at 20kts.
Guns: four 4.5in QF Mk IV; two 40mm (1×2); eight 20mm (4×2).
Torpedoes: eight 21in (2×4).
Complement: 186 (Leader 222).

Design Basically repeat *U* class, this flotilla introduced two important changes to British destroyer design. In the first place, the 4.7-inch gun, which had reigned supreme in Royal Navy destroyers since 1918, finally gave way to the new 4.5-inch which had been successfully tried in *Savage*. Secondly, following the lead of the *W* class, a dual-purpose director was again specified but this time the new Mk VI HA/LA tower. The 4.5-inch gun was the Mk IV on CP Mk V mounting, but still only capable of 55° elevation. In fact, this mounting was almost identical with that of the 4.7-inch gun in the preceding class. Gun disposition was identical with that of the *W* class. Despite orders being placed for eight ships on 12 February 1942, the first ship, *Myngs*, did not commission until June 1944 and even then she was incomplete, lacking her director among other things. The reason for this was that the Mk IV director was well behind schedule and an interim type, known as the Mk I Type K HA/LA director had to be fitted instead. Even this failed to appear on time with the result that most of the class spent weeks in the builders' yards awaiting their directors. This interim director or 'K' tower as it was more commonly known, did not, unfortunately fulfil all that was expected of it and turned out a ton and a half heavier than estimated. Its design was essentially a rework of the tower fitted in the *L* and *M*-class destroyers, with the addition of an HA sight. RPC was fitted for the first time, but the hydraulics were very sensitive and the tower gained an unfavourable reputation. For the close-range AA outfit, the designed four twin Oerlikons were amended to single 2pdrs on power mountings in the light of Pacific war experience. In the event, a mixture of weapons was eventually shipped. *Myngs*, *Zambesi* and *Zest* all completed with the short lattice mast, but the rest had the tall one. Radar 293 had now replaced 271, but 291 was retained on a pole aft.

Modifications Completing so late in the war there were few modifications. *Myngs* had two 2pdrs in the bridge wings, with one 40mm and two single 20mm abaft the funnel, in addition to her Mk IV Bofors. *Zephyr* had four 2pdrs, in the bridge wings and abaft the funnel.

Service After work-up, the *Z* class joined the Home Fleet, spending the remainder of 1944 on carrier raids, offensive cruiser patrols and Russian convoys. In 1945, the flotilla remained on Arctic convoy duty until May, when *Zealous, Zephyr, Zest* and *Zodiac* were part of the force to liberate Denmark. None of these ships went to the Pacific, all remained in home waters. On their sale to Egypt, *Myngs* and *Zenith* became *El Quaher* and *El Fateh* while Israel renamed *Zealous* and *Zodiac, Elath* and *Yaffa* respectively. *Elath* made headlines in 1967 when she was sunk by a surface-to-surface missile launched by an Egyptian FPB. Four years later, Israeli aircraft sank *El Quaher*. Of the three left in the Royal Navy, only *Zest* was converted to a frigate.

Below: *Zest*. (IWM)

Ca CLASS

Ship	Builder	Laid Down	Launched	Commissioned	Fate
R07 *Caesar* (ex-*Ranger*)	John Brown	3 April 43	14 Feb 44	5 Oct 44	Arrived for breaking up 6 Jan 67
R85 *Cambrian* (ex-*Spitfire*)	Scott's	14 Aug 42	10 Dec 43	14 July 44	Arrived for breaking up 3 Sept 71
R01 *Caprice* (ex-*Swallow*)	A. Yarrow	28 Sept 42	16 Sept 43	5 April 44	Arrived for breaking up 5 Oct 79
R30 *Carron* (ex-*Strenuous*)	Scott's	26 Nov 42	28 Mar 44	6 Nov 44	Arrived for breaking up 4 April 67
R25 *Carysfort* (ex-*Pique*)	S. White	12 May 43	25 July 44	20 Feb 45	Arrived for breaking up Nov 1970
R62 *Cassandra* (ex-*Tourmaline*)	A. Yarrow	3 Jan 43	29 Nov 43	28 July 44	Arrived for breaking up 28 April 67
R73 *Cavalier* (ex-*Pellew*)	S. White	28 Feb 43	7 April 44	22 Nov 44	Museum Ship 21 Oct 77
R15 *Cavendish* (ex-*Sibyl*)	John Brown	19 May 43	12 April 44	13 Dec 44	Arrived for breaking up 17 Aug 67

Technical details as *Z* Class.

Design The 11th Emergency Flotilla, ordered on 16 February 1942, were a repeat of the *Z* class. Originally they were to carry a mixture of names but eventually names beginning with 'C' were adopted. *Pellew* and *Pique* were originally ordered from Cammell Laird and were to have been fitted as leaders, but in August 1942, this contract was cancelled and placed instead with J. S. White. Leaders were now to be *Ranger* and *Sybil*. All ships completed with lattice masts, radar 293 and Hazemeyer Bofors (except *Caprice* with a quadruple 2pdr). Light AA generally comprised four single 2pdrs on power-worked mountings in the bridge wings and abaft the funnel.

Modifications No significant alterations were made during the war.

Service On completion, the *C* class destroyers joined the 7th Destroyer Flotilla with the Home Fleet. Their service mostly comprised Arctic convoy duty and offensive carrier sweeps along the Norwegian coast. In November 1944, *Caesar, Cassandra, Caprice* and *Cambrian*, forming the 1st Division of the 7th Flotilla, and *O*-class destroyers of the 17th Flotilla escorted *Bellona* as covering force for Convoy JW62. On 11 December *Cassandra* had her bows blown off by a torpedo from *U365* but managed to reach Murmansk. Temporary repairs were made in Russia, the destroyer being brought home and fully repaired at Gibraltar in late 1945. *Carysfort* took part in the last carrier strike on 4 May 1945. After the end of the war in Europe, the flotilla went to the East Indies returning to reserve in 1946. In the mid 1950s, the flotilla was rebuilt and modernized for ASW duties. *Cavalier* exists today as a museum ship.

Below: *Carron* post-war. (G. Osbourne)

Ch, Co & Cr CLASS

Ship	Builder	Laid Down
R52 *Chaplet*	Thornycroft	29 April 43
R29 *Charity*	Thornycroft	9 July 43
R61 *Chequers* (ex-*Champion)*	Scott's	4 May 43
R90 *Cheviot*	Stephen	27 April 43
R51 *Chevron*	Stephen	18 Mar 43
R36 *Chieftain*	Scott's	27 June 43
R91 *Childers*	Denny	27 Nov 43
R21 *Chivalrous*	Denny	27 Nov 43
R34 *Cockade*	A. Yarrow	11 Mar 43
R26 *Comet*	A. Yarrow	14 June 43
R43 *Comus*	Thornycroft	21 Aug 43

*Hull sub-contracted to V.A. (Tyne).

Displacement: 1,825tons/1,854tonnes (standard); 2,535tons/2,575tonnes (full load).
Length: 362ft 9in/110.5m (oa); 348ft/106m (wl); 339ft 6in/103.4m (pp).
Beam: 35ft 8in/10.9m.
Draught: 10ft/3.05m (mean).
Machinery: two Admiralty 3-drum boilers; 2-shaft Parsons geared turbines.
Performance: 40,000shp; 36kts.
Bunkerage: 615tons/625tonnes.
Range: 4,680nm at 20kts.
Guns: four 4.5in QF Mk IV (4×1); two 40mm (1×2); two 2pdr (2×1); two 20mm (2×1).
Torpedoes: four 21in (1×4).
Complement: 186 (Leaders 222).

Design The original intention had been that this group of destroyers would, once again, be repeats of the *Z* class. However, RPC was becoming much

Above: *Caprice*, still awaiting her 'K' DCT. (IWM)

Above: *Chevron*. (Author's Collection)

Launched	Commissioned	Fate
8 July 44	24 Aug 45	Arrived for breaking up 6 Nov 65
30 Nov 44	19 Nov 45	To Pakistan 16 Dec 58
30 Oct 44	28 Sept 45	Arrived for breaking up 23 July 66
May 44	11 Dec 45	Arrived for breaking up 22 Oct 61
23 Feb 44	23 Aug 45	Arrived for breaking up Dec 1969
26 Feb 45	7 Mar 46	Arrived for breaking up 20 Mar 61
27 Feb 45	19 Dec 45	Arrived for breaking up 22 Sept 63
22 June 45	13 May 46	To Pakistan 29 June 54
Mar 44	29 Sept 45	Arrived for breaking up 1964
22 June 44	6 June 45	Arrived for breaking up 23 Oct 62
4 Mar 45	8 July 46	Arrived for breaking up 12 Nov 58

Ship	Builder	Laid Down	Launched	Commissioned	Fate
R76 *Consort*	Stephen	26 May 43	19 Oct 44	19 Mar 46	Arrived for breaking up 15 Mar 61
R71 *Constance*	Parsons M.S.T.Co.*	18 Mar 43	22 Aug 44	31 Dec 45	Arrived for breaking up 8 Mar 56
R12 *Contest*	S. White	1 Nov 43	16 Dec 44	9 Nov 45	Arrived for breaking up 2 Feb 60
R63 *Concord* (ex-*Corso*)	Thornycroft	18 Nov 43	14 May 45	20 Dec 46	Arrived for breaking up 22 Oct 62
R57 *Cossack*	Parsons M.S.T.Co.*	18 Mar 43	10 May 44	4 Sept 45	Arrived for breaking up 1 Mar 61
R68 *Crispin* (ex-*Cracher*)	S. White	1 Feb 44	23 June 45	10 July 46	To Pakistan 18 Mar 58
R82 *Creole*	S. White	3 Aug 44	22 Nov 45	14 Oct 46	To Pakistan 29 Feb 56
R35 *Cromwell* (ex-*Cretan*)	Scott's	24 Nov 43	6 Aug 45	16 Sept 46	To Norway 1946
R16 *Crescent*	John Brown	16 Aug 43	20 July 44	21 Aug 45	To RCN 1945
R46 *Crown*	Scott's	16 Jan 44	19 Dec 45	17 April 47	To Norway 1946
R27 *Croziers*	A. Yarrow	26 Oct 43	19 Aug 44	30 Nov 45	To Norway 10 Oct 46
R20 *Crusader*	John Brown	15 Nov 43	5 Oct 44	26 Nov 45	To RCN 26 Nov 45
R38 *Crystal*	A. Yarrow	13 Jan 44	12 Feb 45	6 Feb 46	To Norway 10 Oct 46

Below: *Crystal*. Note the Mk VI director and uniform 40mm CRA. (Author's Collection)

more of a requirement for gunnery purposes in order that the advances in radar techniques and gun-direction systems could be fully utilized. This posed problems because RPC involved an extra weight of about eight tons, high in the ship, and the new Mk VI director, now at last becoming available, would weigh about ten tons, i.e., four more than the 'K' tower. The new fire-control radar, Type 275, allowed full blind fire control from the transmitting station. Because of the top-weight problems, there was an urgent need to reduce weight wherever possible and at one stage, it was considered reverting to the R/F Director Mk III (w) as carried by the *W* class. This was a considerably retrograde step which involved giving up all the new advances and it found little favour with most parties including the DNO. Other areas were therefore studied with a view to reducing top-weight, one being the close-range outfit. It had been originally intended to fit the 40mm Bofors STAAG mounting in lieu of the Hazemeyer mount, the STAAG being a newer, much more sophisticated and in fact terribly over-complicated version of the Dutch gun. Its estimated weight was eleven tons (when it belatedly did enter service, it was more like seventeen tons!) and it was proposed to fit the lighter twin Hazemeyer Mk IV, but the DNC decided that even this did not confer sufficient improvement in stability. The only alternative left was to halve the torpedo outfit, saving something like twenty tons. In compensation, the remaining (after) set would be given RPC. The ASW outfit was reduced to two depth-charge throwers with only 35 depth-charges as further economy in top-weight, and for the same reason the bridge wings were generally given only a single manual 20mm Oerlikon. Most units received the Mk IV Hazemeyer, also two single power-operated 2pdr Mk XV abaft the funnel. Later units completed with single Bofors Mk VII in lieu of the 2pdr (*Concord*, *Comus* and probably all the *Cr* group at least). At or very shortly after their completion, the Mk IV twin Bofors began to be replaced by the simpler twin Mk V with RPC.

Contest, built by White, was the first all-welded destroyer in the Royal Navy. The *Ch* and *Co* groups were ordered on 24 July, the *Crs* on 12 September 1942. This latter group were all-welded.

Modifications None within the period covered by this volume.

Service Severe delays caused by the late delivery of director towers prevented any of this group from seeing war service despite the fact, that for example, *Chevron* laid down as early as March 1943, was due to commission in June 1944. Many of the *Cr* group were transferred to Allied Navies, *Cromwell* on completion to Norway as *Bergen*, followed by *Crown* (*Oslo*), *Crystal* (*Stavanger*) and *Croziers* (*Trondheim*). *Crescent* and *Crusader* went to the RCN and retained their names, in 1946.

1942 BATTLE CLASS

Ship	Builder	Laid Down	Launched	Commissioned	Fate
R14 *Armada* (L)	Hawthorn Leslie	29 Dec 42	9 Dec 43	2 July 45	Arrived for breaking up 18 Dec 65
R80 *Barfleur* (L)	Swan Hunter*	28 Oct 42	1 Nov 43	14 Sept 44	Arrived for breaking up 29 Sept 66
R09 *Cadiz*	Fairfield	10 May 43	16 Sept 44	12 April 46	To Pakistan 1 Feb 57
R32 *Camperdown*	Fairfield	3 Oct 42	8 Feb 44	18 June 45	Arrived for breaking up Sept 1970
R55 *Finisterre*	Fairfield	8 Dec 42	22 June 44	11 Sept 45	Arrived for breaking up 12 June 67
R47 *Gabbard*	Swan Hunter*	2 Feb 44	16 Mar 45	10 Dec 46	To Pakistan 24 Jan 57
R24 *Gravelines*	Cammell Laird	10 Aug 43	30 Nov 44	14 June 46	Arrived for breaking up 4 April 61
R74 *Hogue*	Cammell Laird	6 Jan 43	21 April 44	24 July 45	Sold out 7 Mar 62
R44 *Lagos*	Cammell Laird	8 April 43	4 Aug 44	2 Nov 45	Arrived for breaking up June 1967
R65 *St. James* (L)	Fairfield	20 May 43	7 June 45	12 July 46	Arrived for breaking up 19 Mar 61
R18 *St. Kitts*	Swan Hunter*	8 Sept 43	4 Oct 44	21 Jan 46	Arrived for breaking up 19 Feb 62
R84 *Saintes* (L)	Hawthorn Leslie	8 June 43	19 July 44	27 Sept 46	Arrived for breaking up 1 Sept 72
R60 *Sluys*	Cammell Laird	24 Nov 43	28 Feb 45	30 Sept 46	To Iran 26 Jan 67
R70 *Solebay* (L)	Hawthorn Leslie	3 Feb 43	22 Feb 44	11 Oct 45	Arrived for breaking up 11 Aug 67
R77 *Trafalgar* (L)	Swan Hunter*	15 Feb 43	12 Jan 44	23 July 45	Arrived for breaking up July 1970
R31 *Vigo*	Fairfield	11 Sept 43	27 Sept 45	9 Dec 46	Arrived for breaking up 6 Dec 64

*Engined by Wallsend Slipway Co. Ltd.

Right: *Barfleur*. (IWM)

Above: *Armada.* (IWM)

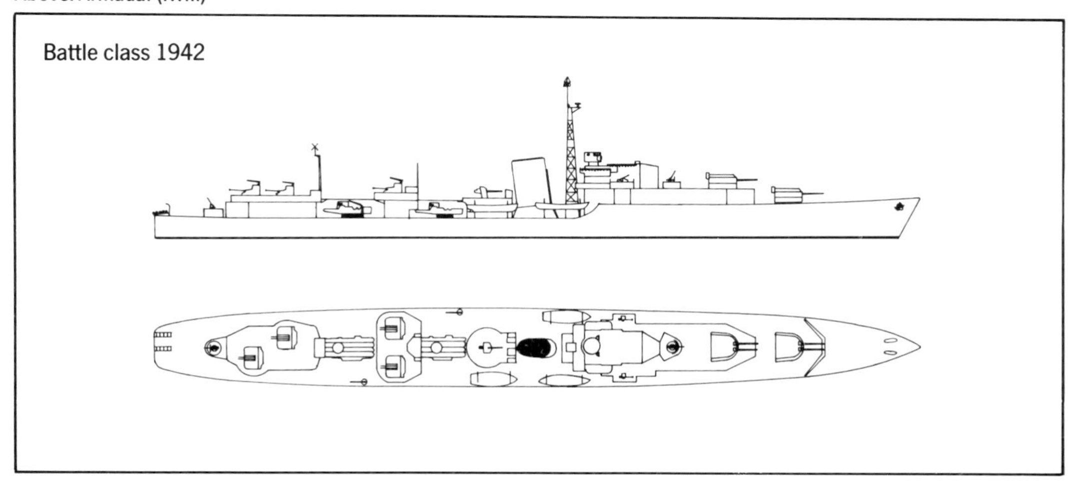

Displacement: 2,315tons/3,252tonnes (standard); 3,361tons/3,415tonnes (full load).
Length: 379ft/115.5m (oa); 364ft/110.9m (wl); 355ft/108.2m (pp).
Beam: 40ft 3in/12.2m.
Draught: 12ft 9in/3.9m (mean).
Machinery: two Admiralty 3-drum boilers; 2-shaft Parsons geared turbines.
Performance: 50,000shp; 35.75kts.
Bunkerage: 766tons/778tonnes.
Range: 4,400nm at 20kts.
Guns: four 4.5in QF Mk III (2×2); one 4in HA Mk XIX; eight 40mm (4×2); six 20mm (2×2, 2×1).
Torpedoes: eight 21in (2×4).
Complement: 247 (Leaders 286).

Design Events in the Mediterranean and home waters had by 1941, forcefully rammed home the need to improve the anti-aircraft defences of all classes of ship, not least destroyers. Not only did the close-range outfit need augmenting, but it was obvious that the main armament of destroyers needed to be given a dual-purpose capability. After all, the Americans and Japanese had had 5-inch DP guns in service for many years and there was really no excuse for the Royal Navy to be without one. A design for a 4.7-inch BD mounting with 85° elevation had been prepared by July 1941, and it was ruled that sketch designs be prepared for ships carrying this gun, fitted with RPC and stabilizers. All the main armament was to be forward 'as experience has shown that we rarely need to fire aft'. Eventually, a design with four 4.7-inch BD 80° mountings, four twin Bofors and six Oerlikons was approved. Two quadruple banks of tubes were fitted despite the very perceptive comment by the ACNS that the torpedo carriers of the future were aircraft, submarines and small, fast craft. Had the torpedoes been omitted, and the weight saved used to ship a third twin mounting aft as was done in the early 1950s for, of all people, the Venezuelan Navy, the *Battle* design would have had few critics. There was in fact some consensus within the Fleet for the addition of a third twin mounting, but this was held to involve a larger ship of new design and the loss of two twin Bofors. As the Venezuelan *Nueva Esparta* later showed, the hull was enlarged a little but the armament was greatly enhanced:

	1942 *Battle* Class	*Nueva Esparta*
Displacement	2,300/3,360shp	2,600/3,300shp
Length	379ft	402ft
Beam	40.25ft	43ft
Draught	12.6ft	12.75ft
4.5in guns	2×2	3×2
40mm guns	4×2	8×2
Torpedo tubes	2×4	1×3

In March 1942, the Admiralty decided that the standard 4.7-inch gun calibre for destroyers would be replaced by a new 4.5-inch gun on several grounds. First, its projectile was 5lb heavier than that of the 4.7-inch, it was ballistically better and, it was believed, a fixed round could be successfully man-handled by the loading numbers. This latter feature was nonsense; a fixed round weighed 85lb and difficulties were already being experienced with the 74lb 4.7-inch round! In the event, common sense prevailed and separate ammunition was developed. Thus the main armament for this class became the 4.5-inch QF Mk III in 80° BD mountings Mk IV, one of which went to sea for trials in *Savage* (q.v.). This gun was given RPC and could fire 20rpg/m. Abaft the funnel, a single utility 4-inch single gun Mk III was fitted for starshell purposes, a somewhat needless addition because it seems futile to waste weight and space for this purpose, when the main guns were equally capable of the task. As for giving astern fire, this was impossible given its location and the presence of all the equipment astern of it.

Four Hazemeyer Mk IV twin Bofors with Type 282 radar control, all aft and six 20mm (two Mk V twin, two single) completed the AA outfit.

The main armament fire-control system was the Mk VI HA/LA director which was electrically-powered and capable of blind fire. This director was fitted with radar 275 in distinctive nacelles as well as a conventional rangefinder unit at the rear. Deliveries were very late and, as recounted in the *C*-class section, resulted in serious delays in these destroyers reaching the fleet. Many ships completed and ran trials without the director and were then laid up for many weeks awaiting its arrival.

The *Battle* design broke new ground not only in armament and fire control, but also as regards machinery, since for the first time since *Acheron* boiler pressures were increased to obtain better efficiency. Pressure was now 400psi at 700°F, but this was still behind US and German practice.

Orders were placed for twelve units on 27 April 1942 and a further four in August. *Camperdown* was the first to lay down, but *Barfleur* was the first afloat. However, the previously mentioned delivery problems associated with guns and directors resulted in *Barfleur*, which was due to complete in March 1944, not running trials until September when she commissioned and laid up to await her DCT.

Modifications Only *Barfleur, Camperdown, Hogue* and *Finisterre* completed before the end of hostilities, and they received no modifications during the war. The 2nd Flotilla (*Gabbard, St. Kitts, Cadiz, St. James, Vigo, Gravelines, Sluys* and *Solebay*) whose completions ran as late as December 1946, generally completed with STAAG 40mm Bofors on the after gun deck and five single Mk 7 Bofors (abaft funnel, bridge wings and before the bridge). None of these received the 4-inch gun whose fitment had been discontinued after *Hogue*. *Sluys* completed with the prototype twin 4.5in mounting Mk 6 in 'B' position.

Service Only *Barfleur* arrived in time to see action with the British Pacific Fleet from mid 1945, taking part in the last carrier operations against the Japanese mainland before being present at the final surrender. The remainder of her flotilla followed her as they completed. Post-war service extended until the late 1960s when armament and equipment was considerably updated. *Cadiz* was sold to Pakistan and renamed *Khaibar*, being sunk on the night of 4/5 December 1971 by Styx missiles launched by Indian Navy *Osa*-class FPBs off Karachi. *Gabbard* was also sold to Pakistan, renamed *Badr*. *Sluys* was sold to Iran and renamed *Artemiz*.

1943 BATTLE CLASS

Ship	Builder	Laid Down	Launched	Commissioned	Fate
I06 *Agincourt*	Hawthorn Leslie	12 Dec 43	29 Jan 45	25 June 47	Arrived for breaking up 27 Oct 74
I22 *Aisne*	Parsons M.S.T.Co.*	26 Aug 43	12 May 45	20 Mar 47	Arrived for breaking up 27 June 70
I17 *Alamein*	Hawthorn Leslie	1 Mar 44	28 May 45	21 May 48	Arrived for breaking up 1 Dec 64
I51 *Albuera*	V.A. (Tyne)	16 Sept 43	28 Aug 45	–	Arrived for breaking up 21 Nov 50
I68 *Barrosa*	John Brown	28 Dec 43	17 Jan 45	14 Feb 47	Arrived for breaking up 1 Dec 78
I88 *Belleisle*	Fairfield	10 Nov 43	7 Feb 46	–	Arrived for breaking up May 1946
I97 *Corunna*	Swan Hunter†	12 April 44	29 May 45	6 June 47	Arrived for breaking up 23 Nov 74
I09 *Dunkirk*	Stephen	19 July 44	27 Aug 45	27 Nov 46	Arrived for breaking up 22 Nov 65
I16 *Jutland* (i)	Hawthorn Leslie	11 Aug 44	2 Nov 45	–	Arrived for breaking up Oct 1957
I62 *Jutland* (ii) (ex-*Malplaquet*)	Stephen	27 Nov 44	20 Feb 46	30 April 47	Arrived for breaking up 14 May 65
I43 *Matapan*	John Brown	11 Mar 44	30 April 45	5 Sept 47	Arrived for breaking up 11 Aug 79
I53 *Mons*	Hawthorn Leslie	9 June 45	–	–	–
I58 *Namur*	Cammell Laird	29 April 44	12 June 45	–	Arrived for breaking up Feb 1951
I82 *Navarino*	Cammell Laird	25 May 44	21 Sept 45	–	Arrived for breaking up April 1946
I98 *Omdurman*	Fairfield	8 Mar 44	–	–	–
I02 *Oudenarde*	Swan Hunter	12 Oct 44	11 Sept 45	–	Arrived for breaking up Dec 1957
I10 *Poictiers*	Hawthorn Leslie	9 Feb 45	4 Jan 46	–	Broken up 1946
I83 *River Plate*	Swan Hunter	11 April 45	–	–	–
I42 *St. Lucia*	Stephen	19 Dec 45	–	–	–
I37 *San Domingo*	Cammell Laird	9 Dec 44	–	–	–
I31 *Somme*	Cammell Laird	24 Feb 45	–	–	–
I72 *Talavera*	John Brown	29 Aug 44	27 Aug 45	–	Sold for breaking up Jan 1946
I59 *Trincomalee*	John Brown	5 Feb 45	8 Jan 46	–	Sold for breaking up Feb 1946
I07 *Waterloo* (ex-*Vimeira*)	Fairfield	14 June 45	–	–	–
G22 *Vimeira*	Cammell Laird	–	–	–	–
G83 *Ypres*	Fairfield	–	–	–	–

*Hull sub-contracted to V.A. (Tyne).

As 1942 *Battle* but:
Displacement: 2,574tons/2,615tonnes (standard); 3,418tons/3,472tonnes (full load).
Beam: 40ft 6in/12.34m.
Guns: five 4.5 QF (2×2 Mk III, 1 Mk IV); eight 40mm (3×2, 2×1).
Torpedoes: ten 21in (2×5).

Design Although originally intended as repeat 1942 *Battles*, these ships were altered in a number of details major and minor. In October 1942, acquisition of the US Mk 37 fire-control system was considered to be of top priority and, if it could be obtained, the destroyers would be designed around it. British radar 275 would be fitted to it in lieu of the US FM type. There was also considerable discussion as to the gun armament to be carried because the lack of astern firepower in the 1942 *Battles* was still being criticized in some quarters. A new twin 4.5-inch mounting of the Upper Deck (UD) type had been designed, and it was being proposed that it be fitted to at least some of the new ships. It was eventually agreed that the last five ships be modified to carry three 4.5-inch twin UD Mk VI mountings, the rest to be as the 1942 type but some were to have an additional single 4.5-inch amidships. This idea was soon altered in that the last five ships were to carry two UD Mk VI mounts, one forward and one aft in a repeat *Battle* hull and machinery. This, however, was not generally liked but in all probability was the genesis of the *G* class. Argument continued over the gun layout and the relative merits of the BD Mk IV and UD Mk VI mountings, but eventually it was agreed that three flotillas (24 ships) were to be repeats of the 1942 class with two (*Waterloo* and *Ypres*) a new design. *Belleisle* and *Omdurman* were to have a greater beam (41 feet) to take the 4.5-inch UD Mk VI, but as a result of objections from their builders this was cancelled and *Talavera* and *Trincomalee* substituted instead. Then it was finally agreed to ship a single 4.5-inch Mk V abaft the funnel in all units, landing one twin 20mm and the 4-inch and fitting an extra twin Bofors between the tubes. This necessitated an increase in beam of 3 inches to 40 feet 6 inches to improve stability. In January 1944, *Waterloo* and *Ypres* were no longer to be new design, merely repeats but with UD mountings in lieu of BD which necessitated an increase in beam of 9 inches.

Torpedo outfit was increased to ten in two pentad mountings Mk III. In March 1944, two STAAG 40mm Bofors replaced the after pair of Mk IV Bofors and a utility Mk V twin the pair between the tubes. Two single and one twin 20mm completed the AA outfit.

Orders were placed for four units in March 1943, fifteen in April and five more in June.

Modifications The ships were not completed in time for war service.

Service Eighteen were cancelled, of which nine had been launched. Of those completed, the first, *Dunkirk*, did not complete until late 1946 and the last, *Alamein*, in mid 1948 some three years after the end of the war in Europe. In the 1960s, four, *Agincourt, Aisne, Barrosa* and *Corunna* were extensively converted to radar pickets. Curiously, *Matapan* after having spent almost her whole life in reserve, was rebuilt as a trials ships, becoming hardly recognizable as a former 'Battle'. She was not broken up until the end of the 1970s, more than thirty years after her completion.

Left: *Corunna*. (MOD)

WEAPON CLASS

Ship	Builder	Laid Down	Launched	Commissioned	Fate
G18 *Battleaxe*	A. Yarrow	22 April 44	12 June 45	23 Oct 47	Arrived for breaking up 20 Oct 64
G31 *Broadsword*	A. Yarrow	20 July 44	4 Feb 46	4 Oct 48	Arrived for breaking up 8 Oct 68
G82 *Carronade*	Scott's	26 April 44	5 April 46	–	Arrived for breaking up 5 April 46
G34 *Claymore*	Scott's	–	–	–	–
G96 *Crossbow*	Thornycroft	26 Aug 44	20 Dec 45	4 Mar 48	Arrived for breaking up 21 Jan 72
G28 *Culverin*	Thornycroft	27 April 44	–	–	–
G74 *Cutlass*	A. Yarrow	28 Sept 44	20 Mar 46	–	Arrived for breaking up Mar 1946
G23 *Dagger*	A. Yarrow	7 Mar 45	–	–	–
G02 *Dirk*	Scott's	–	–	–	–
G53 *Grenade*	Scott's	–	–	–	Cancelled 23 Dec 44
G99 *Halberd*	Scott's	–	–	–	Cancelled 23 Dec 44
G44 *Howitzer*	Thornycroft	26 Feb 45	–	–	–
G55 *Longbow*	Thornycroft	11 April 45	–	–	–
G78 *Musket*	S. White	–	–	–	Cancelled 5 Oct 45
G06 *Poniard*	Scott's	–	–	–	Cancelled 23 Dec 44
G21 *Rifle*	Denny	30 June 44	–	–	Cancelled 27 Dec 45
G30 *Spear*	Denny	28 Sept 44	–	–	Cancelled 27 Dec 45
G85 *Sword* (ex-*Celt*)	S. White	17 Sept 45	–	–	Cancelled 5 Oct 45
G64 *Tomahawk* (ex-*Centaur*)	S. White	16 Dec 44	15 Aug 46	17 Sept 47	Arrived for breaking up 1971

Displacement: 1,955tons/1,986tonnes (standard); 2,820tons/2,865tonnes (full load).
Length: 365ft/111.2m (oa); 350ft/106.7m (wl); 341ft 6in/104m (pp).
Beam: 38ft/11.6m.
Draught: 12ft 6in/3.8m (mean).
Machinery: two Foster-Wheeler boilers; 2-shaft geared turbines.
Performance: 40,000shp; 36kts.
Bunkerage: 630tons/640tonnes.
Guns: six 4in QF Mk XVI (3×2); four 40mm (2×2); four 20mm (2×2).
Torpedoes: eight 21in (2×4).
Complement: 255 (Leader 286).

Design This class was in essence a return to the 4-inch *L* class concept with better fire-control facilities, and its adoption is difficult to comprehend, except in the context of its having been developed to allow construction in yards unable to build *Battle*-class ships. The AA *L*-class ships had, however, acquitted themselves well in their brief careers despite a certain amount of criticism of their 4-inch guns from the surface action protagonists, and since then there had been frequent suggestions of putting the 4-inch HA twin in new destroyers. The hull length was kept roughly similar to that of the 'Emergency Flotillas', but the beam increased to 38 feet to allow retention of two banks of torpedo tubes. Only three twin 4-inch Mk XIX mountings could be accommodated, equipped with RPC and controlled by the Mk VI director and radar 275. Thus the gun armament was no advance on the Type II and IV *Hunt* class although the control facilities were infinitely better. Two predictor-controlled Mk IV twin Bofors (or STAAG when available) and two twin Oerlikon mountings completed the armament. For the first time, a separate barrage director was fitted aft. The most important change adopted by this design was the unit machinery principle, i.e., two separate boiler rooms and engine rooms. This was a significant step forward in damage-control practice and one which had been adopted by the USA years before. It also necessitated a return to two funnels, the first since the *Tribals*, but the fore funnel was hidden in the lattice mast. Boiler pressures were once again the 400psi of the *Battles* at a marginally higher temperature, but some units received 420psi boilers. Turbine gearing remained single reduction but they were the last to be so fitted. Sixteen ships were ordered on 7 April 1943, those built by White to be fully welded, the rest only partially. On 27 May 1943, four more were ordered.

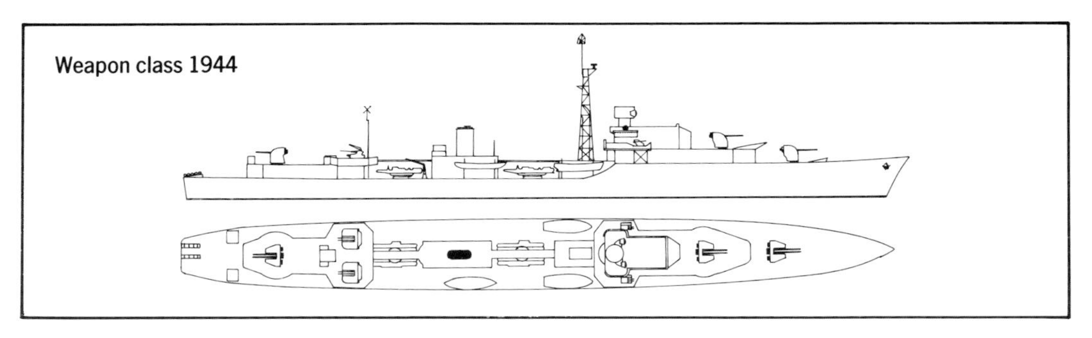

Left: *Scorpion*, converted to a radar picket, here photographed in April 1962. (Pavia)

G CLASS

Ship	Builder	Laid Down
G07 *Gael*	A. Yarrow	ordered 24 July 44, cancelled 27 Dec 45
G03 *Gallant*	A. Yarrow	ordered 24 July 44, cancelled 27 Dec 45
G59 *Gauntlet*	Thornycroft	Cancelled
G19 *Guernsey*	Denny	Cancelled 28 April 45
G45 *Glowworm* (ex-*Gift*)	Thornycroft	Cancelled
G76 *Grafton*	S. White	Cancelled
G88 *Greyhound*	S. White	Cancelled
G67 *Gift* (ex-*Glowworm*, ex-*Guinivere*)	Denny	Cancelled 28 Dec 45

Displacement: 1,995tons/2,027tonnes (standard); 2,740tons/2,783tonnes (full load).
Length: 365ft/111.25m (oa); 341ft 6in/104.09m (pp).
Beam: 39ft 6in/12.04m.
Draught: 14ft 2in/4.32m (mean).
Machinery: As *Weapon* class.
Performance: 40,000shp; 36.75kts.
Bunkerage: 586tons/595tonnes.
Guns: four 4.5in QF Mk 5 (2×2); six 40mm (2×2, 2×1).
Torpedoes: ten 21in (2×5).

Design Something of a mystery design, the precise path which led to the *G* class is rather obscure, buried in the tortuous discussions concerning the destroyers projected for the 1944 programme. As finally developed, the main armament was to be two twin 4.5-inch Mk VI UD mountings disposed one forward, one aft. This arrangement had been considered for some of the 1943 *Battles*, but the general hull layout more closely resembled the *Weapons*. The *Weapons* had a good machinery layout but were poorly armed with only 4-inch guns and it would appear that the two designs coalesced to a certain extent to produce the *G* class. This class therefore may have taken the place of the 6th *Battle* flotilla in the building programme. The hull dimensions conformed to the *Weapon* design except that the beam was increased to 39½ feet to compensate the greater top-weight associated with the heavier Mk VI mountings and US-pattern Mk 37 director. However, it is interesting to note that the 1943 *Battles*, projected to take the 4.5-inch UD mounting, were to have a beam of 41 feet and that the later *Daring* class, with three such mountings, had a 43 feet beam. Orders were placed for eight ships in 1944, Yarrow receiving theirs on 24 July, but all were subsequently cancelled in 1945. It is unlikely that any were laid down. The reason for their cancellation is unclear, but the end of the war obviously had some bearing on the matter. Nevertheless, it is probable that the gun armament, especially forward, was not popular and there is a clear resemblance between the *G* and *Daring* classes, the latter having an extra twin 4.5-inch worked in before the bridge. Orders were placed for the *Darings* on 29 March 1945, the day after the cancellation of at least one *G*. Even some of this class were subsequently cancelled on or about the time of the cancellation of the remainder of the *Gs*.

HUNT (TYPE 1) CLASS

Ship	Builder	Laid Down	Launched	Commissioned	Fate
L05 *Atherstone*	Cammell Laird	8 June 39	12 Dec 39	23 Mar 40	Sold out 23 Nov 57
L17 *Berkeley*	Cammell Laird	8 June 39	29 Jan 40	6 June 40	Lost 19 Aug 42
L24 *Blencathra*	Cammell Laird	18 Nov 39	6 Aug 40	14 Dec 40	Arrived for breaking up 2 Jan 57
L42 *Brocklesby*	Cammell Laird	18 Nov 39	30 Sept 40	9 May 41	Broken up 1959
L35 *Cattistock*	A. Yarrow	9 June 39	22 Feb 40	1 Aug 40	Arrived for breaking up June 1957
L46 *Cleveland*	A. Yarrow	7 July 39	24 April 40	18 Sept 40	Wrecked 28 June 57
L78 *Cottesmore*	A. Yarrow	12 Dec 39	5 Sept 40	29 Dec 40	To Egypt July 1950
L54 *Cotswold*	A. Yarrow	10 Oct 39	18 July 40	16 Nov 40	Arrived for breaking up 11 Sept 57
L87 *Eglington*	Parsons M.S.T.Co.*	8 June 39	28 Dec 39	28 Aug 40	Arrived for breaking up 28 May 56
L61 *Exmoor* (i)	Parsons M.S.T.Co.*	8 June 39	25 Jan 40	18 Oct 40	Lost 25 Feb 41
L100 *Liddesdale*	Parsons M.S.T.Co.*	20 Nov 39	19 Aug 40	28 Feb 41	Sold out 1 Oct 48
L11 *Fernie*	John Brown	8 June 39	9 Jan 40	29 May 40	Arrived for breaking up 7 Nov 56
L20 *Garth*	John Brown	8 June 39	14 Feb 40	1 July 40	Arrived for breaking up 25 Aug 58
L37 *Hambledon*	Swan Hunter	9 June 39	12 Dec 39	8 June 40	Arrived for breaking up Sept 1957
L48 *Holderness*	Swan Hunter	29 June 39	8 Feb 40	10 Aug 40	Arrived for breaking up 20 Nov 56
L60 *Mendip*	Swan Hunter	10 Aug 39	9 April 40	12 Oct 40	To China May 1948
L82 *Meynell*	Swan Hunter	10 Aug 39	7 June 40	30 Dec 40	To Equador 1955
L92 *Pytchley*	Scott's	27 July 39	13 Feb 40	23 Oct 40	Arrived for breaking up 1 Dec 56
L58 *Quantock*	Scott's	26 July 39	22 April 40	6 Feb 41	To Equador 16 Aug 55
L66 *Quorn*	S. White	22 Aug 39	27 Mar 40	3 Aug 40	Lost 2/3 Aug 44
L25 *Southdown*	S. White	22 Aug 39	5 July 40	8 Nov 40	Arrived for breaking up 1 Nov 56
L96 *Tynedale*	Stephens	27 July 39	5 June 40	5 Nov 40	Lost 12 Dec 43
L45 *Whaddon*	Stephens	27 July 39	16 July 40	28 Feb 41	Broken up 1959, Faslane

*Hulls sub-contracted to V.A. (Tyne).

Left: *Berkeley* in April 1942. She was sunk by German aircraft during the Dieppe raid. (G. Ransome)

Displacement: 1,000tons/1,016tonnes (standard); 1,490tons/1,513tonnes (full load).
Length: 280ft/85.3m (oa); 272ft/82.9m (wl); 264ft 3in/80.54m (pp).
Beam: 29ft/8.84m.
Draught: 7ft 9in/2.36m (mean).
Machinery: two Admiralty 3-drum boilrs; 2-shaft Parsons geared turbines.
Performance: 19,000shp; 30kts.
Bunkerage: 280tons/284tonnes.
Range: 2,000nm at 12kts.
Guns: six 4in HA QF (3×2); four 2pdr (1×4) (as designed, but see text).
Complement: 146.

Design The prolific *Hunt* class arose from the need for an escort vessel capable of convoy AA defence but with a good turn of speed so that it might also, when required, undertake a limited number of destroyer functions. The escort vessels of the *Egret* and *Black Swan* types, with eight or six 4-inch HA guns were admirable designs as far as their AA outfits were concerned, but their speed of less than 20 knots was not sufficient for what the Naval staff had in mind. While speed was not strictly important for ASW work, it considerably assisted transit and chasing operations. As for the other extant patrol vessels, the *Puffin* class, they were no faster than the sloops and their armament was pitiful. The other major factor to be taken into consideration was, as usual, cost, for it was necessary to build as many units as possible to give the numbers of destroyer types predicted as needed in the forthcoming war.

A good high-angle main armament was essential. This ruled out the 4.7-inch twin Mk XIX (only 40° elevation) while the 4.7-inch twin Mk XX with 50° elevation would require a much bigger ship than the money could provide and in any case, few were under construction. This left only the 4-inch HA Mk XIX 80° twin mounting. Design work pressed ahead rapidly, other parameters being a speed of 28/31 knots; four 4-inch HA, one quad 2pdr and an endurance of 3,500 nautical miles at 15 knots. Stabilizers were to be fitted and one quadruple bank of tubes on a standard displacement of 810 tons. At the same time, two other escort vessel designs were also proposed, of just over 600 tons, armed with two twin 4-inch but no torpedoes and having a speed of 25 knots.

In the event, none of these designs were acceptable and instead a different design was proceeded with. This added a third twin 4-inch at the expense of torpedoes. Requirements for speed and good seaworthiness pushed up the hull weights and in consequence, displacement, to close on 900 tons. Armament was now six 4-inch HA, two quadruple

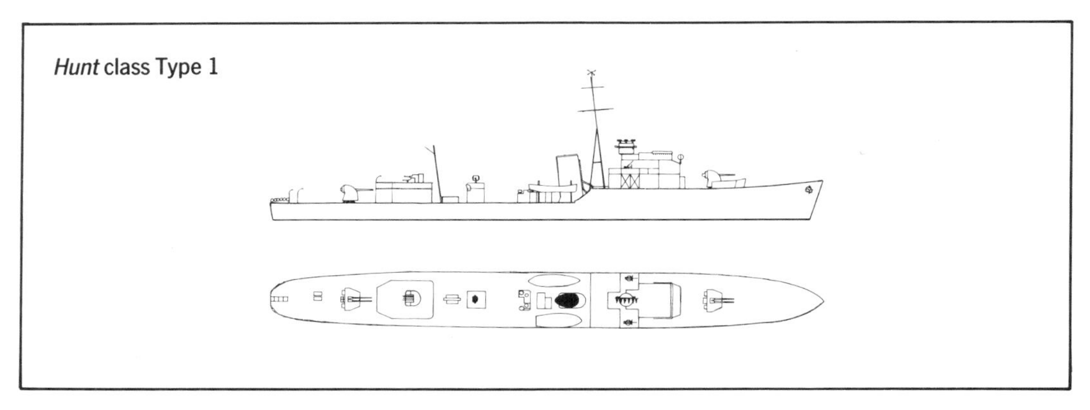

Above: *Hambledon.* **Below:** *Southdown.* (Author's Collection)

.5in machine-guns, two depth-charge throwers one rail and twenty depth-charges. 18,000shp gave a maximum speed of 29 knots at deep load displacement. Later, a quadruple 2pdr supplanted the .5in MGs and depth-charge stowage was increased to 30. This increased displacement once again and SHP was therefore raised to 19,000 to maintain speed.

War was obviously not far off once more and it was essential to get the ships under construction as quickly as possible. Herein lay a flaw, for the design calculations were done in such a rush that an error was made which was not immediately spotted. Verbal orders were placed for the first time in January 1939, being confirmed in March, followed by orders for ten more on 11 April. Nine were laid down in June 1939 and by the outbreak of war, a total of eighteen were on the slipways. When the leading ship *Atherstone* was fitting out, it was realized that a serious error in stability calculations had been made, confirming what had hitherto been only a suspicion in some quarters. The stability was insufficient to accommodate three 4-inch twin. This was a grave error for by now, 23 ships were under construction beyond the point where they could be altered to retain the three mountings. 'X' gun was removed from *Atherstone* and all construction stopped on the remaining ships until trials had been completed on the leading ship. Fortunately, these proved satisfactory, although deep load displacement had by now risen to 1,340 tons with a consequent reduction in speed. The other 22 units were then completed to the same configuration as *Atherstone*.

Modifications In 1941–42, sponsons were built out from the after end of the bridge at shelter deck level to accommodate single 20mm Oerlikons and many also received a single 2pdr hand-worked Mk VIII as a bow-chaser, especially when employed on east coast convoy routes. Radar 286 was fitted at the masthead, later replaced by 290 or 291. Radar 285 was fitted to the HACS. Some, including *Holderness, Fernie, Whaddon* and *Blencathra*, later received radar 271 lanterns on towers between the searchlight platform and the after deck-house. *Meynell* received a twin 40mm Bofors in 1945, replacing the quad. 2pdr.

Service By the end of 1940, there were 19 *Hunt*s operational, based at Sheerness, Harwich and Portsmouth. Their main task was east coast and Channel convoy escort and it was on this duty that *Exmoor* was lost. While escorting Convoy FN417, she was hit aft by a torpedo fired by the German *S30*, caught fire and sank quickly. In 1942, *Atherstone, Cleveland* and *Tynedale* took part in the St-Nazaire raid and in August 1942, *Berkeley, Garth, Brocklesby* and *Fernie* with other *Hunt*s covered the Dieppe raid, when *Berkeley* was sunk by German aircraft and both *Brocklesby* and *Fernie* damaged. *Tynedale, Cottesmore* and *Quorn* were part of the force which intercepted the German raider *Komet* in the English Channel in October 1942. In 1943, several went to the Mediterranean when *Atherstone, Cleveland, Hambledon, Mendip, Quantock, Tynedale* and *Whaddon* were at the invasion of Sicily and, except the last two, Salerno in September 1943. *Tynedale* was torpedoed and sunk by *U593* off Bougie in December. *Cattistock, Cottesmore, Cotswold, Eglinton, Garth, Holderness, Meynell, Pytchley* and *Quorn* were in the Channel for the invasion of Europe in June 1944. *Quorn*, however, was sunk by a *Linsen* explosive motorboat off the invasion area. *Atherstone, Cleveland* and *Blencathra* covered the landings in southern France in August 1944 and later *Clevedon, Liddesdale* and *Whaddon* went to the Aegean.

After the end of the war, most if not all, went into the reserve fleet and saw no more active service. The exception was *Brocklesby* which ran as a trials ship for some time. *Cottesmore* was sold to Egypt as *Ibrahim el Awal* and had a very chequered subsequent career; *Mendip* to Nationalist China as *Lin Fu* (but later returned and resold to Egypt as *Mohamed Ali el Kebir*), and both *Meynell* and *Quantock* to Equador as *Velasco Ybarra* and *Presidente Alfaro*.

HUNT (TYPE 2) CLASS

Ship	Builder	Laid Down	Launched	Commissioned	Fate
L06 *Avon Vale*	John Brown	12 Feb 40	23 Oct 40	17 Feb 41	Arrived for breaking up 15 May 58
L03 *Badsworth*	Cammell Laird	15 May 40	17 Mar 41	18 Aug 41	To Norway 1946
L14 *Beaufort*	Cammell Laird	17 July 40	9 June 41	3 Nov 41	To Norway 1946
L26 *Bedale*	Hawthorn Leslie	25 May 40	23 July 41	18 June 42	To India 1953
L34 *Bicester*	Hawthorn Leslie	29 May 40	5 Sept 41	9 May 42	Arrived for breaking up 22 Aug 56
L43 *Blackmore*	Stephen	10 Feb 41	2 Dec 41	14 April 42	To Denmark 1952
L30 *Blankney*	John Brown	17 May 40	19 Dec 40	11 April 41	Arrived for breaking up Mar 1959
L51 *Bramham*	Stephen	7 April 41	29 Jan 42	16 June 42	To Greece 1943
L08 *Exmoor* (ii) (ex-*Burton*)	Swan Hunter	7 June 40	12 Mar 41	18 Oct 41	To Denmark 1953
L71 *Calpe*	Swan Hunter	12 June 40	28 April 41	11 Dec 41	To Denmark 1952
L31 *Chiddingfold*	Scott's	1 Mar 40	10 Mar 41	16 Oct 41	To India 1954
L52 *Cowdray*	Scott's	30 April 40	22 July 41	29 July 42	Arrived for breaking up 3 Sept 59
L62 *Croome*	Stephen	7 June 40	30 Jan 41	29 June 41	Arrived for breaking up 13 Aug 57
L63 *Dulverton*	Stephen	16 July 40	1 April 41	28 Sept 41	Lost 13 Nov 43
L68 *Eridge*	Swan Hunter	21 Nov 39	20 Aug 40	28 Feb 41	C.T.L. 29 Aug 42
L70 *Farndale*	Swan Hunter	21 Nov 39	30 Sept 40	27 April 41	Arrived for breaking up 4 Dec 62
L77 *Grove*	Swan Hunter	28 Aug 40	29 May 41	5 Feb 42	Lost 12 June 42
L85 *Heythrop*	Swan Hunter	18 Dec 39	30 Oct 40	21 June 41	Lost 20 Mar 42
L84 *Hursley*	Swan Hunter	21 Dec 40	25 July 41	2 April 42	To Greece 1943
L28 *Hurworth*	V.A. (Tyne)	10 April 40	10 April 41	5 Oct 41	Lost 22 Oct 43
L88 *Lamberton*	Swan Hunter	10 April 40	14 Dec 40	16 Aug 41	To India 1953
L95 *Lauderdale*	Thornycroft	21 Dec 39	5 Aug 41	23 Dec 41	To Greece 1946
L90 *Ledbury*	Thornycroft	24 Jan 40	27 Sept 41	11 Feb 42	Arrived for breaking up May 1958
L74 *Middleton*	V.A. (Tyne)	10 April 40	12 May 41	10 Jan 42	Arrived for breaking up 4 Oct 57
L72 *Oakley* (i)	V.A. (Tyne)	22 Nov 39	30 Oct 40	17 June 41	Lost 16 June 42
L108 *Puckeridge*	S. White	1 Jan 40	6 Mar 41	30 July 41	Lost 6 Sept 43
L115 *Silverton*	S. White	5 Dec 39	4 Dec 40	28 May 41	To Poland 1941
L10 *Southwold*	S. White	18 June 40	5 July 41	9 Oct 41	Lost 23 Feb 42
L99 *Tetcott*	S. White	29 July 40	12 Aug 41	11 Dec 41	Arrived for breaking up 24 Sept 56
L98 *Oakley* (ii) (ex-*Tickham*)	Yarrow	19 Aug 40	15 Jan 42	7 May 42	To W. Germany 1958
L122 *Wheatland*	Yarrow	30 May 40	7 June 41	3 Nov 41	Arrived for breaking up 20 Sept 59
L128 *Wilton*	Yarrow	7 June 40	17 Oct 41	18 Feb 42	Arrived for breaking up 30 Nov 59
L59 *Zetland*	Yarrow	2 Oct 40	7 Mar 42	27 June 42	To Norway 1954

Displacement: 1,050tons/1,067tonnes (standard); 1,610tons/1,635tonnes (full load).
Length: 280ft/85.3m (oa); 272ft/82.9m (wl); 264ft 3in/80.54m (pp).
Beam: 31ft 6in/9.6m.
Draught: 7ft 9in/2.36m (mean).
Machinery: two Admiralty 3-drum boilers; 2-shaft Parsons geared turbines.
Performance: 19,000shp; 29kts.
Bunkerage: 345tons/350tonnes.
Range: 3,600nm at 14kts.
Guns: six 4in QF HA (3×2); four 2pdr (1×4).
Complement: 146.

Design Following the experience with *Atherstone*, these ships were altered while on the stocks to increase their beam. This was done by kippering those already laid down by the insertion of extra plates on each side of the keel plate. This increased the beam to 31 feet 6 inches and allowed the retention of the third twin 4in. The 2pdr replaced by this mounting was repositioned abaft the funnel as originally intended.

Modifications These generally followed the pattern of the Type 1 *Hunt*s, except that most completed with 20mm in the bridge wings, surface warning radar and Type 285 on the HACS. Wartime alterations were limited to the addition of radar 271 amidships in some units (including *Avon Vale, Blackmore* and *Blankney*) and a few received HF/DF on pole masts aft. *Eridge* was unusual in that she still had her 286 radar in August 1942 and had her 20mm guns mounted on the forecastle deck at the break. 2pdr bow-chasers were added in some units and power-operated twin 20mm replaced the singles in the bridge wings in 1943–44. Some, including *Exmoor* and *Beaufort*, received two single 40mm Bofors.

Service *Bedale, Oakley* (i) and *Silverton* served as the Polish *Slazak, Kujawiak* and *Krakowiak* from 1941–42, *Bramham* and *Hursley* as the Greek *Themistocles* and *Kriti* on completion (q.v.); *Avon Vale* and *Cowdray* also served briefly in the Greek Navy as *Aegean* and *Admiral Hastings* respectively in 1944.

Practically the whole of this class served in the Mediterranean theatre from the summer of 1941 to the spring of 1945 with the greatest numbers being present for the major landings on Sicily and at Salerno in 1943. A few operated in home waters

Left: *Lamberton*. Note 286 radar and lack of 20mm guns. (Swan Hunter)

Right: *Hursley*. (Swan Hunter)

Below: *Avonvale*. Note radars, HF/DF and 2pdr bow-chaser. (MOD)

prior to their transfer to the Mediterranean, for example, *Wheatland, Lamberton* and *Chiddingfold* participated in the Lofoten Island raid in December 1941, and in June 1942 *Wilton* and *Ledbury* were part of the escort for Russian Convoy PQ17. *Middleton* also covered this duty in February 1943, but this was a task for which they had not been designed and they were not often so employed.

A few operated with the Western Approaches Command where *Croome* sank the Italian submarine *Baraca* in September 1941, *Lamberton* and aircraft *Ferraris* in October, *Exmoor* and *Blankney* assisted in the loss of *U131* in December 1941 and *Blankney* with *Stanley, U431* later in the month. In 1942, *Grove* and *Aldenham* (Type III) with other escorts sank *U587* in March.

In the Mediterranean one of their early tasks was the Malta convoys. *Farndale* sank the Italian submarine *Caracciola* in December 1941, but was herself badly damaged by bombs off Mersa Matruh the following February. A month later, *Heythrop* was torpedoed and sunk by *U652* north of Sollum and *Southwold* was mined outside Malta. *Grove* was torpedoed by *U77* also off Sollum in June and in August *Eridge* was so badly damaged by a torpedo in the Eastern Mediterranean that she could only be used as a depot ship at Alexandria for the remainder of the war. *Badsworth* was twice damaged on Malta convoys. On the positive side, *Croome* and *Tetcott*, in company with other destroyers and aircraft, accounted for *U372* while *Dulverton* and *Hurworth* assisted in the sinking of *U559*, both of these successes being in the eastern Mediterranean.

In the New Year, *Hursley* was involved in the sinking of the Italian submarine *Narvalo* but in that January *Avon Vale* was seriously damaged by an aircraft torpedo. Other successes in February 1943 were *Asteria* sunk by *Wheatland* and *Easton* (Type III), *U562* by *Hursley* once again with other ships and aircraft and finally *U443* by *Bicester, Lamberton* and *Wheatland*. Many units participated in the Invasion of Sicily during July and also the landings at Salerno in September. However, *Puckeridge* was torpedoed and sunk by *U617* off Gibraltar that month also. In the autumn of 1943 the centre of operations shifted to the eastern Mediterranean and the Dodecanese. Here, *Hursley* and *Beaufort* (with *Belvoir*) encountered and sank *UJ2109*, but *Hurworth* was mined off Kalymnos in October. *Dulverton* was sunk by an HS293 glider bomb in November off Leros, but *Calpe* shared the sinking of *U593* in December.

1944 saw some units covering the landings at Anzio while others remained in the Adriatic and Aegean theatres. *Middleton* and *Avon Vale* were in home waters for the Normandy landings, while in November, *Wheatland* and *Avon Vale* fought an

action in the Adriatic sinking the German escorts *TA20, UJ202* and *UJ208*. With the running down of the action in the Mediterranean by 1945, many units returned to home waters for the last months of hostilities.

Only a few units saw post-war service, many being sold or transferred to other Allied nations. *Badsworth, Beaufort* and *Zetland* went to Norway as *Arendal, Haugesund* and *Tromso. Bedale, Chiddingfold* and *Lamberton* to India as *Godavari, Ganga* and *Gomati. Blackmore, Exmoor* and *Calpe* were sold to Denmark and renamed *Esbern Snare, Valdemar* and *Rolf Krake*, and *Lauderdale* to Greece as *Aigaion*. Finally, much later, *Oakley* was transferred to the resurrected German Navy as *Gneisenau*. The survivors on the Navy List dwindled rapidly throughout the 1950s, the last to go being *Farndale* as late as 1962.

HUNT (TYPE 3) CLASS

Ship	Builder	Laid Down	Launched	Commissioned	Fate
L07 *Airedale*	John Brown	20 Nov 40	12 Aug 41	31 Dec 41	Lost 15 June 42
L12 *Albrighton*	John Brown	30 Dec 40	11 Oct 41	22 Feb 42	To W. Germany 1958
L22 *Aldenham*	Cammell Laird	22 Aug 40	27 Aug 41	30 Jan 42	Lost 14 Dec 44
L32 *Belvoir*	Cammell Laird	14 Oct 40	18 Nov 41	29 Mar 42	Arrived for breaking up 21 Oct 57
L47 *Blean*	Hawthorn Leslie	24 Feb 41	15 Jan 42	23 Aug 42	Lost 11 Dec 42
L50 *Bleasdale*	V.A. (Tyne)	31 Oct 40	23 July 41	16 April 42	Arrived for breaking up 14 Sept 56
L65 *Bolebroke*	Swan Hunter	3 April 41	5 Nov 41	10 June 42	To Greece 1942
L67 *Border*	Swan Hunter	1 May 41	3 Feb 42	5 Aug 42	To Greece 1942
L81 *Catterick*	V.A. (Barrow)	1 Mar 41	22 Nov 41	6 June 42	To Greece 1946
L83 *Derwent*	V.A. (Barrow)	29 Dec 40	22 Aug 41	3 April 42	Sold for breaking up Nov 1946
L09 *Easton*	S. White	25 Mar 41	11 July 42	7 Dec 42	Arrived for breaking up Jan 1953
L15 *Eggesford*	S. White	23 June 41	12 Sept 42	29 Jan 43	To W. Germany 1958
L36 *Eskdale*	Cammell Laird	18 Jan 41	16 Mar 42	31 July 42	Lost 14 April 43
L44 *Glaisdale*	Cammell Laird	4 Feb 41	5 Jan 42	12 June 42	To Norway 1946
L27 *Goathland*	Fairfield	30 Jan 41	3 Feb 42	6 Nov 42	Arrived for breaking up Aug 1945
L19 *Haldon*	Fairfield	16 Jan 41	27 April 42	30 Dec 42	To France 1942
L53 *Hatherleigh*	V.A. (Tyne)	12 Dec 40	18 Dec 41	10 Aug 42	To Greece 1942
L75 *Haydon*	V.A. (Tyne)	1 May 41	2 April 42	24 Oct 42	Arrived for breaking up 18 May 58
L56 *Holcombe*	Stephen	3 Mar 41	14 April 42	17 Sept 42	Lost 12 Dec 43
L57 *Limbourne*	Stephen	8 April 41	12 May 42	23 Oct 42	Lost 23 Oct 43
L73 *Melbreak*	Swan Hunter	23 June 41	5 Mar 42	10 Oct 42	Arrived for breaking up 22 Nov 56
L91 *Modbury*	Swan Hunter	5 Aug 41	13 April 42	25 Nov 42	To Greece 1942
L89 *Penylan*	V.A. (Barrow)	4 June 41	17 Mar 42	25 Aug 42	Lost 3 Dec 42
L39 *Rockwood*	V.A. (Barrow)	29 Aug 41	13 June 42	4 Nov 42	C.T.L. 11 Nov 43
L16 *Stevenstone*	S. White	2 Sept 41	23 Nov 42	18 Mar 43	Arrived for breaking up 2 Sept 59
L69 *Tanatside*	A. Yarrow	23 June 41	30 April 42	4 Sept 42	To Greece 1946
L86 *Wensleydale*	A. Yarrow	–	20 June 42	30 Oct 42	C.T.L. Nov 1944
L18 *Talybont*	S. White	28 Nov 41	3 Feb 43	19 May 43	Sold for breaking up 14 Feb 61

Displacement: 1,037tons/1,053tonnes (standard); 1,620tons/1,646tonnes (full load).
Length: 280ft/85.3m (oa); 272ft/82.9m (wl); 264ft 3in/80.54m (pp).
Beam: 31ft 6in/9.6m.
Draught: 7ft 9in/36m (mean).
Machinery: two Admiralty 3-drum boilers; 2-shaft Parsons geared turbines.
Performance: 19,000shp; 29kts.
Bunkerage: 345tons/350tonnes.
Range: 3,700nm at 14kts.
Guns: four 4in HA (2×2); four 2pdr (1×4); three 20mm (3×1).
Torpedoes: two 21in (1×2).
Complement: 168.

Design This group, originally thirty in number, were ordered under the 1940 programme and were intended to be repeat Type-2 ships. However, as a result of representations from the torpedo protagonists, 28 of them were given torpedoes and the remaining two completed to a new design.

To accommodate the torpedoes (a twin trainable mounting), 'Y' gun was deleted to save the necessary top-weight. In its place a third single Oerlikon was fitted and the remaining quarter deck space vacated by the 4-inch mounting was given over to ASW equipment. Apart from the torpedo tubes the other visually different feature was the vertical mast and funnel, the latter with a sharply raked top. There were also two distinctive styles of bridge.

Modifications These followed the lines of the Group 2 ships. Towards the end of the war, those units refitting for transfer to the East Indies including *Easton, Talybont, Haydon* and *Melbreak*, received single Bofors guns before the bridge and on the quarter deck, losing the Oerlikons from the bridge wings as compensation. *Bleasdale* at least received three power-operated 20mm, one of which was mounted on a bandstand on the quarter deck.

Above: *Melbreak*. (Swan Hunter) **Below:** *Albrighton* in February 1943. (MOD)

Below: *Eggesford* in 1946. (MOD)

Below: *Blean* in 1942. (MOD)

Service *Bolebroke, Border, Hatherleigh* and *Modbury* were transferred to the Greek Navy on completion and renamed *Pindos, Adrias, Kanaris* and *Miaoulis* respectively. *Eskdale* was completed for the Royal Norwegian Navy, but retained her name, while *Glaisdale* was Norwegian-manned.

The service of these destroyers was similar to that of the other *Hunt*s, in the Mediterranean, Adriatic and North Seas. However, with their torpedo outfit they were also found useful in sweeps against enemy convoys in the English Channel. *Airedale* was one which went to the Mediterranean and became an early loss when she was sunk by dive-bombers while on Malta convoys. *Albrighton* and *Bleasdale* were at Dieppe in August 1942. In one of the Channel sweeps, *Eskdale* and *Albrighton* with the Norwegian *Glaisdale* were involved in the action during which *Komet* was sunk, but *Penylan* was torpedoed and sunk by *S115* while on convoy duty in the Channel in December. Meanwhile, in the Mediterranean, *Blean*, on passage to Gibraltar, was torpedoed and sunk by *U443*. *Derwent*, after a brief deployment into the Red Sea and Arabian Gulf, was hit by a circling torpedo dropped by an aircraft while she was in harbour at Tripoli on 19 March 1943. Badly damaged, she was declared a constructional total loss. Several units participated in the landings at Sicily and Salerno and many operated in the eastern Mediterranean where *Rockwood* was badly damaged by Hs 293 bombs, then declared a write-off and *Belvoir* was damaged by a mine. Finally, during the mopping-up operations in the Adriatic in 1944, *Aldenham*, returning from a bombardment operation, struck a mine and sank off Pola.

Above: *Haydon*, lacking all radar. (Real Photos)

In home waters, *Melbreak* was badly damaged during a sweep against an enemy convoy off Ushant in July 1943, then *Limbourne* was torpedoed and sunk by *T22* off the coast of Brittany in the *Charybdis* disaster. In 1944, many units were present for 'Overlord', including *Stevenstone, Wensleydale, Belvoir, Goathland* and *Haldon. Goathland*, mined on 24 June 1944, was never repaired. Apart from covering the landings, the *Hunt*s were also used with MGBs against S-boats along the Channel coast. In July, *Melbreak* unsuccessfully attempted to prevent *T28* returning to Germany from Le Havre. *Wensleydale* was badly damaged in a collision in November 1944 and never repaired. Actions against S-boats continued into 1945 but most were inconclusive.

Post-war, *Albrighton* and *Eggesford* went to Germany, being renamed *Raule* and *Brommy. Glaisdale*, Norwegian-manned throughout the war, was transferred to Norway in 1946, being renamed *Narvik. Catterick* and *Tanatside* were sold to Greece becoming *Hastings* and *Adrias* (ii).

HUNT (TYPE 4) CLASS

Ship	Builder	Laid Down	Launched	Commissioned	Fate
L76 *Brecon*	Thornycroft	27 Feb 41	27 June 42	18 Dec 42	Arrived for breaking up 17 Sept 62
L79 *Brissenden*	Thornycroft	28 Feb 41	15 Sept 42	12 Feb 42	Arrived for breaking up 3 Mar 65

Displacement: 1,170tons/1,188tonnes (standard); 1,589tons/1,614tonnes (full load).
Length: 296ft/90.2m (oa); 283ft/86.2m (wl); 276ft/84.1m (pp).
Beam: 33ft 4in/10.15m.
Machinery: two Admiralty 3-drum boilers; 2-shaft Parsons geared turbines.
Performance: 19,000shp; 25kts.
Bunkerage: 286tons/290tonnes (357/362 *Brissenden*).
Range: 2,350nm at 20kts.
Guns: six 4in QF Mk XVI (3×2); four 2pdr (1×4); two 20mm.
Torpedoes: three 21in (1×3).
Complement: 170.

Design The final pair of the 1940 programme were built to a new design based upon proposals from Thornycroft. This had originally been submitted at the request of the Naval Staff in the autumn of 1938, and it incorporated an almost flush deck with a square section hull form. The design as first submitted was not liked by the Construction Department on a number of grounds including stability, hull form and speed, the latter being 2¾ knots slower than the ordinary *Hunt*s (installed power was only 15,000shp). The long forecastle deck was, however, a definite advantage. Revision of the design was called for and a modified design was submitted in May 1940. This too received some criticism and it was not until mid-July that a final design was submitted and accepted. By now, full load displacement had risen to over 1,500 tons and installed power increased to 19,000shp in line with the other *Hunt*s. Beam was more than 2 foot greater than the Type III *Hunt*s, allowing the torpedo outfit to be increased to a triple mounting, carried at forecastle deck level, and three twin 4-inch. Special attention was paid to the design of the bridge to reduce and control air flow over the compass platform. Stabilizers were included in the design, but they were removed from *Brissenden* before completion, and oil stowage correspondingly increased.

Modifications In 1943, power-operated twin 20mm Oerlikons replaced the singles in the bridge wings (*Brissenden* only) and two more were fitted on the

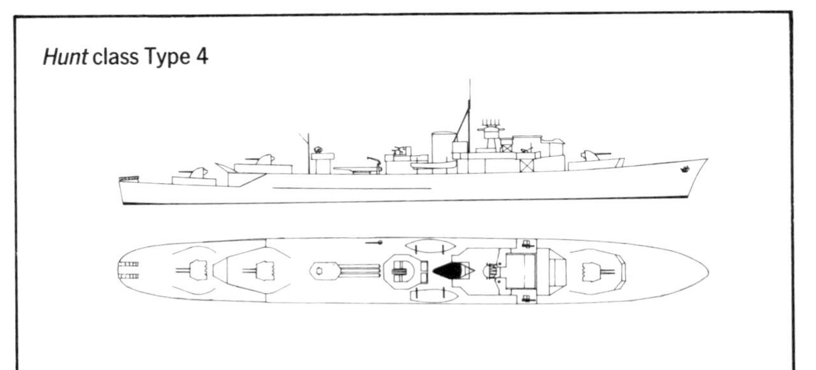

Hunt class Type 4

Below: *Brecon*. (IWM)

Above: *Brissenden*. (IWM)

upper deck abreast the searchlight platform. Radar 271 was fitted in lieu of the searchlight (*Brissenden* only) and 291 at the masthead. *Brissenden* also carried a 2pdr bow-chaser. In 1945, *Brecon* exchanged her twin 20mm amidships for single 40mm Bofors.

Service Both ships served initially in home waters, but in 1943 went to the Mediterranean to support the landings on Sicily in July. *Brecon* remained in these waters, serving at Salerno and Anzio. *Brissenden* meanwhile had returned to home waters. *Brecon* participated in the sinking of *U343* in March 1944 when her sister was in action in the Channel Theatre, and at Normandy in June.

In the Mediterranean, *Brecon* covered the invasion convoys for the landings in the South of France in August 1944, before going to the Aegean in September. Finally in 1945 she went to the East Indies and *Brissenden* came out to the Mediterranean.

After the end of the war, both went into reserve and never saw service again. *Brecon* was broken up at Faslane and her sister at Dalmuir.

CAPTAIN (TURBO-ELECTRIC) CLASS

Ship	Builder	Laid Down	Launched	Commissioned	Fate
K314 *Bentinck* (ex-*DE52*)	Bethlehem (Hingham)	29 June 42	22 Aug 42	19 May 43	Ret USN 5 Jan 46
K315 *Byard* (ex-*DE55*)	Bethlehem (Hingham)	15 Oct 42	13 Mar 43	18 June 43	Ret USN 12 Dec 46
K349 *Calder* (ex-*DE58*)	Bethlehem (Hingham)	11 Dec 42	27 Mar 43	15 July 43	Ret USN 19 Oct 45
K351 *Duckworth* (ex-*DE61*)	Bethlehem (Hingham)	16 Jan 43	1 May 43	4 Aug 43	Ret USN 17 Dec 45
K352 *Duff* (ex-*DE64*)	Bethlehem (Hingham)	22 Feb 43	29 May 43	23 Aug 43	C.T.L. 30 Nov 44
K353 *Essington* (ex-*DE67*)	Bethlehem (Hingham)	15 Mar 43	19 June 43	7 Sept 43	Ret USN 19 Oct 45
K462 *Affleck* (ex-*DE71*)	Bethlehem (Hingham)	5 April 43	30 June 43	29 Sept 43	C.T.L. 26 Dec 44
K463 *Aylmer* (ex-*DE72*)	Bethlehem (Hingham)	12 April 43	10 July 43	20 Sept 43	Ret USN 5 Nov 45
K464 *Balfour* (ex-*DE73*)	Bethlehem (Hingham)	19 April 43	10 July 43	7 Oct 43	Ret USN 25 Oct 45
K465 *Bentley* (ex-*DE74*)	Bethlehem (Hingham)	26 April 43	17 July 43	13 Oct 43	Ret USN 5 Nov 45

CAPTAIN (TURBO-ELECTR

Ship	Builder	Laid Down
K466 *Bickerton* (ex-*DE75*)	Bethlehem (Hingham)	3 May 43
K467 *Bligh* (ex-*DE76*)	Bethlehem (Hingham)	10 May 43
K468 *Braithwaite* (ex-*DE77*)	Bethlehem (Hingham)	10 May 43
K460 *Bullen* (ex-*DE78*)	Bethlehem (Hingham)	17 May 43
K508 *Byron* (ex-*DE79*)	Bethlehem (Hingham)	24 May 43
K509 *Conn* (ex-*DE80*)	Bethlehem (Hingham)	2 June 43
K510 *Cotton* (ex-*DE81*)	Bethlehem (Hingham)	2 June 43
K511 *Cranstoun* (ex-*DE82*)	Bethlehem (Hingham)	9 June 43
K512 *Cubitt* (ex-*DE83*)	Bethlehem (Hingham)	9 June 43
K513 *Curzon* (ex-*DE84*)	Bethlehem (Hingham)	23 June 43
K550 *Dakins* (ex-*DE85*)	Bethlehem (Hingham)	23 June 43
K551 *Deane* (ex-*DE86*)	Bethlehem (Hingham)	30 June 43
K552 *Ekins* (ex-*DE87*)	Bethlehem (Hingham)	5 July 43
K553 *Fitzroy* (ex-*DE88*)	Bethlehem (Hingham)	24 Aug 43
K554 *Redmill* (ex-*DE89*)	Bethlehem (Hingham)	14 July 43
K555 *Retalick* (ex-*DE90*)	Bethlehem (Hingham)	21 July 43
K556 *Halsted* (ex-*Reynolds*, ex-*DE91*)	Bethlehem (Hingham)	10 July 43
K557 *Riou* (ex-*DE92*)	Bethlehem (Hingham)	4 Aug 43
K558 *Rutherford* (ex-*DE93*)	Bethlehem (Hingham)	4 Aug 43
K559 *Cosby* (ex-*Reeves*, ex-*DE94*)	Bethlehem (Hingham)	11 Aug 43
K560 *Rowley* (ex-*DE95*)	Bethlehem (Hingham)	18 Aug 43
K561 *Rupert* (ex-*DE96*)	Bethlehem (Hingham)	25 Aug 43
K562 *Stockham* (ex-*DE97*)	Bethlehem (Hingham)	25 Aug 43
K563 *Seymour* (ex-*DE98*)	Bethlehem (Hingham)	1 Sept 43
K572 *Spragge* (ex-*DE563*)	Bethlehem (Hingham)	15 Sept 43
K573 *Stayner* (ex-*DE564*)	Bethlehem (Hingham)	22 Sept 43
K574 *Thornbrough* (ex-*DE565*)	Bethlehem (Hingham)	22 Sept 43
K575 *Trollope* (ex-*DE566*)	Bethlehem (Hingham)	29 Sept 43

ASS—*continued*

Launched	Commissioned	Fate
24 July 43	17 Oct 43	Lost 22 Aug 44
31 July 43	22 Oct 43	Ret USN 12 Nov 45
31 July 43	13 Nov 43	Ret USN 13 Nov 45
7 Aug 43	25 Oct 43	Lost 6 Dec 44
14 Aug 43	30 Oct 43	Ret USN 24 Nov 45
21 Aug 43	31 Oct 43	Ret USN 26 Nov 45
21 Aug 43	8 Nov 43	Ret USN 5 Nov 45
28 Aug 43	13 Nov 43	Ret USN 3 Dec 45
11 Sept 43	17 Nov 43	Ret USN 4 Mar 46
18 Sept 43	20 Nov 43	Ret USN 27 Mar 46
18 Sept 43	23 Nov 43	C.T.L. 25 Dec 44
29 Sept 43	26 Nov 43	Ret USN 4 Mar 46
2 Oct 43	29 Nov 43	C.T.L. 16 April 45
1 Sept 43	16 Oct 43	Ret USN 5 Jan 46
2 Oct 43	30 Nov 43	C.T.L. 27 April 45
9 Oct 43	8 Dec 43	Ret USN 25 Oct 45
14 Oct 43	3 Nov 43	C.T.L. 10 June 44
23 Oct 43	14 Dec 43	Ret USN 25 Feb 46
23 Oct 43	16 Dec 43	Ret USN 25 Oct 45
30 Oct 43	20 Dec 43	Ret USN 4 Mar 46
30 Oct 43	22 Dec 43	Ret USN 12 Nov 45
31 Oct 43	24 Dec 43	Ret USN 20 Mar 46
31 Oct 43	28 Dec 43	Ret USN 15 Feb 46
1 Nov 43	23 Dec 43	Ret USN 5 Jan 46
16 Oct 43	14 Jan 44	Ret USN 28 Feb 46
6 Nov 43	30 Dec 43	Ret USN 24 Nov 45
13 Nov 43	31 Dec 43	Ret USN 29 Jan 47
20 Nov 43	10 Jan 44	C.T.L. 6 July 44

CAPTAIN (TURBO-ELECTRIC) CLASS—*continued*

Ship	Builder	Laid Down	Launched	Commissioned	Fate
K576 *Tyler* (ex-*DE567*)	Bethlehem (Hingham)	6 Oct 43	20 Nov 43	14 Jan 44	Ret USN 12 Nov 45
K577 *Torrington* (ex-*DE568*)	Bethlehem (Hingham)	22 Sept 43	27 Nov 43	18 Jan 44	Ret USN 11 June 46
K578 *Narbrough* (ex-*DE569*)	Bethlehem (Hingham)	6 Oct 43	27 Nov 43	21 Jan 44	Ret USN 4 Feb 46
K579 *Waldegrave* (ex-*DE570*)	Bethlehem (Hingham)	16 Oct 43	4 Dec 43	25 Jan 44	Ret USN 3 Dec 45
K580 *Whittaker* (ex-*DE571*)	Bethlehem (Hingham)	20 Oct 43	12 Dec 43	28 Jan 44	C.T.L. 1 Nov 44
K581 *Holmes* (ex-*DE572*)	Bethlehem (Hingham)	27 Oct 43	18 Dec 43	31 Jan 44	Ret USN 3 Dec 45
K582 *Hargood* (ex-*DE573*)	Bethlehem (Hingham)	27 Oct 43	18 Dec 43	7 Feb 44	Ret USN 4 Mar 46
K583 *Hotham* (ex-*DE574*)	Bethlehem (Hingham)	5 Nov 43	21 Dec 43	8 Feb 44	Ret USN 13 Mar 56

Displacement: 1,430tons/1,452tonnes (standard); 1,823tons/1,852tonnes (full load).
Length: 306ft/93.27m (oa); 300ft/91.44m (wl).
Beam: 37ft/11.28m.
Draught: 11ft 3in/3.43m (mean).
Machinery: two boilers; 2-shaft GEC turbines with electric drive.
Performance: 12,000shp; 23kts.
Bunkerage: 359tons/364tonnes.
Range: 6,000nm at 12kts.
Guns: three 3in (3×1); two 40mm (2×1); eight 20mm (8×1) (some ten 20mm, nil 40mm).
Complement: 200.

CAPTAIN (DIESEL-ELECTRIC) CLASS

Ship	Builder	Laid Down	Launched	Commissioned	Fate
K310 *Bayntun* (ex-*DE1*)	Boston NYd.	5 April 42	27 June 42	20 Jan 43	Ret USN 22 Aug 45
K311 *Bazely* (ex-*DE2*)	Boston NYd.	5 April 42	27 June 42	18 Feb 43	Ret USN 20 Aug 45
K312 *Berry* (ex-*DE3*)	Boston NYd.	22 Sept 42	23 Nov 42	15 Mar 43	Ret USN 15 Feb 46
K313 *Blackwood* (ex-*DE4*)	Boston NYd.	22 Sept 42	23 Nov 42	27 Mar 43	Lost 15 June 44

Below: *Bazeley*. (Perkins)

CAPTAIN (DIESEL-ELECTRIC) CLASS—*continued*

Ship	Builder	Laid Down	Launched	Commissioned	Fate
K347 *Burges* (ex-*DE12*)	Boston NYd.	8 Dec 42	26 Jan 43	2 June 43	Ret USN 27 Feb 46
K316 *Drury* (ex-*DE46*)	Philadelphia NYd.	12 Feb 42	24 July 42	4 April 43	Ret USN 20 Aug 45
K470 *Capel* (ex-*DE266*)	Boston NYd.	11 Mar 43	22 April 43	16 Aug 43	Lost 26 Dec 44
K471 *Cooke* (ex-*DE267*)	Boston NYd.	11 Mar 43	22 April 43	16 Aug 43	Ret USN 5 Mar 46
K472 *Dacres* (ex-*DE268*)	Boston NYd.	7 April 43	14 May 43	28 Aug 43	Ret USN 26 Jan 46
K473 *Domett* (ex-*DE269*)	Boston NYd.	7 April 43	14 May 43	3 Sept 43	Ret USN 5 Mar 46
K474 *Foley* (ex-*DE270*)	Boston NYd.	7 April 43	19 May 43	8 Sept 43	Ret USN 22 Aug 45
K475 *Garlies* (ex-*DE271*)	Boston NYd.	7 April 43	19 May 43	13 Sept 43	Ret USN 20 Aug 45
K476 *Gould* (ex-*DE272*)	Boston NYd.	23 April 43	4 June 43	18 Sept 43	Lost 1 Mar 44
K478 *Grindall* (ex-*DE273*)	Boston NYd.	23 April 43	4 June 43	23 Sept 43	Ret USN 20 Aug 45
K478 *Gardiner* (ex-*DE274*)	Boston NYd.	20 May 43	8 July 43	28 Sept 43	Ret USN 12 Feb 46
K480 *Goodall* (ex-*DE275*)	Boston NYd.	20 May 43	8 July 43	4 Oct 43	Lost 29 April 45
K480 *Goodson* (ex-*DE276*)	Boston NYd.	20 May 43	8 July 43	9 Oct 43	C.T.L. 25 June 44
K481 *Gore* (ex-*DE277*)	Boston NYd.	20 May 43	8 July 43	14 Oct 43	Ret USN 2 May 46
K482 *Keats* (ex-*DE278*)	Boston NYd.	5 June 43	17 July 43	19 Oct 43	Ret USN 27 Feb 46
K483 *Kempthorne* (ex-*DE279*)	Boston NYd.	5 June 43	17 July 43	23 Oct 43	Ret USN 20 Aug 45
K484 *Kingsmill* (ex-*DE280*)	Boston NYd.	9 July 43	13 Aug 43	29 Oct 43	Ret USN 22 Aug 45
K514 *Lawford* (ex-*DE516*)	Boston NYd.	9 July 43	13 Aug 43	3 Nov 43	Lost 8 June 44
K515 *Luis* (ex-*DE517*)	Boston NYd.	9 July 43	13 Aug 43	9 Nov 43	Ret USN 20 Mar 46
K516 *Lawson* (ex-*DE518*)	Boston NYd.	9 July 43	13 Aug 43	15 Nov 43	Ret USN 20 Mar 46
K564 *Pasley* (ex-*Lindsay*, ex-*DE519*)	Boston NYd.	18 July 43	30 Aug 43	20 Nov 43	Ret USN 20 Aug 45
K565 *Loring* (ex-*DE520*)	Boston NYd.	18 July 43	30 Aug 43	27 Nov 43	Ret USN 7 Jan 47
K566 *Hoste* (ex-*Mitchell*, ex-*DE521*)	Boston NYd.	14 Aug 43	24 Sept 43	3 Dec 43	Ret USN 22 Aug 45
K567 *Moorsom* (ex-*DE522*)	Boston NYd.	14 Aug 43	24 Sept 43	16 Dec 43	Ret USN 25 Oct 45
K568 *Manners* (ex-*DE523*)	Boston NYd.	14 Aug 43	24 Sept 43	6 Dec 43	C.T.L. 26 Jan 45
K569 *Mounsey* (ex-*DE524*)	Boston NYd.	14 Aug 43	24 Sept 43	23 Dec 43	Ret USN 25 Feb 46
K570 *Inglis* (ex-*DE525*)	Boston NYd.	25 Sept 43	2 Nov 43	29 Dec 43	Ret USN 20 Mar 46
K571 *Inman* (ex-*DE526*)	Boston NYd.	25 Sept 43	2 Nov 43	13 Jan 44	Ret USN 1 Mar 46

Displacement: 1,190tons/1,209tonnes (standard); 1,416tons/1,438tonnes (full load).
Length: 289ft 5in/88.22m (oa); 283ft 6in/86.41m (wl).
Beam: 35ft 2in/10.72m.
Draught: 10ft 1in/3.07m (mean).
Machinery: 2-shaft General Motors diesels with electric drive.
Performance: 6,000bhp; 19.5kts.
Range: 6,000nm at 12kts.
Guns: three 3in (3×1); two 40mm (2×1); ten 20mm.
Complement: 200.

Design American destroyer-escorts transferred to the Royal Navy. Classified as 'frigates' by Great Britain, they were given corvette pendant numbers.

Modifications Limited to the addition of a 2pdr bow-chaser in a number of units.

Service Used exclusively in the escort role, mainly in the Atlantic, but many saw service in the English Channel during and after the Invasion of Europe in June 1944. *Gould*, a unit of the 1st Support Group, was torpedoed and sunk by *U358* north of the Azores on 1 March 1944, after a very brief career. *Blackwood* was sunk by *U764* south of Portland in June 1944. *Bickerton*, serving with the 5th Escort Group, was torpedoed by *U354* in the Barents Sea while escorting *JW59* to Russia. She was eventually sunk by *Vigilant*. *Bullen* was sunk by *U775* north-west of Scotland and *Capel* by *U486* off Cherbourg. Finally, *Goodall* was lost to a torpedo from *U968* off the Kola Inlet. By the time of their entry into service, the escort vessel situation had improved considerably and with the end of the war in Europe in sight, these ships were considered expendable. In consequence, several were declared constructive total losses after heavy damage and not repaired. *Halstead*, torpedoed by the German *Jaguar* and *Möwe* off the Normandy beach-head, was towed to Portsmouth and cannibalized. She was subsequently scrapped in Holland in 1947. *Goodson* was torpedoed by *U984* also off Normandy. The following month, *Trollope* was torpedoed by S-boats of the 8th Flotilla in the same area. She was scrapped in Scotland in 1951. *Whittaker* was seriously damaged by *U483* off Malin Head and was scrapped in 1947. *Duff* was mined off the Dutch Coast, as was *Dakins* off Belgium. The latter was scrapped in Holland in January 1947. *Affleck* was badly damaged by *U486* in the attack which sunk *Capel*. In 1945, *Manners* was torpedoed by *U1172* in the Irish Sea and *Ekins* was mined in the North Sea. These ships were responsible in full or part for the losses of thirty U-boats (*U91, U212, U214, U246, U269, U285, U286, U297, U358, U394, U399, U480, U600, U618, U636, U648, U671, U672, U722, U757, U765, U774, U988, U989, U1001, U1021, U1051, U1172, U1278* and *U1279*). Post-war, all were soon returned to the USN with the exception of *Hotham* which was used for experiments.

Greece

Historically, the small Greek Navy had considered its main enemy to be Turkey, and the rivalry between the two Balkan powers dictated the size and composition of their navies. Greece had a long coast-line and a large number of islands to defend, but, despite the presence of Turkey, it was plainly impossible to build more than a small fleet for economic reasons. The war which broke out in the Balkans in 1912, had resulted in the dismemberment of most of Turkey in Europe in 1913. Greece subsequently played only a very small role at sea during the First World War, but in 1921, went to war against defeated Turkey, only to be soundly beaten this time by the Turkish Army in 1922. Between the two world wars, the Greek Navy expanded by the acquisition of five ex-Austrian torpedo-boats in 1921, and during the 1920s, purchased a total of six submarines from French shipyards. The ex-Austrian boats were of wartime vintage and were effective only for coastal defence purposes which, however, suited the Greek Navy. The only other torpedo-craft were six 350-ton ships of 1906 vintage, two 560-ton ships built in 1922 and the four *Aetos*-class ships purchased from Argentina before the First World War. These were completely overhauled in the mid 1920s. In 1929, Greece ordered four destroyers of a modern type from Italy and in 1937 two more from Great Britain. All these had joined the fleet by the outbreak of the Second World War in 1939, but at first, Greece remained neutral despite the threat of Italy, now in occupation of Albania.

Despite the absence of a state of war between the two countries, there were several incidents concerning Italian attacks on Greek warships and auxiliaries from June to October 1940, usually in the form of bombing attacks. These took place while the Greek vessels were in their own territorial waters, but the most flagrant incident was the torpedoing of the old Greek cruiser *Helle* on 15 August 1940 while she lay at anchor off the island of Tinos in the Northern Cyclades. Three torpedoes were fired at the elderly vessel, one of which hit in a boiler room. Fire broke out and *Helle* later sank despite attempts to beach her. One man was killed and nearly thirty injured. A Greek Navy court of inquiry could not establish the nationality of the submarine, but the torpedoes, based on fragment evidence, were definitely Italian. As far as one can ascertain, the identity of the submarine remains a mystery today. Despite this severe provocation, Greece could not afford to go to war with Italy, the disparity between the two were too great, but preparations were begun to put the nation on a war footing. When Italy finally invaded Greece from Albania on 28 October 1940, the army was ready and waiting for them and the navy was poised for action. After the invasion of Greece, the destroyers which managed to escape to Egypt were placed under the command of the C-in-C, Mediterranean (Royal Navy).

AETOS CLASS

Ship	Builder	Laid Down	Launched	Commissioned	Fate
01 *Aetos* (ex-*San Luis*)	Cammell Laird		2 Feb 11	19 Sept 12	Stricken 1945
Iérax (ex-*Santa Fé*)	Cammell Laird		15 Mar 11	19 Sept 12	Stricken 1945
Léon (ex-*Tucuman*)	Cammell Laird		15 July 11	19 Sept 12	Sunk 15 May 41
Panther (ex-*Santiago*)	Cammell Laird		26 April 11	19 Sept 12	Stricken 1945

Displacement: 1,050tons/1,067tonnes (standard); 1,300tons/1,320tonnes (full load).
Beam: 27ft 9in/8.45m.
Draught: 8ft 6in/2.59m (mean).
Machinery: four White boilers; 2-shaft Parsons-Curtis turbines.
Performance: 19,750shp; 32kts.
Bunkerage: 260tons/264tonnes.
Range: 3,000nm at 10kts.
Guns: three 4in (3×1); one 3in; two 2pdr.
Torpedoes: three 21in (1×3).
Mines: 40 (*Aetos* and *Panther*).
Complement: 110.

Design Originally ordered by Argentina before the First World War, these destroyers were purchased by Greece on 12 September 1912 for £148,000 each, just as they were ready to sail for Argentina. As built, they differed considerably from their Second World War form, in that they had five funnels, mixed coal and oil firing and a different disposition of guns and torpedoes. They retained this layout until 1924–35 when they came to Cowes for reconstruction by Samuel White and Co. Ltd. In the course of this, the original coal-fired boilers, were removed and replaced by four new oil-fired boilers, with a consequent reduction in numbers of funnels to two. A new and substantial bridge structure was built on to a forward shelter deck, upon which was also mounted one of the 4-inch guns. This gun had been displaced from forward of the mainmast by a triple bank of torpedo tubes, two

Below: *Aetos* on completion of trials after reconstruction in Great Britain. (Cdr Cremos, RHN)

of which had supplanted the original four single, sided tubes. In line with the current aerial defence thinking, two single 2pdr AA guns were fitted to a platform between the torpedo tubes. This refit, at a cost of some £110,000 each, proved a considerable success, speeds of between 31.1 knots (*Aetos*) and 31.16 knots (*Léon*) being achieved. *Aetos* and *Panther* were further refitted in 1937–38 when they were equipped for minelaying.

Modifications *Léon* was sunk before any modifications could be made to her, but the remaining three landed 'X' and 'Y' 4-inch guns to allow increased depth-charge stowage and lost the after bank of torpedo tubes for a 3-inch HA gun. Three 20mm guns and Type 123A asdic were added.

Service Early operational service included convoy protection between the Aegean Islands and mainland Greece during which time, in October 1940, *Aetos* attacked and (erroneously) claimed sunk an Italian submarine off Skiathos. Several Italian submarines were, however, operating in the Aegean at this time. The other main convoy route covered was between Athens and Crete. When the German Army invaded Greece to bale out the hard-hit Italians, however, the situation changed dramatically, for the Greek Navy was as ill-equipped for the war against aircraft as any other. Up until April 1941, the Greek Navy had lost only one submarine, but thereafter the Luftwaffe took a considerable toll of the British and Greek ships between Greece and Alexandria. Following the damage to *Vasilefs Georgios* on 13 April, *Aetos* became the destroyer flagship for a brief period. All four ships got away from the mainland at the time of the evacuation, but *Léon*, while escorting the liner *Ardenna* to Crete on 17 April, was rammed by her charge. The destroyer lost part of her stern including rudder and propellers and had to be towed into Suda Bay, where she was beached and abandoned. Later, she was sunk by aircraft there on 15 May.

The three survivors reached Egypt safely and operated in the eastern Mediterranean and the Levant until the end of 1941 by which time these old ships were badly in need of refits. *Aetos* was the first to be taken in hand, sailing for India on 12 November and arriving in Madras on 5 December. This refit was completed on 5 March 1942, during which time her armament was modified. After escort duty in the Indian Ocean *Aetos* returned to Alexandria on 4 April. *Iérax* followed her sister on 9 February 1942 bound for Calcutta where she arrived on 19 March. However, due to Japanese activities in the Indian Ocean at this time, her refit was cancelled and the ship left India on 7 May still unfinished, to be completed at Port Sudan where she arrived on 16 May. *Panther* also went to India for refit, on 5 April 1942, arriving on 12 May but due to the conditions in India, this refit was greatly delayed and it was not until October that she returned to service. For the remainder of the year *Panther* served in the Indian Ocean and took part in the surrender of Djibouti.

Back in the Mediterranean in 1943, the ships served on North Africa coastal convoys, but on 29 September 1943 *Panther* was decommissioned at Port Said to release men for new ships. By the end of that year, her two sister ships were also at Port Said with reduced crews under long repair/reserve status.

KONDOURIOTIS CLASS

Ship	Builder	Laid Down	Launched	Commissioned	Fate
Kondouriotis	Odero (Genoa)		29 Aug 31	Nov 1932	Broken up Sept 1946
97 *Ydra*	Odero (Genoa)		21 Oct 31	Nov 1932	Lost 22 April 41
Spetsai	Odero (Genoa)		1932	May 1933	Broken up Sept 1947
Psara	Odero (Genoa)		1932	May 1933	Lost 20 April 41

Displacement: 1,389tons/1,411tonnes (standard); 2,050tons/2,082tonnes (full load).
Length: 303ft/92m (pp).
Beam: 32ft/9.75m.
Draught: 12ft/3.65m (mean).
Machinery: three Yarrow Express boilers; 2-shaft Parsons geared turbines.
Performance: 44,000shp; 38kts.
Bunkerage: 630tons/640tonnes.
Range: 5,800nm at 20kts.
Guns: four 4in (4×1); three 40mm (3×1).
Torpedoes: six 21in (2×3).
Mines: 40.
Complement: 156.

Design The first new destroyers ordered (in October 1929) for the Greek Navy since 1911, these ships countered four modern destroyers ordered in the same period for the Turkish Navy, Greece's hereditary enemy. They were based upon the design of the Italian Navy's latest destroyers of the *Dardo* and *Folgore* classes, but with a shorter hull. Their machinery installation followed the Italian practice and they too had a single funnel, a novelty for the destroyers of the day. Apart from this single funnel, however, their visual appearance differed considerably from that of their Italian contemporaries due to the adoption of single guns instead of twin and the elimination of the heavy director platform atop the bridge. The secondary director between the tubes was replaced by a searchlight in the Greek ships. 4.7-inch, the Italian destroyer calibre, was adopted for the main armament, manufactured by Ansaldo and were their 1926 Model of 50 calibre. Their secondary armament comprised three single 40mm guns grouped abaft the funnel. *Ydra* and *Kondouriotis* were fitted for minelaying and could embark 40 mines. Electric welding was extensively used in the hull and light alloys employed in the superstructure. Like all Italian designs, speed was the keynote, with *Spetsai* returning the fastest trials speed of 41.5 knots on 52,000shp.

Modifications The two survivors after April 1941, *Kondouriotis* and *Spetsai* were modified while working with the Royal Navy. 'Y' gun was landed to increase depth-charge stowage and the after torpedo tubes were replaced by a 3-inch HA gun. Two 20mm guns were also added. Depth-charge throwers were increased to eight, and Type 127 asdic was fitted.

Service *Ydra* was attacked and bombed without effect, by Italian aircraft off Crete in June 1940 even

Below: *Kondouriotis* on 13 September 1943. (Cdr Cremos, RHN)

before Italy and Greece were at war. When Italy did finally attack Greece at the end of October 1940, *Spetsai* and *Psara* were immediately dispatched from the Gulf of Patras to bombard Italian positions on the Albanian coast. Thereafter, other sweeps up the Albanian coast took place by the destroyers, aimed at Italian supply convoys between Italy and Valona. Occasionally, these were combined with further bombardments of enemy-occupied coast. They were also employed on convoy duties in the Aegean and to the Dardenelles, depth-charging suspected Italian submarines on numerous occasions but without success. When British troops were sent to Greece in 1941, the destroyers also escorted convoy traffic to and from Egypt. During the Battle of Cape Matapan, all except *Psara* were in the vicinity and ordered to cut off the retreating Italian forces. Because of coding errors, they were unable to do so although *Hydra* managed to rescue more than one hundred survivors from *Pola*.

During the evacuation of Greece by British forces in April 1941, the Greek destroyers covered the evacuation convoys. On the 21st, Captain (D) shifted his flag to *Ydra* and the following day left the Piraeus with a convoy bound for Alexandria. During the early evening, north of the island of Aegina, they were sighted by a large force of Ju 87 Stuka dive-bombers. *Ydra*'s guns crews were overwhelmed by the size of the attack and within a few minutes, most of her guns were out of action and both engines stopped by near misses. There were many casualties as the stricken destroyer sank. *Psara* had been sunk two days earlier, again by dive-bombers, while lying at anchor off Megara. A heavy bomb blew away the forecastle up to the bridge and the ship slowly sank as bulkheads gave way. *Spetsai* and *Kondouriotis* reached Alexandria from Athens unscathed.

Under British control, *Spetsai* and *Kondouriotis* were employed upon escort duties to Port Said, Cyprus and Haifa, operating from Alexandria until August 1941. In that month, *Spetsai* sailed for refit in India where her armament was modified, being completed on 27 March 1942 at Bombay. *Kondouriotis* followed at the end of December 1941 but her refit was much shorter, being completed on 15 April 1942 with the ship back at Port Said on 30 April. Both ships were then employed on escort duties once more, in the Levant and along the North African coast. *Kondouriotis* took the surrender of Casteloriso in the Dodecanese on 13 September 1943, but *Spetsai* reduced to reserve at Port Said on the 29th of that month. Finally *Kondouriotis* too paid off at Port Said on 13 December 1943. Spares were difficult for these Italian-built ships and their crews were badly needed for new ships on loan from the Royal Navy.

VASILEFS GEORGIOS CLASS

Ship	Builder	Laid Down	Launched	Commissioned	Fate
14 *Vasilefs Georgios*	A. Yarrow	Feb 1937	3 Mar 38	27 Dec 38	Captured April 1941
15 *Vasilissa Olga*	A. Yarrow	Feb 1937	2 June 38	4 Feb 39	Lost 26 Sept 43

Displacement: 1,350tons/1,371tonnes (standard); 1,850tons/1,879tonnes (full load).
Length: 323ft 1in/98.4m (oa); 312ft/95.09m (pp).
Beam: 33ft/10.05m.
Draught: 8ft 3in/2.51m (mean).
Machinery: three Admiralty 3-drum boilers; 2-shaft Parsons geared turbines.
Performance: 34,000shp; 36kts.
Bunkerage: 393tons/399tonnes.
Range: 3,760nm at 20kts.
Guns: four 5in (4×1); four 37mm (4×1); eight .5in MG (2×4).
Torpedoes: eight 21in (2×4).
Complement: 162.

Design The Greek government placed an order for these two ships with Yarrow on 29 January 1937. Their general design dimensions conformed to that of the contemporary British *I* class, with various modifications to suit Greek requirements. In particular, their main gun armament was purchased from Germany and was to comprise the new 12.7cm SKC/34 (5-inch) gun as mounted in the new destroyers of the Kriegsmarine. 192 rounds per gun were allowed. To compensate the extra top-weight, only quadruple torpedo tubes were carried. Their AA outfit was also different and improved in that four 37mm guns were fitted, disposed between the funnels and abaft the after funnel. These were in addition to the quadruple .5in machine-guns. Two depth-charge throwers, one rail and seventeen depth-charges comprised the ASW outfit. The main machinery installation conformed to British practice with Admiralty 3-drum (not Yarrow) boilers operating at 300psi, and Parsons impulse-reaction single reduction geared turbines. Designed power was 34,000shp. Laid down as Yard numbers 1702 and 1703 the first to complete, *Vasilefs Georgios* ran her first trials on 24 October 1938 and on 30 October full-power trials, when a mean speed of 36.58 knots was achieved with 35,109shp. It should be noted however, that no guns were aboard, although the torpedo tubes were. Obviously, Germany was not about to send her newest destroyer guns to England for fitment at this critical period of history! This trial was on a displacement of 1,426 tons. Deep load speed trials returned 33.9 knots with 33,512shp. *Vasilissa Olga* commenced her trials on 19 December 1938, making 36.09 knots with 33,683shp on a mean of 6 hours. After completion at Yarrow's yard, both destroyers proceeded to Greece, where their full armament was installed.

Modifications *Vasilissa Olga* landed her after tubes to accommodate a 3-inch HA gun and had 'Y' gun removed to allow increased depth-charge stowage. Ten Hotchkiss machine-guns and Type 128 asdic were also installed. Four 20mm later replaced the 37mm guns. *Vasilefs Georgios*, after salvage by the Germans, was fitted with four single 20mm MG C/30 guns at the rear end of the forward shelter deck and the forward end of the after shelter deck. A fifth gun was fitted on the forecastle. She was also fitted for minelaying, the torpedo outfit being reduced to six by the simple expedient of removing one tube from each bank.

Service Upon her arrival in Greek waters, *Vasilefs Georgios* became flagship of the Greek Navy's destroyer flotilla. After the sinking of *Helle*, both ships were dispatched to Tinos to escort home the ships lying off the island. En route, Italian bombers attacked them, near-missing *Vasilefs Georgios*. After Italy invaded Greece, both destroyers conducted offensive night sorties and bombardment patrols into the Adriatic against enemy supply routes to and positions in, Albania. They were also employed on escort duties around the Aegean and to the Dardenelles as required.

On 1 March 1941, the two ships were used to evacuate the Greek gold reserves to Crete and, after the British intervention in Greece following the German invasion on 13 April, they were also used to cover convoys to and from Egypt via Crete. Neither ship saw action at the Battle of Cape Matapan because of communications problems.

After Germany had invaded Greece, *Vasilefs Georgios* was moved from Scala Meganon under a policy of dispersing the fleet in the face of Luftwaffe air power. Off Sofiko in the Peloponnese she lay close up against sheer cliffs where deep water came close inshore. Even so, on 14 April, one aircraft managed to get in an attack. Its bombs missed but were close enough to rent the hull on the port quarter and serious flooding took place. Listing up to 30°, *Vasilefs Georgios* limped to Salamis where she was put into floating dock. As repairs were impossible to complete in the face of the German advance, attempts were made to scuttle the dock and destroy the ship. Attempts to move the dock into deep water were to no avail and although demolition charges were used, the ship was not seriously damaged.

Vasilissa Olga had sailed for Crete, with the Greek government and the C-in-C of the Navy, embarked on 22 April, five days before the Germans entered Athens. For the remainder of her career, *Olga* served with British forces in the Mediterranean.

After escort duties in the eastern Mediterranean, *Vasilissa Olga* was ordered to India for refit, sailing on 9 October 1941. During this refit her armament was modified and she returned to service on 5 January 1942. However, on passage to Trincomalee, her stability was found to be suspect and as a result the four 37mm guns were landed and replaced by a like number of 20mm. She was then used for escort work in the Arabian and Red Seas before returning to Alexandria on 22 February. In March, while escorting the oiler *Slavol*, together with the British *Jaguar*, she depth-charged *U652* but in a counter-attack the U-boat sank *Jaguar*. Early in May, she ran aground while escorting a convoy from Alexandria to Tobruk, damaging her propellers. After repairs *Vasilissa Olga* served in the Indian Ocean late in 1942 but was back in the Mediterranean by December.

In company with *Petard*, she sank the Italian submarine *Uarsciek* south of Malta on 15 December 1942. In January 1943, she took part in strikes against the Axis traffic to North Africa with some success, and in February was briefly deployed to the Red Sea. In May and June, further offensive action occurred, during which the Greek destroyer participated in the sinking of transports and the torpedo-boat *Castore*. After covering the landings on Sicily, *Vailissa Olga* had the satisfaction of seeing the surrender of the Italian fleet before covering the landings at Salerno. Following this, she moved into the Aegean for operations in the Dodecanese, when she was caught and sunk in harbour at Leros by Stukas of LGI.

Her sister, captured by the Germans, was refitted and put into service as *ZG3* (q.v.).

TRANSFERRED UNITS

Salamis (ex-*Boreas*)

Formerly a *B*-class destroyer, transferred to Greece by the Royal Navy in April 1944 after a refit at Liverpool. *Salamis* sailed for Mediterranean waters and served with the 12th (Greek) Destroyer Flotilla mostly in Aegean waters until the end of the war. Post-war she was employed on training duties until her return to RN control in September 1951. She was sold for breaking up on 23 November 1951 and scrapped at West of Scotland Shipbreakers (Troon).

Navarinon (ex-*Echo*)

Transferred to Greece by the Royal Navy on 5 April 1944, *Navarinon* also served in the Aegean for the last year of the war with the 12th Flotilla. She did not return to RN control until 1946 at Malta, having been present at the Coronation Review of 1953. She was towed to the UK for dispersal, arriving at Clayton & Davie (Dunston) on 26 April 1956 for scrapping.

Themistocles (ex-*Bramham*), *Kriti* (ex-*Hursley*), *Pindos* (ex-*Bolebroke*), *Adrias* (ex-*Border*), *Kanaris* (ex-*Hatherleigh*), *Miaoulis* (ex-*Modbury*)

Formerly British *Hunt* class destroyers (Type 2 – *Themistocles* and *Kriti*; Type 3 the other four), transferred to Greece on completion, *Pindos, Adrias, Kanaris* and *Miaoulis* in 1942, *Themistocles* and *Kriti* in 1943 after service in the Royal Navy. All six went to the Mediterranean under the Greek ensign, where all except *Kriti* participated in the landings on Sicily. In August 1943, *Pindos* assisted in the sinking of *U458* off Pantellaria. Later in 1943, the flotilla moved to Aegean waters where *Adrias* was so badly damaged by a mine off Calimnos (laid by the German minelayer *Drache*) on 22 October, that she was beyond repair. Laid up until the end of the war, she was eventually brought back to the UK towards the end of 1945 for breaking up. In the Aegean, many operations were carried out among the German-held islands with the occasional deployment elsewhere, such as Anzio in January 1944 (*Themistocles*) and the Invasion of southern France in August 1944 (*Themistocles, Kriti* and *Pindos*). Post-war, the five survivors continued in Greek service until *Kriti, Themistocles, Pindos* and *Kanaris* were returned to Great Britain on 12 December 1959, being subsequently scrapped in Greece. *Miaoulis* was disposed of in 1960.

PROUSSA CLASS

Ship	Builder	Laid Down	Launched	Commissioned	Fate
Proussa (ex-*92F*)	Danubius, Porto Ré	30 Nov 14	29 Sept 15	23 Mar 16	Lost 4 April 41
Pergamos (ex-*95F*)	Danubius, Porto Ré	9 Feb 15	24 June 16	27 Sept 16	Lost 25 April 41

Displacement: 266tons/270tonnes (standard); 330tons/335tonnes (full load).
Length: 192ft 9in/58.8m (oa); 191ft 11in/58.5m (wl); 189ft 7in/57.8m (pp).
Beam: 19ft 2in/5.8m.
Draught: 5ft 1in/1.5m (mean).
Machinery: two Yarrow boilers; 2-shaft AEG turbines.
Performance: 5,000shp; 28kts.
Bunkerage: 20tons/20.3tonnes (coal) + 34tons/34.5tonnes (oil).
Range: 1,200nm at 16kts.
Guns: two 66mm; 2 MG.
Torpedoes: four 18in (2×2).
Complement: 25.

Design Formerly Austro-Hungarian torpedo-boats of First World War vintage, allocated to Greece in 1920. One sister ship, *Panormos* (ex-*95F*) struck a reef off Cape Tourlos in March 1938; others of the class subsequently served in the Portuguese, Roumanian and Yugoslav Navies.
Modifications Probably few if any.
Service *Proussa* was sunk by German bombers off Corfu and *Pergamos* was sunk by bombing off Salamis.

KYZIKOS CLASS

Ship	Builder	Laid Down	Launched	Commissioned	Fate
Kyzikos (ex-*98M*)	C.N.T. Monfalcone	19 Mar 14	18 Nov 14	19 Aug 15	Lost 24 April 41
Kios (ex-*99M*)	C.N.T. Monfalcone	22 Mar 14	17 Dec 14	29 Oct 15	Lost 22 April 41
Kidoniai (ex-*100M*)	C.N.T. Monfalcone	28 Mar 14	15 Jan 15	13 Mar 16	Lost 26 April 41

Displacement: 270tons/274tonnes (standard); 330tons/335tonnes (full load).
Length: 198ft 6in/60.5m (wl); 196ft 6in/59.9m (pp).
Beam: 18ft 4in/5.6m.
Draught: 5ft 1in/1.5m (mean).
Machinery: two Yarrow boilers; 2-shaft Melms & Pfenninger turbines.
Performance: 5,000shp; 28.5kts.
Range: 1,200nm at 16kts.
Guns: two 66mm; 2 MG.
Torpedoes: four 18in (2×2).
Mines: 12.
Complement: 38.

Design A class of three 250-ton High Seas Torpedo-boats built for the Austro-Hungarian Navy during the First World War. They differed from the *Proussa* class only in that they had a longer and beamy hull and were given Melms & Pfenninger turbines.
Modifications Probably none.
Service All three were destroyed by German aircraft during the invasion of Greece in April 1941. *Kios* was lost first, off Athens, followed by *Kyzikos* at Salamis and finally *Kidoniai* south of Morea on the 26th.

Italy

Italy's development as a naval power in reality dates only from 1870 after the unification of the country under Garibaldi. By the end of the century the navy was assisting in Italy's colonial expansion in Abyssinia, and before the First World War supported further territorial gains, this time in North Africa at the expense of the Turks. On the outbreak of the First World War, the Royal Italian Navy possessed dreadnought battleships and a number of pre-dreadnoughts as well as a miscellaneous collection of cruisers. Its strong point, however, was its small submarine force and, more importantly, a large force of destroyers and torpedo-boats. Like France, Italy had been concentrating on torpedo-boat construction since the 1880s using initially Schichau and Thornycroft designs. By the first decade of the twentieth century, these boats had reached about 215 tons displacement, armed with three guns and three torpedoes. Approximately 85 of various designs were available at the commencement of the 1914–18 war. Following the pattern of other navies, however, a parallel line of development had begun in the late 1890s which increased size and fighting power to combat the torpedo-boats of possible enemy nations, i.e., a Torpedo-Boat Destroyer. This type culminated in the *Ardito* class of 1912 which displaced about 700 tons and carried two 18-inch torpedo tubes. The Royal Italian Navy had initially armed its destroyers with 12pdr guns, but in about 1911, had begun to mount 4.7-inch guns in their newer destroyers and from this date all new ships carried one 4.7-inch gun in addition to their 12pdrs. They were thus in advance of Great Britain in this respect, although the 4-inch later became the main armament calibre and full 4.7-inch outfits were not carried until the 1920s. When Italy entered the First World War in 1915, on the side of Britain and France, she had 33 destroyers in service, with sixteen more under construction. Her main task was the containment of the small but powerful Austro-Hungarian Fleet in the Adriatic. The Austrian Fleet itself did not often venture to sea, but her cruisers, destroyers and submarines did. It was against the latter that the Italian destroyers were most active. Two were sunk by Italian ships (*U3* and *U17*), but the destroyers *Impetuoso* and *Nembo* were lost by the Italians. Due to circumstances, war-time construction was limited and slow, the three ships of the *Mirabello* class (laid down 1914–15) were completed in 1916–17, eight *Pilo* class, which had been started before the war, completed in 1915–16, four *Sirtoris* were completed in 1917 and eight *La Masa* class towards the end of the war. Of these, the largest and most powerful were the *Mirabello* class of about 1,800 tons, armed with one 6-inch gun and seven 4-inch. One other destroyer was added during the war; this was the British-built *Intrepido*, formerly the Japanese *Kawakaze*, transferred to the Italian Navy while under construction.

With the surrender of Austro-Hungary in 1918, Italy received four of their *Tatra*-class destroyers, *Tatra, Balaton, Csepel* and *Orzen*, which were commissioned and renamed *Fasana, Zenzon, Muggia* and *Pola* (later *Zenzon* in 1931). Three later *Tatra*-class destroyers were also taken over, *Triglav* (ii), (renamed *Grado*), *Lika* (ii), (*Cortellazzo*) and *Uzsok* (*Monfalcone*). *Fasana* and *Zenzon* were discarded in 1923, while *Muggia* was lost in a typhoon off Amoy in March 1929. The remainder had all been discarded by 1939. Also taken over by Italy were the former German destroyers *V116* (renamed *Premuda*), *B97* (*Cesare Rossarol*) and *S63* (*Ardimentoso*). These were also discarded from 1937 to 1939 but they had in the meantime given the Italian constructors a valuable insight into foreign design practice.

The return of peace slowed down new construction considerably, the four *Palestro* class not completing until 1921–23 although laid down early in 1917. However, the *Generali* class, which were smaller and not laid down until well after the end of the war, were completed by 1921–22. The first true post-war design to be developed was the *Leone* class, originally classified as scouts (*esploradi*). These ships introduced the all 4.7-inch gun armament and were heavily armed with four twin mountings. Their role was more light cruiser than destroyer and it was not until the *Sella* class of 1922 that a return to smaller dimensions was made. The reduction in size allowed a maximum design speed of 35 knots to be attained, but with a considerable reduction in armament. Sixteen ships were built to this general design in three separate classes before a return was made to larger dimensions with the *esploradi* of the *Navigatori* class built 1927–30.

This larger size was only briefly perpetrated, however, for the *Dardo* class of 1929 reverted to the four 4.7-inch gun concept. With their distinctive single funnel layout, this class set the general layout adopted for all future destroyers built for the Royal Italian Navy, the design being refined through several classes until the *Comandanti Medaglie d'Oro* class of 1943.

With the exception of a small force in the Red Sea based in Abyssinia, the Royal Italian Navy's theatre of operations was the Mediterranean and in consequence Italian designs did not have to take account of weather in open oceans such as the Pacific or Atlantic. Thus high endurance was not an overriding priority and designs did not have to be so strongly built as did British and American contemporaries. A combination of light construction, together with a penchant for running trials without armament on board gave Italian ships of all classes often fantastic trial speeds which of course could nowhere near be attained under full load war conditions. Italy's hereditary foe was France and the two nations matched each other's designs fairly closely, but Italy was the one nation which took full advantage of the 600-ton clause of the London Naval Treaty and built large numbers of small torpedo-armed escorts to which the French did not really reply. Britain and her interests in the Mediterranean obviously clashed with those of Italy and, with the collapse of France, Italy found herself facing the British Mediterranean Fleet at war.

Despite a large and well-equipped modern navy, Italy was handicapped by a combination of incompetent High Command and serious shortage of oil fuel, but its ships, in general, fought well, often against heavy odds and technical superiority. Italy was far behind in radar development, but the ASW arm and its ships were very efficient.

Italy's main naval tasks were the containment of the British Mediterranean Fleet, escorting of supply traffic to North Africa and the Aegean and the protection of the Abyssinian colony. The supply routes to and from North Africa gave rise to heavy losses among the escorting destroyers and torpedo-boats. Italy began the war with 59 fleet destroyers, 33 older torpedo-boats and 34 new-type torpedo-boats or destroyer escorts. Of this total, 51 destroyers, 27 old and 25 new torpedo-boats became war losses. New construction was very slow; only five destroyers and an equal number of captured enemy ships were put into commission during the war, and about 16 torpedo-boats. Many of these also became war losses.

MIRABELLO CLASS

Ship	Builder	Laid Down	Launched	Commissioned	Fate
MI *Carlo Mirabello*	Ansaldo, Genoa	21 Nov 14	21 Dec 15	24 Aug 16	Lost 21 May 41
RI *Augusto Riboty*	Ansaldo, Genoa	27 Feb 15	24 Sept 16	5 May 17	To USSR 1946

Displacement: 1,811tons/1,840tonnes (standard); 2,302tons/2,339tonnes (full load).
Length: 340ft 5in/103.75m (oa); 331ft 5in/101m (pp).
Beam: 32ft/9.75m.
Draught: 10ft 6in/3.2m (mean).
Machinery: four Yarrow boilers; 2-shaft Parsons geared turbines.
Performance: 35,000shp; 35kts.
Bunkerage: 350tons/356tonnes.
Range: 2,840nm at 15kts.
Guns: eight 4in (8×1); 2 MG.
Torpedoes: four 17.7in (450mm) (2×2).
Mines: 100.
Complement: 158.

Design These large destroyers dated from the First World War and were originally a class of three. However, *Carlo Alberto Racchia*, completed in 1916, was sunk by a mine while engaged in operations in the Black Sea on 21 July 1920. When first completed, this class was designated *esplorati* (scouts) because of their size. In their day they were powerful and effective ships but by 1939, their design was well out of date, with their beam gun armament and sided paired torpedo tubes.

Modifications During the course of the war, in about 1942–43, *Riboty* landed torpedo tubes and the 4-inch guns were reduced to four with the pair at the after end of the forecastle and on the quarters being removed. The mainmast was removed and the AA outfit increased to eight single 20mm guns. Depth-charge stowage was increased for ASW duties. *Mirabello* was probably lost in her original condition.

Service On the entry of Italy into the war in June 1940, both destroyers were based in the Adriatic at Brindisi, but one of their early tasks was the laying of defensive minefields in the Gulf of Taranto in June and July. By October they were both engaged in escorting troop and supply convoys between Italy and Albania. When the Italian Army invaded Greece from Albania in October, both took part in fire support and bombardment operations, principally against Corfu. The following year, *Mirabello*, whilst escorting a convoy to Greece, struck a mine off Cape Dukato, laid by the British *Abdiel* only a few hours earlier. Her sister spent the remainder of the war mainly on convoy escort duties to and from North Africa until surrendered at Malta in September 1943. After the war, *Riboty* was ceded to the USSR, but remained in Italy and was scrapped in 1951.

Below: *Augusto Riboty*, little modified by war. (Author's Collection)

LEONE CLASS

Ship	Builder	Laid Down	Launched	Commissioned	Fate
LE *Leone*	Ansaldo, Genoa	23 Nov 21	1 Oct 23	1 July 24	Wrecked 1 April 41
PA *Pantera*	Ansaldo, Genoa	19 Dec 21	18 Oct 23	28 Oct 24	Scuttled 3/4 April 41
TI *Tigre*	Ansaldo, Genoa	23 Jan 22	7 Aug 24	10 Oct 24	Scuttled 3/4 April 41

Displacement: 1,743tons/1,771tonnes (standard); 2,648tons/2,690tonnes (full load).
Length: 372ft/113.41m (oa); 359ft 7in/109.6m (pp).
Beam: 34ft/10.36m.
Draught: 10ft 2in/3.1m (mean).
Machinery: four Yarrow boilers; 2-shaft geared turbines.
Performance: 42,000shp; 34kts.
Bunkerage: 393tons/400tonnes.
Range: 2,400nm at 16kts.
Guns: eight 4.7in (4×2); two 40mm (2×1); four 20mm (4×1).
Torpedoes: four 21in (2×2).
Mines: 60.
Complement: 206.

Design Once again a heavily armed scout type, but reclassified as destroyers on 5 September 1938. Like the *Mirabello* class, this was also an Ansaldo design, but this class introduced the twin 4.7-inch gun which was a feature of all Italian destroyers henceforth. The *Leone* class had the old M1918/19 Pattern gun whose mountings had 32° elevation. The hull was larger and beamier, with a corresponding increase in displacement, to accommodate the heavier armament weights. All main guns and torpedo tubes were now axially mounted, but the disposition of the gun mountings was unusual in that only two were placed so as to give bow or stern fire. No. 2 gun was between the funnels and No. 3 between the torpedo tubes. Both of these guns had only restricted arcs of fire. In appearance, therefore, these ships were quite distinctive with two closely spaced vertical funnels and an unusually long forecastle deck. On trials, speeds of over 33 knots were achieved with 45,000hp, and with their eight 4.7-inch guns, these ships were well armed but the fortunes of war did not favour them.

Modifications Probably none in view of their area of employment and early war loss.

Service All three formed the 5th Destroyer Division based in the Red Sea at the outbreak of war. Their initial task was defensive minelaying but from June 1940 to March 1941, they made several unsuccessful attempts to find and intercept British convoys passing through the Red Sea. On 31 March, *Leone* struck an uncharted rock and was destroyed by her consorts, *Pantera* and *Tigre*, which then returned to Massawa. *Pantera* and *Tigre* sailed again on 2 April with three other destroyers to attack Port Sudan, but were attacked by Swordfish aircraft from *Eagle*, operating from Port Sudan. Two of their consorts were sunk but *Pantera* and *Tigre* escaped only to be scuttled off the Arabian coast on the night of 3–4 April.

Above: *Pantera*, seen here at Venice before the war. (Fraccaroli)

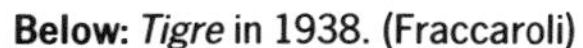

Below: *Tigre* in 1938. (Fraccaroli)

SELLA CLASS

Ship	Builder	Laid Down	Launched	Commissioned	Fate
CP, CR *Francesco Crispi*	Pattison, Naples	21 Feb 23	12 Sept 25	29 April 27	German *TA15* Sept 1943
SE *Quintino Sella*	Pattison, Naples	12 Oct 22	25 April 25	25 Mar 26	Lost 11 Sept 43
RC *Bettino Ricasoli*	Pattison, Naples	11 Jan 23	29 Jan 26	11 Dec 26	To Sweden Mar 1940
NC *Giovanni Nicotera*	Pattison, Naples	6 May 25	24 June 26	8 Jan 27	To Sweden Mar 1940

Displacement: 970tons/985tonnes (standard); 1,480tons/1,503tonnes (full load).
Length: 278ft 6in/84.9m (oa); 275ft 6in/84m (pp).
Beam: 28ft 2in/8.6m.
Draught: 8ft 10in/2.7m (mean).
Machinery: three Thornycroft boilers; 2-shaft Parsons (Belluzzo *Crispi*) turbines.
Performance: 36,000shp; 35kts.
Bunkerage: 220tons/223tonnes.
Range: 1,800nm at 14kts.

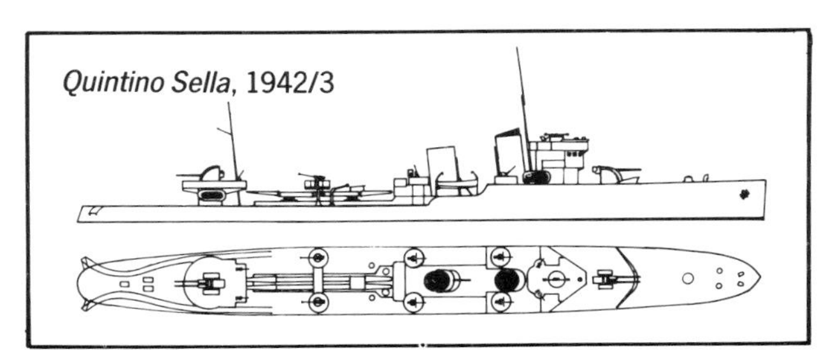

Below: *Crispi* in about 1943–42. (Fraccaroli)

Guns: four 4.7in (2×2); two 40mm (2×1); two 13.2mm.
Torpedoes: four 21in (2×2).
Mines: 32.
Complement: 253.
Design These ships, designed by Pattison of Naples, were enlarged versions of the *Palestro*-class torpedo-boats. However, the standard gun and torpedo calibre of the Italian Navy was now 4.7-inch and 21-inch respectively and to accommodate these heavier weapons the design had to be enlarged. With this larger displacement and an increase in speed of 3 knots, the installed horse power had also to be increased by more than 60 per cent. Each boiler was in a separate space and the two turbines in separate rooms themselves. When originally completed, only a single 4.7-inch gun was shipped on the forecastle, but in 1929 a twin mounting was substituted in lieu. This set the pattern for a number of Italian destroyer designs. The guns were 45 calibre O.T.O. 1926 pattern. In service, these ships proved disappointing as a result of their unreliable machinery. Like all Italians ships, the trials speeds at light displacement were never achieved under loaded wartime conditions and by 1940, maximum speed had fallen to about 33 knots. Because of Italy's desperate need for foreign exchange, *Ricasoli* and *Nicotera* were both sold to Sweden in March 1940, being renamed *Puke* and *Psilander*.
Modifications A clinker screen was fitted to the forward funnel during the war. The second gun director, originally abaft the after funnel, was landed as was the searchlight and platform at the base of the mainmast. The two old-pattern 40mm guns were replaced by new single 20mm guns and two more were fitted on the after end of the forecastle after removal of the sea-boats. The 13.2mm machine-guns were repositioned in place of the former searchlight. Two depth-charge throwers were added.
Service *Crispi* and *Sella* formed the under-strength 4th Division based at Leros in the Dodecanese at the start of Italy's war. Both destroyers spent much of their careers in the Aegean, initially – as in all commands – upon defensive minelaying and later on convoy escort duties. In February 1941 both ships were involved in counter-attacking British attempts to capture Rhodes, and in the following month carried a force of explosive motor-boats to Crete where a successful attack was made, sinking a large tanker and badly damaging the cruiser *York* in Suda Bay. *Sella* herself was badly damaged in error by Stuka bombers during the British evacuation of Greece in the spring of 1941. 1942 and 1943 saw operations in the Aegean continue, but at the time of the Italian surrender in September 1943, *Sella* was in the northern Adriatic where she was torpedoed and sunk by two German S-boats, *S54* and *S61*. *Crispi*, lying in Piraeus, was captured by the Germans who refitted her and recommissioned her as *TA15* (q.v.).

Above: *Sella* before the war. (Fraccaroli)

SAURO CLASS

Ship	Builder	Laid Down	Launched	Commissioned	Fate
BT *Cesare Battisti*	Odero, Sestri Ponente	9 Feb 24	11 Dec 26	13 April 27	Scuttled 3 April 41
MA *Daniele Manin*	C.N.Q. Fiume	9 Oct 24	15 June 25	1 Mar 27	Sunk 3 April 41
NL *Francesco Nullo*	C.N.Q. Fiume	9 Oct 24	14 Nov 25	15 April 27	Lost 21 Oct 40
SU *Nazario Sauro*	Odero, Sestri Ponente	9 Feb 24	12 May 26	23 Sept 26	Lost 3 April 41

Below: *Manin*. (Fraccaroli)

Displacement: 1,058tons/1,056tonnes (standard); 1,600tons/1,625tonnes (full load).
Length: 295ft 10in/90.16m (oa); 294ft/89.6m (wl).
Beam: 30ft 2in/9.2m.
Draught: 9ft 6in/2.9m (mean).
Machinery: three Yarrow Express boilers; 2-shaft Parsons geared turbines.
Performance: 36,000shp; 35kts.
Bunkerage: 230tons/234tonnes.
Range: 2,600nm at 14kts.
Guns: four 4.7in (2×2); two 40mm; two 13.2mm.
Torpedoes: six 21in (2×3).
Mines: 52.
Complement: 156.
Design This class was a development of the previous *Sella* class and was laid down in the following year. Because the forward gun was now to be a twin mounting in lieu of *Sella*'s original single, and torpedo tubes triple instead of twin, beam was increased by 600mm to compensate. The bridge structure was revised with a command position being added above the navigating bridge and the searchlight repositioned at the rear of the bridge. The second rangefinder was moved aft from its

position in *Sella* and fitted amidships between the torpedo tubes. Internally, the machinery, except for the substitution of Yarrow boilers for the Thornycroft type, remained as the *Sella* design and was therefore no more reliable.

Modifications No significant alteration because of their early war loss.

Service All four units formed the 3rd *Squadriglia*, based in the Red Sea for the protection of Italian Somaliland. Early operations comprised mercantile warfare sorties against shipping in the Red Sea, but these were unsuccessful. In the course of the attack upon British Convoy BN7 which was heavily escorted by cruisers, destroyers and sloops, *Nullo*, struggling because of steering defects, was badly damaged by *Kimberley* on withdrawing and was put ashore on Harmi Island under the guns of shore batteries (which in turn damaged *Kimberley*) where she was later destroyed by the RAF. *Manin* and *Sauro*, in the course of another sortie the following April, were attacked by shore-based Swordfish and sunk by bombing. *Battisti* left behind because of machinery defects, scuttled herself on the fall of the Italian colony.

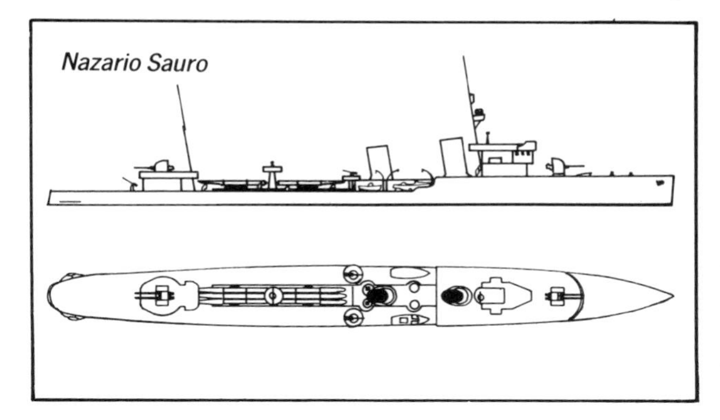

Above: *Nullo*. (Author's Collection)

TURBINE CLASS

Ship	Builder	Laid Down	Launched	Commissioned	Fate
AL *Aquilone*	Odero, Sestri Ponente	18 May 25	3 Aug 27	3 Dec 27	Mined 17 Sept 40
BR *Borea*	Ansaldo, Genoa	29 April 25	28 Jan 27	14 Nov 27	Lost 17 Sept 40
ES *Espero*	Ansaldo, Genoa	29 April 25	31 Aug 27	30 April 28	Lost 28 June 40
ER *Euro*	C.T. Riva Trigoso	24 Jan 25	7 July 27	22 Dec 27	Lost 1 Oct 43
NB *Nembo*	C.T. Riva Trigoso	21 Jan 25	27 Jan 27	14 Oct 27	Lost 20 July 40
OT *Ostro*	Ansaldo, Genoa	29 April 25	2 Jan 28	9 June 28	Lost 20 July 40
TB *Turbine*	Odero, Sestri Ponente	24 Mar 25	21 April 27	27 Aug 27	German *TA14* Sept 1943
ZF *Zeffiro*	Ansaldo, Genoa	29 April 25	27 May 27	15 May 28	Lost 5 July 40

Displacement: 1,070tons/1,090tonnes (standard); 1,670tons/1,700tonnes (full load).
Length: 305ft 9in/93.2m (oa); 299ft 6in/91.3m (pp).
Beam: 30ft 2in/9.2m.
Draught: 9ft 10in/3m (mean).
Machinery: three Express boilers; 2-shaft Parsons geared turbines.
Performance: 40,000shp; 36kts.
Bunkerage: 270tons/274tonnes.
Range: 3,200nm at 14kts.
Guns: four 4.7in (2×2); two 40mm; two 13.2 MG.
Torpedoes: six 21in (2×3).
Mines: 52.
Complement: 179.

Design A further expansion of *Sella* with a slightly larger hull and an 11 per cent increase in designed horse power to give a 1 knot increase in top speed. Bunkerage was increased to give a useful extension in endurance. Armament remained unchanged. Very fast speeds were attained on trials, the fastest being *Turbine* with 39.5 knots with power output 28 per cent over design figures.

Modifications The six ships lost within three months of Italy's entry into the war were probably not modified at all. *Euro* and *Turbine* landed the 1917 Vickers-Terni pattern 40mm/39cal guns and received 20mm guns of modern pattern instead. *Turbine* had one bank of torpedo tubes removed and shipped two single 37mm/54cal in lieu. Her armament was further modified in German hands.

Service These eight destroyers formed the 1st and 2nd *Squadriglie* based at Tobruk in June 1940. Early war operations included the laying of defensive mine barrages off the North African coast in June, and on 14 June the 1st Division shelled Sollum. Supply runs were made between Taranto and Tobruk, foreshadowing the major wartime task of the Royal Italian Navy. In the course of one of these, *Espero*, *Ostro* and *Zeffiro* were intercepted by the British 7th Cruiser Squadron (*Liverpool*, *Gloucester* and *Sydney*) west-south-west of Cape Matapan on the evening of 28 June 1940. *Espero*, fighting a rearguard action to enable the other two to escape, was sunk by gunfire from the Australian cruiser *Sydney*. Then early in

Below: *Ostro*. (Author's Collection)

the next month, *Eagle*'s ever-active Swordfish launched an attack on Tobruk harbour which sank *Zeffiro* and blew the bows off *Euro* so that the latter had to be beached. (She was, however, salvaged and towed to Taranto for repair later). Further losses occurred in the same month when on 20 July, Swordfish aircraft from *Eagle* found *Nembo* and *Ostro* in the Gulf of Bomba and torpedoed both of them. In mid September the British launched an attack on Benghazi where *Aquilone* and *Borea* lay. The former struck an air-laid mine, dropped by aircraft from *Illustrious*, and *Borea* was hit and sunk by bombs from the same carrier's aircraft. Only two of the eight ships now remained afloat after but four months' hostilities. Supply convoys to and from North Africa continued to be the main task throughout the rest of 1940 and all of 1941. *Euro*, at the end of 1941, was one of the few ships to escape the annihilation of a convoy by cruisers of Force K although she was damaged, being hit by six 6-inch shells which did not explode. In 1942, *Turbine* moved to the Adriatic and Aegean Theatre, based upon Piraeus, where she fell into German hands on 9 September at the time of the Italian capitulation. *Euro*, on the other hand, escaped into Allied custody and then operated with Allied naval forces in the eastern Mediterranean. However, her career against her former allies was brief for she was part of the British forces assigned to the defence of Leros where she was sunk in harbour by Stuka dive-bombers. *Turbine* was eventually put into service by the Kriegsmarine as *TA14* (q.v.).

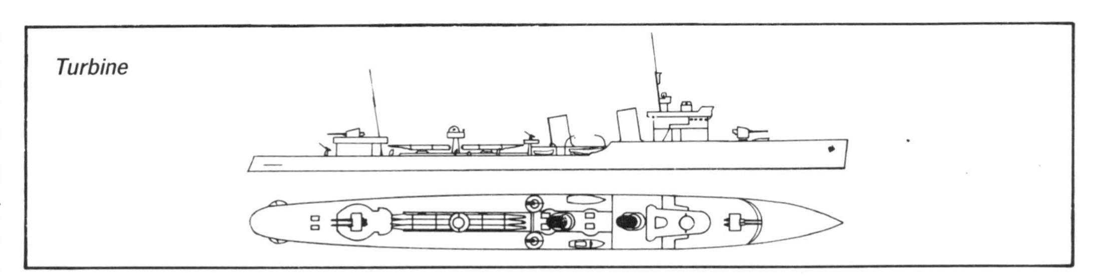

Right: *Espero* in 1936. (Fraccaroli)

NAVIGATORI CLASS

Ship	Builder	Laid Down	Launched	Commissioned	Fate
DM *Alvise Da Mosto*	C.N.Q. Fiume	22 Aug 28	1 July 29	15 Mar 31	Lost 1 Dec 41
DN *Antonio Da Noli*	C.T. Riva Trigoso	25 July 27	21 May 29	29 Dec 29	Lost 9 Sept 43
DR *Nicoloso Da Recco*	C.N.R. Ancona	14 Dec 27	5 Jan 30	20 May 30	Stricken 15 July 54
DV *Giovanni Da Verazzano*	C.N.Q. Fiume	17 Aug 27	15 Dec 28	25 Sept 30	Lost 19 Oct 42
MO *Lanzerotto Malocello*	Ansaldo	30 Aug 27	14 Mar 29	18 Jan 30	Lost 24 Mar 43
PN *Leone Pancaldo*	C.T. Riva Trigoso	7 July 27	5 Feb 29	30 Nov 29	Lost 30 April 43
PS *Emanuele Pessagno*	C.N.R. Ancona	9 Oct 27	12 Aug 29	10 Mar 30	Lost 29 May 42
PI *Antonio Pigafetta*	C.N.Q. Fiume	29 Dec 28	10 Nov 29	1 May 31	German *TA44* Oct 1944
TA *Luca Tarigo*	Ansaldo	30 Aug 27	9 Dec 28	16 Nov 29	Lost 16 April 41
US *Antonio Usodimare*	Odero, Sestri Ponente	1 June 27	12 May 29	21 Nov 29	Lost 8 June 42
VI *Ugolino Vivaldi*	Odero, Sestri Ponente	16 May 27	9 Jan 29	6 Mar 30	Lost 10 Sept 43
ZE *Nicolò Zeno*	C.N.Q. Fiume	5 June 27	12 Aug 28	27 May 30	Lost 9 Sept 43

Displacement: 1,870tons/1,900tonnes (standard); 2,608tons/2,650tonnes (full load).
Length: 352ft/107.3m (oa); 346ft 3in/105.5m (pp).
Beam: 33ft 5in/10,2m.
Draught: 11ft 6in/3.5m (mean).
Machinery: four Odero boilers (except C.N.Q. ships, Yarrow); 2-shaft Parsons geared turbines (except C.N.Q. ships, Belluzo and C.N.R. ships Tosi turbines).
Performance: 50,000shp; 38kts.
Bunkerage: 453tons/460tonnes.
Guns: six 4.7in (3×2); two 40mm; eight 13.2mm.
Torpedoes: four 21in (2×2).
Mines: 56 (except *Da Recco*).
Complement: 224.

Design In 1926, after the construction of a series of sixteen destroyers of moderate dimensions, the Royal Italian Navy decided to revert to a larger *exploratori* type to counter the powerful French *contre-torpilleurs* of the *Jaguar* and *Guépard* classes. In fact they were not originally classified as *esploratori* but as *caccia-torpedinieri*, not being reclassified until 19 July 1929 while still under construction.

(They were rerated *caccia-torpedinieri*, once again, on 5 September 1938). As compared with the earlier *Leone*, this new class was slightly smaller in dimensions but displaced some 200 tonnes more. The main armament was reduced by two guns, there being three twin mountings with one amidships between the funnels. While the main gun calibre was not new (4.7-inch), the guns themselves were, being Ansaldo 1926-pattern 50-calibre weapons. They fired the same 51lb shell as the earlier guns, but had an improved muzzle velocity of 3,117 feet per second as compared with the earlier pattern's 2,789 feet per second. Maximum elevation 45°, rate of fire 6rpm. Two triple torpedo tube banks were fitted, unusual in that the centre tube of each bank was fitted with a reducer and fired 17.7-inch torpedoes, while the wing tubes fired 21-inch torpedoes. Finally, the AA outfit remained two 40mm/30cal and four 13.2mm Breda machine-guns.

The machinery arrangement of this design was noteworthy in that the unit principle was adopted, with two separate boiler room-engine room units. The forward unit drove the port shaft and the after one the starboard shaft. Installed power had to be increased to 55,000shp for a maximum designed speed of 38 knots. On trials, under light load conditions (1,921 tons) 39.58 knots was achieved by *Pigafetta*. *Da Recco* was reported as reaching 41.5 knots with 71,000shp and *Da Mosto* 43.5 knots on trials.

Visually these were distinctive ships with a bridge structure layout which was to be repeated in all subsequent Italian destroyer designs. Atop the bridge was a large tower fitted with two 3m range rangefinders abaft which was a taller tower for the main armament fire-control director which was stepped adjacent to the foremast. A secondary fire-control director was fitted abaft the after funnel. All except *Da Recco* were fitted for minelaying. *Da Recco*, fitted as a flagship had a wider after deck-house and in consequence there was insufficient room for the mine rails.

After their entry into service in 1929–31, it was found that stability was not as good as it should have been and steps were taken to rectify matters. This involved removal of upper fuel bunkers and the construction of three more in the double bottom thereby reducing bunkerage to 460 tons with consequent reduction in endurance. *Pigafetta*, however, had only 405 tons. The upper level of the bridge structure was removed, lowering its height by about 2½ metres, funnels were cut down a little and masting was altered. Later the centre tube in each torpedo tube bank was landed in a further attempt to reduce top-weight. All these steps produced some improvement, but not enough it transpired, for in 1938, further modifications were put in hand to improve stability and reduce wetness forward.

Above: *Da Noli* in 1940. (Fraccaroli) **Below:** *Da Recco*. Note differences in bows, upper bridge and midships compared to *Da Noli*. (Author's Collection)

Below: *Da Verazzano* in August 1942. (Fraccaroli)

This new project involved increasing the beam by extra plating about ½m outside the original hull, raising the bows to improve sea-worthiness and, by utilizing the new hull space, increasing bunkerage to 680 tons. Finally all the machinery was overhauled. *Vivaldi* was the first to start this refit, on 25 October 1938 and *Tarigo* the last on 6 May 1940. *Da Verazzano* was the last to finish the refit, on 30 August 1940, while *Usodimare* and *Da Recco* were never taken in hand at all. This modification reduced the speed to about 28 knots but the unmodified pair kept their higher speed. Displacement of the modified ships was now an average of 2,125 tons (standard).

Modifications After the outbreak of war, *Da Verazzano, Pigafetta, Pessagno, Tarigo* and *Da Mosto* received two new triple banks for 21-inch torpedoes, with the centre tube raised. Towards the end of 1941, seven 20mm/65 Breda guns replaced the older outfit, two on the bridge, two in lieu of the 40mm/39cal guns, one abaft the forward funnel and two abaft the after funnel. *Pancaldo*, however, received an extra two 20mm/65 at the after end of the quarter deck and *Da Noli* had 20mm/70cal weapons in lieu of the 65cal guns. Later *Da Recco* and *Pigafetta* received an extra pair of single 20mm/70 on the quarterdeck. After 1942, the after tubes were removed from *Pigafetta, Da Recco, Malocello, Pancaldo, Da Noli, Vivaldi* and *Zeno*, being replaced by two single 37mm/54cal 1932 guns. *Pancaldo* received an Italian EC3/ter Gufo radar set and *Malocello* a German FuMo 26/40G set by the end of 1942. Several others were fitted for a set but never received one. In 1942, *Da Recco, Da Verazzano, Malocello, Pancaldo* and *Vivaldi* were fitted with an asdic-type set. To accommodate the augmented AA outfit, the after director had been removed by 1942.

Service The twelve ships constituted the 14th, 15th and 16th *Squadriglie* at the outbreak of war, but due to the major refit programme in process, only nine were immediately available for service. All three squadriglie were initially attached to the Fleet with IV, VII and VIII Cruiser Squadrons taking part in minelaying, anti-submarine and bombardment duties.

Vivaldi, Da Noli, Pancaldo, Pigafetta, Zeno, Da Recco, Pessagno and *Usodimare* were present at the action off Calabria in July 1940, but shortly afterwards *Pancaldo* was torpedoed and sunk by Swordfish from *Eagle* while at anchor in Augusta harbour on 10 July. She was not refloated until 26 July 1941 then towed to Genoa for repair, re-entering service on 12 December that year. *Vivaldi* rammed and sank the British submarine *Oswald* off Cape Spartivento on 1 August, and with her sisters *Da Noli* and *Tarigo* laid mines off Cape Bon and Malta in October which caused the loss of the British destroyers *Hyperion* and *Imperial*. In November and December, *Pigafetta, Da Recco* and *Pessagno* were in action off

Above: *Malocello*, fitted with German-pattern radar. (G. Alfano)

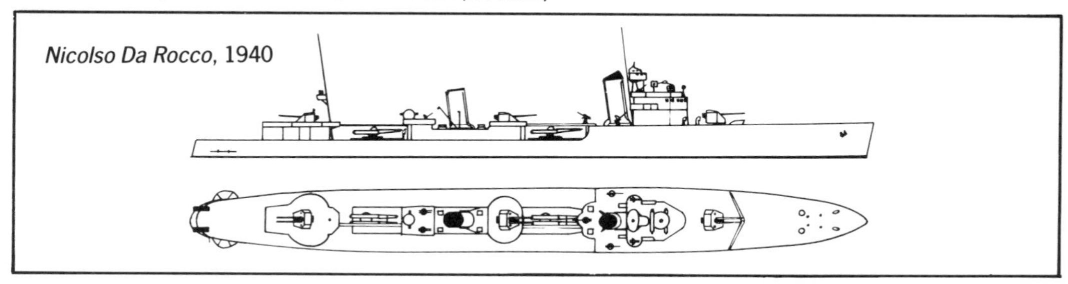

Nicolso Da Rocco, 1940

Corfu and the Greek coast in support of the Italian invasion of Greece.

1941 saw several of the class employed on minelaying sorties, and escorting convoys to North Africa. Only *Da Recco* and *Pessagno* were present with the Italian Fleet at Matapan, but in the following month another loss occurred when *Tarigo* which, with *Lampo* and *Baleno*, was escorting a convoy to Tripoli, was sunk by a force of four British destroyers during darkness. At the same time, however, the Italian destroyer managed to torpedo *Mohawk*. Convoy duty and minelaying continued, with *Pigafetta* and *Zeno* sinking the submarine *Usk* off Sicily early in May. Mines laid off Tripoli in June by an Italian force, including five of this class, caused serious losses to Force K in December. In September, *Da Recco, Da Noli, Pessagno* and *Usodimare* (with *Gioberti*) were the escort to three large passenger liners, of which two were sunk by *Upholder* with very heavy casualties to the troops embarked. At the end of the year, *Da Mosto*, while picking up survivors from a sunken tanker, was intercepted and sunk by the cruiser *Penelope* off the Kerkenah Bank.

The submarine *P38* fell victim to *Usodimare* and *Circe* off Tunisia on 25 February 1942, but in May another loss occurred when *Pessagno* was torpedoed and sunk by *Turbulent*. In June, during the action off Pantellaria in which *Vivaldi* and *Malocello* participated, the former received serious damage in a boiler room and had to be towed away by *Malocello*. *Usodimare*, after a rather unlucky career, was finally torpedoed and sunk in error by the Italian submarine *Alagi*. *Verazzano* was torpedoed and sunk by *Unbending* while escorting a convoy from Naples to Tripoli.

By 1943, the plight of the Axis armies in North Africa was desperate and all available forces were thrown into escorting the supply convoys. *Malocello* was lost on a mine north of Cape Bon in March and *Pancaldo* while operating with *Hermes* (q.v.) was bombed and sunk en route to Tunisia. With *Zeno* having collided with *Da Noli* on 28 February and requiring repair, there was now only *Da Noli, Vivaldi, Pigafetta* and *Da Recco* still operational.

After the loss of North Africa by the Axis forces, the tempo of life for the Italian destroyers slowed down somewhat, until the capitulation in September 1943. *Da Noli* and *Vivaldi* sailed from La Spezia on 8 September to attack German convoy traffic between Sardinia and Corsica, damaging and sinking some lighters, but the former was hit by shore batteries, then mined and sunk. *Vivaldi* also suffered damage and while making for internment in the Balearic Islands, was bombed and sunk by German aircraft. *Pigafetta*, damaged in Tunis in April 1943, was under repair at Fiume where, despite her crew's attempts at sabotage, she was captured by the Germans and recommissioned as *TA44* (q.v.). *Da Recco*, which had only returned to service in July after her damage the previous December, escaped from Italy and survived the war. Finally *Zeno*, still under repair at Trieste, was scuttled on 9 September to avoid capture by the Germans.

FRECCIA CLASS

Ship	Builder	Laid Down	Launched	Commissioned	Fate
DA *Dardo*	Odero, Sestri Ponente	23 Jan 29	6 Sept 30	25 Jan 32	German *TA31* Sept 1943
FR *Freccia*	C.T. Riva Trigoso	20 Feb 29	3 Aug 30	21 Oct 31	Lost 8 Aug 43
SA *Saetta*	C.T. Riva Trigoso	27 May 29	17 Jan 32	10 May 32	Lost 3 Feb 43
ST *Strale*	Odero, Sestri Ponente	20 Feb 29	26 Mar 31	6 Feb 32	Wrecked 21 June 42

Displacement: 1,205tons/1,225tonnes (standard); 2,116/2,150tonnes (full load).
Length: 315ft 5in/96.15m (oa); 302ft 6in/92.2m (pp).
Beam: 32ft/9.75m.
Draught: 10ft 4in/3.15m (mean).
Machinery: three R.It.N. Express boilers; 2-shaft Parsons geared turbines.
Performance: 44,000shp; 38kts.
Bunkerage: 630tons/640tonnes.
Range: 4,600nm at 12kts.
Guns: four 4.7in (2×2); two 40mm; four 13.2mm MG.
Torpedoes: six 21in (2×3).
Mines: 54.
Complement: 185.

Design This was a reversion to the smaller type of Fleet destroyer, essentially an extension of the *Turbine* class and, as originally designed, was similar in visual appearance. The designed horse-power, however, was increased by 10 per cent over that of *Turbine* to give a contract speed of 38 knots in order to have a sufficient margin over the contemporary heavy cruisers of the *Zara* type. The machinery arrangements were identical with that of the *Turbine*, i.e., three boiler rooms and two turbine rooms, but the unit arrangement of the *Navigatori* class was not perpetuated. While under construction, it was decided to trunk all uptakes into one large funnel producing, for the period, a unique appearance. Modifications were also made to the bridgework and hull with the result that, as completed this class was larger and considerably beamier than *Turbine*. This extra hull space was utilized to increase bunkerage and hence endurance considerably. As far as armament was concerned, however, there was no change in either broadside or disposition over that of *Turbine* but they shipped the Ansaldo 50cal 1926-pattern gun as in the *Navigatori*. After entry into service, it was found that the machinery was unreliable, sea-worthiness poor and stability marginal. To rectify matters, bilge keels and nearly 100 tons of permanent ballast had to be added. A system of compensating fuel consumed by seawater in the fuel bunkers exacerbated their problems as fuel contamination resulted.

Modifications The obsolete 40mm guns and the twin 13.2mm guns were removed and replaced by 20mm guns for a total of five or six 20mm/65cal. These were generally fitted on the bridge, abaft the funnel and on the quarter deck. In 1943–44 all except *Strale* had their after tubes removed and replaced by two single 37mm/54cal guns. The after director was landed and two 20mm in a twin mounting fitted instead. Two further twin 20mm were added to port and starboard on the forecastle.

Service All four units belonged to the 7th Squadriglia based at Taranto in June 1940. *Strale* scored an early success by sinking the British submarine *Odin* off Taranto on 13 June 1940. In July all four were with the 7th Division (*Cavour* and *Cesare*) at the action off Calabria, but thereafter most of their service was with the North Africa convoys. However, *Saetta* accompanied the fleet against Malta convoys in February 1942 and with *Freccia* did so again in June against the British 'Harpoon'/'Vigorous' operations. In that month *Strale* ran ashore near Cape Bon on the 21st and was finally destroyed by torpedoes fired by *Turbulent* on 6 August. *Saetta* took part in the evacuation of Tunis but was lost to a mine laid by *Abdiel*. *Freccia* was sunk by bombs at Genoa the month before Italy's capitulation, but *Dardo* was captured by the Germans and recommissioned at Genoa as their *TA31* (q.v.).

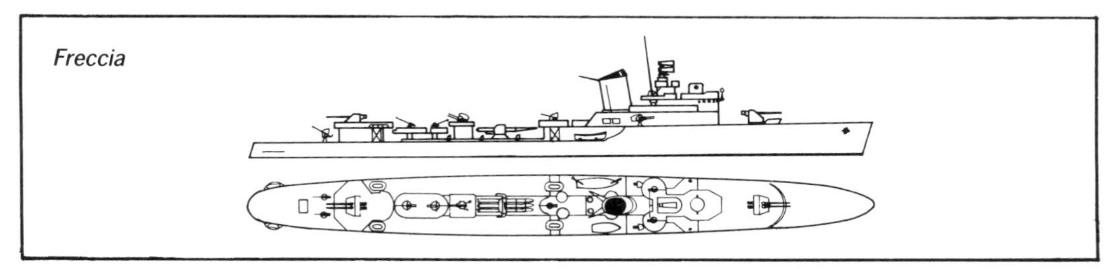

Above: *Strale* in 1938. (Fraccaroli) **Below:** *Dardo*, also in 1938. (Fraccaroli)

FOLGORE CLASS

Ship	Builder	Laid Down	Launched	Commissioned	Fate
BO *Baleno*	C.N.Q. Fiume	1 Oct 29	22 Mar 31	15 June 32	Lost 17 April 41
FG *Folgore*	O.C. Partenopei, Naples	30 Jan 30	26 April 31	1 July 32	Lost 2 Dec 42
FL *Fulmine*	C.N.Q. Fiume	1 Oct 29	2 Aug 31	14 Sept 32	Lost 9 Nov 41
LP *Lampo*	O.C. Partenopei, Naples	30 Jan 30	26 July 31	13 Aug 32	Lost 30 April 43

Displacement: 1,220tons/1,240tonnes (standard); 2,096tons/2,130tonnes (full load).
Length: 315ft 1in/96.05m (oa); 309ft 5in/94.3m (wl).
Beam: 30ft 2in/9.2m.
Draught: 10ft 10in/3.3m (mean).
Machinery: three Thornycroft boilers; 2-shaft Belluzo geared turbines.
Performance: 44,000shp; 38kts.
Bunkerage: 510tons/518tonnes.
Range: 3,600nm at 12kts.
Guns: four 4.7in (2×2); two 40mm; four 13.2mm MG.
Torpedoes: six 21in (2×3).
Mines: 52.
Complement: 183.

Above: *Fulmine* before the war. (Fraccaroli) **Below:** *Folgore* in August 1942. (Fraccaroli)

Design A modification of the *Dardo* class of which they were sometimes referred to as the '2nd Group'. In an attempt to enable them to attain and maintain their designed full speed, beam was reduced by 1½ feet, but all other features remained the same except that the reduced hull volume also reduced bunkerage. In consequence, endurance was reduced by almost 22 per cent at 12 knots. Furthermore, the main machinery was no more reliable than that of the *Dardo*s so that the class was no more successful than the earlier group. They were also given the same modifications to improve stability and seaworthiness as their half-sisters.

Modifications Early in the war, five or six 20mm/65cal replaced the former 40mm and 13.2mm guns. *Folgore* and *Lampo* later also landed the after tubes in exchange for a pair of single 37mm/54cal guns.

Service This group constituted the 8th *Squadriglia* based at Taranto on Italy's entry into the war. The *sqadriglia* took part in the action off Calabria in June 1940, but the majority of their service was on escort duty with the North Africa supply convoys. *Folgore* and *Fulmine* were in action shelling Albania in January 1941. On 16 April 1941, *Baleno* and *Lampo* (with *Tarigo*) were escorting a convoy of five ships when they were intercepted at night by the British *Jervis, Nubian, Mohawk* and *Janus*. The radar-equipped British destroyers sank all the merchantmen, *Lampo* and *Tarigo* at the cost of *Mohawk*. The badly damaged *Baleno* foundered the following day. *Lampo*, aground on the banks, was salvaged on 8 August, towed to Italy and repaired, being recommissioned in May 1942. *Fulmine* and *Folgore* frequently operated together on the convoy routes throughout 1941, but in November the former was sunk by Force K (*Aurora, Penelope, Lance* and *Lively*) together with her seven-ship convoy. Two other destroyers escaped. *Folgore* operated with the Fleet against Malta convoys in 1942, but was eventually sunk by Force Q (*Aurora, Sirius, Agonaut, Quiberon* and *Quentin*) off the Skerki Bank with four merchantmen of her convoy in December. *Lampo*, on returning to service, went to the Aegean briefly but spent all of 1943 in the desperate struggle to supply and finally evacuate the Axis forces trapped in Tunisia. On 30 April during a last-ditch attempt to run ammunition to the army, she and *Pancaldo* were sunk by bombs off Cape Bon.

MAESTRALE CLASS

Ship	Builder	Laid Down	Launched	Commissioned	Fate
GR *Grecale*	C.N.R. Ancona	25 Sept 31	17 June 34	15 Nov 34	Stricken 31 May 64
LI *Libeccio*	C.T. Riva Trigoso	29 Sept 31	4 July 34	23 Nov 34	Lost 9 Nov 41
ML *Maestrale*	C.N.R. Ancona	25 Sept 31	5 April 34	2 Sept 34	Scuttled 9 Sept 43
SC *Scirocco*	C.T. Riva Trigoso	29 Sept 31	22 April 34	21 Oct 34	Foundered 23 Mar 42

Displacement: 1,417tons/1,440tonnes (standard); 2,219tons/2,255tonnes (full load).
Length: 350ft/106.7m (oa); 333ft 4in/101.6m (pp).
Beam: 33ft 7in/10.15m.
Draught: 10ft 10in/3.31m (mean).
Machinery: three Yarrow small tube vertical boilers; 2-shaft Parsons geared turbines.
Performance: 44,000shp; 38kts.
Bunkerage: 521tons/530tonnes.
Range: 4,000nm at 12kts.
Guns: four 4.7in (2×2); two 40mm; four 13.2mm MG.
Torpedoes: six 21in (2×3).
Mines: 56.
Complement: 191.

Design An expansion of the *Dardo* design some 35 feet longer and with a foot more beam than the *Dardo*s, this class sought to rectify the defects of earlier designs. In this they were largely successful and with some minor variations formed the basis of 23 ships of later classes. Main machinery power and speed remained the same as the *Dardo* class, permitted by the increased length and hull form. Endurance, however, was intermediate between that of the two *Dardo* groups. Armament was identical with the previous destroyers except that the O.T.O. pattern 1931 4.7in/50calibre gun was carried. This was lighter, but less robust than the 1926 model. AA defence was stil the venerable 40mm Vickers design of 1917, because the 37mm of modern pattern was only, as yet, available as a twin mounting. No after rangefinder was fitted in this class.

Modifications As in all classes of destroyer, the 40mm and 13.2mm guns were replaced initially by six 20mm single mountings. *Libeccio* and *Scirocco* were probably lost in this condition. Possibly in an effort to reduce the Italian Navy's disadvantage due to lack of radar, some units received a 4.7in/15cal O.T.O. lighting howitzer for starshell. (This gun in *Maestrale* was later replaced by a single 4.7in/50cal Ansaldo gun.) *Grecale* had her after torpedo tubes removed and replaced by two 37mm/54cal single guns and the 20mm outfit increased to about twelve guns in a mixture of twins and singles. It is probable that *Maestrale* was modified likewise when under repair in 1943.

Service Serving with the 10th *Squadriglia* in Sicily, these four destroyers were attached to the 2nd Division (*Bande Nere* and *Colleoni*). In June 1940 they formed the close escort of a convoy to North Africa at the time of the action off Calabria and thus did not get into action. In August, minefields laid by the *squadriglia* accounted for the loss of the British destroyer *Hostile*. Throughout 1940 and 1941 they were mainly attached to the Fleet but conducted a number of convoy and minelaying sorties. *Libeccio* was slightly damaged by bombs during the Fleet Air Arm raid on Taranto in November 1940. Almost exactly a year later she was torpedoed by the submarine *Upholder* while picking up survivors from sunken ships and despite being taken in tow by *Euro*, sank soon afterwards. *Grecale* was badly damaged by British cruisers of Force K on 9 November 1941 but was successfully towed home by *Oriani*. *Grecale*, now repaired, was present at the second battle of Sirte in March 1942, but *Scirocco* which, with *Geniere* had been ordered from Taranto to join *Littorio*, was ordered to turn back after the Italian Fleet disengaged. On passage she lost one engine and later foundered in heavy weather about 100 miles southeast of Cape Spartivento, only two of her company being rescued. *Maestrale* struck a mine laid by *Abdiel* on 9 January 1943, losing her stern abaft the after deck-house. Although she was successfully brought into Genoa for repair, she was still incomplete at the time of the Capitulation and to avoid capture, scuttled by her crew on 9 September. *Grecale* on the other hand, escaped to Malta and subsequently saw service against her former Allies. She was mainly employed as a transport for small battle units. In this role *Maiale*, launched from her in June 1944, penetrated the harbour of La Spezia and sank the heavy cruiser *Bolzano* while undergoing repairs after her capture by the Germans. In another sortie in April 1945, the incomplete aircraft carrier *Aquila* was damaged in Genoa. *Grecale* survived the war and had a long post-war career with the Italian Navy in the A/S role for which she was refitted and modernized.

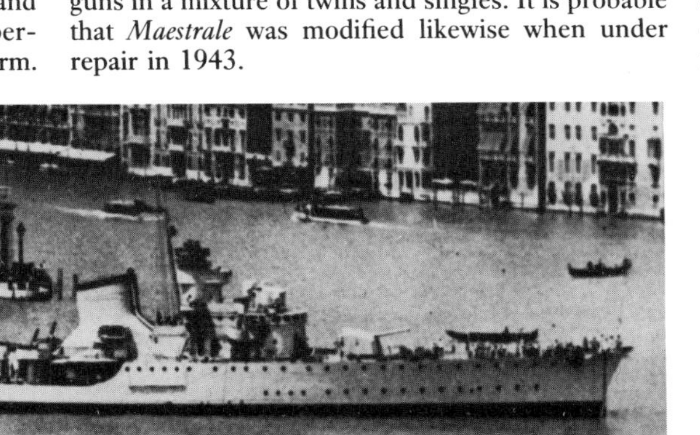

Above: *Maestrale*. (Author's Collection) **Below:** *Grecale*. Note star-shell gun and twin 20mm.

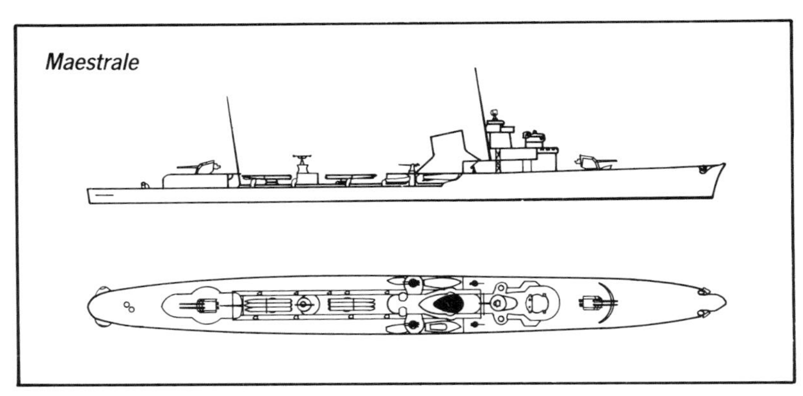

ORIANI CLASS

Ship	Builder	Laid Down	Launched	Commissioned	Fate
AL *Vittorio Alfieri*	O.T.O. Livorno	4 April 36	20 Dec 36	1 Dec 37	Lost 28 Mar 41
CD *Giosue Carducci*	O.T.O. Livorno	5 Feb 36	28 Oct 36	1 Nov 37	Lost 28 Mar 41
GB *Vincenzo Gioberti*	O.T.O. Livorno	2 Jan 36	19 Sept 36	27 Oct 37	Lost 9 Aug 43
OA *Alfredo Oriani*	O.T.O. Livorno	28 Oct 35	30 July 36	15 July 37	To France 1948

Displacement: 1,559tons/1,584tonnes (standard); 2,470tons/2,510tonnes (full load).
Length: 350ft/106.7m (oa); 333ft 4in/101.6m (pp).
Beam: 33ft 7in/10.15m.
Draught: 11ft 2in/3.42m (mean).
Machinery: three Thornycroft 3-drum boilers; 2-shaft Parsons geared turbines.
Performance: 48,000shp; 38kts.
Bunkerage: 502tons/510tonnes.
Range: 2,190nm at 18kts.
Guns: four 4.7in (2×2); four 37mm (2×2); six 13.2mm MG.
Torpedoes: six 21in (2×3).
Mines: 56.
Complement: 207.

Design These four destroyers, all built by O.T.O. at Livorno, were repeat *Maestrale* class except that the installed power was increased by 9 per cent. This move failed to show much improvement on trials, but the sea speed was better by about 1 knot. The only change in the armament was the omission of the 40mm guns and their replacement by a further pair of 13.2mm twin machine-guns abaft the funnel.

Modifications The usual early war alterations were made, i.e., the removal of the 13.2mm guns and their replacement by single 20mm/65cal mountings. Up to eight of these were fitted. No further alterations were made to the pair lost at Matapan, but the two survivors had the after tubes replaced by a pair of single 37mm/54cal Breda guns. Two twin 20mm/70cal Scotte-Isotta Fraschini mountings were added as well as a 4.7-inch/15cal star-shell gun. The ASW outfit was augmented by two depth-charge throwers. Finally, *Oriani* received a German 'Seetakt' radar set in 1942–43, and finished the war with four 4.7-inch, two 37mm and twelve 20mm.

Service All four ships were serving with the battle fleet at the start of the war, their first major operation being the action off Calabria in June 1940 when they formed part of the 1st Cruiser Division (*Zara* and *Fiume*). In November they saw action off Cape Teulada in Sardinia with *Pola, Fiume* and *Gorizia*. All except *Oriani* were involved in shelling Greek positions in Albania in January 1941. The following month, the Italian Admiralty planned a major sweep against British shipping in the Aegean and eastern Mediterranean. This was to be a double-pronged attack both north and south of Crete, involving *Vittorio Veneto*, three heavy cruisers and seven destroyers as the southern group, and a northern group consisting of the 1st Cruiser Division (R-Ad. Cattaneo in *Zara* with *Pola* and *Fiume*) and two light cruisers of the 8th Cruiser Division. The four *Oriani*s of the 9th Squadriglia under Capt. Toscano in *Alfieri* were attached to the heavy cruisers, while *Da Recco* and *Pessagno* screened the light cruisers. This sortie began on 26 March but failed to proceed according to plan due to faulty Intelligence. The two groups were ordered to combine and after *Vittori Veneto* had been damaged by torpedo-bombers from *Formidable* on the 28th, the heavy cruisers and attendant destroyers were ordered to escort the damaged battleship. On the evening of the 28th, *Pola* was hit by an aircraft torpedo amidships and stopped. *Zara, Fiume* and the 9th *Squadriglia* were then detached to assist the crippled cruiser. By the time a tow had been passed it was dark and, unknown to the Italian force, they had been detected by radar of a British force of three battleships (*Warspite, Valiant* and *Barham*) with escorting destroyers. Taken completely by surprise, the Italian ships were annihilated by 15-inch gunfire. The Italian destroyers mounted a counter-attack, but *Alfieri*, having got off four salvoes from her forward guns and three torpedoes, was sunk by gunfire. *Carducci*, which had been repeatedly hit, with serious fires raging onboard, was finished off by the destroyers *Stuart* and *Havock. Oriani*, hit and with one engine disabled, managed to make her escape, and *Gioberti*, after a gallant but unsuccessful counter-attack, also disengaged successfully.

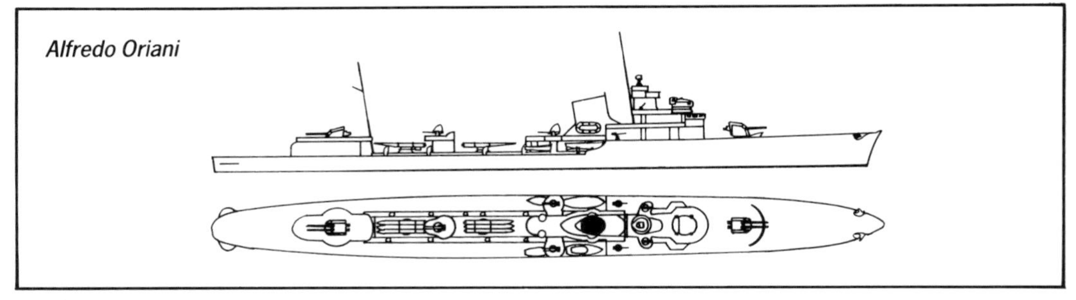
Alfredo Oriani

Below: *Oriani*, pre-war. Note unusual AA gun at break of forecasstle. (Author's Collection)

The two survivors spent the remainder of 1941 and all of 1942 operating with the Fleet, *Gioberti* taking part in both of the Sirte actions in December 1941 and *Oriani* the second. Both sailed with the 7th Cruiser Division to attack the 'Harpoon'/'Vigorous' convoy operation in 1942, but *Gioberti* suffered engine problems and turned back. Convoy cover operations formed much of their work and in the first few months of 1943, *Gioberti* was heavily committed to the support, supply and, finally, evacuation of Axis forces in Tunisia. She was eventually torpedoed and sunk by the British submarine *Simoom* off La Spezia in August 1943. *Oriani* escaped from that port at the time of the Capitulation and sailed with the fleet to Malta. Subsequently she served in the eastern Mediterranean with British forces. In August 1948, *Oriani* was transferred to France and renamed *D'Estaing*, being finally condemned on 12 June 1954.

Above: *Oriani* at the end of the war, with rebuilt bridge, new masting and 37mm guns in lieu of the after tubes. (Author's Collection)

SOLDATI (1st SERIES) CLASS

Ship	Builder	Laid Down	Launched	Commissioned	Fate
AP *Alpino*	C.N.R. Ancona	2 May 37	18 Sept 38	20 April 39	Lost 19 April 43
AR *Artigliere*	O.T.O. Livorno	15 Feb 37	12 Dec 37	14 Nov 38	Lost 12 Oct 40
AI *Ascari*	O.T.O. Livorno	11 Dec 37	31 July 38	6 May 39	Lost 24 Mar 43
AV *Aviere*	O.T.O. Livorno	16 Jan 37	19 Sept 37	31 Aug 38	Lost 17 Dec 42
BG *Bersagliere*	C.N.R. Palermo	21 April 37	3 July 38	1 April 39	Lost 7 Jan 43
CN *Camicia Nera*	O.T.O. Livorno	21 Jan 37	8 Aug 37	30 June 38	To USSR 21 Feb 49
CB *Carabiniere*	C.T. Riva Trigoso	1 Feb 37	23 July 38	20 Dec 38	Stricken 18 Jan 65
CZ *Corazziere* CR	O.T.O. Livorno	7 Oct 37	22 May 38	4 Mar 39	Scuttled 9 Sept 43
FC *Fuciliere*	C.N.R. Ancona	2 May 37	31 July 38	10 Jan 39	To USSR 17 Jan 50
GE *Geniere*	O.T.O. Livorno	26 Aug 37	27 Feb 38	14 Dec 38	Lost 1 Mar 43
GN *Granatiere*	C.N.R. Palermo	5 April 37	24 April 38	1 Feb 39	Stricken 1 July 58
LN *Lanciere*	C.T. Riva Trigoso	1 Feb 37	18 Dec 38	25 Mar 39	Foundered 23 Mar 42

Displacement: 1,620tons*/1,645tonnes (standard); 2,550tons/2,590tonnes (full load).
Length: 350ft/106.7m (oa); 333ft 4in/101.6m (pp).
Beam: 33ft 7in/10.15m.
Draught: 11ft 6in/3.15m (mean).
Machinery: three Yarrow small tube vertical boilers; 2-shaft Belluzzo (O.T.O. Ships, Parsons) geared turbines.
Performance: 48,000shp; 38kts.
Bunkerage: 516tons/525tonnes.
Range: 2,200nm at 20kts.
Guns: four (except *CN, CB, GE* and *LN*, five) 4.7in 2×2 (and 1×1); twelve 13.2mm MG.
Torpedoes: six 21in (2×3).
Mines: 48.
Complement: 206.

Design This class was essentially a repeat *Oriani* and orders were placed for three *squadriglie* in 1936, being named after military professions. In service they were known as the 'Soldati' class. Armament remained two twin 4.7-inch Ansaldo 1936- or 1937-pattern guns disposed one forward, one aft. The machine-gun armament was increased to twelve 13.2mm in four twin and four single mountings. Fire-control equipment was similar to the earlier

*Actually varied up to 1,830tons according to the builder.

Below: *Fuciliere*, before the war. She has a star-shell gun amidships. (Author's Collection)

destroyers, but some ships, including *Aviere, Ascari, Carabiniere* and *Lanciere*, had a second director at the forward end of the after shelter deck and *Alpino* had hers abaft the funnel. *Camicia Nera* and *Artigliere* were among those not so fitted. Amidships, all except *Carabiniere* shipped a 4.7-inch/15cal star-shell gun.

Modifications All units fitted with an after director had it removed in 1940–41. When the new Ansaldo 1940-pattern single 4.7-inch gun became available, this was fitted on the midships platform between the torpedo tubes in *Carabiniere, Ascari, Camicia Nera, Geniere* and *Lanciere*, replacing the 15cal star-shell gun in the last four units. The 13.2mm guns were supplanted by 20mm/65cal twin mountings, generally fitted two on the upper bridge and two abaft the funnel. By 1943, surviving units had received one or two further twin and single mount-ings. At this time also, the midships 4.7-inch gun was removed from *Fuciliere* and she, with *Carabiniere* and *Granatiere*, also lost the after torpedo tubes in exchange for a pair of single 37mm/54cal guns. Only *Fuciliere* received a radar set, of Italian 'Gufo' type, in 1943.

Service All twelve units served with the Fleet at the entry of Italy into the war. *Corazziere* and *Lanciere* were involved in early minelaying operations in June, but in July all the class were present at the action off Calabria when they formed the 12th (*Lanciere, Carabiniere, Corazziere, Ascardi*), 11th (*Artigliere, Camicia Nera, Aviere, Geniere*) and 8th (*Granatiere, Fuciliere, Bersagliere* and *Alpino*) *Squadriglie*. Three months later, the 11th *Squadriglie* was engaged by the British cruiser *Ajax* and the 7th Cruiser Squadron when *Artigliere* was very badly hit and *Aviere* lightly damaged. *Camicia Nera* took *Artigliere* in tow, but after an unsuccessful attack by torpedo-carrying Swordfish aircraft, had to cut loose the tow on the approach of the cruiser *York*. *Artigliere* was sunk by *York* after her crew was taken off. Before the close of the year, *Lanciere* had also been badly damaged, on 27 November, during sorties against the Malta convoys, having to be towed in to Cagliari.

In 1941, the class took part in the various Fleet sorties and seven were present at Matapan (*Alpino, Bersagliere, Fuciliere, Granatiere, Corazziere, Carabiniere* and *Ascari*) but suffered no loss. As the year progressed, the increasing importance of the North Africa supply route led to frequent convoy escort duties or as distant support with the heavy units of the Fleet. It was in the protection of these convoys, particularly at night, that the lack of radar was most acutely felt by the Italians, several convoys being decimated by British light forces, particularly Force K. This task continued into 1942 but *Carabiniere* was torpedoed and badly damaged by the submarine *P36* in February although she was brought safely into port. In the next month, however, *Lanciere* foundered in heavy weather with the loss of all but five men, following the second Battle of Sirte. *Aviere* was sunk by bombs at Palermo in January 1943 and her sister *Geniere* in the same manner and place two months later. *Ascari*, having participated in the evacuation attempts to Tunisia, struck a mine laid by *Abdiel* towards the end of March, and *Alpino* was bombed by US Liberators and sunk at La Spezia in April. In mid 1943 the fascist name *Camicia Nera* (black shirt) fell out of fashion and the ship was renamed *Artigliere* (ii) on 30 July. At the Capitulation, *Corazziere*, under damage repair at Genoa, was scuttled to avoid capture on 9 September, but despite her refloating by the Germans, was sunk finally in an air raid on 4 September 1944. *Fuciliere* and *Carabiniere* escaped to internment in Port Mahon until January 1944 when they sailed for Malta. *Artigliere* and *Granatiere* also escaped to Malta in September 1943.

After the war, *Artigliere* and *Fuciliere* were ceded to the USSR, designated *Z12* and *Z20* respectively, being removed from the effective list in about 1958. The other two survivors were retained by the Italian Navy serving in the A/S role until removed from the effective list on 1 July 1958 (*Granatiere*) and 18 January 1965 (*Carabiniere*).

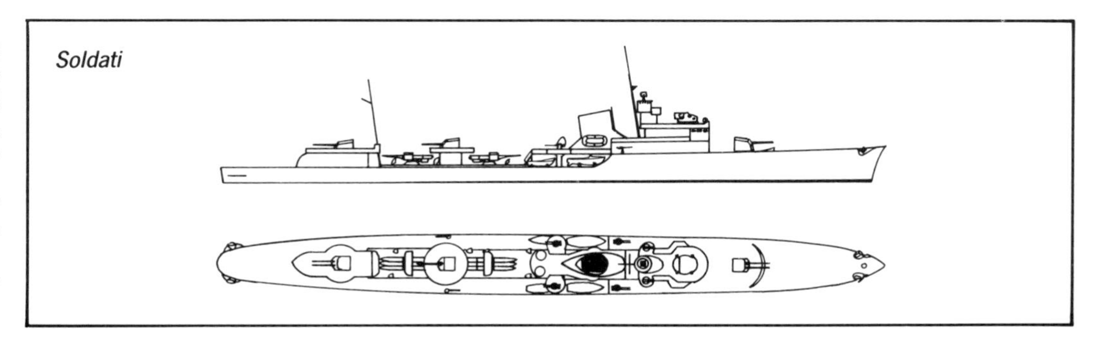

Above: *Aviere*. (Author's Collection) **Below:** *Geniere*, with the midships 4.7-inch gun. (Author's Collection)

SOLDATI (2nd SERIES) CLASS

Ship	Builder	Laid Down	Launched	Commissioned	Fate
BR *Bombardiere*	C.N.R. Ancona	7 Oct 40	23 Mar 42	15 July 42	Lost 17 Jan 43
CR *Carrista*	O.T.O. Livorno	11 Sept 41	–	–	Scrapped on slip
CA *Corsaro*	O.T.O. Livorno	23 Jan 41	16 Nov 41	16 May 42	Lost 9 Jan 43
LG *Legionario*	O.T.O. Livorno	21 Oct 40	16 April 41	1 Mar 42	To France 15 Aug 48
MT *Mitragliere*	C.N.R. Ancona	7 Oct 40	28 Sept 41	1 Feb 42	To France 15 July 48
SQ *Squadrista*	O.T.O. Livorno	4 Sept 41	12 Sept 42	–	German *TA33* Sept 1943
VL *Velite*	O.T.O. Livorno	19 April 41	31 Aug 41	31 Aug 42	To France 24 July 48

Displacement: 1,620tons*/1,645tonnes (standard); 2,550tons/2,590tonnes (full load).
Length: 350ft/106.7m (oa); 333ft 4in/101.6m (pp).
Beam: 33ft 7in/10.15m.
Draught: 11ft 6in/3.15m (mean).
Machinery: three Yarrow small tube vertical boilers; 2-shaft Parsons (O.T.O. ships), others Belluzzo geared turbines.
Performance: 48,000shp; 38kts.
Bunkerage: 516tons/525tonnes.
Range: 2,200nm at 20kts.
Guns: five 4.7in (*VL* four) 5×1; twelve 13.2mm MG.
Torpedoes: six 21in (2×3).
Complement: 228.

Design Repeat *Soldati* class, generally known as *Soldati* (ii). All this class carried five 4.7-inch guns with the single exception of *Velite* which retained instead the star-shell gun. (The single 4.7-inch/50cal gun could be used for star-shell). Rather oddly, in view of the R.It.N.'s four-ship destroyer *squadriglia* formation, only seven units were ordered, none of which were laid down before Italy's entry into the war. Of the four units laid down in 1941, two, *Carrista* and *Squadrista*, remained incomplete at the Italian surrender in 1943, the former not even launched, having been cannibalized to repair the damaged *Carabiniere* (bow) and *Velite* (stern). No after directors were fitted to this class, which had a slightly different bridge form from that of the earlier type.

*Actually varied up to 1,830tons according to the builder.

Modifications Essentially as the *Soldati* (i) type except that 20mm guns were fitted from the outset. *Legionario* and *Velite* landed their after tubes in 1943, receiving two single 37mm/54cal in lieu and the latter also received a further single gun in place of the 4.7-inch/15cal gun (but this was removed once more by 1946). *Legionario* received the first radar outfit in destroyers, a German set, and *Velite* later had an Italian 'Gufo' equipment. *Bombardiere*, an early loss, received no alterations. Light AA was eventually twelve or thirteen 20mm in four twin, four or five single mountings.

Service *Mitragliere* was the first to enter service, followed a month later by *Legionario*. Both took part in operations against the British 'Harpoon'/'Vigorous' Malta convoys as part of the 13th and 7th *Squadriglie* respectively in June 1942. In August, *Legionario* and *Corsaro* operated against 'Pedestal', while *Mitragliere* spent much of the remainder of the year on minelaying sorties and convoy escorting. However, *Legionario, Bombardiere* and *Velite* were intercepted off Naples on 21 November 1942 by the British submarine *P228* (*Splendid*) when the last named lost her stern to a torpedo. In January 1943 *Bombardiere* was torpedoed and sunk off Marettimo by the submarine *United* and *Corsaro* was mined in a field laid by *Abdiel*. After the operations off Tunisia, *Mitragliere* and *Legionario* served in home waters, joined later, after repair, by *Velite*. On the surrender, *Mitragliere* was interned at Port Mahon and the other two joined the Allies at Malta, serving later in the eastern Mediterranean. *Mitragliere* joined her sisters at Malta in January 1944.

Post-war, all three survivors were ceded to France, as *Duchaffault* (*Legionario*), *Jurien de la Gravière* (*Mitragliere*) and *Duperré* (*Velite*). None saw any operational service under the French ensign and all three were stricken from the Navy List on 12 June 1954.

Below: *Bombardiere* in 1942. (Fraccaroli)

Above: *Velite*, fitted with Gufo radar. (Author's Collection)

Above: *Mitragliere*. (Author's Collection)

COMANDANTI MEDAGLIE D'ORO CLASS

Ship	Builder	Laid Down	Launched	Commissioned	Fate
BA *Comandante Baroni*	O.T.O. Livorno	20 Feb 43	–	–	Broken up after 8 Sept 43
BO *Comandante Borsini*	O.T.O. Livorno	29 April 43	–	–	Broken up after 8 Sept 43
Comandante Botti	C.R.D.A. Trieste	1 Aug 43	–	–	Broken up after 8 Sept 43
CN *Comandante Casana*	C.N.R. Ancona	14 Feb 43	–	–	Broken up 1944
Comandante Corsi	C.R.D.A. Trieste	–	–	–	–
DC *Comandante di Cristofaro*	C.T. Riva Trigoso	6 Feb 43	–	–	Damaged on slip, broken up
DL *Comandante Dell'Anno*	C.N.R. Ancona	14 Feb 43	–	–	Broken up 1944
Comandante Esposito	C.R.D.A. Trieste	–	–	–	–
Comandante Fiorelli	C.R.D.A. Trieste	–	–	–	–
FA *Comandante Fontana*	O.T.O. Livorno	–	–	–	–
Comandante Giannattasio	C.R.D.A. Trieste	–	–	–	–
Comandante Giobbe	C.T. Riva Trigoso	–	–	–	–
Comandante Giorgis	C.T. Riva Trigoso	–	–	–	–
MA *Comandante Margottini*	O.T.O. Livorno	18 Mar 43	?	–	Abandoned at La Spezia 1945
Comandante Milano	C.R.D.A. Trieste	–	–	–	–
Comandante Moccagatta	O.T.O. Livorno	–	–	–	–
Comandante Novaro	C.R.D.A. Trieste	–	–	–	–
Comandante Rodocanacchi	O.T.O. Livorno	–	–	–	–
RU *Comandante Ruta*	C.R.D.A. Trieste	16 Aug 43	–	–	Broken up after 8 Sept 43
TO *Comandante Toscano*	C.T. Riva Trigoso	14 Dec 42	–	–	Damaged on slip, broken up
(Plus four not named)					

Displacement: 2,067tons/2,100tonnes (standard); 2,900tons/2,946tonnes (full load).
Length: 396ft/120.7m (oa).
Beam: 40ft 4in/12.30m.
Draught: 11ft 10in/3.6m (mean).
Machinery: three boilers; 2-shaft geared turbines.
Performance: 60,000shp; 35kts.
Guns: four 5.3in (4×1); twelve 37mm (12×1).
Torpedoes: six 21in (2×3).
Mines: 52.
Complement: 272.

Design Like all navies, the Italian fleet found that pre-war anti-aircraft outfits were far too weak and with this class, made determined attempts to remedy the fact. It was also decided to increase the gun calibre to 5.3-inch, the same calibre as carried by the new *Capitani Romani*-class light cruisers. These guns, initially five in number, were at first to be shipped in a similar disposition to that of the *Soldati* classes, i.e., two twin and one single. However, this arrangement was later amended to four guns only, all singles, disposed two forward, two aft, one gun superfiring on the other. The guns were 54cal Ansaldo or O.T.O.-pattern weapons, reportedly dual-purpose. Twelve 37mm guns in single mountings disposed about the ship comprised the AA outfit. These would probably have been the 1939 RM type. No 20mm guns were included in the design, but in all probability would have been added, had the ships been completed. Two triple 21-inch banks of torpedo tubes completed the armament. 'Gufo' radar was to be fitted on the forward director and a second director fitted aft.

As a result of the increased weight of the armament, the hull was more than forty feet longer and almost seven feet beamier to confer the necessary stability and accommodate the superfiring main armament. Displacement rose accordingly by about 400 tons. Speed therefore fell to 35 knots despite a 25 per cent increase in installed power. The machinery arrangements were to be similar to that of the *Soldati* classes except that one unit was to receive her machinery on the unit principle as had been seen in the *Navigatori* class. This ship, *Comandante Esposito*, would therefore have had two funnels and in all probability a lengthened hull compared to her sisters.

Orders were placed with four yards for a total of twenty destroyers and a further four were projected. However, only one had been laid down by the end of 1942 and eight more in 1943, the last barely three weeks before the surrender. The remainder were never laid down. All were broken up on the slips by the Germans or destroyed by Allied bombing after September 1943. Only *Margottini* was launched (by the Germans?) and found broken in two at La Spezia, whence presumably she had been towed, in 1945.

Units not laid down were: *Comandante Corsi, Comandante Esposito, Comandante Fiorelli, Comandante Giannattasio, Comandante Milano, Comandante Novaro* (all CRDA(T)); *Comandante Fontana, Comandante Moccagatta, Comandante Rodocanacchi* (O.T.O.(L)); *Comandante Giobbe, Comandante Giorgis* (CT(RT)).

ORSA CLASS

Ship	Builder	Laid Down	Launched	Commissioned	Fate
ON *Orione*	C.N.R. Palermo	27 April 36	21 April 37	31 Mar 38	Stricken 1 Jan 65
OS *Orsa*	C.N.R. Palermo	27 April 36	21 Mar 37	31 Mar 38	Stricken 1 July 64
PG *Pegaso*	B.S. Napoletani	15 Feb 36	8 Dec 36	30 Mar 38	Scuttled 11 Sept 43
PR *Procione*	B.S. Napoletani	15 Feb 36	31 Jan 37	30 Mar 38	Scuttled 9 Sept 43

Displacement: 840tons/884tonnes (standard); 1,575tons/1,600tonnes (full load).
Length: 293ft/89.3m (oa); 270ft 6in/82.50m (pp).
Beam: 31ft 9in/9.69m.
Draught: 12ft 3in/3.74m (mean).
Machinery: two 3-drum boilers; 2-shaft Tosi geared turbines.
Performance: 16,000shp; 28kts.
Bunkerage: 520tons/528tonnes.
Guns: two 3.9in (2×1); eight 13.2mm MG.
Torpedoes: six 21in (2×3).
Mines: 20.
Complement: 168.

Design In essence these were fast escort vessels of a type not dissimilar to the later British *Hunt* class destroyers and, as such, worthy of inclusion here. Displacing more than the 600-ton limit of the Treaty, they were in consequence limited in size and numbers. The design was a useful one with a maximum speed of 28 knots obtained by a 16,000shp twin shaft turbine arrangement. They therefore possessed a sufficient margin of speed over the submarines of the day, combined with the manoeuvrability of a twin-screw design. In fact, they were originally classed as escort vessels (*Avisi Scorta*), but re-rated torpedo-boats in view of their four 17.7-inch torpedo tubes, paired on each beam. Only two main guns were carried, 3.9-inch/47 O.T.O. in single, shielded handworked mountings. ASW outfit was good, six depth-charge throwers indicating their main role, but no asdic-type equipment was available. Being larger than the *Spica*-type torpedo-boats, they had more bunker space and hence better endurance. In service they proved successful and useful vessels, but only four were constructed and not until 1941 were further vessels of this type begun.

Modifications The 13.2mm machine-guns were replaced by up to eleven 20mm/65 or 70.

Service Convoy escort duties throughout the war. *Pegaso* had a particularly successful career, sinking three British submarines, the famous *Upholder* on 14 April 1942 off Tripoli, *Urge* a fortnight later on the 28th, in the eastern Mediterranean, and *Thorn* off Tobruk on 6 August of that year. At the Capitulation, *Pegaso* escaped to Majorca, but scuttled herself in Pollensa Bay later. *Procione* failed to get away and was scuttled at La Spezia. The other pair survived the war and served the post-war Italian Fleet until 1954–65.

Below: *Pegaso*. (Author's Collection)
Below right: *Orsa*. (Author's Collection)

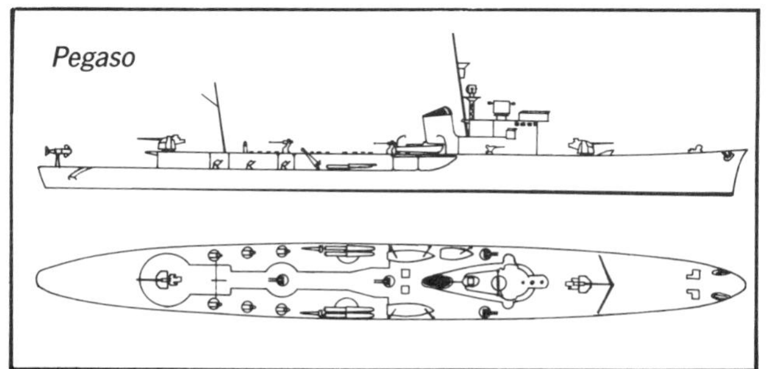

CICLONE CLASS

Ship	Builder	Laid Down	Launched	Commissioned	Fate
AS *Aliseo*	Castellammare di Stabia	16 Sept 41	20 Sept 42	28 Feb 43	To Yugoslavia 1949
AM *Animoso*	Ansaldo, Genoa	3 April 41	15 April 42	14 Aug 42	To USSR 16 Mar 49
AD *Ardente*	Ansaldo, Genoa	7 April 41	27 May 42	30 Sept 42	Lost 12 Jan 43
AZ *Ardimentoso*	Ansaldo, Genoa	7 April 41	28 June 42	14 Dec 42	To USSR 28 Feb 49
AR *Ardito*	Ansaldo, Genoa	3 April 41	14 Mar 42	30 June 42	German *TA26* 19 Dec 43
CI *Ciclone*	C.R.D.A. Trieste	9 May 41	1 Mar 42	21 May 42	Lost 8 Mar 43
FT *Fortunale*	C.R.D.A. Trieste	9 May 41	18 April 42	16 Aug 42	To USSR 1 Mar 49
GH *Ghibli*	Castellammare di Stabia	30 Aug 41	28 Feb 43	24 July 43	Scuttled 9 Sept 43
GP *Groppo*	Castellammare di Stabia	18 June 41	19 April 42	31 Aug 42	Lost 25 May 43
IM *Impavido*	C.T. Riva Trigoso	15 Aug 41	24 Feb 43	30 April 43	German *TA23* 9 Oct 43
IP *Impetuoso*	C.T. Riva Trigoso	15 Aug 41	20 April 43	7 June 43	Scuttled 11 Sept 43
ID *Indomito*	C.R. Riva Trigoso	10 Jan 42	6 July 43	4 Aug 43	To Yugoslavia 1949
IT *Intrepido*	C.T. Riva Trigoso	31 Jan 42	8 Sept 43	–	German *TA25* 16 Jan 44
MS *Monsone*	Castellammare di Stabia	18 June 41	7 June 42	28 Nov 42	Lost 1 Mar 43
TF *Tifone*	C.R.D.A. Trieste	17 June 41	31 Mar 42	11 July 42	Scuttled 7 May 43
UR *Uragano*	C.R.D.A. Trieste	17 June 41	3 May 42	26 Sept 42	Lost 3 Feb 43

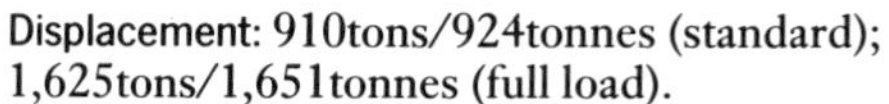

Displacement: 910tons/924tonnes (standard); 1,625tons/1,651tonnes (full load).
Length: 287ft 10in/87.75m (oa); 270ft 8in/82.5m (pp).
Beam: 32ft 6in/9.9m.
Draught: 12ft 4in/3.77m (mean).
Machinery: two Yarrow boilers; 2-shaft Tosi or Parsons geared turbines.
Performance: 16,000shp; 26kts.
Bunkerage: 442tons/449tonnes.
Guns: two or three 3.9in (2/3×1); eight 20mm.
Torpedoes: four 21in (2×2).
Mines: 20.
Complement: 177.

Design With the heavy demands and losses off the North Africa supply route in mind, the Navy revised the design of the 1934–35 programme *Orsa* class and put it into production as the *Ciclone* class of which sixteen units were ordered. In comparison with the earlier class they were shorter, beamier and heavier with the result that designed speed fell to 26 knots because the installed power remained unchanged. Turbine propulsion was also retained. In view of their designed employment, bunkerage was reduced allowing better stability and an increase in the AA outfit which experience had shown to be vital. Better control facilities were also provided for the guns in that a director replaced the simple rangefinder above the bridge. Rather surprisingly, the four torpedo tubes were retained, possibly because a British cruiser/destroyer attack on any convoy being escorted might provide targets of opportunity. Four or six depth-charge throwers were fitted and a minelaying capability of 20 mines was incorporated. Seven units shipped an extra 3.9-inch gun amidships (*Animoso, Ghibli, Impavido, Impetuoso, Indomito, Intrepido* and *Monsone*). The twin 20mm was therefore replaced by two singles on the quarter deck.

Modifications Limited mainly to the addition of a pair of extra 20mm singles on the forecastle and quarter deck for a total of twelve maximum.

Service As the first unit (*Ciclone*) did not enter service until May 1942, and construction was rather

Above: *Ciclone*. (Author's Collection) **Below:** *Fortunale*. (Author's Collection)

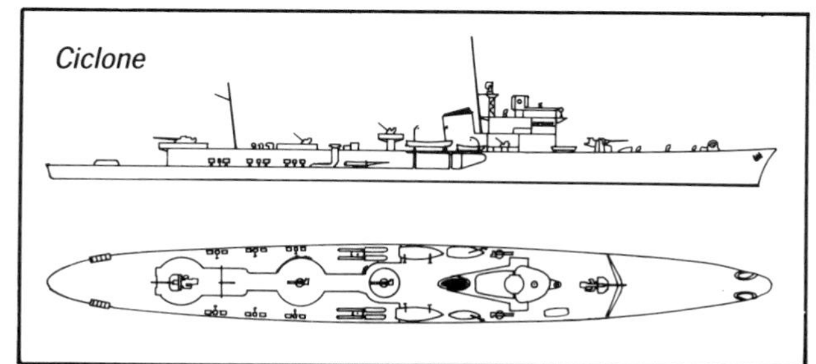

slow, their service life was in the main relatively brief during the Second World War. Ten were completed by the end of 1942 and five more the next year, but *Intrepido* was not commissioned at the time of Italy's surrender. She was captured by the Germans, commissioned as *TA25* and finally torpedoed and sunk by US PT-boats in the Ligurian Sea. Her sister *Indomito* was only days in commission at the time of the surrender. The remainder fulfilled their escort role but only *Ardente* scored a success, sinking the submarine *P48* in the Gulf of Tunis on Christmas Day 1942. In point of fact, North Africa had been lost before five of the ships were completed. *Ardente* survived *P48* by only a couple of weeks, being herself sunk by collision with *Grecale* in January 1943. *Ciclone* was mined in the Tunisia operations, as was *Uragano*, and *Tifone* scuttled at Korbus after damage. *Monsone* was bombed and sunk at Naples and *Groppo* at Messina, while both *Ardito* and *Impavido* were captured by the Germans and renamed *TA26* and *TA23* respectively, at the surrender in September 1943. *Ghibli*, repairing damage, was scuttled at La Spezia on 9 September. Although raised and towed to Genoa, repairs were never completed and she was eventually scuttled finally on 25 April 1945. *Impetuoso* after reaching Pollensa Bay, Majorca, scuttled herself to avoid internment. Of the units which survived the war after escaping from occupied Italy, *Aliseo* became the Yugoslav *Biokovo* on 3 May 1949 and *Indomito, Triglav. Animoso, Ardimentoso* and *Fortunale* were ceded to the USSR, thus none remained to the Italian Navy post-war.

LA MASA CLASS

Ship	Builder	Laid Down	Launched	Commissioned	Fate
BS *Angelo Bassini*	Odero, Sestri Ponente	2 Oct 16	28 Mar 18	1 May 18	Lost 28 May 43
CA *Giacinto Carini*	Odero, Sestri Ponente	1 Sept 16	7 Nov 17	30 Nov 17	Stricken 31 Dec 58
CS *Enrico Cosenz*	Odero, Sestri Ponente	23 Dec 17	6 June 19	13 June 19	Scuttled 27 Sept 43
FB *Nicola Fabrizi*	Odero, Sestri Ponente	1 Sept 16	8 July 18	12 July 18	Stricken 1 Feb 57
LF *Giuseppe La Farina*	Odero, Sestri Ponente	29 Dec 17	12 Mar 19	18 Mar 19	Lost 4 May 41
LM *Giuseppe La Masa*	Odero, Sestri Ponente	1 Sept 16	6 Sept 17	28 Sept 17	Scuttled 11 Sept 43
MD *Giacomo Medici*	Odero, Sestri Ponente	2 Oct 16	6 Sept 18	13 Sept 18	Lost 16 April 43

Displacement: 650tons/660tonnes (standard); 880tons/894tonnes (full load).
Length: 241ft 3in/73.54m (oa); 237ft 11in/72.54m (pp).
Beam: 24ft/7.32m.
Draught: 8ft 4in/2.55m (mean).
Machinery: four Thornycroft boilers; 2-shaft Tosi turbines.
Performance: 15,500shp; 30kts.
Bunkerage: 150tons/152tonnes.
Range: 1,700nm at 15kts.
Guns: four 4in (4×1); two 3in AA (2×1).
Torpedoes: four 17.7in (2×2).
Complement: 96.

Design Further modifications of earlier designs with marginally less beam and draft resulting in slightly lower displacement. Once again designed and built by Odero, the main difference between these ships and the *Sirtori* class was the reduction in 4-inch guns to four, of which the after pair were mounted on the centre-line. Those on the forecastle, however, remained sided. The pair of twin torpedo tube banks was retained, but the deleted 4-inch were replaced by two 3-inch/40 1917 Ansaldo AA guns sided between the after pair of 4-inch guns. Eight units were ordered, all except *Cosenz* and *La Farina* completing in time to see service during the First World War. *Benedetto Cairoli* was lost in collision with *Giacinto Carini* on 10 April 1918. All were reclassified as torpedo-boats on 1 October 1929.

Modifications The 3-inch guns were removed as were one or two of the 4-inch guns, being replaced by up to six 20mm guns. Some units had one pair of tubes removed and the remaining bank repositioned on the centre-line. *Carini* and *La Masa* retained only one 4-inch gun (repositioned on the forecastle centre-line) with eight 20mm guns. These two also had a different arrangement of torpedo tubes with a new triple 21-inch bank fitted axially abaft the third funnel and one of the twin banks for 17.7-inch torpedoes fitted in place of the after 4-inch gun.

Below: *Bassini.* (Author's Collection)

Service *La Farina* was at Naples, *Carini* and *La Masa* at Taranto with the 3rd Division and the other four formed the 7th Torpedo-boat Division in the Adriatic in June 1940. The division in the Adriatic covered the army's supply route to Albania, and shelled Greek positions 1940–41. After the fall of Greece, they escorted supply convoys to and from the Aegean and were also employed, like the others, on the North Africa route. *Cosenz* made an unsuccessful A/S attack on the British *Pandora* off Benghazi in September 1940, but was then badly damaged by air attack in that port. In November, *Fabrizi* had a lucky escape although damaged when her entire convoy was wiped out by a force of British cruisers. *La Farina* was mined off the Kerkenha Bank in May 1941, but no others were lost until 1943 when first *Medici* was sunk by bombing in Catania harbour followed in May by *Bassini* at Livorno by the USAAF. *Cosenz* and *La Masa* were lost during the Capitulation, the former being damaged in collision, then by bombs, and finally being scuttled. *La Masa*, under repair at Naples, was scuttled by her crew. *Carini* and *Fabrizi* survived the war and were converted to minesweepers in 1952–53.

Left: *La Masa.* (Author's Collection)

PALESTRO CLASS

Ship	Builder	Laid Down	Launched	Commissioned	Fate
CF *Confienza*	Orlando, Livorno	10 May 17	18 Dec 20	25 April 23	Lost 20 Nov 40
PT *Palestro*	Orlando, Livorno	12 April 17	23 Mar 19	26 Jan 21	Lost 22 Sept 40
SM *San Martino*	Orlando, Livorno	30 April 17	8 Sept 20	10 Oct 22	Captured 9 Sept 43
SL *Solferino*	Orlando, Livorno	21 April 17	28 April 20	31 Oct 21	Captured 9 Sept 43

Displacement: 862tons/875tonnes (standard); 1,076tons/1,093tonnes (full load).
Length: 268ft 8in/81.9m (oa); 262ft 9in/80.09m (pp).
Beam: 26ft 4in/8.02m.
Draught: 8ft 6in/2.6m (mean).
Machinery: four Thornycroft boilers; 2-shaft Zoelly turbines.
Performance: 22,000shp; 32kts.
Bunkerage: 170tons/172tonnes.
Guns: four 4in (4×1); two 3in (2×1).
Torpedoes: four 17.7in (2×2).
Mines: 10.
Complement: 106.

Design These were the last destroyers laid down by the Italian Navy during the First World War. They were of increased dimensions, being about 25 feet longer and with about 9 inches more beam. In consequence, the displacement rose by about 200 tons. The designed speed was some 2 knots faster, requiring increased installed power now raised to 22,000shp. Four boilers were retained, again in separate spaces, but their uptakes were trunked into only two short, fat funnels. However, the fore funnel was later considerably heightened. In contrast to their earlier designs, Zoelly turbines were fitted instead of the Tosi type and bunkerage was increased, giving better range. Armament remained similar to that of the *La Masa* design, but once again was rearranged. The cumbersome sided guns were retained on the forecastle, but No. 3 gun was moved forward and placed on a bandstand abaft the second funnel where it had a better arc of fire. Likewise the 3-inch AA guns were retained, these being repositioned on the main deck abreast the after funnel. The torpedo calibre remained 17.7-inch, four torpedoes being carried in paired tubes in echelon as previously, except that the port side had the foremost pair. Although laid down in the spring of 1917, they were not completed until 1921–23 because of a general slowing down of military activities after the end of the First World War. They were reclassified as torpedo-boats on 1 October 1938.

Modifications The two early losses received no modifications, but the surviving pair landed two 4-inch guns in 1942 and had six 20mm guns added.

Service In 1940, *Confienza* and *Palestro* formed a detachment of the 15th Torpedo-boat Division for local defence duties based in the Adriatic, while the other pair were at Leros in the Dodecanese also for

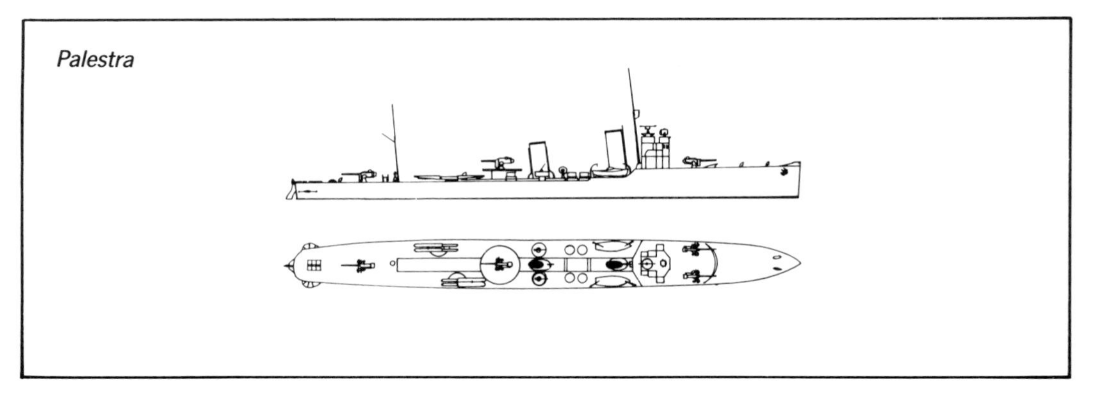

local defence duties. The Division concentrated in the Adriatic in the autumn of 1940, becoming part of the escort forces for the supply convoys to and from Albania. *Palestro* was torpedoed and sunk by the British submarine *Osiris* while escorting a convoy to Durrazo in September. In November, *Confienza* was lost by collision with the armed merchant cruiser *Capitano A. Cecchi*, also in the Adriatic. The two survivors spent the remainder of the war on convoy escort duties and were in the eastern Mediterranean at the time of the Capitulation. *San Martino* was captured at Piraeus and *Solferino* at Corfu, being recommissioned as the German *TA17* and *TA18* respectively.

Below: *Solferino*. (Fraccaroli)

AUDACE

Ship	Builder	Laid Down	Launched	Commissioned	Fate
AD *Audace*	Yarrow	1 Oct 13	27 Sept 16	1 Mar 17	German *TA20* 12 Sept 43

Displacement: 815tons/829tonnes (standard); 995tons/1,011tonnes (full load).
Length: 286ft 3in/87.2m (oa); 284ft 4in/86.6m (wl); 275ft 3in/83.9m (pp).
Beam: 27ft 7in/8.40m.
Draught: 8ft/2.43m (mean).
Machinery: three Yarrow boilers; 2-shaft Brown-Curtis geared turbines.
Performance: 22,000shp; 28kts.
Bunkerage: 248tons/252tonnes.
Range: 1,800nm at 15kts.
Guns: seven 4in (7×1); two 40mm.
Torpedoes: removed.
Complement: 127.

Design An over-age torpedo-boat built originally for the Japanese Navy, but sold to Italy in 1916 while still under construction. In 1929, *Audace* was rerated as a torpedo-boat. Her sister *Urakaze* served in the Japanese fleet until stricken in 1936. They were Japan's first oil-fired torpedo-craft.

Modifications Between the wars, *Audace* had her bridge rebuilt and was partially disarmed to act as a control vessel for the target ship *San Marco*. On the outbreak of war, she was rearmed for escort duties. In 1942 her 4-inch guns were reduced to two and twenty 20mm guns were added.

Service Escort duties until captured by the Germans on 12 September 1943 while inoperational at Venice. After repair she was commissioned as *TA20* (q.v.).

Above: *Audace*. (Author's Collection)

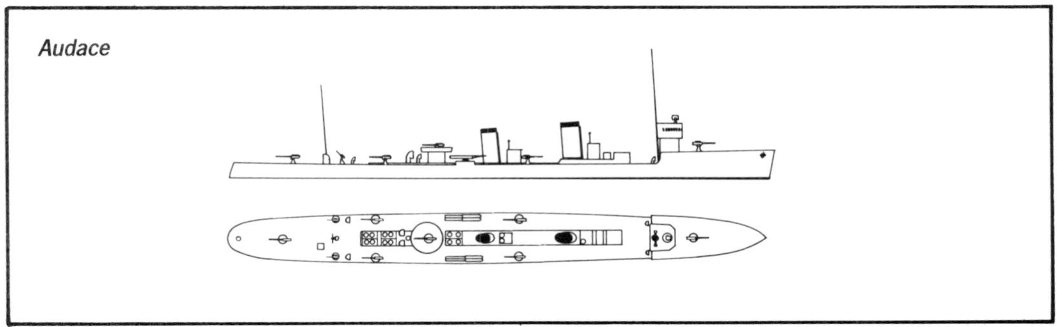

PILO CLASS

Ship	Builder	Laid Down	Launched	Commissioned	Fate
AB *Giuseppe Cesare Abba*	Odero, Sestri Ponente	19 Aug 13	25 May 15	6 July 15	Stricken 1 Sept 58
CL *Fratelli Cairoli*	Pattison, Naples	24 Sept 13	12 Nov 14	1 May 15	Lost 23 Dec 40
DZ *Giuseppe Dezza*	Odero, Sestri Ponente	12 Sept 13	26 Oct 15	1 Jan 16	Scuttled 16 Sept 43
MS *Giuseppe Missori*	Odero, Sestri Ponente	19 Jan 14	20 Dec 15	7 Mar 16	Captured 10 Sept 43
MT *Antonio Mosto*	Pattison, Naples	9 Oct 13	20 May 15	7 July 15	Stricken 15 Dec 58
PL *Rosolino Pilo*	Odero, Sestri Ponente	19 Aug 13	24 Mar 15	25 May 15	Stricken 1 Oct 54
SF *Simone Schiaffino*	Odero, Sestri Ponente	12 Sept 13	11 Sept 15	7 Nov 15	Lost 24 April 41

Displacement: 615tons/625tonnes (standard); 900tons/914tonnes (full load).
Length: 239ft 6in/73m (oa); 236ft 2in/71.9m (pp).
Beam: 24ft 1in/7.34m.
Draught: 8ft 11in/2.72m (mean).
Machinery: four Thornycroft boilers; 2-shaft Tosi turbines.
Performance: 15,500shp; 30kts (Pattison boats 14,500shp).
Bunkerage: 150tons/152tonnes.
Range: 1,700nm at 15kts.
Guns: five 4in (5×1); two 40mm (2×1).
Torpedoes: four 17.7in (4×1).
Mines: 10.
Complement: 95.

Design Originally a class of eight destroyers, re-rated torpedo-boats on 1 October 1929, of which *Ippolito Nievo* had been discarded on 25 April 1938. In their day, they had been quite a respectable design but all had seen service during the First World War and by 1940 they were out-dated in years and concept. Nevertheless, like many old ships in all navies, they gave good service in the escort role although no longer suitable for front-line destroyer tasks. Two of the boats had been built by Pattison and with 1,000shp less, were originally some 2–3 knots slower when built. By 1941 it is doubtful if any were good for more than about 25 knots. Their armament originally comprised five 4-inch/35cal Schneider-Armstrong or Terni guns, two 40mm and four 18-inch torpedoes. Only the forward gun was on the centre-line.

Modifications Except for *Cairoli* and *Schiaffino*, the number of 4-inch guns was reduced to two and six 20mm/65 guns added, with three torpedo tubes being landed.

Service *Pilo, Missori* and *Mosto* were units of the 6th Torpedo-boat Division at Taranto, *Schiaffino, Abba, Dezza* and *Cairoli* the 5th Division at Naples in June 1940, employed as local defence flotillas. During hostilities, their task was convoy escorting, initially on the North Africa supply route. *Cairoli* was lost on a mine north-east of Tripoli before the end of the year, as was *Schiaffino* the following spring off Cape Bon. In 1943, *Mosto* and *Pilo* were able to reach Allied forces at the Capitulation, but their two sisters, *Dezza* and *Missori*, were trapped in the Adriatic. The former was scuttled at Fiume on 16 September, but raised and repaired by the Germans as their *TA35*. *Missori* was captured at Durazzo on 10 September and designated *TA22*. The two boats to survive the war had a surprisingly long career in the post-war Italian Navy and *Pilo* was not removed from the active list until October 1954. *Mosto* served even longer in a new role as a minesweeper from 1953 until stricken on 15 December 1958, 43 years old!

Above: *Abba*. (Author's Collection) **Below:** *Pilo* in 1944. (Author's Collection)

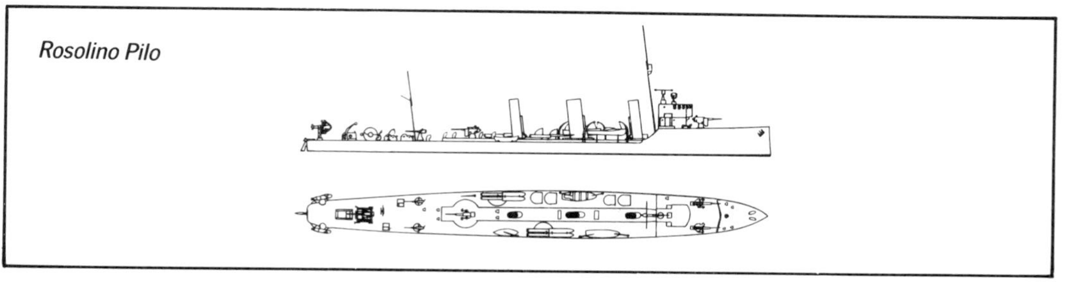

SIRTORI CLASS

Ship	Builder	Laid Down	Launched	Commissioned	Fate
AC *Giovanni Acerbi*	Odero, Sestri Ponente	2 Feb 16	14 Feb 17	26 Feb 17	Lost 4 April 41
OR *Vincenzo Giordano Orsini*	Odero, Sestri Ponente	2 Feb 16	23 April 17	12 May 17	Scuttled 8 April 41
SR *Giuseppe Sirtori*	Odero, Sestri Ponente	2 Feb 16	24 Nov 16	22 Dec 16	Scuttled 25 Sept 43
SO *Francesco Stocco*	Odero, Sestri Ponente	2 Feb 16	5 June 17	19 July 17	Lost 24 Sept 43

Displacement: 669tons/709tonnes (standard); 900tons/914tonnes (full load).
Length: 241ft 3in/73.54m (oa); 238ft/72.54m (pp).
Beam: 24ft/7.34m.
Draught: 8ft 10in/2.7m (mean).
Machinery: four Thornycroft boilers; 2-shaft Tosi turbines.
Performance: 15,500shp; 30kts.
Bunkerage: 150tons/152tonnes.
Range: 1,700nm at 15kts.
Guns: six 4in (6×1); two 40mm (2×1).
Torpedoes: four 17.7in (2×2).
Mines: 10.
Complement: 98.

Design These ships were a modification of the *Pilo* type, but with a different disposition of the armament. General dimensions, power and speed remained the same as the earlier type. Four boilers in separate spaces necessitated three funnels with the thicker second one serving the central two boilers. The main armament was increased to six 4-inch/45cal Schneider-Armstrong 1917-pattern guns (all single), the extra gun being obtained by the simple if unsatisfactory expedient of having two sided mountings on the forecastle. None of the guns was therefore on the centre-line. This class also introduced twin torpedo mountings, in echelon on the beam with the starboard set forward of the port. All saw service during the First World War and by 1940 were about 23 years old.

Modifications The pair lost in Eritrea probably received little or no modifications. The other two no doubt received 20mm guns to augment their AA outfit and may have landed some of their 4-inch guns.

Service These four ships were not serving together at the beginning of the war, for *Acerbi* and *Orsini* were with the Italian forces in the Red Sea for local defence duties. The other pair, *Sirtori* and *Stocco*, were at Taranto with the 6th and 3rd Torpedo-boat Divisions respectively. *Acerbi* was destroyed during a British air raid on Massawa in April 1941 and only a few days later, *Orsini* scuttled herself just prior to the port's fall. *Stocco* saw service on Albania supply convoys in 1940, and both operated on the Africa supply route. Both were casualties of the surrender chaos, being bombed by German aircraft and/or scuttled at Corfu.

Below: *Sirtori*. (Fraccaroli)

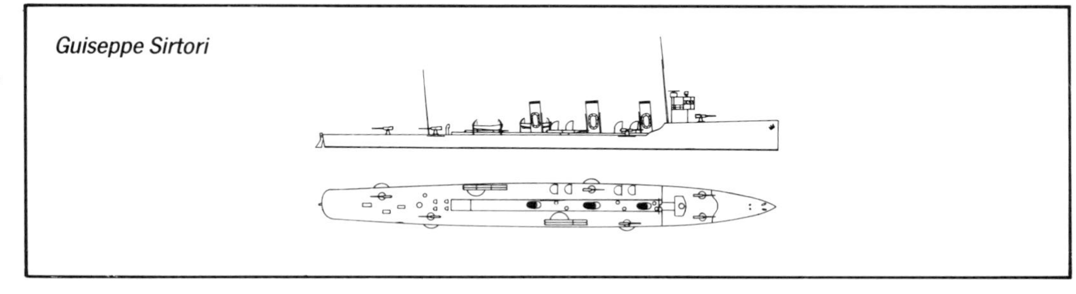

Guiseppe Sirtori

GENERALI CLASS

Ship	Builder	Laid Down	Launched	Commissioned	Fate
CE *Generale Antonio Cantore*	Odero, Sestri Ponente	10 Nov 19	24 Mar 21	1 July 21	Lost 22 Aug 42
CI *Generale Antonio Cascino*	Odero, Sestri Ponente	13 Mar 20	18 Mar 22	8 May 22	Scuttled 9 Sept 43
CH *Generale Antonio Chinotto*	Odero, Sestri Ponente	20 Nov 19	7 Aug 21	26 Sept 21	Lost 28 Mar 41
MN *Generale Carlo Montanari*	Odero, Sestri Ponente	7 June 21	4 Oct 22	9 Nov 22	Scuttled 9 Sept 43
PA *Generale Achille Papa*	Odero, Sestri Ponente	24 Dec 19	8 Dec 21	9 Feb 22	Scuttled 9 Sept 43
PR *Generale Marcello Prestinari*	Odero, Sestri Ponente	23 May 19	4 July 22	17 Aug 22	Lost 31 June 43

Displacement: 635tons/645tonnes (standard); 890tons/904tonnes (full load).
Length: 241ft 3in/73.54m (oa); 238ft/72.54m (pp).
Beam: 24ft/7.32m.
Draught: 7ft 10in/2.4m (mean).
Machinery: four Thornycroft boilers; 2-shaft Tosi turbines.
Performance: 15,500shp; 30kts.
Bunkerage: 150tons/152tonnes.
Range: 2,200nm at 14kts.
Guns: three 4in (3×1); two 3in AA (2×1).
Torpedoes: four 17.7in (2×2).
Mines: 10.
Complement: 106.

Design This class was a slight modification of the earlier *La Masa* design, of similar dimensions, speed and power. The only difference in reality was that the clumsy sided forward gun arrangement was dispensed with, with a resulting reduction of fire power by one 4-inch.

Modifications Probably limited to the addition of 20mm guns and possibly the removal of part of the torpedo outfit.

Service *Papa, Cascino, Chinotto* and *Montanari* formed the 2nd Torpedo-boat Division at La Spezia, *Cantore* was at Naples and *Prestinari* at Taranto on local defence duties in June 1940. The 2nd Division was immediately involved in defensive minelaying and thereafter supply convoy escorting to North Africa. *Prestinari* and *Cantore* escorted Adriatic convoys to Albania in the early months of the war. On the Africa supply route, *Papa* caught the submarine *Cachalot*, surfaced while on a supply run to Malta on 30 July 1940, sinking her by ramming. A month later, *Rorqual* was heavily depthcharged by the same torpedo-boat but escaped. Mines laid by this submarine the following year caused the loss of *Chinotto* off Cape Gallo, west of Sicily, on 28 March 1941. *Cantore* was also lost to mines, this time laid by *Porpoise* off Cyrenaica as was *Prestinare* on a barrage laid by the minelayer *Welshman*. The Italian surrender found the three surviving boats in La Spezia where all were scuttled to avoid capture. *Montanari* and *Papa* were subsequently raised, but neither saw service under Kriegsmarine colours.

Below: *Cascino*. (G. Alfano) **Above:** *Chinotto*, after salvage. (G. Alfano)

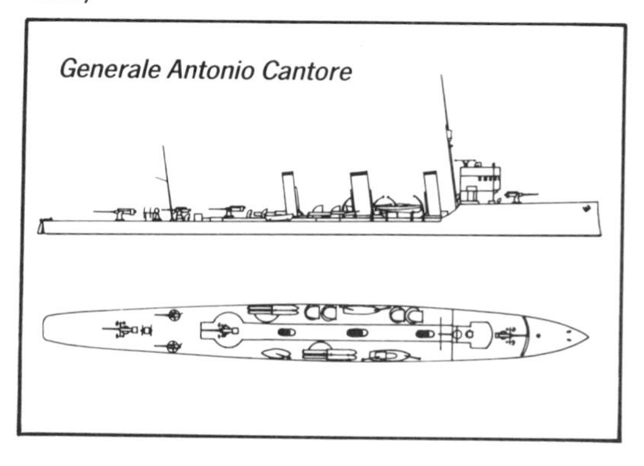

CURTATONE CLASS

Ship	Builder	Laid Down	Launched	Commissioned	Fate
CM *Calatafimi*	Orlando, Livorno	1 Dec 20	17 Mar 23	24 May 24	Captured 9 Sept 43
CD *Castelfidardo*	Orlando, Livorno	20 July 20	4 June 22	7 Mar 24	Captured 9 Sept 43
CT *Curtatone*	Orlando, Livorno	3 Jan 20	17 Mar 22	21 June 23	Lost 20 May 41
MB *Monzambano*	Orlando, Livorno	20 Jan 21	6 Aug 23	4 June 24	Stricken 15 April 51

Displacement: 876tons/890tonnes (standard); 1,210tons/1,229tonnes (full load).
Length: 278ft/84.72m (oa); 277ft 6in/84.6m (pp).
Beam: 26ft 3in/8m.
Draught: 8ft/2.46m (mean).
Machinery: four Thornycroft boilers; 2-shaft Zoelly turbines.
Performance: 22,000shp; 32kts.
Bunkerage: 200tons/203tonnes.
Range: 1,800nm at 15kts.
Guns: four 4in (2×2); two 3in AA.
Torpedoes: six 17.7in (2×3).
Mines: 16.
Complement: 117.

Design This class of destroyers represented a return to the dimensions of the *Palestro* type and were designed by the same shipyard. For the first time in Italian torpedo-craft, all armament was on the centre-line, guns in twin mountings and the torpedoes in triple banks. The main armament consisted of 4-inch Schneider-Armstrong M1919 in a common cradle. This mounting was capable of 35° elevation and unique to this class. It was also the first appearance of twin mountings in any destroyer in the world. Actually the gun mounting was unsuccessful, but this does not detract from the Italian Navy's efforts for it set the pattern for the general adoption of twin mounting (4.7-inch) in all Italian destroyers.

Installed power remained 22,000shp, with Zoelly turbines once again being used. *Curtatone* proved the fastest on trials with 36.6 knots. *Castelfidardo* reached 35.5 knots while the other pair were slower.

Modifications The twin 4-inch mountings were removed and replaced by single guns. Both 40mm/39 guns were landed and replaced by two 20mm AA and two further 20mm added in the bridge wings. Both triple banks of tubes were taken out, the forward bank being replaced by a twin 21-inch bank while a single 20mm was added in the after position. A sixth 20mm was fitted in the bandstand between the former torpedo tube positions. The mainmast was removed, W/T aerials slung from outriggers on the after funnel and the foremast was cut down in height.

Service All four units formed the 16th Torpedo-boat Division based at La Spezia for local defence duties at the outbreak of war. When a strong force of French cruisers and destroyers bombarded Genoa in June 1940 *Calatafimi*, supported only by some MTBs, made a determined counter-attack but without result. By autumn, all had been transferred to the Adriatic to cover the Albania supply route. They served on this task during 1941–43 also in the Aegean, where *Curtatone* was lost to a mine in the Gulf of Athens. Of the remainder, only *Monzambano* reached the Allies to continue escort duties for the rest of the war. *Calatafimi* was captured by the Germans at Piraeus and recommissioned as their *TA19* and *Castelfidardo* at Suda Bay, Crete to become *TA16*. Neither boat survived the war.

Right: *Monzambano.* (Fraccaroli)

Right: *Castelfidardo.* (Author's Collection)

SPICA CLASS

Ship	Builder	Laid Down	Launched	Commissioned	Fate
AO *Airone* (3)	Ansaldo, Genoa	29 Oct 36	23 Jan 38	10 May 38	Lost 12 Oct 40
AC *Alcione* (3)	Ansaldo, Genoa	29 Oct 36	23 Dec 37	10 May 38	Lost 11 Dec 41
AL *Aldebaran* (3)	Ansaldo, Genoa	2 Oct 35	14 June 36	6 Dec 36	Lost 20 Oct 41
AT *Altair* (3)	Ansaldo, Genoa	2 Oct 35	26 July 36	23 Dec 36	Lost 20 Oct 41
AD *Andromeda* (2)	Ansaldo, Genoa	2 Oct 35	28 June 36	6 Dec 36	Lost 17 Mar 41
AN *Antares* (2)	Ansaldo, Genoa	2 Oct 35	19 July 36	23 Dec 36	Lost 28 Mar 43
AU *Aretusa* (3)	Ansaldo, Genoa	29 Oct 36	6 Feb 38	1 July 38	Stricken 1 Aug 58
AE *Ariel* (3)	Ansaldo, Genoa	29 Oct 36	14 Mar 38	1 July 38	Lost 12 Oct 40
CI *Calipso* (3)	Ansaldo, Genoa	29 Sept 37	12 June 38	16 Nov 38	Lost 5 Dec 40
CP *Calliope* (3)	Ansaldo, Genoa	26 May 37	15 April 38	28 Oct 38	Stricken 1 Aug 58
CA *Canopo* (1)	C.T. Riva Trigoso	10 Dec 35	1 Oct 36	31 Mar 37	Lost 3 May 41
CS *Cassiopea* (1)	C.T. Riva Trigoso	10 Dec 35	22 Nov 36	26 April 37	Stricken 31 Oct 59
CT *Castore* (1)	C.N.R. Ancona	25 Jan 36	27 Sept 36	16 Jan 37	Lost 2 June 43
CO *Centauro* (1)	C.N.R. Ancona	30 May 34	19 Feb 36	16 June 36	Lost 4 Nov 42
CG *Cigno* (1)	C.N.R. Ancona	11 Mar 36	24 Nov 36	15 Mar 37	Lost 16 April 43
CC *Circe* (3)	Ansaldo, Genoa	29 Sept 37	29 June 38	4 Oct 38	Lost 27 Nov 42
CE *Climene* (1)	C.N.R. Ancona	25 July 34	7 Jan 36	24 April 36	Lost 28 April 43
CL *Clio* (3)	Ansaldo, Genoa	29 Oct 36	3 April 38	2 Oct 38	Stricken 31 Oct 59
LB *Libra* (3)	C.N.Q. Fiume	7 Dec 36	3 Oct 37	19 Jan 38	Stricken 1 April 64
LC *Lince* (3)	C.N.Q. Fiume	7 Dec 36	15 Jan 38	1 April 38	Lost 28 Aug 43
LR *Lira* (3)	C.N.Q. Fiume	7 Dec 36	12 Sept 37	1 Jan 38	Scuttled 9 Sept 43
LP *Lupo* (3)	C.N.Q. Fiume	7 Dec 36	7 Nov 37	28 Feb 38	Lost 2 Dec 42
PD *Pallade* (3)	B.S. Napoletani	13 Feb 37	19 Dec 37	5 Oct 38	Lost 5 Aug 43
PN *Partenope* (3)	B.S. Napoletani	31 Jan 37	27 Feb 38	26 Nov 38	Scuttled 11 Sept 43
PS *Perseo* (2)	C.N.Q. Fiume	12 Nov 34	9 Oct 35	1 Feb 36	Lost 4 May 43
PL *Pleiadi* (2)	B.S. Napoletani	4 Jan 37	5 Sept 37	4 July 38	Lost 14 Oct 41
PC *Polluce* (3)	B.S. Napoletani	13 Feb 37	24 Oct 37	8 Aug 38	Lost 4 Sept 42
SG *Sagittario* (2)	C.N.Q. Fiume	14 Nov 35	21 June 36	8 Oct 36	Stricken 1 July 64
SI *Sirio* (2)	C.N.Q. Fiume	12 Nov 34	16 Nov 35	1 Mar 36	Stricken 31 Oct 59
VG *Vega* (2)	C.N.Q. Fiume	14 Nov 35	21 June 36	12 Oct 36	Lost 10 Jan 41

Below: *Lince*, August 1942. (Fraccaroli)

Displacement: 640tons/650tonnes (1), 630/640 (2), 670/680 (3) standard); 995tons/1,011tonnes (1), 985/1,000 (2), 1,030/1,046 (3) (full load).
Length: 263ft 4in/80.4m (C.N.R. and Ansaldo boats of Groups (1) and (2), 269/82) (oa); 246ft/75m (pp).
Beam: 26ft 11in/8.2m (except (3), 26/7.92m).
Draught: 9ft 3in–10ft 2in/2.82m–3.09m (mean).
Machinery: two Yarrow boilers; 2-shaft Tosi geared turbines.
Performance: 19,000shp; 34kts.
Bunkerage: 207tons/210tonnes.
Range: 1,200nm at 20kts.
Guns: three 3.9in (3×1); eight 13.2mm (4×2).
Torpedoes: four 17.7in (2×1, 1×2 or 2×2).
Mines: 20.
Complement: 119.

Design The Italian Navy was one of those which took advantage of the 600-ton clause in the international treaties which allowed unlimited numbers of craft to be built below that level. In fact, as other nations found, 600 tons was a very tight restriction and had to be exceeded if a useful design were to be obtained. The role of this craft was both offensive and defensive to which end they were given a combined gun and torpedo armament, hence their classification as torpedo-boats. The offensive role demanded speed, 34 knots designed obtained by a 19,000shp Tosi geared turbine twin shaft arrangement. Main armament comprised three 3.9-inch O.T.O. 47cal 1931 hand-worked guns in open shield mountings. They were not dual-purpose weapons (45° elevation). Two guns were aft, one forward, as they would require maximum defence after a torpedo attack. When it became available, the 1937-pattern version of this gun mounting with 60° elevation was retro-fitted to earlier units of the class and later units completed with it.

The torpedo outfit comprised four 17.7-inch tubes in three differing arrangements. *Astore, Spica, Centauro* and *Climene* had two single tubes on the beam amidships and a twin bank on the centre-line. The remainder of the *Climene* group and the four Quarnaro-built vessels of the *Alcione* group had four single tubes, two on each beam. All the remaining units shipped two twin banks on the centre-line.

The two units of the *Spica* group were armed with two single 40/39 guns on bandstands axially abaft the funnel and two 20mm singles on the forecastle abreast the bridge. Later units shipped 20mm/65 singles as a uniform AA outfit. All were equipped for both minesweeping and minelaying. Initially only two depth-charge throwers were fitted.

Modifications These were restricted almost entirely to the strengthening of both the AA and ASW outfits. The 20mm guns were replaced by 20mm/65cal Breda twin mountings, three or four in number, with single 20mm/70cal single mountings,

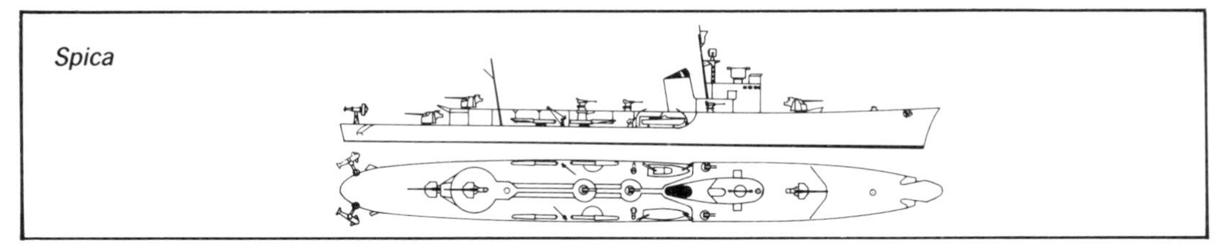

being additionally fitted for a total of up to ten 20mm. Some 13.2mm machine-guns were also fitted, in one or two twin mountings. Depth-charge throwers were increased to four and some units eventually received German 'S Gerät' sets.

Service The first two units, *Spica* and *Astore* were sold to Sweden in 1940. The others formed the 1st (*Airone, Alcione, Aretusa, Ariel*); 8th (*Libra, Lince, Lira, Lupo*); 9th (*Canopo, Cassiopea*); 10th (*Perseo, Sagittario, Sirio, Vega*) 11th (*Castore, Centauro, Cigno, Climene*); 13th (*Calipso, Calliope, Circe, Clio*) and 14th (*Pallade, Partenope, Pleiadi, Polluce*) Torpedo-boat Divisions based respectively at Tripoli, Naples, Sardinia, Naples, Syracuse, La Spezia, Syracuse and Syracuse. All were used for convoy escort tasks during the war when they achieved some success as A/S vessels. *Circe* and *Clio* sank *Grampus* in June 1940, and later *Circe* participated in the sinking of *P38* and also sank *Tempest*. *Clio* was responsible for the sinking of *Triton* in the southern Adriatic in December 1940. *Antares* sank the Greek *Proteus* off Albania that same month. Another success by *Clio* was the Free-French *Narval* in January 1941. *Undaunted* was sunk by *Pleiadi* off Tripoli in May 1941. *Cassiopea* and *Cigno* sank the destroyer *Pakenham* in an engagement in April 1943, but *Cigno* was herself also sunk. *Sagittario* sank *MTB 639* also in April 1943.

Twenty-two of the thirty which served in the R.It.N. during the war were lost under Italian colours and one more after capture by the Germans. The 1st Torpedo-boat Flotilla, consisting of *Airone, Alcione* and *Ariel*, attempted to attack a convoy from Malta on the night of 11/12 October 1940, but ran into the cruiser *Ajax*, part of the screen. In a short-range moonlight action, both *Airone* and *Ariel* were sunk, but not before hitting the cruiser several times, damaging her bridge and radar. Two months later, *Calypso* was mined and sunk east of Tripoli.

In January 1941, the Royal Navy passed a convoy through the Mediterranean bound for Malta and Piraeus, Operation 'Excess'. *Vega* and *Circe* sortied from Pantellaria to attack this convoy, but were driven off by the cruiser *Bonaventure* which heavily hit *Vega*. Stopped and on fire, the crippled Italian ship was sunk by *Hereward* with a torpedo. *Andromeda*, operating in the Adriatic, was sunk by an aircraft torpedo off Valona and two months later *Canopo* by bombing at Tripoli. In May, *Lupo*, defending her convoy from *Dido, Ajax* and *Orion*, received eighteen 6-inch hits but escaped. *Pleiadi* was damaged by bombs on 13 October 1941 then foundered the following day, also in Tripoli harbour. Six days later, both *Aldebaran* and *Altair* were lost in the Gulf of Athens on mines laid by the submarine *Rorqual*. *Alcione* was torpedoed north of Crete by *Truant* and was beached as a total loss. No further losses were incurred until the autumn of 1942 when *Polluce*, escorting a convoy from Piraeus to Tobruk with *Lupo* and *Castore*, was sunk by torpedo-bombers north of Tobruk. *Centauro* was sunk by bombing in Benghazi harbour early in November and later that month *Circe* was lost by collision off Sicily. The final loss of the year was *Lupo*, sunk by aircraft off Kerkenah while picking up survivors.

In 1943, *Cigno* was lost in an engagement with *Paladin* and *Pakenham* as mentioned above, and *Climene* was torpedoed by *Unshaken* off Sicily. *Perseo* was sunk in action with the destroyers *Nubian, Paladin* and *Petard* off Kelibia while engaged on the last Tunis operations. Later in May, *Antares* was bombed and sunk at Livorno by the USAAF. *Castore* was sunk in an engagement with *Jervis* and the Greek *Vasilissa Olga* off Cape Spartivento, *Lince* was torpedoed by *Ultor* while aground in the Gulf of Taranto and finally *Pallade* sank at Naples during an air raid.

At the Capitulation, *Partenope*, in dry dock at Naples, was destroyed by her crew, but *Lira*, scuttled at La Spezia, was raised and renamed *TA49* by the Germans. She was bombed and sunk before completion, on 4 November 1944. The remainder of the survivors served with the Allied forces for the last years of the war and saw extensive post-war service with the reformed Italian Navy.

Below: *Partenope*. (Author's Collection)

Above: *Sirio* in December 1941. (Fraccaroli) **Below:** *Climene.* (Author's Collection)

Right: *Calliope*. (Author's Collection)

ARIETE CLASS

Ship	Builder	Laid Down	Launched	Commissioned	Fate
AB *Alabarda*	C.R.D.A. Trieste	24 Mar 43	–	Completed as German *TA42*	
AE *Ariete*	Ansaldo, Genoa	15 July 42	6 Mar 43	5 Aug 43	To Yugoslavia 30 April 49
AO *Arturo*	Ansaldo, Genoa	15 July 42	27 Mar 43	Completed as German *TA24*	
AG *Auriga*	Ansaldo, Genoa	15 July 42	15 April 43	Completed as German *TA27*	
BL *Balestra*	C.N.Q. Fiume	5 Sept 42	–	German *TA47*. Not completed by 1945	
DG *Daga*	C.R.D.A. Trieste	9 Jan 43	15 July 43	Completed as German *TA39*	
DR *Dragone*	Ansaldo, Genoa	15 July 42	14 Aug 43	Completed as German *TA30*	
ED *Eridano*	Ansaldo, Genoa	15 July 42	12 July 43	Completed as German *TA29*	
FI *Fionda*	C.N.Q. Fiume	26 Aug 42	–	German *TA46*. Never completed	
GL *Gladio*	C.R.D.A. Trieste	9 Jan 43	15 June 43	Completed as German *TA37*	
LN *Lancia*	C.R.D.A. Trieste	24 Mar 43	–	Completed as German *TA41*	
PU *Pugnale*	C.R.D.A. Trieste	9 Jan 43	1 Aug 43	Completed as German *TA40*	
RG Rigel	Ansaldo, Genoa	15 July 42	22 May 43	Completed as German *TA28*	
SD *Spada*	C.R.D.A. Trieste	9 Jan 43	1 July 43	Completed as German *TA38*	
SP *Spica*	C.N.Q. Fiume	14 Jan 42	–	Completed as German *TA45*	
SR *Stella Polare*	C.N.Q. Fiume	1 April 42	11 July 43	Completed as German *TA36*	

Displacement: 745tons/757tonnes (standard); 1,110tons/1,127tonnes (full load).
Length: 274ft/83.5m (oa); 266ft 1in/81.1m (pp).
Beam: 28ft 3in/8.62m.
Draught: 10ft 4in/3.15m (mean).
Machinery: two 3-drum boilers; 2-shaft Parsons geared turbines.
Performance: 22,000shp; 31.5kts.
Bunkerage: 210tons/213tonnes.
Guns: two 3.9in (2×1); ten 20mm (3×2, 4×1).
Torpedoes: six 17.7in (2×3).
Mines: 28.
Complement: 158.

Design Mounting losses in escort vessels on the vital North Africa supply route were beginning to make themselves felt by 1942. To maintain the large Italo-German army in the African desert required huge quantities of supplies which could only be provided in quantity by sea. As a result, the convoys were the life blood of the Army, a fact quite obviously realized by the British who launched a three-pronged assault on them by air, sea and submarine. Losses in convoyed merchantmen were soaring, with the implied loss of the supplies carried. The escorts too were suffering (one third of the *Spica* class had been lost by mid 1942) with the result that the fate of the armies was in doubt. To provide a new supply of escort vessels, the proven *Spica* design was taken and modified in the light of wartime experience.

The main threat to the convoys was by surface attack from cruisers and destroyers based at Malta and elsewhere, plus the ever-present submarines. The escort vessels could not hope to match cruisers or even destroyers in gun power, but the torpedo was much more powerful against the attackers and to this end, the torpedo outfit was increased to six tubes. This was at the expense of one 3.9-inch gun but the removal of the quarter-deck mounting left a large clear space for ASW equipment. The hull was some ten feet longer than that of the *Spica*s' with beam increased by about two feet. Displacement rose accordingly, but despite a 15 per cent increase in installed power, speed dropped by about 2½ knots and endurance fell to 1,500 nautical miles at 16 knots. This latter feature was not of great significance as they were mainly intended for the Africa supply route whose longest passage, say Taranto to Tripoli, was only about 600nm. The AA outfit was planned to comprise two single 37mm guns and twelve 20mm in two twin and eight single mountings, but due to war circumstances this was not achieved.

A total of 42 ships of this design were planned, but Italian yards and industrial capacity could not accommodate such a large programme in a short time and only sixteen units were in fact laid down. These were split equally between west-coast and Adriatic yards. Shortages of materials meant that by the close of 1942, only ten of the sixteen had been laid down and the first unit to join the fleet, *Ariete*, did so only in August 1943. A month later, Italy surrendered, by which time, apart from this one completed unit, ten others were afloat and in the course of fitting out.

Modifications None in Italian hands (See Germany for further details).

Service *Ariete* was the only ship to complete for the Royal Italian Navy, sailing to surrender brand-new.

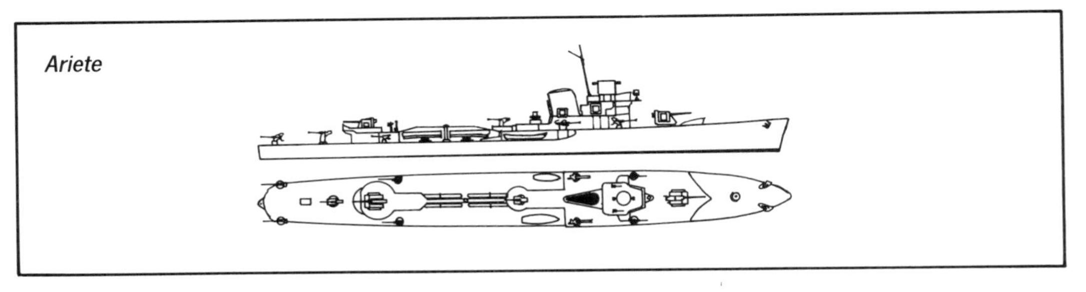
Ariete

Post-war she was transferred to Yugoslavia as war reparations and renamed *Dumitor*. She was not removed from the active list until 1963. All the remaining ships were captured by the Germans in September 1943 in varying stages of completion. All but two were eventually commissioned by the Kriegsmarine (see Germany for details). *Fionda* (German *TA46*) and *Balestra* (German *TA47*) were both seized still incomplete by Yugoslavia in 1945, but only *Ucka* (ex-*Balestra*) was completed in 1949. Construction of *Velebit* (ex-*Fionda*) was eventually abandoned. Both had been damaged by bombing on 20 February 1945 while still on the slipways. None of the units completed by the Kriegsmarine survived the war.

CAPTURED UNITS

T1, T3, T5, T6, T7

All former similarly numbered Yugoslav vessels of considerable vintage, employed on local escort duties in the Adriatic by the Royal Italian Navy, from April 1941 until the Capitulation in 1943. Two 3-inch AA of Italian pattern replaced the main armament in some units and a few 20mm were added. Only *T1* and *T5* escaped in September 1943 and were restituted to Yugoslavia in December that year. Both served until the early 1960s. *T3* was captured by the Germans at Fiume on 16 September 1943 and recommissioned as *TA48*, a unit of the Croatian Navy. *T7* was also captured at Gravosa, in September and turned over to the Croatian Navy at Sebenico in June 1944. *T6* was scuttled 10 miles north of Cesenatico on 11 September 1943 and *T8* was sunk by German bombers at Punta Oliva during the evacuation of Italian troops from the Dalmatians on 11 September 1943.

Spalato

This incomplete destroyer, launched in 1940 as *Split* for the Royal Yugoslav Navy, was captured still incomplete by the Germans on 8 September 1943. Although scuttled by them at the end of the war, she was eventually completed by Yugoslavia in 1958.

Premuda

Formerly the Yugoslav *Dubrovnik*, captured in Kotor on 17 April 1941. In Italian hands she was modified before re-entering service in January 1942. The large deck-house at the forward end of the after shelter deck was removed, being replaced by a bandstand for 20mm guns. In addition, the 3.3-inch twin mounting was removed and replaced initially by a 4.7-inch/15cal star-shell gun. This was eventually replaced by a twin 37mm mounting. A new director tower was fitted on the bridge and the searchlights were replaced by 20mm single guns. A further major modification of her armament was in progress at the time of the Italian surrender when her guns were to be changed for the new 5.3-inch/45cal guns, as carried by the *Capitani Romani* class light cruisers, but in single mountings. She was also to have received an augmented 37mm and 20mm outfit, probably losing the after tubes in the process. *Premuda* served on North Africa convoys from February 1942 and took part in the 7th Division's attacks on the 'Harpoon'/'Vigorous' operation in June of that year. More convoy duties followed, culminating in the Tunisia supply run during the first quarter of 1943. Later in 1943, *Premuda* went for refit and alteration at Genoa where she fell into German hands, on 8 September, being later renamed *TA32*.

Sebenico, Lubiana

These destroyers were formerly the Yugoslav *Beograd* and *Ljubljana* captured on 17 April 1941 at Cattaro and Sebenico respectively. After repairs, *Sebenico* joined the Italian Fleet in August 1941 and her sister in October 1942. In Italian hands, the ships were modified, receiving a new director on the bridge. *Sebenico* appears not to have been altered as much as *Lubiana*; she retained both her searchlight amidships and the after director at least until mid 1942. *Lubiana*, on the other hand, lost her searchlight in exchange for a single 37mm gun and also the after director was landed. She carried five 20mm guns in addition, but the original 40mm guns were removed. *Lubiana* had her funnels tops cut to a more raked angle than her sister.

Both ships served as escorts during 1941–43, but *Lubiana* after operating on the Tunisia supply route from the beginning of 1943, was wrecked on a shoal in the Gulf of Tunis on 1 April 1943. *Sebenico* was in the Adriatic in 1942 and at the time of the Capitulation was in Venice where she was seized by the Germans on 11 September 1943 and later became their *TA43*. It is likely that by this time the after tubes had been removed to augment the AA outfit.

FR21, FR24

FR21 (ex-*Lion*) and *FR24* (ex-*Valmy*) were two of the French *contre-torpilleurs* of the *Guépard* class scuttled at Toulon in November 1942. Both were subsequently raised by the Royal Italian Navy and towed to La Spezia for repairs. While in Italian hands, *FR21* had the forward torpedo tube bank removed, but was otherwise seemingly little altered although she probably received a number of Italian 20mm guns. Only *FR21* was recommissioned by the Italian Navy, on 19 January 1943, but had only just finished work-up by the time of the Surrender when she was scuttled at La Spezia on 9 September 1943. *FR24* was captured by the Germans while still on route to La Spezia in tow. She was scuttled there in 1945, still unrepaired.

FR22, FR23

Ex-French *Panthère* and *Tigre* respectively, both were captured relatively undamaged at Toulon in November 1942. The former was never made operational and scuttled at La spezia on 8 September 1943. *FR23*, on the other hand, was recommissioned by the Royal Italian Navy. She had her forward tubes removed for additional light AA guns, but was little modified in appearance. On 28 October 1943 she was restituted to France.

FR31

Formerly the French *torpilleur Trombe*, she was commissioned by the Royal Italian Navy on 19 January 1943. After running ashore on 2 May 1943 the ship was once again repaired. She returned to French colours on 28 October 1943.

FR32, FR33, FR34, FR35, FR36, FR37

All *Le Hardi*-class French *torpilleurs*, respectively *Scirocco, L'Adroit, Lansquenet, Bison, Foudroyant* and *Le Hardi*, scuttled at Toulon and salvaged by Italy. None was ever recommissioned by the Italian Navy.

FR41, FR42, FR43

Small French torpedo-boats of the 600 tonnes class (*Bombarde, La Pomone, L'Iphigénie*) taken at Bizerta by Germany and later on 28 December 1942 allocated to Italy. However, none saw service with the Royal Italian Navy as they were again repossessed by German and renamed *TA9, TA10* and *TA11* respectively.

Below: *Sebeninico*. (Author's Collection)

Japan

Like that of Italy, Japan's navy was of relatively recent origin, but, as a result of concerted absorption of foreign techniques, particularly from Britain, she had, by the turn of the century, created a well-equipped and well-trained Fleet. During the war with Russia in 1904–05 she had opportunity to employ modern warships and techniques against a nominally equal foe and was thus able to gain invaluable experience in both tactics and material. Against a poorly trained and indifferently led Russian Fleet, the Japanese training paid off, leading to a decisive victory at Tsushima, closely observed by all the major naval powers of the time. Modern battleships armed with 12-inch guns were already being laid down in home dockyards by 1905, signalling the end of reliance upon foreign expertise, and in 1909 the first dreadnoughts were laid down. The last major vessel to be ordered abroad, the battlecruiser *Kongo* went afloat in Britain in 1912, the remainder of her class being constructed in Japan.

Japan had been an early user of torpedo-boats, having decided in 1895 that they would be a powerful weapon against Russia, and had built in home yards several of various designs, including Yarrow, Schichau and Normand, the premier types of the period. These reached 120 tons armed with three guns and three 18-inch torpedo tubes by 1905, after which the larger destroyers were concentrated upon. Construction of these had begun in 1897 with the ordering of twelve ships in Great Britain, but by 1902 home shipyards had begun to build destroyers to Thornycroft plans. At the time of the Russo-Japanese war in 1904, Japan had 30 destroyers of the British '30-knotter' type. Design expertise, already wide as a result of orders placed in Britain, France and Germany, was further enhanced by the capture of modern Russian types after the war of 1904–05. At the outbreak of the First World War, the standard Japanese destroyer displaced about 850 tons full load, was armed with one 4.7-inch gun, two 3-inch and four torpedo tubes, and was capable of 30 knots. Oil firing had not been completely adopted so they were mixed fired, but they proved robust and effective vessels. An indication of the prowess of Japanese designers was the fact that twelve destroyers of similar design were built for the French Navy during 1915–17. Turbine propulsion and 21-inch torpedo tubes were introduced in the *Momi* class (1918 programme), but by the close of 1918 neither full oil firing nor triple tubes had yet been adopted.

During the opening months of the First World War, Japan was actively engaged in the containment and neutralization of German bases in China and later was tasked with the escorting of convoys from Australia to the Mediterranean. In 1917, an important contribution was made to the Allied war effort when a number of destroyers were sent to the Mediterranean. No destroyer losses were incurred during hostilities, but *Sakaki* was badly damaged by an Austrian submarine in June 1917. At peace again, Japan had the opportunity to take over several ex-German ships, but instead had them broken up in Europe unlike other powers such as France and Italy. Also, unlike most other victorious Allies, Japan continued construction of destroyers and did not cancel late war programme orders. Moreover, she continued to place orders in 1919 and 1920. These ships, the 21 vessels of the *Momi* class completed between 1919 and 1920 but most had been relegated to second-line duties by the outbreak of the Pacific war in 1941. It is significant that the USA was the other major power to continue large-scale destroyer construction after 1918.

The 1920s saw the adoption of full oil firing and of triple tubes, but general appearance remained essentially that of the 1914–18 period. Japan retained the torpedoes in the well deck forward of the bridge long after this layout had been abandoned by other powers and its retention is difficult to appreciate. However, a complete rethink of destroyer design was in hand and the middle of the decade witnessed the laying down of the *Fubuki* class. These powerful ships surprised the world's naval circles for they introduced weatherproof gun-houses, dual-purpose guns and, not least importantly, 24-inch calibre torpedoes. This calibre was unique in world navies (only Great Britain had a similar calibre, 24.5-inch and then only in two battleships), but the most telling fact about these torpedoes was that later they were given oxygen propulsion (as opposed to compressed air or electricity) which gave them a range far beyond that of any other rival. This feature was completely unknown to either the USA or Great Britain, and these 'Long Lance' torpedoes, as they were known, were to give the Japanese Fleet a decided advantage in the war to come. Allied to this new weapon was the provision of nine reload torpedoes. Later an effective and well-designed reload system was developed which doubled the punch of subsequent Japanese destroyers. The speed of this system caught the US and Allied Navies by surprise.

Japan was bound by Treaty restrictions at this time and the measures adopted to squeeze such a quart into a pint pot caused problems of stability and structural strength. These were found to affect not only the destroyers, but most of the new cruisers and torpedo-boats as well. To overcome these problems, Japan virtually rebuilt nearly all of her new warships in the years leading up to 1941 and the result was a powerful and effective fighting force. The *Fubuki* design was refined and improved during the intervening years so that at the end of the thirties Japanese destroyers were arguably the most powerful in the world.

Japan's war started on 28 May 1937 when she began her attempted conquest of China and although this was of course predominantly a land war, the navy was involved from the outset. She had thus been at war for more than four years before embarking on a full-scale Pacific conquest.

During the 1941–45 period, many more well-designed destroyers joined the fleet and inflicted serious harm to Allied naval forces in the early years. However, a combination of rising US carrier air power superiority and very effective submarine operation began to extract a heavy toll from all Japanese warships, but especially destroyers, which were often used with almost foolhardy dash and courage, frequently in support of isolated island army garrisons.

This destruction was accelerated by the failure of Japan to develop an effective air warning radar until very late in the war, and the complete absence of any gunnery radar sets. Taken together with Japan's lack of an AA gun heavier than 25mm, it meant that US carrier-borne aircraft had a decisive advantage in the Pacific war. The result was that by the time of Japan's surrender in August 1945, no less than 134 destroyers had been lost in action, leaving only nine modern Fleet destroyers still afloat, with a handful of war-built emergency escort destroyers and pre-special types.

MINEKAZE CLASS

Ship	Builder	Laid Down	Launched	Commissioned	Fate
Akikaze	Mitsubishi (Nagasaki)	7 June 20	14 Dec 20	1 April 21	Lost 3 Nov 44
Hakaze	Mitsubishi (Nagasaki)	11 Nov 18	21 June 20	16 Sept 20	Lost 23 Jan 43
Hokaze	Maizuru NYd.	30 Nov 20	12 July 21	22 Dec 21	Lost 6 July 44
Minekaze	Maizuru NYd.	20 April 18	8 Feb 19	29 Mar 20	Lost 10 Feb 44
Namikaze	Maizuru NYd.	7 Nov 21	24 June 22	11 Nov 22	To China 1947
Nokaze	Maizuru NYd.	16 April 21	1 Oct 21	31 Mar 22	Lost 20 Feb 45
Numakaze	Maizuru NYd.	10 Aug 21	25 Feb 22	24 July 22	Lost 19 Dec 43
Okikaze	Maizuru NYd.	22 Feb 19	3 Oct 19	17 Aug 20	Broken up 1948
Sawakaze	Mitsubishi (Nagasaki)	7 Jan 18	7 Jan 19	16 Mar 20	Broken up 1948
Shiokaze	Maizuru NYd.	15 May 20	22 Oct 20	29 July 21	Lost 17 Feb 44
Tachikaze	Maizuru NYd.	18 Aug 20	31 Mar 21	5 Dec 21	Broken up 1947
Yakaze	Mitsubishi (Nagasaki)	15 Aug 18	10 April 20	19 July 20	Broken up
Yukaze	Mitsubishi (Nagasaki)	24 Dec 20	28 May 21	24 Aug 21	To UK 1947

Displacement: 1,345tons/1,366tonnes (standard); 1,650tons/1,676tonnes (full load).
Length: 336ft 6in/102.5m (oa); 326ft 6in/99.5m (wl); 320ft/97.5m (pp).
Beam: 29ft 8in/9.04m.
Draught: 9ft 6in/2.9m (mean).
Machinery: four Kampon boilers; 2-shaft Parsons geared turbines.
Performance: 38,500shp; 39kts.
Bunkerage: 395tons/401tonnes.
Range: 3,600nm at 14kts.
Guns: four 4.7in (4×1); two 7.7mm.
Torpedoes: six 21in (3×2).
Mines: 20.
Complement: 148.

Design Two units of this design were authorized under the 1917 programme (*Minekaze* and *Sawakaze*). They were essentially developments of earlier classes and retained the generally Germanic appearance and layout of their forebears. Japan had adopted the 4.7-inch gun for destroyers as early as 1907 with the two ships of the *Umikaze* class, but these early destroyers had a mixed calibre gun armament. Uniform 4.7-inch calibre was adopted for the *Amatsukaze* class (1915 programme) and these new destroyers naturally followed suit. Four single 4.7-inch 45cal 3rd Year type (1914) hand-worked mountings were carried, disposed one forward, one each ahead and abaft the second funnel and one on the after deck-house. This gun fired a 45lb projectile with a maximum range of 17,500 yards. The arrangement of the guns cannot be considered ideal, for ahead and astern fire power was only one gun and both midships guns had limited arcs of fire particularly that between the funnels. The six torpedoes were shipped in three twin mountings, all centre-line, which gave a broadside of six tubes, but the forward mounting was liable to be washed out in heavy seas.

Main machinery comprised four Kampon boilers and a twin screw geared turbine arrangement developing 38,500shp. This gave a designed top speed of 39 knots, but *Shimakaze* reached over 40 knots on trials. Contemporary British and US destroyers shipped 27,000shp power plants on roughly the same displacement figure for maximum speeds of about 34–35 knots. Bunkerage was greater than in British ships and considerably in excess of that of the US '4-pipers', but endurance was only roughly 75 per cent of that of the American type, suggesting somewhat inefficient machinery. Both turbines occupied the same space between No. 3 gun and the after tubes.

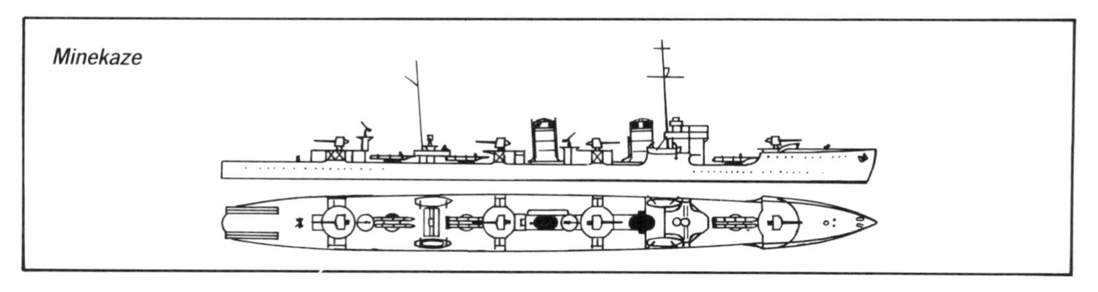

Left: *Nokaze* in the 1930s. (IWM)

A further ten units were ordered, five each under the 1918 and 1919 programmes, with a final trio under the 1920 programme. These last ships, *Nokaze, Namikaze* and *Numakaze*, were given different armament arrangements. No. 3 4.7-inch gun was replaced by the repositioned searchlight and shifted to the after deck-house, where it was placed back to back with No. 4 gun. This improved its arc of fire, although why it was not placed on the quarter deck for even better results is not clear. More importantly, this rearrangement considerably simplified ammunition supply as it now could be served by the after magazine.

Modifications Because these destroyers had become outclassed by the new 'Special Type' (q.v.), a number were modified for other duties between 1937 and 1941. In 1937, *Yakaze* was converted to a control ship for the radio-controlled target ship *Settsu*, her armament being reduced to two 4.7-inch guns and landing the torpedo tubes. Later in September 1942, she herself became a target ship for aircraft with armament reduced to only one 50mm and four 25mm guns.

All the remainder of the class had their bunkerage reduced in 1937–38. Hulls were also strengthened and funnel caps added. *Okikaze* was disarmed and stricken in 1938, but not disposed of and when war broke out again in 1941, was rearmed as a destroyer. Two others, *Nadakaze* and *Shimakaze*, were rerated as patrol vessels in 1939–40 being armed with two 4.7-inch; ten 25mm; two 21-inch TT. Later they were also modified to carry Daihatsu landing craft. The forward boilers were removed, reducing power to 19,250shp and speed to 20 knots. Both were lost, *Nadakaze* (as *Patrol Boat No. 2*) torpedoed by a British submarine on 27 July 1945 and *Shimakaze* (as *Patrol Boat No. 1*) by US submarine *Guardfish* on 13 January 1943.

By 1944, surviving ships had their light AA increased to thirteen–twenty, 25mm guns (*Nadakaze* had sixteen). *Namikaze*, badly damaged by a mine in September 1944, was rebuilt as a *Kaiten* carrier. Her stern was cut down to the waterline and the forward boiler removed, reducing her speed to 28 knots. Armed now with one 4.7-inch; twenty 25mm and eight machine-guns, she could also carry two *Kaiten*. *Shiokaze*, also severely damaged, in January 1945, was modified for similar duties but equipped to carry four *Kaiten*, but her conversion was not finished by the end of the war. *Sawakaze* and *Yukaze* had been converted for air-sea rescue duties by 1945. *Shiokaze* and *Yukaze* received Type 13 radar, *Namikaze* and *Sawakaze*, Type 22. This latter ship had been fitted experimentally with a 9-barrelled 5.9-inch ASW rocket-launcher in place of No. 1 gun. The remaining armament was one 4.7-inch gun (No. 4) and ten 25mm. She was capable of only 16 knots.

Service Used in the main for escort duties, this class suffered the usual heavy losses of all Japanese destroyer classes. *Okikaze* was sunk by the US submarine *Trigger* in home waters, *Hakaze* by *Guardfish* off New Ireland and *Numakaze* by *Greyback* off Okinawa, all in 1943. 1944 saw the losses of *Minekaze* to *Pogy* off Formosa, *Akikaze* torpedoed by *Pintado* west of Luzon, *Hokaze* by *Paddle* in the Celebes Sea and *Tachikaze* by air attack at Truk. *Yakaze* was badly damaged by air attack at Yokosuka, *Nadakaze* torpedoed and *Shiokaze* also badly damaged in 1945. *Shiokaze, Yukaze* and *Namikaze* were all used on repatriation duties post-war, with the latter being transferred to China on 3 October 1947 (as *Shen Yang*). The rest of the survivors were broken up.

KAMIKAZE CLASS

Ship	Builder	Laid Down	Launched	Commissioned	Fate
Asakaze (ex-*No.3*)	Mitsubishi (Nagasaki)	16 Feb 22	8 Dec 22	16 June 23	Lost 23 Aug 44
Asanagi (ex-*No.15*)	Fujinagata	5 Mar 23	21 April 24	29 Dec 24	Lost 22 May 44
Harukaze (ex-*No.5*)	Maizuru NYd.	16 May 22	18 Dec 22	31 May 23	Broken up 1947
Hatakaze (ex-*No.9*)	Maizuru NYd.	3 July 23	15 Mar 24	30 Aug 24	Lost 15 Jan 45
Hayate (ex-*No.13*)	Ishikawajima	11 Nov 22	23 Mar 25	21 Dec 25	Lost 11 Dec 41
Kamikaze (ex-*No.1*)	Mitsubishi (Nagasaki)	15 Dec 21	25 Sept 22	28 Dec 22	Broken up Oct 1947
Matsukaze (ex-*No.7*)	Maizuru NYd.	2 Dec 22	30 Oct 23	5 April 24	Lost 9 June 44
Oite (ex-*No.11*)	Uraga	16 Mar 23	27 Nov 24	30 Oct 25	Lost 17 Feb 44
Yunagi (ex-*No.17*)	Sasebo NYd.	17 Sept 23	23 April 24	24 April 25	Lost 25 Aug 44

Displacement: 1,400tons/1,422tonnes (standard); 1,720tons/1,747tonnes (full load).
Length: 336ft 6in/102.5m (oa); 327ft/99.6m (wl); 320ft/97.5m (pp).
Beam: 30ft/9.1m.
Draught: 9ft 7in/2.9m (mean).
Machinery: four Kampon boilers; 2-shaft Parsons geared turbines.
Performance: 38,500shp; 37.3kts.
Bunkerage: 420tons/426tonnes.
Range: 3,600nm at 14kts.
Guns: four 4.7in (4×1); two 7.7mm.
Torpedoes: six 21in (3×2).
Complement: 148.

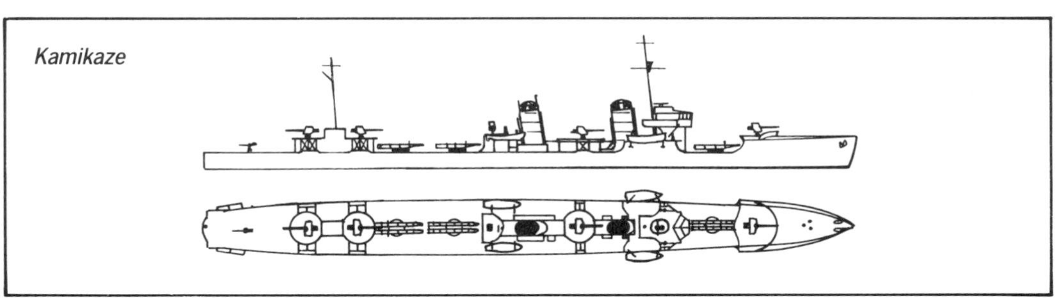

Design Improved *Minekaze* class but with slightly increased beam to compensate modified bridge structures (which increased top-weight). The main machinery remained a 38,500shp twin screw geared turbine installation, but the increased displacement resulted in a reduction of speed to 37¼ knots. Armament was also identical with that of the *Minekaze* except that the same layout was adopted as had been introduced with the last three units of the earlier design. Eleven units were authorized under the 1921/22 programme, but because of the recent signing of the Washington Treaty two, *Okaze* and *Tsumikaze*, were subsequently cancelled. They were all completed with numbers in lieu of names. *Kamikaze* was originally to have been named *Kujokaze* or *Shirushikaze*, and *Asakaze, Karuikaze* or *Suzukaze*.

Modifications During 1941–42, one 4.7-inch gun was landed (No. 4), together with the after bank of tubes and the light AA was increased to ten 25mm guns. Four throwers and eighteen depth-charges were also fitted. Displacement rose to 1,523 tons and speed fell in consequence. AA outfits were progressively improved in survivors during the war and by 1944, the 25mm guns had been increased to between thirteen and twenty. By this time speed had been reduced to 35 knots or less.

Service At the outbreak of the Pacific war, these ships formed two of the Fleet's destroyer divisions, 5th (*Asakaze, Harukaze, Hatakaze* and *Matsukaze*) and 29th (*Oite, Hayate, Yunagi* and *Asanagi*). The 5th Division took part in the assault on the Philippines in December 1941 and then the invasion of Malaya in December and January of 1942. They supported the occupation of the Dutch East Indies in February and March 1942, where *Harukaze* was damaged by the cruisers *Perth* and *Houston*. Her sisters *Asakaze* and *Hatakaze* took part in the counter-attack which sank both Allied cruisers. In April 1942, the division escorted the convoys on the Indian Ocean bound for Rangoon.

The 29th Division, on the other hand, were part of the Task Force detailed to capture Wake Island where *Hayate*, sunk by US coastal batteries became the first Japanese loss of the war. From Wake, the remainder of the division moved to Rabaul in January 1942 and in March to Lae where both *Asanagi* and *Yunagi* were damaged in a raid by US aircraft from *Yorktown* and *Lexington*. In May, *Asanagi* and *Oite* participated in the assault on Port Moresby. By July 1942, following the disaster at Midway, the Fleet was reorganized and the 29th Division formed part of the 4th Fleet based at Truk. From here they supported operations in New Guinea. *Yunagi* was present at the Battle of Savo Island in August and with her sisters, *Asanagi* and *Oite* shelled the Island of Nauru the same month. They also ran transport sorties in the Solomon Islands.

Oite was damaged by a torpedo from *Gudgeon* in September 1943, but she was not lost until February the following year when sunk by carrier aircraft at Truk. *Asanagi* fell victim to a torpedo from *Pollack* off Bonin and the following month *Matzukaze* was sunk by *Swordfish* in the same area. In August both *Asakaze* and *Yunagi* were sunk by submarines (*Haddo* and *Picuda* respectively), both off Luzon. Finally, *Hatakaze* was sunk by aircraft at Takao Formosa.

Kamikaze and *Harukaze* survived the war, but the latter had been twice badly damaged, once by a mine on 4 November 1944 and on the second occasion by aircraft off Formosa on 21 January 1945. Although towed to Japan she remained unrepaired at Sasebo at the surrender. *Kamikaze* was used for repatriation duties but was wrecked on 7 June 1946 and subsequently broken up.

WAKATAKE CLASS

Ship	Builder	Laid Down	Launched	Commissioned	Fate
Wakatake (ex-*No.2*)	Kawasaki (Kobe)	13 Dec 21	24 July 22	30 Sept 22	Lost 30 Mar 44
Asagao (ex-*No.10*)	Ishikawajima	14 Mar 22	4 Nov 22	10 May 23	Broken up June 1948
Huyo (ex-*No.16*)	Fujinagata	16 Feb 22	23 Sept 22	16 Mar 23	Lost 20 Dec 43
Karukaya (ex-*No.18*)	Fujinagata	16 May 22	19 Mar 23	20 Aug 23	Lost 10 May 44
Kuretaka (ex-*No.4*)	Kawasaki (Kobe)	15 Mar 22	21 Oct 22	21 Dec 22	Lost 30 Dec 44
Sanae (ex-*No.6*)	Uraga	5 April 22	15 Feb 23	5 Nov 23	Lost 18 Nov 43

Displacement: 900tons/914tonnes (standard); 1,100tons/1,117tonnes (full load).
Length: 280ft/85.3m (wl); 275ft/83.8m (pp).
Beam: 26ft 6in/8m.
Draught: 8ft 3in/2.5m (mean).
Machinery: three Kampon boilers; 2-shaft Parsons geared turbines.
Performance: 21,500shp; 35.5kts.
Bunkerage: 275tons/279tonnes.
Range: 3,000nm at 15kts.
Guns: three 4.7in (3×1); two 7.7mm.
Torpedoes: four 21in (2×2).
Complement: 110.

Design Built under the 1921 programme, these ships were improved *Momi* class and the last small (second-class) destroyers to be built. Fast and relatively well armed for their size, they had otherwise no special merits. Thirteen units were planned, but the contracts for five were cancelled in 1922. They were equipped for both minelaying and minesweeping. Although originally intended to carry names, numbers were substituted until 1 August 1932 when they were named once more. The cancelled units were *No.14* (*Shian*), *No.20* (*Omodoka*), *No.22* (*Nadeshiko*), *No.24* (*Botan*) and *No.26* (*Basho*). In addition, *Sawarabi* (ex-*No.8*) foundered in a storm north-north-east of Keelung in the Formosa Straits on 5 December 1932.

Modifications *Yugao*, rerated as a patrol boat in 1939–40 was rearmed with two 4.7-inch, eight 25mm and 60 depth-charges, horse-power reduced to 10,000shp and speed to 18 knots. Displacement was now 910–1,130 tons. The ships still rated as destroyers were altered in 1941–42 to carry two 4.7-inch and six 25mm in two triple mounts which replaced No. 2 gun; 13mm guns were also added. Minesweeping and minelaying gear was replaced by four depth-charge throwers and up to 48 depth-charges. *Asagao* had one twin bank of tubes removed. Type 13 radar was fitted in some units.

Service Like the *Mutsuki*-class destroyers, these older and smaller ships were no longer suitable for Fleet duties by 1941. Instead they were used for escort duties and, because of their shallow draft, spent much of their lives in Chinese waters and the Philippines area. *Sanae* was the first loss, torpedoed by *Bluefish* in the northern Celebes Sea. Barely a month later, *Huyo* was sunk by *Puffer* west of Manila. *Karukaya* was also torpedoed and sunk, this time by *Cod* in the South China Sea, west of Luzon, and *Kuretaka* by *Razorback* south-east of Formosa. *Asagao*, which had been badly damaged by a mine in the Straits of Shimonoseki on 22 August 1945, was not repaired. *Wakatake* was sunk by aircraft of *TF58* north of Palau in March 1944.

Below: *Kuri*, *Momi*-class.

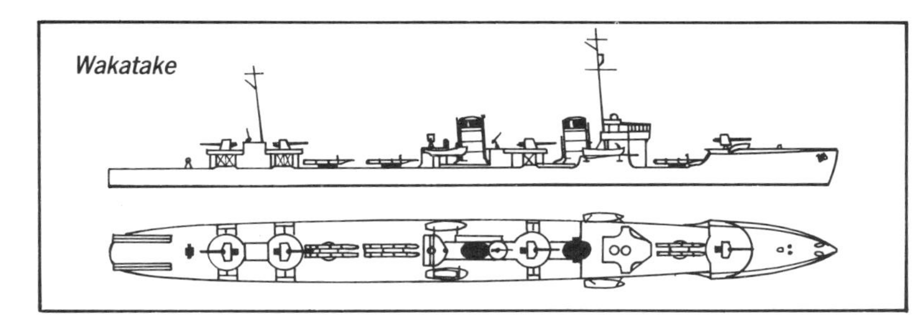

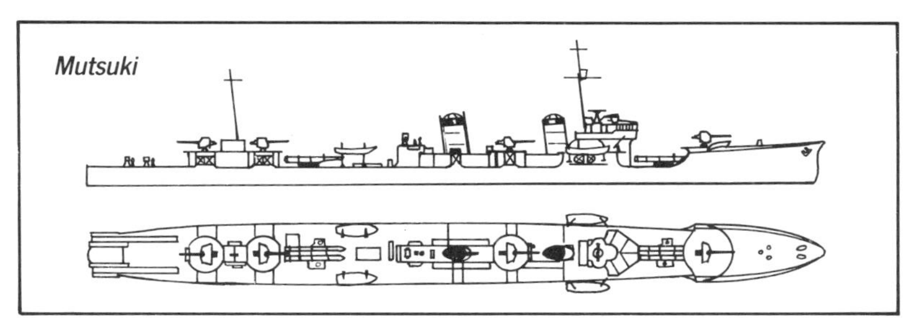

MUTSUKI CLASS

Ship	Builder	Laid Down	Launched	Commissioned	Fate
Fumizuki (ex-*No.29*)	Fujinagata	20 Oct 24	16 Feb 26	3 July 26	Lost 17 Feb 44
Kikuzuki (ex-*No.31*)	Kosakubu	15 June 25	15 May 26	20 Nov 26	Lost 4 May 42
Kisaragi (ex-*No.21*)	Kosakubu	3 June 24	5 June 25	21 Dec 25	Lost 11 Dec 41
Mikazuki (ex-*No.32*)	Sasebo Dkyd.	21 Aug 25	12 July 26	7 May 27	Lost 28 July 43
Minazuki (ex-*No.28*)	Uraga	24 Mar 25	25 May 26	22 Mar 27	Lost 6 June 44
Mochizuki (ex-*No.33*)	Uraga	23 Mar 26	28 April 27	31 Oct 27	Lost 24 Oct 43
Mutsuki (ex-*No.19*)	Sasebo Dkyd.	21 May 24	23 July 25	25 Mar 26	Lost 25 Aug 42
Nagatsuki (ex-*No.30*)	Ishikawajima	16 April 25	6 Oct 26	30 April 27	Lost 6 July 43
Satsuki (ex-*No.27*)	Fujinagata	1 Dec 24	25 Mar 25	15 Nov 25	Lost 21 Sept 44
Uzuki (ex-*No.25*)	Ishikawajima	11 Jan 24	15 Oct 25	14 Sept 26	Lost 12 Dec 44
Yayoi (ex-*No.23*)	Uraga	11 Jan 24	11 July 25	28 Aug 26	Lost 11 Sept 42
Yuzuki (ex-*No.34*)	Fujinagata	27 Nov 26	4 Mar 27	25 July 27	Lost 12 Dec 44

Displacement: 1,315tons/1,336tonnes (standard); 1,772tons/1,800tonnes (full load).
Length: 338ft 9in/100.2m (wl); 320ft/97.54m (pp).
Beam: 30ft/9.16m.
Draught: 9ft 9in/2.96m (mean).
Machinery: four Kampon boilers; 2-shaft Parsons geared turbines.
Performance: 38,500shp; 37.25kts.
Bunkerage: 420tons/426tonnes.
Range: 4,000nm at 15kts.
Guns: four 4.7in (4×1); two 7.7mm.
Torpedoes: six 24in (2×3).
Mines: 16.
Complement: 150.

Design This class, built under the 1923 programme, was an improved *Kamikaze* type. They were the last to retain the torpedo tubes ahead of the bridge, but introduced both triple mountings and the 24-inch torpedo. The adoption of triple tubes allowed the designers to reduce the number of mountings by one yet retain the same number of torpedoes in the broadside (four reloads were carried), while at the same time conserving valuable deck space. Under these circumstances, it is difficult to understand the retention of the forecastle tubes and not one of the midships banks. Apart from this aspect, the armament remained the same as that of the *Kamikaze* type.

Displacement and hull length were marginally increased, the latter as a result of the adoption of a characteristic double curved bow profile. Internally, machinery arrangements were similar to *Kamikaze*, except that two units, *No. 30* (later *Nagatsuki*) and *No. 23* (later *Yayoi*), received foreign turbines for comparison purposes – Zoelly in *No. 30* and Rateau in *No. 23*. On trials, *No. 30* reached36.3 knots with 40,787shp. On full load displacement, speed was a disappointment, none exceeding 33¼ knots.

Twelve units were ordered, as Nos. *19, 21, 23, 25, 27–34*. Previously first-class destroyers had received odd numbers, second-class even numbers, but with the abandonment of the second-class type, all destroyers from No. *27* were numbered consecutively. All were completed with numbers only, not being named until 1928.

Modifications Half the class, *Satsuki, Minazuki, Fumizuki, Nagatsuki, Kikuzuki* and *Mikazuki* were reconstructed 1935–36 when their hulls were strengthened, funnel caps raked and shields fitted to the torpedo tubes. In 1941–42, many were converted to fast transports with armament reduced to two 4.7-inch guns and ten 25mm but retaining their torpedo tubes. By June 1944, the few survivors had their AA outfits increased to ten 25mm and five 13mm guns.

Service *Mutsuki, Yayoi, Mochizuki* and *Kisaragi*, forming the 30th Division of the 6th Destroyer Flotilla were tasked with the capture of Wake Island in December 1941, supported by the 23rd Division consisting of *Kikuzuki, Uzuki* and *Yuzuki*. In the course of this operation, *Kisaragi* was driven ashore and wrecked by US Army coastal batteries to become the second destroyer lost.

Satsuki, Minazuki, Fumizuki and *Nagatsuki*, forming the 22nd Division, were involved in the Malayan campaign during December 1941 and January 1942. Later, from February on, all three divisions were used in the Dutch East Indies. In May, *Uzuki, Mutsuki, Mochizuki* and *Yayoi* operated off New Guinea, *Kikuzuki* and *Yuzuki* at Tulagi. Here, *Kikuzuki* was sunk by aircraft from the US carrier *Yorktown*. After the fleet reorganization of July 1942, *Yuzuki* was a unit of the 29th Division at Truk with the 4th Fleet while the 30th Division (with *Uzuki* replacing the lost *Kisaragi*) belonged to the 8th Fleet. *Uzuki* was damaged by aircraft at New Guinea in July, but was able to participate in bombardment operations at Guadalcanal with *Mutsuki* and *Yayoi* in August. Counter-attacks by US Marine Corps aircraft, however, sank *Mutsuki*. US and Australian aircraft sank *Yayoi* south of New Britain before the close of the year.

Much of the remainder of their careers was involved with the fighting in the Solomon Islands, serving as fast transports for the garrisons ashore. Early in July 1943, *Mochizuki, Mikazuki* and another destroyer, *Hamakaze*, landed troops in the Kula Gulf and then, in a similar operation the following night, joined by other destroyers including *Satsuki* and *Nagatsuki*, the Japanese force came into action with US forces once more, sinking the USS *Helena* but *Nagatsuki* was damaged and wrecked near Bambari harbour where she was destroyed later the same day by American aircraft. *Mikazuki* was yet another loss, to US Marine Corps' aircraft SSW of Rabaul in October 1943.

Over half the class had therefore been lost by the end of 1943, losses which continued into 1944 with *Fumizuki* being sunk at Truk during a raid by US carrier aircraft in February. In June, *Minazuki*, part of the Japanese forces assigned to the defence of the Marianas, was torpedoed and sunk off Tarakan in the Celebes Sea by *Harder*. This was the only loss to submarine attack by this class. *Uzuki* was also involved in this operation. *Satsuki* was sunk by carrier-based aircraft in Manila Bay in September, leaving only two survivors, and neither of these were afloat by the end of the year. While engaged upon operations north of Cebu, *Uzuki* and *Yuzuki* had a brief engagement with the US destroyer *Coghlan* and then *Uzuki* was torpedoed and sunk by *PT490* and *PT492* while *Yuzuki* fell victim to USMC bombers the same day.

SPECIAL TYPE – FUBUKI CLASS

Ship	Builder	Laid Down	Launched	Commissioned	Fate
35 *Fubuki*	Kosakubu	19 June 26	15 Nov 27	10 Aug 28	Lost 11 Oct 42
36 *Shirayuki*	Yokohama	19 Mar 27	20 Mar 28	18 Dec 28	Lost 3 Mar 43
37 *Hatsuyuki*	Kosakubu	12 April 27	29 Sept 28	30 Mar 29	Lost 17 July 43
38 *Miyuki*	Uraga	30 April 27	26 June 28	29 June 29	Lost 29 June 34
39 *Murakumo*	Fujinagata	25 April 27	27 Sept 28	10 May 29	Lost 12 Oct 42
40 *Shinonome*	Sasebo Dkyd.	12 Aug 26	26 Nov 27	27 May 28	Lost 18 Dec 41
41 *Usugumo*	Ishikawajima	21 Oct 26	26 Dec 27	26 July 28	Lost 7 July 42
42 *Shirakumo*	Fujinagata	27 Oct 26	27 Dec 27	28 July 28	Lost 16 Mar 44
43 *Isonami*	Uraga	18 Oct 26	24 Nov 27	30 June 28	Lost 9 April 43
44 *Uranami*	Sasebo Dkyd.	28 April 27	29 Nov 28	30 June 29	Lost 26 Oct 44
45 *Ayanami*	Fujinagata	20 Jan 28	5 Oct 29	30 April 30	Lost 15 Nov 42
46 *Shikinami*	Kosakubu	6 July 28	22 June 29	24 Dec 29	Lost 12 Sept 44
47 *Asagiri*	Sasebo Dkyd.	12 Dec 28	18 Nov 29	30 June 30	Lost 28 Aug 42
48 *Yugiri*	Kosakubu	1 April 29	12 May 30	3 Dec 30	Lost 25 Nov 43
49 *Amagiri*	Ishikawajima	28 Nov 28	27 Feb 30	10 Nov 30	Lost 23 April 44
50 *Sagiri*	Uraga	28 Mar 29	23 Dec 29	31 Jan 31	Lost 24 Dec 41
51 *Oboro*	Sasebo Dkyd.	29 Nov 29	8 Nov 30	31 Oct 31	Lost 16 Oct 42
52 *Akebono*	Fujinagata	25 Oct 29	7 Nov 30	31 July 31	Lost 13 Nov 44
53 *Sazanami*	Kosakubu	21 Feb 30	6 June 31	19 May 32	Lost 14 Jan 44
54 *Ushio*	Uraga	24 Dec 29	17 Nov 30	14 Nov 31	Broken up Aug 1948

Displacement: 1,750tons/1,778tonnes (standard).
Length: 388ft 6in/118.41m (oa); 378ft 3in/115.3m (wl); 367ft/111.86m (pp).
Beam: 34ft/10.36m.
Draught: 10ft 6in/3.2m (mean).
Machinery: four Kampon-type RO boilers; 2-shaft Kampon impulse geared turbines.
Performance: 50,000shp; 35kts.
Bunkerage: 475tons/482tonnes.
Range: 5,000nm at 14kts.
Guns: six 5in (3×2); two 13mm.
Torpedoes: nine 24in (3×3).
Mines: 18.
Complement: 197.

Design In 1922, Japan became a signatory of the Washington Naval Treaty, but was dissatisfied with the terms which she obtained. Thus while outwardly appearing to adhere to the conditions of the treaty, the Naval General Staff set about examining just what vessels the Navy would require, given that the most likely enemy would be the USA and bearing in mind Japan's island status and dependence upon seaborne trade for her existence. As a result of these deliberations, a total of 144 destroyers was deemed necessary which on an aggregate tonnage of 201,600 tons, allowed the designers an individual displacement figure of 1,400 tons. This figure was quite sufficient to produce a usable destroyer design but Japan was determined to off-set her poor tonnage allocation with quality of construction. In addition, she was aiming for a long-ranged fleet capable of operating far out into the Pacific wastes and was not too worried if, like Germany, she exceeded any treaty restrictions while doing so. As early as October 1922, a proposal had been submitted for a 2,000-ton design armed with two twin 4.7-inch torpedo tubes and capable of 40 knots. It was not until February 1924, however, that this proposal was converted into a specific design (F24) and by this time, an extra triple bank of torpedo tubes had been worked in, speed reduced to 39 knots with a radius of action of 4,000 nautical miles at 14 knots. The provision of 24-inch torpedoes was the result of their complete success in *Mutsuki* and were to give these new destroyers a tremendous punch. Nine reload torpedoes further increased their fighting power. This design caused some discussion and dissention within staff circles for the displacement was well in excess of that allowed under the treaty, and the numbers of destroyers which could be built would be far less than the 144 units considered necessary by the Navy. Further studies were then made, which resulted in the displacement being reduced by 250 tons, while at the same time an extra twin 5-inch gun had been worked in although the Navy had merely specified a reduction of displacement at *no loss* of fire-power. There was naturally a cost incurred, for speed was reduced by one knot through the specification of less powerful machinery, and the reduction of magazine capacity by 10 per cent. This design was not approved either and further changes had to be made, principally by installing only 50,000shp for a maximum speed of 35 knots. There was, however, a positive trade-off in that endurance increased by 20 per cent because bunkerage was increased. Armament was now to be six 5-inch in twin mounts, one 3-inch AA, two 40mm, two 7.7mm machine-guns and nine 24-inch torpedo tubes.

There were several noteworthy aspects of this finalized design, known as the 'Special Type'. The main armament was shipped in weatherproof gunhouses with some splinter protection, never before

Below: *Shikinami* in 1929. (IWM)

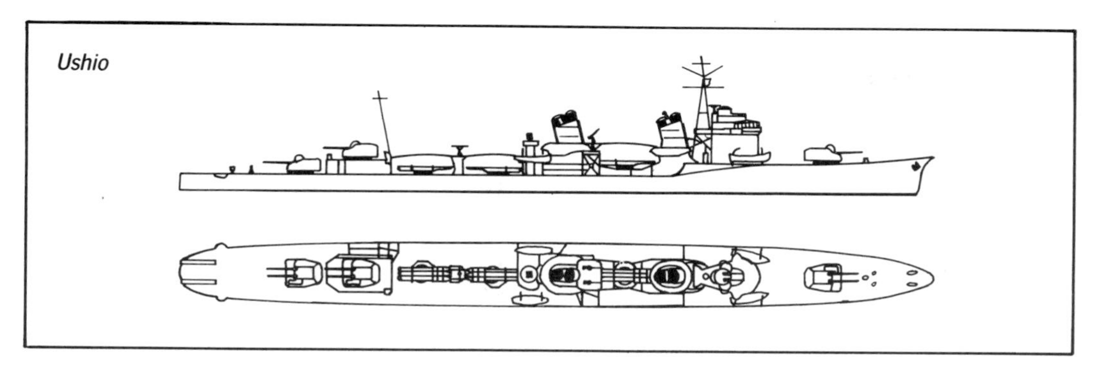

done on destroyer-sized vessels. The guns were of a new calibre for Japanese destroyers, 5-inch, but were themselves a 1914-pattern 50cal model. In the first ten units, the 'Type A' twin mountings were fitted, which had only 40° elevation. Subsequent units received the 'Type B' mounting with 75° elevation. The gun was a B.L. model, firing a 51lb projectile with a range of 20,100 yards. Elevation and training were electro-powered oil-hydraulic, but poor tracking speeds meant that despite the good elevation, the mountings were unsatisfactory for AA purposes. The torpedo tubes hitherto fitted forward of the bridge were moved aft to a far better position between the funnels, where they were much less affected by seawater. The removal of these tubes allowed the forecastle to be extended farther aft which, together with the flare and sheer of the forward ends made for enhanced seakeeping properties. Open ocean employment was further improved by the provision of a covered bridge of considerable height, made necessary by the bulky gun-house on the forecastle.

The main machinery, a single reduction geared turbine installation, developed 50,000shp, i.e., 3 per cent more than the previous standard destroyer machinery. Four boilers, each in its own space, provided steam for the turbines.

While under construction, the elderly 40mm Vickers-pattern guns were deleted, as were the 7.7mm machine-guns and replaced by two 13.2mm guns, but as the latter were not yet available the 7.7mm guns were shipped instead.

Five units were authorized under the 1923 programme as numbers 35 to 39 and four more (40–43) specially authorized in November 1925. After some delay due to financial problems, authorization was finally granted under the 1927 programme for fifteen more ships to be laid down, two 1927–28, five 1928–29, four 1929–30 and 1930–31.

Because construction was extended over a period of more than five years, there were naturally modifications made within that time. The first group (35–44) received the LA 5-inch guns, had lower and less elaborate fire-control systems atop the bridge and had conspicuous boiler room air intakes abreast the funnels. The second group received the modified 'Type B' HA gun-house, more elaborate fire-control stations with an extra level above the bridge, and modified, less conspicuous boiler room air intakes. These ships were Nos. 45–54. Finally, improvements in boiler design by 1927 allowed the last four units to ship only three boilers instead of four, this being outwardly apparent by the thinner forward funnel of this quartet. The forward boiler room could therefore be adapted for other purposes. They also carried shields to the torpedo control platform.

When the first unit, *Fubuki*, came into service in August 1928, the appearance of power given by these destroyers greatly worried contemporary naval powers, particularly the USA and Great Britain, for the former had no destroyers more modern than the 1917-vintage '4-pipers' and the latter's *A*-class destroyers were far outclassed, even without taking into consideration the fact that the USA and Britain had no knowledge of the existence and capabilities of the 24-inch torpedo. All was not as it seemed, however, and although western naval architects must have had some doubts as to the declared displacement of these destroyers, considering their heavy armament, they cannot have been aware of the weaknesses inherent in them.

To achieve the heavy demands made by the Fleet in terms of speed, armament and range on a restricted displacement, the design departments had to exercise great ingenuity. Weight had to be reduced by every possible means, in particular by installing lighter and less powerful machinery, the use of light alloys for superstructures and extensive use of welding for the hulls. Butt jointing was employed for bottom plates in lieu of the more common lap-joint to reduce hull friction and increase speed. However, weight always seems to increase when a ship is building, be it British, American or Japanese, and the 'Special Type' were no exception. The longer forecastle, high bridge and gun-houses resulted in an increase of 200 tons on the designed displacement for Group 1 ships. The matter was even worse in subsequent ships, because the 'Type B' gun-house weight was 20 per cent more than that of the 'Type A' and their bridges had an extra deck level. When shields were added to the tubes a further growth in displacement ensued. Considered together with the lighter weight of machinery low down in the ship and reduced magazine stowage, this increased top-weight must have given rise to concern among Japanese designers, and inclination tests should have shown how close to the wind they were sailing.

That something was manifestly wrong with new Japanese warships did not become obvious until 12 March 1934 when the torpedo-boat *Tomozuru* capsized in heavy weather during exercises only three weeks after her completion. Following examination and investigation of the incident it was concluded that an increase in top-weight combined with an increase in displacement without compensating increase in beam had been responsible for the loss. It was obvious that the new destroyers were also suspect in this respect, but before anything could be done about it, in July 1935, the Fleet began exercises off the east coast of Japan. In the course of these exercises, the 4th Fleet was struck by a typhoon on 26 September when both *Hatsuyuki* and *Yugiri* lost their bows. *Akebono, Murakumo* and *Ushio* suffered severe structural damage and *Shirakumo, Amagiri, Oboro, Shirayuki* and *Usugumo* damage to their hulls to various degrees. Although none were lost, it demonstrated the structural weaknesses in these 'Special Type' destroyers.

The outcome of these experiences was a major and drastic programme of reconstruction applied to all new ships completed in the late 1920s and early 1930s. In the case of the 'Special Type' this involved docking all the destroyers between 1937 and 1938 when bridges and funnels were cut down, magazine stowage reduced and bunkerage increased (to add weight low down). Reload torpedoes were reduced to three only, for the centre tubes, and the eight later units of the class were given a new 'Type C' gun-house which was lighter but had only 55° elevation. In addition to this weight reduction, all hulls had to be greatly strengthened by riveting and rewelding. The result was an increase in displacement to 2,090 tons and a reduction in speed of 1 knot, but the destroyers were now fully effective and some of the best in the world.

Modifications The 'Special Type' were equipped to carry the 24-inch 'long lance' oxygen-fuelled torpedoes from their reconstruction (but it would seem that these were not always shipped), and shields had been fitted to the tubes in 1932–33. During hostilities, the light AA was progressively improved by the addition of numerous 25mm guns. Fitment of this calibre had begun in 1937 when two twin mountings were added. In 1942–43 and probably the latter part of this period, 'X' mount was removed and replaced by two triple 25mm mountings. Total 25mm outfit was now fourteen guns, with four 13.2mm machine-guns. By mid 1944, this had been increased in the survivors (of which there were only twelve), to twenty-two 25mm and six to ten 13.2mm guns, but it is not known if all ever received this outfit in full. Late in the war, radar began to be fitted, *Ushio* receiving a Type 13 set on the mainmast.

Service Only 23 ships started the war because *Miyuki* had been sunk in collision with *Inazuma* on 15 August 1934 while on exercises south-west of the Korean Straits.

Most of these destroyers belonged to the 3rd Destroyer Flotilla at the outbreak of war, tasked with the occupation of Malaya. They were organized as follows: 12th Division (*Murakumo, Shinonome, Shirakumo, Usugumo*), 19th Division (*Isonami, Uranami, Shikinami, Ayanami*), 20th Division (*Isonami, Uranami, Shikinami, Ayanami*), 20th Division (*Amagiri, Asagiri, Yugiri*). Also involved was *Sagiri* and the 11th Division consisting of *Fubuki, Hatsuyuki* and *Shirayuki*. Two others formed a separate group for a different task, the shelling of Midway Island. These were *Akebono* and *Uhio*.

During the Malayan occupation, *Uranami* sank the Dutch submarine *020* on 20 December and her sisters *K XVII* on 24 December. On the other hand, a Dutch flying-boat torpedoed and sank *Shinonome* while *K XV* sank *Sagiri*. Moving to the Dutch East Indies in 1942, the flotilla covered the invasion and became embroiled with Allied counter-attacks when *Perth* and *Houston* raided their bridgehead on 29 February 1942. *Fubuki* launched an unsuccessful torpedo attack on the Allied cruisers then called up reinforcements including the cruisers *Natori, Mikuma* and *Mogami* as well as several of her flotilla mates. *Shirakumo* and *Murakumo* were probably responsible for the crucial torpedo hits on both Allied cruisers and later wrecked the Dutch destroyer *Evertsen* with gunfire before she was driven ashore. Both *Shirakumo* and *Shikinami* were damaged during this action.

After the conquest of the East Indies, the flotilla moved into the Indian Ocean, taking part in anti-shipping strikes into the Bay of Bengal in April. During the course of these, the 20th Division (as listed earlier plus *Shirakumo*) together with heavy cruisers, sank many merchant ships off the Indian coast.

In May 1942, the 7th Division (*Akebono, Sazanami* and *Ushio*) were operating in the Coral Sea, *Sazanami* rescuing the survivors of the sunken *Shoho*. Later this division transferred to the north Pacific and sailed on a diversionary raid to the Aleutian Islands at the time of the Midway actions. The 11th and 12th Divisions formed the screen for Admiral Yamamoto's Midway Support Group, while the 20th Division did likewise for the Aleutian Support Group of Vice-Admiral Takasu. After Midway, the 11th, 19th and 20th Divisions served with the 1st Fleet, *Oboro* and *Usugumo* were with the 5th Fleet in the Aleutians and the 7th Division was with Admiral Yamamoto's Combined Fleet.

In August, while carrying troops from Borneo to Guadalcanal, the 20th Division (*Asagiri, Shirakumo, Yugiri* and *Amagiri*) was attacked by USMC dive-bombers when *Asagiri* was sunk, two others severely damaged and *Amagiri* slightly. The 11th Division also took part in these operations and units of the 19th Division were with the Carrier Force of Admiral Nagumo. These units were all engaged upon the supply line to Guadalcanal into September when *Murakumo, Hatsuyuki* and *Yudachi* engaged and sank the American APDs *Gregory* and *Little*. October proved a fateful month: *Fubuki* was sunk by US cruisers and destroyers of Task Group 64.2 off Cape Esperance and *Hatsuyuki* was damaged. *Murakumo*, loaded with survivors, was sunk by US dive-bombers the next day. Finally to the north, *Oboro*, still in the Aleutians, was bombed and sunk north-east of Kiska.

Action continued off Guadalcanal in November when on 14th/15th, strong US and Japanese forces clashed south of Savo Island, in 'Iron Bottom' Sound. The USN lost three destroyers and the Japanese the battleship *Kirishima* as well as the destroyer *Ayanami* sunk by the USS *Washington*. Operations off Guadalcanal ceased on 9 February 1943. Transport and army support operations continued, however, this time in aid of forces in New Guinea. Escorting a group of transports from

Below: *Ayanami*. (IWM)

Rabaul to Lae, *Shirayuki* was one of four destroyers and eight transports sunk in the Bismarck Sea by US and Australian aircraft in March 1943. *Isonami* was the next to go, this time by torpedoes from the US submarine *Tautog* south-east of Celebes.

In July 1943, *Amagiri* and *Hatsuyuki*, running troops with other destroyers in the Kula Gulf, were engaged and damaged by US TG36.1 and then the former again by the destroyers *Nicholas* and *Radford*. Shortly afterwards, *Hatsuyuki* was sunk by US Navy aircraft off Bougainville. During the course of one of her supply runs, *Amagiri* sank *PT109*. *Yugiri* was another loss on transport operations, sunk in action with five US destroyers off New Ireland. 1944 saw a series of submarine successes against the 'Special Type', over a wide area of the Pacific. First to go was *Sazanami*, torpedoed by *Albacore* south of Yap, then *Shirakumo* off Hokkaido by *Tautog*. *Amagiri* which, with two sisters, had briefly transferred to the Indian Ocean, was mined off Borneo in April and *Usugumo* fell to a torpedo from *Skate* far to the north in the Sea of Okhotsk. *Shikinami* was torpedoed by *Growler* in the South China Sea. *Uranami* and *Akebono* were both lost in the Philippines, the former by US TG 77.4.2 and the latter by aircraft of TF38 in Manila Bay. The day after the loss of *Akebono*, *Ushio* was badly damaged in a repeat attack but towed to Japan for repairs. These were not completed by the surrender and she was broken up in 1948, the only unit of her class to survive hostilities.

SPECIAL TYPE – AKATSUKI CLASS

Ship	Builder	Laid Down	Launched	Commissioned	Fate
55 *Akatsuki*	Sasebo Dkyd.	17 Feb 30	7 May 32	30 Nov 32	Lost 13 Nov 42
56 *Hibiki*	Kosakubu	21 Feb 30	16 June 32	31 Mar 33	To USSR 1947
57 *Ikazuchi*	Uraga	7 Mar 30	22 Oct 31	15 Aug 32	Lost 14 April 44
58 *Inazuma*	Fujinagata	7 Mar 30	25 Mar 32	15 Nov 32	Lost 14 May 44

Displacement: 1,680tons/1,706tonnes (standard).
Length: 388ft 9in/118.4m (oa); 371ft 9in/113.3m (wl); 350ft/106.68m (pp).
Beam: 34ft/10.36m.
Draught: 10ft 9in/3.28m (mean).
Machinery: three Kampon-type RO boilers; 2-shaft Kampon impulse geared turbines.
Performance: 50,000shp; 38kts.
Bunkerage: 475tons/482tonnes.
Range: 5,000nm at 14kts.
Guns: six 5in (3×2); two 13mm.
Torpedoes: nine 24in (3×3).
Mines: 18.
Complement: 197.

Design 'Special Type' destroyers, built under the 1927 programme. They differed from the other 'Specials' by having only three boilers and, in consequence, a thinner forward funnel. They also had shorter hulls and displaced slightly less than the earlier vessels, *Hibiki* being the first fully-welded ship in the IJN. In service they were found to be affected by the same problems as *Fubuki* and were modified in a similar manner.

Modifications Like *Fubuki*, *Hibiki* had twenty-eight 25mm guns in total by the end of the war.

Service All four units formed the 6th Destroyer Division in December 1941. Two, *Ikazuchi* and *Inazuma* were with the battlecruisers *Taruna* and *Kongo* in the South China Sea and the other pair joined later. All served in the invasion of Malaya and in the Dutch East Indies 1941–42 and later at Midway. After Midway, all except *Hibiki* went to the Aleutian Islands, but in September 1942, were back with the 4th Destroyer Flotilla running supplies to Guadalcanal. Still in the Guadalcanal area in November, *Akatsuki*, *Ikazuchi* and *Inazuma* were with Admiral Abe's force which sank the US cruiser *Atlanta* (credited to *Akatsuki*), and four destroyers (*Laffey*, *Barton*, *Monssen* and *Cushing*) in Iron Bottom Sound but at the cost of two destroyers, including *Akatsuki*. In 1943, *Ikazuchi* and *Inazuma* were in the Komandorski Islands and in July, participated with *Hibiki* in the evacuation of the Aleutians. The following year they were relegated to escort duties with the fleet train. *Ikazuchi* was torpedoed and sunk south-south-east of Guam by *Harder*, and *Inazuma* by *Bonefish* east of Borno. *Hibiki*, damaged by a mine on 29 April 1945, survived the war and was later (5 April 1947) ceded to the Soviet Union.

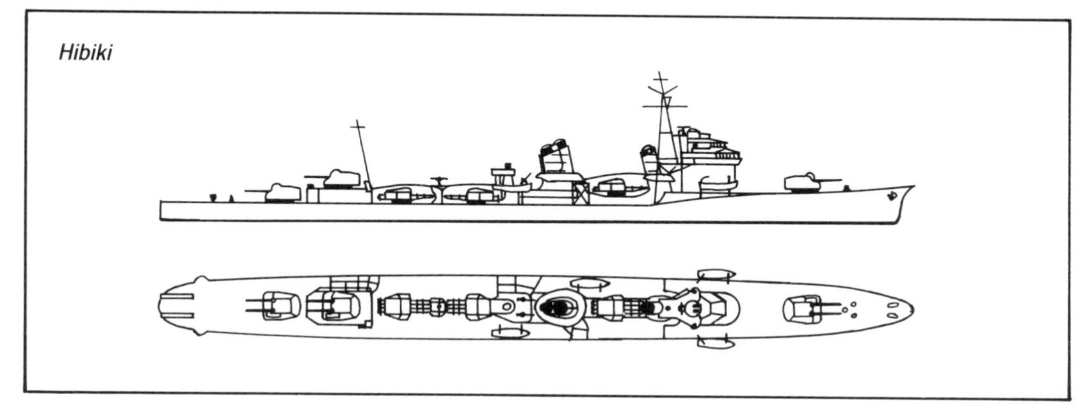
Hibiki

Below: *Inazuma* in 1936. (IWM)

HATSUHARU CLASS

Ship	Builder	Laid Down	Launched	Commissioned	Fate
59 *Ariake*	Kawasaki, Kobe	14 Jan 33	23 Sept 34	25 Mar 35	Lost 28 July 43
60 *Hatsuharu*	Sasebo Dkyd.	14 May 31	27 Feb 33	30 Sept 33	Lost 13 Nov 44
61 *Hatsushimo*	Uraga	31 Jan 33	4 Nov 33	27 Sept 34	Lost 30 July 45
62 *Nenohi*	Uraga	15 Dec 31	22 Dec 32	30 Sept 33	Lost 4 July 42
63 *Wakaba*	Sasebo Dkyd.	12 Dec 31	18 Mar 34	31 Oct 34	Lost 24 Oct 44
64 *Yugure*	Kosakubu	9 April 33	6 May 34	30 Mar 35	Lost 20 July 43

Displacement: 1,490tons/1,513tonnes (standard); 1,802tons/1,830tonnes (full load).
Length: 359ft 3in/109.5m (oa); 346ft 1in/105.5m (wl); 339ft 7in/103.5m (pp).
Beam: 32ft 10in/10m.
Draught: 9ft 11in/3.03m (mean).
Machinery: three Kampon boilers; 2-shaft geared turbines.
Performance: 42,000shp; 36.5kts.
Bunkerage: 500tons/508tonnes.
Range: 6,000nm at 15kts.
Guns: five 5in (2×2, 1×1); two 13mm.
Torpedoes: nine 24in (3×3).
Complement: 200.

Design The *Hatsuharu* class was essentially a product of the London Naval Treaty of 1930, for this restricted maximum individual destroyer tonnage to 1,850 tons, but allowed only 16 per cent to be of this figure. The remainder had to be 1,500 tons maximum. This meant that building of the 'Special Type' could no longer be continued, a serious blow to Japanese naval planning. However, by dint of great ingenuity and detailed attention to weight saving, the designers succeeded in producing a design which carried only one gun less than the 'Special Type' and, moreover, was fitted with a properly designed system for reloading the torpedo tubes. Nevertheless, despite all the attention given to reduction in weight, displacement exceeded the design limits. Light displacement was some 260 tons less than that of the 'Special Type', with a shorter and less beamy hull. Visually, these destroyers, as first completed, looked top-heavy and so they were, for not only was the high built-up bridge retained, but a superimposed (single) gun-house was added forward of it (the first time in Japanese destroyers), and the third bank of tubes was fitted in a raised position on the after shelter deck where, with its reloads, it virtually negated the weight saving of the removal of No. 2 gun-house. The *Hatsuharu* class were, incidentally, the first destroyers to be equipped with the oxygen-propelled version of the 24-inch torpedo. All this top-weight allied to a narrower hull should have caused the stability to be questioned, but it would appear that when completed, the stability of the leading ships was judged satisfactory.

The *Hatsuharu* class introduced the Type 'B' gun-house for their 5-inch guns, allowing 55° elevation, but at some cost to weight. Otherwise, the armament remained as in *Fubuki* except, as noted earlier, the reduction of one 5-inch gun and the provision of oxygen-fuelled torpedoes.

Lighter and less powerful machinery was adopted with 16 per cent less shaft horse power resulting in a drop in speed of 1½ knots. Radius of action, however, increased on the same bunker capacity.

Twelve units were provided for under the 1931 programme. At the time of the *Tomozuru* disaster, only *Hatsuharu* and *Nenohi* had been completed, whereupon their stability was at once re-examined and found wanting. Two others were well advanced and the others less so. Construction of this class was halted after six units and the design was recast.

Modifications The major structional alterations applied to *Hatsuharu, Nenohi, Wakaba* and *Hatsushimo* during 1935–37 involved the removal of the single superfiring gun and deck-house forward and the after bank of tubes. Superstructure, funnels and masting were cut down and 84 tonnes of ballast resorted to. The after deck-house was rebuilt and shortened to allow the single gun-house to be reshipped on the upper deck, back to back with the after twin mounting. Displacement increased to

Left: *Hatsushimo*. (IWM)

Top right: *Nenohi* after reconstruction. (A. D. Baker)

Bottom right: *Ariake* in 1938. (A. D. Baker)

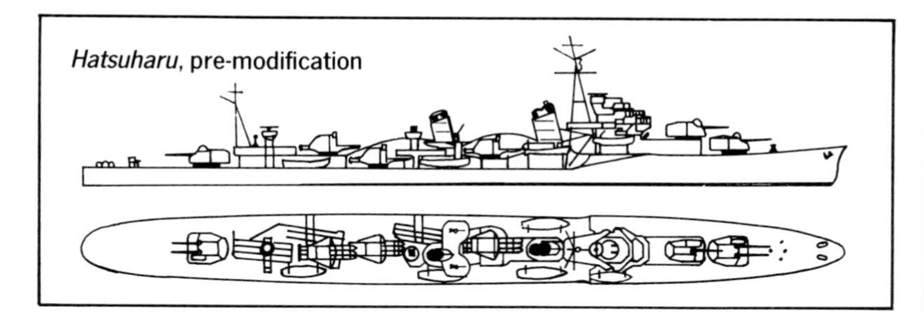
Hatsuharu, pre-modification

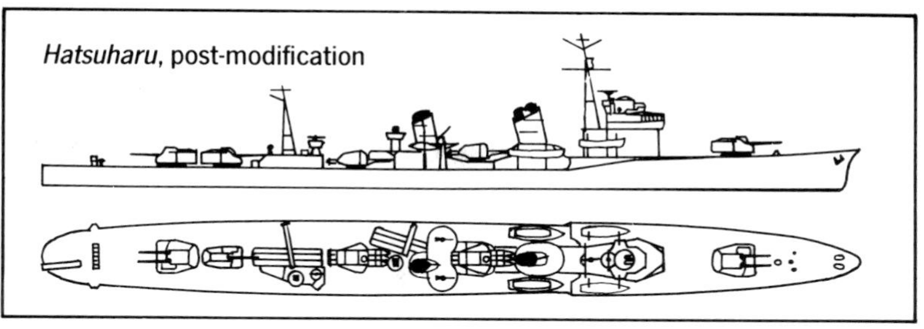
Hatsuharu, post-modification

2,099 tons full load and in consequence, speed dropped a further three knots. The last two units (*Arake* and *Yugure*) were completed to a slightly modified version of this refit.

These modifications raised the metacentric height from .588m to .80m and lowered the centre of gravity from 1.232m to .486m. Draught increased by .34m.

During the war, all except *Nenohi* had the single gun removed, when it was supplanted by two triple 25mm mountings, and the 25mm outfit increased to a total of between thirteen and twenty-one guns. The reload gear for the after tubes were also landed. Type 13 radar was added on some units.

Service These destroyers formed the 21st and (*Ariake* and *Yugure*) 18th Destroyer Divisions at the end of 1941. The 21st Division took part in operations in the Philippines early in 1942, where *Hatsuharu* was damaged by US aircraft off Celebes in January. In February and March, the 18th Division participated in the invasion of Java and in May were part of Rear-Admiral Hara's carrier force in the New Guinea/Tulagi area. The 21st Division went to the Aleutians in May, while the 18th Division ships escorted the Midway Invasion Fleet. In the Aleutians, *Nenohi* was torpedoed and sunk by *Titon* at Agatt in July.

After the Fleet reorganization of July 1942, *Ariake* and *Wakaba* now became part of the 27th Division of the 4th Destroyer Flotilla with Admiral Kondo's 2nd Fleet. Their sisters remained in Aleutian waters. For the remainder of 1942, the 27th Division operated in support of the Guadalcanal actions latterly as part of the 2nd Destroyer Flotilla. In 1943, they continued operations in the Solomon Islands. *Yugure* was damaged in May by a torpedo from *Grayback* but following repair, saw action at the battle of Kolombangara in July. Both were lost in July; *Ariake* ran ashore on a reef near Cape Gloucester and was destroyed by US bombers the following day, while *Yugure* was sunk by USMC aircraft in Vella Lavella Gulf.

To the north, in the Aleutians, *Wakaba* and *Hatsushimo* were present at the action off the Komandonski Islands in March 1943, when they unsuccessfully launched twelve torpedoes at the damaged US cruiser *Salt Lake City*. Upon the evacuation of the islands in July, when both destroyers were damaged in accidents, the surviving members of the class moved south to operate in the Formosa/Philippines/Leyte area, taking part in the defence of the Marianas and the battle of the Philippine Sea. In October 1944, *Wakaba* was sunk by aircraft from *Franklin* off the west coast of Panay at the time of the Suriago Strait action. The following month, *Hatsuharu* was lost to US carrier aircraft of *TF38* in Manila Bay. The last survivor, *Hatsushimo*, took part in the last sortie by the battleship *Yamato* in April 1945, before falling victim to a mine off Maizuru in July.

SHIRATSUYU CLASS

Ship	Builder	Laid Down	Launched	Commissioned	Fate
Shiratsuyu	Sasebo Dkyd.	14 Nov 33	5 April 35	20 Aug 36	Lost 14 June 44
Shigure	Uraga	9 Dec 33	18 May 35	7 Sept 36	Lost 24 Jan 45
Murasame	Fujinagata	1 Feb 34	20 June 35	7 Jan 37	Lost 6 Mar 42
Yudachi	Sasebo Dkyd.	16 Oct 34	21 June 36	7 Jan 37	Lost 13 Nov 42
Samidare	Uraga	19 Dec 34	6 July 35	29 Jan 37	Lost 25 Aug 44
Harusame	Uraga	3 Feb 35	21 Sept 35	26 Aug 37	Lost 8 June 44
Yamakaze	Uraga	25 May 35	21 Feb 36	30 Jan 37	Lost 25 June 42
Kawakaze	Fujinagata	25 April 35	1 Nov 36	30 April 37	Lost 6 Aug 43
Umikaze	Kosakubu	4 May 35	27 Nov 36	31 May 37	Lost 1 Feb 44
Suzukaze	Uraga	9 July 35	11 Mar 37	31 Aug 37	Lost 26 Jan 44

Displacement: 1,685tons/1,712tonnes (standard); 1,980tons/2,011tonnes (full load).
Length: 352ft 8in/107.5m (wl); 339ft 7in/103.5m (pp).
Beam: 32ft 6in/9.9m.
Draught: 11ft 6in/3.5m (mean).
Machinery: three Kampon boilers; 2-shaft geared turbines.
Performance: 42,000shp; 34kts.
Bunkerage: 500tons/508tonnes.
Range: 6,000nm at 15kts.
Guns: five 5in (2×2, 1×1); two 13mm.
Torpedoes: eight 24in (2×4).
Complement: 180.

Design Formerly intended as *Hatsuharu*-class destroyers, these ships were redesigned in the light of the *Tomozuru* incident and emerged as a separate class to which four more units were added under the 1934 programme. They were very similar to the *Hatsuharu* class, but had less beam and greater draft. Bridge structures were considerably reduced and the design included the single gun aft of the rebuilt *Hatsuharu*s. Torpedo armament, however, was improved in that for the first time quadruple tubes were carried. Reload torpedoes for the forward tubes were now stowed two on each side of the after funnel thus eliminating the characteristic asymmetrical funnel placings of the *Hatsuharu*s. Gun-houses were Type 'C' with 55° elevation. The 42,000shp power plant was retained for a maximum speed of 34 knots. The last four (1934) ships incorporated various improvements making them somewhat similar to the following *Asashio* class.

Modifications As *Hatsuharu*.

Service Initially employed escorting forces bound for the invasion of the Philippines, this class formed two full and one part destroyer divisions, the 2nd (*Murasame, Yudachi, Harusame* and *Samidare*) and 22nd (*Umikaze, Yamakaze, Kawakaze* and *Suzukaze*) with the two spare ships being *Shigure* and *Shiratsuyu*, later part of the 27th Division. Early in 1942, during operations in the Dutch East Indies, *Yamakaze* sank the Dutch minelayer *Prins Van Orange* near Tarakan, but in February *Suzukaze* was damaged by a torpedo from the US submarine *Salmon*. The 2nd Division, plus *Umikaze, Kawakaze* and *Yamakaze*, participated in the invasion of Java in February 1942. There, in the course of the Battle of the Java Sea, *Yamakaze, Kawakaze, Murusame, Samidare* and *Yudachi* made torpedo attacks on the Allied squadron but without success. All units participated in the Midway operations, the 2nd Division with the main body of the Invasion Fleet, the remainder with the Aleutians Support Group. *Yamakaze* returned to home waters in June only to be torpedoed and sunk by *Nautilus* off Yokosuka. In recompense, *Kawakaze* torpedoed *Blue* in Savo Sound in August. Before the end of the year, the fighting around Guadalcanal claimed another victim, *Yudachi*, part of a bombardment force of Japanese ships which fought a night engagement south-east of Savo Island with a US cruiser and destroyer group. *Yudachi* was badly hit by gunfire and abandoned by her crew who were rescued by *Samidare*. At daybreak, the shattered

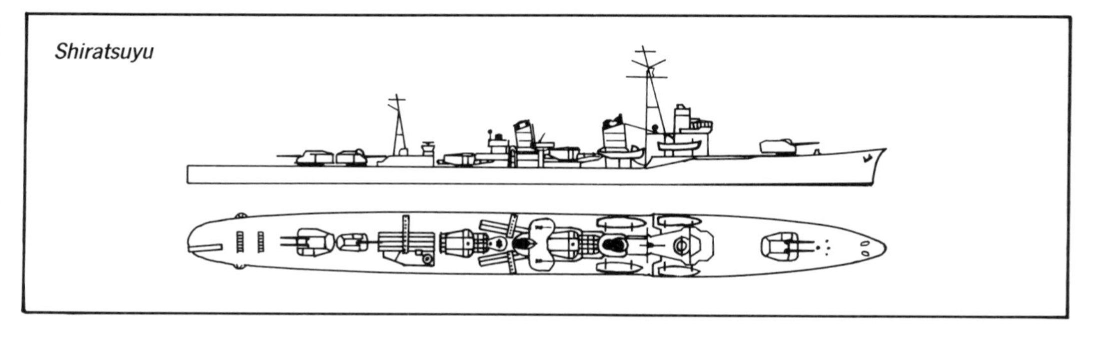
Shiratsuyu

Below: *Umikaze*. (IWM)

hulk was shelled and sunk by the cruiser *Portland*. *Murasame* which, with *Minegumo*, had left Faisi to run supplies to Vila, sank the US submarine *Grampus*, but was caught by a US cruiser-destroyer force in the Kula Gulf in March 1943. Shelled to a wreck, *Murasame* was finally sent to the bottom by a torpedo from *Waller*. *Minegumo* was also sunk.

In August 1943, *Kawakaze* was one of four destroyers running supplies and troops from Bougainville to Kolombangara. This force was intercepted by radar-equipped US destroyers of Destroyer Divisions 12 and 15 in Vella Gulf. Taken by surprise, the Japanese force was decimated, with only *Shigure* escaping. *Kawakaze* hit by torpedoes and shells, capsized and sank. 1944 saw the loss of all but one of the remaining units of the class, *Suzukaze* being torpedoed and sunk by the submarine *Skipjack* south of New Britain in January and *Umikaze* south of Truk in February by *Guardfish*. US aircraft sank *Harusame* near the Dampier Straits off New Guinea and *Shiratsuyu* was lost by collision with the tanker *Seiyo Maru* off the Surigao Strait, both in June. *Shigure*, as part of Vice-Admiral Nishimura's Southern Force at the battle of Leyte, fought in the action in the Surigao Strait on 24/25 October 1944 when she was the only survivor of a force of two battleships, a cruiser and four destroyers. She was not finally sunk until January 1945, by a torpedo from *Blackfin* off the east coast of Malaya, near Khota Bharu.

ASASHIO CLASS

Ship	Builder	Laid Down	Launched	Commissioned	Fate
Asashio	Sasebo Dkyd.	7 Sept 35	16 Dec 36	31 Aug 37	Lost 4 Mar 43
Oshio	Kosakubu	5 Aug 36	19 April 37	31 Oct 37	Lost 20 Feb 43
Michishio	Fujinagata	5 Nov 35	15 Mar 37	31 Oct 37	Lost 25 Oct 44
Arashio	Kawasaski, Kobe	1 Oct 35	26 May 37	20 Dec 37	Lost 4 Mar 43
Natsugumo	Sasebo Dkyd.	1 July 36	26 May 37	10 Feb 38	Lost 12 Oct 42
Yamagumo	Fujinagata	4 Nov 36	24 July 37	15 Jan 38	Lost 25 Oct 44
Minegumo	Fujinagata	22 Mar 36	4 Nov 37	30 April 38	Lost 5 Mar 43
Asagumo	Kawasaki, Kobe	23 Dec 36	5 Nov 37	31 Mar 38	Lost 25 Oct 44
Arare	Kosakubu	5 Mar 37	16 Nov 37	15 April 38	Lost 5 July 42
Kasumi	Uraga	1 Dec 36	18 Nov 37	28 June 38	Lost 7 April 45

Displacement: 1,961tons/1,992tonnes (standard); 2,370tons/2,512tonnes (full load).
Length: 388ft/118.26m (oa); 377ft 4in/115m (wl); 364ft 2in/111m (pp).
Beam: 33ft 11in/10.35m.
Draught: 12ft 1in/3.69m (mean).
Machinery: three Kampon boilers; 2-shaft geared turbines.
Performance: 50,000shp; 35kts.
Bunkerage: 500tons/508tonnes.
Range: 5,700nm at 10kts.
Guns: six 5in (3×2); four 25mm.
Torpedoes: eight 24in (2×4).
Complement: 200.

Design With the weight and stability problems of the 'Special Type' having been rectified in the *Shirasuyu* class at some cost in speed and fire power, the Japanese naval staff decided to consolidate this success by regaining the properties sacrificed. This could naturally only be done by an increase in displacement beyond the limits of the London Naval Treaty, but because Japan had made the (unpublished) decision to withdraw from this treaty, this presented no particular problems. The new destroyers were designed to carry the same battery as the 'Special Type', i.e., six 5-inch in twin gunhouses (Type 'C' 55°) and, to ensure stability and strength, beam was increased by almost 1½ feet with displacement rising by about 400 tons. They were nearly 25 feet longer on the waterline and the increased beam allowed the after guns to be superfiring. Installed power was once again pushed back up to 50,000shp with more advanced turbines giving an increase in maximum speed to 35 knots. The torpedo battery remained eight 24-inch, with eight reload torpedoes, but the AA outfit was enhanced by the shipping of the new 25mm Hotchkiss gun in two twin mountings abreast the after funnel.

Japan had not, however, produced the perfect destroyer. Two defects were to manifest themselves with the *Asashio* class. In the first place, the rudder design was inefficient leading to very poor manoeuvrability and a large turning circle. To rectify this, the stern shape was altered to transom giving at the same time a slight increase in speed. Later, further problems were found with the new-design turbines, when blade stripping was experienced. Not until 1943 was the root cause of this defect established. Ten ships were ordered to this design under the 1934 programme.

Modifications In about 1941, the stern was altered to cure the problems described above. By 1943–44 survivors had No. 2 gun-house removed and AA outfits increased to fifteen 25mm, but by June 1944 the 25mm fit had risen to about 28 guns. Displacement rose to 2,635 tons full load, despite the removal of the reload torpedoes. Four depth-charge throwers and 36 depth-charges were added.

Service In November 1941, *Arare* and *Kasumi* formed part of the screen for the aircraft carriers bound for Pearl Harbor. The following month, the 4th Division (*Asagumo, Minegumo* and *Natsugumo*) covered the Philippines assault force while the 8th Division (*Asashio, Oshio, Michishio* and *Arashio*) were in the South China Sea with the Malay Assault force. Finally *Yamagumo* was part of the Bataan invasion group. Early in 1942, both divisions transferred to the Dutch East Indies. Here, on 19 February 1942, *Asashio, Oshio* and *Michishio* sank the Dutch *Piet Hein* in Bandoeng Strait while defending the invasion fleet from a Dutch/US force. Both *Oshio* and *Michishio* were damaged on this occasion. Later, several units participated in the main Java Sea action, 27/28 February, when *Asagumo* and *Minegumo* launched unsuccessful torpedo attacks. However, they engaged the British *Electra* and *Encounter* when *Asagumo* was badly hit by *Electra* but in turn so badly damaged *Electra* that the British destroyer sank.

Units of the 8th and 9th (formerly the 4th) Divisions supported the Midway operations in June 1942, but in July *Arare* and *Kasumi* were in the Aleutian Islands where they were hit by torpedoes from *Growler* when *Arare* sank. In October, *Natsugumo* was a casualty of the Guadalcanal battles when she was sunk by US dive-bombers while rescuing survivors of *Furutaka* and *Fubiki* off Savo Island.

Early in 1943, *Oshio* was torpedoed and sunk by *Albacore* north-west of Manus Island, but a more

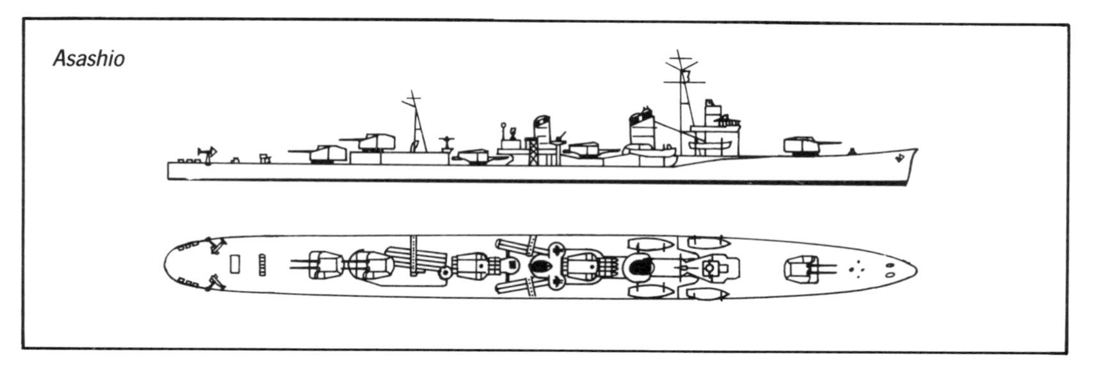
Asashio

Above: *Asagumo.* (IWM)

serious disaster overtook these destroyers in March. *Arashio* and *Asahio* were part of a force of eight destroyers and eight transports running troops from Rabaul to Lae which was caught and annihilated by US and Australian aircraft in the Bismarck Sea. Both these destroyers and all the transports as well as two other destroyers were sunk. Two days later *Minegumo*, running supplies to Vila, was sunk in the Kula Gulf by *TF68*.

Only *Asagumo, Michishio* and *Yamagumo* now remained afloat. *Michishio* one of a force of four destroyers running supplies to New Georgia in May 1943, was the only ship to escape, albeit heavily damaged by aircraft, after the others had run on to a mine barrage. *Asagumo* was involved in the evacuation of the Aleutians in July, but by the autumn of the year, all three survivors were transferred to the Rabaul area to support the Solomons campaign. *Yamagumo* was slightly damaged by carrier aircraft on New Year's Day, 1944 while so employed. All three units were involved in the defence of the Marianas in the late spring and early summer of 1944, *Michishio* and *Yamagumo* with the 4th Destroyer Division and *Asagumo* with the 10th, attached to the 3rd Aircraft Carrier Squadron. These three destroyers were also with Vice-Admiral Nishimura's Southern Force at the Leyte Gulf engagements, where, in the battle of the Surigao Strait on the night of 25/25 October 1944, all were sunk. These were first, *Yamagumo*, torpedoed in the opening minutes, sinking quickly afterwards, then *Michishio*, also struck by a torpedo, staggered out of line but continued northwards for a while until sunk later by *Hutchins. Asgumo*, also badly damaged and limping southwards, was finally sunk by gunfire from the cruiser *Denver*.

KAGERO CLASS

Ship	Builder	Laid Down	Launched	Commissioned	Fate
Kagero	Maizuru NYd.	30 Sept 37	27 Sept 38	6 Nov 39	Lost 8 May 43
Kuroshio	Fujinagata	31 Aug 37	25 Oct 38	27 Jan 40	Lost 7/8 May 43
Oyashio	Maizuru NYd.		29 Nov 38	20 Aug 40	Lost 8 May 43
Hatsukaze	Kawasaki, Kobe	3 Dec 37	24 Jan 39	15 Feb 40	Lost 2 Nov 43
Natsushio	Fujinagata		23 Feb 39	31 Aug 40	Lost 8 Feb 42
Yukikaze	Sasebo Dkyd.	2 Aug 38	24 Mar 39	20 Jan 40	To China 6 July 47
Hayashio	Uraga		19 April 39	31 Aug 40	Lost 24 Nov 42
Maikaze	Uraga		15 Mar 41	15 July 41	Lost 17 Feb 44
Isokaze	Sasebo Dkyd.		19 June 39	30 Nov 40	Lost 7 April 45
Shiranui	Uraga	30 Aug 37	28 June 38	20 Dec 39	Lost 27 Oct 44
Amatsukaze	Uraga		19 Oct 39	26 Oct 40	Lost 6 April 45
Tokitsukaze	Maizuru NYd.		10 Nov 39	15 Jan 40	Lost 3 April 43
Urakaze	Uraga		10 April 40	15 Dec 40	Lost 21 Nov 44
Hamakaze	Fujinagata		25 Nov 40	30 June 41	Lost 7 April 45
Nowaki	Maizuru NYd.		17 Sept 40	28 April 41	Lost 26 Nov 44
Arashi	Maizuru NYd.		22 April 40	27 Jan 41	Lost 6/7 Aug 43
Hagikaze	Fujinagata		18 June 40	31 Mar 41	Lost 6/7 Aug 43
Tanikaze	Fujinagata		1 Nov 40	25 April 41	Lost 9 June 44

Displacement: 2,033tons/2,065tonnes (standard); 2,490tons/2,529tonnes (full load).
Length: 388ft 9in/118.5m (oa); 381ft 3in/116.2m (wl); 364ft 2in/111m (pp).
Beam: 35ft 5in/10.8m.
Draught: 12ft 4in/3.76m (mean).
Machinery: three Kampon boilers; 2-shaft geared turbines.
Performance: 52,000shp; 35kts.
Range: 5,000nm at 18kts.
Guns: six 5in (3×2); four 25mm.
Torpedoes: eight 24in (2×4).
Complement: 240.

Design Having withdrawn from the London Naval Treaty in 1937, Japan was able to consolidate all her design experience with destroyers of all classes from the 'Special Type' to the *Asashio* class, to draw up a specification which would fully meet the strategic and tactical requirements of the Imperial Japanese Navy. This could now be done without regard to tonnage restrictions and, in the current political climate in Japan, without financial restrictions either. The Navy specified four main requirements: (i) speed greater than 36 knots; (ii) range 5,000 nautical miles at 18 knots; (iii) armament as the 'Special Type'; (iv) hull not larger than the 'Special Type'. As usual, however, a compromise had to be reached, with 35 knots being finally accepted. Great attention was paid to stability, beam being increased by 1½ feet and draft increasing slightly. Bridge structures were reduced and welding extensively employed on frames and internal structures as well as superstructures but not for the shell plating. The hull form was modified, particularly at the stern, to reduce propulsion resistance.

The power plant was improved, lightened and made more efficient, with power output increased and standardized on 52,000shp. Three boilers, now improved with air pre-heaters, were fitted in three separate spaces, the forward and centre rooms being served by the forward funnel. *Amatsukaze* received experimental boilers of a newer and smaller type, developing higher temperatures and pressures than the standard type. Both turbines were fitted abreast each other in the main turbine room. Fuel stowage was mainly in the double bottom spaces with a large bunker immediately forward of the first boiler room.

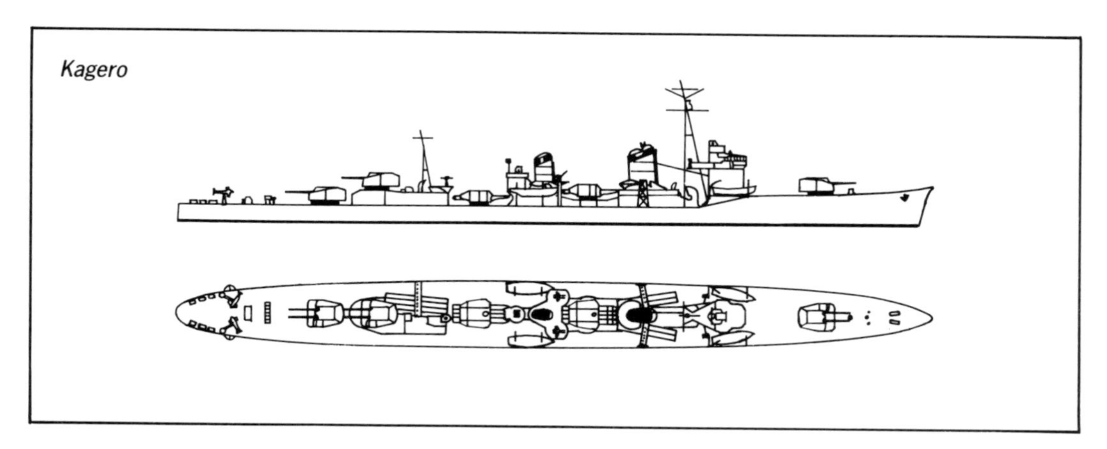

Above: *Isokaze.* (IWM) **Below:** *Arashi.* (IWM)

Main armament remained the 5-inch/50cal 3rd-year gun in twin gun-houses Type 'C' with 55° elevation, but the improved stability allowed the single gun of the *Hatsuharu* class to be replaced by a twin, in a superfiring position over No. 3 gun. The torpedo outfit remained eight 24-inch in two quadruple banks, but the reloading arrangements were improved and the layout altered once more. The reloads for the forward bank were moved ahead of the tubes and placed symmetrically about the forward funnel. There was no improvement in either the AA or A/S outfits.

Fifteen ships were authorized under the 1937 programme and a further three under that for 1939.

Modifications By mid 1943, the AA outfit had been enhanced by the fitting of a twin 25mm on a stand before the bridge and changing the twin 25mm abreast the after funnels for triple mountings (surviving ships only). Towards the end of 1943, the after, superfiring gun-house was landed and replaced by two triple 25mm for a total of fourteen guns. Radar began to be fitted from this time (Types 13 and 22). By mid 1944, the AA was being further augmented by fourteen single 25mm mountings on the upper deck and forecastle.

Service At the outbreak of the Pacific War, the eighteen units of this class formed the 15th (*Hayashio, Kuroshio, Natsushio* and *Oyashio*), 16th (*Amatsukaze, Hatsukaze, Tokitsukaze* and *Yukikaze*), 17th (*Hamakaze, Isokaze, Tanikaze* and *Urakaze*) and 4th Destroyer Divisions (*Arashi, Hagikaze, Maikaze* and *Nowaki*) with *Kagero* and *Shiranui* part of the 18th Division. These divisions were attached to the 1st Destroyer Flotilla (17th Division plus *Kagero* and *Shiranui*), 2nd Flotilla (15th and 16th Divisions) and 3rd Flotilla (4th Division).

The units attached to the 1st Destroyer Flotilla screened the Pearl Harbor Carrier Task force in November 1941, and thereafter many of the class served during the occupation of the Philippines, Rabaul and Dutch East Indies. Here, the 16th Division fought at the Battle of the Java Sea, 26–28 February 1942, but their torpedoes were fired at too great a range, scoring no hits. One of this Division, *Yukikaze*, sank the US submarine *Perch* off northern Surabaya on 3 March by gunfire but another submarine, *S37*, had already scored the first loss of the class, torpedoing *Natsushio* off Eastern Borneo in early February. *Shiranui* had her bows blown off by a torpedo from *Growler* off Kiska on 5 July 1942 and spent most of the remainder of that year under repair at Maizuru.

The 4th and 17th Divisions formed part of the destroyer group at the Battle of Midway in July 1942, *Tanikaze* escaping a mass US dive-bomber attack unscathed. In August 1942, US troops landed on Guadalcanal and Tulagi to forestall Japanese intentions towards Port Moresby, thus precipitating a long series of local actions in the Solomon Islands as the Japanese tried to counter-attack and run supplies to island garrisons. Both *Yukikaze* and *Amatsukaze* were in action off Guadalcanal on 13 November when the former sank the US destroyers *Barton* and *Laffey*. *Amatsukaze* was damaged and the battleship *Hiei* had to be sunk by a torpedo from *Yukikaze*. *Oyashio* sank the US cruiser *Northampton* off Tassafaronga on 1 November 1942. *Hayashio* was the first casualty in this region, caught and sunk by US bombers in November while on a supply mission in the Huon gulf, and in the following March *Tokitsukaze* suffered the same fate when a transport force was destroyed by US and Australian aircraft south-east of Finchhafen. Taking part in the 'Tokyo Express' supply run down the slot was a hazardous undertaking for the Japanese destroyers as three of the class found at dawn on 8 May. Three US destroyer-minelayers (*Preble, Gamble* and *Breese*) had laid a minefield in the Blackett Strait between Arundel Island and Kolombangara the previous day on to which a force of four Japanese destroyers ran. *Oyashio* received severe damage, *Kuroshio* sank quickly and *Kagero* was also badly damaged. Only *Michishio* escaped. The two cripples were later sunk by US naval and marine air-strikes.

Tanikaze and *Susukaze* took part in the engagement in Kula Gulf on 5/6 July 1943, when their torpedoes sank the *Helena*. Both received minor

Above: *Amatsukaze* in May 1941. (Shizuo Fukui)

damage. *Yukikaze* and *Hamakaze* fought at Kolombangara on 13 July 1943, when the cruiser *Leander* was damaged by a torpedo. *Arashi* and *Hagikaze*, running supplies from Bougainville to Kolombangara on the night of 5/6 August, had an engagement with US Destroyer Divisions 12 and 15 when both were sunk, the former by torpedoes and gunfire, the latter by torpedoes. *Isokaze* was present at the Battle of Vella Lavella on 6/7 October and *Hatsukaze* sailed with Rear-Admiral Omori's force of cruisers and destroyers sent to bombard Bougainville on 2 November, but in an engagement with US cruisers and destroyers, the destroyer was rammed by *Myoko* and later sunk by *Dunlap, Craven* and *Maury* off Kolombangara. When Truk was evacuated, on 4 February 1944, *Maikaze* was damaged by aircraft and later sunk by the ships of TG50.3 about 40 nautical miles north-west of that island.

Only six of the original eighteen ships were afloat by the time of the Battle of Leyte Gulf in October 1944, in which *Shiranui* took part only to be sunk by aircraft from the carrier *Essex* off Panay on the 27th. Less than a month later, the submarine *Sealion* torpedoed and sank *Urakaze* off Formosa. Thus at the turn of the year, only *Amatsukaze, Isokaze, Hamakaze* and *Yukikaze* remained in service. Now operating in the South China Sea area, *Amatsukaze* was sunk by US aircraft east of Amoy in April 1945, and the following day, *Hamakaze* was sunk by carrier aircraft in home waters, south of Nagasaki. *Isokaze*, badly damaged on the same occasion, sunk later that day. Both had formed part of the screen for the battleship *Yamato*'s last sortie against US forces in the Pacific. *Yukikaze*, also present on this occasion, escaped undamaged and returned to Japan where she was surrendered in August. After use on repatriation duties, *Yukikaze* was eventually ceded to China and renamed *Tang-Ten*. In 1970 she was damaged by grounding and later broken up.

SHIMAKAZE

Ship	Builder	Laid Down	Launched	Commissioned	Fate
Shimakaze	Maizuru NYd.	8 Aug 41	18 July 42	10 May 43	Lost 11 Nov 44

Displacement: 2,567tons/2,608tonnes (standard); 3,048tones/3,096tonnes (full load).
Length: 413ft 5in/125m (wl); 395ft 4in/120.5m (pp).
Beam: 36ft 9in/11.2m.
Draught: 13ft 7in/4.14m (mean).
Machinery: three Kampon boilers; 2-shaft geared turbines.
Performance: 75,000shp; 39kts.
Range: 1,400nm at 30kts.
Guns: six 5in (3×2); six 25mm.
Torpedoes: fifteen 24in (3×5).

Design An experimental prototype design utilizing high-pressure steam boilers of a new type, possibly as a result of German influence. In comparison with the *Kagero* ships, *Shimakaze* displaced 410 tons more, was 25 feet longer and had her beam increased by more than four feet. This increase in beam allowed the torpedo battery to be increased to fifteen tubes in three quintuple mounts, the first (and only) occasion that quintuple tubes were used by the IJN. She is also credited with five reload torpedoes, but drawings published do not show the usual reload facilities of Japanese destroyers of the period. Armament otherwise remained similar to the *Kagero* class except that she was completed with a 25mm mount before the bridge and had the Type 'D' 75° elevation gun-house. *Shimakaze* received a new design of turbine developing nearly 50 per cent more power than the standard destroyer turbine set, while her new boilers generated steam at 400°C and 571psi. On trials, she developed 79,240shp and a speed of 40.9 knots. Construction was fairly slow and sixteen sister ships due to be built under the 1942 programme were never ordered. These would have displaced 2,750 tons standard and were Nos. 733–748 of that programme.

Modifications The forward 25mm was made a twin in 1944 and No. 2 gun-house was landed and replaced by two triple 25mm. The twins abreast the funnel were also converted to triple mounts for a total of fourteen 25mm guns. By mid 1944, fourteen single 25mm on the upper and main decks brought this total up to 28 guns. Type 22 radar was also added on the foremast.

Service *Shimakaze* participated in the evacuation of the Aleutians in July 1943, following which, she was attached to the Combined Fleet at Truk. In 1944, she took part in the defence of the Marianas, the Battle of the Philippine Sea and Leyte Gulf. She was sunk by carrier aircraft north-east of Cebu while running reinforcements to Ormoc.

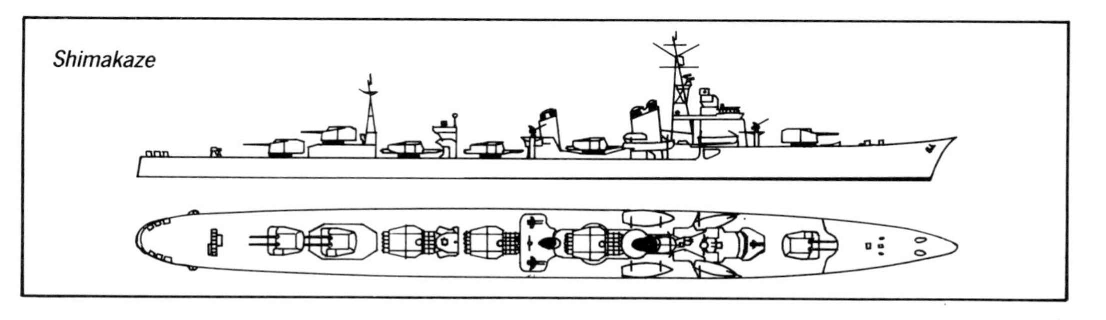

Above: *Shimakaze* in May 1943. (Shizuo Fukui)

YUGUMO CLASS

Ship	Builder	Laid Down	Launched	Commissioned	Fate
Yugumo	Maizuru NYd.		16 Mar 41	5 Dec 41	Lost 6/7 Nov 43
Akigumo	Uraga		11 April 41	27 Sept 41	Lost 11 April 44
Kazekumo	Uraga		26 Sept 41	18 Mar 42	Lost 8 June 44
Makikumo	Fujinagata		5 Nov 41	14 Mar 42	Lost 1 Feb 43
Makinami	Maizuru NYd.		27 Dec 41	18 Aug 42	Lost 25 Nov 43
Takanami	Uraga		16 Mar 42	31 Aug 42	Lost 1 Dec 42
Naganami	Fujinagata		5 Mar 42	30 June 42	Lost 11 Nov 44
Tamanami	Fujinagata		26 Dec 42	30 April 43	Lost 7 July 44
Suzunami	Uraga		12 Mar 43	27 July 43	Lost 11 Nov 43
Onami	Fujinagata		13 Aug 42	29 Dec 42	Lost 25 Nov 43
Fujinami	Fujinagata		20 April 43	31 July 43	Lost 27 Oct 44
Kishinami	Uraga		19 Aug 43	3 Dec 43	Lost 4 Dec 44
Hayanami	Maizuru NYd.		19 Dec 42	31 July 43	Lost 7 June 44
Kiyonami	Uraga		17 Aug 42	25 Jan 43	Lost 20 July 43
Okinami	Maizuru NYd.		18 July 43	10 Dec 43	Lost 13 Nov 44
Hamanami	Maizuru NYd.		18 April 43	5 Oct 43	Lost 11 Nov 44
Asashimo	Fujinagata		18 July 43	27 Nov 43	Lost 7 April 45
Kiyoshimo	Uraga		29 Feb 44	15 May 44	Lost 26 Dec 44
Hayashimo	Maizuru NYd.		Nov 1943	20 Feb 44	Lost 26 Oct 44
Akishimo	Fujinagata		5 Dec 43	11 Mar 44	Lost 13 Nov 44

Cancelled units: *Umigiri, Yamagiri, Tanigiri, Kawagiri, Taekaze, Kiyokaze, Satokaze, Murakaze* (not ordered).

Displacement: 2,077tons/2,110tonnes (standard); 2,520tons/2,560tonnes (full load).
Length: 391ft/119.17m (oa); 383ft 10in/117m (wl); 366ft/111.55m (pp).
Beam: 35ft 5in/10.8m.
Draught: 12ft 4in/3.76m (mean).
Machinery: three Kampon boilers; 2-shaft geared turbines.
Performance: 52,000shp; 35kts.
Guns: six 5in (3×2); four 25mm.
Torpedoes: eight 24in (2×4).
Complement: 228.

Design Essentially repeat *Kagero*-class ships, but with marginally longer hull. Armament remained as *Kagero*, but the Type 'D' gun-house allowing 75° elevation was fitted. Ordered in 1939 and 1941, only one was completed before the outbreak of war and eight were subsequently deleted from the programme.

Modifications Early units received an extra twin 25mm before the bridge and later units landed No. 2 gun-house and received two triple 25mm in lieu, making fourteen 25mm in all. In 1944, the usual fourteen single 25mm were added, making 28 guns in all. Despite this removal of two 5-inch guns from some units, ships completing in 1943–44 still received six 5-inch guns, possibly because two triple 25mm mountings were fitted on bandstands just aft of the forward funnel thereby eliminating the necessity of landing No. 2 gun-house. It is reported that a few units landed the after 5-inch Type 'D' twin gun-house and received a twin 5-inch/40cal. Type 89 AA mounting as fitted in the later *Matsu*-class escort destroyers, possibly in recognition of the poor tracking speeds of the normal destroyer gun and the 90° elevation of the 40cal weapon. Type 22 radar was fitted from about 1943 and later units completed with it.

Service Only *Akigumo* was fully operational when Japan opened hostilities with Britain and the USA, forming part of the Pearl Harbor carrier strike force destroyer screen. She moved to Truk later with the 1st Destroyer Flotilla, covering the Rabaul landings in January 1942, then participated in the carrier raid against Port Darwin in February and the raid into the Indian Ocean in March/April 1942. By the time of Midway, she had been joined by her sisters *Makikumo, Kazekumo* and *Yugumo*, forming the 10th Destroyer Division. After the Fleet reorganization, this division was part of the 10th Destroyer Flotilla with the 3rd Fleet. They took part in the Guadalcanal landings and the later support operations, joined in October by the new ships of the 31st Division, *Naganami, Takanami* and *Makinami*. These seven ships played an active role in the Solomons, escorting bombardment forces as well as

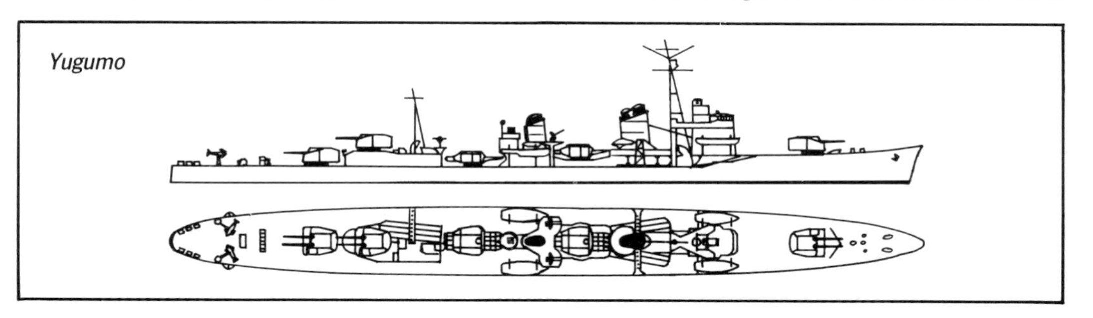

running troops and supplies. They fought at the battle of Santa Cruz in October when *Akigumo* and *Makikumo* finished off the damaged US carrier *Hornet*. In November, both *Takanami* and *Naganami* were damaged by dive-bombers while on a supply run to Guadalcanal. At the end of that month, the 31st Division were three of eight destroyers running supplies to Guadalcanal when they were intercepted by a force of five US cruisers and six destroyers. In the action which followed, known as the Battle of Tassafaronga, *Takanami* was very badly damaged and later foundered after only three months' service.

By the turn of the year, the decision had been made to evacuate the island of Gaudalcanal and, in the final evacuation runs, *Makinami* was damaged by aircraft at the beginning of February and *Makikumo* sunk by a mine off Savo Island.

Kiyonami was present at the battle of Kolombangara in July 1943, but her sisters *Akigumo, Naganami, Yugumo* and *Kazekumo* had moved to the North Pacific, covering the evacuation of Kiska. *Kiyonami* became yet another destroyer lost on a supply mission when, in mid-July, she was sunk by air attack off Kolombangara, en route to Villa. In September, during the evacuation of the Solomons, *Yugumo, Kazekumo, Akigumo* and three other destroyers fought an engagement with US destroyers in which *Yugumo* was sunk by *Chevalier* and *Selfridge* but not before she had damaged the former so badly that she too sank.

The autumn of 1943 saw most of the class attached to the carrier group in the Rabaul area. The new *Onami* had now replaced the lost *Takanami* in the 31st Division, while the newly formed 32nd Division comprised *Tamanami, Suzunami, Fujinami* and *Hayanami* with *Akigumo* and *Kazekumo* as the 10th Division. *Naganami* was present at the battle of Empress Augusta Bay at the beginning of November. A couple of days later she was torpedoed by aircraft of TG50.3 but remained afloat. *Suzunami* was not so lucky, however, the torpedo which hit her sent her to the bottom of Rabaul harbour. *Fujinami*, also hit by a torpedo, escaped because it failed to explode. Towards the end of November five US destroyers of Desron 23 attacked a force of six Japanese destroyers, of which *Onami* and *Makinami* were part. Both succumbed to gunfire and torpedoes from the US destroyers off Cape St. George.

1944 saw the first loss to a submarine, when *Akigumo* was torpedoed and sunk by *Redfin* in the Sulu Archipelago. In the operations in defence of the Marianas during the early summer of 1944, the three divisions comprised *Okinami, Kishinami, Naganami* and *Asashimo* (31st Division), *Tamanami, Hamanami, Fujimami* and *Hayanami* (32nd Division) and *Kazekumo* of the 10th Division. *Akishimo* was also attached. However, *Kazekumo* was sunk by the submarine *Rake* near the Davao Gulf in early June, *Hayanami* by *Harder* east of Borneo and *Tamanami* the following month by *Mingo* off Manila. The survivors took part in the Leyte Gulf engagements but *Hayashimo* was wrecked south-east of Mindoro then sunk by air attack later. The following day, *Fujinami* was also sunk by aircraft from TG38.3 north of Ilo Ilo. Operations in the Philippines during November resulted in further losses to air attack, *Hamanami* and *Naganami* both to TF38 north-east of Cebu and two days later, aircraft from the same Task Force sank *Akishimo* and *Okinami* west of Manila. After the loss of *Kishinami* to torpedoes from *Flasher* off the Luzon Straits, only *Kiyoshimo* and *Asashimo* survived. Withdrawn to Camhran Bay, the former was lost to a torpedo from *PT223* south of Manila during the last sortie into Philippine waters. *Asashimo*, back in home waters, and almost immobilized through lack of fuel, sailed with *Yamato* on her last suicidal sortie in April 1945, only to be sunk by aircraft of TF58 150 miles south-west of Nagasaki. Thus a combination of aggressive spirit, poor AA and ASW defence and lack of good radar, led to the wiping out of a whole class of twenty modern destroyers, but it was typical of the IJN's destroyer story.

Left: *Hayanami.* (IWM)

AKIZUKI CLASS

Ship	Builder	Laid Down	Launched	Commissioned	Fate
Akizuki	Maizuru, NYd.	July 1940	2 July 41	11 June 42	Lost 25 Oct 44
Teruzuki	Mitsubishi, Nagasaki	13 Nov 40	21 Nov 41	31 Aug 42	Lost 12 Dec 42
Suzutsuki	Mitsubishi, Nagasaki	15 Mar 41	4 Mar 42	29 Dec 42	Broken up 1948
Hatsutsuki	Maizuru NYd.		3 April 42	29 Dec 42	Lost 25 Oct 44
Niizuki	Mitsubishi, Nagasaki	8 Dec 41	29 June 42	31 Mar 43	Lost 6 July 43
Wakatsuki	Mitsubishi, Nagasaki	9 Mar 42	24 Nov 42	31 May 43	Lost 11 Nov 44
Shimotsuki	Mitsubishi, Nagasaki	6 July 42	7 April 43	31 Mar 44	Lost 24 Nov 44
Fuyutsuki	Maizuru NYd.		20 Jan 44	25 May 44	Broken up 1948
Hanatsuki	Maizuru NYd.		10 Oct 44	26 Dec 44	USN 28 Aug 47
Yoizuki	Uraga	25 Aug 43	25 Sept 44	31 Jan 45	To China 29 Aug 47
Harutsuki	Sasesbo Dkyd.		3 Aug 44	29 Dec 44	To USSR 28 Aug 47
Natsuzuki	Sasebo Dkyd.		2 Dec 44	8 Aug 45	To RN 3 Sept 47
Mochizuki	Sasebo Dkyd.	3 Jan 45	–	–	Broken up
Kiyotsuki	Maizuru NYd.	Cancelled			
Ozuki	Mitsubishi, Nagasaki	Cancelled			
Hazuki	Maizuru NYd.	Cancelled			

Improved units cancelled (2,980 tons, light): *Arashikaru, Asahikari, Chugao, Hikugumo, Hikushio, Hitonozi, Kaosame, Karuiyuki, Kitakaze, Natsukaze, Nishikaze, Nobikaze, Shimushio, Soragumo, Yugachio, Yugao.*

Improved units cancelled (2,701 tons): *Yamatsuki, Amagumo, Aogumo, Asagochi, Fuyukaze, Fuyugumo, Hae, Harugumo, Hatsunatsu, Hatsuaki, Hayaharu, Hayakaze, Kitakaze, Kochi, Natsukaze, Nishikaze, Okitsugumo, Okaze, Shimokaze, Uruzuki, Yaegumo, Yukigumo.*

Displacement: 2,701tons/2,744tonnes (standard); 3,700tons/3,759tonnes (full load).
Length: 440ft 3in/134.2m (oa); 433ft 1in/132m (wl); 413ft 5in/126m (pp).
Beam: 38ft 1in/11.6m.
Draught: 13ft 7in/4.15m (mean).
Machinery: three Kampon boilers; 2-shaft Kampon geared turbines.
Performance: 52,000shp; 33kts.
Bunkerage: 1,097tons/1,114tonnes.
Range: 8,300nm at 18kts.
Guns: eight 3.9in (4×2); four 25mm.
Torpedoes: four 24in (1×4).
Complement: 300.

Design This design was arguably the most useful destroyer produced by the Japanese and it was certainly well regarded in the Fleet. It was originally conceived as an AA screening vessel for the fast carrier groups, but the design was modified to meet demands for a more general-purpose destroyer. The design centred around the new 3.9-inch

(10cm) 65cal gun, Type 98 of 1938, firing a 29lb projectile. Fixed ammunition was employed (weight 62lb) and the gun had a vertical range of 14,220 yards. These guns were in twin weatherproof electro-hydraulic mountings, and for the first time in Japanese destroyers four mounts were to be shipped, two each forward and aft with Numbers 2 and 3 superfiring. 90° elevation made these guns, with a rate of fire of 15–20 rounds per minute, an effective dual-purpose weapon.

Although originally intended to be pure gun-carriers, the general-purpose requirement led to the shipping of a single quadruple bank of 24-inch torpedo tubes and four spares in the usual quick reload system. Six depth-charge throwers and a capacity for 72 depth-charges were also added. Size naturally increased considerably because the new gun mountings were a little heavier than the standard 5-inch twin destroyer gun-house and an extra mounting was carried in a high position. In consequence, beam increased by 2½ feet and length by nearly 50 feet over the other 1939 programme destroyers of the *Yugumo* class. The increased displacement (*Suzutsuki*, 3,478 tons, trials displacement) entailed a reduction in speed despite the greater length because the standard 52,000shp turbine set was retained.

While designed for AA purposes, the light guns remained only two twin 25mm fitted on platforms between the funnel and the torpedo tubes. However, the main battery was controlled by the excellent Type 94 *Kosha Sochi* AA fire-control system with one director for each of the forward and after groups of armament. Originally each mounting was also equipped with a somewhat complicated local director sight and computer, but this was later replaced by a simpler type of sight.

Six ships were authorized under the 1939 programme and ten further units under the 1941 programme. The improved *Arashikaru* group (16 units) were authorized under the 1942 programme and the 22 *Yamatsuki* group under that for the 1942 'M' programme. All the improved units of the 1942 and 1942 'M' programmes were cancelled due to shortages of raw materials and, in addition, the last four of the 1941 programme were also cancelled. Of these latter, *Mochizuki* had been laid down. Building was stopped in March and the hull broken up to allow the construction of suicide-craft.

Modifications Early units completed with the designed light AA outfits, no radar and normal tripod foremasts. From 1943, with the fitting of a Type 21 radar aerial on the foremast, the mast structure was altered to accommodate it. Some units received two extra triple 25mm abreast the funnel. By 1944, the after AA director had been landed and replaced by a triple 25mm mounting and two more fitted abreast the searchlight. Twelve single 25mm guns were added on the upper deck making a total in *Fuyutsuki* at this date of twenty-seven 25mm guns. This was further improved in surviving units in 1945 with *Suzutsuki* having six triple mountings (forward of the tubes, abreast funnel and abreast the bridge) and thirty single mountings for a total of forty-eight guns without reduction in main armament. Radar Types 13 and 22 were also fitted.

Service *Akizuki*, the leading ship, did not enter service until the summer of 1942 and only three sisters had joined her by the turn of the year. *Teruzuki* and *Akizuki* were thrown into the Guadalcanal fighting in the autumn of 1942, the former being damaged by a torpedo from an aircraft in October, but the following month while attached to the 10th Destroyer Flotilla with the 2nd Fleet at Truk, this ship was sunk by *PT37* and *PT40* when running supplies to Guadalcanal. *Akizuki* took part in the final battles for that island, and its evacuation, but on 19 January 1943 while on an ASW hunt, she struck a mine, flooding one boiler room and the bows. After temporary repairs at Truk, *Akizuki* sailed for Saipan, but on leaving that island the bows threatened to break off and she had to return. After the bows had been cut off (including the bridge) she sailed for Sasebo and was repaired by Mitsubishi at Nagasaki, completing in July 1943.

Suzutsuki, with Admiral Shima's 2nd Striking Force in the South China Sea, was damaged by a torpedo from *Besugo* on 15 October 1944. *Wakatsuki* was another loss on supply runs, being sunk by air attack north of Cebu while making for Ormoc. *Fuyutsuki* and *Suzutsuki* accompanied *Yamato* on her last sortie when the latter was damaged by hits and near misses. The last units completed too late to see any real war service, *Natsuzuki* being brand-new at the surrender.

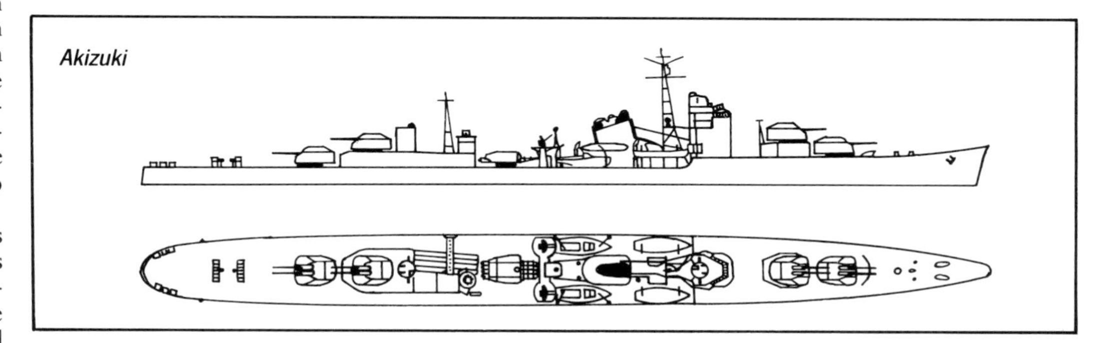

Above: *Akizuki.* (IWM) **Below:** *Hatsutzuki.* (IWM)

Above: *Natsuzuki*, post-war. (A. D. Baker)

MATSU CLASS

Ship	Builder	Laid Down	Launched	Commissioned	Fate
Matsu	Maizuru NYd.		3 Feb 44	29 April 44	Lost 4 Aug 44
Momo	Maizuru NYd.		25 Mar 44	10 June 44	Lost 15 Dec 44
Take	Yokosuka Dkyd.		28 Mar 44	16 June 44	RN 16 July 47
Ume	Fujinagata		24 April 44	28 June 44	Lost 31 Jan 45
Kuwa	Fujinagata		25 May 44	25 July 44	Lost 3 Dec 44
Maki	Maizuru NYd.		10 June 44	10 Aug 44	RN 14 Aug 47
Kiri	Yokosuka Dkyd.		27 May 44	14 Aug 44	USSR 29 July 47
Sugi	Fujinagata		3 July 44	25 Aug 44	To China 31 July 47
Momi	Yokosuka Dkyd.		16 June 44	3 Sept 44	Lost 5 Jan 45
Hinoki	Yokosuka Dkyd.		4 July 44	3 Sept 44	Lost 7 Jan 45
Kashi	Fujinagata		13 Aug 44	30 Sept 44	USN 7 Aug 47
Kaya	Maizuru NYd.		30 July 44	30 Sept 44	To USSR 5 July 47
Kaede	Yokosuka Dkyd.		25 July 44	30 Oct 44	To China 6 July 47
Sakura	Yokosuka Dkyd.		6 Sept 44	25 Nov 44	Lost 11 July 45
Nara	Fujinagata		12 Oct 44	26 Nov 44	Broken up July 48
Tsubaki	Maizuru NYd.		30 Sept 44	30 Nov 44	Broken up July 48
Keyaki	Yokosuka DYd.		30 Sept 44	15 Dec 44	USN 5 July 47
Yanagi	Fujinagata		25 Nov 44	8 Jan 45	Broken up April 47

11 more cancelled in 1944 before laying down.

Displacement: 1,262tons/1,282tonnes (standard); 1,530tons/1,554tonnes (full load).
Length: 328ft 1in/100m (oa); 321ft 6in/98m (wl); 302ft 3in/92.1m (pp).
Beam: 30ft 8in/9.35m.
Draught: 10ft 10in/3.3m (mean).
Machinery: two Kampon boilers; 2-shaft Kampon geared turbines.
Performance: 19,000shp; 27.8kts.
Range: 4,680nm at 16kts.
Guns: three 5in (1×2, 1×1); twenty-four 25mm (4×3, 12×1).
Torpedoes: four 24in (1×4).

Design The crippling losses caused by the fierce fighting in the Solomon Islands during 1942, forced the Imperial Staff radically to re-think its design policy for destroyers. The standard *Yugumo* design was an excellent destroyer, but took far too long to build, probably the primary consideration of naval staff at that time. Speed of construction was therefore the main demand. Secondly, good damage survival was demanded bearing in mind the nature of their probable employment (although Japanese damage-control techniques were very poor). A good AA armament and torpedo ability was also required. To enable the ships to be built as quickly as possible, the hull was designed as simply as possible, all unnecessary curves being eliminated. Electric welding was used extensively. For the first time in Japanese destroyers, the machinery was arranged on the unit principle with boiler rooms and engine rooms alternating (the port turbine occupied the forward engine room). This arrangement would normally have caused an increase in length, but because only two boilers were shipped, the *Matsu* class were more than sixty feet shorter than the *Yugumo*s. Installed power, however, was reduced by more than 60 per cent to 19,000shp leading to a drop in speed to 28 knots. As their role was intended to be escort and supply missions, this did not matter to much because they would not be called upon to operate with the Fleet.

The *Matsu* class represented another departure for Japanese destroyers in that for the first time since the appearance of the 'Special type', the twin 5-inch weatherproof gun-house and 50cal 3rd year gun was abandoned, to be replaced by a more AA-capable 5-inch 40cal Type 89 gun in one single and

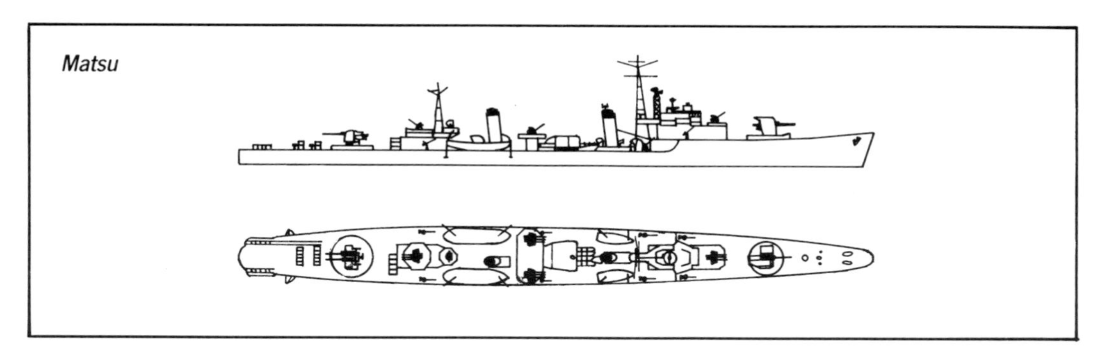

Above: *Tsubaki.* (IWM) **Below:** *Momo.* (IWM)

one twin mounting. This gun fired the same weight projectile as the standard destroyer gun, but with a lower muzzle velocity of 2,362 feet per second. It had a vertical range of 30,970 feet at the maximum elevation of 90°. Mountings were electro-hydraulic. The after, twin, mountings were only partially, often completely, unshielded, while the single mounting forward received a simple shield, probably more for spray purposes than splinter protection. Recognizing the fact that in close-quarters engagements, torpedoes were often decisive, it was originally intended to carry a single sextuple bank of 24-inch tubes, but this did not materialize and a standard quadruple bank was fitted. No reloads were carried. Light AA comprised four triple 25mm disposed fore, aft and amidships with twelve single guns. Radar 13 and 22 were fitted.

Twenty-nine units were ordered under the 1942 'M' programme, but the last eleven were cancelled before laying down and replaced by the modified type described later.

Modifications Not known with certainty, but in all probability light AA would have been augmented. *Take* and others were modified to transport *kaiten*.

Service As the leading ship, *Matsu*, did not complete until April 1944, this class missed the brunt of the fighting around the Solomon Islands but was committed to the Philippines from the autumn of that year. *Matsu*, herself, became the first casualty, sunk by gunfire of the destroyers *Ingersoll, Knapp* and *Cogswell* off Chichijima Retto in the Bonin Islands. *Maki, Kiri, Kuwa, Sugi, Ume* and *Take* supported Japanese troops at Ormoc on Leyte when US forces invaded the island. During the course of these operations *Kuwa* and *Take*, loaded with reinforcements for General Yamashita, encountered the destroyers *Sumner, Moale* and *Cooper* in Ormoc Bay on 3 December. The US destroyers shelled *Kuwa* to a wreck when she sank. However, a torpedo from *Take* hit *Cooper*, which broke in two and sank with heavy casualties. On 7 December, both *Ume* and *Sugi* were damaged by aircraft at Ormoc (and the latter again at Takao, Formosa in January 1945). *Maki*, steaming south of Nagasaki in the East China Sea, was badly damaged by torpedoes from the US submarine *Plaice* on 9 December, but *Momo* was even more unfortunate. She was sunk by *Hawkbill* west-south-west of Cape Bolinao, Luzon on 15 December. *Hinoki* and *Momi* remained in the Philippines in January 1945 as the US forces completed their capture of Luzon. In an engagement with *Bennion* and two Australian minesweepers off Manila, *Momi* was damaged by the US destroyer and later sunk by aircraft from TF38 west-south-west of Manila. Two days later, *Hinoki* fought the last naval engagement in Philippine waters, when she was caught alone at the entrance to Manila Bay by the destroyers *Ausburne, Shaw, Braine* and *Russell*. Outnumbered, her torpedoes having missed, *Hinoki* was sunk by gunfire shortly before midnight. The last attempted sortie into Philippine waters, from Indo China, had taken place on Christmas Eve and included *Kaya, Sugi* and *Kashi*, but this was aborted. Finally *Ume* was bombed and sunk south of Formosa at the end of January.

As the US forces pressed ever closer to the home-land, Japan's defensive perimeter shrank with the forcus of naval action centering upon the Iwo Jima and Okinawa areas. By February 1945, all the *Matsu* class had been completed, but only eleven ships remained. *Maki* and *Kiri* had been damaged by submarine and aircraft respectively; *Kashi* was also damaged by aircraft at Takao on 21 January as was *Kaede* on 31 January south-west of Formosa. Virtually withdrawn to home waters, one last loss was *Sakura*, mined in Osaka harbour.

After the surrender, Great Britain and the USA scrapped their allocated ships (or used them as targets) after brief examination. The Soviet Union retained hers for some time, but only China commissioned any into her navy. *Sugi* was renamed *Hwei Yang* and *Kaede, Hen Yang*.

TACHIBANA CLASS

Ship	Builder	Laid Down	Launched	Commissioned	Fate
Tachibana	Yokosuka Dkyd.		14 Oct 44	20 Jan 45	Lost 14 July 45
Nire	Maizuru NYd.		25 Nov 44	31 Jan 45	Broken up April 1948
Tsuta	Yokosuka Dkyd.	31 July 44	2 Nov 44	8 Jan 45	To China 31 July 47
Hagi	Yokosuka Dkyd.		27 Nov 44	1 Mar 45	RN 16 July 47
Kaki	Yokosuka Dkyd.		11 Dec 44	5 Mar 45	USN 12 April 47
Shii	Maizuru NYd.		13 Jan 45	13 Mar 45	USSR 5 July 47
Nashi	Kawasaki, Kobe	1 Sept 44	17 Jan 45	15 Mar 45	Lost 28 July 45
Sumire	Yokosuka Dkyd.		27 Dec 44	26 Mar 45	RN 20 Aug 47
Enoki	Maizuru NYd.		27 Jan 45	31 Mar 45	Lost 26 June 45
Kusunoki	Yokosuka Dkyd.		18 Jan 45	28 April 45	RN 16 July 47
Odake	Maizuru NYd.		10 Mar 45	15 May 45	USN 4 July 47
Hatsuzakura	Yokosuka Dkyd.		10 Feb 45	28 May 45	To USSR 29 July 47
Kaba	Fujinagata		27 Feb 45	29 May 45	USN 4 Aug 47
Hatsuume	Maizuru NYd.		25 May 45	18 June 45	To China 6 July 47
Yaezakura	Yokosuka Dkyd.		17 Mar 45	–	Lost 18 July 45
Tochi	?		28 May 45	–	Broken up 1946–48
Yadake	Yokosuka Dkyd.		1 May 45	–	Broken up 1946–48
Katsura	Fujinagata		23 June 45	–	Broken up 1946–48
Wakazakura	Fujinagata	15 Jan 45	–	–	Broken up
Azura	Yokosuka Dkyd.	29 Dec 44	–	–	Broken up
Sakaki	Yokosuka Dkyd.	29 Dec 44	–	–	Broken up
Kuzu	Yokosuka Dkyd.	2 Mar 45	–	–	Broken up
Hishi	Maizuru NYd.	10 Feb 45	–	–	Broken up

10 more cancelled in March 1945. 80 improved versions projected but never ordered.

Displacement: 1,289tons/1,309tonnes (standard).
Length: 328ft 1in/100m (oa); 321ft 6in/98m (wl); 302ft 4in/92.15m (pp).
Beam: 30ft 8in/9.35m.
Draught: 11ft 1in/3.37m (mean).
Machinery: two Kampon boilers; 2-shaft Kampon geared turbines.
Performance: 19,000shp; 27.8kts.
Range: 4,680nm at 16kts.
Guns: three 5in (1×2, 1×1); twenty-four 25mm.
Torpedoes: four 24in (1×4).

Design This design was a further simplification of the *Matsu* class with all unnecessary curves eliminated and a slightly modified bridge and mast structure. Constructed entirely of mild steel, the displacement rose accordingly by about 50 tons. Thirty-three units were ordered under the 1942 'M' and 1943–4 programmes, but ten of the latter programme were subsequently cancelled and eighty improved units projected under the 1944–45 programme were never ordered. The last eight of the 1942 'M' programme were also cancelled to expedite construction of midget submarines and suicide-craft.

Modifications Probably as *Matsu* class.

Service This class came too late for extensive war service, and in the end merely provided targets for US air raids since fuel was in such short supply. *Nire* was damaged at Kure on 22 June 1945, *Hagi* two days later in the same port; *Kaba*, damaged by aircraft at Osuka on 19 March was never repaired, while *Shii* was badly damaged by a mine in the Bungo Straits on 5 June. *Tachibana* was sunk by aircraft at Hakodate on 14 July, *Nashi* also by aircraft at Mitajirizaki on 28 July and *Enoki* by a mine at Obama Wan on 26 June. The incomplete *Yaezakura* was also destroyed by an air raid on 18 July. After service on repatriation duty (operational units only) the survivors were divided up between the Allies. Great Britain and the USA immediately disposed of their allocations, but China renamed *Tsuta*, *Hua Yang* and *Hatsuume*, *Hsin Yang*. *Hatsuzakura* (launched as *Susuki*) was renamed *TSL24* by the Soviet Union who used her as a trials ship. Curiously enough, *Nashi*, which had been sunk during the war, was raised in 1955, rebuilt and recommissioned on 31 May 1956 as *Wakaba* for the new Japanese Self Defence Force. Used for training initially, she later became a radar trials ship and was not broken up until the early 1970s.

Below: *Kaba*, post-war. (A. D. Baker)

TOMOZURU CLASS

Ship	Builder	Laid Down	Launched	Commissioned	Fate
Tomozuru	Maizuru NYd.	11 Nov 32	1 Oct 33	24 Feb 34	Lost 24 Mar 45
Chidori	Maizuru NYd.	13 Oct 31	1 April 33	20 Nov 33	Lost 24 Dec 44
Manazuru	Fujinagata	22 Dec 31	11 July 33	31 Nov 34	Lost 1 Mar 45
Hatsukari	Fujinagata	6 April 33	19 Dec 33	15 July 34	Broken up 1946

Displacement: 535tons/543tonnes (standard); 737tons/748tonnes (full load).
Length: 269ft/82m (oa); 259ft 2in/79m (wl); 254ft 3in/77.5m (pp).
Beam: 24ft 3in/7.4m.
Draught: 8ft 2in/2.5m (mean).
Machinery: two Kampon boilers; 2-shaft geared turbines.
Performance: 11,000shp; 30kts.
Bunkerage: 150tons/152tonnes.
Range: 9,000nm at 10kts.
Guns: three 5in (3×1); one 40mm.
Torpedoes: three 21in (1×3).
Complement: 113.

Design Built under the 1931 programme, these were small torpedo-boats designed to fall into the 600-ton category of the London Naval Treaty. Like all Japanese design of the period, they were given the maximum fighting power on the minimum dimensions possible. Armed with three 5-inch guns, in one twin and one single gun-house, together with four 21-inch torpedoes and a speed of 30 knots, these small vessels were, on paper, quite formidable and appeared to outclass the equivalent French and

Italian designs built to the same Treaty restrictions. Indeed they were as heavily armed as some destroyers. In fact, the top-weight problem was serious and unappreciated. Armament represented 22.7 per cent of her weight on a beam of only 24½ feet and a shallow draught of eight feet. *Tomozuru* capsized and sank in a storm on 12 March 1934 precipitating an immediate investigation into the stability problem. While this was being carried out, construction of the last two ships was suspended. Drastic measures were necessary to make the ships battle and seaworthy. Both 5-inch gun-houses were landed as well as the after pair of torpedo tubes. The bridge structure was cut down by one level and the ships were regunned with three single 4.7-inch hand-worked 11th year Type 'M' in single shielded mountings. These replaced the former 5-inch and one was shipped in lieu of the after tubes, reducing the armament weight by more than 60 tons. The modifications increased displacement from 737 to 815 tons (98 tonnes of ballast were added) and reduced speed to 28 knots. Stability was improved by the reduction in the centre of gravity from 1.09m to 0.28m.

Modifications The after gun was landed and the light AA increased to ten 25mm. Depth-charge stowage was increased to forty-eight.

Service After service in Chinese waters before the outbreak of the Pacific war, these ships were mainly used for anti-submarine duties. However, in December 1941 all four covered the invasion of the northern Philippines, sailing from their bases in Formosa. *Chidori*, assisted by *Submarine Chaser No. 18*, sank the US submarine *Amberjack* off Rabaul on 16 February 1943. This ship was herself torpedoed and sunk by *Tilefish* off Yokosuka in December 1944. *Manazuru* was lost to air attack off Okinawa in March 1945 and *Tomozuru* the same month to air attack in the East China Sea. *Hatsukari* was surrendered at Hong Kong and broken up there after the war.

Below: *Chidori*. (IWM)

OTORI CLASS

Ship	Builder	Laid Down	Launched	Commissioned	Fate
Otori	Maizuru NYd.	8 Nov 34	25 April 35	10 Oct 36	Lost 12 June 44
Kasasagi	Osaka Iron Works	4 Mar 35	28 Oct 35	15 Jan 37	Lost 26 Sept 43
Hiyodori	Ishikawajima	26 Nov 34	25 Oct 35	20 Dec 36	Lost 17 Nov 44
Hayabusa	Yokohama Dkyd.	19 Dec 34	28 Oct 35	7 Dec 36	Lost 24 Sept 44
Hato	Ishikawajima	28 May 36	25 Jan 37	7 Aug 37	Lost 16 Oct 44
Sagi	Harima K.K.	20 May 36	30 Jan 37	31 July 37	Lost 8 Nov 44
Kari	Mitsubishi, Yokohama	11 May 36	20 Jan 37	20 Sept 37	Lost 16 July 45
Kiji	Tama, Okayama	24 Oct 35	26 Jan 37	31 July 37	To USSR 1947

Displacement: 840tons/853tonnes (standard); 1,040tons/1,056tonnes (full load).
Length: 290ft 4in/88.5m (oa); 284ft 9in/86.8m (wl); 278ft 10in/85m (pp).
Beam: 26ft 10in/8.18m.
Draught: 9ft 1in/2.76m (mean).
Machinery: two Kampon boilers; 2-shaft geared turbines.
Performance: 19,000shp; 30.5kts.
Bunkerage: 150tons/152tonnes.
Range: 4,000nm at 14kts.
Guns: three 4.7in (3×1); one 40mm.
Torpedoes: three 21in (1×3).
Complement: 113.

Design This class benefited from the mistakes made with *Tomozuru* and in consequence were designed with the reduced armament and lower bridges to start with. To further improve their stability, beam was increased by more than 2½ feet and displacement (hence draught) rose considerably. Design speed was maintained, even very slightly increased, by a 72 per cent increase in installed power.

Authorized under the 1934 programme, eight of the sixteen units were subsequently cancelled in favour of submarine-chasers Nos. 4 to 11, a wise if inadequate decision. The cancelled units were: *Hatsutaka, Aotaka, Wakataka, Kumataka, Yamadori, Mizudori, Umidori* and *Komadori*.

Modifications As *Tomozuru*. Radar was added in some units.

Service Mainly used for escort duties, half the class were lost to submarine attack, three to aircraft and only *Kiji* survived hostilities. *Kasasagi* was the first loss, torpedoed by *Bluefin* in the Flores Sea. *Otori* was sunk by carrier aircraft north-west of Saipan in June 1944, *Hayabusa* in September off Manila and *Hato* in October by aircraft in the South China Sea, east of Hong Kong. Both *Sagi* and *Hiyodori* were lost in November 1944, the former torpedoed by *Gunnel* west of Luzon and the latter by the same submarine off Cape Tourane. *Kari* was torpedoed by the submarine *Baya* off Macassar in July 1945, leaving only *Kiji*, surrendered at Soerabaja in the Dutch East Indies. This ship was transferred to the Soviet Union after service on repatriation duties.

Below: *Otori*, August 1937.

The Netherlands

The Netherlands had a long seafaring history developed in direct connection with her colonial expansion in the East. In fact, by the turn of the century, in 1900, the bulk of her fleet was designed for service in her most valuable possession, The Dutch East Indies, and would continue to be so until the colonies were lost. By the outbreak of war in 1914, the fleet was comprised of nine 'battleships' of which the newest dated from 1909, armed with only two 11-inch guns. None was capable of more than 16 knots and all were completely outclassed by contemporary British, German and even French designs. The torpedo-craft possessed by the Royal Netherlands Navy were fairly numerous and included about fifty torpedo-boats, ranging from the 39-ton *Hobein*-class of 1890, armed with two small guns and two torpedoes, to the *G13* design of 1914, which displaced 180 tons, armed with two 3-inch guns and three torpedoes. Larger destroyers had been built, in home yards but to Yarrow designs, from about 1909. These displaced about 485 tons and were armed with four 12pdr guns and two 18-inch torpedoes. Known as the *Wolf* and *Fret* types, these eight ships represented the most modern torpedo-craft in the navy in 1914. Four new destroyers had, however, been ordered from German yards in 1914 and named *Z1* to *Z4*. These would have displaced 420 tons, armed with two guns, and two torpedoes. Unfortunately, the outbreak of war in August 1914 resulted in their being requisitioned by the Imperial German Navy for its own use but in recompense, plans were passed to the Dutch to allow four ships to be constructed in Holland. These four destroyers, known as *Z1–Z4*, did not enter service until the beginning of the 1920s by which time they were hopelessly outdated. Nevertheless, *Z3* was still extant in 1939 on secondary duties. Four further ships, *Z5–Z8* of slightly modified design with reciprocating machinery were also built during the war years.

The Netherlands remained neutral throughout the First World War and in consequence there was no great expansion of her fleet, nor were there any technical advances. After the war, financial restraints prevented any new construction being started until the middle years of the 1920s when, with assistance from Yarrow, the eight new destroyers of the *Van Ghent* and *Van Galen* classes were built. Once again, all were intended for use in the Dutch East Indies where Japanese naval strength was an obvious threat. These destroyers were similar to contemporary British types, but had the novel idea of shipping a sea-plane for reconnaissance purposes. They were followed by four larger ships of the *Callenburgh* class, but before all these could be completed, the Second World War had erupted and this time, Holland was overrun by German forces. Three out of the four new ships were lost or fell into German hands as was one of the earlier ships which happened to be in home waters at the time.

Until the Japanese entry into the war, the seven destroyers in the East Indies led a fairly uneventful existence cut off from their homeland. This quickly changed in December 1941, and by February 1942, the Dutch destroyer force in the East had been wiped out by superior Japanese forces and the colonies lost.

The Royal Netherlands Navy, after the débâcle in the East, now possessed only one destroyer, *Isaac Sweers*, which had been completed to a modified design in Britain following her escape from Holland in 1940, and she too was lost in November 1942. Following the losses of early 1942, however, the Royal Navy transferred two destroyers which were under construction, to the Royal Netherlands Navy in February (*Van Galen*) and May 1942 (*Tjerk Hiddes*). These two destroyers, after the loss of *Isaac Sweers*, remained the only Dutch destroyers in service until the end of hostilities.

VAN GHENT CLASS

Ship	Builder	Laid Down	Launched	Commissioned	Fate
GT *Van Ghent* (ex-*De Ruyter*)	K.M. de Schelde	28 Aug 25	23 Oct 26	31 May 28	Wrecked 15 Feb 42
EV *Evertsen*	Bergerhout	5 Aug 25	29 Dec 26	31 May 28	Lost 1 Mar 42
KN *Kortenaer*	Bergerhout	24 Aug 25	30 June 27	3 Sept 28	Lost 27 Feb 42
PH *Piet Hein*	Bergerhout	16 Aug 25	2 April 27	25 Jan 28	Lost 19 Feb 42

Displacement: 1,316tons/1,337tonnes (standard); 1,640tons/1,666tonnes (full load).
Length: 322ft/98.15m (oa); 307ft/93.57m (pp).
Beam: 31ft 2in/9.53m.
Draught: 9ft 9in/2.97m (mean).
Machinery: three Yarrow boilers; 2-shaft geared turbines.
Performance: 31,000shp; 36kts.
Bunkerage: 300tons/305tonnes.
Range: 3,200nm at 15kts.
Guns: four 4.7in (4×1); two 75mm AA (2×1); four .5in MG; one aircraft.
Torpedoes: six 21in (2×3).
Mines: 24.
Complement: 129.

Design Like many other nations, the Dutch turned to Yarrow, one of the foremost destroyer builders of the day, when it was decided to replace its ageing First World War-designed destroyers. Yarrow provided the plans for a design based broadly upon the British *Ambuscade* to be constructed in Dutch yards. The displacement was a little greater than the British prototype and the installed power less. In appearance, there was no mistaking their British design, but there were a number of detail differences in the outward appearance.

Main armament was the Bofors 1924-pattern 4.7-inch, 50cal QF gun firing a 53lb shell, disposed two forward, two aft in single mountings. Maximum elevation was 30° to 35°. Shields were not fitted to 'B' to 'Y' guns, and 'A' and 'X' guns carried only a simple curved front shield. Two rangefinders were fitted, one on the upper bridge, the second on the port side of the midships deck-house. Two 3-inch

AA guns were shipped on bandstands between the funnels, giving heavy calibre, if slow-firing anti-aircraft defence. Four rifle calibre machine-guns completed the AA outfit. Six 21-inch torpedo tubes in two triple mountings was standard for the day. An unusual feature was the provision of a sea-plane for reconnaissance purposes, a very sensible arrangement in pre-radar days. The Dutch East Indies, their intended deployment area, was a maze of islands and an aircraft was of immense benefit in any search operation. To accommodate the aircraft, a flying-deck was built over the after tubes and the aircraft was handled by a derrick on the mainmast. This necessitated stepping the mainmast on the centre deck-house, displacing the searchlight. In consequence, two searchlights had to be fitted, one each side of the forward funnel. The aircraft carried was the Fokker C VII-W, first flown in 1926, a two-seat biplane with a speed of 100 knots. It was armed with machine-guns and could carry a couple of light bombs.

Finally, to complete their offensive potential, all were equipped for minelaying and could accommodate twenty-four mines.

Modifications The second funnel was reduced in

Above: *Kortenaer*. (RNethN) **Below:** *Evertsen*. Note only No. 1 gun with shield. (RNethN)

height before the war and the sea-plane equipment landed prior to the outbreak of the Pacific war. Other modifications are not known, but in view of the circumstances they were few before their loss.

Service All four ships were in the Dutch East Indies in 1940 and remained there until 1941 when the Japanese invaded Malaya. Employed on escort and defensive duties, it was not until February 1942 that serious action took place. *Piet Hein* and *Van Ghent* were with Admiral Doorman's strike force on 3/4 February during an abortive attack on invasion vessels at Balikpapan. During a similar sortie with Dutch, British and Australian cruisers on the night of 13/14 February, aimed at Japanese forces in the Banka Strait, *Kortenaer, Piet Hein* and *Van Ghent* sailed from Batavia. Unfortunately, *Van Ghent* ran aground in the narrow harbour mouth of Tjilatjap and became a wreck, being destroyed by *Banckert* and her crew. On 18 February, both *Kortenaer* and *Piet Hein* screened Admiral Doorman's cruisers once more in an attack on Japanese invasion forces at Bali. In a very confused night action, *Piet Hein*, steaming directly astern of *De Ruyter* and *Java*, caught the brunt of the Japanese defensive fire. Her main assailants were the destroyers *Asashio, Oshio* and *Michishio* and, not inconceivably, *Pope* and *Ford*, her own consorts. Her after magazine exploded and she eventually went down in the Badoeing Strait. *Kortenaer*, part of Admiral Doorman's ABDA Force at the Battle of the Java Sea on 27 February, could make only 25 knots as one boiler was out of action. At the start of the action, she was on the disengaged side and could only watch the cruiser gun duel, but later under a sharp turn, *Kortenaer* was struck by a torpedo which broke her in two and she quickly sank. The fatal torpedo is considered to have come from the heavy cruiser *Haguro*. *Evertsen* was attached to the Allied Western Force which searched unsuccessfully for Japanese invasion convoys before passing through the Lombok Strait and thence to Ceylon. The Dutch destroyer, however, put into Batavia and then attempted to join the cruisers *Perth* and *Hobart* but before she could do so, ran into Japanese forces and was severely damaged by the destroyers *Shirakumo* and *Murakumo* in the Sunda Straits on 28 February 1942. She was deliberately beached on Sebuku Besar Island by her crew on 1 March 1942.

VAN GALEN CLASS

Ship	Builder	Laid Down	Launched	Commissioned	Fate
VG *Van Galen*	Fijenoord	28 May 27	28 June 28	22 Oct 29	Sunk 10 May 40
WW *Witte de With*	Fijenoord	28 May 27	11 Sept 28	20 Feb 30	Scuttled 2 Mar 42
BK *Banckert*	Bergerhout	15 Aug 28	14 Nov 29	14 Nov 30	Sunk as target Sept 1949
VN *Van Ness*	Bergerhout	15 Aug 28	20 Mar 30	12 Mar 31	Sunk 17 Feb 42

Displacement: 1,316tons/1,337tonnes (standard); 1,650tons/1,676tonnes (full load).
Length: 322ft/98.15m (oa); 307ft/93.57m (pp).
Beam: 31ft 2in/9.53m.
Draught: 9ft 10in/2.97m (mean).
Machinery: three Yarrow boilers; 2-shaft Parsons geared turbines.
Performance: 31,000shp; 36kts.
Bunkerage: 330tons/335tonnes.
Range: 3,300nm at 15kts.
Guns: four 4.7in (4×1); one 75mm; four 40mm; four .5in MG; one aircraft.
Torpedoes: six 21in (2×3).
Complement: 120.

Design Modified *Van Ghent*-class, once again produced from Yarrow plans. They differed mainly in adopting higher pressure boilers (370psi instead of 250) and with 30 tons more fuel, had increased endurance. While the main armament remained 4.7-inch calibre they were Wilton-Fijenoord Mk 5 versions. Once again, shields were only fitted to 'A' and 'X' guns. The 3-inch outfit was reduced to one gun, repositioned on the centre-line between the funnels, and the two searchlights were placed also on the centre-line ahead and abaft of it. Although these ships are usually credited with two twin 40mm guns, they do not seem to have ever carried them, their normal outfit being four single guns on the main deck amidships. Like their earlier sisters, they could embark a sea-plane but were fitted for minesweeping and not minelaying.

Modifications Apart from the removal of the aircraft, little modification was done to these ships.

Service *Van Galen* was the only destroyer in home waters in 1940. At Den Helder at the time of the German invasion, she was dispatched to Rotterdam to assist in its defence. In the Nieuwe Waterweg and the port itself, she was in action against German Army and Luftwaffe units. In the confined waters, she could not manoeuvre well enough to avoid all the air attacks and was finally hit by bombs from Heinkels of KG4 and sank in the Merwede Haven. The three in the East Indies faced the Japanese invasion in 1941 and saw action with the ABDA forces in 1942. *Van Ness* was sunk by shore-based naval aircraft while escorting the merchantman *Sloet van de Beele* in the Banka Straits before the Java Sea action in which *Witte de With* participated until ordered to escort the damaged *Exeter* to Soerabaya. The destroyer had received minor damage. In Soerabaya, she was damaged in an air raid on 1 March, and as she was non-operational, was scuttled to avoid capture. *Banckert*, also damaged by bombing on 24 and 28 February, was under repair in the floating dock at Soerabaya and was scuttled together with the dock on 2 March. This destroyer was subsequently salvaged by the Imperial Japanese Navy and reclassified as *Patrol Vessel No. 16* on 20 April 1944. However, she remained incomplete in August 1945 at Soerabaya and was repossessed by the Royal Netherlands Navy, only to be sunk as a target in September 1949, in the Madura Straits.

Below: *Van Galen*. Note different AA arrangements between the funnels. (RNethN)

Below right: *Van Ness*. (RNethN)

TJERK HIDDES CLASS

Ship	Builder	Laid Down	Launched	Commissioned	Fate
Gerard Callenburgh	R.D.M. Rotterdam	12 Oct 38	12 Oct 39	–	See Germany *ZH1*
Isaac Sweers	K. M. de Schelde	26 Nov 38	16 Mar 40	29 May 41	Lost 13 Feb 42
Philips Van Almonde	K. M. de Schelde	2 Mar 39	–	–	Broken up on stocks
Tjerk Hiddes	R.D.M. Rotterdam	26 Nov 38	12 Oct 39	–	Scuttled 15 May 40

Displacement: 1,604tons/1,629tonnes (standard); 2,228tons/2,263tonnes (full load).
Length: 351ft/107m (oa); 344ft 6in/105m (pp).
Beam: 34ft 9in/10.6m.
Draught: 9ft 2in/2.8m (mean).
Machinery: three Yarrow boilers; 2-shaft Parsons geared turbines.
Performance: 45,000shp; 37.5kts.
Bunkerage: 560tons/568tonnes.
Guns: five 4.7in (2×2, 1×1); four 40mm (2×2); four .5in MG.
Torpedoes: eight 21in (2×4).
Complement: 158.

Design The existing destroyers of the *Van Ghent* and *Van Galen* classes being poorly armed in comparison with contemporary Japanese destroyers which they would most probably have to face, led to the demand for a larger, more heavily armed destroyer. Designed once again with the assistance of Yarrow & Co. Ltd., this new design was approximately 300 tons heavier in displacement, with a longer and more beamy hull. The increased dimensions permitted the main armament to be increased by one gun by the expedient of fitting twin mountings in 'A' and 'Y' positions with the single superfiring on 'X' position. A new 4.7-inch gun was carried, a 40cal QF weapon, using 71lb fixed ammunition, reportedly capable of AA use, although the elevation is not known. Two twin 40mm Bofors guns with the advanced Hayemeyer control were fitted, one in 'B' position, the second between the torpedo tubes. This was far and away more advanced than anything else in the world at the time. Finally, for the first time in Dutch destroyers, quadruple 21-inch torpedo tubes were shipped. Like the previous classes, an aircraft was accommodated, but to avoid its masking the arcs of fire of the 40mm guns, it was moved forward and carried between the funnels where it was handled by a derrick stepped against the forward funnel. Mines could also be accommodated. Three boilers in two spaces (the aftermast housing two boilers) and a single turbine space comprised the main machinery. With an increase in installed power of 45 per cent, speed rose by 1½ knots and an increase in bunkerage gave a corresponding increase in range. Two units were ordered under the 1937 programme (*Tjerk Hiddes* and *Callenburgh*) and the other pair under that for the following year.

Modifications The incomplete *Callenburgh* was captured and eventually entered service with the Kriegsmarine in slightly modified form as *ZH1*

(q.v.). *Isaac Sweers* was the only unit to commission in the Netherlands Navy but not until she reached a British yard. Lack of the intended Dutch equipment therefore forced a modified design to be adopted. In particular, the 4.7-inch guns were unobtainable and in lieu she was fitted with standard 4-inch QF Mk XVI in twin mountings Mk XIX, on 'A', 'X' and 'Y' positions. Both Bofors mountings were carried and two quadruple .5in MG mounts replaced the aircraft equipment between the funnels. British fire-control equipment was shipped, Mk V rangefinder director for HA/LA use and radar 285 fitted to it. She was given a tripod mast with HF/DF at the truck. Both sets of tubes were retained. By the time of her loss, it is probable that the HF/DF set had been moved aft to the mainmast and surface warning radar taken its place at the foremast truck. Two single 20mm later replaced the .5in MG equipments.

Service None had been completed at the time of Holland's surrender, but it proved possible to tow away *Isaac Sweers* with the tug *Zwarte Zee* on 11 May 1940 to be completed in Britain. *Tjerk Hiddes* and *Gerard Callenburgh*, both further advanced than *Sweers*, were scuttled by the Navy on 15 May 1940 in their builders' yards as it was impossible to tow them away with any chance of success in the face of the German advance, Rotterdam having fallen the previous day. *Tjerk Hiddes* was salvaged and raised on 12 June 1942, but repairs were impossible and she was broken up at Hendrik-Ido, Ambacht. *Gerard Callenburgh*, on the other hand, was raised on 14 June 1940 and completed as *ZH1* for the Kriegsmarine. *Philips Van Almonde*, still on the slipway, could not be launched, despite attempts to do so, and was destroyed on the slip on 17 May 1940 being broken up later.

After completion in Britain, *Isaac Sweers* served briefly in the Atlantic, but spent the greater part of her distinguished career in the Mediterranean theatre. From September 1941, she escorted supply convoys to Malta and the dispatching of aircraft reinforcements to the island from aircraft carriers in the western Mediterranean. In December 1941, as a member of a division of four destroyers (the others were *Sikh, Legion* and *Maori*), she intercepted and assisted in the sinking of two Italian cruisers, *Alberico da Barbiano* and *Alberto di Guissano* in a night action off Cape Bon. 1942 saw further Malta convoy duty and in January she towed the torpedoed *Gurkha* out of burning fuel oil thus enabling many of her crew to escape certain death when the ship sank. *Isaac Sweers* was dispatched to the Indian Ocean for duty with the Eastern Fleet early in 1942 when the Japanese thrust towards the Dutch East Indies, India and Ceylon. She saw no action in the Eastern theatre where she was replaced by the new *Tjerk Hiddes* (ii) ex-*Nonpareil*. Later in the year, she returned to Britain and began escort duty for the North Africa invasion. In November 1942, she sailed with a convoy to Gibraltar, then brought in another from the Azores before rescuing the survivors of a sunken ship sixty miles off the Rock. She returned to her flotilla in the Mediterranean and was almost immediately torpedoed by *U431* and sank with heavy casualties.

Above: *Banckert* with her sea-plane. (Navpic) **Below:** *Isaac Sweers*, as completed with British modifications. (IWM)

TRANSFERRED UNITS

Van Galen, Tjerk Hiddes

Design British *N*-class destroyers transferred to the Royal Netherlands Navy, *Van Galen* on 11 February 1942 (ex-*Noble*) and *Tjerk Hiddes* on 27 May 1942 (ex-*Nonpareil*).

Modifications As British *N*-class destroyers.

Service Both went out to the Indian Ocean in 1942 and were present at the occupation of Madagascar towards the end of that year. *Tjerk Hiddes* went to Australia in December and assisted in the evacuation of Timor in three journeys. She remained in Australian waters into 1943 but by 1944 both were once more in the Indian Ocean. *Van Galen* participated in the Sabang and Soerabaya carrier raids in April and May and later bombarded the Nicobar Islands. After the war, both continued in service with the Royal Netherlands Navy until *Tjerk Hiddes* was sold to Indonesia on 1 March 1951 being renamed *Gadjah Mada*. She was reported to have been scrapped in 1961. *Van Galen* was eventually sold for scrapping on 8 February 1957.

Norway

Considering the length of the coastline and the size and importance of her merchant marine, Norway paid astonishingly little attention to naval defence. Her fleet was, by 1939, little more than a collection of museum pieces unfit to take part in any action and, moreover, death-traps for their own crews. No new surface ships had been added to the fleet between 1921 and 1937, with the exception of one minelayer. The only new fighting units completed between the wars were the six submarines, *B1* to *B6*, built from 1923 to 1930 and even these were not the equal of contemporaries. In addition, six 600-ton and two 1,200-ton destroyers had been authorized but this modest programme was far from complete when German forces invaded Norway in April 1940, taking full advantage of the defenceless nature of their opponent.

In the débâcle of April 1940, Norway's motley fleet was destroyed by sinking or capture with only a few units escaping to Britain. The Royal Norwegian Navy offered little resistance to the invading forces, with the exception of a few brave patrol vessels and this failure, particularly by the submarines, led to a post-war Board of Inquiry, the results of which were suppressed by the King.

The destroyers laid down in 1933 and subsequently were but small ones, inferior in fighting power to the German *Möwe* type, being more comparable to the French 600-tonne *torpilleur* design. The larger type was a more true destroyer, but by the standards of the day, carried a poor torpedo outfit. Only one modern vessel, *Sleipner*, escaped to fight with the Allies from 1940 to 1945. During the war, four former US 'flush-deckers', *Mansfield, Bath, St Albans* and *Newport* and later *Lincoln* were transferred to the Royal Norwegian Navy. Two *Hunt*-class destroyers raised the Norwegian ensign in 1942 and eventually two new Fleet destroyers of the *S* class were received by the Norwegians. With these new ships (plus corvettes, submarines and coastal craft), the Royal Norwegian Navy played an active role in the North Sea and Atlantic.

SLEIPNER CLASS

Ship	Builder	Laid Down	Launched	Commissioned	Fate
Sleipner	Horten NYd.		7 May 36		Stricken 1956
Aeger	Horten NYd.		25 Aug 36		Sunk 9 April 40
Gyller	Horten NYd.	1936	7 July 38	1 Aug 39	Captured 11 April 40

Displacement: 597tons/606tonnes (standard); 708tons/719tonnes (full load).
Length: 243ft 9in/74.3m (oa); 236ft 3in/72m (pp).
Beam: 25ft 7in/7.8m.
Draught: 6ft 11in/2.1m (mean).
Machinery: three Yarrow boilers; 2-shaft de Laval geared turbines.
Performance: 12,500shp; 30kts.
Bunkerage: 100tons/102tonnes.
Range: 1,500nm at 15kts.
Guns: three 4in (3×1); one 40mm; two MG.
Torpedoes: two (*Gyller* four) 21in (1×2 or 2×2).
Complement: 75.

Design These were the first modern torpedo-craft built for the Royal Norwegian Navy since the end of the First World War, and except for *Garm*, built in 1914, the first with turbine propulsion. If considered as true destroyers they compared badly with foreign contemporaries, for the standard destroyer gun abroad was 4.7-inch or 5-inch calibre, of which between four and eight were carried. Similarly, torpedo armament was usually between six and twelve tubes. Thus they are more properly to be regarded as torpedo-boats and as such contemporaries of the French 600-tonnes type or Italian *Spica* class. Nevertheless, they had a good turn of speed and were new, a direct contrast to all of the remainder of Norway's fleet. Unfortunately, their construction was overtaken by events and they had hardly entered service before they were fighting a war. The main armament of this class was the 4-inch 40cal Bofors QF gun, which used fixed ammunition. In common with many other contemporaries, these were disposed one forward and two aft in single, shielded mountings. A single 40mm Bofors and two .5in machine-guns completed the gunnery department. One twin bank of 21-inch tubes was shipped, except *Gyller* which had two twin banks. Three units were ordered from the naval yard at Horten and laid down between 1933 and 1936, entering service between 1937 and 1939.

Modifications *Aeger* was never modified and *Gyller* fell into German hands; her modifications are detailed under the German section. Operating with British forces, *Sleipner* had No. 2 gun removed and the others changed for British-pattern guns. These appear to have been 4-inch QF Mk V on HA mountings. Two 20mm guns were also added.

Service At the time of the German invasion in April 1940, *Sleipner* and *Aeger* formed the 1st Destroyer Division originally based at Bergen while *Gyller* was

Below: *Aeger*.

stationed at the naval base of Marvika near Kristiansand. *Aeger* operated off Bokenfjord in defence of Stavanger where she sank a large transport of the invasion force. However, when Sola airfield fell, leaving the Luftwaffe in control, she was bombed by aircraft of 111 KG4. Hit in the engine room, *Aeger* was run ashore in Amøyfjorden and scuttled. *Sleipner* fought on during the Allied operations in April, eventually escaping to Britain where she arrived at Lerwick on 27 April. *Gyller* offered no resistance to the German invasion force at Kristiansand, where she surrendered on 11 April subsequently being taken over as the Kriegsmarine's *Löwe*. *Sleipner* served with the Royal Navy on escort duty throughout the war, mostly on the east coast. From 28 June 1940 she was stationed at Rosyth until laid up on 27 February 1944 and paid off on 10 March 1944. *Sleipner* returned to Norway in 1945 and in 1948 was converted to a frigate, being finally scrapped in 1959.

ODIN CLASS

Ship	Builder	Laid Down	Launched	Commissioned	Fate
Odin	Horten NYd.	1938	17 Jan 39	17 Nov 39	Captured 11 April 40
Balder	Horten NYd.	1938	11 Oct 39	–	Captured April 1940
Tor	Fredrikstad M.V.	1938	9 Sept 39	9 April 40	Captured April 40

Displacement: 632tons/642tonnes (standard).
Length: 242ft 9in/74m (pp).
Beam: 25ft 7in/7.8m.
Draught: 9ft 10in/3m (mean).
Machinery: three Yarrow boilers; 2-shaft de Laval geared turbines.
Performance: 12,500shp; 30kts.
Bunkerage: 100tons/102tonnes.
Guns: two 4in (2×1); one 40mm; two MG.
Torpedoes: two 21in (1×2).
Complement: 75.

Design Modified versions of *Sleipner* with increased length, but only two 4-inch guns.

Modifications None in Norwegian hands.

Service Only *Odin* had been completed by the outbreak of war in April 1940. She was based at Kristiansand where, like *Gyller*, she offered no resistance to the German forces and surrendered at Marvika on 11 April. She was subsequently incorporated into the Kriegsmarine as *Panther* (q.v.). *Balder* was captured at Horten while fitting out and *Tor* (still running trials) scuttled at Fredrikstad on 9 April also fitting out. These two ships became the German *Leopard* and *Tiger* respectively (q.v.). Both were found at Korsor in Denmark in May 1945 and returned to Norway, as was *Panther* the same year. In 1948 they were converted to frigates and stricken in 1959. *Balder* was broken up in 1961.

AALESUND CLASS

Ship	Builder	Laid Down	Launched	Commissioned	Fate
(i)	Horten NYd.	April 1939	29 May 41	–	Captured April 1940
(ii)	Horten NYd.	April 1939	30 June 43	–	Captured April 1940

Displacement: 1,220tons/1,239tonnes (standard).
Length: 328ft/100m (oa); 311ft 8in/95m (pp).
Beam: 32ft 6in/9.9m.
Draught: 9ft 2in/2.8m (mean).
Machinery: two Yarrow boilers; 2-shaft de Laval geared turbines.
Performance: 30,000shp; 34kts.
Bunkerage: 300tons/305tonnes.
Range: 3,100nm at 19kts.
Guns: four 4.7in (1×2, 2×1); two 40mm; two 13mm.
Torpedoes: four 21in (2×2).
Complement: 130.

Design The first true destroyer-type ships designed for the Royal Norwegian Navy, albeit still underarmed in comparison with foreign types. They were considerably larger than the *Sleipners* and armed with 4.7-inch guns. These would probably have been of Bofors manufacture similar to those shipped by the minelayer *Olav Tryggvason*. The torpedo outfit still comprised only two twin banks of 21-inch tubes, rather surprisingly in view of the opportunities for this form of warfare in the Norwegian coastal waters. They were only in the initial stages of construction when captured on the stocks in April 1940. The German Navy was unable to complete them although both reached the launching stage. Postwar, one was resumed by the Norwegians and named *Aalesund*, but was later abandoned. The incomplete vessel was finally sold to Høvding Skibsopphugning in 1956 for breaking up.

MISCELLANEOUS UNITS

Of the other destroyers and torpedo-boats, the three *Draug* class of 1908–14 (540 tons; six 3-inch guns; three TT) *Draug, Garm* and *Troll* were with the 1st Destroyer Division originally at Bergen. *Draug*, after action against enemy transport ships, escaped to England, arriving in Sullom Voe in the Shetlands on 10 April. Subsequently she was used by the Royal Navy on subsidiary duties. *Garm* was sunk by German aircraft at Bjordal in Sognefjord on 26 April and *Troll*, ordered to Shetland, was abandoned by her crew and surrendered at Floro on 18 May 1940. She was subsequently used as a condenser vessel and heating barge at the yard in Laksevaag. The three *Snoegg*-class torpedo-boats (220 tons; two 3-inch guns; four TT) dating from 1919/21, *Snoegg, Stegg* and *Trygg*, were also originally at Bergen as the 1st Torpedo-boat Division. *Snoegg* was with *Troll* at Floro and her crew deserted under similar conditions. *Stegg* was sunk by the German *Bremse* at Heroysund on 20 April and *Trygg* near Andalesnes on 26 April by German aircraft. *Snoegg* was later taken over by the Kriegsmarine as *Zack* for use as a patrol boat. Later she became *V5504* then *V5502* before being lost by stranding off Bergen on 6 September 1943.

TRANSFERRED UNITS

The Royal Norwegian Navy manned four of the ex-USN 'flush-deckers', *Mansfield, Bath, St Albans* and *Newport*. *Bath* was torpedoed in the North Atlantic by *U204* on 19 August 1941 and replaced by *Lincoln*. Most of their work was on the Atlantic convoys, but *Mansfield* took part in the Lofoten Raid. *Mansfield* went to the RCN in 1942 and *Lincoln* to Russia in 1944, as did *St Albans*. *Newport* reverted to RN control in 1942. Two *Hunt*-class destroyers, *Eskdale* and *Glaisdale*, were also taken over by the Norwegian Navy. These two ships served in the Channel theatre on convoy duties and also on offensive sweeps against enemy coastal traffic. *Eskdale* had her bows blown off by a torpedo from *S90* off the Lizard on 14 April 1943, and a second torpedo blew the stern off. She remained afloat for some time but later further torpedoes from *S112* and *S65* blew up a magazine and she finally sank. *Glaisdale* survived the war and was renamed *Narvik* after hostilities. The final destroyer transfers to the Royal Norwegian Navy were the former *Success* in 1943 to replace *Eskdale*, renamed *Stord* and the following year, *Shark* was also transferred as *Svenner*. These two destroyers served with the Home Fleet, *Stord* taking part in the hunting and sinking of *Scharnhorst* in December 1943. Both ships were at the Normandy landings with the 23rd Destroyer Flotilla where *Svenner* was torpedoed and sunk by German torpedo-boats of the 5th Torpedo-boat Flotilla (*T28, Möwe, Jaguar* and *Falke*) on the night of 6 June off 'Sword' Beach. *Stord* survived the war and was retained by the RNN until scrapped in 1959.

Peru

Despite her long Pacific coastline, Peru has never maintained much of a naval force and such vessels as were obtained were mainly of a riverine nature for operations far in the hinterland at the headwaters of the Amazon. Here, based on Iquitos, the Peruvian Navy supported their national interests far inland on the borders of Equador, Colombia and Brazil during the nineteenth century. Tension with Colombia peaked once more in 1933, and two destroyers, the first ever possessed by Peru, were hurriedly bought from Estonia, sailed to South America and sent 3,000 miles up the Amazon to defend Iquitos. To control the mouth of the Amazon, the cruiser *Almirante Grau* and two submarines were dispatched into the Atlantic, no mean feat for such a small and ill-equipped navy, as it involved a passage of more than 4,000 miles to the other side of the continent where Peru had no possessions or bases. When it was known that Colombia had bought two destroyers from Portugal, the two Peruvian destroyers were sent back down the Amazon and dispatched to patrol the Colombian coast in the Caribbean, where they remained on patrol for two months, based at Martinique and Trinidad. The situation with Colombia was resolved diplomatically and no action was seen by the destroyers which were thereafter based in the Pacific at Callao. Peru remained neutral during the Second World War and her destroyer force was not altered during that period.

VILLAR

Ship	Builder	Laid Down	Launched	Commissioned	Fate
Villar	Putilov, St. Petersburg	23 Oct 14	27 Aug 15	1917	Discarded 1955

Displacement: 1,260tons/1,280tonnes (standard); 1,620tons/1,646tonnes (full load).
Length: 321ft 6in/98m (oa).
Beam: 30ft 9in/9.34m.
Draught: 12ft 9in/3.9m (mean).
Machinery: four Normand boilers; 2-shaft A.E.G. turbines.
Performance: 31,500shp; 24kts.
Bunkerage: 500tons/508tonnes.
Range: 1,253nm at 16kts.
Guns: four 4in (4×1); two 20mm.
Torpedoes: nine 18in (3×3).
Mines: 60.
Complement: 142.

Design Like her half-sister, *Guise*, this destroyer was also of Russian origin, one of a class of seven ships built during the First World War. Laid down as *Kapitän Kingsbergen*, she was renamed *Miklucha-Maklaj* on 27 June 1915. Taken over by the Bolshevik fleet, she was renamed once more on 18 December 1918 as *Spartak*. She was captured by British forces on 26 December 1918, after a token bombardment of Reval when she ran aground while withdrawing. Given to Estonia on 4 January 1919, *Spartak* now became *Vambola* until sold to Peru in 1933.

GUISE

Ship	Builder	Laid Down	Launched	Commissioned	Fate
Guise	Bocker, Reval	27 Oct 13	31 Dec 14	30 July 17	Discarded 1947

Displacement: 1,354tons/1,375tonnes (standard); 2,200tons/2,235tonnes (full load).
Length: 351ft/107m (oa).
Beam: 31ft 3in/9.5m.
Draught: 16ft/4.9m (mean).
Machinery: four Normand boilers; 2-shaft Parsons turbines.
Performance: 32,700shp; 28kts.
Bunkerage: 570tons/579tonnes.
Range: 1,565nm at 16kts.
Guns: five 4in (5×1); two 20mm.
Torpedoes: nine 18in (3×3).
Mines: 60.
Complement: 142.

Design One of a class of five 1,350-ton destroyers laid down for the Imperial Russian Navy during the First World War to plans by the French shipbuilder Augustin Normand. They were developments of the famous *Novik* of 1911. She was completed as *Avtroil* and in 1918, fought with the Bolshevik fleet in the Gulf of Finland against the Royal Navy. Captured by British forces on 27 December 1918, the ship was presented to the Estonian Navy on 4 January 1919. Renamed *Lennuk*, she served with the Estonians until sold to Peru in 1933.

Below: *Villar.* (A. D. Baker)

Below: *Guisse.* (A. D. Baker)

Poland

Poland's naval situation was essentially an artificial creation resulting from her acquisition of the Polish Corridor following the First World War. This gave her access to the Baltic Sea on the western shore of the Gulf of Danzig and for a few miles to the west of Hela. Danzig itself was a 'free city' and the only port available to Poland was Gdynia which was developed as a major commercial harbour and naval base. With such a short coastline (about 90 miles in all), the naval needs of independent Poland were small, satisfied initially by a handful of former First World War ex-German and Russian torpedo-boats and gunboats. There were, in addition, small flotillas of river gunboats on the Dnieper and Vistula.

In 1920, the Marine Department prepared a 10-year plan, which called for the construction of two battleships, six cruisers and 28 destroyers, as well as smaller craft. This was never achieved, but the mid 1920s saw a small programme of new construction with orders being placed in French yards for two destroyers (*Burza* and *Wicher*) and three submarines (*Wilk* class). Ten years later, a further expansion was planned, with two destroyers ordered in Great Britain (*Grom* and *Blyskawica*) and two more submarines, this time from Dutch yards (the famous *Orzel* and *Sep*). France received the order for a large minelayer/training ship, and for the first time, orders were placed in Polish yards for small warships, six minesweepers. Then in 1931, the Naval Staff saw a requirement for among other things, 34 destroyers, but nothing came of this. In 1936–37, a large naval programme was drawn up which included, among other ships, three 25,000-ton battleships, one aircraft-carrying cruiser, twelve destroyers and twelve submarines. This grandiose programme (never approved by the Polish Parliament), far beyond the needs of Poland, was mainly a political exercise designed to secure a place for Poland in international negotiations and had little or no chance of reaching fruition. At the same time, the Naval Staff had prepared a realistic (as opposed to political) plan which envisaged the navy with a strength of eight destroyers, twelve submarines, a minelayer, twelve minesweepers and some torpedo-boats by 1942.

Prior to the outbreak of war, the Polish Naval Staff, recognizing priorities, sailed three of their destroyers to Britain where they were free to fight outside the narrow confines of the Baltic. Of the submarines, *Sep, Zbik* and *Rys* eventually were interned in Stockholm. *Wilk* managed to escape from the Baltic after many adventures and reached Britain in late September. *Orzel*, interned in Reval, broke out later and also reached Britain safely. The remainder of the Polish Navy was sunk or captured during the German and Soviet invasions. The ships of the Free Polish Navy fought in exile with spirit and aggression until the end of the war in Europe, but with the advent of a Communist government in post-war Poland, the return of surviving units was protracted due to political problems.

BURZA CLASS

Ship	Builder	Laid Down	Launched	Commissioned	Fate
B *Burza*	C.N. Français (Blainville)	1 Nov 26	16 April 29	10 Aug 32	Museum Ship 1962
W *Wicher*	C.N. Français (Blainville)	19 Feb 27	10 July 28	8 July 30	Lost 3 Sept 39

Displacement: 1,540tons/1,564tonnes (standard); 2,430tons/2,468tonnes (full load).
Length: 351ft 9in/109.6m (oa); 344ft/104.8m (wl); 331ft/100.9m (pp).
Beam: 29ft/8.8m.
Draught: 9ft 9in/2.97m (mean).
Machinery: three boilers; 2-shaft Parsons geared turbines.
Performance: 35,000shp; 33kts.
Bunkerage: 300tons/305tonnes.
Range: 3,000nm at 15kts.
Guns: four 5.1in (4×1); two 40mm (2×1); four 13.2mm MG.
Torpedoes: six 21in (2×3).
Mines: 60.
Complement: 155.

Design These two ships were built in France, one of the by-products of the close links which existed between Poland and France following the First World War. They were slightly modified *Bourrasque*-class '1500-tonne' *torpilleurs* and differed only in detail such as having 40mm guns in lieu of the 37mm aboard their French counterparts and were equipped for minelaying. For political reasons, the order was placed with a yard having little or no experience in building destroyer-type vessels and in consequence, construction was extended over a long period, because of materials and industrial problems.

Modifications *Wicher*, lost on the third day of the war, received no modifications. *Burza* on the other hand escaped to Britain where some modifications were made to her armament. The after tubes were landed and replaced by a 12pdr AA gun. 'X' gun was also replaced by a quadruple 2pdr. When they became available, single 20mm Oerikons were fitted in the bridge wings, abreast the third funnel and on the after deck-house making six in all. The search-

Below: *Bruza* in 1937. (Wright & Logan)

light above the bridge was removed and replaced by radar 271. During the middle war years, 'A' gun was also landed and a hedgehog fitted in lieu. It is likely that her remaining guns were changed for 4.7-inch weapons. Radar 291 was also fitted.

Service *Burza* sailed for Britain with *Grom* and *Blyskawica* on 30 August 1939, as part of Operation 'Pekin' and thus missed the opening events in the Baltic. *Wicher* remained behind and on 1 September was ordered from Gdynia to Hela. Despite heavy air attacks, *Wicher* reached Hela where, on 3 September, she was in action with the German destroyers *Maass* and *Zenker*. *Wicher* received some damage and about two hours later, Stuke dive-bombers of 4/Trägergruppe 186 made a massed attack which sank the destroyer at its moorings. She was later raised by the Kriegsmarine and renamed *Serose*, but not refitted. After reaching Britain, *Burza* moved to Plymouth and operated in the south-western approaches and then joined the 1st Destroyer Flotilla at Harwich, patrolling the southern North Sea. In April, 1940, she moved to Scapa and then participated in the Norway operations during April and early May. Moving south to Harwich once more, as the German armies reached the Channel coast, she was, on 24 May 1940, ordered to Dover for support operations off Calais. While bombarding enemy positions, *Burza* came under air attack and had her bows badly damaged. Towed to Plymouth for repairs, she was back in service again by mid-August. Atlantic convoy duties followed before returning to Plymouth in September. Operating in the south-western approaches, *Burza* assisted in the rescue of survivors from *Empress of Britain* in October. By late 1941, *Burza* was beginning to show the strain and went in for re-arming and a long refit, her crew manning the new *Slazak*. Her French equipment was unreliable and spares impossible to obtain. By December 1942, *Burza* was permanently on Atlantic convoy duty, initially with Escort Group B6, later B3. In February 1943, she assisted in the sinking of *U606*. By the autumn of 1943, *Burza* was with *Fencer* and the 8th Support Group, operating in the Azores and South Atlantic, becoming the first Polish warship to cross the Equator. Built for cold Baltic conditions, she was uncomfortable in hot climes. 1944 saw her back on Atlantic duties with Escort Group B3. After the war, *Burza* remained laid up in Britain until returned to Poland in March 1951.

Left: *Burza* in 1942.

GROM CLASS

Ship	Builder	Laid Down	Launched	Commissioned	Fate
Blyskawica H34	S. White (Cowes)	1 Oct 35	1 Oct 36	1 Oct 37	Museum Ship 1 May 76
G *Grom* H71	S. White (Cowes)	20 July 35	20 July 36	March 1937	Lost 5 May 40

Displacement: 2,144tons/2,178tonnes (standard); 3,383tons/3,437tonnes (full load).
Length: 374ft/114m (oa); 357ft/109m (pp).
Beam: 37ft/11.3m.
Draught: 10ft 6in/3.1m.
Machinery: four 3-drum boilers; 2-shaft Parsons geared turbines.
Performance: 54,000shp; 39kts.
Range: 3,573nm at 15kts (*Blyskawica*).
Guns: seven 4.7in (3×2, 1×1); four 40mm (2×2); eight 13.2mm (4×2).
Torpedoes: six 21in (2×3).
Mines: 44.
Complement: 180.

Design Despite the close links with France, it was Great Britain who won the contract for two new destroyers to be built for the Polish Navy in the mid-1930s. This may have reflected certain dissatisfaction with the *Burza*-class ships or just a recognition of the firms in Great Britain as leading destroyers designers. Whatever the reasons, these new destroyers were large and powerful vessels which were superior to the neighbouring German and Russian destroyers. They were also bigger than the British *Tribal*s with a very respectable turn of speed.

The main armament calibre of the previous *Burza* class, 5.1-inch, was changed to the standard British destroyer calibre of 4.7-inch. The guns, however, were not of British manufacture, being Swedish Bofors 50cal QF M34/36, which had also been installed in the minelayer *Gryf*. Unlike British 4.7-inch guns, the Bofors fired a 90lb fixed round. The single mounting was carried in 'A' position, presumably to reduce bow weight. The two 40mm twin Bofors guns were fitted on a stand between the torpedo tubes and just abaft the funnel, while the twin 13.2mm machine-guns were mounted at the after end of the upper bridge and the forward end of the after shelter deck. The torpedo outfit was unusual in that by means of special adaptors, 18-inch torpedoes could be used as well as the normal 21-inch type. Both ships were fitted for minelaying, an important task in the shallow waters of the Baltic, and ASW capability was provided by two chutes and forty depth-charges. Two range-finders were fitted for the main armament, one being on the after shelter deck.

This class had a designed maximum speed of 39 knots, provided by two 27,000shp single reduction geared turbine sets and four boilers with an operating pressure of 385psi. On trials, they achieved 39.26 knots (*Grom*) and 39 knots (*Blyskawica*).

Two ships were ordered from White in 1935 and two more were ordered for construction at Gdynia in May 1939, but these were overtaken by the outbreak of war and they were never laid down.

Modifications Being designed for Baltic operations, these ships experienced difficulties in the North Sea and Atlantic and in consequence, both received

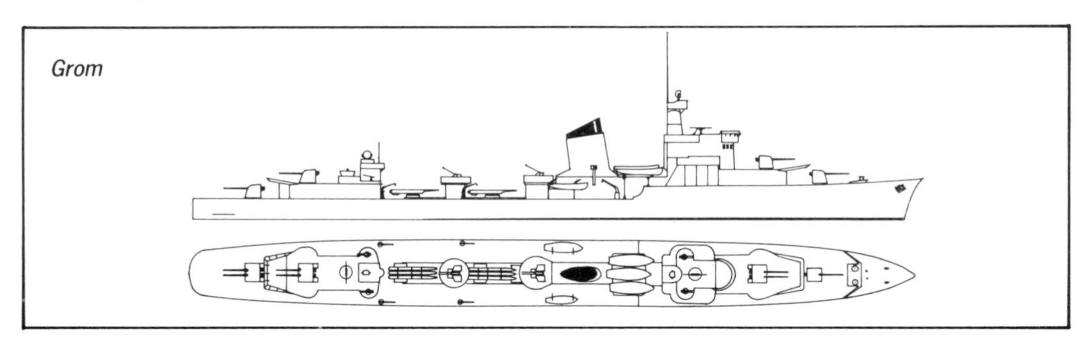

Grom

initial modifications to improve stability after they reached Great Britain in 1939. These involved the removal of the searchlight tower on the foremast as well as the searchlight and deck-house aft. Boats not at davits were landed as were the after torpedo tubes, but the latter were replaced by a 4-inch HA gun. The distinctive funnel cap was also removed. *Grom* was lost in this state. In December 1941, the original 4.7-inch guns were taken out and replaced by eight 4-inch Mk XVI in twin mountings Mk XIX. Her after tubes were replaced and four 20mm guns added in lieu of the 13.2mm machine-guns. In 1941–42, radar 271 was added instead of the after rangefinder and Type 291 fitted at the foremast truck. A high-angle director replaced the former rangefinder on the bridge and two depth-charge throwers were added. By mid-1942, the forward tubes were landed and radar 284 added to the HA director; by 1945, type 293 radar was fitted on the foremast.

Service Both ships reached Great Britain after Operation 'Pekin' on 1 September 1939 and on Britain's entry into the war, formed the Polish Flotilla with *Burza*. This flotilla moved to the south-western approaches in late autumn but were found unsuitable for Atlantic conditions and brought back to Harwich for operations in the North Sea. In April, both were dispatched to Rosyth for operations in Norway where they worked with the fleet. Both ships bombarded communications and enemy positions at Vestfjord, Skjelfjord and Narvik. *Grom* was hit by a 75mm shell from a shore battery which pierced an oil bunker and damaged one boiler on 3 May, but after silencing it, was caught in Rombaksfjord the following day by Heinkel 111s of KG100. These aircraft, flying extremely high, managed to hit *Grom* with two bombs, one on the torpedo casing and one on the ship's side. Broken in two, *Grom* sank with heavy casualties. *Blyskawica* returned to Scapa Flow on 12 May then sailed for Harwich and saw service in the Channel on Operation 'Dynamo' until 1 June 1940, when ordered back to Harwich. A period in dockyard hands followed until late summer, when she sailed north once more for a brief spell on convoys. In September, she was back at Plymouth on offensive patrols off the Brittany coast and in October, was present at the bombardment of Cherbourg. More Atlantic duty followed, based on the Clyde before a major refit in 1942. After the North Africa landings and further convoy duty, *Blyskawica* went to the Mediterranean in 1943 and by May of that year, was with Force Q at Bone. Returning to Britain, served on Arctic duty in the first few months of 1944 and took part in carrier strikes against the Norwegian coast in May and June. The Invasion of Normandy in June, brought her south once more where she was in action as part of the 10th Destroyer Flotilla along the coast of Brittany. In one action, with the German 8th Destroyer Flotilla, two of the Germans, *ZH1* and *Z32* were sunk. In others, German patrol vessels were sunk. She remained in the Channel area until the end of hostilities. After the war, *Blyskawica* took part in Operation 'Deadlight', the disposal of German U-boats in the Atlantic before being turned over to the Royal Navy on 28 May 1946 by the Free Polish Forces. On 1 July 1947, she sailed for Poland and had a long career with the Communist fleet of Poland until finally paid off in October 1974.

TRANSFERRED UNITS

Ouragan

Design French '1500-tonne' *torpilleur* taken over from the Free French Forces. Name was not changed; see page 47.
Modifications See France.
Service Manned by the Polish Navy from 18 July 1940 to 30 April 1941, when she was returned to the Free French Forces.

Garland

Design British *G*-class destroyer, name unchanged. See Great Britain.
Modifications As *G* class.
Service Transferred to Poland on 3 May 1940, while lying at Malta, serving with the Mediterranean fleet in the eastern basin and off Greece. Returned to Great Britain on 3 September and served the rest of 1940 in the Channel with the Polish Flotilla and latterly on the Clyde for Western Approaches Command. From 1941 to 1944 she served on Atlantic and Arctic convoys, but by April 1944, she was in the Mediterranean where in September, with *Terpsichore* and *Troubridge*, she sank *U407*. Later that year, she returned to Great Britain, serving in home waters until May 1945. She reverted to RN control in 1947.

Piorun

Design British *N* class (q.v.).
Modifications As *N* class.
Service Formerly the British *Nerissa* transferred to Poland in October 1940 and renamed. Served initially in the Clyde with other Polish destroyers but she was with Captain Vian's 4th Destroyer Flotilla when the attacks were made on *Bismarck* in May 1941. In September, *Piorun* was in the Mediterranean covering Operation 'Halberd' to Malta, but by June the following year, was part of Escort Group B2 in the North Atlantic. Returning to the Mediterranean, *Piorun* joined other Polish destroyers in the 'Husky' landings on Sicily in July 1943 before moving to the Adriatic for shore bombardment support operations in August and September. The Salerno landings were her next major operation, in September, but in 1944 she returned to the North Sea for sorties against the Norwegian coastal supply traffic. During the Normandy operations she served with the 10th Destroyer Flotilla when she saw action with German destroyers and coastal forces, until the end of 1944. In September 1946, *Piorun* was returned to the Royal Navy.

Orkan

Design British *M* class (q.v.).
Modifications As *M* class.
Service Formerly *Myrmidon*, taken over by Poland in December 1942 prior to completion. She served mainly on Arctic and Atlantic convoy duty except for a brief Biscay deployment in June 1943. In October she was torpedoed and sunk by *U378* while escorting Convoy SC143 as part of the 3rd Support Group.

Slazak, Kujawiak, Krakowiak

Design British *Hunt* Type II (q.v.).
Modifications Standard *Hunt* modifications.
Service Formerly *Bedale* (*Slazak*), taken over in April 1942, *Oakley* (i) (*Kujawiak*) taken over in June 1941 and *Silverton* (*Krakowiak*) in May 1941. *Kujawiak* and *Krakowiak* took part in the Lofoten Raid in December 1941 and then served in the Channel and Western Approaches. *Kujawiak* was dispatched to the Mediterranean in June 1942 for a Malta convoy operation but was mined and sank outside Grand Harbour when attempting to assist *Badsworth*, also mined. *Slazak* was manned by the crew of *Burza*. Her first major operation was the Dieppe Raid of August 1942 following which, both she and *Krakowiak* served in the Channel theatre before going to the Mediterranean in 1943. Both participated in the landings on Sicily and at Salerno. *Krakowiak* also served in the Aegean towards the end of 1943, but both were back in the Channel for duty with the 'Overlord' Invasion forces in June 1944. Thereafter, they served in the Channel and southern North Sea until the end of hostilities. *Krakowiak* reverted to Royal Navy control in September and *Slazak* in November 1946.

Below: *Blyscawicia* as re-armed with twin 4-inch guns, four 20mm and radars 291, 285 and 271. (IWM)

Portugal

Although Portugal has a long seafaring history of exploration and colonization, her navy has never been large or of international importance, nor has it ever been capable of defending even the homeland from sea-borne attack. In 1912 a new programme was authorized for the construction of three battleships, three cruisers, 24 destroyers and six submarines, but lack of financial resources prevented any progress being made. By 1914 the navy consisted of only a handful of old gunboats or cruisers, three destroyers of about 660 tons, four ancient torpedo-boats and one submarine. Portugal remained neutral throughout the First World War during which period only three submarines were added. The destroyers of the *Guadiana* class were armed with one 4-inch and two 3-inch guns as well as four 18-inch torpedo tubes. They were of Yarrow design, very broadly equivalent to the British *H* or *Acorn* class of 1910–11, but with a heavier torpedo armament and turbine propulsion. Two, *Douro* and *Guadiana*, had been discarded by the 1930s. After the end of the First World War, Portugal reinforced her flotilla by obtaining six former Austrian torpedo-boats, of which two were of nineteenth-century vintage. The other four had been completed just prior to, or during, the early war years. All had been discarded by 1940.

In 1930, a new construction programme envisaged the addition of two 5,000-ton cruisers, twelve destroyers and a similar number of submarines and escorts over a period of ten years. A start was made by the ordering of five destroyers, three submarines and six escorts of which all but three destroyers and two escorts were ordered from British yards. The submarines and two of the escorts were originally ordered in Italy. The destroyers, named the *Douro* class, were designed by Yarrow and were of typical British design. While they were under construction, the war between Colombia and Peru led to the sale of two to the former country and two repeats constructed to replace them. None of the rest of the 1930 programme was ever completed, but in May 1938 it was decided to build three more destroyers in Portugal as well as a similar number of submarines and minor war vessels. The destroyers were not, as far as is known, ever laid down and remained only projected.

Neutral once more during the Second World War, Portugal built no more destroyers and the five *Douro*s served into the 1960s as the largest ships of the Portuguese fleet.

DOURO CLASS

Ship	Builder	Laid Down	Launched	Commissioned	Fate
D *Dao*	Lisbon Dkyd.		30 July 34	5 Jan 35	Stricken 29 Nov 60
DR *Douro* (i)	Lisbon Dkyd.		18 Nov 33	16 May 34	To Colombia 1934
DR *Douro* (ii)	Lisbon Dkyd.		16 Aug 35	11 Feb 36	Stricken 1959
L *Lima*	Yarrow		29 May 33	12 Oct 33	Stricken 1960s
T *Tejo* (i)	Lisbon Dkyd.		10 May 33	24 Feb 34	To Colombia 1934
T *Tejo* (ii)	Lisbon Dkyd.		4 May 35	12 Oct 35	Stricken 9 Feb 65
V *Vouga*	Yarrow		25 Jan 33	24 June 33	Stricken 1960s

Displacement: 1,219tons/1,238tonnes (standard); 1,563tons/1,588tonnes (full load).
Length: 323ft/98.45m (oa); 307ft/93.57m (pp).
Beam: 31ft/9.45m.
Draught: 11ft/3.35m (mean).
Machinery: three Yarrow boilers; 2-shaft Parsons-Curtis geared turbines.
Performance: 33,000shp; 36kts.
Bunkerage: 311tons/316tonnes.

Below: *Vouga*. (Courtesy Mr W. C. McMillan)

Range: 5,400nm at 15kts.
Guns: four 4.7in (4×1); three 40mm (3×1).
Torpedoes: eight 21in (2×4).
Mines: 20.
Complement: 127.

Design Designed by Yarrow, these destroyers were typical of the standard British destroyer of the 1920–30 period. Main armament consisted of four 4.7-inch Vickers-Armstrong Mk G 50cal QF guns (although Yarrow records show BL guns), two forward, two aft in single shielded mountings. A total of 140 rounds per gun were carried. Light armament consisted of three 40mm pom-poms in single 85° mountings, two on the after shelter deck and one between the funnels. Two quadruple banks of torpedo tubes and two depth-charge throwers with twelve depth-charges completed the armament. All were fitted for minelaying.

The main machinery included three Yarrow side-fired boilers working at 400psi and equipped with air pre-heaters. The twin-shaft turbine installation had Curtis HP and cruising stages with Parsons LP turbines. This was a similar arrangement to the British *Ambuscade* and the installed power of 33,000shp was identical.

Yarrow received the contract for two destroyers and four sets of machinery on 12 June 1931 as their yard Nos. 1624–1627. These were *Vouga, Lima, Tejo* (i) and *Douro* (i) respectively, of which the latter two were to be built in Portugal at Lisbon. On 18 January 1933, the contract for the machinery of *Dao* was placed with Yarrow as their yard No. 1635. *Vouga* was the first to complete and after inclining tests on 1 April 1933, showed a metacentric height of 16¼ feet. In the fully loaded condition with mines aboard the GM was 2.57 feet. On the official full-power trial on 6 June 1933, *Vouga* reached 36.17 knots (mean) on the Arran Mile with a mean of 32,255shp. Her fastest run was 36.55 knots with 33,050shp. *Lima* made 36.36 knots with 31,110shp on 12 September 1933. As completed, the ship's complement had been increased to 147.

Two ships building in Portugal, *Douro* (Yarrow yard No. 1627) and *Tejo* (Yarrow yard No. 1626) were sold to Colombia while under completion and renamed *Caldas* and *Antioquia* respectively [sic]. This was to counter the two Peruvian destroyers *Guise* and *Villar* purchased from Estonia in 1933 at a time of tension between Colombia and Peru. Two new ships were ordered as replacements, being given the same names. Once again, Yarrow's engined these ships as their yard Nos. 1654 and 1655, but the hulls were built at Lisbon.

Modifications During the middle war years, having noted the experience of the combatant navies, Portugal augmented the anti-aircraft defence of these ships by the addition of three 20mm guns, in the bridge wings and abaft the second funnel. The forward tubes were landed and two 20mm added in lieu and the 40mm removed. Two of the 40mm, on the after shelter deck were replaced by 20mm guns. Further modifications were made post-war.

Service Local defence and neutrality patrols during the war years.

Note: Also extant during the Second World War was the old destroyer *Tamega*, launched in January 1922, but she was not effective as a fighting unit any longer.

Below: *Lima* on trials in the Clyde. (Courtesy Mr W. C. McMillan)

Romania

Romania maintained a small naval force primarily for coast defence and coastguard duties together with some river gunboats, for use on the Danube. Being backward, with no industrial base, and lacking strong financial resources, Romania could pay little attention to seaward defence and could not hope to counter the strong Russian Black Sea Fleet. The largest ship in the fleet, the old Elswick cruiser, *Elizabetha*, was over-aged even in 1914 and the only other warships, apart from river monitors, were the three *Nalucca* class torpedo-boats, which were as old as the cruiser. These torpedo-boats (of French design) dated from 1888, displaced only 56 tons and were armed with two torpedoes. In 1914, a start was made on modernizing the Navy and providing it with some effective fighting ships. To this end, an order was placed with an Italian yard for four 1,700-ton destroyers, but like many other minor neutral powers in 1914, Romania suffered the disappointment of having her order comandeered by a beligerent power, in this case, Italy. Although Romania did declare war on 27 August 1916, joining the Allies against the central powers, she did not get her destroyers back immediately. On land, a disastrous campaign saw the Romanian Army defeated and thereafter, during the war, the army received priority in re-equipment and the navy played little part.

After the end of the First World War, Romania did succeed in recovering two of the four destroyers and, at the same time, she also acquired seven former Austrian torpedo-boats as war reparations. One of these, *Fulgerul* (ex-*84F*) foundered in the Bosphorus en route to Romania. Of the remainder, *Vartejul* (ex-*75T*), *Viforul* (ex-*74T*) and *Vijelia* (ex-*80T*) were discarded in 1932.

During the mid-1920s, a modest new construction programme was put in hand, consisting of four destroyers and two submarines, but in the end only two of the destroyers and one submarine materialized. Ten years or so later, in 1937, a further programme was projected, which would have built a cruiser, four small destroyers, three submarines and some smaller ships. Only two of the submarines and a minelayer were actually completed.

As in the earlier conflict, Romania remained neutral initially during the Second World War but during 1940 she was forced to cede Bessarabia under Soviet pressure and also concluded a treaty with Germany, allowing the latter to move troops through Romania. This was needed to facilitate the German thrust against Yugoslavia, and German troops first entered the country on 7 October, a month after the abdication of King Carol. The net result of these manoeuvres was that when Romania did enter the war, it was, unlike 1916, on the side of the Axis Powers, for she saw a chance of regaining her lost territory.

The main task of the Romanian Navy was to secure the supply routes of the advancing Axis armies along the western and northern coasts of the Black Sea. This, in the main, involved escorting convoys to and from the Bosphorus to Varna (in Bulgaria) and Constanza, an important route for oil supplies to Axis forces in the Mediterranean. A second major route was from Constanza to the Crimea, when the advance extended that far. Thus, the navy's role was essentially anti-submarine and the only offensive action performed was by the submarine arm and they were few in number. As the war progressed and Axis fortunes reversed, the navy helped cover the evacuation from Sevastopol in 1944 until Romania agreed terms with the Soviet Union on 23 August 1944. Thereafter, Romanian forces fought the retreating Germans and only the riverine forces saw any further action. With the Soviet occupation of Romania, most of the fleet was, in 1944, taken over by the Red Navy and in some cases, not returned for many years.

MARASTI CLASS

Ship	Builder	Laid Down	Launched	Commissioned	Fate
Mărăşti	Pattison, Naples	29 Jan 14	26 Mar 17	15 July 17	Discarded 1963
Mărăşeşti	Pattison, Naples	15 July 14	30 Jan 18	15 May 18	Discarded 1963

Displacement: 1,410tons/1,432tonnes (standard); 1,723tons/1,750tonnes (full load).
Length: 309ft/94.18m (pp).
Beam: 31ft/9.47m.
Draught: 11ft 6in/3.5m (mean).
Machinery: five Thornycroft boilers; 2-shaft Tosi turbines.
Performance: 45,000shp; 34kts.
Bunkerage: 260tons/264tonnes.
Range: 1,700nm at 15kts.
Guns: five 4.7in (2×2, 1×1); four 3in (4×1); two 13.2mm.
Torpedoes: four 18in (2×2).
Complement: 139.

Design Originally a class of four ordered in Italy in 1913 as *Vifor, Viscol, Vartei* and *Vijelia*, but requisitioned by the Royal Italian Navy in 1915. They were renamed *Aquila, Falco, Nibbio* and *Sparviero*. Large, fast and well armed for their time, these ships originally mounted three single 6-inch guns of Armstrong 1899-pattern, as well as four 3-inch guns. Their torpedo layout was a little unusual in that the two twin banks of tubes were shipped to port and starboard of the midships funnel, while the deck abaft the after funnel remained unused. In comparison with contemporary Italian destroyers, they were much larger and carried more heavy calibre guns. As a result they were classified as *esploratori* or scouts and in the Black Sea would have been well matched with the existing Imperial Russian destroyers. They adopted turbine propulsion, proving very fast on trials, *Mărăşeşti* making 38.04 knots on 48,020shp. Later she was credited with achieving more than 40 knots. After war service with the Royal Italian Navy, *Sparviero* and *Nibbio* were returned to the Royal Romanian Navy as *Mărăşti* and *Mărăşeşti* respectively, arriving in Constanza on 1 July 1920. The other pair were not returned (one of which was not completed until 1920) and remained in Italian service until sold to

Left: *Marasti*. Note damaged barrel on No. 1 gun. (Nordmark Film, Kiel) **Above:** *Marasesti*. (Romanian Naval Museum)

Spain in 1937 (q.v.). Both were extensively refitted and re-armed in Italy in 1925–26 when the 6-inch guns were landed, being replaced by twin 4.7-inch 45cal Schneider-Canet-Armstrong M1918/19 twin mountings forward and aft with a single M1918 gun amidships. The two quarter-deck 3-inch guns were also landed.

Modifications In 1939 the armament was further modified by the removal of the midships 4.7-inch gun when it was replaced by two twin 13.2mm Hotchkiss machine-guns. The two remaining 3-inch guns were also landed and two single Rheinmetall 37mm fitted in lieu. Depth-charge equipment was shipped aft and an Italian-pattern depth-charge projector added. During the war four single 20mm guns were added, on the forecastle, quarter deck and bridge wings, and the 37mm outfit was increased to four.

Service These old but still powerful ships were seldom offensively employed by the Romanians, but used instead for escort duties between Constanza and the Crimea as well as to the Bosphorus to safeguard the vital oil route to the Mediterranean Sea. They also covered minelaying sorties off the Romanian and occupied Soviet coasts. *Mărăşti* suffered damage to her turbine rotor cover in 1941–42 and was thereafter only capable of 22 knots. During 1943 much of their work was on the Constanza-Sevastopol route and in the course of one such convoy, *Mărăşeşti* depth-charged and sank the submarine *M31* on 7 July 1943. Both ships covered the supply traffic to the surrounded Axis forces in the Crimea during the spring of 1944, but *Mărăşti* ran aground in April 1944, badly damaging her propellers, and remained out of action at Constanza until the end of the war. Her sister was damaged in the heavy air raids by the USAAF at Constanza on 20 August 1944 and Romania capitulated three days later, declaring war on her former Allies the following day. When the Red Army occupied that port on 30 August, both destroyers were seized and put into service with the Red Navy as *Lovky* (ex-*Mărăşti*) and *Lyogky* (ex-*Mărăşeşti*). They were eventually returned to the Romanian Navy in 1946 and renamed yet again, *D11* and *D12* respectively. Well over-aged, they served as training ships until scrapped in the 1960s.

REGELE FERDINAND CLASS

Ship	Builder	Laid Down	Launched	Commissioned	Fate
RF *Regele Ferdinand*	Pattison, Naples	June 1927	2 Dec 28	7 Sept 30	Discarded 1960s
RM *Regina Maria*	Pattison, Naples	1927	2 Mar 29	7 Sept 30	Discarded 1960s

Displacement: 1,400tons/1,422tonnes (standard); 1,850tons/1,879tonnes (full load).
Length: 334ft 4in/101.9m (oa).
Beam: 31ft 6in/9.6m.
Draught: 11ft 6in/3.51m (mean).
Machinery: four Thornycroft boilers; 2-shaft Parsons geared turbines.
Performance: 52,000shp; 37kts.
Range: 3,000nm at 15kts.
Guns: five 4.7in (5×1); one 3in AA; two 40mm; two MG.
Torpedoes: six 21in (2×3).
Mines: 50.
Complement: 212.

Design When Romania had sufficient funds for a further small expansion of her fleet, she once again placed orders with the Pattison yard at Naples. This yard had connections with English shipyards and their designs were often based on British practice. Like many minor powers, Romania required powerful ships but could only afford them in penny numbers so it was natural that she chose one of the most effective destroyer designs of the era, a British flotilla leader type. Designed by Thornycroft and visually comparable to the *Shakespeare* class of 1918, these ships carried a similar armament of five 4.7-inch guns to the *Mărăşti* class, but being a British design, the guns were single shielded mountings. Two were forward, two aft and one abaft the second funnel. These guns were 50cal Bofors-pattern QF model (45° elevation). Bofors

Below: *Regele Ferdinand*. (Nordmark Film Kiel)

also supplied the single 3-inch HA gun, carried between the funnels on a bandstand. Bofors may well have supplied the light AA guns too, a pair of single, shielded 40mm guns on the main deck, abreast the after funnel. (Romanian sources quote four 40mm, but only two appear to have been fitted). Minelaying equipment was fitted with accommodation for fifty mines. The German company, Siemens, supplied the fire-control equipment, separate rangefinders being fitted for the forward and after armament groups. Two triple banks of tubes for 21-inch torpedoes were fitted, the first time this calibre had been used in the Royal Romanian Navy. The armament was completed by a single depth-charge rail aft.

Internally, the machinery layout differed from that of *Shakespeare* in that the turbine rooms were en-echelon, and unlike the direct drive plant in *Mărăşti*, these destroyers adopted single reduction geared turbines of Parsons' design, built by Stabilimento Technico of Trieste. A speed of 38 knots was achieved on trials. Both arrived in Constanza and were officially named on 7 September 1930.

Modifications In 1939 the 40mm were replaced by two Rheinmetall 37mm guns and two 13.2mm Hotchkiss. Two trainable Italian-pattern depth-charge mortars which elevated to 45° were fitted to port and starboard just abaft the after gun. These fired 200lb depth-charges and resembled large coal-scuttles! Visually appearance was altered by the addition of a clinker screen to the forward funnel. Light AA was increased by about four 20mm and the 3-inch gun was landed. In 1944, 'A' gun was replaced by a short-calibre 88mm DP gun.

Service Despite the obvious potential of these relatively modern destroyers, they, like their older consorts, were never used on offensive duties despite the occasional sweeps by the Soviet warships against the western coast of the Black Sea. The reasons for this are unclear, but in all probability it was due to the relatively low state of training of the Royal Romanian Navy and possibly a degree of imprecise co-operation with their German Allies. As by far the most powerful surface units available to the Axis forces, perhaps more could have been expected of them, but it should be remembered that there were only two of them facing the whole Soviet Black Sea Fleet. Their war service was spent on convoy duty on the two main supply routes, i.e., that between the Bosphorus and Constanza and to the Crimea. *Regele Ferdinand* scored an early success in 1941 when she depth-charged and sank the Soviet submarine *M54* off the Romanian coast in November. Both ships participated in the evacuation of the Crimea in 1944, but *Regele Ferdinand* was one of the ships damaged in the great air raid on Constanza on 20 August. After the Romanian collapse, both destroyers were taken over by the Soviet Navy, being renamed *Likhoi* (*Regele Ferdinand*) and *Letuchy* (*Regina Maria*). They were not given back to Romania until 1953, when they were renamed *D22* and *D21* respectively. Later still, they were renumbered as *D10* and *D9* before being discarded during the 1960s.

Above: *Regina Maria* during the war. (Bundesarchiv)

Below: *Regina Maria* in May 1937. (Wright & Logan)

NALUCA CLASS

Ship	Builder	Laid Down	Launched	Commissioned	Fate
Naluca (ex-*82F*)	Danubius, Porto Ré	30 Oct 13	11 Aug 14	16 Aug 16	Lost 20 Aug 44
Smeul (ex-*83F*)	Danubius, Porto Ré	17 Nov 13	7 Nov 14	7 Aug 15	Broken up 1960

Displacement: 266tons/270tonnes (standard); 330tons/335tonnes (full load).
Length: 192ft 9in/58.8m (oa); 191ft 11in/58.5m (wl); 189ft 7in/57.8m (pp).
Beam: 19ft 2in/5.8m.
Draught: 5ft 1in/1.5m (mean).
Machinery: two Yarrow boilers; 2-shaft A.E.G. turbines.
Performance: 5,000shp; 28kts.
Bunkerage: 20tons/20.3tonnes (coal) + 34tons/34.5tonnes (oil).
Range: 1,200nm at 16kts.
Guns: two 66mm; 2 MG.
Complement: 38.

Design Built originally for the Austro-Hungarian Fleet during the First World War, these two ships were transferred to Romania in 1920. A third ship, *Fulgerul* (ex-*84F*) was also transferred but foundered in the Bosphorus en route to Romania. Six sister-ships went to Portugal and four to Yugoslavia, but only the Yugoslav vessels survived into the Second World War. By 1939, they were obsolete but useful for escort duties.

Modifications In 1939 one 66mm was replaced by a 37mm gun and a 20mm was added amidships. During the war, both were rearmed with two single 88mm guns and two 20mm, landing both the banks of torpedo tubes. *Smeul* may have later lost the forward gun for another 20mm plus a machine-gun.

Service Both ships were employed as convoy escorts along the western coast of the Black Sea 1941–44 and also to the Crimea. On occasions, they covered various minelaying operations by Romanian and German minelayers. *Naluca* was sunk in a Soviet air raid on Constanza, but *Smeul* survived to be taken over by the Soviet Navy as *Toros*, being returned to Romania on 22 September 1945. Refitted at Galatz from October 1945, *Smeul* re-entered service in 1948. She was finally discarded in 1959–60.

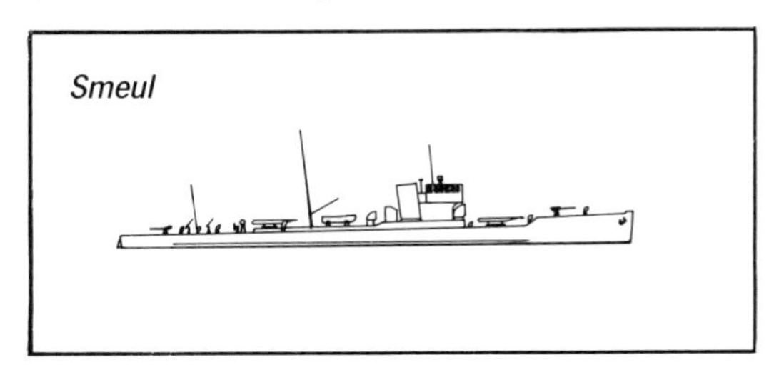

SBORUL CLASS

Ship	Builder	Laid Down	Launched	Commissioned	Fate
Sborul (ex-*81T*)	Stabilimento, Trieste	6 Feb 14	6 Aug 14	1 Dec 14	Stricken 1960

Displacement: 262tons/266tonnes (standard); 320tons/325tonnes (full load).
Length: 190ft 9in/58.2m (wl); 188ft/57.3m (pp).
Beam: 18ft 9in/5.7m.
Draught: 5ft 1in/1.5m (mean).
Machinery: two Yarrow boilers; 2-shaft Parsons turbines.
Performance: 5,000shp; 28kts.
Bunkerage: 24tons/24.3tonnes (coal) + 18tons/18.2tonnes (oil).
Range: 980nm at 16kts.
Guns: two 66mm; 2 MG.
Torpedoes: four 18in (2×2).
Complement: 38.

Design One of a class of eight 250-ton High Seas Torpedo-boats built for the Austro-Hungarian Navy during the First World War of which half were allocated to Romania post-war. Four others went to Yugoslavia, but only two of the Yugoslav and one Romanian boat were still extant in 1939. Like all her sisters *Sborul* was over-aged but still useful for patrol and escort work.

Modifications As *Naluca* and *Smeul*.

Service Employed in similar fashion to *Naluca* and *Smeul*. Renamed *Musson* when captured by the Soviets in 1944, but returned at the same time as *Smeul* and reverted to her original Romanian name. Re-entered service after refit at Galatz in 1946 and finally stricken in 1959–60.

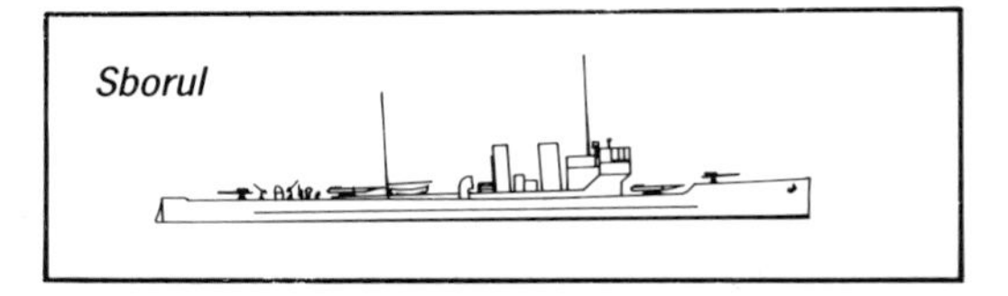

Left: *Smeul.* (Nordmark Film, Kiel) **Above:** *Sborul*, with *Smeul*-class boat in background. (W. B. Bilddienst) **Below:** *Phuket*, post-1939–45 with 40mm guns. (Royal Thai Navy)

Siam

Until the early years of the twentieth century, the small Siamese coastal defence fleet was comprised mostly of small gunboats and armed merchantmen commanded, surprisingly enough, mainly by Scandinavian officers. However, before the First World War, Siam purchased two 375-ton destroyers from Japan and four 90-ton torpedo-boats, all of which served until the late 1930s. Siam did not declare war until July 1917, on the side of Great Britain and the Allies, and her participation was limited to the seizure of enemy merchant ships trapped in her ports. After the war, Siam obtained one modern destroyer from Great Britain which served under the Siamese ensign for almost forty years! The first post-war new construction was a coast defence ship armed with two 6-inch guns, ordered from Armstrong's in 1924. The order for a sister ship followed in 1928. It was 1934, however, which saw the beginning of a large expansion of the navy, for in that year, a major programme was initiated which included two more coast defence ships, nine torpedo-boats, three small torpedo-boats, four submarines and several escorts, minelayers, etc. Construction was shared between Japan and Italy. The nine torpedo-boats were ordered in Italy while the smaller craft were built in Japan. All of this programme was completed, but the two light cruisers ordered in 1938 from Italian yards were eventually requisitioned by the Royal Italian Navy at the end of 1941. Neither was ever completed.

Siam was not initially affected by the outbreak of hostilities in 1939, but in 1941 friction with Vichy Indo-China led to an engagement which left her navy rather crippled. When war broke out in the Pacific theatre in December 1941, Siam was invaded by the Japanese from French Indo-China and the Navy fell under the control of the IJN. It seems to have played little part in the war and emerged in 1945 with almost all its ships intact.

THORNYCROFT R CLASS

Ship	Builder	Laid Down	Launched	Commissioned	Fate
Pra Ruang	Thornycroft	9 Dec 15	25 Nov 16	28 Feb 17	Stricken July 1959

Displacement: 1,035tons/1,051tonnes (standard).
Length: 274ft/83.5m (oa); 265ft/80.77m (pp).
Beam: 27ft 4in/8.32m.
Draught: 11ft/3.3m (mean).
Machinery: three Yarrow boilers; 2-shaft Brown-Curtis geared turbines.
Performance: 29,000shp; 35kts.
Bunkerage: 285tons/289tonnes.
Range: 1,940nm at 10kts.
Guns: three 4in; one 3in; two 20mm.
Torpedoes: four 21in (2×2).
Complement: 113.

Design A Thornycroft variant of the R-class destroyer built for the Royal Navy during the First World War and sold by the Admiralty back to Thornycroft on 21 June 1920 for resale to Siam. She was formally renamed *Pra Ruang* in September 1920.
Modifications Not known.
Service Used mainly for training duties by the time of the Second World War.

TRAD CLASS

Ship	Builder	Laid Down	Launched	Commissioned	Fate
11 *Trad*	C.R.D.A. Monfalcone	9 Feb 34	29 Sept 35	19 Mar 35	Paid off 26 Nov 75
12 *Phuket*	C.R.D.A. Monfalcone	7 Jan 34	26 Oct 35	19 Mar 35	Paid off 26 Nov 75
13 *Pattani*	C.R.D.A. Monfalcone	31 Mar 35	28 Nov 36	5 Oct 38	Paid off 26 Nov 75
21 *Surasdra*	C.R.D.A. Monfalcone	31 Mar 35	14 Nov 36	5 Oct 38	Paid off 23 Nov 77
22 *Chandaburi*	C.R.D.A. Monfalcone	6 June 36	28 Nov 36	5 Oct 38	Paid off 16 Dec 76
23 *Rayong*	C.R.D.A. Monfalcone	6 June 36	16 Dec 36	5 Oct 38	Paid off 16 Dec 76
31 *Chumporn*	C.R.D.A. Monfalcone	7 July 36	12 Jan 37	5 Oct 38	Paid off 26 Nov 75
32 *Cholburi*	C.R.D.A. Monfalcone	22 Aug 36	18 Jan 37	5 Oct 38	Lost 17 Jan 41
33 *Songkla*	C.R.D.A. Monfalcone	29 Aug 36	10 Feb 37	5 Oct 38	Lost 17 Jan 41

Displacement: 318tons/323tonnes (standard); 470tons/477tonnes (full load).
Length: 223ft/67.97m (oa); 219ft/66.75m (pp).
Beam: 21ft/6.4m.
Draught: 7ft/2.13m (mean).
Machinery: two Yarrow boilers; 2-shaft Parsons geared turbines.
Performance: 9,000shp; 31kts.
Bunkerage: 102tons/103tonnes.
Range: 1,700nm at 15kts.
Guns: three 3in (3×1); two 20mm (2×1); four 8mm MG.
Torpedoes: six 18in (2×2, 2×1).
Complement: 70.

Design Diminutive versions of the contemporary *Spica*-class torpedo-boats, these ships were fast and well armed for their size. Their torpedo tubes were disposed with the twin banks on the centre-line abaft No. 2 gun and the singles to port and starboard of the forecastle break. The main armament was supplied by Vickers-Armstrong. Like all Italian construction of this period, fast speeds were obtained on trials with *Trad* reaching 32.54 knots.
Modifications Apparently none during hostilities.
Service *Trad*, *Cholburi* and *Songkla* were escorting the coast defence ships *Dhonburi* and *Sri Ayuthia* in Koh-Chang roads in the Gulf of Siam on 17 January 1941, when they were attacked by the Vichy French Far East Squadron consisting of the light cruiser *Lamotte-Piquet* and several sloops. During the engagement, *Cholburi* and *Songkla* were sunk as was *Dhonburi*, and *Trad* was badly damaged. The remainder of the class survived the war under Japanese control.

Soviet Union

From early Imperial days, Russia had interested herself in the development of the mine, which was an ideal weapon for the shallow waters of the Baltic and Black Seas. When, therefore, a self-propelled mine, i.e., a torpedo, was invented, it was natural that this new weapon be adopted also because, in the Gulf of Finland at least, the long approaches to the main naval base at Kronstadt could be easily defended by torpedo-boats in and around the myriad islands off the Finnish coast. Russian torpedo-craft had their origins in the spar torpedo-boats used in the 1870s, but by the end of that decade, the true Whitehead torpedo had made its appearance in the Black Sea, being used for the first time against the Turkish Fleet. Encouraged by the success obtained in the war with Turkey, the Russian Admiralty instigaged a crash programme of torpedo-boat construction. Such was the rate of this programme that by 1878 no less than 110 of these craft had been completed. All, however, were very small, displacing between 20 and 30 tonnes with the majority at the lower end of this range. Most were built in Russian yards, with foreign assistance notably from Yarrow, while a few were built by Thornycroft and some by German yards. In service, however, this huge 'mosquito' fleet proved a distinct disappointment due to lack of seaworthiness and unreliability. Weather conditions in winter in the Baltic did nothing to improve matters either. Most were employed in the Baltic with some being sent to the Black Sea and nine sent to the Siberian Flotilla. Nine more boats were sent out to Vladivostock by rail in 1904, when tension rose between Russia and Japan. The majority had been struck off the Navy List by 1908, or used for subsidiary duties.

The answer to the problems lay in larger and more sea-worthy boats and Russia, like all other sea powers, followed this route. Tonnage gradually rose to about 200 tons with the *Lastochka* type of 1904, which carried three torpedo tubes and were capable of 30 knots. Thereafter, displacement increased to 300 tons with the *Twerdi* class of 1905–06, but, as with other navies of this period, classification became confused by the appearance of the Torpedo-boat Destroyer which at first differed little from the torpedo-boat itself. Foreign influence and assistance from Yarrow, Normand, Schichau and Germania remained strong into the first decade of the twentieth century, but thereafter declined somewhat and more designs were home-grown. War with Japan in 1904 gave opportunity for the torpedo-craft to demonstrate their merits, but the performance on both sides failed to live up to expectations. After the Russo-Japanese war, destroyer construction lapsed with the four *Kondratenko*-class ships of 625-tons displacement, which were coal-fired, reciprocating-engined ships, armed with two 4-inch guns and three torpedo tubes. Attractive two-funnelled ships with a pronounced ram bow, this class were contemporaries of the British *River* class and German *S120* design. In comparison with the British type, the Russian ships were larger with fewer but larger calibre guns and one more torpedo tube. The German destroyers (actually still classified as 'torpedo-boats') were considerably smaller, only lightly gunned but were armed also with three torpedo tubes. They were also considerably faster than the Russian boats. In technical terms, however, both Britain and Germany were beginning to install turbine propulsion and the former was intending to change to oil fuel with the 1905-programme *Tribal* class.

During the decade leading up to the First World War, no further destroyer or torpedo-boat construction was undertaken by the Imperial Russian Navy except for one ship. Nevertheless, this one ship was of extreme importance for it involved doubling the displacement of *Kondratenko* and at the same time adopting both turbine propulsion and full oil-firing. Installed power was quintupled to give a speed of 36 knots. Completed in 1913, this boat (*Novik*) out-gunned contemporary German destroyers and shipped eight torpedoes to the Germans' six. From 1914, a further 53 destroyers of a similar type were ordered, divided into a number of sub-types, displacing between 1,100 and 1,350 tons, capable of 33 to 35 knots. As with most Russian shipbuilding, the pace of construction was slow and of these, only thirty were completed. One, *Grom*, became a war loss on 14 October 1917 and twelve others were lost or scuttled during the Civil War of 1918–20. Six went to Bizerte with the White Russian forces in 1920 and were later scrapped there. Nine more were cancelled incomplete. Of the other destroyers, eleven became war losses before the Revolution and many others were scuttled or taken by the Whites afterwards.

Following the end of the Civil War, the country, now Soviet Russia, remained in turmoil and was unable to continue warship design because the skills had been lost, either by emigration or execution. Foreign assistance was entirely lacking and in the period 1920 to 1930, Russia was able to complete only six destroyers, all of which had been laid down during the war years. Thus by 1930, the Soviet Navy could dispose only seventeen destroyers, all First World War *Novik* type, including the former *Novik* herself (since renamed). In 1932, shipbuilding and industrial capacity had been somewhat restored, enough to allow new destroyer construction, albeit with Italian assistance. This design, the Type 7 with the later modification type 7U, formed the backbone of the Soviet Navy's destroyer force during the Second World War. Also constructed were a class of six large flotilla leaders of the *Leningrad* class, an extension of the *Novik* concept. This idea was perpetuated by the *Tashkent*, built in Italy, but construction of her successors and many of the Type 7, 7U and later classes was severely disrupted by the German invasion in June 1941. Many destroyers were captured incomplete, destroyed on the slips or just suspended due to other pressing (army) priorities.

Wartime service by Soviet destroyers led initially to heavy losses for little return, particularly in the Baltic, followed in this theatre by enforced inactivity bottled up at Leningrad. In the Arctic, the destroyers of the Northern Fleet led a relatively uneventful existence, when their presence in force on the Russian convoys would have been of inestimable benefit to the Allies. The Black Sea Fleet destroyers were fairly active in shore support operations, but, as in the Baltic, early losses and the withdrawal to bases on the eastern shore led to a sharp drop in activity, despite an overwhelming superiority in strength. Here and in the Arctic, Soviet Naval forces could and should have achieved far more than they did, but in the Baltic the collapse of the Red Army left the Navy in a precarious position which would have taxed any navy. When the Red Army went on the offensive in 1944, clearing the German forces from the Gulf of Finland and Baltic shores, the Soviet Navy's surface ships in the main, remained inactive, despite the weakness of the Kriegsmarine by that time. Today, it is evident that, despite the poor showing of the Soviet Navy, the importance of sea power has been fully appreciated by the Kremlin and it is now a force to be reckoned with throughout the world.

LENINGRAD CLASS

Ship	Builder	Laid Down	Launched	Commissioned	Fate
Leningrad	Zhdanov, Leningrad	Nov 1932	1933	Dec 1936	?
Minsk	Zhdanov, Leningrad	5 Oct 34	6 Nov 35	23 Feb 39	Auxiliary 1959
Moskva	Marti, Nikolaiev	1932	1935	Aug 1937	Lost 26 June 41
Kharkov	Marti, Nikolaiev	1932	1936	15 Sept 38	Lost 6 Oct 43
Tbilisi	Nikolaiev-Dalzavod	1936	1938	1939	?
Baku	Nikolaiev-Komsomolsk	1936	25 July 38	6 May 40	?

Displacement: 2,150tons/2,184tonnes (standard); 2.582tons/2,623tonnes (full load).
Length: 418ft 3in/127.5m (oa).
Beam: 38ft 5in/11.7m.
Draught: 13ft 4in/4.06m (mean).
Machinery: three boilers; 2-shaft geared turbines.
Performance: 66,000shp; 36kts.
Bunkerage: 600tons/610tonnes.
Range: 2,100nm at 20kts.
Guns: five 5.1in (5×1); two 3in (2×1); two 45mm (2×1).
Torpedoes: eight 21in (2×4).
Mines: 70 to 80.
Complement: 250.

Design These large flotilla leaders were the first new construction undertaken by Soviet Russia since 1920. Three were authorized under the first Five Year Building Programme and were built to a design known as 'Projekt 1'. Armed with five 5.1-inch guns in single mountings, these ships were contemporaries of the French *contre-torpilleurs*, but with a different position for No. 3 gun, which was shipped between the bridge and forefunnel. It is possible that some design assistance was received from French or Italian sources. Displacing more than 2,500 tons at full load displacement, the machinery arrangement comprised a 3-shaft layout using, for the first time, geared turbines. Visually, they were heavy looking, distinctive ships with large raked funnels and a massive bridge structure. The fore ends had noticeably little sheer and this fact, combined with the weighty bridge, made them poor sea-boats in service.

The main armament of five guns was good, but No. 3 gun had a very restricted arc of fire and its omission would have benefited the design by a reduction in top-weight for little actual loss in useful fire-power. Two single 3-inch/55cal guns comprised the heavy AA outfit, a common calibre for the period, before the speed of aircraft rose much above 120mph. Similar guns were carried by British and US destroyers. These guns were shipped on the after shelter deck where they commanded fairly good arcs of fire. On the after end of the forward shelter deck were two single semi-automatic 45mm/46 guns, fulfilling the role of the contemporary 2pdr fitted in British destroyers. Quadruple torpedo tubes were shipped for the first time in Soviet destroyers and, like all Soviet ships, they were capable of minelaying.

Under the first programme, one unit (*Leningrad*) was laid down for the Baltic Fleet and two (*Moskva* and *Kharkov*) for the Black Sea Fleet in 1932. Construction proceeded fairly slowly, not surprisingly, since these were the first large ships built under the Soviet rule. Three more ships were authorized under the second Five Year Plan and laid down in 1934, for the Baltic and Pacific fleets. These were *Minsk, Baku* and *Tbilisi* respectively, and completed to a modified design known as Projekt 38. *Baku* was originally named *Kiev* and laid down as such, but renamed successively *Sergyei Ordzhonikidze* and *Ordzhonikidze* in 1939 before receiving the name *Baku* on 25 September 1940, i.e., after completion. Visual differences between the two groups appear to have been minimal. *Leningrad* was the first to complete and reportedly achieved 36.30 knots on trials, but other sources credit her with more than 39 knots.

Modifications It is unlikely that the two Baltic units, *Minsk* and *Moskva*, received much in the way of modification before their early loss, and it is probable also that alterations to *Kharkov* were limited to some additional AA guns. The ships serving with the Northern Fleet appear to have received the most attention with *Baku* having six single 37mm added and six .5in machine-guns. She also received US-pattern surface warning radar in a PT-boat type

Above: *Moskova* in 1939. (Author's Collection)

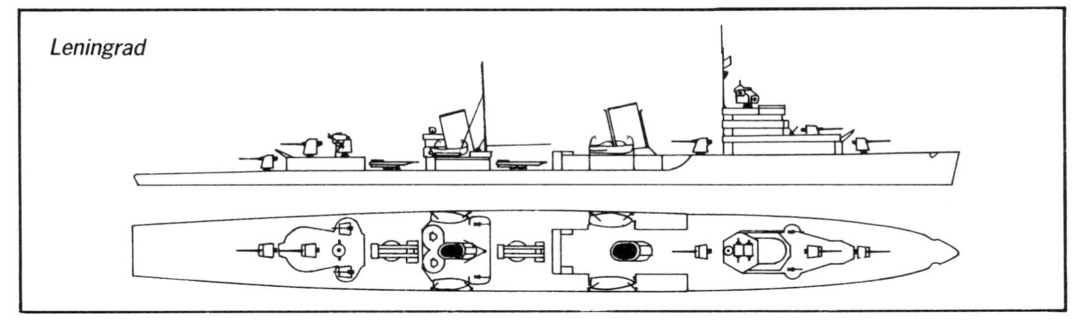

dome at the foremast truck, and British-pattern gunnery radar fitted to her forward gun director. In addition, the mainmast was removed and the W/T aerials led to the after funnel. Some units had No. 3 5.1-inch gun removed.

Service In the Baltic, *Minsk* participated in bombardment operations during the war with Finland in 1939. With the German invasion in 1941, both destroyers supported Soviet forces in Reval and elsewhere, but as the Red Army fell back, they covered the evacuation of the city in August when *Minsk* was badly damaged by mines while forcing her way back to Leningrad. *Leningrad* took part in the evacuation of the Soviet base at Hangö, but she too was badly damaged by mines en route to her name city in November. After the fleet had been blockaded in Leningrad, *Minsk* was sunk by Stuka dive-bombers off Kronstadt on 23 September 1941. However, she was refloated and repaired, being recommissioned in November 1942, but neither she nor her sister took any further active sea-going part in the war except for bombardment support of the Red Army from within the approaches to Leningrad.

The destroyers of the Black Sea Fleet were some of the most active of the Soviet vessels, but *Moskva* was an early loss when mined off Constanza while on a bombardment raid with *Kharkov*. They had effectively shelled ammunition depots, but when attempting to evade the reply from an 11-inch railway gun battery, *Moskova* ran into a Romanian defensive field. Although her paravanes caught a mine, they did not sever the wire and it swung in, hitting her amidships, whereupon *Moskva* broke in two and sank. *Kharkov* continued a very active career, supporting the retreating Red Army from the Romanian frontier, first to Odessa, then Nikolaiev and finally Sevastopol. From November 1941 to June 1942, *Kharkov* was continuously employed running supplies and troops to the encircled fortress interspersed with bombardments of the attacking Axis troop positions. On 18 June she was damaged and had to be towed away. After Sevastopol had fallen *Kharkov*, off the eastern coast in support of troops at Novorossisk in September, took part in an offensive sortie against Axis shipping traffic off the Romanian coast at the end of November. The following month she shelled Yalta and continued shore support duties into 1943. Finally, she was dispatched to shell Yalta once more in October 1943, but on withdrawal accompanied by *Sposobny* and *Besposhchadny*, was attacked by Stukas of St.G.77. *Kharkov* was hit in the first attack and taken in town by *Sposobny*. A second attack hit all three ships and a third sank first *Besposhchadny* then *Kharkov* and finally *Sposobny*.

Tbilisi and *Baku* in the Pacific were not affected by hostilities until July 1942 when, on the 15th, *Baku* sailed for service with the Northern Fleet via the Siberian seaway. After an arduous passage across the northern coast of Russia, she finally arrived at Kola on 14 October, a three-month journey. In Arctic waters, she performed local escort duties between Kola and the White Sea and short-range escort of the occasional Russian convoy. In January 1943, she and *Razumny* had a brief engagement west of Varanger Fjord with the German minelayer *Skagerrak* and two minesweepers, but failed to inflict damage. By 1944, she was engaged in bombarding Axis army positions on the Arctic front and finished the war on this task.

Above: *Leningrad* in about 1948. (Author's Collection)

TASHKENT CLASS

Ship	Builder	Laid Down	Launched	Commissioned	Fate
Tashkent	O.T.O. Livorno	Jan 1937	21 Nov 37	May 1939	Lost 2 July 42
Modified Units:					
Kiev	Marti, Nikolaiev	Oct 1939	12 Dec 40	–	Not completed
Ochakov	61 Kommunar Yd.	1940	–	–	Scrapped on slip
Perekop	61 Kommunar Yd.	1940	–	–	Scrapped on slip
Yerevan	Marti, Nikolaiev	Dec 1939	29 June 41	–	Not completed

Displacement: 2,893tons/2,939tonnes (standard); 3,200tons/3,251tonnes (full load).
Length: 458ft 6in/139.7m (oa).
Beam: 45ft/13.7m.
Draught: 12ft 3in/3.7m (mean).
Machinery: two Yarrow boilers; 2-shaft geared turbines.
Performance: 110,000shp; 42kts.
Range: 4,000nm at 20kts.
Guns: six 5.1in (3×2); six 45mm (6×1); six .5in MG.
Torpedoes: nine 21in (3×3).
Mines: 80.
Complement: 250.
Above data refers to *Tashkent*.

Design This large flotilla leader was ordered from Italy in 1937, under the second Five Year Plan, almost certainly with a view to gaining experience of foreign construction despite marked political differences between the two countries. In comparison with the home-designed *Leningrad* class, this ship was considerably larger with nearly 6½ feet more beam and more than forty feet longer. Designed power was almost doubled for a maximum speed of 39 knots although on trials, *Tashkent* achieved 44.2 knots with 116,000shp albeit without armament on board. Her designed main armament was three twin 5.1-inch guns in weatherproof gun-houses, but these were not ready in time and the ship had to be delivered without armament. The light AA was increased to six 45mm, all in single mountings. Her torpedo outfit was unusual in that three triple axial

Below: *Tashkent* as completed without armament. (WSS)

banks of tubes were carried. This was a very successful design and it is believed that a further twelve units of a modified design were authorized under the third Five Year Plan as 'Projekt B1'. This differed in a number of ways, in particular, a lower displacement, two 3-inch replacing three 45mm AA and only two banks of tubes, either quadruple or quintuple. Only four had been laid down prior to the German invasion, all on the Black Sea.

Modifications The only completed unit, *Tashkent*, was fitted on an interim basis with three single 5.1-inch guns when she arrived in Russia until her twin gun-houses were ready in 1940–41. It is probable that her 45mm guns were replaced by 37mm. During the war, one bank of tubes was replaced by two 3-inch AA.

Service *Tashkent* was actively employed during the whole of her brief period of service, mainly on supply runs to Sevastopol. In total, she made forty round trips, but on the last was bombed off the Crimea by German aircraft on 28 June 1942. Taken in tow by *Bditelnyi*, she was successfully brought into Novorossisk although many compartments were flooded. On 2 June she foundered and was abandoned when the German Army took the port. Her twin gun-houses were salvaged and later installed in *Ognyevoi*. Of the improved units, about eight were cancelled prior to laying-down. *Ochakov* and *Perekop* were captured on the stocks at Nikolaiev by the German Army and later demolished. *Kiev* and *Yerevan* were towed out to Poti and Batum in August 1941 where they lay incomplete throughout the war. Neither was ever completed and both were broken up post-war.

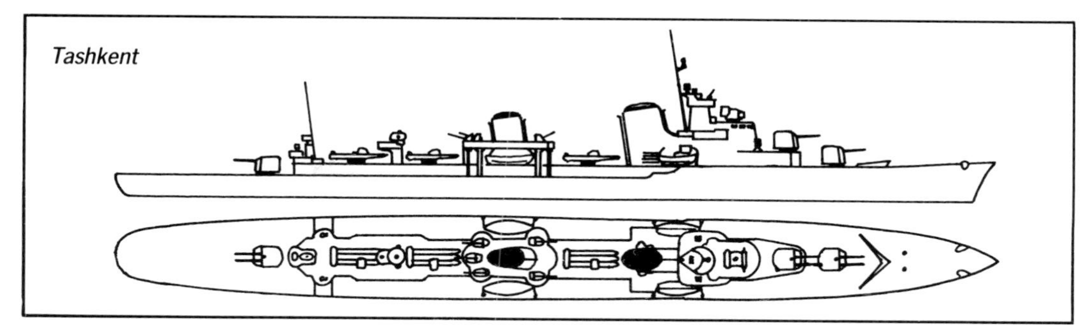

Below: *Tashkent* with extemporized armament. (A. D. Baker)

Below: *Tashkent* with designed armament. (Author's Collection)

NOVIK CLASS

Ship	Builder	Laid Down	Launched	Commissioned	Fate
Yakov Sverdlov	Putilov, St. Petersburg	19 July 10	26 June 11	22 Aug 13	Lost 28 Aug 41

Displacement: 1,271tons/1,291tonnes (standard); 1,801tons/1,829tonnes (full load).
Length: 336ft/102.43m (oa).
Beam: 31ft 3in/9.53m.
Draught: 11ft 6in/3.53m (mean).
Machinery: six Vulcan boilers; 3-shaft A.E.G. turbines.
Performance: 36,500shp; 36kts.
Bunkerage: 430tons/437tonnes.
Range: 1,800nm at 16kts.
Guns: five 4in (5×1); one 3in AA; one 37mm; two MG.
Torpedoes: nine 18in (3×3).
Mines: 60.
Complement: 168.

Design This ship, completed as *Novik* for the Imperial Russian Navy, was the prototype for a large series of powerful destroyers. The design was based upon German plans and much of the equipment was supplied from abroad with the Putilov yard assembling the ship rather than building it. The major advance as far as Russian destroyers were concerned, was the use of turbine propulsion for the first time and a three-shaft machinery layout. The main armament consisted of four 4-inch 60cal Obuchov guns in single, partially shielded mountings disposed in a rather peculiar fashion, with one forward and three on the quarterdeck. These after guns were very closely spaced and all axial. As a result, only one gun could bear directly astern and even that was later

Below: *Novik* later became *Yakov Sverdlov*. (W. B. Bilddienst)

'wooded' by an old 1915-pattern 3-inch AA gun added right astern. Thus, while the weight of firepower was good for its day, its disposition was very poor. Originally, *Novik* was completed with two twin banks of tubes. As in all Russian ships, this new destroyer was fitted for minelaying.

The machinery arrangement was also a new one for Russian destroyers in that a three-shaft turbine layout was adopted. To obtain the specified 36 knots, the designed power installed was increased fivefold compared to the previous destroyers of the *Kondratenko* class. However, the increase in displacement due to the additional guns and other growth while under construction, was about 140 tons which fact remained concealed from the builders of the machinery, Vulcan. Thus when *Novik* achieved only 35.8 knots initially on trials, the unfortunate German company was committed to rectify matters. Actually they succeeded in giving the ship a trial speed of 37.2 knots eventually.

Modifications After the Bolshevik Revolution, *Novik* was laid up and later had the armament altered by the addition of an old 1915-pattern 3-inch gun right aft on the quarterdeck where it masked the arc of fire of No. 4 gun. The twin tubes were removed and replaced by three triple banks. Her appearance was altered by the cutting down of the after three funnels and a tripod foremast was fitted. The bridge structure was enlarged and the forecastle extended a little farther aft. At the same time, the after deck-house was moved and the mainmast had a searchlight platform fitted to it. This remained her appearance until the Second World War and she was now renamed *Yakov Sverdlov*. By this time it is doubtful if her speed exceeded 30 knots. It is unlikely that any further alterations were made during the war before her loss.

Service A unit of the Baltic Fleet, *Yakov Sverdlov* participated in the occupation of the Baltic states and Poland in 1939–40. When war with Germany broke out, she covered the evacuation of these countries until August 1941 when she was sunk by mines while attempting to break through the barrages off Cape Juminda on passage from Reval to Kronstadt.

FRUNZE CLASS

Ship	Builder	Laid Down	Launched	Commissioned	Fate
Frunze	Metal Wks. Kherson	16 Oct 13	25 May 14	18 April 15	Lost 21 Sept 41

Displacement: 1,100tons/1,117tonnes (standard); 1,300tons/1,320tonnes (full load).
Length: 305ft 3in/93m (oa).
Beam: 30ft 6in/9.3m.
Draught: 9ft 3in/2.8m (mean).
Machinery: five Thornycroft boilers; 2-shaft Parsons turbines.
Performance: 29,800shp; 25kts.
Bunkerage: 350tons/355 tonnes.
Range: 1,800nm at 21kts.
Guns: four 4in (4×1); one 75mm; one 37mm; two MG.
Torpedoes: nine 18in (3×3).
Mines: 60.
Complement: 160.

Design *Frunze*, completed for the Imperial Navy as *Bystry*, was a slightly smaller version of *Novik*, one of a class which originally numbered five destroyers. Sister ships, *Gromky* and *Stchastlivy*, were lost during the Civil War and the other two, *Pospiechny* and *Pylky*, interned and subsequently scrapped at Bizerte. She differed from *Novik* in that she had one less boiler, a twin-shaft machinery arrangement and only three funnels. Her armament was also arranged differently. While three of the four 4-inch guns remained aft, No. 2 gun was made superfiring, an improvement in disposition. Her torpedoes were arranged in three banks, one each forward and aft of the forward funnel, with the third bank aft of the third funnel. By 1941, it is doubtful if she could exceed 28 knots.

Modifications Not known, but may have had extra machine-guns fitted. One 3-inch AA was added aft on the quarter deck before the Second World War.

Service *Frunze* served in the Black Sea where her early operations included shore bombardment in support of the defence of Odessa against German and Romanian forces in August 1941. The following month, she escorted transports to Odessa with reinforcements for the army. In the course of a landing operation on 21/22 September wearing the flag of Rear-Admiral Vladiminski, *Frunze* was sunk by Luftwaffe dive-bombers off Tendra Island while attempting to assist another Russian warship.

Above: *Frunze*, in 1928. (Author's Collection)

KALININ CLASS

Ship	Builder	Laid Down	Launched	Commissioned	Fate
Kalinin	Böcker, Reval	27 Oct 13	27 July 15	20 July 27	Lost 28 Aug 41
Karl Marx	Böcker, Reval	27 Oct 13	9 Nov 14	16 June 16	Lost 8 Aug 41

Displacement: 1,354tons/1,375tonnes (standard); 2,200tons/2,235tonnes (full load).
Length: 351ft/107m (oa).
Beam: 31ft 3in/9.5m.
Draught: 16ft/4.9m (mean).
Machinery: four Normand boilers; 2-shaft Parsons turbines.
Performance: 32,700shp; 28kts.
Bunkerage: 570tons/579tonnes.
Range: 1,565nm at 16kts.
Guns: five 4in (5×1); one 75mm; one 37mm; two MG.
Torpedoes: six 18in (2×3).
Mines: 80.
Complement: 168.

Design Another variant of the *Novik* concept, but built to designs from the French yard of Augustin Normand, who also supplied much of the equipment. Ordered under the 1912 programme, the design underwent many changes of armament before a five-gun, three triple torpedo tubes layout was finalized. In consequence of this heavier arma-

Above: *Karl Marx* as completed. (M. Bar)

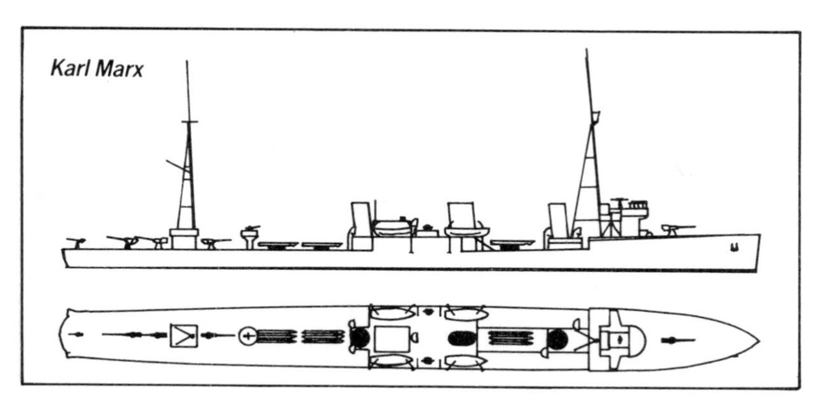

ment, the hull length was increased over that of *Novik* and displacement rose accordingly. The guns were arranged with two in tandem on the forecastle and three aft, No. 3 gun being moved forward a little and a deck-house being built between Nos. '3' and '4' guns. The main machinery included five Normand boilers with Brown-Boveri turbines developing about 9 per cent more power for a maximum speed of 33 knots. Five ships were ordered, all from Böcker & Lange of Reval, named *Avtroil, Bryachislav, Fedor Stratilat, Gromonosets* and *Pryamyslav*. The outbreak of war presented immediate problems, however, for Brown-Boveri were prevented from delivering the turbines for any except *Avtroil* and *Gromonosets*. New orders were placed in Great Britain and the USA for turbines for *Pryamyslav* and the remaining pair, but the delays incurred meant that only *Avtroil* and *Gromonosets* (renamed *Izyaslav* in 1915) commissioned with the Imperial Navy. The other three were incomplete at the time of the Revolution and both *Bryachislav* and *Fedor Stratilat* were subsequently broken-up incomplete. *Izyaslav*, laid-up post-war, was eventually renamed *Karl Marx* in 1922 and – even later – in 1927, *Pryamyslav* was finally completed as *Kalinin. Avtroil*, captured by the Royal Navy in 1919, eventually ended up in the Peruvian Navy (q.v.). Like all the other old destroyers, it is unlikely that their speed exceeded 28 knots by 1941.

Modifications Probably none in view of their early losses.

Service Both destroyers belonged to the Baltic Fleet in 1939. *Karl Marx* bombarded Finnish positions during the 'Winter War' of 1939. Later when war with Germany commenced, they were in the Baltic states taking part in the Soviet withdrawal in the face of the German advance. *Karl Marx* was finally sunk in Loksa Bay near Reveal by German aircraft on 8 August and her sister became one of the many victims of the Cape Juminda minefields that same month.

DZERZHINSKI CLASS

Ship	Builder	Laid Down	Launched	Commissioned	Fate
Dzerzhinski	Ryssuab Sbdg. Co. (Nikolaiev)	29 Oct 15	14 Aug 16	1917	Lost 14 May 42
Nyesamozhnik	Ryssuab Sbdg. Co. (Nikolaiev)	1915	1917	7 Nov 23	Scrapped post-1945
Shaumyan	Ryssuab Sbdg. Co. (Nikolaiev)	1915	1925	10 Dec 25	C.T.L. April 1942
Zhelezniakov	Ryssuab Sbdg. Co. (Nikolaiev)	1915	1924	10 June 25	Scrapped 1956

Displacement: 1,308tons/1,329tonnes (standard); 1,700tons/1,729tonnes (full load).
Length: 334ft 6in/102m (oa).
Beam: 31ft 3in/9.5m.
Draught: 9ft 9in/3m (mean).
Machinery: five Thornycroft boilers; 2-shaft Parsons turbines.
Performance: 32,500shp; 26kts.
Bunkerage: 390tons/396tonnes.
Range: 1,800nm at 20kts.
Guns: four 4in (4×1); two 45mm; two 37mm; twelve MG.
Torpedoes: six 18in (2×3).
Mines: 45.
Complement: 168.

Design Approved under the 1914 programme, this class originally numbered eight ships and were intended for service with the Black Sea Fleet. As initially designed,they were to carry three 4-inch guns and no less than twelve 18-inch torpedo tubes in four triple banks all mounted axially, an extremely heavy battery. With a design displacement of 1,570 tons, they were expected to reach 35 knots. An unusual feature for the day was the provision of a pair of 40mm AA guns. However, cost considerations ruled otherwise and instead the design was recast as an improved and enlarged *Bespokoiny* with four 4-inch guns. Designed power was reduced to 29,000shp giving a speed of 33 knots. The eight ships, all ordered from the Ryssuab yard at Nikolaiev, were originally named *Fidonisi, Gadzhibei, Kaliakryia, Kerch, Korfu, Levkos, Tserigo* and *Zante*. Four of these names being of Greek islands for some unaccountable reason. Only the first four units

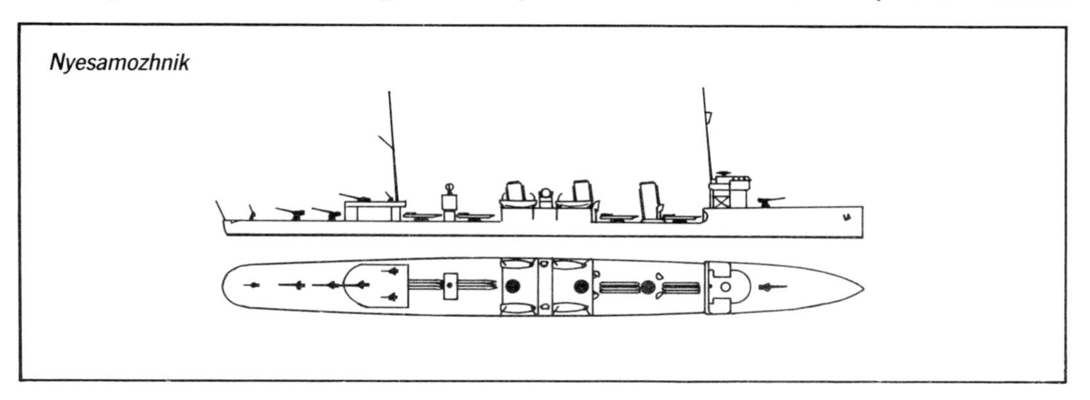

had been completed by the Revolution when they were scuttled by Red forces at Novorossisk on 18 June 1918. Those units still incomplete were passed to the White forces by the Germans, but only *Tserigo* was completed. She was interned at Bizerte in 1920 and subsequently scrapped. *Zante, Korfu* and *Levkos* were resumed and completed by the Soviets in the 1920s while *Kaliakryia* was raised in 1925 and recommissioned in 1929. In Soviet service, *Zante* was renamed *Nezamozhnyi* (later *Nezamozhnik*), *Korfu* became *Petrovski* (later *Zheleznyakov*), and *Levkos, Shaumyan. Kaliakryia* was renamed *Dzerzhinski.*

Modifications Unknown.

Service All were in the Black Sea at the start of the Second World War. In June 1941, *Dzerzhinski* assisted in the laying of defensive minefields off Batum, but in July and August she, *Shaumyan* and *Nyesamozhnik* operated in the north-western Black Sea, supporting the Soviet Army in the face of German and Romanian pressure towards the Crimea. Initially, these operations were off the Danube and border coastal areas, but in August *Dzerzhinski* and *Nyesamozhnik* were dispatched to assist in the evacuation of Nikolaiev and in October, now with *Shaumyan*, the evacuation of Odessa. With increasing Axis pressure on Sevastopol, all four destroyers were thrown into its defence, running supplies and troops into the beleaguered city until it fell. In the course of these operations, *Dzerzhinski* was mined and sunk off Sevastopol. The three survivors took part in army fire-support and landing operations in December at Feyodosia when all received damage and thereafter continued their support duties as the Red Army fell back eastwards. *Nyesamozhnik* was damaged by air attack at Novorossisk in April 1942 but not seriously. Operating from Novorossisk all three ships ran support to Sevastopol but after that town had been lost, Novorossisk was itself threatened by the German V Army Corps, thrusting south from Rostov-on-Don, finally falling on 10 September 1942. After fire-support operations in and around the front line at Novorossisk, all three destroyers fell back to the south-eastern corner of the Black Sea. Here, they had only the ports of Batum and Poti, which lacked the facilities required by a fleet and in consequence serviceability deteriorated especially in these old destroyers. Thereafter, their major task was troop transporting with occasional fire-support duties when the Red Army finally went over to the offensive in 1943–44.

Above: *Nesamozhnik.* (Author's Collection)

ARTEM CLASS

Ship	Builder	Laid Down	Launched	Commissioned	Fate
Artem	Metal Works, St. Petersburg	July 1915	22 May 16	10 Oct 16	Lost 28 Aug 41
Engels	Metal Works, St. Petersburg	15 June 15	22 Oct 15	12 Aug 16	Lost 24 Aug 41
Stalin	Metal Works, St. Petersburg	July 1915	23 May 16	21 Nov 16	Broken up 1953
Uritzky	Metal Works, St. Petersburg	6 Sept 14	6 Mar 15	11 Nov 15	Broken up 1953
Volodarski	Metal Works, St. Petersburg	1913	23 Oct 14	23 Oct 15	Lost 28 Aug 41

Displacement: 1,440tons/1,463tonnes (standard); 1,800tons/1,829tonnes (full load).
Length: 312ft 6in/98m (oa).
Beam: 30ft 6in/9.3m.
Draught: 10ft 6in/3.2m (mean).
Machinery: four Thornycroft boilers; 2-shaft Parsons turbines.
Performance: 32,000shp; 24kts.
Bunkerage: 500tons/508tonnes.
Range: 2,800nm at 15kts.
Guns: four 4in (4×1); two 45mm (2×1); two 37mm; twelve MG.
Torpedoes: six 18in (2×3).
Mines: 60.
Complement: 160.

Design Enlarged *Novik*s of German design, the survivors of a class of eight ships ordered from the St. Petersburg Metal Works under the 1912 Programme. All were completed for service during the First World War when *Grom* was lost on 14 October 1917, and *Lietoun* was also a casualty. *Azard* was renamed first *Zinoviev* then *Artem* while the Soviet names for the rest of the ships were as follows: *Desna* (*Engels*), *Samson* (*Stalin*), *Zabiyaka* (*Uritzky*) and *Pobiedityel* (*Volodarski*).

Modifications Not known.

Service *Stalin*, in the Pacific, saw little or no war service. *Artem, Engels* and *Volodarski* of the Baltic Fleet were all casualties of the early months of the German invasion. *Artem* and *Engels* were both lost in the Cape Juminda minefields while their sister was mined off Seiskari island in the inner Gulf of Finland. *Uritzky* was part of the Arctic Fleet where she was active against German and Finnish positions in the Petsamo area in the summer of 1941. In 1942–3 she assisted the local escort of PQ18 and JW53 in the White Sea and also operated in the Kara Sea on escort duty. She remained in the Arctic for the whole of her wartime career.

KARL LIEBKNECHT CLASS

Ship	Builder	Laid Down	Launched	Commissioned	Fate
Karl Liebknecht	Putilov, St. Petersburg	16 Nov 13	10 Oct 15	3 Aug 28	Scrapped post-1945
Kuibishev	Putilov, St. Petersburg	21 Nov 13	14 Aug 15	15 Oct 27	Scrapped post-1945
Lenin	Putilov, St. Petersburg	16 Nov 13	21 Oct 14	11 July 16	Lost 24 June 41
Voikov	Putilov, St. Petersburg	16 Nov 13	15 Nov 14	29 Nov 16	Scrapped post-1945

Displacement: 1,260tons/1,280tonnes (standard); 1,620tons/1,646tonnes (full load).
Length: 321ft 6in/98m (oa).
Beam: 30ft 9in/9.34m.
Draught: 12ft 9in/3.9m (mean).
Machinery: four Normand boilers; 2-shaft A.E.G.

turbines.
Performance: 31,500shp; 24kts.
Bunkerage: 500tons/508tonnes.
Range: 1,253nm at 16kts.
Guns: four 4in (4×1); one 3in; two 45mm AA; two 37mm; twelve MG.
Torpedoes: nine 18in (3×3).
Mines: 60.
Complement: 168.

Design A further class of *Novik*-type ships, originally eight in number of which two, *Kapitan Krodun* and *Kapitan Konon Zotov*, were cancelled. Another was never completed (*Leitenant Doubasov*) and a fourth, *Kapitan Kingsbergen* (later *Kapitan I Rang Mikloukha Maklai*), captured by the Royal Navy when serving as the Soviet *Spartak* in 1918. She was eventually given to Estonia and finally was sold to Peru (q.v.). Only two of the remaining four ships were completed by 1917, these being *Kapitan Isylmetiev* and *Leitenant Ilin*. These were eventually renamed *Lenin* and *Voikov* in Soviet service. The final pair, *Kapitan Belli* and *Kapitan Kern*, were not completed until the 1920s as *Karl Liebknecht* and *Kuibishev* respectively, although *Kapitan Kern* had, in the meantime borne the names *Rykov* and then *Zhadanov*. This design was very similar to the *Kalinin* sub-type, but had one gun fewer. Only a single gun was carried before the bridge.

Modifications Not known.

Service *Lenin*, in the Baltic Fleet, was under repair at Libau at the start of the German invasion and was scuttled there to avoid capture. *Voikov* remained in the Pacific, having been transferred there in the 1930s. *Karl Liebknecht* and *Kuibishev* supported the Soviet attack on Finland's Arctic coast in December 1939 and in 1941, *Kuibishev* operated against German and Finnish positions in the Petsamo area. She also gave limited local support to incoming Russian convoys (PQ15, 16 and 18) 1941–42, served in the White Sea 1943–44 and finished the war on local defence duties in the Arctic. *Karl Liebknecht* seems to have been strangely inactive during this period, possibly she was under repair, but Soviet sources claim that she sank *U286* in April 1945. This is not accepted by Allied research, however, giving the sinking to the British 19th Escort Group.

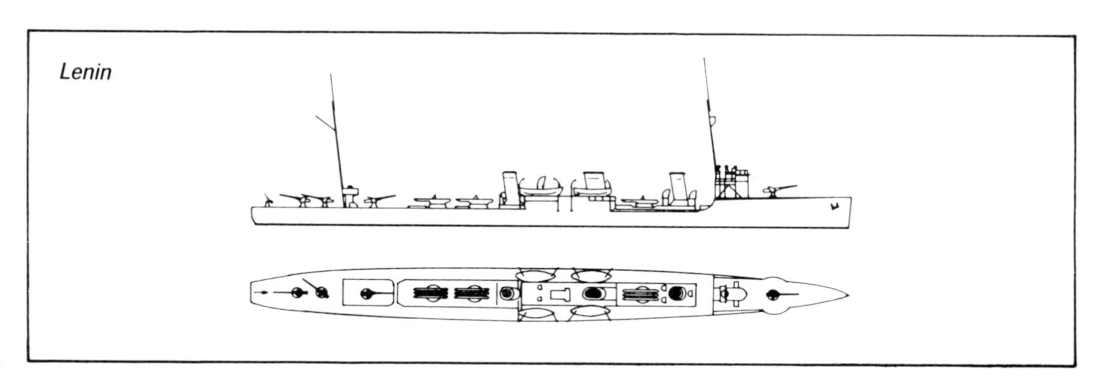

Above: *Karl Libknecht.* (Author's Collection)

TYPE 7 CLASS

Ship	Builder	Laid Down	Launched	Commissioned	Fate
Bodry	Marti, Nikolaiev	27 Nov 35	1936	Nov 1938	Scrapped
Bystry	Marti, Nikolaiev	1935	1936	1938	Lost 1 July 41
Bezuprechny	61 Kommunar, Nikolaiev	31 Dec 35	1936	1938	Lost 26 June 42
Bditelny	61 Kommunar, Nikolaiev	1935	1936	1938	Lost 2 July 42
Boiky	Marti, Nikolaiev	17 April 36	29 Oct 36	1 May 39	Paid off 1958
Bezposhchadni	Sevastopol NYd.	1936	1937	Sept 1939	Lost 6 Oct 43
Gnevnyj	Zhdanov, Leningrad	27 Nov 35	13 June 36	31 Jan 39	Lost 23 June 41
Gordyj	Baltic Yd., Leningrad	1935	1936	1938	Lost 14 Nov 41
Gromki	Baltic Yd., Leningrad	29 April 36	6 Dec 37	23 Feb 39	Scrapped
Grozny	Zhdanov, Leningrad	21 Dec 35	31 July 36	21 Feb 39	Scrapped
Gremyashchy	Zhdanov, Leningrad	23 July 36	12 Mar 37	11 Nov 39	Paid off 1958
Grozyashtchi	Zhdanov, Leningrad	1935	18 Aug 36	1938	Scrapped
Smetlivy	Baltic Yd., Leningrad	1936	1937	Feb 1939	Lost 4 Nov 41
Sokrushitelny	Zhdanov, Leningrad	1935	15 Aug 36	13 Aug 38	Lost 22 Nov 42
Steregushchy	Zhdanov, Leningrad	1936	1937	1939	Lost 21 Sept 41
Stremitelny	Zhdanov, Leningrad	1935	1936	1938	Lost 20 July 41

Displacement: 1,695tons/1,722tonnes (standard); 2,100tons/2,133tonnes (full load). *Gremyashchy* (WW2) 1,850tons/1,879tonnes (standard); 2,080tons/2,113tonnes (normal); 2,380tons/2,418tonnes (full load).
Length: 370ft 3in/112.86m (oa); 357ft 7in/109m (wl).
Beam: 33ft 6in/10.2m.
Draught: 12ft 6in/3.8m (mean); 13ft 5in/4.1m (max.).
Machinery: three boilers; 2-shaft geared turbines.
Performance: 48,000shp; 38kts.
Bunkerage: 540tons/548tonnes.
Range: 2,600nm at 19kts. (Actually not better than 1,700nm/16kts.).
Guns: four 5.1in (4×1); two 76mm (2×1); two 45mm; two .5in MG.

TYPE 7 CLASS—*continued*

Ship	Builder	Laid Down	Launched	Commissioned	Fate
Rezvy	Dalzavod, Nikolaiev	1936	June 1937	Dec 1939	Scrapped
Ryany	Dalzavod, Nikolaiev	Dec 1936	Oct 1937	1940	Scrapped
Reshitelny (i)	Komsomolsk, Nikolaiev	1936	Oct 1938	–	Lost 7 Nov 38
Raztoropny	Komsomolsk, Nikolaiev	1937	1939	1941	Scrapped
Redki	Komsomolsk, Nikolaiev	1937	1940	1941	Lost 1940s ?
Razyashtchi	Dalzavod, Nikolaiev	1937	1938	1940	To China 1955 ?
Reshitelny (ii)	Dalzavod, Nikolaiev	1938	1939	Aug 1941	To China 1955
Retivy	Komsomolsk, Nikolaiev	1938	1940	Oct 1941	To China 1955
Rezki	Komsomolsk, Nikolaiev	1937	1939	1941	To China 1955
Revnostny	Komsomolsk, Nikolaiev	1938	1940	1941	Scrapped
Razyaryonny	Komsomolsk, Nikolaiev	Sept 1937	May 1941	Dec 1941	Expended 15 Nov 58
Razumny	Dalzavod, Nikolaiev	1938	1940	1941	Foundered 1960s
Rekordny	Dalzavod, Nikolaiev	1939	1941	April 1941	Scrapped

Storozhevoi, Silny, completed as type 7U.

Torpedoes: six 21in (2×3).
Mines: 60.
Complement: 240.

Design By the early 1930s, Soviet Russia felt able enough to plan the construction of new destroyers following the commencement of the *Leningrad*-class flotilla leaders, albeit with foreign assistance, from Italy. Forty-eight ships were projected under the second Five Year Plan to provide eight flotillas which would be stationed with the Baltic, Black Sea and Pacific Fleets. The Italian influence led to the adoption of a single-funnel design, a feature then prevalent in contemporary Royal Italian Navy destroyers. On the other hand, the Italian preference for the twin gun mountings was not acceptable to the Soviet Union nor was the 4.7-inch gun calibre. Instead, single 5.1-inch/50cal guns in simple shields were fitted disposed two forward, two aft with Nos. '2' and '3' superfiring. This was essentially a low-angle weapon firing a shell of about 75lb. These guns were of a different and shorter calibre pattern from those mounted in the *Leningrad* class. Like this class of flotilla leaders, a heavy AA outfit of two 3-inch guns were provided, but these were moved to the deck-house between the torpedo tubes where they were clear of the firing arcs of No. '3' gun. Two single 45mm guns were carried at forecastle deck level between bridge and funnel. Quadruple tubes were not adopted, two triple banks being fitted. Like all Soviet warships, they were equipped for minelaying.

The single funnel dictated the machinery layout with three boiler rooms ahead of the two turbine rooms. It was in the machinery that these destroyers were, initially at least, found wanting, because the turbines suffered from serious vibration and blade breakage problems. As a result, difficulties were experienced in obtaining the designed speed. Several in fact had to have their turbines replaced after trials.

Another failing of this design could be attributable to the Italian influence, for the destroyers in the Arctic and Pacific regions had to contend with much more demanding weather than that experienced in the Mediterranean. Thus there were problems with structural strength, possibly exacerbated by inexperience in construction techniques, which led to at least one ship losing her bows and another foundering in heavy weather. Despite the design having been completed in 1933 and finalized in the autumn of 1934, the first ship was not laid down until late 1935 and the first to enter service (*Bodry*) did not commission until late 1938. Because of shipbuilding constraints in the Pacific region, much of the work was prefabricated at Nikolaiev, on the Black Sea, and dispatched to Komsomolsk for erection. The latter yard, on the River Amur, was handicapped by the shallowness of this river, which necessitated towing the incomplete destroyers down to Vladivostock for fitting out and completing. This itself was not without its hazards and one ship, *Reshitelny*, was lost by stranding on this passage in November 1938.

When the limitations and problems associated with the 'Type 7' destroyers became apparent in the summer of 1936, a modified design known as the 'Type 7U' was prepared by early summer of 1937 and construction of the 'Type 7' ships stopped at that time after thirty units. Two of these, however, were converted to the modified design while still under construction and one extra ship (*Rekordny*) was built by converting a 'Type 7U' in order to utilize some of the equipment intended for *Reshitelny*.

Modifications As far as is known, generally restricted to the augmentation of the AA outfits from 1942 by the removal of the 45mm guns, exchanged for two new-pattern 37mm/67 M39, a third 76mm AA and several machine-guns. Two depth-charge throwers were fitted and some received asdic from Allied sources later in the war. British Type 286 radar was fitted to a few units in the Arctic in 1944–45.

Service By June 1941, ten units had been completed in the Baltic and six in the Black Sea with a few more in the Pacific. In the Baltic, mines claimed a heavy toll of this class, commencing with *Gnevnyj*, lost on the second day of hostilities off the Oleg Bank, on which occasion, both *Gordyj* and *Steregushchy* were damaged. Towards the end of the month, *Grozyashtchi* and *Smetlivy* with 'Type 7U' ships participated in minelaying operations designed to defend the entrance to the Gulf of Riga, but only a few days later Riga was evacuated and these two ships passed through Moon Sound into the Gulf of Finland. From Reval, they made attempts to intercept German supply traffic to Riga but without success. *Steregushchy* was also involved in this activity and later commenced the escorting of evacuation traffic from Reval to Kronstadt. From the end of August 1941, this operation continued and resulted in heavy damage by mining to *Gordyj* on 28 August. By this time, *Grozyashtchi* was in use as a floating battery at Leningrad, while *Gordyj, Smetlivy* and *Steregushchy* were similarly employed at Kronstadt. The latter, however, was bombed and sunk by St.G.2 on 21 September (she was refloated in 1944 and recommissioned in 1945). *Gordyj* and *Grozyashtchi* received damage, the last named also again in a later attack. With the decision to evacuate the base at Hango on the western end of the Gulf of Finland, the destroyers went to sea once more in November when *Smetlivy* was mined and sunk off Hango on the return trip to Krondstadt. Ten days later *Gordyj*, similarly employed, also fell victim to mines. Of the original ten Leningrad-built destroyers, only *Grozyashtchi* now remained in service in the Baltic, for *Gromki, Grozny, Gremyashchy* and *Sokrushitelny* had been transferred via the internal waterways to the Arctic Fleet in 1939 as was *Stremitelny* the following year. *Grozyashtchi* with reduced crew served in fire-support duties for the remainder of the war, immobile at Kronstadt.

With the Northern Fleet in June 1941 were *Gromki, Grozny, Gremyashchy, Sokrushitelny* and *Stremitelny*. Initial operations involved covering army movements on the Russo-Finnish boder and counter-bombardment of German positions on the front. *Stremitelny*, however, was sunk very early on by Ju 88 bombers of 5/KG30 while in Ekaterinskaya Bay near Polyarnoe in the Kola inlet. In July, *Grozny* and *Sokrushitelny* laid defensive mine barrages at the entrance to the White Sea, and in September a similar operation was participated in by all four destroyers. Most of their service was on local defence duty with very occasional co-operation with British Naval forces off the Polar coast and a few short-ranged sorties escorting inbound and outbound convoys. From July to October 1942, *Razyaryonny* and *Razumny* transitted the Arctic seaway from the Pacific to reinforce the Northern Fleet, but this did not signal any measurable increase in Soviet destroyer activity on the Russian convoy route for *Sokrushitelny* broke in two and sank in heavy weather while escorting out QP15. No further losses were incurred by the Arctic Flotilla during the remainder of the war.

In the Black Sea, the initial task was the laying of defensive minefields, but on 22/23 June *Bystry* was sunk by an air-laid magnetic mine off Sevastopol and, at the same time, *Bditelny* was badly damaged. The other four units took part in army support and supply operations as well as offensive strikes against enemy shipping in July. This task continued as the Red Army evacuated the northern shores of the Black Sea in 1941–42. *Bezuprechny*, having made many supply runs into Sevastopol during May and June of 1942, was sunk south of the Crimea by Ju 88 bombers, during the last journey in the final days before the fall of Sevastopol. She had played an important role in this task with her sister *Bditelny*, who was also bombed and sunk later by aircraft of 1/KG100 at Novorossisk. *Bodry* too was later badly damaged by an air raid on Poti on 16 July. *Boiky* took part in the shelling of Yalta in October 1942 and, early in December with *Bezposhchadni*, made one defensive sweep against shipping on the Romanian coast, but without success. In February 1943, the survivors supported the Army's offensive at Novorossisk and bombarded German positions. On 29 September, a sortie was mounted against the German evacuation traffic south of the Crimea, but achieved no results. In the following strike a week later in October, *Bezposhchadni* was one of three destroyers sunk by Ju 87 bombers off the Crimea. This had a severe effect on surface operations thereafter and the destroyers were subsequently used only with great caution.

The Pacific units had an inactive war. As mentioned, two were transferred to the Northern Fleet in 1942 and a third, *Revnostny*, had to turn back to Vladivostock because of damage. Even the declaration of war against Japan in August 1945 did not see them used in action as far as is known.

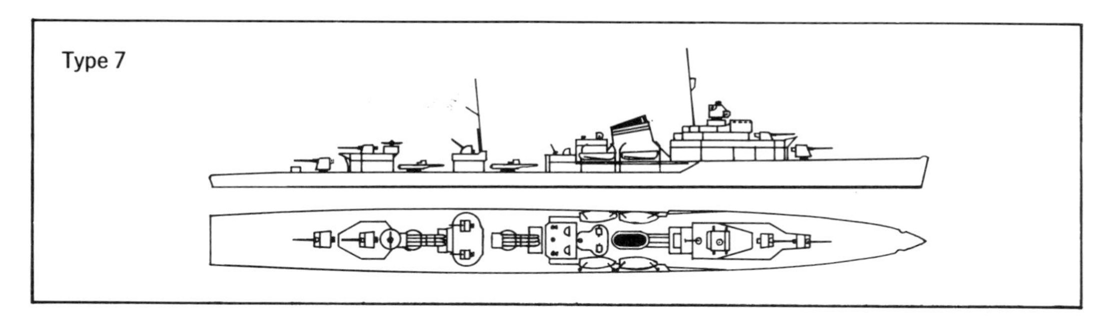

Above: *Gordy* in 1938. (Author's Collection) **Below:** A *Type 7* destroyer. (Navpic)

OPYTNYI

Ship	Builder	Laid Down	Launched	Commissioned	Fate
Opytnyi	Zhdanov, Leningrad	1935	Dec 1935	June 1941	Broken up 1955–56

Displacement: 1,570tons/1,595tonnes (standard); 1,870tons/1,899tonnes (full load).
Length: 372ft 4in/113.5m (oa).
Beam: 34ft 9in/10.6m.
Draught: 13ft 9in/4.2m (max.).
Machinery: four Ramzin boilers; 2-shaft geared turbines.
Performance: 70,000shp; 42kts.
Bunkerage: 400tons/406tonnes.
Guns: six 5.1in (3×2); four 45mm (4×1); three 37mm (3×1).
Torpedoes: eight 21in (2×4).
Mines: 60.
Complement: 197.

Design This destroyer was of experimental design and intended to serve as a prototype for future Soviet destroyer construction. Compared with the Type 7 design, installed power was increased by 48 per cent for a contract speed of 42 knots. Her armament was increased to six 5.1-inch guns, in three twin mountings, one forward and two aft, and the torpedo outfit raised to eight tubes by the adoption of quadruple mountings. The projected displacement figure of 1,570 tons, somewhat less than that of the Type 7 destroyers, was found to be unrealistic and in fact the normal displacement turned out at a round 2,170 tons. The new machinery installation caused considerable problems and delays to the construction programme as the Ramzin boilers were unavailable until 1939.

Modifications The twin 5.1-inch gun mountings did not become available until 1940 and were then fitted to *Tashkent*. In consequence *Opytnyi* received three single guns in lieu of the twin. Other modifications were probably few and limited to perhaps an increase in AA outfit.

Service This ship was completed in 1939, well before the war with Germany broke out. Her original name was *Sergei Ordzhonikidze* being renamed on 1 January 1941. From 1939 to 1941, she remained in a trials status because of severe vibration problems caused by the new machinery and light hull construction. In fact she never reached 36 knots before June 1941. Even so, she

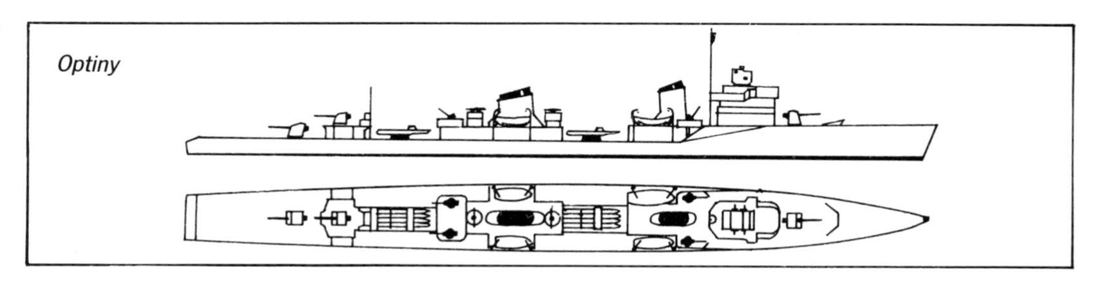

was hurriedly commissioned when the Germans invaded, but was only employed as a battery at Leningrad (like the remainder of the fleet), a task she remained in for the rest of the war. Trials continued from 1947 to 1949, when she was renamed *N20*. She was finally broken up 1955–56.

TYPE 7U CLASS

Ship	Builder	Laid Down	Launched	Commissioned	Fate
Storozhevoi	Zhdanov, Leningrad	Dec 1936	2 Oct 38	1940	Broken up 1959
Silny	Zhdanov, Leningrad	Dec 1936	Oct 1938	1941	–
Surovy	Zhdanov, Leningrad	1937	1939	1941	Lost 13 Nov 41
Serdity	Zhdanov, Leningrad	1937	1939	1941	Lost 19 July 41
Smely	Ordzhonikidze, Leningrad	1937	1939	1941	Lost 27 July 41
Stoiky	Ordzhonikidze, Leningrad	Aug 1938	26 Dec 38	1 May 41	Broken up 1959
Strashny	Zhdanov, Leningrad	1937	1939	23 June 41	–
Slavny	Ordzhonikidze, Leningrad	1937	1939	21 June 41	–
Skory	Zhdanov, Leningrad	1937	1939	18 July 41	Lost 28 Aug 41
Statny	Zhdanov, Leningrad	1937	1939	27 June 41	Lost 18 Aug 41
Svirepy	Zhdanov, Leningrad	1937	1940	23 June 41	–
Strogy	Zhdanov, Leningrad	Nov 1938	1939	Aug 1942	–
Stroiny	Zhdanov, Leningrad	Nov 1938	1940	31 Aug 41	Paid off 1959
Smyshleny	61 Kommunar, Nikolaiev	1937	1939	June 1941	Lost 6 Mar 42
Soobrazitelny	61 Kommunar, Nikolaiev	3 May 39	26 Aug 40	7 June 41	Museum 1966
Sposobny	Sevastopol NYd.	1937	1939	June 1941	Lost 6 Oct 43
Sovershenny	Sevastopol NYd.	1937	1939	–	Lost 4 April 42
Svobodny	Marti, Nikolaiev	1937	1939	Jan 1942	Lost 10 June 42

Displacement: 1,686tons/1,712tonnes (standard); 2,246tons/2,282tonnes (full load).
Length: 370ft 3in/112.86m (oa).
Beam: 33ft 6in/10.2m.

Below: *Soobrazitelny*. (Author's Collection)

Draught: 13ft 3in/4m (mean).
Machinery: four boilers; 2-shaft geared turbines.
Performance: 54,000shp; 36kts. (ex-Type 7 ships, 48,000shp).
Bunkerage: 500tons/508tonnes.
Range: 2,700nm at 19kts.
Guns: four 5.1in (4×1); two or three 76mm (2/3×1); three 37mm; four MG.
Torpedoes: six 21in (2×3).
Mines: 60.
Complement: 207.

Design In 1937, before any 'Type 7' destroyer had been completed, modifications were made to the design, which resulted in the 'Type 7U' (U= *Uluchshenny*=improved). The main change concerned the machinery which was given increased power, with the modified turbines being rated at 54,000shp, made possible by the installation of a fourth boiler. The adoption of en-echelon or unit machinery layout necessitated the twin funnel layout which visually distinguished them from the 'Type 7' destroyers. A rearrangement of the torpedo tubes had to be made in consequence. Despite this increase in power the hull dimensions remained similar to that of the 'Type 7' ships. Considerable attention was paid to the saving of weight in non-strength areas to compensate the strengthened hull and heavier machinery as compared to the 'Type 7' ships. Oil stowage was reduced by 40 tons which together with less economical turbines led to a reduction in endurance. Displacement increased only marginally but designed speed was something less than the 'Type 7' ships.

The main armament remained the same as the earlier ships, disposed in similar fashion, but the AA outfit was modified. The two 76mm guns were displaced by the after funnel and repositioned at the forward end of the after shelter deck, in a similar fashion to that of *Leningrad*, where they commanded good arcs of fire. The as-designed light AA gun remained the 45mm/46 weapon of which three single mountings were carried when the ships were completed, all abaft the forward funnel, but there were several variations on this during the war.

A complete set of reload torpedoes could be accommodated, carried on racks, one each port and starboard of the forward funnel and two each side of the after funnel. No quick reload facilities were provided, however.

Eighteen ships were ordered and two more converted from 'Type 7' ships. The two flotillas intended for the Baltic Fleet were to be built in Leningrad yards, while those for the Black Sea would be constructed at Nikolaiev and Sevastopol. It was originally intended that one of the Baltic flotillas would receive 'L' names but only two are known, *Letuhiy* (renamed *Smely*) and *Likhoi* (renamed *Stoiky*). Similarly, the Black Sea boats were to receive 'P' names but only *Prozorlivyi* is known and she became *Soobrazitelny*. Thus all the class eventually received 'S' names. One unit, building in the Black Sea, was dismantled and sent to the Pacific, where she was converted to a 'Type 7' ship, to utilize components and equipment intended for the lost *Reshitelny*.

When Germany invaded, seven destroyers had been completed in the Baltic and two in the Black Sea. After the invasion four more were commissioned in the Baltic before trials and two more in the autumn but these two, *Strogy* and *Stroiny*, were only used as floating batteries at Leningrad throughout the war. In the Black Sea, three more ships were completed in 1941–42.

Modifications Generally confined to the AA outfits, which were augmented by a third 76mm gun and, after 1941 but generally 1942, some ships received about four of the new 37mm/67 M39 air-cooled automatic AA guns, which became the standard Soviet weapon in this category. Up to eight .5-inch machine-guns were also fitted. Depth-charge throwers were fitted and a few units received asdic sets from Allied sources. Radar of Allied manufacture was also fitted to a small number of ships. *Storozhevoi*, during repair of her torpedo damage in 1941–43, was fitted with a twin 5.1-inch forward, originally intended for an *Ognyevoi*-class destroyer.

Service During the brief period of open water operations by the Baltic Fleet before it was blockaded in Leningrad, five ships were lost. *Serdity*, having participated in defensive minelaying operations in the Gulf of Riga and Irben Straits during June, fought an indecisive engagement with the German depot ship *MRS11* at the beginning of July and operated against German invasion traffic off Riga two weeks later. In the course of another attack on supply traffic to Dunamünde, *Serdity* was bombed by K.Fl.Gr.806 in Moon Sound on 19 July and had to be abandoned. Eight days later, *Smely* was torpedoed and sunk by the German *S54* on 27 July, in the northern part of the Gulf of Riga. During the evacuation of the Baltic States, *Statny* and *Surovy* bombarded German positions in Moon Sound, but the former was mined and sunk in the Sound a few days later. On 27 June *Storozhevoi* was hit by a torpedo from *S31* while in the Irben Straits, losing her bows, but she was successfully towed back to Leningrad. She eventually recommissioned in 1943. *Skory* was one of the many casualties in the Juminda minefield during the evacuation of Hango as was *Surovy* on 13 November. The survivors, *Silny*, *Stoiky*, *Strashny*, *Slavny*, *Svirepy*, *Strogy* and *Stroiny* all saw the rest of the war out, blockaded in Leningrad. (*Spokoiny*, often quoted as a unit of this class, never existed.)

The Black Sea Flotilla saw much active service in 1941–43 against the advancing Axis armies, but, like the Baltic destroyers, suffered heavy losses in action to aircraft and mines. *Sovershenny* struck a mine while running trials off Sevastopol on 30 September 1941, but was brought into the dockyard with heavy damage. While under repair, she was again damaged by bombing on 12 November when she capsized. Salvage was begun but the ship was finally destroyed by German army gunfire in April 1942. *Svobodny*, after taking part in supply and support operations in Sevastopol in 1942, was eventually sunk by Ju 88 bombers in South Bay, Sevastopol. Two months earlier, *Smyshleny* had been mined and sunk off the Crimea. In October 1943, *Sposobny* was one of three destroyers sunk by Luftwaffe bombers also off the Crimea. Only *Soobrazitelny*, in the Black Sea, survived the war.

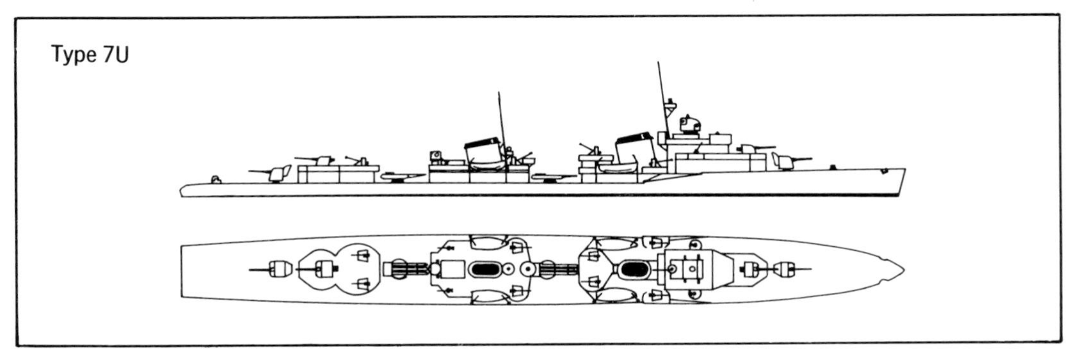
Type 7U

OGNYEVOI CLASS

Ship	Builder	Laid Down	Launched	Commissioned	Fate
Ognyevoi	61 Kommunar, Nikolaiev	1939	1940	1943	–
Ozornoi	61 Kommunar, Nikolaiev	1939	1941	1949	To Bulgaria 1956
Otverzhdyonny	Sevastopol NYd.	1939	1940	1947	–
Opasny	61 Kommunar, Nikolaiev	1940	–	–	–
Osmotritelny	Ordzhonikidze, Leningrad	1939	Aug 1944	1947	–
Otlichny	Zhdanov, Leningrad	1939	1940	1947	–
Obraztsovy	Zhdanov, Leningrad	1939	1940	1948	–
Otvazhny	Zhdanov, Leningrad	1939	1940	1949	–
Odyaryonny	Zhdanov, Leningrad	1940	July 1941	1949	–
Otchetlivy	Leningrad-Molotovsk	1941	1947	1949	–
Stalin	Leningrad-Molotovsk	1941	1947	1949	–
Vnushityelny	Nikolaiev-Komsomolsk	1940	1944	1944	–
Vlastny	Nikolaiev-Komsomolsk	1940	1947	1948	–
Vynoslivy	Nikolaiev-Komsomolsk	1941	1947	1948	–

One unidentified unit scrapped on slipway at Nikolaiev with *Opasny*. Three unidentified units scrapped on slipway at Molotovsk. Bows of two of these units used to repair *Storozhevoi* and *Strashy* in 1942. Six unidentified units scrapped incomplete at Zhdanov 1945–47.

Displacement: 1,800tons/1,829tonnes (standard); 2,650tons/2,692tonnes (full load).
Length: 383ft 9in/117m (oa.)
Beam: 38ft/11.6m.
Draught: 13ft 9in/4.2m (mean).
Machinery: three boilers; 2-shaft geared turbines.
Performance: 60,000shp; 36kts.
Guns: four 5.1in (2×2); two 85mm (1×2); six 37mm.
Torpedoes: eight 21in (2×4).
Mines: 80.
Complement: 250.

Design As the seaworthiness of the 'Type 7' destroyers had proved inadequate, probably due to their Mediterranean origin, design work on a new destroyer, known as 'Projekt 30' was commenced in 1937 under the third Five Year Plan. The basic dimensions of the '7U' design were enlarged, but

Above: *Otlichnyy*-class destroyer. (Author's Collection)

not to the size of *Opitny*, while displacement rose by more than 500 tons at full load as compared with the '7U' type. To improve stability, the main armament was shipped in two twin gun-houses, one forward, one aft, at forecastle and main deck levels. This reduced top-weight, which, allied to a 2½-foot increase in beam, conferred much wanted extra stability. This increased stability allowed the load to be increased by 50 per cent. The power plant remained similar to that of the '7U' destroyers for a maximum speed of 37 knots. It is not known for certain how many of these destroyers were planned, but it is believed that at least 24 were laid down, two at Molotovsk in the Arctic, three in the Pacific, four in the Black Sea, twelve at Leningrad and three more unknown. The outbreak of war almost destroyed this programme for two of those building at Nikolaiev were destroyed incomplete in 1941 and three more under construction at Leningrad were never finished. At least two incomplete hulls were cannibalized to repair damaged ships of earlier classes, while many others were cancelled and broken up on the slipways either during or just after the war. Only two completed before the end of hostilities, *Ognyevoi* in the Black Sea in 1943 after her evacuation incomplete from Nikolaiev in 1941, and *Vnushityelny* in the Pacific in 1944. Twelve others are estimated to have been completed between 1945 and 1949.

Modifications In 1945, *Ognyevoi* had six single 37mm and four .5in MG (2×2).

Service None during hostilities.

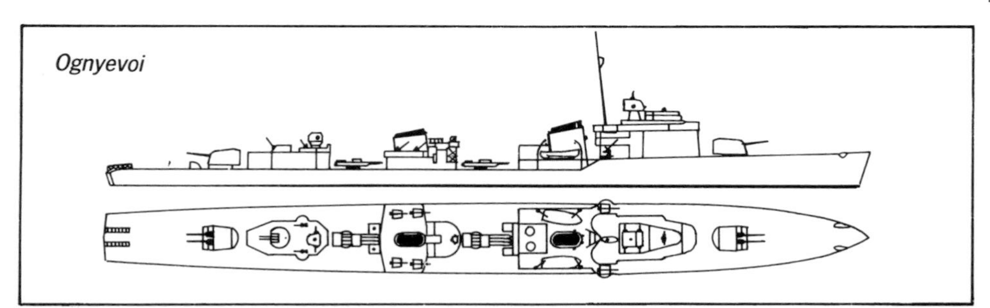

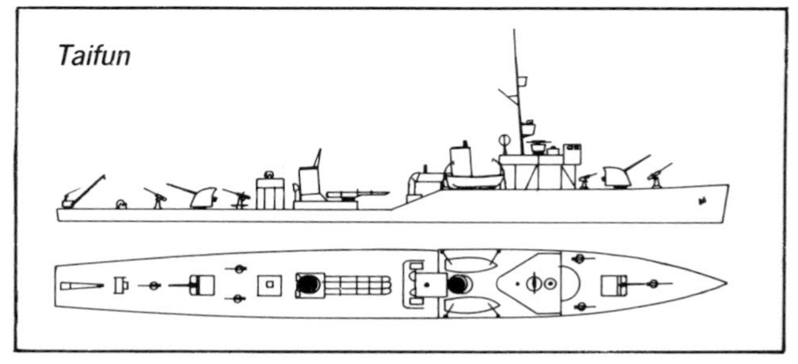

URAGAN (SERIES I) CLASS

Ship	Builder	Laid Down	Launched	Commissioned	Fate
16 *Uragan*	Zhdanov, Leningrad	13 Aug 27	4 Sept 28	12 Sept 31	Broken up 1959
Tajfun	Zhdanov, Leningrad	13 Aug 27	1 June 29	14 Sept 31	Stricken 1959
15 *Smerch*	Zhdanov, Leningrad	13 Aug 27	1929	Sept 1932	Training ship 1950
Tsiklon	Zhdanov, Leningrad	24 Oct 27	1930	8 July 32	Lost 28 Aug 41
Vikhr'	Zhdanov, Leningrad	24 Oct 27	1930	12 Sept 32	Stricken 1959
10 *Groza*	Zhdanov, Leningrad	24 Oct 27	1930	22 July 32	Broken up 1959
*Metel'**	Zhdanov, Leningrad	18 Dec 31	1934	18 Sept 34	Training ship 1950
*V'yuga**	Zhdanov, Leningrad	1932	June 1934	18 Nov 34	Broken up 1959

*Assembled by Dalzavod, Vladivostok.

Displacement: 450tons/457tonnes (standard); 619tons/629tonnes (full load).
Length: 234ft 7in/71.5m (oa); 229ft 8in/70m (wl).
Beam: 24ft 3in/7.4m.
Draught: 8ft 6in/2.6m (mean).
Machinery: two 3-drum boilers; 2-shaft geared turbines.
Performance: 7,500shp; 29kts.
Bunkerage: 48tons/48.7tonnes (160 max.).
Range: 1,500nm at 14kts.
Guns: two 4in (2×1); three 2pdr (3×1); three MG.
Torpedoes: three 18in (1×3).
Mines: 50.
Complement: 90.

Design Known in the Soviet Navy as 'guard ships', a term which encompassed patrol and escort work, these ships are included because of their torpedo armament. Eighteen guard ships were authorized by the Soviet of Work and Defence on 26 November 1926, to replace the over-aged torpedo-boats then being used for this task by the GPU and the Navy. Initial staff requirements were for a design of less than 300 tons, powered by two diesel engines and armed with two 4-inch guns and three torpedo tubes. Political difficulties prevented the purchase of diesel engines from Great Britain and, in the end, a turbine-driven design was adopted. The initial design did not meet with approval and further difficulties were experienced because of the lack of qualified naval architects. As a result, numerous designs were investigated and rejected, so that it was not until the summer of 1927 that the design was finalized. This was actually the twelfth version and known as 'Projekt 2'.

By this time, the design had reached more than 600 tons full load displacement, but the armament remained as originally envisaged. The power plant comprised two boilers and two geared steam turbines arranged on the unit principle with boiler room alternating with engine room. Main armament consisted of two single 4-inch/60cal Obuchov guns as carried originally by *Novik* in 1912. This was disposed one on the forecastle, one aft. No shields were fitted as completed. Three Vickers 2pdr guns and three .5in machine-guns were intended for the AA outfit, but the Vickers guns were never fitted because of a trade embargo by Great Britain. The single triple bank of tubes was fitted between the funnels. A feature of these ships was the very long quarter-deck used for minesweeping or minelaying equipment.

URAGAN (SERIES II) CLASS

Ship	Builder	Laid Down	Launched	Commissioned	Fate
Shkval	Marti, Nikolaiev	24 Sept 27	1 July 29	13 Oct 32	Stricken 1959
Shtorm	Marti, Nikolaiev	24 Sept 27	1 Sept 29	5 Mar 33	Stricken 1959
Buran	Marti, Nikolaiev*	22 April 32	1934	1935	Stricken 1959
Grom	Marti, Nikolaiev*	22 April 32	1934	1935	Stricken 1959

*Assembled by Dalzavod, Vladivostock.

URAGAN (SERIES III) CLASS

Ship	Builder	Laid Down	Launched	Commissioned	Fate
Burya	Zhdanov, Leningrad	1933	1935	6 Nov 36	Lost 24 Aug 42
Molniya	Zhdanov, Leningrad	1933	1935	1936	Stricken 1959
Purga	Zhdanov, Leningrad	1933	1935	4 Sept 36	Lost 1 Sept 42
Zarnitsa	Marti, Nikolaiev	1933	1935	1936	Stricken 1959

URAGAN (SERIES IV) CLASS

Ship	Builder	Laid Down	Launched	Commissioned	Fate
Sneg	Zhdanov, Leningrad	1934	1936	Oct 1937	Lost 28 Aug 41
Tucha	Zhdanov, Leningrad	27 April 35	20 Oct 36	18 Sept 38	Stricken 1959

Because of the conditions in Soviet shipyards at this time, the eighteen ships had to be ordered in four series and it was soon found that if the vessels were to be built in an acceptable time, even by Soviet standards, it would be necessary to purchase much equipment abroad. Eventually turbine sets for eight ships had to be ordered in Germany, but even so, problems in the yards and Soviet industry led to the laying-down of the first three units being delayed nine months. In the meantime, structural strength and vibration problems due to calculation errors had been identified and rectified. Further delays were incurred because of problems with the design, and construction of turbines was running far behind schedule. The culmination of all these difficulties led to the first ship, *Uragan*, not being accepted for sea trials until December 1930. On trials, the ship was revealed as being top-heavy, a poor sea boat and overweight. This in turn led to a low free board, wet decks and a maximum speed of only 26.5 knots. *Uragan* was the first entirely Soviet-built warship to be completed.

Because of the shortcomings of the first series ships, improvements were urged but proved impossible to carry out because no suitable machinery was available. All that could be done was to effect some economy in weight. Some revision of the hull lines was made and minor improvements made to the turbines of the Series III (known as 'Projekt 39') and the Series IV. These later ships were also to receive the newer 3.9-inch/56cal DP gun.

Modifications Before the war, the ships eventually received their .5in machine-guns, each side of the bridge and one on the quarter deck. When the new 45mm/46 Model 1932 AA gun became available, two were generally fitted, forward and abaft the after 4-inch gun. Some units had their second 45mm on the forecastle instead of abaft the after 4-inch gun. After 1939, units in the Baltic and Northern theatres received a pair of 37mm/67 1939 guns, one each side of the bridge but retained the 45mm guns. *Uragan* and *Tajfun*, however, landed both their 45mm guns. As the war progressed, further changes were made, including the fitting of shields to the main armament. In the Black Sea, *Shtorm* and *Shkval* were fitted with 37mm guns in lieu of their after pair of 45mm, and several machine-guns were added. Final armament was two or three 37mm and three or four .5in machine-guns, but some retained a 45mm gun forward. *Smerch* was an exception, however, with one 3-inch and one 4-inch forward together with three 3-inch and two machine-guns on the quarter deck.

Service *Uragan, Smerch* and *Groza* were dispatched to the Northern Fleet via the Stalin Canal in 1933. Here, *Groza* saw service in the Russo-Finnish war of 1939. In 1941, she and *Smerch* covered landing operations and bombarded enemy positions along the Arctic coast as the German Army attempted to press eastwards. *Uragan*, however, had suffered turbine damage and lay unserviceable at Polyarnoe until 1944 when spares could be sent out from Leningrad. The other pair carried out local defence work and short-range convoy escort duties in 1941–42. *Smerch* had a refit in 1942, but while undergoing post-refit trials, was sunk by German bombers, on 8 December 1942. The wreck was raised in 1943, repaired and recommissioned in 1944. *Groza* was employed on local defence duties until 1943 when, badly in need of a refit, she was paid off until 1945.

The ships in the Baltic saw limited service in the Russo-Finnish war of 1939 and later, in 1941, covered the withdrawal from the Baltic states. During the evacuation of Reval in August, both *Sneg* and *Tsiklon* were mined and sunk in the Cape Juminda mine barrage. Blockaded in Leningrad, *Vikhr'* was sunk by air attack on 21 September 1941 and *Tajfun* badly damaged two days later. *Purga* was detached for service on Lake Lagoda when the ice permitted. She was eventually lost on the lake to air attack on 1 September 1942, but was raised in 1943 and cannibalized to repair *Vikhr'* but was herself eventually repaired and recommissioned in 1944. *Burya* was sunk by mines while on a sortie to bombard Suursaari Island in the inner Gulf of Finland.

The units of the Black Sea Fleet played an active role in the supporting of the Soviet ground forces on the northern coast and in particular in the Crimea and the support of Sevastopol. After the loss of this base, *Shkval* and *Shtorm* assisted in the defence of first Novorossisk and later Tulapse, when the former port was lost. In 1943, both ships performed fire-support operations and supply duties, but by this time their efficiency had declined drastically and they saw little further war service.

In the Far East, the guard ships saw no active service until August 1945, when they participated in the Army operations against Japanese forces in Korea and the Kurile Islands.

TRANSFERRED UNITS

Dierzky (ex-*Chelsea*), *Dyeyatelny* (ex-*Churchill*), *Doblestny* (ex-*Roxborough*), *Dostoiny* (ex-*St Albans*), *Druzhny* (ex-*Lincoln*), *Zharky* (ex-*Brighton*), *Zhostky* (ex-*Georgetown*), *Zhguchi* (ex-*Leamington*), *Zhivuchi* (ex-*Richmond*)

Design All former US 'flush-deckers' transferred from the Royal Navy on 30 May 1944 to meet the Soviet demand for a share of the surrendered Italian Fleet. *Druzhny*, handed over on 26 August 1944 for spares, was also commissioned by the Red Navy on 23 September. Thse old ships gave the Russians their first good look at modern radar and ASW equipment.

Modifications None.

Service All served on local defence duties in the Arctic, where *Dyeyatelny* was torpedoed and sunk by *U997* on 16 January 1945 on passage between Kola Inlet and the White Sea. The survivors were retroceded to the Royal Navy from 4 February 1949 (*Doblestny*) to 8 September 1952 (*Zhostky*).

Spain

With the end of the Napoleonic Era, and the divesting of the South-American colonies towards the end of the nineteenth century, the Spanish Navy fell into decline, so that it fought the Spanish-American War of 1898 with a motley collection of obsolete vessels. This conflict resulted in heavy losses to the Spanish fleet, including some of her early destroyers, *Destructor, Furor* and *Pluton* at the Battle of Santiago on 3 August 1898. In fact, *Destructor* was claimed to be the world's first destroyer by Spanish historians as she predated *Havock* by several years. By the turn of the century, there was a strong movement in political and naval circles to rebuild the Navy, and the keystone to the twentieth-century renaissance of the Spanish fleet was the naval programme of 1908, master-minded by Admiral Ferrandiz, then Minister of the Navy. Part of this programme envisaged the setting up of joint ventures with leading foreign shipbuilders of the day, principally British, at Ferrol and Cartagena. Larger ships such as battleships and cruisers would be built at the former and destroyers and smaller craft at the latter. As far as destroyers were concerned, the programme of January 1908 authorized the construction of three destroyers, the *Bustamante* class. These, however, were already obsolete when under construction, because, apart from their turbine propulsion, they were little more advanced than the *Terror* class of 1896–7. Displacing about only 400 tons, armed with five 6pdr guns and two torpedo tubes, they were completely outclassed by the contemporary British *L* class of 965 tons, armed with three 4-inch gun and four torpedo tubes. As a result they could only be classed as coastal torpedo-boats. Nevertheless, they gave the Spanish yard valuable experience and were completed from 1914 to 1916. All were discarded in 1930–31. Also authorized under the 1908 Ferrandiz Programme was a series of 24 180-ton torpedo-boats of the French *Cyclone* high-seas type. Twenty-two numbered units were built from 1911 to 1921 and two more (Nos. *23* and *24*) were abandoned in 1919. These boats were armed with three 3pdr guns and three 18-inch torpedo tubes. Ten were scrapped before the Civil War and one (No. *2*) was lost during it. Five more were scrapped in 1938–39, but Nos. *7, 9, 14, 16, 17* and *19* were extant during the Second World War. Nos. *14* and *17* at least survived into the early 1950s as training hulks.

The 1915 programme authorized three further destroyers, once again of British design but this time, the modern *M* class. However, the First World War prevented their laying-down until 1920, by which time the design had become obsolete. These ships, completed in 1924–25 were the Spanish Navy's first real sea-going destroyers and gave sterling service for many years. Three other destroyers were also authorized under the 1915 programme, but because of the inability to obtain British assistance due to the war, these three were not proceeded with and were held over until the 1922 programme when they were reauthorized and refinanced. These became *Churruca* (i), *Alcala Galiano* (i) and *Sanchez Barcaiztegui*. The delay did, however, allow a more modern design to be chosen and the powerful British *Scott*-class flotilla leader type was adopted.

The *Churruca* design proved very successful and popular in the Spanish Navy, so much so in fact that a series of eighteen ships were built from 1922 to 1936 although the last two were considerably delayed by the Civil War and later the Second World War. These ships had a service life of nearly thirty years.

The Civil War of 1936–39 tore the navy apart, but as far as the destroyers were concerned, most, sixteen in fact, sided with the Republican Fleet; only *Velasco* was available to the Nationalists. To redress the balance, the Nationalists purchased four old destroyers from Italy in July 1937 and commissioned them in October. These ships were old, well-worn and unsuitable for front-line duties. During the Civil War, two destroyers were lost and one seriously damaged (all Republican ships), but one of the sunken ships was later raised and recommissioned.

Having only just returned to peace in 1939, Spain was in no mood to open hostilities again by participation in the Second World War, despite the persuasion of Adolf Hitler and Mussolini. She remained neutral throughout and in that period made no additions to the navy except for the purchase of one or two interned German submarines and MTBs.

ALSEDO CLASS

Ship	Builder	Laid Down	Launched	Commissioned	Fate
A *Alsedo*	S.E.C.N. Cartagena	1920	26 Oct 22	1924	Stricken 1960
L *Lazaga*	S.E.C.N. Cartagena	1920	Mar 1924	1925	Stricken 1961
V *Velasco*	S.E.C.N. Cartagena	1920	June 1923	1925	Stricken 1961

Displacement: 1,044tons/1,060tonnes (standard); 1,315tons/1,336tonnes (full load).
Length: 283ft/86.25m (oa); 275ft/83.82m (oa).
Beam: 27ft/8.23m.
Draught: 15ft/4.57m (mean).
Machinery: four Yarrow boilers; 2-shaft Parsons geared turbines.
Performance: 33,000shp; 34kts.
Bunkerage: 272tons/276tonnes.
Range: 2,500nm at 15kts.
Guns: three 4in (3×1); two 47mm (2×1).
Torpedoes: four 21in (2×2).
Complement: 86.

Design Authorized under the 1915 programme, these destroyers were essentially of British design although built in Spain. In appearance, they resembled the Hawthorn Leslie *M*-class destroyers, *Mansfield* and *Mentor* completed early in 1915. Their main armament consisted of three single 4-inch/40 Vickers-Carraca guns in half-shielded pedestal mountings. No. 2 gun was fitted between the second and third funnels. Two 47mm AA guns were shipped to port and starboard on the forecastle at the break. The torpedo outfit comprised two twin banks on the centreline for 21-inch torpedoes, the first use by the Spanish Navy of this calibre. Like the original Hawthorn Leslie boats, four boilers were installed, hence the four-funnelled layout. In contrast to the British destroyers, however, the turbines were rated at 33,000shp for a maximum speed of 34 knots, but 37.2 knots was attained by *Alsedo* on trials, admittedly without armament, while the others made 36 knots with about 37,000shp. All three ships were built by S.E.C.N. at Cartagena, but although modern enough at the time of authorization, the delay caused by the First World War made them hopelessly obsolete by the time of their completion in 1924–25.

Modifications All three were modernized in 1940–43 when one 4-inch was removed and replaced by a 3.5-inch AA gun and four 20mm added.

Service When the fleet divided at the opening of the Civil War in July 1936, *Velasco* sided with the Nationalists while her sisters remained loyal to the Government of the Republican Fleet. Because *Velasco* was in fact the only destroyer available to the Nationalists for some time, her career was rather more active than that of her sisters. *Velasco* was initially based in the north and scored an early success when she sank the Republican submarine *B6* which had made a surfaced attack on the auxiliary *Galacia* off Cabo Peñas on 19 September 1936. In the same month, she was employed minelaying off Bilbao in anticipation of the arrival of the Republican Fleet which had left the Mediterranean. By February 1937, *Velasco* was herself in the Mediterranean, operating with the heavy cruisers *Baleares* and *Canarias*, bombarding Malaga. After her return north, she participated in the northern blockade in April and at the end of the month, rescued the survivors of the battleship *España*, sunk by a drifting mine off Santander. She operated with the Nationalist Fleet throughout the war and was one of the escort destroyers for the two heavy cruisers during the action on 6 March 1938 when *Baleares* was torpedoed and sunk. *Alsedo* and *Lazaga* were mainly employed on escort duties because the Republican forces had a number of more modern destroyers. *Lazaga* rendered assistance to the British destroyer *Hunter* which had been mined off Almeria in May 1937, helping tow the casualty to Gibraltar. Without *Lazaga*'s assistance, the British destroyer might well have been lost. In the course of 1938, these two elderly destroyers were paid off to man new construction and were finally surrendered at Cartagena in March 1939. All three destroyers rejoined the post-war fleet and served for many years into the 1960s.

Above: *Lazaga* showing her typical WWI British origin. (NMM)

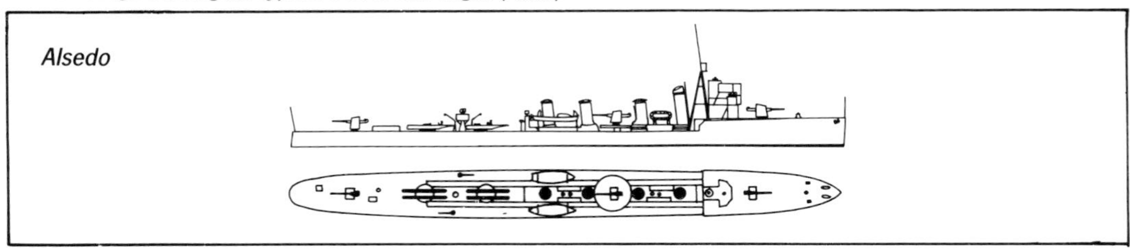

CHURRUCA (1st GROUP) CLASS

Ship	Builder	Laid Down	Launched	Commissioned	Fate
CH *Churruca* (ii)	S.E.C.N. Cartagena	–	June 1929	1932	Stricken 1960s
AG *Alcalá Galiano* (ii)	S.E.C.N. Cartagena	–	12 April 30	1932	Stricken 1957
SB *Sanchez Barcaiztegui*	S.E.C.N. Cartagena	–	24 July 26	1929	Stricken 1960s
AF *Almirante Ferrandiz*	S.E.C.N. Cartagena	–	21 May 28	1930	Lost 29 Sept 36
DZ *José Luis Diez*	S.E.C.N. Cartagena	–	25 Aug 28	1930	Stricken 1960s
LO *Lepanto*	S.E.C.N. Cartagena	–	7 Nov 29	1931	Stricken Aug 57
VS *Almirante Valdés*	S.E.C.N. Cartagena	–	8 Sept 30	1932	Stricken 1957

Displacement: 1,536tons/1,560tonnes (standard); 2,087tons/2,120tonnes (full load).
Length: 333ft/101.5m (oa); 320ft/97.52m (pp).
Beam: 31ft 9in/9.68m.
Draught: 10ft 6in/3.2m (mean).
Machinery: four Yarrow boilers; 2-shaft Parsons geared turbines.
Performance: 42,000shp; 36kts.
Bunkerage: 500tons/508tonnes.
Guns: five 4.7in (5×1); one 3in; four MG.
Torpedoes: six 21in (2×3).
Complement: 175.

Right: *Sanchez Barcaiztegui*. Compare her with British leaders of the 1919 period. (Courtesy Spanish Embassy)

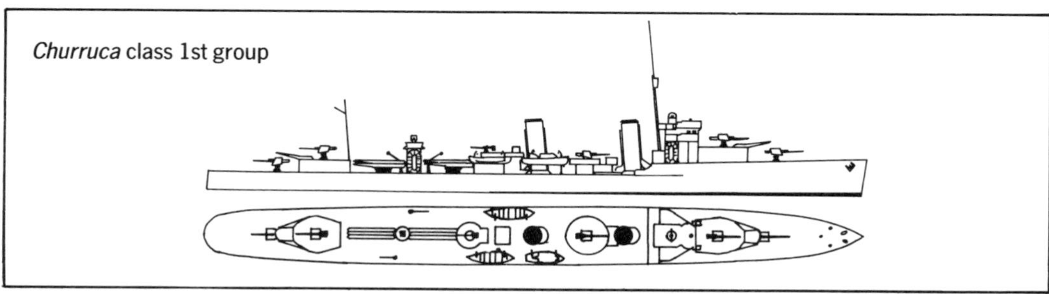
Churruca class 1st group

Below: *Alcalá Galiano*. Note funnel cap and only four 4.7-inch guns. (Courtesy Spanish Embassy)

CHURRUCA (2nd GROUP) CLASS

Ship	Builder	Laid Down	Launched	Commissioned	Fate
AA *Almirante Antequera*	S.E.C.N. Cartegena		29 Dec 30	July 1936*	Stricken 1960s
MA *Almirante Miranda*	S.E.C.N. Cartagena		20 June 31	July 1936	Stricken 2 Mar 70
GA *Gravina*	S.E.C.N. Cartagena		24 Dec 31	Sept 1936	Stricken 1960s
EO *Escaño*	S.E.C.N. Cartagena		28 June 32	Sept 1936	Stricken 1960s
UA *Ulloa*	S.E.C.N. Cartagena		24 July 33	1937	Stricken 1960s
JJ *Jorge Juan*	S.E.C.N. Cartegena		28 Mar 33	1937	Stricken 1959
CR *Ciscar*	S.E.C.N. Cartagena		26 Oct 33	1937	Wrecked 17 Oct 57

*trials

Displacement: 1,519tons/1,543tonnes (standard); 2,175tons/2,209tonnes (full load).
Length: 333ft/101.5m (oa); 320ft/97.52m (pp).
Beam: 31ft 9in/9.68m.
Draught: 10ft 6in/3.2m (mean).
Machinery: four Yarrow boilers; 2-shaft Parsons geared turbines.
Performance: 42,000shp; 36kts.
Bunkerage: 540tons/548tonnes.
Range: 4,500nm at 14kts.
Guns: five 4.7in (5×1); one 3in; four MG.
Torpedoes: six 21in (2×3).
Complement: 175.

Design Of these destroyers, three, *Sanchez Barcaiztegui, Churruca* (i) and *Alcalá Galiano* (i) had originally been authorized under the 1915 programme, in all probability as further *Alsedo*-class ships. Financial and war restrictions led to their being held over until reauthorized in 1922. By this time their design had been altered and they were instead to be constructed to the design of the British *Scott*-class flotilla leaders, then one of the most powerful destroyers in the world. Their layout was in fact almost exactly that of the British flotilla leaders except that the main machinery developed 42,000shp. The main armament, five 4.7-inch/45 guns of Vickers pattern were built at the Carraca ordnance factory in Spain and were fitted with the breast shields then common on British destroyers. All three were laid down in 1923, but *Churruca* (i) and *Alcalá Galiano* (i) were, surprisingly, sold to Argentina (q.v.) in May 1927 before their completion. Their sale was probably due to a pressing need for foreign exchange or for political reasons associated with ties between Spain and the former South American colony. In any event, the Navy almost certainly regretted the loss of two-thirds of their new destroyers. Three repeats were ordered under the 1926 programme (*Almirante Ferrandiz, José Luis Diez* and *Lepanto*) and one more under that for January 1928 (*Almirante Valdés*). At the same time, replacements for the two sold ships were also authorized, taking the same names. The last of these first-series ships completed in 1932.

In 1929, because this class had proved most successful, seven more units were ordered, once again all from Cartegena. They differed only in detail from the earlier group, having rounded bridge fronts and a tripod foremast. In addition their guns were given full shields similar to those in the contemporary British *A–I*-class destroyers. Otherwise, their armament was unchanged and was therefore, like countless contemporaries, extremely weak in AA defence.

Service On or just prior to the rebellion in Morocco, several of these destroyers, including *Churruca, Lepanto, Almirante Valdés* and *Sanchez Barcaiztegui* were ordered into the Straits of Gibraltar to prevent rebel troops from reaching mainland Spain. *Churruca*, however, went over to the rebels at Ceuta and ferried troops to Cadiz on 19 July. After this however, the destroyer's crew arrested their officers and reverted to the Republican cause. In the final event, all these destroyers fought on the side of the Republican forces. *Lepanto* forced the rebels to surrender at Almeria and *Sanchez Barcaiztegui* those at Malaga. In August, *Lepanto*, on patrol in the Straits of Gibraltar, was damaged by a bomb and had to put into Gibraltar for repairs. This allowed the Nationalists to run a convoy from Africa to Spain but even so it was attacked by *Alcalá Galiano* which damaged the gunboat *Dato* before being driven off by aircraft.

On 21 September 1936, the Republican Fleet was ordered north, a major error which left the Straits virtually unguarded. With the Fleet went *Almirante Valdés, José Luis Diez, Almirante Antequera, Almirante Miranda, Lepanto* and *Escaño*. Nothing was achieved in support of the Basques but in the meantime, the Nationalists struck at the weakened destroyer patrols in the Straits. *Almirante Ferrandiz* and *Gravina* were caught unprepared on the night of 28/29 September by the cruisers *Canarias* and *Almirante Cervera* when *Ferrandiz* was shelled to a wreck and sunk by the heavy cruiser while *Cervera* hit and damaged *Gravina*. The damaged destroyer put into Casablanca for repairs. This action opened the Straits for the passage of General Franco's troops to Spain.

In October, the destroyers returned from the north with the Republican Fleet. The following year in February, six of the ships, led by *Almirante Valdés*, made a half-hearted and abortive attempt to lift the Nationalist blockade of Malaga, following which the town fell, giving the rebels their first Mediterranean port. Shortly afterwards, six ships bombarded Ceuta in the absence of the Nationalist cruisers.

While attempting to get two merchantmen through the Nationalist blockade in the north, *José Luis Diez* was damaged by the cruiser *Almirante Cervera* in March 1937 but escaped to the Gironde. *Ciscar*, also in the north at Bilbao, escaped to La Pallice on the fall of that port to the Nationalists in June. Several inconclusive brushes took place with the Nationalist cruisers, particularly the ever-active *Canarias* in the early months of 1937 and in August, *Ciscar* fought an inconclusive action off Gijon with the Nationalist minelayer *Jupiter* and the AMC *Ciudad de Palma*. Santander fell on 26 August when all Government warships left, *José Luis Diez* fleeing to Falmouth for repairs. *Churruca* was torpedoed on 12 August by the Italian submarine *Rubino*, but managed to reach Cartagena although badly damaged and *Almirante Valdés* was damaged by a mine. In September, *Sanchez Barcaiztegui* was damaged in an action with *Canarias* while escorting a convoy from Barcelona to Minorca. Her sisters. *Almirante Antequera* and *Gravina* were driven off and both merchantmen captured by the cruiser. *Escaño* had been damaged by air attack the previous day and was not present.

When Gijon fell in October, *Ciscar* was sunk on 19 October, hit by seven bombs while attempting to evacuate the Government High Command. The wreck was captured by the Nationalists and raised on 21 March 1938, being subsequently commissioned by them early in 1939.

In March 1938, *Sanchez Barcaiztegui, Almirante Antequera, Gravina, Jorge Juan, Escaño, Almirante Valdés, Ulloa* and *Lepanto* (with the cruisers *Libertad* and *Mendez Nuñez*) left Cartagena to attack the Nationalist Fleet which had left Palma for a sweep off Cartagena. The latter force comprised the cruisers *Canarias, Baleares* and *Almirante Cervera* with three destroyers and two minelayers. In a night action, the Republican destroyers *Sanchez Barcaiztegui, Almirante Antequera* and *Lepanto* fired torpedoes which sank *Baleares* at no cost to themselves.

José Luis Diez, having moved from Falmouth to Le Havre for repairs, sailed for Cartagena in August 1938. On 27 August, she encountered *Canarias* in the Straits of Gibraltar and was badly damaged by the cruiser but limped into Gibraltar. Repaired once more by November, the destroyer slipped out in the darkness on 31 December only to immediately run into four Nationalist minelayers off Europa Point. In a confused close-quarters night action in which the destroyer was so close to *Vulcano* that she collided with her, three torpedoes fired by *Diez* passed *over* the minelayer's deck. Although they did not explode, some structural damage was caused. Gunfire from the minelayers badly damaged the destroyer again, when she was beached with some difficulty in Catalan Bay and was later towed back to Gibraltar. Here she was immobilized and her crew sent to Almeria.

At the end of the Civil War, *Churruca* and the damaged *Sanchez Barcaiztegui* (bombed and sunk in shallow water at Cartagena on 4 or 5 March 1939) with *Alcalá Galiano* were surrendered at Cartagena and *José Luis Diez* was at Gibraltar. All the others sailed for Bizerta where they were interned.

Post-war, these destroyers served for many years until broken up, but *Ciscar* ran aground in fog off El Ferrol in October 1957 and was stricken the following year after salvage was abandoned. *Churruca, Escaño, Gravina* and *Ulloa* were offered for sale by auction on 29 December 1964 but failed to reach their reserve price of 5,600,00 pesetas each.

Above: *Almirante Antequera*. Note absence of No. 3 gun. She has full shields to the main armament, and tripod masts. (M. Bar) **Below:** *Gravina*. (A. D. Baker)

CHURRUCA (3rd GROUP) CLASS

Ship	Builder	Laid Down	Launched	Commissioned	Fate
Alava	Bazán, Cartagena	21 Dec 44	19 June 47	21 Dec 50	Stricken 2 Nov 78
Liniers	Bazán, Cartagena	1 Jan 45	1 May 46	27 Jan 51	–

Displacement: 1,650tons/1,676tonnes (standard); 2,170tons/2,205tonnes (full load).
Length: 333ft/101.5m (oa); 320ft/97.52m (pp).
Beam: 31ft 9in/9.68m.
Draught: 10ft 6in/3.2m (mean).
Machinery: four Yarrow boilers; 2-shaft Parsons geared turbines.
Performance: 42,000shp; 36kts.
Bunkerage: 540tons/548tonnes.
Range: 4,500nm at 14kts.
Guns: four 4.7in (4×1); six 37mm (3×2); three 20mm.
Torpedoes: six 21in (2×3).
Complement: 224.

Design Modified *Churruca*-class ships, authorized in 1936, but because of the Civil War they were suspended for the duration of hostilities. Work commenced again in 1939 but was again suspended in 1940. They were to have been identical with the earlier groups except that quadruple tubes were to be fitted at the expense of the midships 4.7-inch gun and two 25mm twin mountings fitted to improve AA defence. The 4.7-inch guns were to have had 45° elevation. During the war years, the design was amended and the ships both relaid down and completed with triple tubes, three twin 37mm and three 20mm guns. Neither was completed until long after the war.

(VELASCO) MELILLA CLASS

Ship	Builder	Laid Down	Launched	Commissioned	Fate
(Velasco) Melilla	Pattison, Naples	11 Mar 14	26 July 16	8 Feb 17	Stricken 1949
(Velasco) Ceuta	Pattison, Naples	19 Aug 16	16 Aug 19	20 Jan 20	Stricken 1947

Displacement: 1,410tons/1,432tonnes (standard); 1,723tons/1,750tonnes (full load).
Length: 310ft 6in/94.7m (oa); 309ft/94.18m (pp).
Beam: 31ft/9.47m.
Draught: 11ft 6in/3.5m (mean).
Machinery: five Thornycroft boilers; 2-shaft Tosi turbines.
Performance: 45,000shp; 34kts.
Bunkerage: 260tons/264tonnes.
Range: 1,700nm at 15kts.
Guns: four 4.7in (2×2); two 3in; two MG.
Torpedoes: four 18in (2×2).
Mines: 50.
Complement: 139.

Design Half of a class of four destroyers originally ordered by Romania before the First World War, all of which were commandeered by the Royal Italian Navy while under construction. Two were eventually returned to Romania (q.v.), but the other pair, *Aquila* and *Falco*, were retained until 1937 when, with two other Italian destroyers, they were transferred to Nationalist Spain as *Melilla* and *Ceuta* respectively. Commissioned on October 1937 they were, however, just as obsolete and worn out as the other pair. For subterfuge reasons, both these ships operated under the name *Velasco* (hence *Velasco Melilla*) and a fourth, dummy funnel was often carried to resemble the real *Velasco*.

Modifications Probably none.

Service These ships saw only restricted service due to their age and condition.

HUESCA CLASS

Ship	Builder	Laid Down	Launched	Commissioned	Fate
Huesca	Ansaldo, Genoa	25 Mar 13	4 Aug 14	25 May 15	Stricken 1953
Teruel	Ansaldo Genoa	2 July 13	17 Sept 14	20 Aug 15	Stricken 1947

Displacement: 1,028tons/1,044tonnes (standard); 1,216tons/1,236tonnes (full load).
Length: 278ft 10in/85m (oa); 272ft 8in/83.1m (wl).
Beam: 26ft 3in/8m.
Draught: 9ft 2in/2.8m (mean).
Machinery: three Yarrow boilers; 2-shaft Belluzzo turbines.
Performance: 20,000shp; 32kts.
Range: 3,000nm at 15kts.
Guns: four 4in (2×2); four MG.
Torpedoes: four 18in (2×2).
Mines: 42.
Complement: 129.

Design Built during the First World War for the Royal Italian Navy as a class of three, but one was a war loss. Originally intended to ship four twin banks of 17.7-inch torpedo tubes, they actually completed with only two twin, but carried six 4-inch guns. Classed as 'scouts' when completed, they were reclassified as destroyers in 1921, and in June 1937 removed from the effective list, being purchased by the Spanish Nationalists in July. *Alessandro Poerio* was renamed *Huesca* and *Guglielmo Pepe* became *Teruel*, commissioning in October 1937.

Modifications Probably none.

Service Due to their age and poor condition, neither of these vessels saw much service, but both were in company with the Nationalist cruisers on 6 March 1938 when *Baleares* was lost. In May they were in collision with each other off the Catalan coast when *Teruel* was badly damaged about the bows. Their service thereafter is obscure and it is likely that they were laid up from the end of the Civil War until their final disposal.

Left: *Liniers.* (A. D. Baker) **Above:** *Alava.* (Author's Collection) **Below:** *Wachtmeister.* (RSwN)

Sweden

Sweden was essentially a Baltic power, except during the period from 1814 to 1905 when Norway and Sweden were a combined kingdom. During the latter half of the nineteenth century, the Swedish fleet was built up into a powerful force which, unlike Norway, it maintained after partition. She maintained a neutral stance although her main potential adversaries were naturally Germany and Russia. This stance was continued throughout the First World War and by the 1930s Sweden had once again begun to rearm in the face of the rise of German nationalism after a very lean post-First World War period of disarmament.

During the late 1880s, Sweden, like most sea-powers, had begun construction of small torpedo-boats which were ideal for short-ranged coastal operations in the summer Baltic. The iced-up winter was of course a different matter! From 1884 until 1910, more than thirty first-class torpedo-boats were built and thirteen second-class boats. The final first-class boats displaced about 120 tons, most lasting until the 1940s before being stricken and, in some instances, until the mid 1950s before being broken up. By the time of the Second World War, all had been reduced to subsidiary duties. Just after the turn of the century, the first destroyers joined the Swedish Fleet. These displaced only about 420 tons. Both were built in England, but in 1908 the Swedish-built *Wale* was commissioned. She was not much larger than the prototypes and armed with two 3-inch guns, four 57mm and two 18-inch torpedo tubes. Five more destroyers were built up to the First World War, all of broadly similar dimensions, but the last two, *Hugin* and *Munin*, introduced turbine propulsion. All served until the end of the 1940s before being scrapped, their later years in service as patrol vessels and minelayers. Four destroyers were authorized at the beginning of the First World War, but because of financial problems, two, *Ehrensköld* and *Nordenskjöld*, were cancelled. Coal-firing was retained, but both completed ships, *Wrangel* and *Wachtmeister*, were converted to oil-firing in the mid 1920s. Like their earlier sisters, these two destroyers were long-lived and served until 1947.

The first new post-war construction was not begun until the 1920s, when the two *Ehrensköld*-class ships were ordered. Two improved versions were ordered in 1929 and a series of six similar but enlarged *Göteborg* class followed, but only half had been completed by the time the Second World War broke out. To augment the fleet, two destroyers and two torpedo-boats were purchased from Italy in 1940, but the former proved very much a mixed blessing. The torpedo-boats, however, were liked, and four similar ships were built in Sweden during the war. Domestic construction continued, with the four *Visby* class ordered in 1942, two of which were replacements for the two *Klas Horn*-class destroyers sunk in the disastrous explosion at Haarsfjarden. These ships had improved AA outfits. The final design put in hand during the war was the two-ship *Oland* class which introduced twin DP guns and even better AA defence. Neither was completed until after 1945.

As Sweden remained neutral during the Second World War, no losses were sustained to the destroyer flotillas.

WRANGEL CLASS

Ship	Builder	Laid Down	Launched	Commissioned	Fate
9 *Wrangel*	Lindholmen, Göteborg		25 Sept 17	4 May 18	Expended 1960
10 *Wachtmeister*	Lindholmen, Göteborg		19 Dec 17	19 Oct 18	Sold out 1950

Both stricken 13 June 47.

Displacement: 465tons/472tonnes (standard).
Length: 232ft 9in/70.9m (oa).
Beam: 22ft/6.7m.
Draught: 9ft 3in/2.8m (mean).
Machinery: four Yarrow boilers; 2-shaft de Laval geared turbines.
Performance: 11,000shp; 34kts.
Bunkerage: 104tons/105tonnes.
Guns: four 3in (4×1); one 25mm; two MG.
Torpedoes: four 18in (2×2).
Complement: 81.

Design This pair of destroyers were actually improved versions of earlier classes, construction of which had begun with *Wale* in 1908. In comparison with contemporary destroyers of the combatant powers, these ships were very small; the *V* class of Great Britain were approximately three times their displacement and armed with 4-inch guns. The discrepancy between Swedish and German destroyers of the period was not so great, but the destroyers of the other Baltic Power, Russia, far outclassed the *Wrangel*. The main armament of four 3-inch guns was disposed one forward, one aft and one on each beam, a clumsy arrangement retained only by the US Navy. The torpedo battery was a respectable six tubes of which two were singles, sided abreast the second and third funnels. The main machinery was originally coal-fired, but by 1939 had been converted to oil fuel. Four boilers were fitted, of similar pattern to the earlier destroyers, each with its own uptake. De Laval turbines were used, in two separate engine rooms, of which the foremost propelled the starboard shaft. Designed power was 11,000shp and single-reduction geared turbines were employed for the first time in Swedish destroyers. The increased displacement of *Wrangel* as compared to earlier boats was in part due to the increased weight (15 tons) and power of

the machinery. On trials, 34.8 knots was achieved and despite poor war-time coal, *Wrangel* showed a marked increase in machinery efficiency compared to the earlier direct-drive boats.
Modifications The two single tubes were removed and one 25mm gun added, in place of the mainmast.
Service Neutrality patrols 1939–45. *Wrangel* was sunk in tests.

Right: *Malmö*. (RSwN)

Below: *Ehrenskold* with neutral stripes. (RSwN)

Below: *Klas Horn*, with midships rangefinder replaced by a 25mm gun. (RSwN)

Below: *Klas Uggla*. (RSwN)

Below: *Stockholm*. (RSwN)

Below: *Göteborg*. (RSwN)

EHRENSKOLD CLASS

Ship	Builder	Laid Down	Launched	Commissioned	Fate
1 *Ehrensköld*	Kockums, Malmö	1924	25 Sept 26	Dec 1927	Stricken 1 April 63
2 *Nordenskjöld*	Götaverken	1924	19 June 26	Sept 1927	Stricken 1 April 63

Displacement: 974tons/989tonnes (standard).
Length: 292ft/89m (pp).
Beam: 20ft 2in/8.88m.
Draught: 12ft 6in/3.8m (mean).
Machinery: three Penhoët boilers; 2-shaft de Laval geared turbines.
Performance: 34,000shp; 36kts.
Bunkerage: 150tons/153tonnes.
Range: 1,600nm at 20kts.
Guns: three 4.7in (3×1); two 40mm (2×1).
Torpedoes: six 21in (2×3).
Mines: 20.
Complement: 120.

Design These were the first modern Swedish destroyers to be built which could compare with their contemporaries. They introduced the 4.7-inch gun, Bofors Mk M24 calibre weapons with 45° elevation, better than the British 4.7-inch guns then in service. Unfortunately only three guns were carried of which No. 2, between the funnels, had a restricted arc of fire. The torpedoes were new 21-inch calibre models in two triple mountings on the centre-line. As completed the AA armament comprised two elderly Vickers-pattern 40mm pom-poms, but these were later replaced by Bofors models. Like most Baltic navy ships, these destroyers were also equipped for minelaying. Improvements in naval boilers allowed a reduction in boilers from four to three, but the power plant output had to be trebled compared to *Wrangel* because of the increased displacement.
Modifications The 40mm guns were replaced by two twin 25mm guns during the war.
Service Neutrality patrols 1939–45. Post-war, both were converted for ASW duties when they were rearmed with four 40mm and one 20mm guns as well as improved ASW weapons. Only the forward 4.7-inch gun was retained. Both sets of tubes were landed and a lattice mast fitted. After being discarded, both were used as target vessels until broken up in 1974 (*Ehrensköld*) and 1964 (*Nordenskjöld*).

KLAS HORN CLASS

Ship	Builder	Laid Down	Launched	Commissioned	Fate
3 *Klas Horn*	Kokums, Malmö		13 June 31	1932	Stricken 15 Aug 58
4 *Klas Uggla*	Karlskrona Dkyd.		18 June 31	1932	Lost 17 Sept 41

Displacement: 1,020tons/1,036tonnes (standard).
Length: 298ft 7in/91m (pp).
Beam: 29ft 2in/8.9m.
Draught: 12ft 2in/3.7m (mean).
Machinery: three Penhoët boilers; 2-shaft de Laval geared turbines.
Performance: 26,000shp; 36kts.
Bunkerage: 150tons/153tonnes.
Range: 1,600nm at 20kts.
Guns: three 4.7in (3×1); two 40mm (2×1).
Torpedoes: six 21in (2×3).
Mines: 20.
Complement: 130.

Design Improved *Ehrensköld* design with a slightly longer hull and increased displacement.
Modifications Light AA increased to six 25mm in *Klas Horn*, one replacing the after rangefinder.
Service Both destroyers were sunk in a still as yet unexplained explosion at the Haarsfjarden naval base near Stockholm on 17 September 1941. *Klas Uggla* was damaged beyond effective salvage, stricken 30 July 42 and broken up, but her sister was raised and repaired. Post-war she was used as a training hulk until sold for breaking up on 14 November 1967.

GOTEBORG CLASS

Ship	Builder	Laid Down	Launched	Commissioned	Fate
5 *Göteborg*	Götaverken	1934	14 Oct 35	Oct 1936	Stricken 15 Aug 58
6 *Stockholm*	Karlskrona Dkyd.	1934	24 Mar 36	27 Nov 37	Stricken 1 Jan 64
7 *Malmö*	Eriksberg	1937	22 Sept 38	15 Aug 39	Stricken 1 Jan 64
8 *Karlskrona*	Karlskrona Dkyd.	1937	19 June 39	12 Sept 40	Stricken 1 July 74
10 *Norrköping*	Eriksberg	1939	25 Sept 40	9 April 41	Stricken 1 Feb 65
9 *Gävle*	Götaverken	1939	23 Sept 40	30 June 41	Stricken 6 Dec 68

Displacement: 1,040tons/1,056tonnes (standard); 1,200tons/1,219tonnes (full load).
Length: 310ft 4in/94.6m (oa); 305ft 1in/93m (pp).
Beam: 29ft 6in/9m.
Draught: 12ft 6in/3.8m (mean).
Machinery: three Penhoët boilers; 2-shaft de Laval geared turbines.
Performance: 32,000shp; 39kts.
Bunkerage: 150tons/152tonnes.
Range: 1,200nm at 20kts.
Guns: three 4.7in (3×1); six 25mm (3×2).
Torpedoes: six 21in (2×3).
Mines: 20.
Complement: 130.

Design Further development of the *Ehrensköld* design with the same layout but of increased displacement and dimensions. The bridge structure was modified and improved director-control facilities fitted. AA armament was six 25mm from completion. They all proved extremely fast ships with *Malmö* exceeding 42 knots on full load trials.
Modifications Few if any, 1939–45.
Service Neutrality patrols 1939–45. *Göteborg* was sunk in the explosion at Haarsfjarden, but was salvaged and recommissioned. Post-war, all except *Göteborg* and *Malmö* were rebuilt as ASW frigates. *Göteborg* and *Norrköping* were eventually expended as targets in 1962.

VISBY CLASS

Ship	Builder	Laid Down	Launched	Commissioned	Fate
11 *Visby*	Götaverken	1942	16 Oct 42	10 Aug 43	Stricken 1 July 82
12 *Sundsvall*	Eriksberg	1942	20 Oct 42	17 Sept 43	Stricken 1 July 82
13 *Hälsingborg*	Götaverken	1942	23 Mar 43	30 Nov 43	Stricken 1 July 82
14 *Kalmar*	Eriksberg	1942	20 July 43	2 Feb 44	Stricken 1 July 82

Displacement: 1,135tons/1,153tonnes (standard); 1,320tons/1,341tonnes (full load).
Length: 321ft 6in/98m (oa); 311ft 2in/95m (pp).
Beam: 29ft 6in/9m.
Draught: 12ft 6in/3.8m (mean).
Machinery: three 3-drum boilers; 2-shaft de Laval geared turbines.
Performance: 36,000shp; 39kts.
Bunkerage: 150tons/153tonnes.
Range: 1,600nm at 20kts.
Guns: three 4.7in (3×1); four 40mm (2×2); four 20mm.

Left: *Kalmar.* (W. B. Bilddienst)
Right: *Uppland.* (RSwN)

Torpedoes: six 21in (2×3).
Mines: 20.
Complement: 140.
Design Enlarged versions of the *Göteborg* design with improved AA outfits, but without any increase in main armament which remained at only three 4.7-inch guns. However, the main armament disposition was improved by the resiting of No. 2 gun aft, to superfire on No. 3 gun. Its removal from between the funnels allowed these to be much closer together than in the *Göteborg* design. The 40mm guns were carried in one twin mounting between the torpedo tubes, and two singles on the upper deck abreast the searchlight platform. Two ships were originally planned, but two further ships were ordered to replace the two sunk in the Haarsfjarden explosion. All were laid down in 1942.
Modifications Probably few, if any, during the war.
Service These were the last new destroyers to be completed for the Swedish Navy during the Second World War. They had a long post-war career, latterly re-armed for ASW duties and re-classed as frigates on 1 January 1965. *Hälsingborg* and *Kalmar* carried one set of quintuple tubes for a time, the only vessels to do so in the whole of the Swedish Fleet. *Sundsvall* and *Visby* had one 4.7-inch gun and all tubes removed, being fitted with two 57mm and a more extensive ASW outfit. They were also equipped to operate a helicopter. *Kalmar* was eventually used as a target. *Sundsvall* was towed to Spain for scrapping in May 1985. *Visby* was also broken up in Spain.

OLAND CLASS

Ship	Builder	Laid Down	Launched	Commissioned	Fate
16 *Oland*	Kockums, Malmö	1943	15 Dec 45	15 Dec 47	Stricken 1 July 78
17 *Uppland*	Karlskrona Dkyd.	1943	15 Nov 46	31 Jan 49	Stricken 1 July 78

Displacement: 1,880tons/1,910tonnes (standard); 2,400tons/2,438tonnes (full load).
Length: 367ft 6in/112m (oa); 351ft/107m (pp).
Beam: 36ft 9in/11.2m.
Draught: 11ft 2in/3.4m (mean).
Machinery: two Penhoët boilers; 2-shaft de Laval geared turbines.
Performance: 44,000shp; 35kts.
Bunkerage: 300tons/305tonnes.
Range: 2,500nm at 20kts.
Guns: four 4.7in (2×2); six or seven 40mm; eight 25mm.
Torpedoes: six 21in (2×3).
Mines: 60.
Complement: 210.
Design These ships represented a considerable advance over the previous class both in terms of size and armament. They were armed with four 4.7-inch guns of a new Mark in two twin mountings, one forward, one aft, which were capable of dual-purpose use and 80° elevation. Both mountings were in enclosed gun-houses. Completing so late in the war, these ships benefitted from Sweden's observations of Soviet air power in the Baltic and in consequence, were given heavier AA defence and some armouring of command and machinery spaces. The 40mm outfit was increased to seven guns, with one twin mounting forward of the bridge and two on the after deck-house, giving very good arcs of fire. The single gun, right in the eyes of the ship in a gun-pit must have been of questionable effectiveness in heavy weather. Six of the 20mm guns were disposed in single mountings around the bridge and the other pair aft of the funnel. Much more powerful machinery was fitted and the number of boilers reduced to two, resulting in a single-funnelled layout, unique at that time to Swedish destroyers. Neither completed before the end of the Second World War.
Service Both underwent several modernizations in their service careers and were reclassified as frigates in 1974. *Uppland* left Lyeskil on 10 January 1981 in tow for the breakers at Gijon, Spain.

Below: *Öland.* (RSwN)

EX-ITALIAN CLASS

Ship	Builder	Laid Down	Launched	Commissioned	Fate
Psilander (ex-*Giovanni Nicotera*)	Pattison, Naples	1925	24 June 26	8 Jan 27	Stricken 13 June 47
Puke (ex-*Bettino Ricasoli*	Pattison, Naples	1925	29 Jan 26	4 Oct 26	Stricken 13 June 47

Both commissioned by R.Sw.N. 27 Mar 40.
Displacement: 1,250tons/1,270tonnes (standard); 1,480tons/1,504tonnes (full load).
Length: 278ft 6in/84.9m (oa); 275ft 7in/84m (pp).
Beam: 28ft 3in/8.6m.
Draught: 8ft 6in/2.6m (mean).
Machinery: three Thornycroft boilers; 2-shaft Parsons geared turbines.
Performance: 36,000shp; 35kts.
Bunkerage: 255tons/259tonnes.
Guns: four 4.7in (2×2); two 40mm (2×1).
Torpedoes: four 21in (2×2).
Mines: 32.
Complement: 152.

Design Former Italian destroyers of the *Sella* class, purchased by Sweden for rather obscure reasons, in March 1940. They were aged ships, designed for Mediterranean conditions and proved to be a poor buy for the more demanding northern conditions. Both underwent several refits to fit them for Swedish service, but they were not successful.
Modifications Their 40mm guns were exchanged for Bofors-pattern weapons during the war.
Service Both ships sailed from Naples on 18 April 1940 bound for Sweden, but their passage was delayed en route and by the time that they had reached the Faeroes, Italy was at war with Great Britain. Obviously suspicious of this purchase, the Royal Navy seized both in Skaalefjord and brought them into Kirkwall, where they were held until diplomatic moves brought about their release on 1 July. Both were stricken very shortly after the end of the war.

ROMULUS CLASS

Ship	Builder	Laid Down	Launched	Commissioned	Fate
Romulus (ex-*Spica*)	B&S, Naples		11 Mar 34	30 May 35	Stricken 15 Aug 58
Remus (ex-*Astore*)	B&S, Naples		22 April 34	1935	Stricken 15 Aug 58

Both commissioned R.Sw.N. 27 Mar 40.
Displacement: 870tons/883tonnes (standard).
Length: 267ft/81.4m (oa); 255ft 11in/78m (pp).
Beam: 26ft/7.9m.
Draught: 10ft 6in/3.2m (mean).
Machinery: two boilers; 2-shaft Tosi geared turbines.
Performance: 19,000shp; 34kts.
Guns: three 3.9in (3×1); six 20mm.
Torpedoes: four 18in (2×2).
Mines: 20.
Complement: 94.

Design Early *Spica*-class units, purchased from Italy in 1940 with the two *Sella*-class destroyers. Unlike the destroyers, they were modern, useful ships and after some modifications for northern conditions, gave good service to their new owners.
Modifications None during 1940–45.
Service Sailed from Italy with the destroyers and were seized with them. After release to Sweden, these ships served throughout the war and in 1953, were reclassified and re-armed as frigates. Both were sold out on 5 August 1959 and scrapped in 1961.

MJOLNER CLASS

Ship	Builder	Laid Down	Launched	Commissioned	Fate
29 *Mode*	Götaverken	Sept 1941	11 April 42	12 Nov 42	Stricken 1 July 70
30 *Magne*	Götaverken	Sept 1941	25 April 42	26 Nov 42	Stricken 1 Jan 66
32 *Mjölner*	Eriksberg	Sept 1941	9 April 42	12 Nov 42	Stricken 1 April 66
31 *Munin*	Oresundsvarvet	Sept 1941	27 May 42	3 Jan 43	Stricken 12 June 68

Displacement: 750tons/762tonnes (standard); 960tons/975tonnes (full load).
Length: 255ft 11in/78m (oa).
Beam: 26ft 7in/8.1m.
Draught: 8ft 10in/2.7m (mean).
Machinery: two 3-drum boilers; 2-shaft de Laval geared turbines.
Performance: 16,000shp; 30kts.
Bunkerage: 190tons/193tonnes.
Range: 1,200nm at 20kts.
Guns: three 4.1in (3×1); two 40mm; two 20mm.
Torpedoes: three 21in (1×3).
Complement: 100.

Design As the purchased Italian torpedo-boats had proved popular and useful, a modified design was prepared by the Swedish Navy in 1940. They were given more beam for better sea-worthiness and had reduced speed compared to their Italian predecessors. The Italian 3.9-inch guns were replaced by Bofors 4.1-inch 41cal M25 guns and four 20mm were exchanged for two 40mm Bofors, but otherwise the gunnery outfit was similar to *Romulus* and *Remus*. A single triple torpedo tube mount replaced the earlier ships' two twin banks.
Modifications None during hostilities.
Service These four ships were converted to ASW frigates in 1953, with armament being reduced by one 4.1-inch gun and the torpedoes. *Mode* and *Magne* were broken up in 1973, *Munin* in 1970 and *Mjölner* sold out on 3 November 1969.

Turkey

The Ottoman Empire was in decline by the beginning of the twentieth century, but it still comprised large areas of the Balkans as well as parts of the near east as far as Egypt. A large army was maintained, but the navy was comprised mostly of old and outdated vessels of limited fighting value. Turkey's geographical position, astride the Bosphorous, enabled it to control the Imperial Russian Black Sea Fleet's access to the open Mediterranean, and her extensive coast-line in the Black Sea made Russia an obvious adversary. Greece too was an hereditary enemy and the newly unified Italy was another contender for Turkey's Mediterranean possessions. It was with this latter State that war first broke out in September 1911, whereupon a number of ships including four destroyers were hurriedly purchased from Germany to bolster the weak Turkish Fleet. The destroyers, built by Schichau, were fast, modern ships, thrown in by Germany to secure the sale of two obsolete battleships. None of the destroyers had been commisssioned by Germany at the time of their sale. Their acquisition was a major reinforcement of the Turkish Fleet for their only other torpedo craft were four 280-ton boats of the French *Durandal* type, built a couple of years previously, and fifteen torpedo-boats of between 98 and 165 tons. During the Italian war, Turkey lost five of the torpedo-boats. In 1911, orders were placed for a major expansion of the fleet, including the purchase of dreadnought capital ships in Britain. The Balkan Wars of 1912–13 intervened, which lost Turkey almost all of her territory in Europe by the Treaty of Bucharest. Then in 1914, further orders were placed in Great Britain for a capital ship and four destroyers, in France for another four destroyers and in Italy for six destroyers. None of these or of those ordered in 1911 were to reach Turkey, all being either requisitioned by Great Britain or cancelled. Thus in August 1914, only four modern, effective destroyers (the Schichau boats) were available.

When war broke out in August 1914, Turkey was ranged on the side of the Central powers, but did not become involved in war with Great Britain until November that year, after Germany had encouraged the Turks to bombard Sevastopol and Novorossisk on 30 October. This act predictably brought Imperial Russia to war with Turkey. The navy's involvement in the First World War was limited and such active participation as occurred was mainly carried out by the Turkish-flagged German-manned *Goeben* and *Breslau* with other Turkish units in the Black Sea. In the Sea of Mamora, however, British submarine activities caused severe disruption of traffic and the navy's torpedo-craft were deployed against them and employed in escort duties. One of their successes was the sinking of the Australian submarine *AE2*, but two Schichau boats and four torpedo-boats were lost during the First World War.

After the surrender of the Turkish forces on 30 October 1918 the situation became complicated by a period of Civil War during which Mustapha Kemel rose to power and assumed leadership of the nation. By 1922, this fact had been recognized by the Allies and among other concessions, Turkey was allowed to keep what fleet remained to her. Of the destroyers, only two of the Schichau boats had survived and these, together with a few torpedo-boats, constituted the Turkish Navy's torpedo flotilla until the late 1920s. As usual, financial restraints prevented their replacement for many years.

In 1929, part of the proposed new construction programme included four destroyers which were ordered in Italy, but it was not until 1939, ten years later, that any more were ordered. This time the orders went to Great Britain, but the outbreak of war led to their requisition by the Royal Navy. Only two of these four destroyers were actually put into service by the British. The other pair were delivered to Turkey in 1942, a move which was in all probability a political one, given the progress of the Axis campaign along the Black Sea littoral at that time. It was not until August 1944, after the German withdrawal from the Black Sea, that Turkey felt able to cut diplomatic relations with her, but did not declare war on the side of the Allies until six months later by which time her naval forces had no opportunity for active participation.

KOCATEPE CLASS

Ship	Builder	Laid Down	Launched	Commissioned	Fate
A *Adatepe*	Ansaldo, Genoa	5 Jan 30	19 Mar 31	18 Oct 31	Stricken 27 Feb 54
K *Kocatepe*	Ansaldo, Genoa	5 Jan 30	7 Feb 31	18 Oct 31	Stricken 27 Feb 54

Displacement: 1,250tons/1,270tonnes (standard); 1,650tons/1,676tonnes (full load).
Length: 328ft 8in/100.2m (oa); 321ft 6in/98m (pp).
Beam: 30ft 9in/9.37m.
Draught: 9ft 6in/2.9m (mean).
Machinery: three Thornycroft boilers; 2-shaft Parsons geared turbines.
Performance: 40,000shp; 36kts.
Bunkerage: 360tons/365tonnes.
Range: 3,500nm at 15kts.
Guns: four 4.7in (4×1); three 40mm (3×1).
Torpedoes: six 21in (2×3).
Complement: 149.

Design Ordered from Italy in 1930, these two ships were modified *Folgore*-type destroyers with their length increased to accommodate the 4.7-inch guns being fitted in single mountings as in contemporary British and French destroyers. They differed also in that they had twin funnels instead of the one as in current Italian practice. On trials they achieved about 41 knots on 52,000shp, but without armament on board.

Modifications Not known.

Service Both were stricken in 1954 after having served in a training role since 1947.

TINAZTEPE CLASS

Ship	Builder	Laid Down	Launched	Commissioned	Fate
T *Tinaztepe*	C.T. Riva Trigoso	5 Jan 30	27 July 31	6 June 32	Stricken 27 Feb 54
Z *Zafer*	C.T. Riva Trigoso	5 Jan 30	20 Sept 31	6 June 32	Stricken 27 Feb 54

Displacement: 1,206tons/1,225tonnes (standard); 1,610tons/1,635tonnes (full load).
Length: 315ft/96m (oa); 307ft/93.57m (pp).
Beam: 30ft 6in/9.3m.
Draught: 10ft 9in/3.28m (mean).
Machinery: three Thornycroft boilers; 2-shaft Parsons geared turbines.
Performance: 35,000shp; 36kts.
Bunkerage: 350tons/355tonnes.
Range: 3,500nm at 15kts.
Guns: four 4.7in (2×2); two 40mm; two MG.
Torpedoes: six 21in (2×3).
Complement: 149.

Design Once again, designed and built in Italy, this pair, bought while under construction for Italy, were reduced-power versions of *Folgore* with two funnels in lieu of one.

Modifications Not known.

Service Both discarded in 1954.

GAYRET CLASS

Ship	Builder	Laid Down	Launched	Commissioned	Fate
Demirhisar	Denny	1939	1941	1942	Stricken 1960
Gayret	V.A. (Barrow)	24 May 39	–	–	To Great Britain 1939
Muavenet	V.A. (Barrow)	24 May 39	–	–	To Great Britain 1939
Sultanhisar	Denny	1939	1941	1942	Stricken 1960

Displacement: 1,360tons/1,381tonnes (standard); 1,880tons/1,910tonnes (full load).
Length: 323ft/98.45m (oa); 312ft/95.1m (pp).
Beam: 33ft/10.06m.
Draught: 8ft 6in/2.59m (mean).
Machinery: three Admiralty 3-drum boilers; 2-shaft Parsons geared turbines.
Performance: 34,000shp; 35.5kts.
Bunkerage: 455tons/462tonnes.
Guns: four 4.7in (4×1); four 20mm (4×1).
Torpedoes: eight 21in (2×4).
Complement: 145.

Design British *I*-class destroyers, but armed with quadruple and not quintuple torpedo tubes. Both were commissioned temporarily as HM ships for the passage to Turkey in 1942 (*Demirhisar*, H80 and *Sultanhisar*, H87).

Modifications Unknown.

Service Both served until discarded in 1960.

Above: *Tinaztepe*. (M. Bar)

Below: *Kocatepe* in May 1937. (Wright & Logan)

United States of America

Above: *Jacob Jones* (DD130), showing typical 1939 'flush-decker' layout. (USN)

It was not until 1898, with the advent of the Spanish-American War, that the United States began to think in terms of a fleet for other than coast-defence purposes. Victory in this late nineteenth-century conflict brought the responsibility of colonial possessions a considerable distance from the continental USA and, as a result, the necessity for their defence. Thus the early years of the twentieth century saw the beginnings of a build-up of the US Navy which was to continue until, two world wars and forty-five years later, the US Fleet was the most powerful in the world and America had overtaken Britain as the premier naval power. From 1900 until 1914, the emphasis was on the construction of battleships, thirteen pre-dreadnoughts and fourteen dreadnought-type units being authorized during this period. However, only thirteen cruisers of various types were authorized in the same period. The material and equipment of the US ships was good and frequently in advance of that of Great Britain; for example, the first American dreadnoughts were laid down in 1905 and thus pre-dated the British prototype although the latter commissioned first.

Before the war with Spain, torpedo-boat construction had begun with the Herreshoff boat, *Lightning*, of 1876, followed much later by *Stiletto*, purchased in 1887. The first true torpedo-boat listed, however, was *Cushing*, completed in 1890. By the time of the outbreak of war on 25 April 1898, there were only a handful of boats in service, but both peace and war-time service showed them to be inadequate in terms of strength and seaworthiness. Construction of torpedo-boats was therefore not proceeded with, only about fifteen more being completed before the First World War.

The immediate effect of the declaration of war in 1898 was the realization that the USA did not possess a fleet suitable for fighting a distant war. It had, for example, practically no auxiliaries or support ships nor did it have any sea-going torpedo-boats to defend its capital ships. To rectify matters, the Naval Act of 4 May 1898 authorized sixteen destroyers of about 400 tons, comprised of six different classes, but all broadly similar. None were completed until long after the end of the Spanish war. From these boats was developed a series of modified designs beginning with the *Smith* class (which introduced turbine propulsion) and continuing with the ten *Pauldings* completed in 1910, which were the first US destroyers to employ oil-firing. These latter ships were also given a heavy (for the time) torpedo outfit of six 18-inch tubes. Eleven repeats were constructed in 1910–12 but in March 1911, a new class of larger destroyer was authorized for sea-going employment with the fleet. This entailed an increase in dimensions and the *Cassin* class were nominal 1,000-tonners. They received 4-inch guns and their torpedo outfit was increased yet again to eight 18-inch in four twin mountings. 21-inch torpedoes were introduced with the succeeding class so that by 1914, US destroyers were better armed in terms of both guns and torpedoes as compared with British destroyers. Further construction was continued until the last of the 1,000-tonners (*Sampson* class) to be built, authorized in June 1914, carried no less than twelve 21-inch tubes in four triple mountings, and also shipped the first AA guns. They compared very favourably with the Russian *Novik* type in fact.

The United States remained neutral until 6 April 1917 by which time she had built 68 modern destroyers with the first ships of a new and important class on the stocks. Her involvement in the naval war was, in the case of the destroyers, limited to the dispatch of a large flotilla to assist anti-submarine operations in the south-western approaches to the British Isles, based on Queenstown, Ireland from May 1917. Most of these were of the 750-ton 'flivver' type or 1,000-tonners, and all of the *Sampson, Tucker* and *O'Brien* classes served in UK waters at some time during this period. One, *Jacob Jones*, became a war loss, torpedoed in December 1917, while *Cassin* was also torpedoed but survived. On the other hand, *U58* was destroyed by *Fanning*. Towards the end of the war, the first destroyers of a new design began to cross the Atlantic as well.

These new destroyers were the first of the famous 'flush-deckers' which were, in fighting power, little different from their predecessors. Six *Caldwell* class were followed by the mass production, during the last years of the First World War, of the *Wickes* and *Clemson* classes which together totalled 266 units. The majority of these were not completed until well after hostilities had ceased, when their existence together with financial restraints, had a considerable effect upon US destroyer planning and construction. They were, in fact, outclassed by the new British destroyers of the *V & W* classes, not to mention the flotilla leaders, but mass production meant in turn mass obsolescence and there was no money for their replacement. Thus, despite many design studies during the 1920s, no material construction transpired until the early 1930s, when the design of the *Farragut* class was developed. This displaced 1,500 tons, and was armed with five 5-inch guns. They represented a radical departure from the 'flush-deckers' in many respects, not least the adoption of dual-purpose main armament, with advanced fire-control systems. A year later, contracts were signed for the first 'leaders' in the USN, although they were not classified as such.

These were 1,850-ton ships armed with eight 5-inch guns, but in low-angle mounts, and their development was associated with the absence of cruisers in the US Fleet at that time. Prior to 1939, they were in fact used as leaders for the destroyer squadrons. They were overloaded ships, with little margin for the additions found so necessary during the First World War. Five modified versions were built in 1936–38, the *Somers* class, but the leader concept was not popular in the USN and by that time, cruiser construction programmes were under way, so that this type of ship was not perpetuated beyond this class.

The 1,500-tonne destroyer was continued through several classes with increasing displacement, great emphasis being placed on the torpedo battery, and all retained the dual-purpose main armament. Advances in machinery design were incorporated where possible and there was less conservatism than across the Atlantic when it came to the adoption of higher-pressure boilers for example. US destroyers were designed to fight a war against the most likely opponent, Japan, which involved the vast distances of the Pacific Basin. In consequence, any increase in machinery efficiency was to be valued and US destroyers were far more long-legged than their British counterparts, which were designed to fight under somewhat different conditions. In one other respect, they were rather unsatisfactory; stability was borderline in one or two classes, which affected their ability to accept augmented AA outfits later.

When war broke out in Europe in September 1939, the USA had completed more than sixty new destroyers, built since 1932, and retained many of the older 'flush-deckers'. Large numbers of these older destroyers had been scrapped or converted to subsidiary duties, but those that remained were to see service in the new war. In fact, there was still one example of the 1,000-ton design which pre-dated even the 'flush-deckers'. Under construction were the *Benson* and *Gleaves* classes which carried four or five 5-inch DP guns and five or ten 21-inch torpedo tubes. Unit arrangement of the main propulsion machinery gave these destroyers a good damage-control facility. As the war in Europe continued, large repeat orders were placed for this design until that for the *Fletcher* class was finished. The famous *Fletcher* class became the epitome of US destroyer design during the Second World War and they were built in larger numbers than any other class. They were larger and faster than earlier designs and incorporated much of the experience gained from observation of events in the North Sea and Mediterranean, particularly when it came to AA defence. Designed for the Pacific war which the American were sure would come, most obviously served in that theatre, but some served in the Atlantic, Mediterranean and Normandy theatres.

The *Fletcher* design was, in its turn, improved by the introduction of a twin 5-inch DP mount on a larger hull, to become the *Allen M. Sumner* class. Armed with two twin mountings forward, these ships drew criticism for being bow heavy. Fifty-eight units were completed as destroyers and a further twelve converted to fast minelayers, before construction switched to the longer-hulled *Gearing* class. This design was equal in offensive power to the *Sumner*s but had a greater range. However, the reduced threat from the Japanese by 1945 made the end of the Pacific war seem feasible and many of these ships were cancelled. Construction on others slowed down and of the large programme proposed, only about forty saw war service.

The progress of US destroyer design followed a different path from that across the Atlantic, in that between the wars, there had been much experimentation with high steam pressures, turbine improvements and the adoption of double reduction gearing. This resulted in several different classes being built up to the start of the Second World War, but had the advantage that all the best features could be put together to produce a standard destroyer for high-volume wartime construction, the *Fletcher* and its successors. In contrast, Britain had stuck with a standard design during the inter-war period, the *A* to *I* types, and then began experimenting with different types just as the war clouds were looming. As far as armament was concerned, the major advantage of US destroyers was the 5-inch 38DP gun and its director system, arguably the best destroyer weapon system of its day. Also, it is as well to remember that the US destroyers of the war-built types and the earlier ones for that matter, were big ships and able to accommodate much heavier weights of additional AA outfits than their smaller British counterparts, although it would appear also that Britain and the USA had different views on stability margins.

Wartime US destroyer service was world-wide, with the emphasis on the Pacific from 1942 onwards. In this theatre, the early reverses in the Solomon Islands were later avenged and US destroyers saw more surface action than any others. As the war progressed, and the Japanese perimeter shrank, there was less opportunity for surface action and the emphasis shifted to countering air attacks, particularly Kamikaze suicide attempts. This was reflected in the changing armaments of US destroyers, for hitherto there had been a reluctance to land torpedo tubes to augment AA defences. The experiences of Okinawa quickly altered this view and by the war's end, many destroyers had lost all their torpedoes for greatly augmented CRA batteries.

The end of the war saw the USN, as in the First World War, with huge numbers of destroyers built or building. However, unlike 1919, many on order were cancelled and all pre-war destroyers were soon discarded or expended at Bikini. Even so, huge numbers remained to present the USN of the 1960s and 1970s with the similar mass obsolescence problems that they had in the 1930s.

SAMPSON CLASS

Ship	Builder	Laid Down	Launched	Commissioned	Fate
DD66 *Allen*	Bath Iron Works	10 May 15	5 Dec 16	24 Jan 17	Scrapped 1946

Displacement: 1,100tons/1,117tonnes (standard); 1,225tons/1,244tonnes (full load).
Length: 315ft 3in/96.1m (oa); 310ft/94.5m (wl).
Beam: 29ft 10in/9.1m.
Draught: 9ft 6in/2.9m (mean).
Machinery: four Yarrow boilers; 2-shaft Curtis turbines.
Performance: 17,500shp; 29.5kts.
Bunkerage: 290tons/294tonnes.
Guns: four 4in (4×1).
Torpedoes: six 21in (4×1).
Complement: 145.

Design This ship was the last survivor of the pre-flush-decked 1,000-ton designs, her five sisters having been scrapped in the mid 1930s.

Modifications During the Second World War, *Allen* was armed with four 4-inch guns and only six tubes, the after pair having been landed. Extra depth-charges and throwers were fitted in their place. Six single 20mm guns comprised the AA outfit and radar was fitted to the foremast truck.

Service *Allen* was based at Pearl Harbor and used for training duties throughout the war.

Below: *Allen* (DD66) in 1943. (USN)

WICKES CLASS

Ship	Builder	Laid Down	Launched	Commissioned	Fate
DD103 *Schley*	Union Iron Works	29 Oct 17	28 Mar 18	20 Sept 18	Scrapped 1946
DD106 *Chew*	Union Iron Works	2 Jan 18	26 May 18	12 Dec 18	Scrapped 1946
DD109 *Crane*	Union Iron Works	7 Jan 18	4 July 18	18 April 19	Scrapped 1947
DD113 *Rathburne*	Cramp	12 July 17	27 Dec 17	24 June 18	Scrapped 1947
DD114 *Talbot*	Cramp	12 July 17	20 Feb 18	20 July 18	Scrapped 1946
DD115 *Waters*	Cramp	26 July 17	9 Mar 18	8 Aug 18	Scrapped 1947
DD116 *Dent*	Cramp	30 Aug 17	23 Mar 18	9 Sept 18	Scrapped 1946
DD118 *Lea*	Cramp	18 Sept 17	20 April 18	2 Oct 18	Scrapped 1945
DD125 *Tattnal*	New York Sbdg.	1 Dec 17	5 Sept 18	26 June 19	Scrapped 1947
DD126 *Badger*	New York Sbdg.	9 Jan 18	24 Aug 18	26 May 19	Scrapped 1945
DD128 *Babbit*	New York Sbdg.	19 Feb 18	30 Sept 18	24 Oct 19	Scrapped 1946
DD130 *Jacob Jones*	New York Sbdg.	21 Feb 18	20 Nov 18	20 Oct 19	Lost 28 Feb 42
DD137 *Kilty*	Mare Island	15 Dec 17	25 April 18	17 Dec 18	Scrapped 1946
DD138 *Kennison*	Mare Island	14 Feb 18	8 June 18	2 April 19	Scrapped 1947
DD139 *Ward* (ex-*Cowell*)	Mare Island	15 May 18	1 June 18	24 July 18	Lost 7 Dec 44
DD142 *Tarbell*	Cramp	31 Dec 17	28 May 18	27 Nov 18	Scrapped 1945
DD144 *Upshur*	Cramp	19 Feb 18	4 July 18	23 Dec 18	Scrapped 1947
DD145 *Greer*	Cramp	24 Feb 18	1 Aug 18	31 Dec 18	Scrapped 1945
DD147 *Roper*	Cramp	19 Mar 18	17 Aug 18	15 Feb 19	Scrapped 1946
DD148 *Breckinridge*	Cramp	11 Mar 18	17 Aug 18	27 Feb 19	Scrapped 1946
DD149 *Barney*	Cramp	26 Mar 18	5 Sept 18	14 Mar 19	Scrapped 1946
DD150 *Blakeley*	Cramp	26 Mar 18	19 Sept 18	8 May 19	Scrapped 1945
DD151 *Biddle*	Cramp	22 April 18	3 Oct 18	22 April 19	Scrapped 1947
DD152 *Du Pont*	Cramp	2 May 18	22 Oct 18	30 April 19	Scrapped 1947
DD153 *Bernadou*	Cramp	4 June 18	7 Nov 18	19 May 19	Scrapped 1945
DD154 *Ellis*	Cramp	8 July 18	30 Nov 18	7 June 19	Scrapped 1947
DD155 *Cole*	Cramp	25 June 18	11 Jan 19	19 June 19	Scrapped 1947
DD156 *J. Fred Talbott*	Cramp	8 July 18	14 Dec 18	30 June 19	Scrapped 1947
DD157 *Dickerson*	New York Sbdg.	25 May 18	12 Mar 19	3 Sept 19	Lost 4 April 45
DD158 *Leary*	New York Sbdg.	6 Mar 18	18 Dec 18	5 Dec 19	Lost 24 Dec 43
DD159 *Schenck*	New York Sbdg.	26 Mar 18	23 April 19	30 Oct 19	Scrapped 1947
DD160 *Herbert*	New York Sbdg.	9 April 18	8 May 19	21 Nov 19	Scrapped 1946
DD164 *Crosby*	Bethlehem, Quincy	23 June 18	28 Sept 18	24 Jan 19	Scrapped 1947

Displacement: 1,090tons/1,107tonnes (standard); 1,047tons/1,063tonnes (full load).
Length: 314ft 4in/95.8m (oa); 310ft/94.5m (wl).
Beam: 30ft 10in/9.4m.
Draught: 9ft 2in/2.8m (mean).
Machinery: four White-Foster boilers; 2-shaft Parsons turbines.
Performance: 24,200shp; 35kts.
Range: 2,500nm at 20kts.
Guns: four 4in (4×1); one 3in AA.
Torpedoes: twelve 21in (4×3).
Complement: 150.

Design The *Wickes* class was an extension of the *Caldwell* design (whose three destroyer survivors had been transferred to Great Britain in 1940), but incorporated more powerful machinery as they were intended to operate with the 34-knot *Omaha*-class scout cruisers, and the new programme battle-cruisers of the *Constellation* class. The increase in machinery power also resulted in an increase in displacement without any increase in fighting power over the *Caldwell*s. The machinery varied depending upon the builder concerned, which led in service to widely differing performance especially in terms of range. There were, in fact, two variants of the basic design, of which one was prepared by Bethlehem and the other by Bath Iron Works. A total of 111 ships were built, the first fifty being authorized in 1916. Two ships saw service at Queenstown, Ireland in 1918, but most were not completed until after the war. Large-scale disposals began in the 1930s as newer destroyers finally began to join the fleet. By 1940, 32 had been stricken, mainly for scrap and in that year, a further 22 had been transferred to the Royal and Canadian Navies. Prior to the war, six had been converted to high-speed transports and four more to fast minelayers.

Modifications Having seen the need for more ASW vessels in the Atlantic in the event of America entering the war, the conversion of a number of these flush-deckers to an escort configuration was authorized in December 1940. This involved the removal of all 4-inch guns and the after banks of torpedo tubes. The new armament was six 3-inch

DP guns shipped in lieu of the 4-inch with the two extra guns replacing the torpedo tubes. Extra depth-charge equipment was fitted and the machine-gun outfit was raised to four .5in MG. This conversion was applied mainly to east-coast ships, but the programme was interrupted by the declaration of hostilities in December 1941. By this time, fifteen of the class had been so altered (*DD118, 126, 130, 142, 144, 145, 147, 152–155, 157–160*). A further alteration authorized at the outbreak of war was aimed at increasing the endurance of these ships. This involved the removal of the after boiler and installing extra fuel bunkers, but was not applied to the Asiatic Fleet units. 'Hegehog' was fitted to seven of the ships (*DD109, 118, 128, 142, 144, 145, 152*) and all received radar. When they became more readily available, 20mm guns were added, six in all (five in 3-inch gunned units).

From October 1942 to December 1943, twelve (*DD103, 113–116, 125, 137, 139, 147, 157, 160* and *164*) were converted to fast transports (APD) in which role all torpedoes were landed and replaced by davits for four LCP (R). Three of these were 3-inch gunned ships (*DD147, 157* and *160*), the remainder 4-inch. Later, all received the 3-inch gun plus two single 40mm and five 20mm. APD conversions had their forward boilers removed, and speed in consequence was much reduced.

The nine units converted to Destroyer Minesweepers (DMS) (*DD117, 119, 136, 141, 146, 161, 178, 179* and *180*) in 1940–42 had a square false stern built on to allow the working of the M/S gear and were armed with four 3-inch guns, a twin 40mm Bofors with three to five 20mm guns. Later the 3-inch outfit was reduced by one or two guns. These ships were renumbered *DMS1, 2, 3, 18* and *4–8* respectively.

Ships converted to Destroyer Minelayers (DM) prior to the war (*DD121–124*) originally kept their 4-inch guns, but landed all torpedo tubes for 80 mines. Finally they too received four 3-inch guns and about four 20mm.

Service When the United States entered the war on 7 December 1941, twenty of these destroyers were in the Atlantic Fleet, *D118, 126, 128, 130, 142, 144, 145* and *147–160*. In point of fact, the USN had been active long before this, patrolling the Neutrality Zone and setting up bases in Newfoundland and Iceland. In doing so, there had been numerous brushes with U-boats and German merchantmen. In one of these, *Greer*, holding contact on *U652*, was attacked by the German boat and in turn used her depth-charges, but neither caused any damage to the other. In the Atlantic, the main duty was convoy escort throughout 1941 to 1945 for these old destroyers. *Roper* sank *U85* off Cape Hatteras on 14 April 1942, *Schenck, U645* on 24 December 1943 and *Dupont* assisted in the destruction of *U172*. By 1944, however, they had, in the main, been replaced by new DEs for escort duties. *Jacob Jones* was lost to a torpedo from *U578* off Cape May in February 1942, and *Leary* was sunk by *U275* in the Atlantic in December 1943.

In the Pacific theatre in December 1941 there were seven destroyers attached to the Fleet (*DD103, 106, 113–116* and *139*) one of which, *Ward DD139* attacked and sank a Japanese midget submarine off Pearl Harbor a few hours before the main attack. Six other ships were attached to local Naval Districts on the West Coast – *Crane, Crosby, Kennison* and *Kitty* at San Diego, with *Tattnell* and *J. Fred Talbott* in the Canal Zone. The flood of new construction reaching the Pacific soon displaced these elderly ships to other duties as described above. *Ward*, after her spell at Pearl Harbor was one of the ships converted to an APD (*APD16*) and was eventually lost to a Kamikaze attack off Leyte at Ormoc on 7 December 1944. Her sister, *Dickerson* (*APD21*), was badly damaged by Japanese aircraft off Okinawa on 2 April 1945 and was scuttled on the 4th.

Eleven ships were reclassified for auxiliary duties by 1945 (*DD128, 138, 144, 148, 149, 151, 152, 154–156* and *159*) and by this time, eight of the minesweeper conversions were also serving in this role.

Like the 'flivers' and '1,000-tonners' in 1918, these old destroyers were quickly discarded after the end of the war and the new *Fletchers* and *Gearings* formed the mainstay of the fleet as they themselves had done nearly thirty years earlier.

Above: *Lea* (DD118), modified for escort duties. (INRO)

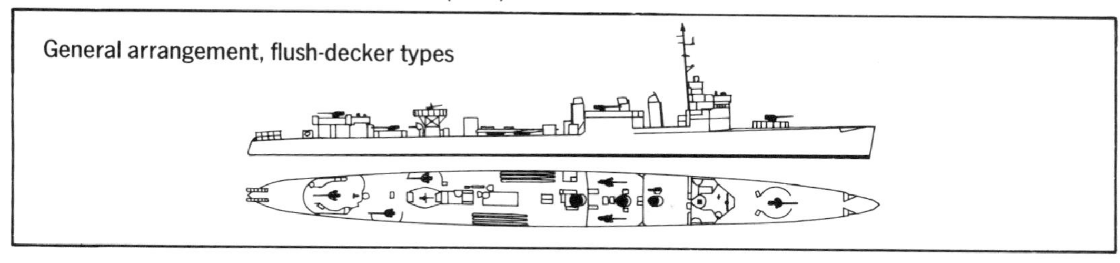

General arrangement, flush-decker types

CLEMSON CLASS

Ship	Builder	Laid Down	Launched	Commissioned	Fate
DD186 *Clemson* (ex-*AVD4*)	Newport News	11 May 18	5 Sept 18	29 Dec 19	Scrapped 1946
DD187 *Dahlgren*	Newport News	8 June 18	20 Nov 18	6 Jan 20	Scrapped 1946
DD188 *Goldsborough* (ex-*AVD5*)	Newport News	8 June 18	20 Nov 18	26 Jan 20	Scrapped 1946
DD196 *George E. Badger* (ex-*AVD3*)	Newport News	24 Sept 18	6 Mar 20	28 July 20	Scrapped June 1946

Displacement: 1,190tons/1,209tonnes (standard); 1,308tons/1,328tonnes (full load).
Length: 314ft 4in/95.8m (oa); 310ft/94.5m (wl).
Beam: 30ft 10in/9.4m.
Draught: 9ft 10in/3m (mean).
Machinery: four White-Foster boilers; 2-shaft Westinghouse geared turbines.
Performance: 27,000shp; 35kts.
Bunkerage: 375tons/381tonnes.

CLEMSON CLASS—*continued*

Ship	Builder	Laid Down	Launched	Commissioned	Fate
DD199 *Dallas*	Newport News	25 Nov 18	31 May 19	30 April 20	Scrapped 1946
DD210 *Broome*	Cramp	8 Oct 18	14 May 19	30 Oct 19	Scrapped 1946
DD211 *Alden*	Cramp	24 Oct 18	7 June 19	24 Nov 19	Scrapped 1945
DD213 *Barker*	Cramp	30 April 19	11 Sept 19	27 Dec 19	Scrapped 1945
DD215 *Borie*	Cramp	30 April 19	4 Oct 19	24 Mar 20	Lost 2 Nov 43
DD216 *John D. Edwards*	Cramp	21 May 19	18 Oct 19	6 April 20	Scrapped 1945
DD217 *Whipple*	Cramp	12 June 19	6 Nov 19	23 April 20	Scrapped 1946
DD218 *Parrott*	Cramp	23 July 19	25 Nov 19	11 May 20	Lost 2 May 44
DD219 *Edsall*	Cramp	15 Sept 19	29 July 20	26 Nov 20	Lost 1 Mar 42
DD220 *MacLeish*	Cramp	19 Aug 19	18 Dec 19	2 Aug 20	Scrapped 1947
DD221 *Simpson*	Cramp	9 Oct 19	28 April 20	3 Nov 20	Scrapped 1946
DD222 *Bulmer*	Cramp	11 Aug 19	22 Jan 20	16 Aug 20	Scrapped 1947
DD223 *McCormick*	Cramp	11 Aug 19	14 Feb 20	30 Aug 20	Scrapped 1947
DD224 *Stewart*	Cramp	9 Sept 19	4 Mar 20	15 Sept 20	Lost 2 Mar 42
DD225 *Pope*	Cramp	9 Sept 19	23 Mar 20	27 Oct 20	Lost 1 Mar 42
DD226 *Peary*	Cramp	9 Sept 19	6 April 20	22 Oct 20	Lost 19 Feb 42
DD227 *Pillsbury*	Cramp	23 Oct 19	3 Aug 20	15 Dec 20	Lost 1 Mar 42
DD228 *John D. Ford*	Cramp	11 Nov 19	2 Sept 20	30 Dec 20	Scrapped 1947
DD229 *Truxton*	Cramp	3 Dec 19	28 Sept 20	16 Feb 21	Lost 18 Feb 42
DD230 *Paul Jones*	Cramp	23 Dec 19	30 Sept 20	19 April 21	Scrapped 1947
DD231 *Hatfield*	New York Sbdg.	10 June 18	17 Mar 19	16 April 20	Scrapped 1947
DD232 *Brooks*	New York Sbdg.	11 June 18	24 April 19	18 June 20	Lost 6 Jan 45
DD233 *Gilmer*	New York Sbdg.	25 June 18	24 May 19	30 April 20	Scrapped 1947
DD234 *Fox*	New York Sbdg.	25 June 18	12 June 19	17 May 20	Scrapped 1947
DD235 *Kane*	New York Sbdg.	3 July 18	12 Aug 19	11 June 20	Scrapped 1946
DD236 *Humphreys*	New York Sbdg.	31 July 18	28 July 19	21 July 20	Scrapped 1946
DD237 *McFarland* (ex-*AVD14*)	New York Sbdg.	31 July 18	30 Mar 20	30 Sept 20	Scrapped 1946
DD239 *Overton*	New York Sbdg.	30 Oct 18	10 July 19	30 June 20	Scrapped 1945
DD240 *Sturtevant*	New York Sbdg.	23 Nov 18	29 July 20	21 Sept 20	Lost 26 April 42
DD242 *King*	New York Sbdg.	28 April 19	14 Oct 20	16 Dec 20	Scrapped 1946
DD243 *Sands*	New York Sbdg.	22 Mar 19	28 Oct 19	10 Nov 20	Scrapped 1946
DD244 *Williamson* (ex-*AVD2*)	New York Sbdg.	27 Mar 19	16 Oct 19	29 Oct 20	Scrapped 1946
DD245 *Reuben James*	New York Sbdg.	2 April 19	4 Oct 19	24 Sept 20	Lost 31 Oct 41
DD246 *Bainbridge*	New York Sbdg.	27 May 19	12 June 20	9 Feb 21	Scrapped 1945
DD247 *Goff*	New York Sbdg.	16 June 19	2 June 20	19 Jan 21	Scrapped 1945
DD248 *Barry*	New York Sbdg.	26 July 19	28 Oct 20	28 Dec 20	Lost 25 May 45
DD250 *Lawrence*	New York Sbdg.	14 Aug 19	10 July 20	18 April 21	Scrapped 1946
DD251 *Belknap* (ex-*AVD8*)	Bethlehem, Fore River	3 Sept 18	14 Jan 19	28 April 19	Lost 11 Jan 45
DD255 *Osmond Ingram* (ex-*AVD9*)	Bethlehem, Fore River	15 Oct 18	28 Feb 19	28 June 19	Scrapped 1946
DD266 *Greene* (ex-*AVD13*)	Bethlehem, Squantum	3 June 18	2 Nov 18	9 May 19	Lost 9 Oct 45
DD336 *Litchfield*	Mare Island	15 Jan 19	12 Aug 19	12 May 20	Scrapped 1946
DD341 *Decatur*	Mare Island	15 Sept 20	29 Oct 21	9 Aug 22	Scrapped 1945
DD342 *Hulbert* (ex-*AVD6*)	Norfolk NYd.	18 Nov 18	28 June 19	27 Oct 20	Scrapped 1946
DD343 *Noa*	Norfolk NYd.	18 Nov 18	28 June 19	15 Feb 21	Lost 14 Sept 44

Range: 2,500nm at 20kts.
Guns: four 4in (4×1); one 3in.
Torpedoes: twelve 21in (4×3).
Complement: 150.

Design This class was a modification of the *Wickes* class in an attempt to rectify the gross inconsistencies in the endurance of the earlier class, but were otherwise very similar. Wing tanks were fitted in the boiler rooms to increase bunkerage. Five ships were given 5-inch guns (*Hatfield, Brooks, Gilmer, Fox* and *Kane*) although all were strengthened to take them and two, *Hovey* and *Long*, received four twin 4-inch mountings.

A total of 144 ships were built, of which seven (*Chauncey, Delphy, Fuller, Woodbury, Lee, Nicholas* and *Young*) ran aground in fog on the Californian coast on 8 September 1923 in what surely must be the biggest peacetime disaster to the USN. Two others were lost in collisions between the wars, and 57, all Bethlehem and Union Iron Works boats, were scrapped before 1940. This was in the main due to the deterioration of their Yarrow-pattern boilers. *Dahlgren* was used as a test-bed for a high-pressure steam system utilizing 1,300psi Babcock & Wilcox boilers and new General Electric geared turbines. The boilers were installed in the after boiler rooms and appear to have proved successful. She remained in this role until June 1940. Fourteen ships had been converted to seaplane tenders (AVD) during 1938–40, but nine of these reverted to destroyer status in November 1943. Four others had been converted to minelayers in 1930–37 and nine to fast minesweepers, 1940–42. Twenty were transferred to Great Britain in 1940.

Modifications Essentially similar to those applied to the *Wickes* class. The pre-war escort destroyer conversion programme had rearmed eleven units with 3-inch guns (*DD199, 210, 220, 221, 223, 229, 239, 240, 245, 246, 341*). The others, with 4-inch guns, were given increased endurance by the removal of a boiler, but the Asiatic units were not modified except for *Parrott* after her escape from the East in the summer of 1942. Nine ships, converted to small seaplane tenders (AVD) prior to the war, were re-rated as destroyers in November 1943 to meet an escort vessel crisis. These ships had only two boilers and were generally armed with two 3-inch guns. At least *McFarland* had sixteen single 20mm guns. *MacLeish* and *McCormick*, employed in the Mediterranean, were given two single 40mm army-type Bofors in lieu of their remaining, forward, tubes.

Service In Atlantic waters in 1941, were *Dallas* leading DesRon 30* composed of eight *Wickes*-class destroyers and DesRon 31 led by *MacLeish* composed of *DD210, 221, 223, 229, 239, 240, 245*, and *246*. *Dallas* took part in the first USN escort to a British convoy, HX150 in September, the start of a number of such operations by the, as yet 'at peace' navy. This led to tragic consequences the following month, when *Reuben James* was torpedoed and sunk by *U562* south-west of Ireland while escorting HX156. By a strange coincidence, her First World War namesake had been the first US ship sunk in that war too. *Truxton* was wrecked in February 1942 when she ran ashore in Newfoundland in atrocious weather while escorting a navy transport to Argentina. Few of her people survived. In March *Sturtevant*, now in the Caribbean area, was mined and sunk off Marquesas Key.

In 1943, *George E. Badger* sank *U613* while operating with the escort carrier *Bogue* south of the

*Destroyer Squadron 30.

Above: *MacLeish* (DD220), also modified for escort duties. (INRO)

Above: *Barker* (DD213) In January 1943. The after tubes have been landed and extra ASW equipment and six 20mm guns added. She also has radar. **Below:** *Clemson* (DD186), shown here in October 1942 as AVD4. (USN)

Azores on 23 July and *Borie*, escorting *Card*, sank *U405* in a close-quarters gun battle on 1 November. Unfortunately the destroyer was so badly damaged in the action that she foundered the following day, after her crew had been taken off by *Goff* and *Barry*. In December *Clemson*, operating with the escort group assigned to the carrier *Bogue*, assisted in the destruction of *U172*. *Parrott*, a survivor of the battles in the Dutch East Indies and now returned to the USA for duty in the Atlantic, had the misfortune to be rammed by the merchant ship *John Morton* at the Norfolk Navy base in May 1944. Subsequently towed to Portsmouth Navy Yard, she was found to be not worth repair and paid off on 16 June 1944.

Thirteen of these ships formed DesRon 29, the only destroyers attached to the Asiatic Fleet in December 1941. Led by *Paul Jones*, they comprised DesDiv 50† (*Peary, Pope, John D. Ford* and *Pillsbury*), DesDiv 57 (*Whipple, Alden, John D. Edwards* and *Edsall*) and DesDiv 58 (*Stewart, Parrott, Bulmer* and *Barker*). All managed to escape from the Philippines in December 1941 and covered the Allied withdrawal to Australia. *Edsall*, in company with Australian corvettes, sank the Japanese submarine *I124* on 20 January 1942, the first to be destroyed by US forces. In 1942, the thirteen ships of DesRon 29 joined the combined Australian-British-Dutch-American (ABDA) force formed for the defence of the Dutch East Indies. In the months that followed, this squadron was extremely active, four (*John D. Ford, Pope, Parrott* and *Paul Jones*) making a strike against Japanese transports in Balikpapan in January in which some success was achieved. *Barker* and *Bulmer* were damaged by near misses from aircraft bombs on 15 February and were withdrawn to Australia, thus avoiding the fate of most of their compatriots. *Peary*, caught in Port Darwin during a Japanese air-raid was bombed and sunk leaving only ten destroyers available to the US forces.

The survivors operated with the combined Allied forces, *Stewart* being damaged in an action in the Badoeng Strait on 18 February. Sent to Soerabaja to repair, she was still unfinished when the Japanese closed in and to avoid capture her crew set off demolition charges. Unfortunately these were not as effective as hoped and the destroyer was repaired by the Japanese. She survived the war as *Patrol Vessel No. 2* and was finally recaptured by the USN on 28 October 1945. Of the others, *Pillsbury* and *Parrott* had defects and were withdrawn, while *Pope* was also in Soerabaja for repairs. Thus only *John D. Edwards, Paul Jones, Alden* and *Ford* were present at the Battle of the Java Sea. Despite courageous torpedo attacks, they scored no hits, but survived the action and eventually returned to the USA. *Edsall*, having been ordered to escort the aircraft transport *Langley*, was then sent to rendezvous with the oiler *Pecos* after which she was never seen agan by the USN. Information about her end is not altogether conclusive, but it would appear that she was sunk by gunfire from the battleships *Hiei* and *Kirishima* as well as the heavy cruiser *Ashigari* south of Java. *Pillsbury* was sunk by the heavy cruisers *Atago* and *Maya* south of Bali having sailed from Tjilatjap in an attempt to reach Australia. *Parrott*, however, got through. *Pope* was not so lucky. She had sailed from Soerabaja with HMSs *Exeter* and *Encounter* on 28 February, steaming for Borneo, making for the Sunda Strait. Trapped by Japanese cruisers in the Java Sea, both British ships were sunk, but *Pope* survived for a while but was eventually damaged by near misses from Japanese dive-bombers. Badly damaged and settling, the destroyer had just been abandoned when the cruisers *Atago* and *Takao* arrived finally to shell her under.

For the remainder of the war, these old destroyers were employed on escort duties. The conversions had some success against Japanese submarines, *Gamble* (*DM 15*) sinking *I123* in August 1942, *Southard* (*DMS10*), *I172* in November 1942 and *Chandler* (*DMS9*), *I185* off Saipan in June 1944.

The end of hostilities brought an end to their already over-extended lives and all were soon disposed of.

†Destroyer Division 50.

FARRAGUT CLASS

Ship	Builder	Laid Down	Launched	Commissioned	Fate
DD348 *Farragut*	Bethlehem, Quincy	20 Sept 32	15 Mar 34	8 June 34	Scrapped 1947
DD349 *Dewey*	Bath Iron Works	16 Dec 32	28 July 34	3 Oct 34	Scrapped 1947
DD350 *Hull*	New York NYd.	7 Mar 33	31 Jan 34	24 May 35	Lost 18 Dec 44
DD351 *MacDonough*	Boston NYd.	15 May 33	22 Aug 34	28 June 35	Scrapped 1947
DD352 *Worden*	Puget Sound NYd.	29 Dec 32	27 Oct 34	1 Mar 35	Lost 12 Jan 43
DD353 *Dale*	New York NYd.	10 Feb 34	23 Jan 35	19 July 35	Scrapped 1947
DD354 *Monaghan*	Boston NYd.	21 Nov 33	9 Jan 35	30 Aug 35	Lost 18 Dec 44
DD355 *Aylwin*	Philadelphia NYd.	23 Sept 33	10 July 34	1 May 35	Scrapped 1947

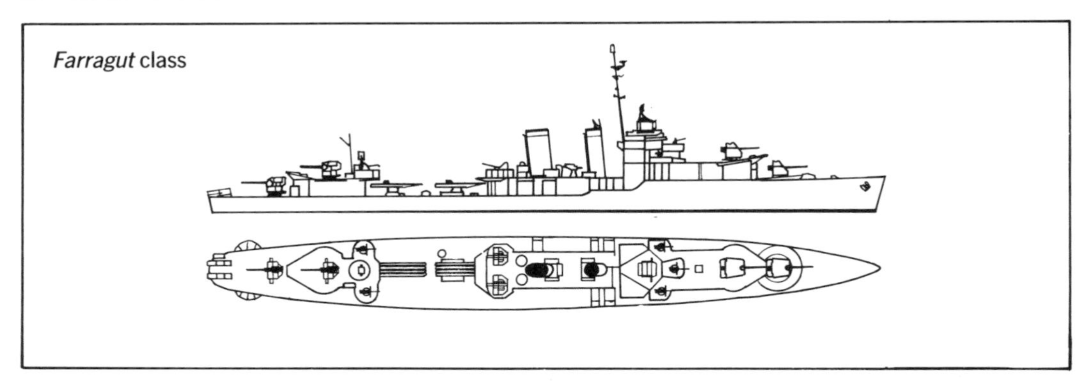
Farragut class

Displacement: 1,395tons/1,417tonnes (1,365/1,386 *Farragut*; 1,345/1,366 *Dewey*; 1,375/1,397 *Aylwin*; 1,410/1,432 *Worden*) (standard); 2,335tons/2,372tonnes (full load).
Length: 341ft 3in/104m (oa); 331ft/100.8m (330/100.5 *Farragut*; 329/100.2 *Dewey*) (wl).
Beam: 34ft 3in/10.44m.
Draught: 8ft 10in/2.69m (8ft 8in/2.64m *Farragut*; 8ft 7in/2.62m *Dewey*) (mean).
Machinery: four Yarrow (Bethlehem) boilers; 2-shaft geared turbines.
Performance: 42,800shp; 36.5kts.
Bunkerage: 400tons/406tonnes.
Range: 5,800nm at 15kts.
Guns: five 5in (5×1); four .5in MG.
Torpedoes: eight 21in (2×4).
Complement: 250.

Design Although much discussion had taken place during the 1920s regarding new destroyer construction, the existence of the old 'flush-deckers' in large numbers, combined with the national financial position, caused all these schemes to come to nothing. However, by the beginning of the 1930s it had become imperative to make a start on new construction partly because of the ageing condition of the *Wickes* and *Clemson* classes, but also because foreign navies, including potential enemies such as Japan, had long since resumed destroyer construction after the war. Several projects were studied of 1,350, 1,500 and 1,850 tons, all armed with four 5-inch guns and, in the case of the 1,500-ton scheme, three triple banks of tubes. Experience with the 'flush-deckers' resulted in a raised forecastle being re-introduced to reduce the wetness forward and to make fighting the forward guns easier.

The gun initially considered was the 5-inch/51cal, low-angle weapon, with one 3-inch AA gun. In keeping with modern thinking, all guns were to be centre-line mounted. The same reasoning led to the demand for the torpedoes also to be centre-line mounted, but this caused problems of deck space and at one time a novel six-tube (three over three) mounting was considered but later discarded because of weight problems. The USA early appreciated the possibilities of air power and this thinking led to the alteration of the main battery to dual-purpose 5-inch/25cal guns in place of the 51cal surface-use weapons. As the 5-inch gun had a greater range than that of the flush-deckers' 4-inch which itself could not be controlled at maximum range, the new ships were to be given an effective fire-control system which also had to be capable of HA use if the full potential of the ship were to be realized. Eventually, the short 25cal 5-inch gun was discarded in favour of the longer 38cal 5-inch Mk 24 weapon, and a fifth gun replaced the originally projected 3-inch AA. The latter was in any event rendered superfluous by the DP nature of the main armament. With five 5-inch guns, the torpedo outfit had to be reduced and only two quadruple tubes were fitted, both on the centre-line. Weight economy was of paramount importance and to this end longitudinal framing and welded construction was adopted. For the same reason, only Nos. 1 and 2 guns were given shields and then more as a weather or spray protection than anything else. Fire control for the main armament was the Mk 33 DP director, developed especially for the new destroyers and the combination of this and the DP 5-inch gun began a line of development which later gave US destroyers an excellent main armament DP capability. There were some problems with this director, especially its ability to accept weighty radar additions later, but despite this, it was in advance of that aboard foreign contemporaries. Light AA comprised only four .5in machine-guns, two forward and two aft. Weight considerations restricted the ASW outfit to sonar installation only, but provision was made for depth-charge racks in wartime.

The main machinery consisted of four Yarrow boilers operating at 400psi and 648°F installed in one large (forward) and one smaller (after) boiler rooms. Two single-reduction geared turbines occupied the one engine room abaft the boiler rooms. 600 tons of oil fuel gave a design endurance of 6,500 nautical miles at 12 knots. Thus the steam conditions were more advanced than contemporary British destroyers, which operated at 300psi and 620°F, but do not appear to have given noticeable improvement in endurance in the Pacific operations context.

This final design, produced by Bethlehem, was considered superior to that of the 'flush-deckers' on many counts, including sea-worthiness, manoeuvrability, fire power and gunnery control, and moreover had an advantage in speed of more than 3 knots. Five ships were authorized on 28 February 1931 for the 1932 programme and three more in September 1932 for the 1933 programme. Two were ordered from private yards, the others from various Navy yards in order to provide work at a time of low industrial activity.

When they entered service,they were an advance on the old 'flush-deckers' and became known as 'Gold Platers', attracting, as always the case, criticism of their 'over-lavish facilities'.

Modifications Early in 1942, No. 3 gun was landed and four single 20mm guns fitted in lieu and around the second funnel. Four more single guns replaced the original .5in machine-guns and the mainmast was removed. By the end of that year, radar had been added, generally SC, SG and FD, and the 20mm guns around the after funnel had been replaced by a pair of 40mm twin mountings and a single 20mm added on a bandstand in front of the bridge. Final authorized armament was five 5-inch, four 40mm (2×2) and five 20mm (5×1).

Service All eight ships were serving with the Pacific Fleet in December 1941, *Aylwin, Dale, Farragut* and *Monaghan* forming DesDiv 2 when the last named sank a Japanese midget submarine during the atack on Pearl Harbor. The other four destroyers formed DesDiv 1.

Dewey, Aylwin, Farragut and *Monaghan* took part

Above: *Hull* (DD350), with eight 20mm guns added, but as yet without radar. (USN) **Below:** *Dale* (DD353), with 40mm and 20mm guns as well as SC2 and SG radars on the mast and a Mk 28 set on the director. No. 3 gun has been removed. (USN)

in the Battle of the Coral Sea in May 1942 as a component of Task Force 11 and later combined with the carriers in Task Force 17. *Worden* escorted the fuelling group. At the Battle of Midway *Dewey*, *Worden*, *Monaghan* and *Aylwin* served with DesRons 1 and 6, but this was essentially a carrier aircraft battle although *Monaghan* assisted in the hunt for *I168* following her sinking of *Yorktown* and the destroyer *Hamman*. In the autumn of 1942, *Farragut*, *Worden* and *Macdonough* (DesRon 1) served in the Solomons but in the new year, *Worden* was attached to the escort forces for the landings in the Aleutian Islands, where she ran ashore and became a total loss at Amchitka. *Dale* and *Monaghan* saw action at the Battle of the Komandorski Islands in March 1943 against a Japanese cruiser and destroyer force and by this time, all seven survivors were in the Aleutians as DesRon 1 and DesDiv 1. Here, *MacDonough* was rammed by the destroyer/minelayer *Sicard* in fog on 10 May 1943, flooding engine room and after boiler room, but *Monaghan* destroyed *I7* by radar-directed gunfire on 22 June.

The end of 1943 saw the repaired *MacDonough*, *Dewey*, *Hull* and *Dale* in the Gilbert Islands, and in January 1944 all except *Dewey* and *Hull* were in the Marshall Islands operations, escorting the Fleet and conducting shore bombardments. In April, *MacDonough* took part in the destruction of *I174* south of Truk. The Marianas operations followed in June, in which all seven ships participated.

Hull and *Monaghan* were both lost in a typhoon off the Philippines while screening the fuelling group attached to Task Force 38. Heavy casualties were caused to their crews in the mountainous seas. *Aylwin* and *Dewey* were also damaged but survived. *Farragut* and *MacDonough* remained with TF38 and entered the South China Sea in January 1945.

All five surviving destroyers were sold for scrapping on 20 December 1946, except *Farragut* on 14 August the following year.

PORTER CLASS

Ship	Builder	Laid Down	Launched	Commissioned	Fate
DD356 *Porter*	New York Sbdg.	18 Dec 33	12 Dec 35	25 Aug 36	Lost 26 Oct 42
DD357 *Selfridge*	New York Sbdg.	18 Dec 33	18 April 36	25 Nov 36	Sold for breaking up 19 Nov 46
DD358 *McDougal*	New York Sbdg.	18 Dec 33	17 July 36	23 Dec 36	Stricken 15 Aug 49
DD359 *Winslow*	New York Sbdg.	18 Dec 33	21 Sept 36	17 Feb 37	Sold for breaking up 23 Feb 59
DD360 *Phelps*	Bethlehem, Quincy	2 Jan 34	18 July 35	26 Feb 36	Stricken 28 Jan 47
DD361 *Clark*	Bethlehem, Quincy	2 Jan 34	15 Oct 35	20 May 36	Sold for breaking up 29 Mar 46
DD362 *Moffett*	Bethlehem, Quincy	2 Jan 34	11 Dec 35	28 Aug 36	Stricken 28 Jan 47
DD363 *Balch*	Bethlehem, Quincy	16 May 34	24 Mar 36	20 Oct 36	Scrapped 1946

Displacement: 1,834tons/1,863tonnes (standard); 2,597tons/2,638tonnes (full load).
Length: 381ft 1in/116.15m (oa); 372ft/113.4m (wl).
Beam: 37ft/11.28m.
Draught: 13ft/3.96m (mean).
Machinery: four Babcock & Wilcox boilers; 2-shaft geared turbines.
Performance: 50,000shp; 37kts.
Bunkerage: 635tons/645tonnes.
Range: 6,500nm at 12kts.
Guns: eight 5in (4×2); eight 1.1in (2×4); two .5in MG.
Torpedoes: eight 21in (2×4).
Complement: 194.

Design The leader category had no real precedent in the USN as it did in the Royal Navy, neither did America possess much in the way of light cruisers either for the traditional cruiser role or as flotilla leaders. In fact, sketch designs for a leader type had been prepared as early as 1917, and by 1919, a 2,000-ton ship carrying five 5-inch guns and twelve tubes had been designed, but Congress refused to fund five ships in the FY1921 programme. There matters rested until new studies were commenced in 1927. Eventually in January 1932 a requirement was tabled for 35 knots minimum, five 5-inch guns and eight torpedo tubes, with light protective plating to bridge, guns and machinery. The main armament was to be 5-inch/38 guns, but from 1927 to 1932, single-purpose 5-inch/51 and 5-inch/25 AA guns had been discussed and in the meantime, the Ordnance Office had produced the 5-inch/38 which had advantages over both. Displacement was fixed at 1,850 tons which, in fact, was the maximum allowed under the London Naval Treaty.

The disposition of the 5-inch guns provoked some discussion and several schemes were prepared of which one showed three single superfiring guns forward, and another retained wing guns on the break of the forecastle. Another showed six guns with three superfiring on the centre-line, forward and aft. In the end, a completely different option was chosen and the DP gun was abandoned in this class for a low-angle outfit of eight 5-inch/38 on base ring mountings in four twin gun-houses. Fire control consisted of the Mk 35 director atop the bridge. Like the destroyers of the *Farragut* class, these heavy destroyers carried eight torpedo tubes in quadruple mountings on the centre-line, but were able in addition to ship eight reload torpedoes around the base of the funnel. The .5in MG outfit was reduced to two, but this was (in theory) more than compensated by the provision of two of the new quadruple 1.1-inch mountings, one superfiring on each of Nos. 2 and 3 gun-houses. With a weight of about 4½–6½ tons, this heavy mounting could not be accommodated on the 1,500-ton destroyers, at least without weight compensation. It was an unsuccessful weapon, however, and eventually was superseded in most ships by the 40mm of Bofors design.

The hull was almost forty feet longer than that of the destroyers which, with an installed power of 50,000shp, enabled a design speed of 37 knots to be achieved, compared to the *Farraguts*' 36.5 knots, despite the increased displacement. The steam plant was similar to that of the *Farraguts* with two boiler rooms, but separate engine rooms were provided for each turbine. A step forward was the installation of two diesel generators for emergency power supply.

Eight ships, *DD 356–363* were authorized to this design under the FY33 programme, the design being prepared by New York Shipbuilding Corp.

Modifications The war in Europe soon illustrated the importance of good AA batteries and consideration was given to rearming the *Porters* with dual-purpose main guns. This initially proved impossible on weight grounds, among others. Even the provision of an extra 1.1-inch mounting would have cost the after director, but in any case, enough DP 5-inch guns were not immediately available. In 1941, the after superstructure was cut down and the heavy tripod mainmast removed, as was the torpedo reload stowage. Gun-tubs for light AA weapons were built just forward of No. 3 gun, accommodating the 1.1-inch mounting to starboard with three single 20mm guns. Two more were added abreast the after funnel. Depth-charge equipment was augmented and FC or Mk 3 fire-control radar added to the forward director (the after one having been landed). Search radar was also fitted at the foremast truck. *Porter* was probably lost in this condition, but in 1943 the remainder received two twin 40mm aft in lieu of the 1.1-inch and 20mm guns. In about 1944, No. 3 5-inch gun-house was landed, to be replaced by a quadruple 40mm mounting; the Atlantic ships being last in line for treatment, *Moffett* not being so fitted until after March 1944. Armament was now six 5-inch/38 SP guns, ten 40mm (1×4, 3×2) and six 20mm guns. The intention was still to replace

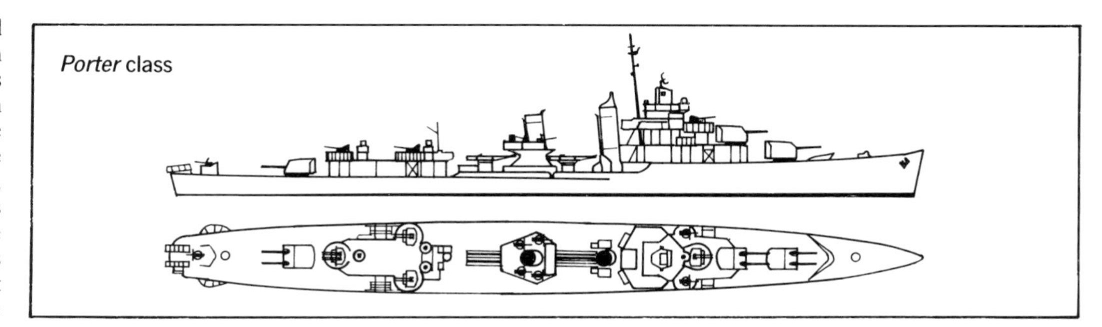

Above: *Porter* (DD356). She has received 20mm guns, SC1 and fire-control radars. (USN) **Below:** *Moffett* (DD362), in July 1944, re-armed with ten 40mm and six 20mm. No. 3 gun has been landed. She retains the old SC radar, but has received radar SG and HF/DF. (USN)

the main armament with 5-inch DP guns, but because of delays and other priorities, this modification was not begun until late 1944, when *Selfridge* and *Phelps* were converted. In this refit, a new, low, Admiralty-style bridge was fitted and both funnels cut down in height with new caps. Twin 5-inch/38 DP Mk 38 mountings were shipped at Nos. 1 and 4 positions, with a single 5-inch/38 Mk 30 DP gunhouse displacing the quadruple 40mm at No. 3 position. This quad was resited forward of the bridge in place of No. 2 gun. The armament of *Phelps* was now five 5-inch DP, eight 40mm (1×4, 2×2) and six 20mm. A new DP Mk 37 main director with Mk 12 and 22 radars was also fitted. *Winslow* was also converted by 1945, but by the August of that year both she and *Phelps* had received the anti-Kamikaze AA refit when both banks of torpedoes were landed, allowing the after pair of twin 40mm to be replaced by a pair of quadruple 40mm Mk 2 mountings and the four 20mm guns abreast the funnel were exchanged for a pair of twin 40mm Mk 1 Mod 6. Finally, the 20mm outfit was reduced to a pair of twin Mk 24 Mod 5 mountings abreast the bridge. ASW equipment was now only a single track and two throwers. The final close-range armament of these two ships was sixteen 40mm (3×4, 2×2) and four 20mm (2×2). This corresponded very closely with some of the late-war 'Barbara' refits applied to German destroyers, but the significant factor was that the US ships had sophisticated fire-control systems for the CRA which the Germans did not. In the case of *Winslow* these were the 40mm directors Mk 51 Mod 2, but *Phelps* had the more advanced Mk 63 GFCS with Mk 29 gunsights and Mk 28 radar on the mountings. *Clark*, *Moffett* and *Balch* never received this outfit, while *McDougal* did receive DP guns, but retained her two banks of quadruple tubes and carried two twin and one quadruple 40mm.

Service In December 1941, three of the class, *Moffett*, *Winslow* and *McDougal*, were serving with the Atlantic Fleet, the remainder in the Pacific. *Winslow* had in fact been transferred from the Pacific in May, and the following month began neutrality patrols with *Moffett* working from Recife in Brazil. These three destroyers spent their entire career in the North and South Atlantic engaged upon convoy escort and anti-blockade runner duties.

Of the Pacific Fleet destroyers, *Phelps* was flagship of DesRon 1, *Selfridge* of DesRon 4, *Porter* of DesRon 5 and *Balch* DesRon 6. *Balch* took part in the raid on Wake Island in February 1942 and *Phelps*, the carrier raid on Papua New Guinea in March. *Balch* accompanied the carriers on the famous Tokyo raid in April and both she and *Phelps* were at Midway. Most of the Pacific units served in the Solomons and at Guadalcanal between July and December 1942. *Porter*, flagship of DesRon 5, was torpedoed and sunk by *I21* during the Battle of the Santa Cruz Islands while screening the carrier *Hornet*. *Selfridge* spent much of her time in 1942 with TF44, an Australian-American-New Zealand formation in Australian and New Guinea waters. She was at the landings in New Georgia in June and July 1943, but at the Battle of Vella Lavella on the night of 6/7 October 1943 was hit by a torpedo from either *Samidare* or *Shigure* and had her bows blown off. After repairs both she and *Phelps* returned to action in the Gilbert Islands, Kwajalein, the Marianas and Saipan when *Phelps* was damaged by gunfire off the latter. All except *Porter* survived the war and, with the exception of *Winslow*, converted for experimental purposes, then scrapped very shortly afterwards.

MAHAN CLASS

Ship	Builder	Laid Down	Launched	Commissioned	Fate
DD364 *Mahan*	Bethlehem, Staten Is.	12 June 34	15 Oct 35	16 Nov 36	Lost 7 Dec 44
DD365 *Cummings*	Bethlehem, Staten Is.	26 June 34	11 Dec 35	26 Jan 37	Scrapped 1947
DD366 *Drayton*	Bath Iron Works	20 Mar 34	26 Mar 36	1 June 37	Scrapped 1947
DD367 *Lamson*	Bath Iron Works	20 Mar 34	17 June 36	4 Jan 37	Expended 2 July 46
DD368 *Flusser*	Federal Sbdg. Co.	4 June 34	29 Sept 35	1 Dec 36	Scrapped 1948
DD369 *Reid*	Federal Sbdg. Co.	25 June 34	11 Jan 36	4 Jan 37	Lost 11 Dec 44
DD370 *Case*	Boston NYd.	19 Sept 34	14 Sept 35	19 Mar 37	Scrapped 1948
DD371 *Conyngham*	Boston NYd.	19 Sept 34	14 Sept 35	10 April 37	Expended 2 July 48
DD372 *Cassin*	Philadelphia NYd.	1 Oct 34	28 Oct 35	6 April 37	Scrapped 1948
DD373 *Shaw*	Philadelphia NYd.	1 Oct 34	28 Oct 35	20 April 37	Scrapped 1946
DD374 *Tucker*	Norfolk NYd.	15 Aug 34	26 Feb 36	30 Mar 37	Lost 4 Aug 42
DD375 *Downes*	Norfolk NYd.	15 Aug 34	22 April 36	26 Mar 37	Scrapped 1948
DD376 *Cushing*	Puget Sound NYd.	15 Nov 34	31 Dec 35	10 Dec 36	Lost 13 Nov 42
DD377 *Perkins*	Puget Sound NYd.	15 Nov 34	31 Dec 35	10 Dec 36	Lost 29 Nov 43
DD378 *Smith*	Mare Island NYd.	27 Oct 34	20 Feb 36	31 Dec 36	Scrapped 1947
DD379 *Preston*	Mare Island NYd.	27 Oct 34	22 April 36	23 Jan 37	Lost 14 Nov 42
DD384 *Dunlap*	Bethlehem, Staten Is.	10 April 35	18 April 36	7 July 38	Scrapped 1948
DD385 *Fanning*	Bethlehem, State Is.	10 April 35	18 Sept 36	4 Aug 38	Scrapped 1948

Displacement: 1,488tons/1,512tonnes (standard); 2,103tons/2,136tonnes (full load).
Length: 341ft 4in/104.04m (oa); 334ft/101.8m (wl).
Beam: 35ft 5in/10.67m.
Draught: 12ft 4in/3.76m (mean).
Machinery: four Babcock & Wilcox boilers; 2-shaft G.E.C. geared turbines.
Performance: 49,000shp; 36.5kts.
Bunkerage: 522tons/530tonnes.
Range: 6.500nm at 12kts.
Guns: five 5in (5×1); four .5in MG.
Torpedoes: twelve 21in (3×4).
Complement: 158.

Design The *Farragut* class were well regarded but there was pressure to increase the torpedo battery even at the expense of one 5-inch gun. The fleet, however, also wanted the retention of the dual-purpose capability main armament which the Construction & Repair Bureau felt could not be done if five guns and twelve tubes were to be carried. In the event, this armament and a DP capability were retained by an increase in beam of 15 inches. There was also a move to more advanced machinery practice both in respect of boilers and turbines, and the *Mahan* class showed a modest increase in steam temperature to 700°F from the *Farragut*s' 648° although a temperature of 850°F had been originally proposed. The well-known firm of naval architects, Gibbs & Cox, were awarded the design contract to encourage new thinking on machinery and the result was the adoption of economisers on the boilers and for the first time, double reduction geared turbines. Surprisingly, perhaps, the machinery weights were about 30 tons heavier than the *Farragut*s' despite these advances, and they incurred some criticism for the cramped nature of the machinery spaces. On the other hand, their economy is illustrated by the fact that their designed endurance was the same as *Farragut* on 50 tons less bunkerage, and an increase in power to 46,000shp gave an increase of ½ knot over the earlier class.

Although the main gun armament was similar to that of *Farragut*, the position of No. 3 gun was altered, being moved aft to the shelter deck ahead of No. 4 gun. The forward bank of tubes, the only one on the centre-line, was mounted on the top of a deck-house between the funnels in what was a relatively high location. The other eight tubes were carried in two beam quadruple mountings on the main deck forward of No. 3 gun to give a broadside of eight torpedoes. A heavy tripod foremast was fitted and, in common with *Farragut*, only Nos.1 and 2 guns had shields. Four single .5in machine-guns comprised the light AA outfit. Sixteen ships were ordered under the 1933 programme and two modified units, *DD384* and *DD385*, under that for

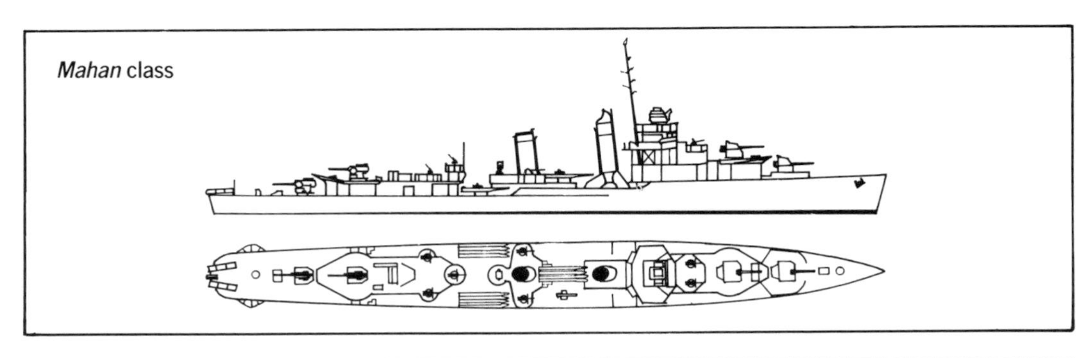

Above: *Preston* (DD379), as she appeared pre-war. (USN) **Below:** *Case* (DD370). (M. Bar)

Below: *Reid* (DD369), with radars, 20mm and 40mm guns added and No. 3 gun landed. (USN)

1934. The latter two, *Dunlap* and *Fanning*, differed in that their forward guns were prototype single enclosed DP base ring mountings and they had pole foremasts.

Modifications From about 1942, search radar was being fitted at the masthead and four or five single 20mm guns added, two or three before the bridge and two abreast the second funnel. The heavy boats and cranes aft were removed. In that year, No. 3 gun was also landed and replaced initially by a pair of single 20mm guns. Later, these were replaced by a pair of twin 40mm. Mk 4 fire-control radar was fitted to the front of the Mk 33 director except in *Cummings* which had it fitted on top of her fully enclosed Mk 33. All excess top-weight was landed to compensate these additions.

In January 1945, the Kamikaze threat forced a further augmentation of destroyer CRA and the *Mahans* were scheduled to land the wing torpedo tubes as compensation for converting the twin 40mm into a pair of quadruples. Only *Lamson* was so altered, retaining the forward, centre-line tubes, and shipping eight 40mm (2×4) and five single 20mm. On August 1945, a further refit was promulgated in which the remaining tubes would be landed to allow a pair of twin 40mm to be fitted abreast the after funnel. Two twin 20mm before the bridge and two more on the main deck between the funnels would complete the CRA outfit. In fact, only *Shaw* received this modification after which her stability was so suspect that No. 4 5-inch gun had to be landed leaving only three 5-inch guns. *Lamson* also lost her remaining tubes in August 1945. *Conyngham* was the only other non-standard conversion in that in 1942 she received four twin and two single .5in machine-guns and two single 20mm. The twin .5in MG were carried on the forward crew shelter and on a deck-house on the after shelter deck abaft No. 4 gun. No. 3 gun was removed and, pending availability of twin 40mm, two single 20mm were fitted in their tubs. Two single .5in MG were fitted abreast the after funnel. By mid 1944, however, she had received the standard four 40mm, five 20mm fit.

Following their destruction at Pearl Harbor, *Cassin* and *Downes* had their machinery and equipment stripped out and fitted in new hulls built at Mare Island and launched on 25 June 1943 (*Cassin*)

and 22 May 1943 (*Downes*). Completed in 1944, they emerged with a new-style low bridge, only eight (centre-line) torpedo tubes, on deck-houses, and Mk 37 directors. Two twin 40mm and six 20mm were fitted as well as an augmented radar suite. Like all her sisters at this time, No. 3 gun had been landed.

Service All eighteen destroyers served with the Pacific Fleet. *Shaw* was in floating dock at the time of Pearl Harbor and was hit by three bombs forward. Set on fire and badly damaged, she lost her bows but was eventually patched up, sent back to the United States and repaired. *Cassin* and *Downes*, both in dry dock under refit, were also bombed and set afire. Almost totally destroyed, their machinery was salvaged and put into new hulls built at Mare Island in 1943–44. *Fanning* and *Dunlap*, serving with DesRon 6, took part in the attempt to relieve Wake Island towards the end of December and, a month later, *Drayton* participated in the abortive raid on the island after its surrender. *Lamson* and *Perkins* were attached to the Anzac Squadron in February 1942, and in April *Fanning* was one of the escorting destroyers for the Tokyo raid. *Conyngham* was with the US carrier forces at the Battle of Midway. In June, *Reid* and *Case* were attached to TF8 for operations in the Aleutian Islands when the former, assisted by aircraft, sank *RO61* off Atka Island on 31 August. Many of the class were employed on escort duties and in the course of one such mission *Tucker* sank, having ran into a minefield laid by the destroyer/minelayers *Gamble, Breese* and *Tracy* off the entrance to Espiritu Santo in the New Hebrides.

DesRon 5, *Smith, Cushing, Preston, Shaw, Mahan* and *Conyngham*, screened the carrier *Enterprise* (TF16) in the Solomons in the autumn of 1942 when *Smith* was struck on the forecastle by a Japanese aircraft in a very early form of Kamikaze attack. Although not lost, she was badly damaged and suffered heavy casualties. *Mahan* was also damaged in collision with *South Dakota*, and *Shaw* had the unhappy task of finishing off *Porter*. In November, *Cushing*, a unit of TG67.4, was in action with the battleship *Hiei* north of Guadalcanal and was one of four destroyers lost in that battle. The following night, *Preston* was lost in the same area in action with Japanese cruisers, destroyers and the battleship *Kirishima*. She was shelled and sunk by the cruiser *Nagara*.

Destroyer action was lively in the Guadalcanal and Solomons area in 1942–43 with many of the class seeing action. *Lamson, Perkins* and *Drayton* were in the action off Tassafaronga on 30 November 1942 when US forces suffered once more at the hands of the Japanese. However, in the summer of 1943, DesRon 5, *Perkins, Conyngham, Smith* and *Mahan*, supported the Allied offensive in the New Guinea area, as did *Smith, Drayton, Reid, Flusser* and *Lamson*. Unfortunately, *Perkins*, en route for Buna, was rammed and sunk by the Australian trooper *Duntroon* as a result of human error aboard the destroyer. *Conyngham, Shaw, Drayton, Reid, Smith, Lamson, Flusser* and *Mahan* were involved in the assault on New Britain in December 1943 where *Shaw* was damaged by aircraft bombs.

In the Vella Gulf on 5/6 August 1943 *Dunlap*, one of a force of six US destroyers in the area, took part in an action which resulted in the loss of three Japanese destroyers, *Kawakaze, Hagikaze* and *Arashi*, at no cost to the US ships.

Dunlap, Fanning and *Cummings* escorted *Saratoga* on her detachment to the British Eastern Fleet in the Indian Ocean between March and May 1944 then returned to the Central Pacific in October, joined by *Case*, and took part in the Marshall Islands campaign. Eventually, the rebuilt *Cassin* and *Downes* also joined them. *Case, Conyngham, Downes* and *Shaw* participated in the assault on the Marianas in 1944 while others moved towards the Philippines, including *Flusser, Drayton, Lamson, Smith, Reid* and *Mahan*. In the landings at Leyte, *Mahan* was struck by three Kamikaze aircraft and had to be sunk, while *Lamson* was badly damaged by another. *Reid*, running supplies to the Ormoc bridgehead, was hit and sunk by two Kamikaze in the Suriago Straits. *Shaw* ran aground at Leyte on 2 April and was so badly damaged that she was not repaired despite being salvaged.

In January 1945, *Dunlap, Fanning* and *Cummings* bombarded Iwo Jima and by the summer, the first named was operating against enemy traffic in the Bonin Islands while her sisters, *Drayton, Flusser, Conyngham* and *Smith*, were covering the 7th Fleet's assault at Tarakan in the Dutch East Indies.

When Japan finally surrendered, the veteran *Flusser* was given the honour of being one of the first destroyers to enter Tokyo.

None saw post-war service, *Lamson* being expended at Bikini Atoll and the rest broken up.

SOMERS CLASS

Ship	Builder	Laid Down	Launched	Commissioned	Fate
DD381 *Somers*	Federal Sbdg.	27 June 35	13 Mar 37	30 June 38	Scrapped 1947
DD383 *Warrington*	Federal Sbdg.	10 Oct 35	15 May 37	12 Aug 38	Lost 13 Sept 44
DD394 *Sampson*	Bath Iron Works	8 April 36	16 April 38	3 Oct 38	Scrapped 1946
DD395 *Davis*	Bath Iron Works	28 July 36	30 July 38	16 Dec 38	Scrapped 1947
DD396 *Jouett*	Bath Iron Works	26 Mar 36	24 Sept 38	7 Mar 39	Scrapped 1946

Displacement: 2,047tons/2,079tonnes (standard); 2,767tons/2,811tonnes (full load).
Length: 381ft/116.13m (oa); 372ft/113.39m (wl).
Beam: 36ft 11in/11.25m.
Draught: 12ft 5in/3.78m (mean).
Machinery: four Babcock & Wilcox boilers; 2-shaft G.E.C. turbines.
Performance: 52,000shp; 37kts.
Bunkerage: 627tons/637tonnes.
Range: 7.500nm at 15kts.
Guns: eight 5in (4×2); eight 1.1in (2×4); two .5in MG.
Torpedoes: twelve 21in (3×4).
Complement: 294.

Design Originally proposed as repeat *Porters*, *DD381* and *383* were authorized under the FY34 programme. However, as a result of the moves described earlier to modernize the navy's machinery practices, they were instead built to a Gibbs and Cox design utilizing newly developed air-encased superheated boilers, operating at 850°F and 600psi. General Electric double reduction geared turbines provided the motive power with 52,000shp giving an increase in design speed of ½ knot over that of *Porter*. The new machinery weighed 65 tons more than that of the earlier leaders. Main armament remained identical with that of *Porter*, but by the elimination of the after director and heavy tripod mainmast, sufficient weight was saved to enable a third quadruple bank of torpedoes to be added. As

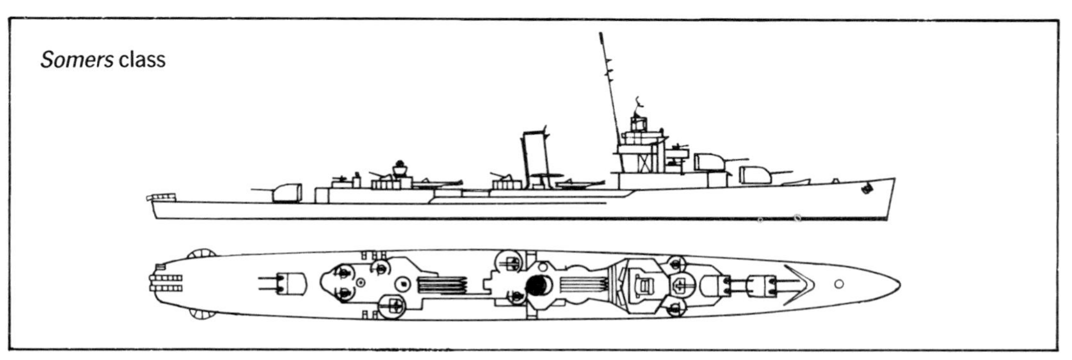
Somers class

the new design was only a single-funnelled one, all three banks of tubes could be accommodated on the centre-line. In service they were found to be very close to the acceptable limits of stability and in consequence were limited in what wartime additions they could accommodate. Three further units were authorized under FY35 (*DD394–396*).

Modifications Because of the stability problem with this class, the possible alterations were restricted initially to the removal of the after deck-house, searchlight platform and 1.1-inch quad as well as the middle bank of torpedo tubes. The searchlight was refitted in a lower position, flanked by a pair of 20mm guns, with two more being fitted in place of the midships torpedo tubes and a further pair before the bridge in lieu of the 1.1-inch quad. The usual search and gunnery control radar outfit was also added. In 1943, No. 3 5-inch gun-house was removed and replaced by two single 20mm with a twin 40mm in a tub offset to starboard just forward of them, balanced by another tub for a single 20mm to port. Abaft the second funnel, the opposite arrangement applied, with the twin 40mm being offset to port and the single 20mm on the starboard side. A third twin 40mm superfired over No. 2 gun-house, with a pair of single 20mm flanking it on the shelter deck. *Jouett*, at least, received a fourth twin 40mm superfiring on No. 4 gun. Only *Jouett* and *Davis* received any further modification, undergoing the Kamikaze refit in mid 1945 and late 1944 respectively. In the course of this, a new low bridge and DP main director were fitted and all remaining tubes removed. She was rearmed with five 5-inch DP guns as in the modified *Porters*, fourteen 40mm (2×4, 3×2) and four 20mm (2×2). Radar fire control was provided for the quadruple 40mm guns. *Jouett*, however, only completed this refit in mid-August 1945 and then saw no action in this guise.

Above: *Jouett* (DD396) in April 1944, having lost No. 3 gun and been re-armed with 40mm and 20mm guns. (USN)

Above: *Warrington* (DD383), after re-arming. Note untypical US camouflage. (USN)

Service All initially served in the Atlantic Fleet prior to the American entry into the war. In April 1941, *Somers, Jouett, Davis* and *Warrington* formed part of DesRon 9 operating with TF3 in the South Atlantic based upon Brazil. In this task, *Somers* seized the German blockade-runner *Odenwald*, despite not being at war with Germany. *Sampson*, in the North Atlantic, covered the occupation of Iceland by US forces in September 1941. She, however, later went to the Pacific while her sisters remained in the South Atlantic. Some success was obtained against Axis blockade-runners and submarines, for *Somers* and *Jouett* intercepted the *Anneliese Essberger* in September 1942 and *Jouett* participated in the destruction of *U128* in May 1943. Then in January 1944, *Somers* scored another success with the interception of *Wesserland. Somers, Davis* and *Jouett* went to the English Channel in June 1944 for 'Overlord' then, less *Davis* (sent home to rearm) transferred to the Mediterranean for the landings in the South of France. Here *Somers* sank the German corvette *UJ6081. Warrington* still on escort duties in home waters, foundered in a hurricane while on passage from Norfolk Va. to the Panama Canal in September 1944. *Jouett* also returned to home waters to rearm and saw no further war service. All four survivors were broken up in the immediate post-war years.

GRIDLEY CLASS

Ship	Builder	Laid Down	Launched	Commissioned	Fate
DD380 *Gridley*	Bethlehem, Quincy	3 June 35	1 Dec 36	24 June 37	Sold for breaking up 20 Aug 47
DD382 *Craven*	Bethlehem, Quincy	3 June 35	25 Feb 37	2 Sept 37	Sold for breaking up 2 Oct 47
DD400 *McCall*	Bethlehem, S. Francisco	17 Mar 36	20 Nov 37	22 June 38	Stricken 27 Jan 47
DD401 *Maury*	Bethlehem, S. Francisco	24 Mar 36	14 Feb 38	5 Aug 38	Sold for breaking up 23 May 46

Displacement: 1,590tons/1,615tonnes (standard); 2,219tons/2,254tonnes (full load).
Length: 340ft 10in/103.89m (oa); 334ft/101.8m (wl).
Beam: 35ft 10in/10,67m.
Draught: 12ft 9in/3.89m (mean).
Machinery: four Yarrow boilers; 2-shaft Bethlehem geared turbines.
Performance: 50,000shp; 38.5kts.

Bunkerage: 525tons/533tonnes.
Range: 6,500nm at 12kts.
Guns: four 5in (4×1); four .5in MG.
Torpedoes: sixteen 21in (4×4).
Complement: 158.

Design Because of strong protagonists within the Navy for heavy torpedo batteries, the question of a further increase in torpedo outfits over that of the twelve-tube *Mahan*s was raised even before that class had entered service. This presented a problem in deck space quite apart from stability, but the USN had never refused to consider the employment of beam torpedo tube mountings despite the theoretical loss of half of the broadside in this disposition. Furthermore, advances in torpedo technology, particularly in gyro control and angling, meant that in theory it would be possible to fire a sixteen-torpedo broadside at a single target. Some sacrifice in gun power would, however, be necessary if the displacement were to be kept to a reasonable limit in view of Treaty (and financial) restrictions. Thus on a hull of the same dimensions as *Mahan* only four 5-inch guns were carried, of which the two forward guns were shielded base ring mountings pioneered in *Dunlap* and *Fanning*. All four banks of tubes were mounted on the upper deck, very close to the ship's side because of reservations about the height of the tubes in *Mahan* and the ability of the torpedoes to clear the deck when fired. In appearance, these destroyers were distinguished by their large single funnel and prominent funnel uptake. The design was prepared by Bethlehem with two ships, *DD380* and *382*, being built under the 1934 programme and two under the following year's programme. Once again, their machinery was of a more advanced nature, with steam pressures being raised to 565psi in four Yarrow-pattern boilers.

Above: *Craven* (DD382) in December 1943. She now has SC2 (fitted at the end of November) as well as Mk 4 fire-control radar and one extra 20mm gun. (USN)

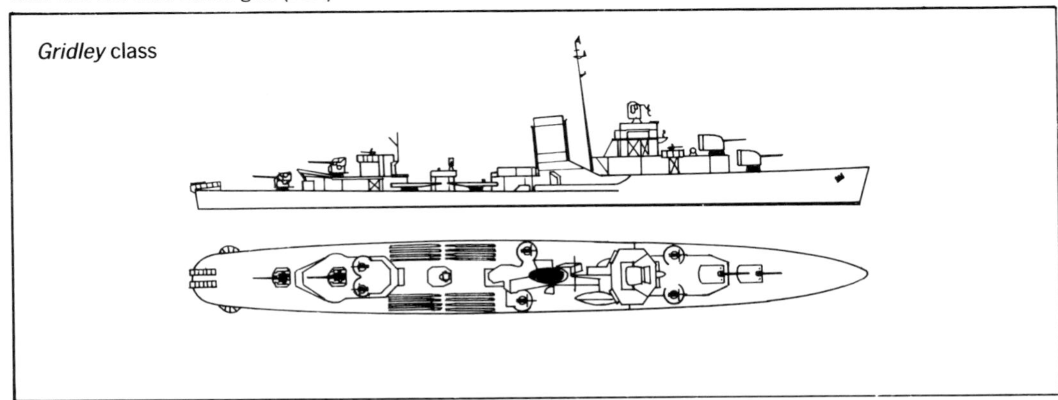

Below: *Craven* (DD382) in May 1942. She has SC radar and six 20mm. (USN)

Modifications Initial modifications comprised the fitting of four 20mm guns in place of the .5in machine-guns and an additional pair abreast the funnel. In mid-1943, another single gun was fitted on the funnel platform and a little later an eighth was shipped forward of the bridge in all except *Maury*. Stability problems prevented the fitting of 40mm guns and the *Gridley*s were the only modern destroyers not to be so armed. Even the modest augmentation of the AA outfit as was completed necessitated the landing of the crow's nest, the removal of the blast shields from the torpedo tubes and the fitting of ten tons of permanent ballast. No further alterations were made until the after tubes were landed when the ships deployed to the Atlantic Fleet in 1945.

Service All four ships formed DesDiv 11, part of DesRon 6 based at Pearl Harbor. Early in 1942, *Maury* participated in the raid on Taroa Atoll and defended the cruiser *Chester* from Japanese aircraft. *McCall* was with *Enterprise* on her raid into the Gilberts and Marshall Islands and both *Maury* and *Craven*, the raid on Wake Island. *Maury* was at Midway, but her sisters *Gridley* and *McCall* went to the Aleutians in June 1942. *Maury* later served in the Guadalcanal campaign where, at the end of November 1942, she was with DesDiv 9 during the Battle of Tassafarona in which US forces were severely mauled, losing one cruiser, sunk, and three badly damaged. In June 1943, all four destroyers covered the carrier group of USS *Saratoga* and HMS *Victorious* during the landings in New Georgia. Then in August, *Craven* and *Maury* with four other destroyers fought an action in the Vella Gulf in which Japanese destroyers *Hagikaze, Arashi* and *Kawakaze* were sunk. *Gridley* and *Maury* covered the Gilbert Islands assault in November 1943 and all four, the landings in the Marshalls the following January and February, as well as the Marianas campaign in June. *Maury, Gridley* and *McCall* served with TG38.4 in sorties against Formosa and Luzon in October 1944, in which month, *Gridley*, with *Helm* sank *I46* on the 28th. By January, DesRon 6 had moved to the Philippines with the escort carriers, but as the dangers of Kamikaze attack became more serious, the weak AA outfits of these destroyers led to their transfer to the Atlantic, where they finished the war. *Maury* was stricken on 1 November 1945, but the other three not until January and February 1947.

BAGLEY CLASS

Ship	Builder	Laid Down	Launched	Commissioned	Fate
DD386 *Bagley*	Norfolk NYd.	31 July 35	3 Sept 36	12 June 37	Scrapped 1947
DD387 *Blue*	Norfolk NYd.	25 Sept 35	27 May 37	14 Aug 37	Lost 22 Aug 42
DD388 *Helm*	Norfolk NYd.	25 Sept 35	27 May 37	16 Oct 37	Scrapped 1947
DD389 *Mugford*	Boston NYd.	28 Oct 35	21 Oct 36	16 Aug 37	Scuttled 22 Mar 48
DD390 *Ralph Talbot*	Boston NYd.	28 Oct 35	31 Oct 36	14 Oct 37	Scuttled 8 Mar 48
DD391 *Henley*	Mare Island NYd.	28 Oct 35	12 Jan 37	14 Aug 37	Lost 3 Oct 43
DD392 *Patterson*	Puget Sound NYd.	23 July 35	6 May 37	22 Sept 37	Scrapped 1947
DD393 *Jarvis*	Puget Sound NYd.	21 Aug 35	6 May 37	27 Oct 37	Lost 9 Aug 42

Above: *Bagley* (DD386) with 40mm guns aft, in April 1944. (USN)

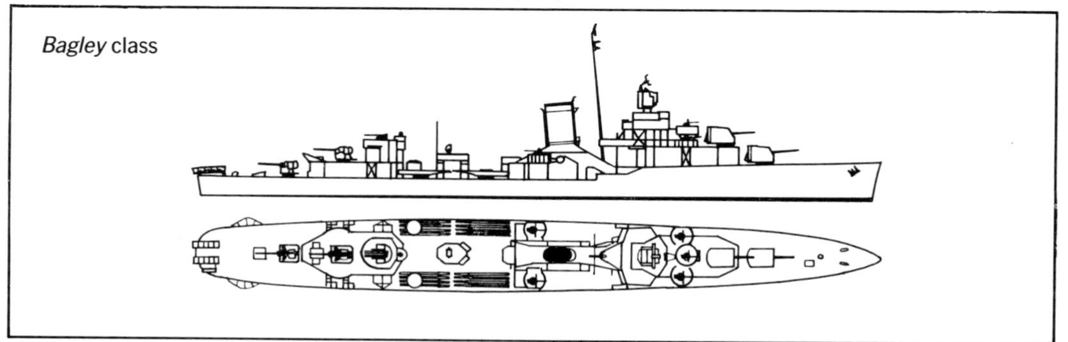

Displacement: 1,646tons/1,672tonnes (standard); 2,245tons/2,280tonnes (full load).
Length: 341ft 4in/104.04m (oa); 334ft/101.8m (wl).
Beam: 35ft 6in/10.82m.
Draught: 12ft 10in/3.91m (mean).
Machinery: four Babcock & Wilcox boilers; 2-shaft G.E.C. geared turbines.
Performance: 49,000shp; 38.5kts.
Bunkerage: 504tons/512tonnes.
Range: 6,500nm at 12kts.
Guns: four 5in (4×1); four .5in MG.
Torpedoes: sixteen 21in (4×4).
Complement: 158.

Design These destroyers, part of the FY35 programme, were of Navy as opposed to Bethlehem design, but were externally similar to the *Gridley* class. They did not have the more advanced boilers of this class, however, and reverted to the machinery plant used for the earlier *Mahan*. Thus their designed power was 46,000shp for a maximum speed of 37 knots. Trial speeds were about 36.8 knots as opposed to the nearly 39 knots reached by the *Gridley*s. Their armament was similar to that of the Bethlehem ships.

Modifications The *Bagley*s had rather better stability than the *Gridley* class and were able to have their AA outfits augmented further. By the spring of 1942, six 20mm single guns had been added, two below the bridge on the forward shelter deck, two just abaft the funnel and fire-control radar to the gun director. When supplies of 40mm guns began to improve, all except *Blue* and *Jarvis* received one twin mounting on the after shelter deck forward of No. 3 gun. The after pair of 20mm, displaced by the 40mm, were later refitted on an enlarged platform at the after end of the funnel. All four banks of tubes were retained. Like all destroyers, their radar suite was progressively modernized as the war progressed.

Service All eight destroyers formed DesRon 4 at Pearl Harbor in December 1941, seeing action against the attacking Japanese aircraft and midget submarines, sinking at least two of the latter. After taking part in some of the early carrier raids against Wake, the Gilberts, Marcus and the Marshall Islands in the opening months of 1942, DesRon 4 was transferred to Australian waters with TF44 in June. They operated with US and Australian cruisers and in July went to Guadalcanal as TG62.2. *Mugford* was damaged during the Guadalcanal landings, but *Jarvis*, screening transports in Lunga Roads, was struck by an aircraft torpedo which badly damaged her, on 8 August. She attempted to return to Sydney where a destroyer tender could effect repairs, and sailed without escort at midnight. Unluckily, she ran into the Battle of Savo Island, when she appears to have been further damaged by the destroyer *Yumagi*, but got through Savo Sound. She was last sighted by US aircraft south-west of Guadalcanal down by the head and leaking oil. On the afternoon of 9 August, she was sunk by torpedo-bombers of 25 Air Flotilla. There were no survivors – all rafts and boats had been left in Lunga Roads to lighten the ship.

The remainder of the class served in the Solomons area throughout the summer of 1942, *Patterson*, *Helm* and *Ralph Talbot* all being damaged to varying degrees. However, in August, *Blue*, *Henley* and *Helm* were escorting supplies to Guadalcanal when the first named pair were ordered to intercept a Japanese destroyer also bound for Guadalcanal. In fact, the Japanese ship, *Kamikaze*, surprised the Americans and torpedoed *Blue*. Taken in tow by her sister, she had almost reached Tulagi harbour when, on 22 August, she was ordered to be scuttled to avoid capture.

The squadron served with TF44 throughout 1942, and in March 1943 became part of the newly constituted 7th Fleet, still serving the US-Australian Squadron. Service was mainly in the New Georgia and New Guinea area where *Patterson* sank *Ro35* on 25 August. *Henley*, escorting an LST convoy with other destroyers, bound for Finschafen, was attacked by Japanese aircraft off the bridgehead but escaped unhurt despite fierce attacks. However, a week later, whilst on an ASW sweep in the Vitiaz Strait, she was torpedoed and sunk by *Ro108*. The survivors remained in the south-west Pacific throughout 1943, then went to the Marianas in July 1944 and were with the 3rd Fleet off the northern Philippines by October. *Helm* assisted in the sinking of *I46* but *Mugford* was damaged by Kamikaze aircraft off Ormoc in December. Now forming DesRon 6, the remainder of the class fought at Leyte, Lingayen and Okinawa in the first months of 1945, *Ralph Talbot* being hit and badly damaged by a Kamikaze off Okinawa on 27 April. *Helm* finished the war in Borneo and the south-west Pacific.

Both Kamikaze-damaged destroyers, *Mugford* and *Ralph Talbot*, were used for the Bikini trials in 1946, despite having been repaired. *Mugford* was scuttled on 22 March 1948 and *Ralph Talbot* on 8 March. The other three were scrapped.

Below: *Mugford* (DD389), 1944. (USN)

SIMS CLASS

Ship	Builder	Laid Down	Launched	Commissioned	Fate
DD409 *Sims*	Bath Iron Works	13 July 37	8 April 38	1 Aug 39	Lost 7 May 42
DD410 *Hughes*	Bath Iron Works	15 Sept 37	17 June 39	21 Sept 39	Scuttled 16 Oct 48
DD411 *Anderson*	Federal Sbdg. Co.	15 Nov 37	4 Feb 39	19 May 39	Expended 2 July 46
DD412 *Hammann*	Federal Sbdg. Co.	17 Jan 38	4 Feb 39	11 Aug 39	Lost 6 June 42
DD413 *Mustin*	Newport News	20 Dec 37	8 Dec 38	15 Sept 39	Scuttled 18 April 48
DD414 *Russell*	Newport News	20 Dec 37	8 Dec 38	3 Nov 39	Scrapped 1947
DD415 *O'Brien*	Boston NYd.	31 May 38	20 Oct 39	2 Mar 40	Lost 19 Oct 42
DD416 *Walke*	Boston NYd.	31 May 38	20 Oct 39	27 April 40	Lost 14 Nov 42
DD417 *Morris*	Norfolk NYd.	7 June 38	1 June 39	5 Mar 40	Scrapped 1947
DD418 *Roe*	Charleston NYd.	23 April 38	21 June 39	5 Jan 40	Scrapped 1947
DD419 *Wainwright*	Norfolk NYd.	7 June 38	1 June 39	15 April 40	Scuttled 2 July 48
DD420 *Buck*	Philadephia NYd.	6 April 38	22 May 39	15 May 40	Lost 9 Oct 43

Displacement: 1,764tons/1,792tonnes (standard); 2,313tons/2,350tonnes (full load).
Length: 348ft 4in/106.17m (oa); 341ft/103.94m (wl).
Beam: 36ft/10.97m.
Draught: 12ft 10in/3.91m (mean).
Machinery: three Babcock & Wilcox boilers; 2-shaft Westinghouse geared turbines.
Performance: 50,000shp; 35kts.
Bunkerage: 459tons/466tonnes.
Range: 6,500nm at 12kts.
Guns: five 5in (5×1); four .5in MG.
Torpedoes: eight 21in (2×4).
Complement: 192.

Design For the destroyers of the 1937 programme, a number of initial schemes were proposed, based on the *Benham* design. All had dual-purpose 5-inch guns and quadruple tubes. One layout was identical with *DD 397* but with less endurance and 0.6 knots more speed, a second shipped only three 5-inch guns on a reduced tonnage of 1,400 tons (so that more ships could be built), while a third had four 5-inch guns disposed in two twin mountings, one forward, one aft and had one of the three banks of tubes right aft on the quarter deck. Yet another scheme was a combination of two of these, mixing single 5-inch guns forward with a twin aft. During 1936, the various schemes were discussed and opinions sought from the Fleet. One of the major questions was over which weapon, gun or torpedo, would be most decisive in a war with Japan. While these discussions were continuing, a new naval treaty was signed, in London, which removed individual limits on destroyer tonnage and replaced it with a total tonnage limit which allowed the possibility of 3,000-ton destroyers. Although this figure was considered too high, some extra tonnage could be utilized to strengthen the hull and improve sea-worthiness. The final design carried five single 5-inch guns and three banks of quadruple tubes, of which the two after banks were carried on the main deck on the beam. Four reload torpedoes were also to be included in the design. A new fire-control system for the 5-inch guns was introduced, the Mk 37 director, which had its separate computer installed below decks for the first time.

The machinery was identical with that of the *Benhams* except that diesel generating capacity was increased to accommodate the power requirements of the 5-inch guns. The guns themselves were in fully enclosed gun-houses, except for Nos. 3 and 4 guns, which were in open mounts to save weight. AA armament remained only four .5in machine-guns when other nations were carrying 37mm, 40mm or 2pdr guns.

When the first units were completed, they were found to be seriously overweight and top-heavy, due to a number of reasons, despite the beam having been increased by 6 inches over that of *Benham*. This over-weight condition (nearly 120 tons) had to be remedied by drastic measures, including the removal of one of the beam tube banks and re-mounting the other on the centre-line deck-house. This did have the advantage of better shelter from heavy seas, however. The tall searchlight tower on the after shelter deck was removed and the two heavy motor-boats relocated lower down on the main deck in place of the beam tubes. This too had an additional side effect over and above the reduction in top-weight as it cleared the firing arcs of No. 3 gun which hitherto had been badly masked by them. Finally, the splinter protection to bridge and director was removed and 60 tons of fixed ballast added. Many of the class were still under construction when these modifications were approved and they completed to this standard.

Modifications Employment in winter Atlantic conditions caused icing problems on the exposed Nos. 3 and 4 5-inch guns. As a result, a half-height gun-house was fitted to these mountings which, to save weight, was given a canvas top. This was, from a distance, very similar in appearance to the fully enclosed gun-house. Depth-charge capacity was increased from six to twelve in stern tracks and a thrower with ten charges added. Four more .5in machine-guns were added to Atlantic units, two on the forward shelter deck and two in place of No. 3 gun, in 1941, pending the availability of 20mm guns, which were installed towards the end of that year. Radar installation was FD-SC. By mid-1943, surviving units began to receive 40mm guns with enlarged platforms on No. 3 gun deck, being fitted with a pair of twin 40mm mountings, with Mk 51 directors. One of the displaced 20mm guns was relocated on the searchlight platform, the other forward of the bridge above the original 20mm, for a total AA outfit of four 40mm and four 20mm guns. No. 4 gun lost its gun-house as weight compensation. *Wainwright*, however, was unique in that she lost the after bank of tubes in September 1944, for a trio of single army-pattern Mk 3 40mm guns and

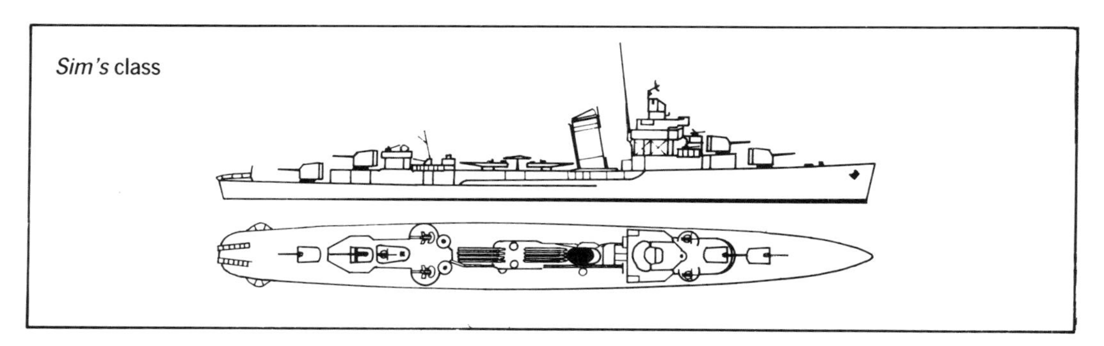

Above: *Hughes* (DD410) in August 1942, at Mare Island. (USN) **Below:** *Wainwright* (DD419) in July 1944. (USN)

had three single 20mm in a two-level arrrangement forward of the bridge. The single Bofors were removed and the after torpedoes restituted by June 1945. All the class was scheduled to receive the Kamikaze refit, but only *Mustin, Russell* and *Morris* in fact received it. All torpedoes were removed and the AA outfit was increased to four 40mm in tubs to port and starboard, between the funnel and No. 3 gun. *Mustin* and *Morris* had four single 20mm while *Russell* had two twin and two single 20mm. Mk 28 radar replaced the Mk 4 on the director, and the ASW outfit was two depth-charge tracks and four throwers. All were completed too late to see action in this configuration.

Above: *Buck* (DD420) in 1942. (USN)

Service By December 1941, all the class were serving with the Atlantic Fleet, having been transferred from the Pacific during April and May that year. Their duties were mainly Neutrality Patrol, convoy escort and tasks in connection with the US occupation of Iceland, but the Japanese attack on Pearl Harbor saw all but *Wainwright, Buck* and *Roe* returned to the Pacific by January 1942. In the Atlantic, *Buck* was rammed by the transport *Awatea* off Halifax and badly damaged in August 1942, but her two sisters were part of the invasion forces for the North Africa landings in November, *Wainwright* wearing the pennant of DesRon 8 and *Roe* DesRon 11. The former was at Casablanca, the latter Port Lyantey. All three then served in the Mediterranean, *Roe* and *Wainwright* with DesRon 13 at Sicily for Operation 'Husky'. *Buck* sank the Italian submarine *Argento* off Pantelleria on 3 August 1943 but she herself was torpedoed and sunk by *U616* with heavy casualties two months later off Salerno. *Roe* returned to the USA later in 1943 and was subsequently transferred to the Pacific, seeing action off Iwo Jima in February 1945. *Wainwright* assisted in the destruction of *U593* in December 1943, and was at Anzio in January 1944. She returned to the USA and was refitted at Brooklyn in September 1944 and in early 1945 was sent to the Pacific theatre.

The Pacific Fleet destroyers, operating with TF17, participated in the early carrier raids on the Caroline Islands and Makin in February 1942, while in March *Anderson, Sims, Hammann* and *Hughes* saw service with the US-Australian forces in New Guinea. Three of these with *Russell* (replacing *Sims*) and *Morris* were with *TF17* and *Yorktown* at the battle of the Coral Sea in May. *Sims* was with the tanker force and was sunk by Japanese dive-bombers, with three direct hits, while attempting to protect the oiler *Neosho. Morris, Hammann* and *Anderson* attempted to assist the torpedoed *Lexington* but were, in the end, forced to evacuate her crew before she was sunk by *Phelps*. DesRon 2 served at the Battle of Midway, losing *Hammann* to a torpedo from *I168*, which boat also sank the damaged *Yorktown*. From the autumn of 1942 the DesRon was involved in the Guadalcanal campaign, escorting supplies between Espiritu Santo and that island. On 15 September, while screening the carrier *Hornet, O'Brien* was torpedoed by *I15* which had actually fired a salvo at *Wasp*, but several of these had missed and run on for five miles to hit *O'Brien* and the battleship *North Carolina*, but only the destroyer sank although not immediately. *O'Brien* managed to return to Espiritu Santo and then to Noumea for makeshift repair. Considered safe to return to the USA for full repairs, *O'Brien* sailed on 10 October, but nine days later off Samoa, she finally broke up and sank. Task Force 17 continued to operate in the Solomon Islands where, on 26 October, the damaged *Hornet* was ordered to be sunk by *Mustin* and *Anderson*. However, despite vast expenditure of torpedoes and shells, the wreck did not go down and was later dispatched by *Akigumo* and *Makigumo*.

The final Pacific loss was *Walke*, sunk in action off Savo Island on the night of 14/15 November 1942. She was leading a column of three destroyers and the battleships *Washington* and *South Dakota* sent to intercept a Japanese bombardment force bound for Henderson Field on Guadalcanal. In the course of this action, *Walke* was heavily hit by shells, probably from the cruiser *Nagara* and then struck by a torpedo, probably fired by one of the cruisers escorting the destroyers (*Shirayuki, Hatsuyuki, Samidare* and *Ikazuchi*).

All except *Russell* were in the Aleutians in July 1943, but by November were back in the Central Pacific participating in the Gilberts Campaign, Kwajalein (where *Anderson* was hit by shore batteries), Eniwetok, Hollandia, Biak and Morotai. In November 1944, *Anderson* was damaged again, this time by a Kamikaze off Panaon Island in the Philippines which badly damaged her boilers. The squadron remained in the Philippines into early 1945, *Russell* seeing action with three other destroyers, sinking the escort destroyer *Hinoki* off Manila Bay. In April 1945, *Morris, Martin* and *Russell* covered the Okinawa landings where *Morris* was hit forward of the bridge on 6 April by a Kamikaze which damaged her so badly that she was not judged worth repair. *Hughes* and *Anderson* served in the Kurile Islands between June and August, then went to Japan on the surrender.

BENHAM CLASS

Ship	Builder	Laid Down	Launched	Commissioned	Fate
DD397 *Benham*	Federal Sbdg. Co.	1 Sept 1936	16 April 38	2 Feb 39	Lost 15 Nov 42
DD398 *Ellet*	Federal Sbdg. Co.	3 Dec 36	11 June 38	18 April 39	Scrapped 1947
DD399 *Lang*	Federal Sbdg. Co.	5 April 37	27 Aug 38	26 May 39	Scrapped 1947
DD402 *Mayrant*	Boston NYd.	15 April 37	14 May 38	1 Nov 39	Scuttled 4 April 48
DD403 *Trippe*	Boston NYd.	15 April 37	14 May 38	15 Dec 39	Scuttled 3 Feb 48
DD404 *Rhind*	Philadelphia NYd.	22 Sept 37	28 July 38	15 Jan 40	Scuttled 22 Mar 48
DD405 *Rowan*	Norfolk NYd.	25 June 37	5 May 38	31 Oct 39	Lost 10 Sept 43
DD406 *Stack*	Norfolk NYd.	25 June 37	5 May 38	3 Jan 40	Scuttled 24 April 48
DD407 *Sterett*	Charlestown NYd.	2 Dec 36	27 Oct 38	15 Sept 39	Scrapped 1947
DD408 *Wilson*	Puget Sound NYd.	22 Mar 37	12 April 39	14 Aug 39	Scuttled 8 Mar 48

Displacement: 1,637tons/1,683tonnes (standard); 2,250tons/2,286tonnes (full load).
Length: 340ft 9in/103.86m (oa); 344ft/101.8m (wl).
Beam: 35ft 6in/10.82m.
Draught: 12ft 10in/3.91m (mean).
Machinery: three Babcock & Wilcox boilers; 2-shaft Westinghouse geared turbines.
Performance: 50,000shp; 38.5kts.
Bunkerage: 484tons/492tonnes.
Range: 6,500nm at 12kts.
Guns: four 5in (4×1); four .5in MG.
Torpedoes: sixteen 21in (4×4).

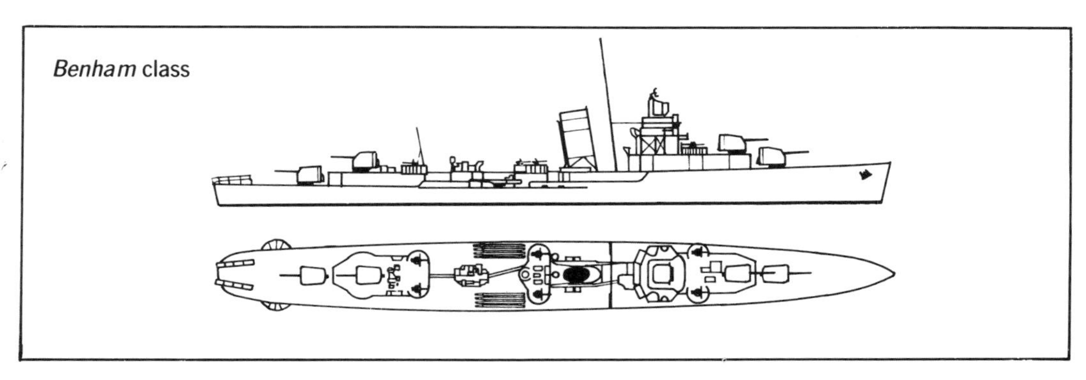

Above: *Meyrandt* (DD402) in Atlantic waters, 1942. She has only SC radar, but has received six 20mm guns. (IWM)
Below: *Lang* (DD399) at the end of October 1943, leaving Mare Island. (USN)

Complement: 184.

Design The growth in weight demanded by the adoption of DP guns, new machinery and four torpedo tube mountings was becoming a serious problem in the context of the 1,500-ton Treaty Limit for destroyers. By the time the *Mahans* had been designed, all the Treaty 1,500-ton allowance had been absorbed and there were also difficulties in that it was found that more men were required to man the ships than had been predicted. This in turn needed more space and weight. The DP gun and its director system was one of the main culprits and it was seriously suggested in 1935 that the DP concept be abandoned and low-angle guns be fitted instead. The Fleet, however, was of the opposite opinion and in any case, there was no SP 5-inch single gun available. It was finally decided to build the *Benham* class to the same hull lines as *Gridley*, with similar armament and fire-control systems. A Gibbs & Cox design was adopted, utilizing only three high-pressure boilers with, once again, a further increase in steam pressure to 600psi. Installed power was also increased to 50,000shp for a maximum speed of 38½ knots. Weights and hence displacement rose considerably and the *Benhams* were considered over-weight, certainly over 1,500 tons at light ship displacement and as much as 1,656 tons at standard displacement. As far as the treaties went, however, this did not now matter so much, because the 1936 London Naval Treaty expressed the restriction on total and not individual destroyer tonnage. Even so, a proposal to carry shields on the after 5-inch guns, now all on base ring mountings, was vetoed at first because it would have involved an extra nine tons top-weight. Ten ships were ordered to this design under the FY1936 programme, all but three from Navy yards.

Modifications Those units in the Atlantic in December 1941, i.e., all but *Benham* and *Ellet*, landed the after tubes on each beam for an increased depth-charge outfit and the light AA increased to six (or seven in some ships) .5in machine-guns, two forward of the bridge, two just abaft the funnel and two more at the forward end of the after shelter deck. In 1942, single 20mm guns were fitted in lieu of the machine-guns, and radar was added. Some ships, including *Trippe*, retained one of the .5in MG on the centre-line abaft the funnel. No. 4 gun was given a full gun house and No. 3 a half-shield with canvas top.

The two Pacific units retained four banks of tubes, four .5in machine-guns and had received radar (but not FC) by the spring of 1942. In 1943, the Atlantic units received two twin 40mm on the after deck-house with Mk 51 directors, SC, SG and FD radar. Pacific units received the same refit. In the summer of 1945, two units, *Sterett* and *Lang*, received the Kamikaze refit, landing the remaining torpedoes and shipping a CRA of four twin 40mm Mk 1 Mod 6 and four twin 20mm Mk 24. Two depth-charge racks and four throwers comprised the ASW outfit. Both after 5-inch guns were now open mounts to compensate the extra top-weight of the AA outfit.

Service *Benham* and *Ellet* served in the Atlantic from September 1939, on neutrality patrols, initially in the Halifax NS area, and later *Benham* with *Lang* were involved in the shadowing of the German liner *Columbus* in December. They returned to the Pacific, but in April 1940 all except *Benham* and *Ellet* were transferred to the Atlantic (DesRon 8). The Atlantic Fleet destroyers were involved in the Neutrality Patrol, convoy escort duties and the occupation of Iceland. In March 1943, *Lang, Sterett* and *Wilson* were sent to Scapa Flow with other US units to replace Royal Navy forces detached to the Indian Ocean for the Madagascar operation. A month later, in April, *Lang* went to the Mediterranean with *Wasp* to fly reinforcements to Malta, and in May both *Lang* and *Sterett* escorted the repeat operation. However, after this sortie *Wasp* returned to the United States in June together with *Lang, Sterett, Stack* and *Wilson* (DesDiv 15), being now based at San Diego as TF18. Of those left in Atlantic waters, *Mayrant, Rhind* and *Rowan* were involved in the PQ17 operation of June 1942 and in November went to North Africa for the 'Torch' operations off Casablanca. These three, with *Trippe*, served at the landings in Sicily in July 1943 where *Mayrant* was badly damaged by air attack on 26 July. She was further damaged later when an ammunition ship blew up while the destroyer was under repair. Her three sisters went to Salerno, but *Rowan* was torpedoed and sunk by German S-boats while escorting a convoy. As compensation, *Trippe* assisted in the destruction of *U73* on 16 December off Oran and then returned to Italy for Anzio.

Serving with DesRon 6, *Benham* and *Ellet* were at sea off Hawaii at the time of Pearl Harbor. In April 1942, both escorted the carriers on the Tokyo Raid and both were involved in the Midway action. For much of the remainder of 1942, these Pacific units of the class were engaged in and around the Solomons and particularly Guadalcanal. *Ellet* had the unhappy task of sinking the badly damaged Australian cruiser *Canberra* on 9 August off Savo Island, and *Sterett* was badly damaged in action with the battleship *Hiei* and other Japanese warships off the same island in a disastrous action on 13 November. A day later, *Benham* was struck by a torpedo in yet another confused night action off Savo Island and despite being towed away towards Espiritu Santo, she finally foundered the following afternoon. *Lang, Sterett* and *Stack* were involved in the action in the Gulf of Vella Lavella in August 1943, in which three Japanese destroyers were sunk without loss to the US force, and the following month, *Ellet* sank the submarine *I168*, north-west of Espiritu Santo on 3 September 1943. These destroyers followed the action throughout 1943 and 1944, serving in the Marshalls, the attack on Truk and the Marianas. In January 1945, *Lang, Sterett, Stack* and *Wilson* were at Leyte, while *Ellet* was at Iwo Jima. The four at Leyte went to Okinawa in April, in which month, *Sterett* (9 April) and *Wilson* (15 April) were both damaged by Kamikaze attack.

Like all the pre-war destroyers, the survivors of this class were soon disposed of after the end of hostilities.

BENSON CLASS

Ship	Builder	Laid Down	Launched	Commissioned	Fate
DD421 *Benson*	Bethlehem, Quincy	16 May 38	15 Nov 39	25 July 40	To Taiwan 26 Feb 54
DD422 *Mayo*	Bethlehem, Quincy	16 May 38	26 Mar 40	18 Sept 40	Stricken 1 Dec 70
DD423 *Gleaves*	Bath Iron Works	16 May 38	9 Dec 39	14 June 40	Stricken 1 Nov 69
DD424 *Niblack*	Bath Iron Works	8 Aug 38	18 May 40	1 Aug 40	Stricken 31 July 68
DD425 *Madison*	Boston NYd.	19 Dec 38	20 Oct 39	6 Dec 40	Stricken 1 June 68
DD426 *Lansdale*	Boston NYd.	19 Dec 38	20 Oct 39	17 Sept 40	Lost 20 April 44
DD427 *Hilary P. Jones*	Charleston NYd.	16 Nov 38	14 Dec 39	7 Sept 40	To Taiwain 26 Feb 54
DD428 *Charles F. Hughes*	Puget Sound NYd.	3 Jan 39	16 May 40	18 Oct 40	Stricken 1 June 68
DD429 *Livermore* (ex-*Grayson*)	Bath Iron Works	6 Mar 39	3 Aug 40	7 Oct 40	Sold for breaking up 3 Mar 61
DD430 *Eberle*	Bath Iron Works	12 April 39	14 Sept 40	4 Dec 40	To Greece April 1951
DD431 *Plunkett*	Federal Sbdg. Co.	1 Mar 39	9 Mar 40	16 July 40	To Taiwan 16 Feb 59
DD432 *Kearny*	Federal Sbdg. Co.	1 Mar 39	9 Mar 40	13 Sept 40	Stricken 1 June 71
DD433 *Gwin*	Boston NYd.	1 June 39	25 May 40	15 Jan 41	Lost 13 July 43
DD434 *Meredith*	Boston NYd.	1 June 39	24 April 40	1 Mar 41	Lost 15 Oct 42
DD435 *Grayson* (ex-*Livermore*)	Charleston NYd.	17 July 39	7 Aug 40	15 April 41	Stricken 1 June 71
DD436 *Monssen*	Puget Sound NYd.	12 July 39	16 May 40	15 Mar 41	Lost 13 Nov 42
DD437 *Woolsey*	Bath Iron Works	9 Oct 39	12 Feb 40	7 May 41	Sold for breaking up 29 May 74
DD438 *Ludlow*	Bath Iron Works	18 Dec 39	11 Nov 40	5 Mar 41	To Greece 21 Jan 51
DD439 *Edison*	Federal Sbdg. Co.	18 Mar 40	23 Nov 40	30 Jan 41	Stricken 1 April 66
DD440 *Ericsson*	Federal Sbdg. Co.	18 Mar 40	23 Nov 40	11 Mar 41	Stricken 1 June 70
DD441 *Wilkes*	Boston NYd.	1 Nov 39	31 May 40	12 June 41	Stricken 1 Mar 70
DD442 *Nicholson*	Boston NYd.	1 Nov 39	31 May 40	3 June 41	To Italy 15 Jan 51
DD443 *Swanson*	Charleston NYd.	15 Nov 39	2 Nov 40	15 July 41	Stricken 1 Mar 71
DD444 *Ingraham*	Charleston NYd.	15 Nov 39	15 Feb 41	17 July 41	Lost 22 Aug 42

Displacement: 1,839tons/1,868tonnes (standard); 2,395tons/1,433tonnes (full load).
Length: 348ft 4in/106.17m (oa); 341ft/103.9m (wl).
Beam: 36ft 1in/11m.
Draught: 13ft 2in/4.01m (mean).
Machinery: four Babcock & Wilcox boilers; 2-shaft Westinghouse geared turbines.
Performance: 50,000shp; 35kts.
Bunkerage: 453tons/460tonnes.
Range: 6,500nm at 12kts.
Guns: five 5in (5×1); six .5in MG.
Torpedoes: ten 21in (2×5).
Complement: 208.

Design Eight destroyers were included in the 1938 programme. They were to be improved versions of the preceding *Sims* class with the same armament of five 5-inch and three quadruple banks of torpedo tubes. Improvements in machinery design had allowed the Engineering Bureau to adopt the unit principle in laying out the machinery spaces to the obvious advantage of damage control and survival in the event of action damage. The wide separation of the two boiler rooms also necessitated a reversion to a two-funnel layout. For the first time, an emergency diesel generator was installed on the main deck, where it would be well clear of any lower deck flooding. Displacement rose by about 50 tons as compared with *Sims*, due to the heavier machinery and a stronger hull. Two companies tendered for the design work, Gibbs & Cox and Bethlehem. The former produced the plans for *Gleaves* and *Niblack*, built by Bath Iron Works, while Bethlehem designed and built *Benson* and *Mayo*. This split led in fact to some controversy. The Bureau of Engineerinh wished to install the new high-pressure machinery as developed from the *Mahan* class in all the new ships, but after receiving the contract Bethlehem asked to be allowed to put their own machinery in their boats, which would entail two different plants in the same class. Although not happy about it, the Engineering Bureau accepted this if only to enable a comparison of the two types to be made. Of the rest of the 1938 ships, *DD425* to *DD428* were contracted to Bethlehem and built to their design. The general design and layout of these ships was one of rugged usefulness, but the surprising factor was the poor AA armament of (initially) four .5in MG only. British destroyers at this time had twice this number of the same calibre, plus a quadruple 2pdr (40mm) gun and Japanese ships were beginning to ship twin 25mm guns. The 1.1-inch quadruple weapon being developed was thought too heavy for the new 1,620-ton destroyers.

The 1939 programme of eight more destroyers were to be similar, but with two more .5-inch machine-guns and two centre-line quintuple banks of tubes. They were also to receive a new 850° steam plant. In fact, because the 1938 programme had been delayed, it proved possible to incorporate the new design changes into the earlier eight ships as well. Thus all received six machine-guns and quintuple tubes, with *Gleaves* and *Niblack* also getting the new steam plant. All eight of the 1939 programme were built to the Navy/Gibbs & Cox design, as were a further eight (*DD437–DD444*) approved on 19 December 1939 under the 1940 programme. The two versions could be distinguished by their funnels: round in Bath ships, flat-sided in Bethlehem ships. As completed, all proved very over-weight.

Modifications Early in 1942, modifications comprised the fitting of six 20mm single guns in tubs forward of the bridge (or a mixture of .5in MG and 20mm until the latter became more available), abreast the after funnel and in lieu of No. 3 gun which was landed, as were the after torpedo tubes. The after superstructure was removed and the searchlight was fitted abaft the after funnel. Both remaining after guns were given canvas-topped shields in the interest of weight-saving. Six depth-charge throwers were fitted and HF/DF added to some Atlantic units. SC and FD radars were added. There were some variations, for *Benson* retained five 5-inch guns with six 20mm as late as 1943 and *Gleaves* five 5-inch guns in 1942.

In January 1941, it had been decided to fit twin 40mm guns aboard the *Benson*s, replacing the pair of 20mm on the former No. 3 gun deck. These were given director control, Mk 49 in a few ships, but as this proved unsuccessful, Mk 51 was fitted later. Nine ships, the 1938 programme (*DD421–428*) and *DD431* had an alternative armament of four 20mm on a demountable platform in place of the after tubes, and some actually carried this fit for a time. The half-shield of No. 3 gun and a sea-boat were removed as compensation for the additional weight of the 40mm guns. Shortages and production delays caused this programme to be put back and it was not until late 1942 that the programme could be commenced. While supplies of 40mm guns were awaited, some ships received a quadruple 1.1-inch gun on No. 3 gun deck, off-set and balanced by a single 20mm gun-tub. Thus the whole question of AA batteries was in a state of flux from 1940 until 1942 and the result was many variations in armament. Torpedo tubes varied between five and ten, 5-inch guns four or five in open, half-shielded or full enclosed gun-houses, while light AA was anything between twelve .5-inch machine-guns, six 20mm guns, one quad 1.1-inch plus five 20mm or a combination of these. By 1943, however, the majority if not all of the ships were armed with two twin 40mm, four 20mm and four 5-inch guns together with ten torpedo tubes.

In March 1944, sixteen ten-tube ships in Atlantic waters belonging to DesDivs 13 (*DD421–424* and *431*), 14 (*DD425–428*), 21 (*DD429, 430, 432* and *440*) and 25 (*437–439*) landed one (after) bank of tubes for two single army-pattern Bofors guns without director control. These were eventually removed in November 1944 after the Normandy landings and they reverted to the above layout.

This outfit remained basically unchanged until the Kamikaze menace forced a further revision in 1945 when, in May, it was proposed to fit two quadruple Bofors in addition to the pair of twins already aboard, reducing the 20mm outfit to a pair of twins forward of the bridge. In addition, a pair of single 20mm would be temporarily carried on the main deck aft until blind-fire capability could be given to the 40mm guns. A great deal of compensation was required including the removal of all torpedoes, one boat, one anchor and cable as well as the fitting of lighter (Mk 28) radar. The twin 40mm aft were replaced by the quadruples and repositioned in tubs between the funnels. Only twelve ships in fact received this refit: DDs *423, 424, 429–432, 435, 437–440* and *443*.

Service None of these destroyers had been completed by the outbreak of war in Europe in 1939, but all 24 had joined the Fleet before the Japanese strike on Pearl Harbor. They formed the DesRons 7 (*DD421–428* and *431*), 11 (*DD429, 430, 432–436* and *440*) and 13 (*DD437–439, 441–444*), all serving

Above: *Charles F. Hughes* (DD428), with peacetime rig. (USN) Below: *Livermore* (DD429) in September 1943. Note open top to No. 3 gun. (USN)

in the Atlantic. DesRon 7 served with the Atlantic Convoy Support Forces, formed on 1 March 1941 and operated in Iceland. DesRon 11 was attached to the Central Atlantic Neutrality Patrol in April 1941. *Kearny*, escorting Convoy SC48 prior to the US declaration of hostilities, was torpedoed on 17 October 1941 by *U568*. The torpedo hit the forward boiler room, but despite severe damage the destroyer reached Iceland and was repaired there by *Vulcan*. When the USA entered the war, four ships, *Gwin, Meredith, Grayson* and *Monssen* (DesDiv 22) were sent to the Pacific, but all the remainder served with the Atlantic Fleet. Their duties were mainly ASW convoy escort and patrol work. *Ingraham* was lost by collision with the oiler *Chemung* off Halifax NS, while escorting Convoy AT20. In a huge explosion, caused by her own depth-charges, the destroyer quickly sank. There were only eleven survivors. The invasion of North Africa saw units of DesRons 11 and 13 as well as DesDivs 19 and 26 in action off Morocco, nine of the class in all. *Woolsey* and *Swanson*, with *Quick*, sank *U173* off North Africa on 16 November. In July 1943, DesRon 13 supported the Sicily landings (*Woolsey, Ludlow, Edison, Wilkes, Nicholson* and *Swanson*), while five ships of DesRon 7 and four of DesRon 3 took part in the Invasion of Italy. *Wolsey* with the British *Calpe* sank *U73* off Oran on 16 December 1943. *C. F. Hughes, Madison* and *Lansdale* joined nine of their sisters off the Anzio beach-head in February 1944 where *Madison* with British *Hunt*-class destroyers sank *U450* in March. However, in April *Lansdale*, equipped for glider-bomb jambing duties, was escorting a convoy off Algeria when she was attacked by aircraft and torpedoed. Damage-control efforts could not save her and she sank about a quarter of an hour later. The following month, *Gleaves* and *Hilary P. Jones* were two of eight US destroyers which sank *U616* off Cape Termes on 12 May and on the 19th, *Ludlow* and *Niblack* accounted for *U960*.

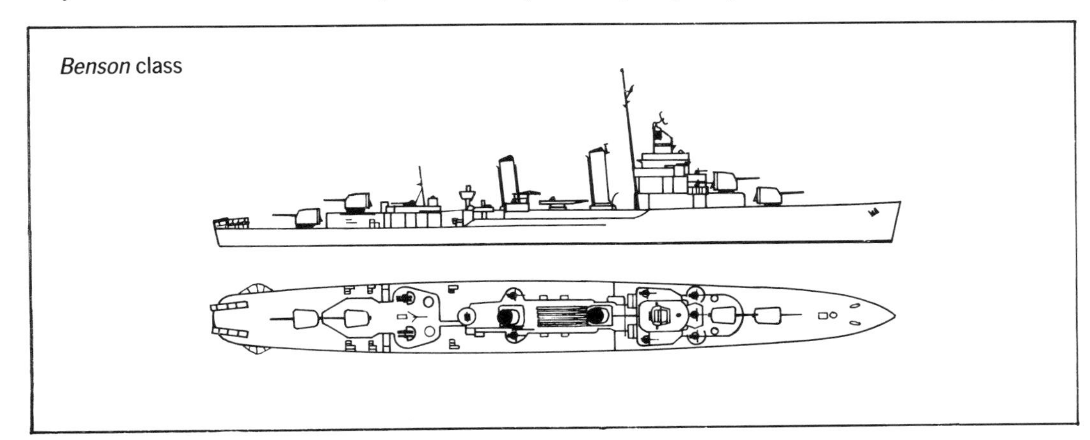

Above: *Gleaves* (DD423) on 13 April 1944. (USN) **Below:** *Mayo* (DD422) showing her layout in August 1944. (USN)

Plunkett alone went north for the Normandy Invasion in June 1944, but returned to the Mediterranean with thirteen of the class for the invasion of the South of France in August. Here, in addition to shore bombardments, the ships had encounters with MTBs, one-man submarines and explosive motorboats. With the run down of the war in Europe, most returned to the USA to refit for Pacific deployment.

The four Pacific Fleet destroyers formed part of the escort for the Tokyo Carrier raid in May 1942 and later that month, *Monssen* and *Gwin* participated in the Midway operation. In June, these destroyers were serving with DesRon 6 at Pearl Harbor and in the summer of 1942, supported the Guadalcanal operations and the Solomons. *Meredith* was the first casualty when escorting a convoy with aviation fuel bound for Guadalcanal. She was attacked by aircraft and overwhelmed by bombs and machine-gun fire. *Monssen*, when part of a US cruiser and destroyer force, was lost between Savo Island and Guadalcanal in action with Japanese battleships and destroyers. After launching five torpedoes at *Hiei*, the destroyer was torn apart and sunk by shellfire.

Gwin was damaged in another action in Iron Bottom Sound on the night of 14/15 November in which engagement she had to give the *coup de grâce* to *Benham*. In July 1943, she was at Rendova and then fought in the Battle of Kolombangara as flagship of DesRon 12 and DesDiv 23. *Gwin*, leading her division astern of the cruisers *Honolulu, Leander* and *St Louis*, was hit by a 'long lance' torpedo, sinking later that morning. The only ship of DesDiv 22 left, *Grayson* remained in the south Pacific, covered the landings at Aitape in April 1944, escorted carrier raids against Formosa and Luzon and eventually returned to the USA to receive the Kamikaze AA refit.

BRISTOL CLASS

Ship	Builder	Laid Down	Launched	Commissioned	Fate
DD453 *Bristol*	Federal Sbdg. Co.	2 Dec 40	25 July 41	22 Oct 41	Lost 12 Oct 43
DD454 *Ellyson*	Federal Sbdg. Co.	2 Dec 40	25 July 41	28 Nov 41	To Japan 19 Oct 54
DD455 *Hambleton*	Federal Sbdg. Co.	16 Dec 40	26 Sept 41	22 Dec 41	Stricken 1 June 71
DD456 *Rodman*	Federal Sbdg. Co.	2 Dec 40	26 Sept 41	27 Jan 42	To Taiwan 28 July 55
DD457 *Emmons*	Bath Iron Works	14 Nov 40	23 Aug 41	5 Dec 41	Lost 6 April 45
DD458 *Macomb*	Bath Iron Works	30 Sept 40	22 Sept 41	26 Jan 42	To Japan 19 Oct 54
DD459 *Laffey*	Bethlehem, S. Francisco	13 Jan 41	29 Nov 41	31 Mar 42	Lost 13 Nov 42
DD460 *Woodworth*	Bethlehem, S. Francisco	13 Jan 41	29 Nov 41	30 April 42	To Italy 25 May 51
DD461 *Forrest*	Boston NYd.	6 Jan 41	14 June 41	13 Jan 42	Scrapped 1946
DD462 *Fitch*	Boston NYd.	6 Jan 41	14 June 41	3 Feb 42	Stricken 1 July 71
DD463 *Corry*	Charleston NYd.	4 Sept 40	28 July 41	18 Dec 41	Lost 6 April 44
DD464 *Hobson*	Charleston NYd.	14 Nov 40	8 Sept 41	22 Jan 42	Lost 27 April 52
DD483 *Aaron Ward*	Federal Sbdg. Co.	11 Feb 41	22 Nov 41	4 Mar 42	Lost 7 April 43
DD484 *Buchanan*	Federal Sbdg. Co.	11 Feb 41	22 Nov 41	21 Mar 42	To Turkey 28 April 49
DD485 *Duncan*	Federal Sbdg. Co.	31 July 41	20 Feb 42	16 April 42	Lost 12 Oct 42
DD486 *Lansdowne*	Federal Sbdg. Co.	31 July 41	20 Feb 42	29 April 42	To Turkey 28 April 49
DD487 *Lardner*	Federal Sbdg. Co.	15 Sept 41	20 Mar 42	13 May 42	To Turkey 28 April 49

Below: *Emmons* (DD457) in November 1943, showing the four-gun, five-tube configuration. (USN)

Design Although the 1941 programme was to consist of the new *Fletcher* design, events in Europe and the increased belligerency of Japan in its conflict with China, caused the General Board to propose continuing the construction of the *Benson/Gleaves* design to maintain the impetus of destroyer building. This was concurred with and on 23 May 1940 approval was given to build *DD453–464*; another flotilla, *DD483–497*, was ordered in September. In December 1940, 41 more units were ordered (*DD598–628* and *DDD632–641*) which were to have an improved AA outfit obtained by the sacrifice of No. 3 5-inch gun and its replacement by a quadruple 1.1-inch mounting. This was eventually amended to a pair of twin Bofors and four 20mm, but this could not be implemented immediately. However, the four-gun layout was retrospectively applied to all the repeats from *DD453*. Finally, a last quartet (*DD645–648*) were ordered in February 1941.

The majority of these four-gun repeats were ordered from yards other than Bethlehem and hence received 'Navy' machinery and not the Bethlehem design.

Demands for destroyers equipped for Atlantic ASW work soon led to investigations as to how the depth-charge stowage (originally only 10) could be improved, and it was eventually decided to land the after tubes for thirty 600lb and a similar number of 300lb depth-charges plus six throwers. Where possible, beam was to be increased by 1 foot 4 inches to compensate the increased top-weight. In the event, only *Doran* and *Earle* had extra beam, and then only 37 feet. In service, the depth-charge outfit was less than this standard and only a few units had eight throwers.

To speed construction, simplifications were made to the design by eliminating curves in the superstructure, but only the Seattle-Tacoma ships and *DD618–623* and *645–648* were so completed. They also had the heavy Mk 37 gun director fitted on a lower trunk. The last four from Federal had their 40mm staggered in tubs abreast and aft of the second funnel.

Modifications Delays in the production of 40mm guns meant that many units completed without them, shipping instead six single 20mm in all. Radar was added for search and gunnery-control purposes, and some Atlantic units received HF/DF. Quadruple 1.1-inch guns were carried in the 40mm tub on the starboard side, counter-balanced by a 20mm gun to port in some units. Eventually the 40mm guns were fitted and three more 20mm added, one before the bridge and, unusually, in US destroyers, two in the bridge wings for a total of seven. Atlantic destroyers by the late-war period carried two stern racks for depth-charges with a total of 22 DCs. Twelve ships, (*DD493, 609, 620, 622, 623, 635, 637–639, 646–648*) were fitted with 'mousetrap' launchers as an experiment, but this was not successful. Pacific units carried a smaller ASW battery. When the Kamikaze threat was recognized, the intention was to replace the twin 40mm with quadruple, and the displaced twins were to be fitted between the funnels when the torpedo tubes had been landed, giving twelve 40mm. The 20mm outfit was to comprise two twin before the bridge and a pair of singles in the waist, pending blind-fire capability being fitted to the 40mm. Actually, only sixteen received this refit, *DD497, 600, 601, 603, 604, 608, 610, 612–617, 623, 624* and *628* (but *McLanahan* had only four twin Bofors).

In 1944, twelve units in the Atlantic were converted to Destroyer/Minesweepers, *DMS*. These were *DD454–458, 461 , 462, 464, 621, 625, 636* and *627*, redesignated *DMS19–30*. For this task, they landed the after 5-inch gun, receiving sweeping gear in lieu. Twelve more were converted in 1945, *DD489, 490, 493–496, 618, 627, 632–635*, as *DMS31–42*. These last dozen were given the increased AA outfits by the substitution of quadruple 40mm for the twins, two twin 20mm forward and two singles in the waist. Only *Hobson* of the earlier dozen was likewise treated.

Service When completed, the majority of this class served in the Atlantic, with 24 (*DD459, 460, 483–488, 491, 492, 598, 599, 602, 605–609, 611, 619, 628* and *645–647*) going to the Pacific theatre. In the course of convoy duties during 1942, *Landsdowne* sank *U153* in Caribbean waters in July and *Quick* assisted in the destruction of *U173* in November. Twenty of the Atlantic units covered the 'Torch' landings in North Africa at the end of 1942, then moved into Mediterranean waters, where 28

BRISTOL CLASS—*continued*

Ship	Builder	Laid Down	Launched	Commissioned	Fate
DD488 *McCalla*	Federal Sbdg. Co.	15 Sept 41	20 Mar 42	27 May 42	To Turkey 28 April 49
DD489 *Mervine*	Federal Sbdg. Co.	3 Nov 41	3 May 42	16 June 42	Stricken 1 July 68
DD490 *Quick*	Federal Sbdg. Co.	3 Nov 41	3 May 42	2 July 42	Sold for breaking up Aug 1973
DD491 *Farenholt*	Bethlehem, Staten Is.	11 Dec 40	19 Nov 41	2 April 42	Sold for breaking up Oct 1972
DD492 *Bailey*	Bethlehem, Staten Is.	29 Jan 41	19 Dec 41	11 May 42	Stricken 1 June 68
DD493 *Carmick*	Seattle-Tacoma	29 May 41	8 Mar 42	28 Dec 42	Stricken 1 July 71
DD494 *Doyle*	Seattle-Tacoma	29 May 41	17 Mar 42	27 Jan 43	Stricken 1 Dec 70
DD495 *Endicott*	Seattle-Tacoma	1 May 41	5 April 42	25 Feb 43	Stricken 1 Nov 69
DD496 *McCook*	Seattle-Tacoma	1 May 41	3 May 42	15 Mar 43	Sold for breaking up Aug 1973
DD497 *Frankford*	Seattle-Tacoma	15 June 41	17 May 42	31 Mar 42	Stricken 1 June 71
DD598 *Bancroft*	Bethlehem, Quincy	20 May 41	31 Dec 41	30 April 42	Stricken 1 June 71
DD599 *Barton*	Bethlehem, Quincy	30 May 41	31 Jan 42	29 May 42	Lost 13 Nov 42
DD600 *Boyle*	Bethlehem, Quincy	30 Dec 41	15 June 42	15 Aug 42	Stricken 1 June 71
DD601 *Champlin*	Bethlehem, Quincy	31 Jan 42	25 July 42	12 Sept 42	Stricken 2 Jan 71
DD602 *Meade*	Bethlehem, Staten Is.	25 Mar 41	15 Feb 42	22 June 42	Stricken 1 June 71
DD603 *Murphy*	Bethlehem, Staten Is.	19 May 41	29 April 42	25 July 42	Stricken 1 Nov 70
DD604 *Parker*	Bethlehem, Staten Is.	9 June 41	12 May 42	29 Aug 42	Stricken 1 July 71
DD605 *Caldwell*	Bethlehem, S. Francisco	24 Mar 41	15 Jan 42	10 June 42	Sold for breaking up 4 Nov 66
DD606 *Coghlan*	Bethlehem, S. Francisco	28 Mar 41	16 Feb 42	10 July 42	Sold for breaking up 29 May 74
DD607 *Frazier*	Bethlehem, S. Francisco	5 July 41	17 Mar 42	30 July 42	Stricken 1 July 71
DD608 *Gansevoort*	Bethlehem, S. Francisco	16 June 41	11 April 42	25 Aug 42	Stricken 1 July 71
DD609 *Gillespie*	Bethlehem, S. Francisco	16 June 41	8 May 42	16 Sept 42	Stricken 1 July 71
DD610 *Hobby*	Bethlehem, S. Francisco	30 June 41	4 June 42	8 Nov 42	Stricken 1 July 71
DD611 *Kalk*	Bethlehem, S. Francisco	30 June 41	18 July 42	17 Oct 42	Stricken 1 June 68
DD612 *Kendrick*	Bethlehem, San Pedro	1 May 41	2 April 42	12 Sept 42	Stricken 1 May 66
DD613 *Laub*	Bethlehem, San Pedro	1 May 41	1 June 42	24 Oct 42	Sold for breaking up 12 June 75
DD614 *Mackenzie*	Bethlehem, San Pedro	1 May 41	27 June 42	21 Nov 42	Stricken 1 July 71
DD615 *McLanahan*	Bethlehem, San Pedro	29 May 41	7 Sept 42	19 Dec 42	Sold for breaking up 29 May 74

ships covered the Sicily landings in mid-1943. During this operation, *Maddox* was bombed off Gela and sank within two minutes. Only *Bristol* saw service off Salerno, but she was torpedoed and sunk by *U371* in October while escorting a convoy between Algiers and Tunis. *Beatty* was sunk by an aircraft torpedo when similarly employed. Operations in the Mediterranean began to run down in 1944 in preparation for the invasion of Europe, 'Overlord', with eight of the Salerno destroyers being transferred to England where they joined seventeen others in the naval forces.

Further Atlantic anti-submarine successes were the sinking of *U182* by *Mackenzie* in May 1943, *Hobson* played a part in the destruction of *U575* in March 1944, *Corry* and aircraft sank *U801* in the same month, while *Champlin* and a destroyer-escort sank *U856* in April. Finally, in the Mediterranean a group of destroyers, including *Nields, Macomb, Hambleton, Rodman* and *Emmons*, sank *U616* in May 1944. On the debit side however, *Turner* blew up and sank while lying at anchor off Ambrose Light in January, possibly as a result of an ammunition explosion.

During the 'Overlord' invasion in June 1944, 25 members of the class participated in the covering operations. *Corry*, a unit of DesDiv 20 assigned to Task Force 'U', struck a mine off Utah beach, broke in two and sank, and *Glennon* also mined off Quineville on 8 June, was eventually sunk by shore batteries while stranded after the mining on 10 June.

The invasion of the South of France followed in September 1944 with many of the Normandy destroyers returning to the Mediterranean for this operation, the final major task of the US destroyers in European waters. Altogether, 29 of the class were at 'Anvil' of which all but ten had been involved in 'Overlord'.

None of the class were completed at the outbreak of the Pacific War, but a number arrived in time to take part in the Guadalcanal campaign, *Aaron Ward* and *Laffey* with DesRon 12 and *Buchanan* with DesRon 1 in August 1942. Five, *Farenholt, Buchanan, Laffey, Duncan* and *McCalla* (DesRon 12) were with four US cruisers at the Battle of Cape Esperance in October 1942 when the Japanese destroyer *Fubuki* was sunk, as was the cruiser *Furutaka* for the loss of *Duncan* to gunfire and heavy damage to *Farenholt*. Several other US and Japanese ships were damaged to varying degrees, the destroyer *Murakumo* being later sunk. *McCalla* sank the Japanese submarine *I15* in the Solomons on 2 November but on the 13th, there began a series of engagements off Guadalcanal which were to be costly for the US destroyer forces. *Buchanan* was badly damaged by friendly AA fire on 11 November and had to be detached. *Laffey, Aaron Ward* and *Barton* were members of TG67.4, comprised of five US cruisers and eight destroyers which fought an engagement with the Japanese battleships *Hiei* and

BRISTOL CLASS—*continued*

Ship	Builder	Laid Down	Launched	Commissioned	Fate
DD616 *Nields*	Bethlehem, Quincy	15 June 42	1 Oct 42	15 Jan 43	Stricken 5 Sept 70
DD617 *Ordronaux*	Bethlehem, Quincy	25 July 42	9 Nov 42	13 Feb 43	Stricken 1 July 71
DD618 *Davison*	Federal Sbdg.Co.	26 Feb 42	19 July 42	11 Sept 42	Sold for breaking up Aug 1973
DD619 *Edwards*	Federal Sbdg. Co.	26 Feb 42	19 July 42	17 Sept 42	Stricken 1 July 71
DD620 *Glennon*	Federal Sbdg. Co.	25 Mar 42	26 Aug 42	8 Oct 42	Lost 10 June 44
DD621 *Jeffers*	Federal Sbdg. Co.	25 Mar 42	26 Aug 42	4 Nov 42	Stricken 1 July 71
DD622 *Maddox*	Federal Sbdg. Co.	7 May 42	15 Sept 42	31 Oct 42	Lost 10 July 43
DD623 *Nelson*	Federal Sbdg. Co.	7 May 42	15 Sept 42	25 Nov 42	Stricken 1 Mar 68
DD624 *Baldwin*	Seattle-Tacoma	16 July 41	1 June 42	30 April 42	Scuttled 5 June 61
DD625 *Harding*	Seattle-Tacoma	22 July 41	28 June 42	25 May 43	Scrapped 1947
DD626 *Satterlee*	Seattle-Tacoma	10 Sept 41	17 July 42	1 July 43	Stricken 1 Dec 70
DD627 *Thompson*	Seattle-Tacoma	22 Sept 41	10 Aug 42	10 July 43	Stricken 1 July 71
DD628 *Welles*	Seattle-Tacoma	27 Sept 41	7 Sept 42	16 Aug 43	Stricken 1 Mar 68
DD632 *Cowie*	Boston NYd.	18 Mar 41	27 Sept 41	1 June 43	Stricken 1 Dec 70
DD633 *Knight*	Boston NYd.	18 Mar 41	27 Sept 41	23 June 42	Stricken 1 June 67
DD634 *Doran*	Boston NYd.	14 June 41	10 Dec 41	4 Aug 42	Sold for breaking up Aug 1973
DD635 *Earle*	Boston NYd.	14 June 41	10 Dec 41	1 Sept 42	Stricken 1 Dec 69
DD636 *Butler*	Philadelphia NYd.	16 Sept 41	12 Feb 42	15 Aug 42	Scrapped 1948
DD637 *Gherardi*	Philadelphia NYd.	16 Sept 41	12 Feb 42	15 Sept 42	Stricken 1 June 71
DD638 *Herndon*	Norfolk NYd.	26 Aug 41	5 Feb 42	20 Dec 42	Stricken 1 July 71
DD639 *Shubrick*	Norfolk NYd.	17 Feb 42	18 April 42	7 Feb 43	Scrapped 1947
DD640 *Beatty*	Charleston NYd.	8 Sept 41	20 Dec 41	7 May 42	Lost 6 Nov 43
DD641 *Tillman*	Charleston NYd.	8 Sept 41	20 Dec 41	4 June 42	Stricken 1 June 70
DD645 *Stevenson*	Federal Sbdg. Co.	23 July 42	11 Nov 42	14 Dec 42	Sold for breaking up April 1970
DD646 *Stockton*	Federal Sbdg. Co.	24 July 42	11 Nov 42	9 Jan 43	Stricken 1 July 71
DD647 *Thorn*	Federal Sbdg. Co.	15 Nov 42	28 Feb 43	31 Mar 43	Stricken 1 July 71
DD648 *Turner*	Federal Sbdg. Co.	15 Nov 42	28 Feb 43	15 April 43	Lost 3 Jan 44

Kirishima, supported by a cruiser and nine destroyers in Iron Bottom Sound. *Laffey* was hit by 14-inch shells and a torpedo, then blew up and sank while *Barton* sank after being hit by two torpedoes. *Aaron Ward* was badly damaged by gunfire. Two other US destroyers and the cruisers *Atlanta* and *Juneau* were sunk, as were the Japanese *Hiei, Yudachi* and *Akatsuki*. *Aaron Ward* was eventually sunk by air attack off Guadalcanal while escorting a convoy for Tulagi in March 1943.

In early 1943, *Gillespie* (DesRon 14), *Bancroft, Caldwell, Frazier* and *Coghlan* served in the

Aleutian Islands as did *Meade*, and in March *Bailey* and *Coghlan* participated in the Battle of the Komandorski Islands when the former was badly damaged by 8-inch shellfire. *Frazier* sank *I31* off Kiska on 13 June 1943. In the final operations in the Aleutians during August 1943, *Coghlan, Caldwell, Gansevoort, Edwards, Frazier* and *Meade* served with the invasion covering groups.

Moving south once more, *Frazier* and *Meade* sank *I35* in the Gilbert Islands in November 1943, when they were employed in the assault on these islands accompanied by *Caldwell, Bancroft, Coghlan, Bailey, Gansevoort* and *Edwards*. The next step was the Marshalls which involved the same ships less *Gansevoort* and *Edwards*. Another anti-submarine success was the sinking of *Ro37* by *Buchanan* south-west of the Solomons on 22 January 1944. *Bailey, Bancroft, Coghlan, Edwards, Lansdowne, Lardner* and *McCalla* all covered the Marianas assault in the summer of 1944.

In 1945, *Farenholt, Shubrick* and *Lansdowne* were at Okinawa, joined by the former Atlantic unit, *Herndon*, as well as some of the destroyer-mine-sweeper conversions, of which *Emmons* was sunk, hit by five Kamikaze aircraft. The fast minesweepers formed TG52.2 and consisted of *Forrest, Hobson, Macomb, Ellyson, Hambleton, Rodman, Emmons, Butler, Gherardi, Jeffers* and *Harding*. Of this group, all ex-Atlantic ships, *Harding* was damaged beyond repair by Kamikaze attack on 16 April, *Butler* similarly on 25 May and *Forrest* also irreparably damaged by the same means two days later. *Shubrick* was another constructional total loss, to Kamikaze attack on 29 May, but these were the final losses of the war.

Post-war, only the minesweeper conversions were retained in the active fleet. Some were transferred to Allied navies but most were broken up in the 1960s and 1970s.

Above: *Emmons* (DMS18) in 1945, converted for fast minesweeping. (USN)

FLETCHER CLASS

Ship	Builder	Laid Down	Launched	Commissioned	Fate
DD445 *Fletcher*	Federal Sbdg. Co.	2 Oct 41	3 May 42	30 June 42	Stricken 1 Aug 67
DD446 *Radford*	Federal Sbdg. Co.	2 Oct 41	3 May 42	21 July 43	Stricken 15 July 69
DD447 *Jenkins*	Federal Sbdg. Co.	22 Nov 41	21 June 42	31 July 42	Stricken 2 July 69
DD448 *La Vallette*	Federal Sbdg. Co.	27 Nov 41	21 June 42	11 Aug 42	Stricken 1 Feb 74
DD449 *Nicholas*	Bath Iron Works	3 Mar 41	19 Feb 42	4 June 42	Stricken 30 Jan 70
DD450 *O'Bannon*	Bath Iron Works	3 Mar 41	14 Mar 42	26 June 42	Stricken 30 Jan 70
DD451 *Chevalier*	Bath Iron Works	30 April 41	11 April 42	20 July 42	Lost 7 Oct 43

Displacement: 2,325tons/2,362tonnes (standard); 2,924tons/2,970tonnes (full load).
Length: 376ft 5in/114.73m (oa); 369ft 1in/112.5m (wl).
Beam: 39ft 7in/12.07m.
Draught: 13ft 9in/4.19m (mean).
Machinery: four Babcock & Wilcox boilers; 2-shaft G.E.C. geared turbines.
Performance: 60,000shp; 38kts.
Bunkerage: 492tons/500tonnes.
Range: 6,500nm at 15kts.
Guns: five 5in (5×1); four 1.1in (1×4); four 20mm.
Torpedoes: ten 21in (2×5).
Complement: 273.

Below: *Radford* (DD446) on 15 January 1944. Note bridge style and 40mm directors atop the pilot-house. (USN)

FLETCHER CLASS—*continued*

Ship	Builder	Laid Down	Launched	Commissioned	Fate
DD465 *Saufley*	Federal Sbdg. Co.	27 Jan 42	19 July 42	28 Aug 42	Stricken 1 Sept 66
DD466 *Waller*	Federal Sbdg. Co.	19 Feb 42	15 Aug 42	30 Sept 42	Stricken 15 July 69
DD467 *Strong*	Bath Iron Works	30 April 41	17 May 42	7 Aug 42	Lost 5 July 43
DD468 *Taylor*	Bath Iron Works	28 Aug 41	7 June 42	28 Aug 42	To Italy 2 July 69
DD469 *De Haven*	Bath Iron Works	27 Sept 41	28 June 42	21 Sept 42	Lost 1 Feb 43
DD470 *Bache*	Bethlehem, Staten Is.	19 Nov 41	27 July 42	14 Nov 42	Stricken 1 Mar 68
DD471 *Beale*	Bethlehem, Staten Is.	19 Dec 41	24 Aug 42	23 Dec 42	Stricken 1 Oct 68
DD472 *Guest*	Boston NYd.	27 Sept 41	20 Feb 42	15 Dec 42	To Brazil 5 June 59
DD473 *Bennett*	Boston NYd.	10 Dec 41	16 April 42	9 Feb 43	To Brazil 15 Dec 59
DD474 *Fullam*	Boston NYd.	10 Dec 41	16 April 42	2 Mar 43	Expended 7 July 62
DD475 *Hudson*	Boston NYd.	23 Feb 42	3 June 42	13 April 43	Stricken 1 Dec 72
DD476 *Hutchins*	Boston NYd.	27 Sept 41	20 Feb 42	17 Nov 42	Scrapped 1948
DD477 *Pringle*	Charleston NYd.	31 July 41	2 May 42	15 Sept 42	Lost 16 April 45
DD478 *Stanly*	Charleston NYd.	30 Dec 41	2 May 42	15 Oct 42	Stricken 1 Dec 70
DD479 *Stevens*	Charleston NYd.	30 Dec 41	24 June 42	1 Feb 43	Stricken 1971
DD480 *Halford*	Puget Sound NYd.	3 June 41	29 Oct 42	1 May 43	Stricken 1 May 68
DD481 *Leutze*	Puget Sound NYd.	3 June 41	29 Oct 42	4 Mar 44	Scrapped 1947
DD498 *Philip*	Federal Sbdg. Co.	7 May 42	13 Oct 42	20 Nov 42	Stricken 1 Oct 68
DD499 *Renshaw*	Federal Sbdg. Co.	7 May 42	13 Oct 42	4 Dec 42	Stricken 14 Jan 70
DD500 *Ringgold*	Federal Sbdg. Co.	25 June 42	11 Nov 42	23 Dec 42	To Germany 14 July 59
DD501 *Schroeder*	Federal Sbdg. Co.	25 June 42	11 Nov 42	31 Dec 42	Stricken 1 Oct 72
DD502 *Sigsbee*	Federal Sbdg. Co.	22 July 42	7 Dec 42	22 Jan 43	Stricken 1 Dec 74
DD503 *Stevenson*		Cancelled			
DD504 *Stockton*		Cancelled			
DD505 *Thorn*		Cancelled			
DD506 *Turner*		Cancelled			
DD507 *Conway*	Bath Iron Works	5 Nov 41	16 Aug 42	9 Oct 42	Stricken 15 Nov 69
DD508 *Cony*	Bath Iron Works	24 Dec 41	16 Aug 42	30 Oct 42	Stricken 2 July 69
DD509 *Converse*	Bath Iron Works	23 Feb 42	30 Aug 42	20 Nov 42	To Spain 15 July 59
DD510 *Eaton*	Bath Iron Works	17 Mar 42	20 Sept 42	4 Dec 42	Stricken 2 July 59
DD511 *Foote*	Bath Iron Works	14 April 42	11 Oct 42	22 Dec 42	Stricken 1 Oct 72
DD512 *Spence*	Bath Iron Works	18 May 42	27 Oct 42	8 Jan 43	Lost 18 Dec 44

FLETCHER CLASS—*continu*

Ship	Builder	Laid Down
DD513 *Terry*	Bath Iron Works	8 June 42
DD514 *Thatcher*	Bath Iron Works	29 June 42
DD515 *Anthony*	Bath Iron Works	17 Aug 42
DD516 *Wadsworth*	Bath Iron Works	18 Aug 42
DD517 *Walker*	Bath Iron Works	31 Aug 42
DD518 *Brownson*	Bethlehem, Staten Is.	15 Feb 42
DD519 *Daly*	Bethlehem, Staten Is.	29 April 42
DD520 *Isherwood*	Bethlehem, Staten Is.	12 May 42
DD521 *Kimberly*	Bethlehem, Staten Is.	27 July 42
DD522 *Luce*	Bethlehem, Staten Is.	24 Aug 42
DD526 *Abner Read*	Bethlehem, S. Francisco	30 Oct 41
DD527 *Ammen*	Bethlehem, S. Francisco	29 Nov 41
DD528 *Mullany* (ex-*Beatty*)	Bethlehem, S. Francisco	15 Jan 42
DD529 *Bush*	Bethlehem, S. Francisco	12 Feb 42
DD530 *Trathen*	Bethlehem, S. Francisco	18 July 42
DD531 *Hazelwood*	Bethlehem, S. Francisco	1 April 42
DD532 *Heermann*	Bethlehem, S. Francisco	8 May 42
DD533 *Hoel*	Bethlehem, S. Francisco	4 June 42
DD534 *McCord*	Bethlehem, S. Francisco	17 Mar 42
DD535 *Miller*	Bethlehem, S. Francisco	18 Aug 42
DD 536 *Owen*	Bethlehem, S. Francisco	17 Sept 42
DD537 *The Sullivans*	Bethlehem, S. Francisco	10 Oct 42
DD538 *Stephen Potter*	Bethlehem, S. Francisco	27 Oct 42
DD539 *Tingey*	Bethlehem, S. Francisco	22 Oct 42
DD540 *Twining*	Bethlehem, S. Francisco	20 Nov 42
DD541 *Yarnall*	Bethlehem, S. Francisco	5 Dec 42
DD544 *Boyd*	Bethlehem, San Pedro	2 April 42
DD545 *Bradford*	Bethlehem, San Pedro	28 April 42

FLETCHER CLASS—*continued*

Launched	Commissioned	Fate
22 Nov 42	26 Jan 43	Stricken April 1974
6 Dec 42	10 Feb 43	Scrapped 1948
20 Dec 42	26 Feb 43	To Germany 17 Jan 58
10 Jan 43	16 Mar 43	To Germany 6 Oct 59
31 Jan 43	2 April 43	To Italy 2 July 69
24 Sept 42	3 Feb 43	Lost 26 Dec 43
24 Oct 42	9 Mar 43	Sold for breaking up 22 April 76
24 Oct 42	10 April 43	To Peru Oct 1961
4 Feb 43	22 May 43	To Taiwan 1 June 67
6 Mar 43	21 June 43	Lost 3 May 45
18 Aug 42	5 Feb 43	Lost 1 Nov 44
17 Sept 42	12 Mar 43	Scrapped 1961
10 Oct 42	23 April 43	To Taiwan 6 Oct 71
27 Oct 42	10 May 43	Lost 6 April 45
22 Oct 42	28 May 43	Expended 1 Nov 72
20 Nov 42	18 June 43	Sold for breaking up 14 April 76
5 Dec 42	6 July 43	To Argentina 1 Aug 61
19 Dec 43	29 July 43	Lost 25 Oct 44
10 Jan 43	19 Aug 43	Expended 1 Nov 72
7 Mar 43	31 Aug 43	Stricken 1 Dec 74
21 Mar 43	20 Sept 43	Stricken 15 April 73
4 April 43	30 Sept 43	Memorial 1974
28 April 43	21 Oct 43	Stricken 1 Dec 72
28 May 43	25 Nov 43	Stricken 1 Nov 65
11 July 43	1 Dec 43	To Taiwan 6 Oct 71
25 July 43	30 Dec 43	To Taiwan 10 June 68
29 Oct 42	8 May 43	To Turkey 1 Oct 69
12 Dec 42	12 June 43	To Greece 27 Sept 62

Ship	Builder	Laid Down	Launched	Commissioned	Fate
DD546 *Brown*	Bethlehem, San Pedro	27 June 42	22 Feb 43	10 July 43	To Greece 27 Sept 62
DD547 *Cowell*	Bethlehem, San Pedro	7 Sept 42	18 April 43	28 Aug 43	To Argentina 17 Aug 71
DD550 *Capps*	Bethlehem, San Pedro	12 June 41	31 May 42	23 June 43	To Spain 1 July 57
DD551 *David W. Taylor*	Gulf Sbdg.	12 June 41	4 July 42	18 Sept 43	To Spain 1 July 57
DD552 *Evans*	Gulf Sbdg.	21 July 41	4 Oct 42	11 Dec 43	Scrapped 1947
DD553 *John D. Henley*	Gulf Sbdg.	21 July 41	15 Nov 42	2 Feb 44	Scrapped 1970
DD554 *Franks*	Seattle-Tacoma	8 Mar 42	7 Dec 42	30 July 43	Sold for breaking up Aug 1973
DD555 *Haggard*	Seattle-Tacoma	27 Mar 42	9 Feb 43	31 Aug 43	Scrapped 1946
DD556 *Hailey*	Seattle-Tacoma	11 April 42	9 Mar 43	3 Sept 43	To Brazil 20 July 61
DD557 *Johnston*	Seattle-Tacoma	6 May 42	25 Mar 43	27 Oct 43	Lost 25 Oct 44
DD558 *Laws*	Seattle-Tacoma	19 May 42	22 April 43	18 Nov 43	Stricken 15 April 73
DD559 *Longshaw*	Seattle-Tacoma	16 June 42	4 June 43	4 Dec 43	Lost 18 May 45
DD560 *Morrison*	Seattle-Tacoma	30 June 42	4 July 43	18 Dec 43	Lost 3 May 45
DD561 *Prichett*	Seattle-Tacoma	20 July 42	31 July 43	15 Jan 44	To Italy 10 Jan 70
DD562 *Robinson*	Seattle-Tacoma	12 Aug 42	28 Aug 43	31 Jan 44	Stricken 1 Dec 74
DD563 *Ross*	Seattle-Tacoma	7 Sept 42	10 Sept 43	21 Feb 44	Stricken 1 Dec 74
DD564 *Rowe*	Seattle-Tacoma	7 Dec 42	30 Sept 43	13 Mar 44	Stricken 1 Dec 74
DD565 *Smalley*	Seattle-Tacoma	9 Feb 43	27 Oct 43	31 Mar 44	Scrapped 1966
DD566 *Stoddard*	Seattle-Tacoma	10 Mar 43	19 Nov 43	15 April 44	Expended 1 June 75
DD567 *Watts*	Seattle-Tacoma	26 Mar 43	31 Dec 43	29 April 44	Sold for breaking up 24 July 74
DD568 *Wren*	Seattle-Tacoma	24 April 43	29 Jan 44	20 May 44	Sold for breaking up 21 Sept 75
DD569 *Aulick*	Consolidated, Orange	14 May 41	2 Mar 42	27 Oct 42	To Greece 21 Aug 59
DD570 *Charles Ausburne*	Consolidated, Orange	14 May 41	16 Mar 42	24 Nov 42	To Germany 12 April 60
DD571 *Claxton*	Consolidated, Orange	25 June 41	1 April 42	8 Dec 42	To Germany 15 Dec 59
DD572 *Dyson*	Consolidated, Orange	25 June 41	15 April 42	30 Dec 42	To Germany 17 Feb 60
DD573 *Harrison*	Consolidated, Orange	25 July 41	7 May 42	25 Jan 43	To Mexico 19 Aug 70
DD574 *John Rodgers*	Consolidated, Orange	25 July 41	7 May 42	9 Feb 43	To Mexico 19 Aug 70
DD575 *McKee*	Consolidated, Orange	2 Mar 42	2 Aug 42	31 Mar 43	Stricken 1 Oct 72
DD576 *Murray*	Consolidated, Orange	16 Mar 42	16 Aug 42	20 April 43	Scrapped 1966

FLETCHER CLASS—*continued*

Ship	Builder	Laid Down	Launched	Commissioned	Fate
DD577 *Sproston*	Consolidated, Orange	1 April 42	31 Aug 42	19 May 43	Stricken 1 Oct 68
DD578 *Wickes*	Consolidated, Orange	15 April 42	13 Sept 42	16 June 43	Expended 1 Nov 72
DD579 *William D. Porter*	Consolidated, Orange	7 May 42	27 Sept 42	6 July 43	Lost 10 June 45
DD580 *Young*	Consolidated, Orange	7 May 42	11 Oct 42	31 July 43	Stricken 1 May 68
DD581 *Charrette*	Boston NYd.	20 Feb 41	3 June 42	18 May 43	To Greece 15 June 59
DD582 *Conner*	Boston NYd.	16 April 42	18 July 42	18 June 43	To Greece 15 Sept 59
DD583 *Hall*	Boston NYd.	16 April 42	18 July 42	6 July 43	To Greece 9 Feb 60
DD584 *Halligan*	Boston NYd.	9 Nov 42	19 Mar 43	19 Aug 43	Lost 26 Mar 45
DD585 *Haraden*	Boston NYd.	13 June 42	19 Mar 43	16 Sept 43	Expended 1 Nov 72
DD586 *Newcomb*	Boston NYd.	19 Mar 43	4 July 43	10 Nov 43	Scrapped 1947
DD587 *Bell*	Charleston NYd.	24 Feb 42	24 June 42	4 Mar 43	Expended 1 Nov 72
DD588 *Burns*	Charleston NYd.	9 May 42	8 Aug 42	3 April 43	Expended 1 Nov 72
DD589 *Izard*	Charleston NYd.	9 May 42	8 Aug 42	15 May 43	Stricken 1 May 68
DD590 *Paul Hamilton*	Charleston NYd.	20 Jan 43	7 April 43	15 Nov 43	Stricken 1 May 68
DD591 *Twiggs*	Charleston NYd.	20 Jan 43	7 April 43	4 Nov 43	Lost 16 June 45
DD592 *Howorth*	Puget Sound NYd.	26 Nov 41	10 Jan 43	1 May 44	Expended 8 Mar 62
DD593 *Killen*	Puget Sound NYd.	26 Nov 41	10 Jan 43	1 June 44	Sold for breaking up 15 April 75
DD594 *Hart* (ex-*Mansfield*)	Puget Sound NYd.	10 Aug 43	25 Sept 44	1 Dec 44	Stricken 15 April 73
DD595 *Metcalfe*	Puget Sound NYd.	10 Aug 43	25 Sept 44	15 Dec 44	Stricken 2 Jan 71
DD596 *Shields*	Puget Sound NYd.	10 Aug 43	25 Sept 44	22 Feb 45	To Brazil 1 July 72
DD597 *Wiley*	Puget Sound NYd.	10 Aug 43	25 Sept 44	14 Mar 45	Stricken 1 May 68
DD629 *Abbot*	Bath Iron Works	21 Sept 42	17 Feb 43	23 April 43	Stricken 1 Dec 74
DD630 *Braine*	Bath Iron Works	12 Oct 42	7 Mar 43	11 May 43	To Argentina 1 Aug 61
DD631 *Erben*	Bath Iron Works	28 Oct 42	21 Mar 43	28 May 43	To S. Korea 1 May 63
DD642 *Hale*	Bath Iron Works	23 Nov 42	4 April 43	15 June 43	To Colombia 23 Jan 61
DD643 *Sigourney*	Bath Iron Works	7 Dec 42	24 April 43	29 June 43	Stricken 1 Dec 74
DD644 *Stembel*	Bath Iron Works	21 Dec 42	8 May 43	16 July 43	To Argentina 1 Aug 61
DD649 *Albert W. Grant*	Charleston NYd.	30 Dec 42	29 May 43	24 Nov 43	Stricken 14 April 71
DD650 *Caperton*	Bath Iron Works	11 Jan 43	24 July 43	30 July 43	Stricken 1 Dec 74
DD651 *Cogswell*	Bath Iron Works	1 Feb 43	5 June 43	17 Aug 43	To Turkey 1 Oct 69

FLETCHER CLASS—*continu*

Ship	Builder	Laid Down
DD652 *Ingersoll*	Bath Iron Works	18 Feb 43
DD653 *Knapp*	Bath Iron Works	8 Mar 43
DD654 *Bearss*	Gulf Sbdg. Co.	14 July 42
DD655 *John Hood*	Gulf Sbdg. Co.	12 Oct 42
DD656 *Van Valkenburgh*	Gulf Sbdg. Co.	15 Nov 42
DD657 *Charles J. Badger*	Bethlehem, Staten Is.	24 Sept 42
DD658 *Colahan*	Bethlehem, Staten Is.	24 Oct 42
DD659 *Dashiell*	Federal Sbdg. Co.	1 Oct 42
DD660 *Bullard*	Federal Sbdg. Co.	16 Oct 42
DD661 *Kidd*	Federal Sbdg. Co.	16 Oct 42
DD662 *Bennion*	Boston NYd.	19 Mar 43
DD663 *Heywood L. Edwards*	Boston NYd.	4 July 43
DD664 *Richard P. Leary*	Boston NYd.	4 July 43
DD665 *Bryant*	Charleston NYd.	30 Dec 42
DD666 *Black*	Federal Sbdg. Co.	14 Nov 42
DD667 *Chauncey*	Federal Sbdg. Co.	14 Nov 42
DD668 *Clarence K. Bronson*	Federal Sbdg. Co.	9 Dec 42
DD669 *Cotten*	Federal Sbdg. Co.	8 Feb 43
DD670 *Dortch*	Federal SBdg. Co.	2 Mar 43
DD671 *Gatling*	Federal Sbdg. Co.	3 Mar 43
DD672 *Healy*	Federal Sbdg. Co.	4 Mar 43
DD673 *Hickox*	Federal Sbdg. Co.	12 Mar 43
DD674 *Hunt*	Federal Sbdg. Co.	31 Mar 43
DD675 *Lewis Hancock*	Federal Sbdg. Co.	31 Mar 43
DD676 *Marshall*	Federal Sbdg. Co.	19 April 43
DD677 *McDermut*	Federal Sbdg. Co.	14 June 43
DD678 *McGowan*	Federal Sbdg. Co.	30 June 43
DD679 *McNair*	Federal Sbdg. Co.	30 June 43
DD680 *Melvin*	Federal Sbdg. Co.	6 July 43

Launched	Commissioned	Fate
28 June 43	31 Aug 43	Stricken 20 Jan 70
10 July 43	15 Sept 43	Sold for breaking up Aug 1973
25 July 43	12 April 44	Sold for breaking up 14 April 76
23 Oct 43	7 June 44	Sold for breaking up 12 April 76
19 Dec 43	2 Aug 44	To Turkey 28 Feb 67
3 April 43	23 July 43	Stricken 1970
2 May 43	23 Aug 43	Stricken 1 Aug 66
6 Feb 43	20 Mar 43	Sold for breaking up 21 Sept 75
28 Feb 43	9 April 43	Stricken 1 Dec 72
28 Feb 43	23 April 43	Stricken 1 Dec 74
4 July 43	14 Dec 43	Stricken 15 April 71
6 Oct 43	26 Jan 44	To Japan 10 Mar 59
6 Oct 43	23 Feb 44	To Japan 10 Mar 59
29 May 43	4 Dec 43	Stricken 1 June 68
28 Mar 43	21 May 43	Stricken 21 Sept 69
28 Mar 43	31 May 43	Stricken 1 Oct 72
18 April 43	11 June 43	To Turkey 14 Jan 67
12 June 43	24 July 43	Stricken 1 Dec 74
20 June 43	7 Aug 43	To Argentina 1 Aug 61
20 June 43	19 Aug 43	Stricken 1 Dec 74
4 July 43	3 Sept 43	Sold for breaking up 12 April 76
4 July 43	10 Sept 43	To S. Korea 15 Nov 68
1 Aug 43	22 Sept 43	Sold for breaking up 14 Aug 75
1 Aug 43	29 Sept 43	To Brazil 2 Aug 67
29 Aug 43	16 Oct 43	Stricken 12 July 69
17 Oct 43	19 Nov 43	Sold for breaking up 21 Jan 66
14 Nov 43	20 Dec 43	To Spain 31 Nov 60
14 Nov 43	30 Dec 43	Sold for breaking up 29 Aug 75
17 Oct 43	24 Nov 43	Sold for breaking up 14 Aug 75

FLETCHER CLASS—*continued*

Ship	Builder	Laid Down	Launched	Commissioned	Fate
DD681 *Hopewell*	Bethlehem, San Pedro	29 Oct 42	2 May 43	30 Sept 43	Stricken 2 Jan 70
DD682 *Porterfield*	Bethlehem, San Pedro	12 Dec 42	13 June 43	30 Oct 43	Expended 1 Mar 75
DD683 *Stockham*	Bethlehem, S. Francisco	19 Dec 42	25 July 43	11 Feb 44	Stricken 1 Dec 74
DD684 *Wedderburn*	Bethlehem, S. Francisco	10 Jan 43	1 Aug 43	9 Mar 44	Stricken 1 Oct 69
DD685 *Picking*	Bethlehem, Staten Is.	24 Nov 42	31 May 43	21 Sept 43	Expended 1 Mar 75
DD686 *Halsey Powell*	Bethlehem, Staten Is.	4 Feb 43	30 June 43	25 Oct 43	To S. Korea 27 April 68
DD687 *Uhlmann*	Bethlehem, Staten Is.	6 Mar 43	30 July 43	22 Nov 43	Stricken 15 July 72
DD688 *Remey*	Bath Iron Works	22 Mar 43	24 July 43	30 Sept 43	Sold for breaking up 29 Aug 75
DD689 *Wadleigh*	Bath Iron Works	5 April 43	7 Aug 43	19 Oct 43	To Chile July 1962
DD690 *Norman Scott*	Bath Iron Works	26 April 43	28 Aug 43	5 Nov 43	Stricken 15 April 73
DD691 *Mertz*	Bath Iron Works	10 May 43	11 Sept 43	19 Nov 43	Stricken 1 Oct 70
DD792 *Callaghan*	Bethlehem, San Pedro	21 Feb 43	1 Aug 43	27 Nov 43	Lost 28 July 45
DD793 *Cassin*	Bethlehem, San Pedro	18 Mar 43	12 Sept 43	31 Dec 43	Stricken 1 Dec 74
DD794 *Irwin*	Bethlehem, San Pedro	2 May 43	31 Oct 43	14 Feb 44	To Brazil 10 May 68
DD795 *Preston*	Bethlehem, San Pedro	13 June 43	12 Dec 43	20 Mar 44	To Turkey 15 Nov 69
DD796 *Benham*	Bethlehem, Staten Is.	3 April 43	29 Aug 43	20 Dec 43	To Peru 8 Oct 61
DD797 *Cushing*	Bethlehem, Staten Is.	3 May 43	30 Sept 43	17 Jan 44	To Brazil 20 July 61
DD798 *Monssen*	Bethlehem, Staten Is.	1 June 43	29 Oct 43	12 Feb 44	Scrapped 1964
DD799 *Jarvis*	Seattle-Tacoma	7 June 43	14 Feb 44	3 June 44	To Spain 3 Nov 60
DD800 *Porter*	Seattle-Tacoma	6 July 43	13 Mar 44	24 June 44	Stricken 1 Oct 72
DD801 *Colhoun*	Seattle-Tacoma	3 Aug 43	10 April 44	8 July 44	Lost 6 April 45
DD802 *Gregory*	Seattle-Tacoma	31 Aug 43	8 May 44	29 July 44	Stricken 1 May 66
DD803 *Little*	Seattle-Tacoma	13 Sept 43	22 May 44	19 Aug 44	Lost 3 May 45
DD804 *Rooks*	Seattle-Tacoma	27 Oct 43	6 June 44	2 Sept 44	To Chile 26 July 62

Cancelled: *DD523–525, 542, 543, 548, 549, DD452 Percival* and *DD482 Watson*

Below: *La Vallette* (DD448). Note lack of radar and only four 20mm guns fitted in this August 1942 shot. (USN)

Design The *Fletcher* class, perhaps the most famous of all US destroyers (and certainly the most numerous) were the first American destroyers to be designed free from Treaty restrictions. Consideration of their design characteristics had begun barely a month after the outbreak of the European war, but quite obviously, too early for that to affect the initial studies. However, it was to be almost two years before the first ship would be commissioned and, in the meantime, a good deal had been learned from both British and US experience at war. In early discussions, there was a strong hope that size could be reduced and hence greater numbers purchased, but this demand soon proved impossible and the upwards spiral of destroyer size continued. As usual, there was also considerable discussion as to the precise role of a destroyer and whether guns or torpedoes were to be its main offensive weapon. The first proposals envisaged a five 5-inch gun ship of not more than 1,600 tons carrying two quintuple banks of tubes, 28 depth-charges and two throwers at a trial speed of 36 knots. Four or six .5in machine-guns were the only AA outfit requested. The early studies, about six in number, were based on the previous *Benson/Gleaves* and *Sims* designs, but by the end of 1939 size was already growing and by the turn of the year three new proposals were under consideration which all reverted to the 'flush-deck' concept for extra strength. Much of the increase in displacement was due to demands for protective plating to bridge, command and machinery spaces. This increase in size did, however, permit an increase in the AA battery and it was proposed to fit a director-controlled quadruple 1.1-inch gun as well as four .5-inch machine-guns. Installed power was to be increased to 60,000shp (with machinery arranged on the unit principle) for a trial speed of 38 knots.

Compared to the previous *Benson/Gleaves* type, the new *Fletchers* displaced almost 1,000 tons more, were 28 feet longer and most importantly, had their beam increased by more than 3½ feet. Thus, while their initial AA outfit could be described as very weak for a ship of this size, the reserve of weight and stability existed to allow a phenomenal growth in CRA battery in a short time, as will be seen.

Orders were placed for the first 24 ships on 28 June and 1 July 1940 (*DD445–451, 465–481*). Further orders were placed on 9 September for *DD498–502, DD507–541, DD544–547, DD550–597* and *DD542/543, DD548/549*. In December though, seven were cancelled *DD523–525, 542/543* and *548/549*, but on the 16th, six more were ordered *DD629–631* and *642–644*. Two ships, *Percival* and *Watson*, were to be built to explore new machinery concepts, very extreme boiler pressures in the former case and diesel propulsion in the latter, but neither was ever laid down. Fifty-six more repeat ships were ordered when the USA entered the war, *DD649–691* and *DD792–804*.

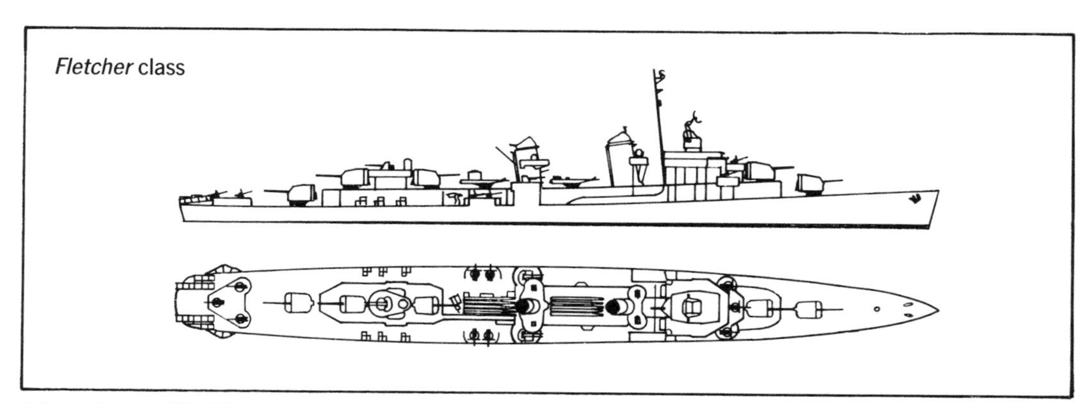

Below: *Isherwood* (DD520), armed with six 40mm and ten 20mm guns. Note also the depth-charge arrangements. (IWM)

By 1941, the experiences of the war at sea in the Mediterranean and North Sea had clearly demonstrated the dangers of air attack and the consequent necessity for a good AA outfit. A spin-off from this was the need for a redesigned bridge to allow all-round vision; hitherto, US destroyers had had a closed pilot house, only the wings being open, unlike British practice in which the ship was conned by the officer of the watch from an open upper bridge. This new-style bridge was incorporated in late-production ships from about *DD518* and in all the FY42 programme ships *DD649–691* and *DD792–804*. Only a few very early ships received the 1.1-inch guns and few if any only .5-inch MGs as both twin 40mm and single 20mm guns were available in numbers by the time these destroyers began to complete. By late 1941, the designed AA outfit for the *Fletchers* had been revised to a twin 40mm (in lieu of the 1.1-inch) and six 20mm. Weight would be compensated by the lowering of the after superstructure and the removal of protective plating to bridge areas. Later units had a lower director trunk for a further weight economy, which was to allow the fitting of a pair of 40mm twins.

Modifications These were concerned solely with augmenting the AA outfit. Ships with closed bridges received one 20mm atop it, another forward of the bridge and two more on the forward shelter deck. Four more were fitted in the waist, making eight 20mm guns in all. Some ships carried a second twin 40mm on the quarter deck between the depth-charge racks, but this was not popular and by 1943 it was being replaced by a trio of 20mm guns. By the mid-war period, ships were being converted to or completed with three twin 40mm (one aft, two abreast the after funnel) and ten or eleven 20mm guns (authorized in February 1943). In June 1943, the standard authorized CRA battery was raised to five twin 40mm, the extra pair being fitted in lieu of the 20mm guns on the forward shelter deck, and many ships completed to this standard. For completed units, these refits were carried out wherever possible and at any one time there were, of course, variations. However, by the end of 1944, 157 out of 166 operational *Fletcher*s had five twin 40mm and seven 20mm.

The Kamikaze refit involved the substitution of the midships twin 40mm by a pair of quadruple 40mm with GFCS 63 blind-fire control, converting the four waist 20mm guns to twin mountings (for a total of eleven) and the landing of the forward bank of tubes as compensation. At the end of the war, however, only 57 ships had received this refit and of these, *Leutze* and *Newcomb* (both still repairing Kamikaze damage) were not yet finished. In fact, both of these ships were stricken unrepaired.

One unusual modification was the requirement for six of the class to be completed with aircraft and catapult. This involved the landing of No. 3 gun and the after tubes to allow room for the catapult. Only one twin 40mm was carried (on the quarter deck) and the 20mm outfit was restricted to seven single guns. Of the conversions ordered (*DD476–481*), only *Halford, Pringle* and *Stevens* were so fitted because the experiment proved unsuccessful and the equipment was soon landed.

Service The sheer number of this class precludes any detailed description of their service careers apart from some comments on their successes and losses. In contrast to the *Benson/Gleaves* destroyers, whose service was predominantly Atlantic based, the *Fletcher*s were used in the Pacific. They saw action in almost every operation from the autumn of 1942 onwards and eighteen were sunk in action. *De Haven* was the first loss, sunk by air attack off Savo Island while escorting landing craft to Tulagi. *Strong* was torpedoed while bombarding Bairoko Harbour New Georgia by the Japanese destroyers *Mochitsuki, Mikatsuki* and *Hamakaze*. *Chevalier*, damaged by depth-charge explosions on the occasion of the loss of *Strong*, was herself sunk in October by a torpedo from the destroyer *Yugumo* off Vella Lavella. The final loss of the year was *Brownson* sunk by air attack off Cape Gloucester, New Britain in December. Ten months passed before the next ship was sunk. This was *Johnston*, sunk in an heroic battle with the main Japanese Fleet at the Battle of Leyte Gulf together with her sister *Hoel* as they successfully defended the escort carriers in their charge. *Spence*, low on fuel and riding high at low draught, was one of three destroyers lost in a typhoon off Luzon when her steering jammed. Only 23 of her crew could be rescued in the mountainous seas. *Halligan* was mined off Okinawa, but the most serious losses in that campaign were caused by devastating waves of Kamikaze attacks. *Colhoun, Luce, Little, Morrison, Longshaw, William D. Porter* and *Callaghan* were all sunk off Okinawa by this weapon. *Bache, Braine, Bryant, Bennett, C. J. Badger, Cassin, Young, Evans**, Franks, Gregory, Haggard**, Hutchins**, Hazelwood, Hudson, Isherwood, Kimberly, Kidd, Leutze**, Murray, Mullany, McDermut, Newcomb**, Sigsbee, Stanly, Thatcher** and *Twiggs* were all very badly damaged, some* beyond repair. Several others were less seriously damaged.

On the credit side, *Fletcher*-class destroyers were directly or partly responsible for the destruction of ten Japanese destroyers (*Hatsukaze, Makinami, Matsu, Hinoki, Michishio, Nowaki, Onami, Yugure* and *Yamagumo*) and 21 Japanese submarines (*I2, 8, 10, 18, 38, 39, 40, 56, 175, 176, 182* and *Ro39, 41, 49, 56, 101, 105, 107, 114, 115* and *117*).

Post-war, these destroyers were retained in the active fleet for a period then saw service in Korea. Many were subsequently sold to other nations and some are extant today.

Below: *Nicholas* (DD449) showing the early *Fletcher*-design with the tall after deck-house, topped by a quad 1.1in gun. (USN)

Below: *Hoel* (DD533) on 25 October 1943, at San Francisco. (USN)

533

ALLEN M. SUMNER CLASS

Ship	Builder	Laid Down	Launched	Commissioned	Fate
DD692 *Allen M. Sumner*	Federal Sbdg. Co.	7 July 43	15 Dec 43	26 Jan 44	Sold for breaking up 13 Nov 74
DD693 *Moale*	Federal Sbdg. Co.	5 Aug 43	16 Jan 44	28 Feb 44	Sold for breaking up 13 Nov 74
DD694 *Ingraham*	Federal Sbdg. Co.	4 Aug 43	16 Jan 44	10 Mar 44	To Greece 15 June 71
DD695 *Cooper*	Federal Sbdg. Co.	30 Aug 43	9 Feb 44	27 Mar 44	Lost 3 Dec 44
DD696 *English*	Federal Sbdg. Co.	19 Oct 43	27 Feb 44	4 May 44	To Taiwan 11 Aug 70
DD697 *Charles S. Sperry*	Federal Sbdg. Co.	19 Oct 43	13 Mar 44	17 May 44	To Chile 8 Jan 74
DD698 *Ault*	Federal Sbdg. Co.	15 Nov 43	26 Mar 44	31 May 44	Stricken 16 July 73
DD699 *Waldron*	Federal Sbdg. Co.	16 Nov 43	26 Mar 44	8 June 44	To Colombia 30 Oct 73
DD700 *Haynsworth*	Federal Sbdg. Co.	16 Dec 43	15 April 44	22 June 44	To Taiwan 12 May 70
DD701 *John W. Weeks*	Federal Sbdg. Co.	17 Jan 44	21 May 44	21 July 44	Stricken 12 Aug 70
DD702 *Hank*	Federal Sbdg. Co.	17 Jan 44	21 May 44	28 Aug 44	To Argentina 1 July 72
DD703 *Wallace L. Lind*	Federal Sbdg. Co.	14 Feb 44	14 June 44	8 Sept 44	To S. Korea Dec 1973
DD704 *Borie*	Federal Sbdg. Co.	29 Feb 44	4 July 44	21 Sept 44	To Argentina 1 July 72
DD705 *Compton*	Federal Sbdg. Co.	29 Mar 44	17 Sept 44	4 Nov 44	To Brazil 27 Sept 72
DD706 *Gainard*	Federal Sbdg. Co.	28 Mar 44	17 Sept 44	23 Nov 44	Sold for breaking up 20 Mar 74
DD707 *Soley*	Federal Sbdg. Co.	18 April 44	8 Sept 44	7 Dec 44	Stricken 13 Feb 70
DD708 *Harlan R. Dickson*	Federal Sbdg. Co.	23 May 44	17 Dec 44	17 Feb 45	Stricken 1 July 72
DD709 *Hugh Purvis*	Federal Sbdg. Co.	23 May 44	17 Dec 44	1 Mar 45	To Turkey 15 Feb 72
DD722 *Barton*	Bath Iron Works	24 May 43	10 Oct 43	30 Dec 43	Stricken 1 Oct 68
DD723 *Walke*	Bath Iron Works	7 June 43	27 Oct 43	21 Jan 44	Sold for breaking up 19 Mar 75
DD724 *Laffey*	Bath Iron Works	28 June 43	21 Nov 43	8 Feb 44	Expended 29 Mar 77
DD725 *O'Brien*	Bath Iron Works	12 July 43	8 Dec 43	25 Feb 44	Stricken 18 Feb 72
DD726 *Meredith*	Bath Iron Works	26 July 43	21 Dec 43	14 Mar 44	Lost 9 June 44
DD727 *De Haven*	Bath Iron Works	9 Aug 43	9 Jan 44	31 Mar 44	To S. Korea Dec 1973
DD728 *Mansfield*	Bath Iron Works	28 Aug 43	29 Jan 44	14 April 44	To Argentina 1974
DD729 *Lyman K. Swenson*	Bath Iron Works	11 Sept 43	12 Feb 44	2 May 44	Stricken 1 April 74
DD730 *Collett*	Bath Iron Works	11 Oct 43	5 Mar 44	16 May 44	To Argentina April 1974
DD731 *Maddox*	Bath Iron Works	28 Oct 43	19 Mar 44	2 June 44	To Taiwan 6 July 72

ALLEN M. SUMNER CLASS

Ship	Builder	Laid Down
DD732 *Hyman*	Bath Iron Works	22 Nov 43
DD733 *Mannert L. Abele*	Bath Iron Works	12 Sept 43
DD734 *Purdy*	Bath Iron Works	22 Dec 43
DD741 *Drexler*	Bath Iron Works	24 April 44
DD744 *Blue*	Bethlehem, Staten Is.	30 June 43
DD745 *Brush*	Bethlehem, Staten Is.	30 July 43
DD746 *Taussig*	Bethlehem, Staten Is.	30 Aug 43
DD747 *Samuel N. Moore*	Bethlehem, Staten Is.	30 Sept 43
DD748 *Harry E. Hubbard*	Bethlehem, Staten Is.	30 Oct 43
DD752 *Alfred A. Cunningham*	Bethlehem, Staten Is.	23 Feb 44
DD753 *John R. Pierce*	Bethlehem, Staten Is.	24 Mar 44
DD754 *Frank S. Evans*	Bethlehem, Staten Is.	21 April 44
DD755 *John A. Bole*	Bethlehem, Staten Is.	20 May 44
DD756 *Beatty*	Bethlehem, Staten Is.	4 June 44
DD757 *Putnam*	Bethlehem, S. Francisco	11 July 43
DD758 *Strong*	Bethlehem, S. Francisco	25 July 43
DD759 *Lofberg*	Bethlehem, S. Francisco	4 Nov 43
DD760 *John W. Thomason*	Bethlehem, S. Francisco	21 Nov 43
DD761 *Buck*	Bethlehem, S. Francisco	1 Feb 44
DD762 *Henley*	Bethlehem, S. Francisco	8 Feb 44
DD770 *Lowry*	Bethlehem, San Pedro	1 Aug 43
DD774 *Hugh W. Hadley*	Bethlehem, San Pedro	6 Feb 44
DD775 *Willard Keith*	Bethlehem, San Pedro	5 Mar 44

Displacement: 2,610tons/2,651tonnes (standard); 3,218tons/3,269tonnes (full load).
Length: 376ft 6in/114.76m (oa); 369ft/112.48m (wl).
Beam: 40ft 10in/12.45m.
Draught: 14ft 2in/4.32m (mean).
Machinery: four Babcock & Wilcox boilers; 2-shaft G.E.C. geared turbines.
Performance: 60,000shp; 36.5kts.
Bunkerage: 504tons/512tonnes.

continued

Launched	Commissioned	Fate
8 April 44	16 June 44	Scrapped 1970
23 April 44	4 July 44	Lost 12 April 45
7 May 44	18 July 44	Sold for breaking up 29 May 74
3 Sept 44	14 Nov 44	Lost 28 May 45
28 Nov 43	20 Mar 44	Stricken 1 Feb 74
28 Dec 43	17 April 44	To Taiwan 2 Dec 69
25 Jan 44	20 May 44	To Taiwan 6 May 74
23 Feb 44	24 June 44	To Taiwan 2 Dec 69
24 Mar 44	22 July 44	Scrapped 1970
3 Aug 44	23 Nov 44	Stricken 1 Dec 74
1 Sept 44	30 Dec 44	Sold for breaking up 6 Nov 74
3 Oct 44	3 Feb 45	Casualty 2 June 69
1 Nov 44	3 Mar 45	Stricken 1 April 74
30 Nov 44	31 Mar 45	Stricken Aug 1972
26 Mar 44	12 Oct 44	Sold for breaking up 11 June 74
22 April 44	8 Mar 45	To Brazil 31 Oct 73
12 Aug 44	26 April 45	Stricken 1 April 74
30 Sept 44	11 Oct 45	To Taiwan 6 May 74
11 Mar 45	28 June 46	To Brazil 16 July 73
8 April 45	8 Oct 46	Sold for breaking up 11 June 74
6 Feb 44	23 July 44	To Brazil 29 Oct 73
16 July 44	25 Nov 44	Scrapped 1947
29 Aug 44	27 Dec 44	To Colombia 1 July 72

Range: 3,300nm at 20kts.
Guns: six 5in (3×2); twelve 40mm (2×4, 2×2); eleven 20mm.
Torpedoes: ten 21in (2×5). (Not in DM conversions).
Mines: 120 (DM conversions only).
Complement: 336.

ALLEN M. SUMNER CLASS—*continued*

Ship	Builder	Laid Down	Launched	Commissioned	Fate
DD776 *James C. Owens*	Bethlehem, San Pedro	4 Sept 44	1 Oct 44	17 Feb 45	To Brazil 16 July 73
DD777 *Zellars*	Todd-Pacific, Seattle	24 Dec 43	19 July 44	25 Oct 44	To Iran 19 Mar 71
DD778 *Massey*	Todd-Pacific, Seattle	14 Jan 44	19 Aug 44	24 Nov 44	Sold for breaking up 13 Nov 74
DD779 *Douglas H. Fox*	Todd-Pacific, Seattle	31 Jan 44	30 Sept 44	26 Dec 44	To Chile 8 Jan 74
DD780 *Stormes*	Todd-Pacific, Seattle	25 Feb 44	4 Nov 44	27 Jan 45	To Iran 16 Feb 71
DD781 *Robert K. Huntington*	Todd-Pacific, Seattle	29 Feb 44	5 Dec 44	3 Mar 45	To Venezuela 31 Oct 73
DD857 *Bristol*	Bethlehem, San Pedro	5 Mar 44	20 Oct 44	17 Mar 45	To Taiwan 22 Sept 69

ALLEN M. SUMNER CLASS (Minelayer Conversions)

Ship	Builder	Laid Down	Launched	Commissioned	Fate
DM23 *Robert H. Smith* (ex-*DD735*)	Bath Iron Works	10 Jan 44	25 May 44	4 Aug 44	Stricken 26 Feb 71
DM24 *Thomas E. Fraser* (ex-*DD736*)	Bath Iron Works	31 Jan 44	10 June 44	22 Aug 44	Stricken 1 Nov 70
DM25 *Shannon* (ex-*DD737*)	Bath Iron Works	14 Feb 44	24 June 44	8 Sept 44	Stricken 1 Nov 70
DM26 *Harry F. Bauer* (ex-*DD738*)	Bath Iron Works	6 Mar 44	9 July 44	22 Sept 44	Stricken 15 Aug 71
DM27 *Adams* (ex-*DD739*)	Bath Iron Works	20 Mar 44	23 July 44	10 Oct 44	Stricken 1 Dec 70
DM28 *Tolman* (ex-*DD740*)	Bath Iron Works	10 April 44	13 Aug 44	27 Oct 44	Stricken 1 Dec 70
DM29 *Henry A. Wiley* (ex-*DD749*)	Bethlehem, Staten Is.	28 Nov 43	21 April 44	31 Aug 44	Stricken 15 Oct 70
DM30 *Shea* (ex-*DD750*)	Bethlehem, Staten Is.	28 Dec 43	20 May 44	30 Sept 44	Stricken 1 Sept 73
DM31 *J. William Ditter* (ex-*DD751*)	Bethlehem, Staten Is.	25 Jan 44	4 July 44	28 Oct 44	Scrapped 1946
DM32 *Lindsey* (ex-*DD771*)	Bethlehem, San Pedro	12 Sept 43	5 Mar 44	20 Aug 44	Stricken 1 Oct 70
DM33 *Gwin* (ex-*DD772*)	Bethlehem, San Pedro	30 Oct 43	9 April 44	30 Sept 44	To Turkey 22 Oct 71
DM34 *Aaron Ward* (ex-*DD773*)	Bethlehem, San Pedro	12 Dec 43	5 May 44	28 Oct 44	Scrapped 1946

Technical details as destroyer versions except where noted.

Design Criticism of the high silhouette of the *Gleaves*-class destroyers, together with demands for a yet more powerful destroyer, led to the consideration of the adoption of a twin 5-inch mounting for destroyer use. These demands ran in parallel with the development of the *Fletcher* class, but that design could not accommodate the twin mounting. Twin mountings were not new to US destroyers as the *Porter* and *Somers* class testified, but hitherto no suitable dual-purpose mount had been available and it had become accepted in the USN that DP was a vital facility. By 1939, enclosed DP base ring mountings were in production for numerous classes of ship, and given suitable excess production could also be allocated for destroyers. The twin mounting did raise a problem in that it was incapable of being trained by hand, and sufficient emergency electrical power would have to be incorporated to ensure no major failure of the main armament in case of action damage.

As usual, many sketch designs were considered and debated during the period 1940 to 1942 before a six-gun, ten-tube sketch was agreed upon. This was also to carry two twin 40mm and four 20mm guns. An unusual feature was the ability of the after 5-inch twin mounting to fire dead ahead, over masts and bridge. To accommodate the twin 5-inch mountings, beam had to be increased over that of *Fletcher* by 1 foot 2 inches, but length was not altered

Above: *Alan M. Sumner* (DD692) in February 1944. (USN) **Below:** *Hank* (DD702) at completion. (USN)

Below: *Gearing* (DD710) in May 1945. (USN)

(despite some overcrowding) in order not to lose manoeuvrability. To this end, twin rudders were also fitted. The main machinery operated at reduced pressures compared with that of *Fletcher*, but generating capacity was increased to 800kW plus 200kW diesel standbys to power the twin mountings. Displacement rose by nearly 200 tons and as a result, speed fell by more than a knot. In practice, speed fell considerably, for *Barton* only reached 34.2 knots on 2,880 tons and *Moale* 33.6 knots on 2,865 tons.

Sixty-nine destroyers of this type, known as the *Sumner* class, were ordered on 7 August 1942 and one more (*Bristol*) completed as a *Sumner* although ordered on 14 June 1943 as a *Gearing*.

Experiences in the Solomon Islands had demonstrated the value of minelaying for offensive purposes, but only old 'flush-deckers' were available for this purpose. Admiral Nimitz recommended that a dozen *Sumner*s be converted for this task on 24 June 1944. Both banks of tubes, three 20mm guns and two depth-charge throwers had to be landed to compensate the additional weight of 120 mines. None actually operated in this role.

Barton DD722, was the first to complete, at the end of 1943 and was immediately subject to criticism. In particular, the low bridge was extremely cramped because of the director base as were the living quarters due to the large increase in on-board electronic equipment. Little could be done about the internal congestion, but the bridge structure was modified on completed units and also incorporated in ships still under construction. After a number of the class had entered service, complaints began to come in from sea, concerning damage to the forward guns in heavy weather. It was felt that the design was bow heavy and the ships did not lift themselves from the sea as easily as did the *Fletcher*s. Investigations by the Naval Staff found much of this to be based on rumour and steps were taken to whiten their reputation! Nevertheless, they were very wet forward.

Modifications In April 1943, an extra pair of twin 40mm were authorized to be fitted on large box sponsons each side of the bridge and one more 20mm was added. Later still, the twin 40mm abaft the second funnel were replaced by quadruple mountings, giving a CRA outfit of twelve 40mm (2× 4, 2×2) and eleven 20mm guns. Finally, the after bank of tubes was replaced by a third 40mm quadruple mounting and the 20mm outfit increased to ten twin 20mm. The latter were fitted four on the forward shelter deck below the bridge, two on a sponson on the port side of the after funnel, one to starboard abreast the middle quad 40mm and three on the quarter deck. The usual comprehensive radar suite was fitted.

Service As the first ship did not complete until the end of 1943, the *Sumner*s missed the risky operations at Guadalcanal and the Solomons in the main, but saw service in the vast US offensive thrust towards Japan in the Central Pacific. Three units, however, saw no active duty during the war because they were not completed in time (*John W. Thompson*, *Buck* and *Henley*). One division, DesDiv 119, part of DesRon 60, consisting of *Barton, Walke, Laffey, O'Brien* and *Meredith* were sent to Europe for the Normandy landings, but the remainder of the class served in Pacific waters. *Meredith* in fact became an early loss when she struck a mine off Normandy and was later sunk by German aircraft. The division was later sent to the Pacific.

In the Pacific, *Sumner*-class destroyers served in the Philippines, where *Sumner* herself, with *Moale* and *Cooper*, sank the Japanese destroyer *Kuwa* off Ormoc, but not before the Japanese ship had torpedoed and sunk *Cooper*. It was the Okinawa campaign which exacted the greatest toll however, as it did with the *Fletcher*s. *Mannert L. Abele* was hit by a Kamikaze and then a Baka bomb, sinking very quickly. *Drexler* too was hit by two Kamikaze and sank, while eight others, *O'Brien, Hyman, Haynsworth, Purdy, Laffey, Hugh W. Handley, D. H. Fox* and *Stormes* were badly damaged. Of these, only *Hugh W. Hadley* was judged beyond repair, despite the fact that *Laffey* had been hit by no less than six Kamikaze aircraft.

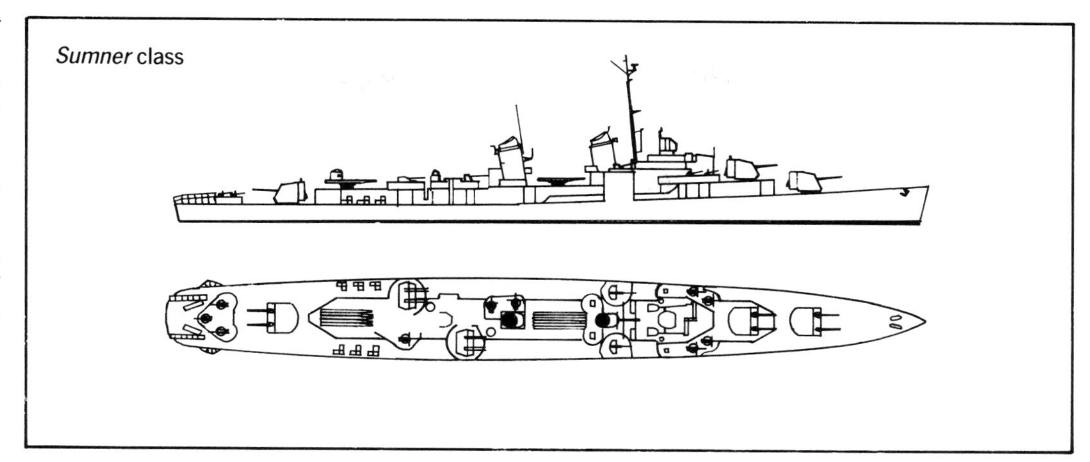

Above: *Hyman* (DD732) on 20 July 1945. Her after tubes have been supplanted by 40mm guns and associated directors, Mk 63 radar controlled the foremost two quads. (USN)
Below: *Lyman K. Swenson* (DD729) in January 1946, as a ten TT unit. (USN)

GEARING CLASS

Ship	Builder	Laid Down	Launched	Commissioned	Fate
DD710 *Gearing*	Federal Sbdg. Co.	10 Aug 44	18 Feb 45	31 May 45	Sold for breaking up 6 Nov 74
DD711 *Eugene A. Greene*	Federal Sbdg. Co.	17 Aug 44	18 Mar 45	8 June 45	To Spain 31 Aug 72
DD712 *Gyatt*	Federal Sbdg. Co.	7 Sept 44	15 April 45	2 July 45	Stricken 22 Oct 69
DD713 *Kenneth D. Bailey*	Federal Sbdg. Co.	21 Sept 44	17 June 45	31 July 45	To Iran 13 Jan 75
DD714 *William R. Rush*	Federal Sbdg. Co.	19 Oct 44	8 July 45	21 Sept 45	To S. Korea 1 July 78
DD715 *William W. Wood*	Federal Sbdg. Co.	22 Nov 44	29 July 45	23 Nov 45	Stricken 1 Dec 76
DD716 *Wiltsie*	Federal Sbdg. Co.	13 Mar 45	31 Aug 45	11 Jan 46	To Pakistan 29 April 77
DD717 *Theodore E. Chandler*	Federal Sbdg. Co.	23 April 45	20 Oct 45	21 Mar 46	Sold for breaking up 1 Dec 75
DD718 *Hamner*	Federal Sbdg. Co.	25 April 45	24 Nov 45	11 July 46	To Taiwan 17 Dec 80
DD719 *Epperson*	Federal Sbdg. Co.	20 June 45	22 Dec 45	18 Mar 49	To Pakistan 29 April 77
DD720 *Castle*	Federal Sbdg. Co.	11 July 45	1946 (cancelled 11 Dec 45)		Sold for breaking up 29 Aug 55
DD721 *Woodrow R. Thompson*	Federal Sbdg. Co.	1 Aug 45	1946 (cancelled 11 Dec 45)		Sold for breaking up 29 Aug 55
DD742 *Frank Knox*	Bath Iron Works	8 May 44	17 Sept 44	11 Dec 44	To Greece 30 Jan 71
DD743 *Southerland*	Bath Iron Works	27 May 44	5 Oct 44	22 Dec 44	To Equador
DD763 *William C. Lawe*	Bethlehem, S. Francisco	12 Mar 44	21 May 45	18 Dec 46	To Uraguay
DD764 *Lloyd Thomas*	Bethlehem, S. Francisco	26 Mar 44	5 Oct 45	21 Mar 47	To Taiwan 12 Oct 72
DD765 *Keppler*	Bethlehem, S. Francisco	23 April 44	24 June 46	23 May 47	To Turkey 30 June 72
DD766 *Lansdale*	Bethlehem, S. Francisco	2 April 44	20 Dec 46	(cancelled 7 Jan 46)	Stricken 9 June 58
DD767 *Seymour D. Owens*	Bethlehem, S. Francisco	3 April 44	24 Feb 47	(cancelled 7 Jan 46)	Stricken 9 June 58
DD768 *Hoel*	Bethlhem, S. Francisco	21 April 44	–	–	Cancelled 13 Sept 46
DD769 *Abner Read*	Bethlehem, S. Francisco	21 May 44	–	–	Cancelled 13 Sept 46
DD782 *Rowan*	Todd-Pacific, Seattle	25 Mar 44	29 Dec 44	31 Mar 45	To Taiwan 18 Dec 75
DD783 *Gurke*	Todd-Pacific, Seattle	1 July 44	15 Feb 45	12 May 45	To Greece 17 Mar 77
DD784 *McKean*	Todd-Pacific, Seattle	15 Sept 44	31 Mar 45	9 June 45	To Turkey 12 Oct 82
DD785 *Henderson*	Todd-Pacific, Seattle	27 Oct 44	28 May 45	4 Aug 45	To Pakistan 30 Sept 80
DD786 *Richard B. Anderson*	Todd-Pacific, Seattle	1 Dec 44	7 July 45	28 Sept 45	To Taiwan 10 June 77
DD787 *James E. Kyes*	Todd-Pacific, Seattle	27 Dec 44	4 Aug 45	8 Feb 46	To Taiwan 18 April 73
DD788 *Hollister*	Todd-Pacific, Seattle	18 Jan 45	9 Oct 45	29 Mar 46	Stricken 31 Aug 79

GEARING CLASS—*continue*

Ship	Builder	Laid Down
DD789 *Eversole*	Todd-Pacific, Seattle	21 Mar 45
DD790 *Shelton*	Todd-Pacific, Seattle	31 May 45
DD791 *Seaman*	Todd-Pacific, Seattle	10 July 45
DD805 *Chevalier*	Bath Iron Works	12 June 44
DD806 *Higbee*	Bath Iron Works	26 June 44
DD807 *Benner*	Bath Iron Works	10 July 44
DD808 *Dennis J. Buckley*	Bath Iron Works	24 July 44
DD817 *Corry*	Consolidated, Orange	5 April 45
DD818 *New*	Consolidated, Orange	14 April 45
DD819 *Holder*	Consolidated, Orange	23 April 45
DD820 *Rich*	Consolidated, Orange	16 May 45
DD821 *Johnston*	Consolidated, Orange	5 June 45
DD822 *Robert H. McCard*	Consolidated, Orange	20 June 45
DD823 *Samuel B. Roberts*	Consolidated, Orange	27 June 45
DD824 *Basilone*	Consolidated, Orange	7 July 45
DD825 *Carpenter*	Consolidated, Orange	30 July 45
DD826 *Agerholm*	Bath Iron Works	19 Sept 45
DD827 *Robert A. Owens*	Bath Iron Works	29 Oct 45
DD828 *Timmerman*	Bath Iron Works	1 Oct 45
DD829 *Myles C. Fox*	Bath Iron Works	14 Aug 44
DD830 *Everett F. Larson*	Bath Iron Works	4 Sept 44
DD831 *Goodrich*	Bath Iron Works	18 Sept 44
DD832 *Hanson*	Bath Iron Works	7 Oct 44
DD833 *Herbert J. Thomas*	Bath Iron Works	30 Oct 44
DD834 *Turner*	Bath Iron Works	13 Nov 44
DD835 *Charles P. Cecil*	Bath Iron Works	2 Dec 44
DD836 *George K. Mackenzie*	Bath Iron Works	21 Dec 44
DD837 *Sarsfield*	Bath Iron works	15 Jan 45

GEARING CLASS—*continued*

Launched	Commissioned	Fate
8 Jan 46	10 May 46	To Turkey 11 July 73
8 Mar 46	21 June 46	To Taiwan 18 April 73
20 Mar 46	(cancelled 7 July 46)	Scrapped 1962
29 Oct 44	9 Jan 45	To S. Korea 5 July 72
12 Nov 44	27 Jan 45	Stricken 15 July 79
30 Nov 44	13 Feb 45	Sold for breaking up 19 Mar 75
20 Dec 44	2 Mar 45	Sold for breaking up 28 Mar 74
28 July 45	26 Feb 46	To Greece May 1981
18 Aug 45	4 April 46	To S. Korea 23 Feb 77
25 Aug 45	17 May 46	To Equador 1 Sept 78
5 Oct 45	2 July 46	Stricken 15 Dec 77
19 Oct 45	22 Aug 46	To Taiwan 27 Feb 81
9 Nov 45	22 Oct 46	Stricken 1 Oct 80
30 Nov 45	19 Dec 46	Stricken 2 Nov 70
22 Dec 45	21 July 49	Stricken 1 Nov 77
28 Dec 45	15 Dec 49	To Turkey 27 Feb 81
30 Feb 46	20 June 46	Stricken 1 Dec 78
15 July 46	5 Nov 49	Stricken 1 Oct 79
19 May 51	26 Sept 52	Scrapped 1959
13 Jan 45	20 Mar 45	To Greece 2 Aug 80
28 Jan 45	6 April 45	To S. Korea 23 Feb 77
25 Feb 45	24 April 45	Sold for breaking up Aug 1977
11 Mar 45	11 May 45	To Taiwan 18 April 73
25 Mar 45	29 May 45	To Taiwan 1 Feb 74
8 April 45	12 June 45	Stricken 26 June 69
22 April 45	29 June 45	Stricken 1 Oct 69
13 May 45	13 July 45	Expended 17 Oct 76
27 May 45	31 July 45	To Taiwan 1 Oct 77

Ship	Builder	Laid Down	Launched	Commissioned	Fate
DD838 *Ernest G. Small*	Bath Iron Works	30 Jan 45	14 June 45	21 Aug 45	To Taiwan 13 April 71
DD839 *Power*	Bath Iron Works	26 Feb 45	30 June 45	13 Sept 45	To Taiwan 1 Oct 77
DD840 *Glennon*	Bath Iron Works	12 Mar 45	14 July 45	4 Oct 45	Stricken 1 Oct 76
DD841 *Noa*	Bath Iron Works	26 Mar 45	30 July 45	1 Nov 45	To Spain 31 Oct 73
DD842 *Fiske*	Bath Iron Works	9 April 45	8 Sept 45	28 Nov 45	To Turkey 1980
DD843 *Warrington*	Bath Iron Works	23 April 45	27 Sept 45	20 Dec 45	Stricken 1 Oct 72
DD844 *Perry*	Bath Iron Works	14 May 45	25 Oct 45	17 Jan 46	Sold for breaking up 11 June 74
DD845 *Baussell*	Bath Iron Works	28 May 45	19 Nov 45	7 Feb 46	Stricken 30 May 78
DD846 *Ozbourn*	Bath Iron Works	16 June 45	22 Dec 45	5 Mar 46	Sold for breaking up 1 Dec 75
DD847 *Robert L. Wilson*	Bath Iron Works	2 July 45	5 Jan 46	28 Mar 46	Stricken 30 Sept 74
DD848 *Witek*	Bath Iron Works	16 July 45	2 Feb 46	25 April 46	Stricken 17 Sept 68
DD849 *Richard E. Kraus*	Bath Iron Works	31 July 45	2 Mar 46	23 May 46	To S. Korea 30 Oct 72
DD850 *Joseph P. Kennedy Jr.*	Bethlehem, Quincy	2 April 45	26 July 46	14 Dec 46	Stricken 2 July 73
DD851 *Rupertus*	Bethlehem, Quincy	2 May 45	21 Sept 45	8 Mar 46	To Greece 10 July 73
DD852 *Leonard F. Mason*	Bethlehem, Quincy	6 Aug 45	4 Jan 46	28 June 46	To Taiwan 10 Mar 78
DD853 *Charles H. Roan*	Bethlehem, Quincy	27 Sept 45	15 Mar 46	12 Sept 46	To Turkey 21 Sept 73
DD858 *Fred T. Berry*	Bethlehem, San Pedro	16 July 44	28 Jan 45	12 May 45	Stricken 15 Sept 70
DD859 *Norris*	Bethlehem, San Pedro	29 Aug 44	25 Feb 45	9 June 45	To Turkey 7 July 74
DD860 *McCaffery*	Bethlehem, San Pedro	1 Oct 44	12 April 45	26 July 45	Sold for breaking up 29 May 74
DD861 *Harwood*	Bethlehem, San Pedro	29 Oct 44	22 May 45	28 Sept 45	To Turkey 17 Dec 71
DD862 *Vogelgesang*	Bethlehem, Staten Is.	3 Aug 44	15 Jan 45	28 April 45	To Mexico 24 Feb 82
DD863 *Steinaker*	Bethlehem, Staten Is.	1 Sept 44	13 Feb 45	26 May 45	To Mexico 24 Feb 82
DD864 *Harold J. Ellison*	Bethlehem, Staten Is.	3 Oct 44	14 Mar 45	23 June 45	To Pakistan 1 Aug 83
DD865 *Charles R. Ware*	Bethlehem, Staten Is.	1 Nov 44	12 April 45	21 July 45	Stricken 12 Dec 74
DD866 *Cone*	Bethlehem, Staten Is.	30 Nov 44	10 May 45	17 Aug 45	To Pakistan 1 Oct 82
DD867 *Stribling*	Bethlehem, Staten Is.	15 Jan 45	8 June 45	29 Sept 45	Stricken 1 July 76
DD868 *Brownson*	Bethlehem, Staten Is.	13 Feb 45	7 July 45	17 Nov 45	Stricken 30 Sept 76
DD869 *Arnold J. Isbell*	Bethlehem, Staten Is.	13 Mar 45	6 Aug 45	5 Jan 46	To Greece 4 Dec 73

GEARING CLASS—*continued*

Ship	Builder	Laid Down	Launched	Commissioned	Fate
DD870 *Fechteler*	Bethlehem, Staten Is.	12 April 45	19 Sept 45	2 Mar 46	Stricken 11 Sept 70
DD871 *Damato*	Bethlehem, Staten Is.	10 May 45	21 Nov 45	27 April 46	To Pakistan 30 Sept 80
DD872 *Forrest Royal*	Bethlehem, Staten Is.	8 June 45	17 Jan 46	28 June 46	To Turkey 27 Mar 71
DD873 *Hawkins*	Consolidated, Orange	14 May 44	7 Oct 44	10 Feb 45	Stricken 1 Oct 79
DD874 *Duncan*	Consolidated, Orange	22 May 44	27 Oct 44	25 Feb 45	Stricken 1 Sept 73
DD875 *Henry W. Tucker*	Consolidated, Orange	29 May 44	8 Nov 44	12 Mar 45	To Brazil 3 Dec 73
DD876 *Rogers*	Consolidated, Orange	3 June 44	20 Nov 44	26 Mar 45	To S. Korea 25 July 81
DD877 *Perkins*	Consolidated, Orange	19 June 44	7 Dec 44	5 April 45	To Argentina 15 Jan 73

Displacement: 2,616tons/2,657tonnes (standard); 3,460tons/3,516tonnes (full load).
Length: 390ft 6in/119.03m (oa); 383ft/116.74m (wl).
Beam: 40ft 10in/12.45m.
Draught: 14ft 4in/4.37m (mean).
Machinery: four Babcock & Wilcox boilers; 2-shaft G.E.C. geared turbines.
Performance: 60,000shp; 36.8kts.
Bunkerage: 740tons/752tonnes.
Range: 4,500nm at 20kts.
Guns: six 5in (3×2); twelve 40mm (2×4, 2×2); eleven 20mm.
Torpedoes: ten 21in (2×5).
Complement: 336.

Design Disappointing endurance performance of the *Sumner*-class destroyers led to the lengthening of the hull by fourteen feet to increase bunkerage

Left: *Chevalier* (DD805), modified for radar picket duties. (USN)

Right: *Steinaker* (DD863) in June 1945. The after tubes have been replaced by quadruple 40mm guns. (USN)

GEARING CLASS—*continued*

Ship	Builder	Laid Down	Launched	Commissioned	Fate
DD878 *Vesole*	Consolidated, Orange	3 July 44	29 Dec 44	23 April 45	Stricken 1 Dec 76
DD879 *Leary*	Consolidated, Orange	11 Aug 44	20 Jan 45	7 May 45	To Spain 31 Oct 73
DD880 *Dyess*	Consolidated, Orange	17 Aug 44	26 Jan 45	21 May 45	To Greece May 1981
D881 *Bordelon*	Consolidated, Orange	9 Sept 44	3 Mar 45	5 June 45	To Iran 1 Feb 77
DD882 *Furse*	Consolidated, Orange	23 Sept 44	9 Mar 45	10 July 45	To Spain 31 Aug 72
DD883 *Newman K. Perry*	Consolidated, Orange	10 Oct 44	17 Mar 45	26 July 45	To S. Korea 1981
DD884 *Floyd B. Parks*	Consolidated, Orange	30 Oct 44	31 Mar 45	31 July 45	Sold for breaking up 28 Mar 74
DD885 *John R. Craig*	Consolidated, Orange	17 Nov 44	14 April 45	20 Aug 45	Stricken 27 July 79
DD886 *Orleck*	Consolidated, Orange	28 Nov 44	12 May 45	15 Sept 45	To Turkey 1 Oct 82
DD887 *Brinkley Bass*	Consolidated, Orange	20 Dec 44	26 May 45	14 Sept 45	To Brazil 3 Dec 73
DD888 *Stickell*	Consolidated, Orange	5 Jan 45	16 June 45	26 Sept 45	To Greece 1 July 72
DD889 *O'Hare*	Consolidated, Orange	27 Jan 45	22 June 45	29 Nov 45	To Spain 31 Oct 73
DD890 *Meredith*	Consolidated, Orange	27 Jan 45	28 June 45	31 Dec 45	To Turkey 7 Dec 79

and relieve internal congestion somewhat, although the extra length contained no berthing space. At the same time, it was expected that the extra length would raise the speed and compensate the increased displacement to a degree. Armament, machinery and general layout were otherwise similar to the *Sumner* class. The *Gearing* was, in fact, merely a production variant of the *Sumner*, 152 ships being ordered as *Gearing*s. However, with the end of the war, many units were cancelled as the destroyer-programme was cut back. *DD809–816, DD854–856* and *DD891–926* were all cancelled before laying down, two were broken up on the slip (*DD768/9*) and nine delivered incomplete and laid up (*DD719–721, DD766–767, DD791, DD824, DD825* and *DD827*). One ship, *Timmerman* (*DD828*), was completed as an experimental engineering test-bed and some of the incomplete units were completed to a revised design long after the war.

Forty-five units of the class (which eventually reached 93 ships) were completed before the end of the Pacific war, but as the first ship did not commission until the end of 1944 and many of the others not until the last months of the war, their service during hostilities was brief.

Modifications The most significant modification made was the conversion of 24 ships to Radar Picket destroyers for the anticipated Invasion of Japan. This involved the removal of the forward torpedo tubes to allow the installation of height-finding SP radar, IFF and an ECM system. Internally, alterations had to be made to accommodate the extra space needed for men and equipment for this new role. The after torpedo tubes were also removed later to allow installation of the third quadruple 40mm as in the *Sumners*. *Chevalier* (*DD805*) was the first to complete conversion in May 1945.

Twelve ships had been selected for conversion in January 1945, being *DD742, 743, 805–808, 829* and *873–877*, of which only three had yet been completed. Twelve more were selected in May, *DD830–835, DD878–883*.

Service Few saw any significant war service due to their late completion and the conversion to Radar Picket duty. As the most modern US Fleet destroyers, however, they did have a long post-war service, some into the 1980s.

EVARTS (GMT) CLASS

Ship	Builder	Laid Down	Launched	Commissioned	Fate
DE5 *Evarts*	Boston NYd.	17 Oct 42	7 Dec 42	15 April 43	Scrapped July 1946
DE6 *Wyffels*	Boston NYd.	17 Oct 42	7 Dec 42	21 April 43	To China 1945
DE7 *Griswold*	Boston NYd.	27 Nov 42	9 Jan 43	28 April 43	Scrapped Jan 1947
DE8 *Steele*	Boston NYd.	27 Nov 42	9 Jan 43	4 May 43	Scrapped Jan 1947
DE9 *Carlson*	Boston NYd.	27 Nov 42	9 Jan 43	10 May 43	Scrapped Dec 1946
DE10 *Bebas*	Boston NYd.	27 Nov 42	9 Jan 43	15 May 43	Scrapped Feb 1947
DE11 *Crouter*	Boston NYd.	8 Dec 42	26 Jan 43	25 May 43	Scrapped Dec 1946
DE13 *Brennan*	Mare Island NYd.	28 Feb 42	22 Aug 42	20 Jan 43	Scrapped Aug 1946
DE14 *Doherty*	Mare Island NYd.	28 Feb 42	29 Aug 42	6 Feb 43	Scrapped Dec 1946
DE15 *Austin*	Mare Island NYd.	14 Mar 42	25 Sept 42	13 Feb 43	Scrapped Feb 1947
DE16 *Edgar G. Chase*	Mare Island NYd.	14 Mar 42	26 Sept 42	20 Mar 43	Scrapped April 1947
DE17 *Edward C. Daly*	Mare Island NYd.	1 April 42	21 Oct 42	3 April 43	Scrapped Feb 1947
DE18 *Gilmore*	Mare Island NYd.	1 April 42	22 Oct 42	17 April 43	Scrapped Mar 1947
DE19 *Burden R. Hastings*	Mare Island NYd.	14 April 42	20 Nov 42	1 May 43	Scrapped Mar 1947
DE20 *Le Hardy*	Mare Island NYd.	15 April 42	21 Nov 42	15 May 43	Scrapped Jan 1947
DE21 *Harold C. Thomas*	Mare Island NYd.	30 April 42	18 Dec 42	31 May 43	Scrapped Feb 1947
DE22 *Wileman*	Mare Island NYd.	30 April 42	19 Dec 42	11 June 43	Scrapped Feb 47
DE23 *Charles R. Greer*	Mare Island NYd.	7 Sept 42	8 Jan 43	25 June 43	Scrapped Mar 1947
DE24 *Whitman*	Mare Island NYd.	7 Sept 42	19 Jan 43	3 July 43	Scrapped Feb 1947
DE25 *Wintle*	Mare Island NYd.	1 Oct 42	18 Feb 43	10 July 43	Scrapped Aug 1947
DE26 *Dempsey*	Mare Island NYd.	1 Oct 42	19 Feb 43	24 July 43	Scrapped May 1947
DE27 *Duffy*	Mare Island NYd.	29 Oct 42	16 April 43	5 Aug 43	Scrapped Aug 1947
DE28 *Emery* (ex-*Eisner*)	Mare Island NYd.	29 Nov 42	17 April 43	14 Aug 43	Scrapped Aug 1947
DE29 *Stadtfield*	Mare Island NYd.	26 Nov 42	17 May 43	26 Aug 43	Scrapped Aug 1947
DE30 *Martin*	Mare Island NYd.	26 Nov 42	18 May 43	4 Sept 43	Scrapped July 1947
DE32 *Sederstrom* (ex-*Gillette*)	Mare Island NYd.	24 Dec 42	15 June 43	11 Sept 43	Scrapped Feb 1948
DE32 *Fleming*	Mare Island NYd.	24 Dec 42	16 June 43	18 Sept 43	Scrapped Feb 1948
DE33 *Tisdale*	Mare Island NYd.	23 Jan 43	28 June 43	11 Oct 43	Scrapped Mar 1948
DE34 *Eisele*	Mare Island NYd.	23 Jan 43	29 June 43	18 Oct 43	Scrapped Feb 1948
DE35 *Fair*	Mare Island NYd.	24 Feb 43	27 July 43	23 Oct 43	Sold out June 1947
DE36 *Manlove*	Mare Island NYd.	24 Feb 43	28 July 43	8 Nov 43	Scrapped Mar 1948
DE37 *Greiner*	Puget Sound NYd.	7 Sept 42	20 May 43	18 Aug 43	Scrapped Mar 1947
DE38 *Wyman*	Puget Sound NYd.	7 Sept 42	3 June 43	1 Sept 43	Scrapped June 1947
DE39 *Lovering*	Puget Sound NYd.	7 Sept 42	18 June 43	17 Sept 43	Scrapped Jan 1947
DE40 *Sanders*	Puget Sound NYd.	7 Sept 42	18 June 43	1 Oct 43	Scrapped June 1947
DE41 *Brackett*	Puget Sound NYd.	12 Jan 43	1 Aug 43	18 Oct 43	Scrapped June 1947
DE42 *Reynolds*	Puget Sound NYd.	12 Jan 43	1 Aug 43	1 Nov 43	Scrapped May 1947
DE43 *Mitchell*	Puget Sound NYd.	12 Jan 43	1 Aug 43	17 Nov 43	Scrapped Jan 1947
DE44 *Donaldson*	Puget Sound NYd.	12 Jan 43	1 Aug 43	1 Dec 43	Scrapped Aug 1946
DE45 *Andres*	Philadelphia NYd.	12 Feb 42	24 July 42	15 Mar 43	Scrapped Feb 1946
DE47 *Decker*	Philadelphia NYd.	1 April 42	24 July 42	3 May 43	To China Aug 1945
DE48 *Dobler*	Philadelphia NYd.	1 April 42	24 July 42	17 May 43	Scrapped July 1946
DE49 *Doneff*	Philadelphia NYd.	1 April 42	24 July 42	10 June 43	Scrapped Jan 1947
DE50 *Engstrom*	Philadelphia NYd.	1 April 42	24 July 42	21 June 43	Scrapped Jan 1947
DE256 *Seid*	Boston NYd.	10 Jan 43	22 Feb 43	11 June 43	Scrapped Feb 1947
DE257 *Smartt*	Boston NYd.	10 Jan 43	22 Feb 43	18 June 43	Scrapped Aug 1946
DE258 *Walter S. Brown*	Boston NYd.	10 Jan 43	22 Feb 43	25 June 43	Scrapped Aug 1946
DE259 *William C. Miller*	Boston NYd.	10 Jan 43	22 Feb 43	2 July 43	Scrapped May 1947
DE260 *Cabana*	Boston NYd.	27 Jan 43	10 Mar 43	9 July 43	Scrapped June 1947
DE261 *Dionne*	Boston NYd.	27 Jan 43	10 Mar 43	16 July 43	Scrapped July 1947
DE262 *Canfield*	Boston NYd.	23 Feb 43	6 April 43	22 July 43	Scrapped July 1947

EVARTS (GMT) CLASS

Ship	Builder	Laid Down
DE263 *Deede*	Boston NYd.	23 Feb 43
DE264 *Elden*	Boston NYd.	23 Feb 43
DE265 *Cloues*	Boston NYd.	23 Feb 43
DE301 *Lake*	Mare Island NYd.	22 April 43
DE302 *Lyman*	Mare Island NYd.	22 April 43
DE303 *Crowley*	Mare Island NYd.	24 May 43
DE304 *Rall*	Mare Island NYd.	24 May 43
DE305 *Halloran*	Mare Island NYd.	21 June 43
DE306 *Connolly*	Mare Island NYd.	31 June 43
DE307 *Finnegan*	Mare Island NYd.	5 July 43
DE308 *Creamer*	Mare Island NYd.	1943
DE309 *Ely*	Mare Island NYd.	1943
DE310 *Delbert W. Halsey*	Mare Island NYd.	1943
DE311 *Keppler*	Mare Island NYd.	–
DE312 *Lloyd Thomas*	Mare Island NYd.	–
DE313 *William C. Lawe*	Mare Island NYd.	–
DE314 *Willard Keith*	Mare Island NYd.	–
DE315 –	–	–
DE527 *O'Toole*	Boston NYd.	25 Sept 43
DE528 *John J. Powers*	Boston NYd.	25 Sept 43
DE529 *Mason*	Boston NYd.	14 Oct 43
DE530 *John M. Bermingham*	Boston NYd.	14 Oct 43

Displacement: 1,192tons/1,211tonnes (standard); 1,416tons/1,438tonnes (full load).
Length: 289ft 5in/88.22m (oa); 283ft 6in/86.4m (wl).
Beam: 35ft 2in/10.72m.
Draught: 10ft 1in/3.07m (mean).

—continued

Launched	Commissioned	Fate
6 April 43	29 July 43	Scrapped July 1947
6 April 43	5 Aug 43	Scrapped July 1947
6 April 43	10 Aug 43	Scrapped June 1947
18 Aug 43	5 Feb 44	Scrapped Jan 1947
19 Aug 43	19 Feb 44	Scrapped Jan 1947
22 Sept 43	25 Mar 44	Scrapped Jan 1947
23 Sept 43	8 April 44	Scrapped April 1947
14 Jan 44	27 May 44	Scrapped April 1947
15 Jan 44	8 July 44	Scrapped June 1946
22 Feb 44	19 Aug 44	Scrapped June 1946
23 Feb 44	–	Cancelled Sept 1944
10 April 44	–	Cancelled Sept 1944
11 April 44	–	Cancelled Sept 1944
–	–	Cancelled Mar 1944
–	–	Cancelled Mar 1944
–	–	Cancelled Mar 1944
–	–	Cancelled Mar 1944
–	–	Cancelled Mar 1944
2 Nov 43	22 Jan 44	Scrapped Mar 1946
2 Nov 43	29 Feb 44	Scrapped Feb 1946
17 Nov 43	20 Mar 44	Scrapped April 1947
17 Nov 43	8 April 44	Scrapped Mar 1946

Machinery: 2-shaft General Motors diesels.
Performance: 6,000bhp; 19.5kts.
Range: 6,000nm at 12kts.
Guns: three 3in (3×1); nine 20mm.
Complement: 156.

Below: *Donaldson* (DE44) in December 1943. Note quad 1.1in gun aft. (USN)

BUCKLEY (TE) CLASS

Ship	Builder	Laid Down	Launched	Commissioned	Fate
DE51 *Buckley*	Bethlehem, Hingham	21 July 42	9 Jan 43	30 April 43	Stricken 1 June 68
DE53 *Charles Lawrence*	Bethlehem, Hingham	1 Aug 42	16 Feb 43	31 May 43	*Stricken Sept 1964
DE54 *Daniel T. Griffin*	Bethlehem, Hingham	7 Sept 42	23 Feb 43	9 June 43	*To Chile 1 Dec 66
DE56 *Donnell*	Bethlehem, Hingham	27 Nov 42	13 Mar 43	26 June 43	Sold for breaking up April 1946
DE57 *Fogg*	Bethlehem, Hingham	4 Dec 42	20 Mar 43	7 July 43	Stricken 1 April 65
DE59 *Foss*	Bethlehem, Hingham	31 Dec 42	10 April 43	23 July 43	Stricken 1 Nov 65
DE60 *Gantner*	Bethlehem, Hingham	31 Dec 42	17 April 43	29 July 43	*To Taiwan May 1966
DE62 *George W. Ingram*	Bethlehem, Hingham	6 Feb 43	8 May 43	11 Aug 43	*To Taiwan July 1967
DE63 *Ira Jeffery*	Bethlehem, Hingham	13 Feb 43	15 May 43	15 Aug 43	*Stricken 1960
DE65 *Lee Fox*	Bethlehem, Hingham	1 Mar 43	29 May 43	30 Aug 43	*Scrapped 1966
DE66 *Amesbury*	Bethlehem, Hingham	8 Mar 43	5 June 43	31 Aug 43	*Stricken 1960
DE68 *Bates*	Bethlehem, Hingham	29 Mar 43	6 June 43	12 Sept 43	*Lost 25 May 45
DE69 *Blessman*	Bethlehem, Hingham	22 Mar 43	19 June 43	19 Sept 43	*To Taiwan July 1967
DE70 *Joseph E. Campbell*	Bethlehem, Hingham	29 Mar 43	26 June 43	23 Sept 43	*To Chile 1 Dec 66
DE153 *Reuben James*	Norfolk NYd.	7 Sept 42	6 Feb 43	1 April 43	Stricken June 1968
DE154 *Sims*	Norfolk NYd.	7 Sept 42	6 Feb 43	24 April 43	*Stricken 1960
DE155 *Hopping*	Norfolk NYd.	15 Dec 42	10 Mar 43	21 May 43	*Scrapped 1966

Below: *Buckley* (DE51) in May 1943. She is fitted with a twin 40mm, but has only a light 20mm outfit. Note the triple tubes. (USN)

BUCKLEY (TE) CLASS—*continued*

Ship	Builder	Laid Down	Launched	Commissioned	Fate
DE156 *Reeves*	Norfolk NYd.	7 Feb 43	22 April 43	9 June 43	*Stricken 1960
DE157 *Fechteler*	Norfolk NYd.	7 Feb 43	22 April 43	1 July 43	Lost 4 May 44
DE158 *Chase*	Norfolk NYd.	16 Mar 43	24 April 43	18 July 43	*Sold for breaking up Nov 1946
DE159 *Laning*	Norfolk NYd.	23 April 43	4 July 43	1 Aug 43	*Stricken 1 Mar 75
DE160 *Loy*	Norfolk NYd.	23 April 43	4 July 43	12 Sept 43	*Scrapped 1966
DE161 *Barber*	Norfolk NYd.	27 April 43	20 May 43	10 Oct 43	*To Mexico 17 Feb 69
DE198 *Lovelace*	Norfolk NYd.	22 May 43	4 July 43	7 Nov 43	Stricken 1 July 67
DE199 *Manning*	Charleston NYd.	15 Feb 43	1 June 43	1 Oct 43	Stricken 30 July 68
DE200 *Neuendorf*	Charleston NYd.	15 Feb 43	1 June 43	18 Oct 43	Expended July 1967
DE201 *James E. Craig*	Charleston NYd.	15 April 43	22 July 43	1 Nov 43	Stricken June 1968
DE202 *Eichenberger*	Charleston NYd.	15 April 43	22 July 43	17 Nov 43	Stricken 1 Dec 72
DE203 *Thomason*	Charleston NYd.	5 June 43	23 Aug 43	10 Dec 43	Stricken June 1968
DE204 *Jordan*	Charleston NYd.	5 June 43	23 Aug 43	17 Dec 43	Scrapped July 1947
DE205 *Newman*	Charleston NYd.	8 June 43	9 Aug 43	26 Nov 43	*Scrapped 1966
DE206 *Liddle*	Charleston NYd.	8 June 43	9 Aug 43	6 Dec 43	*Stricken April 1967
DE207 *Kephart*	Charleston NYd.	12 May 43	6 Sept 43	7 Jan 44	*To S. Korea Aug 1967
DE208 *Cofer*	Charleston NYd.	12 May 43	6 Sept 43	19 Jan 44	*Scrapped 1968
DE209 *Lloyd*	Charleston NYd.	26 July 43	23 Oct 43	11 Feb 44	*Scrapped 1968
DE210 *Otter*	Charleston NYd.	26 July 43	23 Oct 43	21 Feb 44	Stricken Nov 1969
DE211 *Joseph C. Hubbard*	Charleston NYd.	11 Aug 43	11 Nov 43	6 Mar 44	*Stricken Nov 1969
DE212 *Hayter*	Charleston NYd.	11 Aug 43	11 Nov 43	16 Mar 44	*To S. Korea Dec 1966
DE213 *William T. Powell*	Charleston NYd.	26 Aug 43	27 Nov 43	28 Mar 44	Scrapped 1966
DE214 *Scott*	Philadelphia NYd.	1 Jan 43	3 April 43	20 July 43	Scrapped 1967

Below: *Edsal* (DE129) in May 1943. Note paucity of AA guns. (USN)

BUCKLEY (TE) CLASS

Ship	Builder	Laid Down
DE215 *Burke*	Philadelphia NYd.	1 Jan 43
DE216 *Enright*	Philadelphia NYd.	22 Feb 43
DE217 *Coolbaugh*	Philadelphia NYd.	22 Feb 43
DE218 *Darby*	Philadelphia NYd.	22 Feb 43
DE219 *J. Douglas Blackwood*	Philadelphia NYd.	22 Feb 43
DE220 *Francis M. Robinson*	Philadelphia NYd.	22 Feb 43
DE221 *Solar*	Philadelphia NYd.	22 Feb 43
DE222 *Fowler*	Philadelphia NYd.	5 April 43
DE223 *Spangenberg*	Philadelphia NYd.	5 April 43
DE575 *Ahrens*	Bethlehem, Hingham	5 Nov 43
DE576 *Barr*	Bethlehem, Hingham	5 Nov 43
DE577 *Alexander J. Luke*	Bethlehem, Hingham	5 Nov 43
DE578 *Robert J. Paine*	Bethlehem, Hingham	5 Nov 43
DE633 *Foreman*	Bethlehem, S. Francisco	9 April 43
DE634 *Whitehurst*	Bethlehem, S. Francisco	21 Mar 43
DE635 *England*	Bethlehem, S. Francisco	4 April 43
DE636 *Witter*	Bethlehem, S. Francisco	28 April 43
DE637 *Bowers*	Bethlehem, S. Francisco	28 May 43
DE638 *Willmarth*	Bethlehem, S. Francisco	25 June 43
DE639 *Glendreau*	Bethlehem, S. Francisco	1 Aug 43
DE640 *Fieberling*	Bethlehem, S. Francisco	1943
DE641 *William C. Cole*	Bethlehem, S. Francisco	5 Sept 43
DE642 *Paul G. Baker*	Bethlehem, S. Francisco	26 Sept 43
DE643 *Damon M. Cummings*	Bethlehem, S. Francisco	17 Oct 43
DE644 *Vammen*	Bethlehem, S. Francisco	1 Aug 43
DE665 *Jenks*	Dravo, Pittsburg	12 May 43
DE666 *Durik*	Dravo, Pittsburg	22 June 43
DE667 *Wiseman*	Dravo, Pittsburg	26 July 43

—continued

Launched	Commissioned	Fate
3 April 43	20 Aug 43	*To Colombia June 1968
29 May 43	21 Sept 43	*To Equadaor 14 July 67
29 May 43	15 Oct 43	Stricken 1 July 72
29 May 43	15 Nov 43	Stricken Sept 1968
29 May 43	15 Jan 44	Stricken Jan 1970
29 May 43	15 Jan 44	Stricken 1 July 72
29 May 43	15 Feb 44	Lost 30 April 46
3 July 43	15 Mar 44	Sold for breaking up 29 Dec 67
3 July 43	15 April 44	Sold for breaking up 3 Oct 66
21 Dec 43	12 Feb 44	Scrapped 20 June 67
28 Dec 43	15 Feb 44	*Stricken 1960
28 Dec 43	19 Feb 44	Stricken May 1970
30 Dec 43	28 Feb 44	Stricken June 1968
1 Aug 43	22 Oct 43	Stricken 1 May 65
5 Sept 43	19 Nov 43	Stricken 12 July 69
29 June 43	10 Dec 43	Scrapped Nov 1946
17 Oct 43	29 Dec 43	Scrapped Nov 1946
31 Oct 43	27 Jan 44	*To Philippines April 1961
21 Nov 43	13 Mar 44	Scrapped 1968
12 Dec 43	7 April 44	Stricken 1 Dec 72
2 April 44	11 April 44	Stricken 1 Mar 72
29 Dec 43	12 May 44	Stricken 1 Mar 72
12 Mar 44	25 May 44	Scrapped 1970
18 April 44	29 June 44	Stricken 1 Mar 72
21 May 44	27 July 44	Expended 1971
11 Sept 43	19 Jan 44	Scrapped 1968
9 Oct 43	24 Mar 44	Scrapped 1967
6 Nov 43	4 April 44	Stricken 15 April 73

BUCKLEY (TE) CLASS—*continued*

Ship	Builder	Laid Down	Launched	Commissioned	Fate
DE675 *Weber*	Bethlehem, Quincy	22 Feb 43	1 May 43	30 June 43	*Stricken 1960
DE676 *Schmitt*	Bethlehem, Quincy	22 Feb 43	29 May 43	24 July 43	*To S. Korea May 1967
DE677 *Frament*	Bethlehem, Quincy	1 May 43	28 June 43	15 Aug 43	*Sold 1961
DE678 *Harmon*	Bethlehem, Quincy	31 May 43	25 July 43	31 Aug 43	Scrapped 1967
DE679 *Greenwood*	Bethlehem, Quincy	29 June 43	21 Aug 43	25 Sept 43	Scrapped 1967

Above: *Bowers* (DE637). (Real Photos) **Below:** *Poole* (DE151) armed with one quad and two twin 40mm in June 1945. (USN)

BUCKLEY (TE) CLASS—*continued*

Ship	Builder	Laid Down	Launched	Commissioned	Fate
DE680 *Loeser*	Bethlehem, Quincy	27 July 43	11 Sept 43	10 Oct 43	Stricken Sept 1968
DE681 *Gillette*	Bethlehem, Quincy	24 Aug 43	25 Sept 43	27 Oct 43	Stricken 1 Dec 72
DE682 *Underhill*	Bethlehem, Quincy	16 Sept 43	15 Oct 43	15 Nov 43	Lost 24 July 45
DE683 *Henry R. Kenyon*	Bethlehem, Quincy	29 Sept 43	30 Oct 43	30 Nov 43	Stricken Dec 1969
DE693 *Bull*	Defoe, Bay City	15 Dec 42	25 Mar 43	12 Aug 43	*To Taiwan Aug 1966
DE694 *Bunch*	Defoe, Bay City	22 Feb 43	29 May 43	21 Aug 43	*Scrapped 1965
DE695 *Rich*	Defoe, Bay City	27 Mar 43	22 June 43	1 Oct 43	Lost 8 June 44
DE696 *Spangler*	Defoe, Bay City	28 April 43	15 July 43	31 Oct 43	Stricken 1 Mar 72
DE697 *George*	Defoe, Bay City	22 May 43	14 Aug 43	20 Nov 43	Scrapped 1970
DE698 *Raby*	Defoe, Bay City	7 June 43	4 Sept 43	7 Dec 43	Stricken June 1968
DE699 *Marsh*	Defoe, Bay City	23 June 43	25 Sept 43	12 Jan 44	Stricken 15 April 73
DE700 *Currier*	Defoe, Bay City	21 July 43	14 Oct 43	1 Feb 44	Stricken Jan 1966
DE701 *Osmus*	Defoe, Bay City	17 Aug 43	4 Nov 43	23 Feb 44	Stricken 1 Dec 72
DE702 *Earl V. Johnson*	Defoe, Bay City	7 Sept 43	24 Nov 43	18 Mar 44	Scrapped 1968
DE703 *Holton*	Defoe, Bay City	28 Sept 43	15 Dec 43	1 May 44	Stricken 1 Nov 72
DE704 *Cronin*	Defoe, Bay City	19 Oct 43	5 Jan 44	5 May 44	Stricken June 1970
DE705 *Frybarger*	Defoe, Bay City	8 Nov 43	25 Jan 44	18 May 44	Stricken 1 Dec 72
DE789 *Tatum*	Consolidated, Orange	22 April 43	7 Aug 43	22 Nov 43	*Scrapped 1960
DE790 *Borum*	Consolidated, Orange	28 April 43	14 Aug 43	30 Nov 43	Stricken 1 Aug 65
DE791 *Maloy*	Consolidated, Orange	10 May 43	18 Aug 43	13 Dec 43	Scrapped 1966
DE792 *Haines*	Consolidated, Orange	17 May 43	26 Aug 43	27 Dec 43	*Stricken 1960

Below: *Osmus* (DE701). (Real Photos)

BUCKLEY (TE) CLASS

Ship	Builder	Laid Down
DE793 *Runels*	Consolidated, Orange	7 June 43
DE794 *Hollis*	Consolidated, Orange	5 July 43
DE795 *Gunason*	Consolidated, Orange	9 Sept 43
DE796 *Major*	Consolidated, Orange	16 Aug 43
DE797 *Weeden*	Consolidated, Orange	18 Aug 43
DE798 *Varian*	Consolidated, Orange	27 Aug 43
DE799 *Scroggins*	Consolidated, Orange	4 Sept 43
DE800 *Jack W. Wilke*	Consolidated, Orange	18 Oct 43

*Converted to APD after completion. *DE668–DE673* converted to APD before completion.

Displacement: 1,432tons/1,455tonnes (standard); 1,823tons/1,852tonnes (full load).
Length: 306ft/93.27m (oa); 300ft/91.44m (wl).
Beam: 37ft/11.28m.
Draught: 11ft 3in/3.43m (mean).
Machinery: two Foster-Wheeler, Babcock & Wilcox or Combustion Engineering boilers; 2-shaft G.E.C. turbines.

CANNON (DET) CLASS

Ship	Builder	Laid Down
DE99 *Cannon*	Dravo, Wilmington	14 Nov 42
DE100 *Christopher*	Dravo, Wilmington	7 Dec 42
DE101 *Alger*	Dravo, Wilmington	2 Jan 43
DE102 *Thomas*	Dravo, Wilmington	16 Jan 43
DE103 *Bostwick*	Dravo, Wilmington	6 Feb 43
DE104 *Breeman*	Dravo, Wilmington	20 Mar 43
DE105 *Burrows*	Dravo, Wilmington	24 Mar 43
DE112 *Carter*	Dravo, Wilmington	9 Nov 43
DE113 *Clarence L. Evans*	Dravo, Wilmington	23 Dec 43
DE162 *Levy*	Federal, Newark	19 Oct 42
DE163 *McConnell*	Federal, Newark	19 Oct 42
DE164 *Osterhaus*	Federal, Newark	11 Nov 42
DE165 *Parks*	Federal, Newark	11 Nov 42

—continued

Launched	Commissioned	Fate
4 Sept 43	3 Jan 44	*Stricken 1960
11 Sept 43	24 Jan 44	*Stricken 15 Sept 74
16 Oct 43	1 Feb 44	Stricken 1 Sept 73
23 Oct 43	12 Feb 44	Stricken 1 Dec 72
27 Oct 43	19 Feb 44	Stricken 30 June 68
6 Nov 43	29 Feb 44	Stricken 1 Dec 72
6 Nov 43	30 Mar 44	Stricken 1 July 65
18 Dec 43	7 Mar 44	Stricken 1 Aug 72

Performance: 12,000shp; 23kts.
Bunkerage: 340tons/344tonnes.
Range: 5,000nm at 15kts.
Guns: three 3in (3×1); four 1.1in (1×4); eight 20mm.
Torpedoes: three 21in (1×3).
Complement: 186.

Launched	Commissioned	Fate
25 May 43	26 Sept 43	To Brazil Dec 1944
19 June 43	23 Oct 43	To Brazil Dec 1944
8 July 43	12 Nov 43	To Brazil Mar 1945
31 July 43	21 Nov 43	To China 31 Oct 48
30 Aug 43	1 Dec 43	To China 31 Dec 48
4 Sept 43	12 Dec 43	To China 31 Oct 48
2 Oct 43	19 Dec 43	To Netherlands 1 June 50
29 Feb 44	2 May 44	To China 31 Dec 48
22 Mar 44	25 June 44	To France 29 Mar 52
28 Mar 43	13 May 43	Stricken 1 Aug 73
28 Mar 43	28 May 43	Stricken 1 Oct 72
18 April 43	12 June 43	Stricken 1 Nov 72
18 April 43	22 June 43	Stricken 1 July 72

CANNON (DET) CLASS—*continued*

Ship	Builder	Laid Down	Launched	Commissioned	Fate
DE166 *Baron*	Federal, Newark	30 Nov 42	9 May 43	5 July 43	To Uruguay May 1952
DE167 *Acree*	Federal, Newark	30 Nov 42	9 May 43	19 July 43	Stricken 1 July 72
DE168 *Amick*	Federal, Newark	30 Nov 42	27 May 43	26 July 43	To Japan 14 June 55
DE169 *Atherton*	Federal, Newark	14 Jan 43	27 May 43	29 Aug 43	To Japan 14 June 55
DE170 *Booth*	Federal, Newark	30 Jan 43	21 June 43	19 Sept 43	To Philippines 15 Dec 67
DE171 *Carroll*	Federal, Newark	30 Jan 43	21 June 43	24 Oct 43	Stricken 1 Aug 65
DE172 *Cooner*	Federal, Newark	22 Feb 43	25 July 43	21 Aug 43	Sold for breaking up Oct 1973
DE173 *Eldridge*	Federal, Newark	22 Feb 43	25 July 43	27 Aug 43	To Greece 15 Jan 51
DE174 *Marts*	Federal, Newark	26 April 43	8 Aug 43	3 Sept 43	To Brazil Mar 1945
DE175 *Pennewill*	Federal, Newark	26 April 43	8 Aug 43	15 Sept 43	To Brazil Aug 1944
DE176 *Micka*	Federal, Newark	3 May 43	22 Aug 43	23 Sept 43	Stricken 1 Aug 65
DE177 *Reybold*	Federal, Newark	3 May 43	22 Aug 43	29 Sept 43	To Brazil Aug 1944
DE178 *Herzog*	Federal, Newark	17 May 43	5 Sept 43	6 Oct 43	To Brazil Aug 1944
DE179 *McAnn*	Federal, Newark	17 May 43	5 Sept 43	11 Oct 43	To Brazil Aug 44
DE180 *Trumpeter*	Federal, Newark	7 June 43	19 Sept 43	16 Oct 43	Stricken 1 Aug 73
DE181 *Straub*	Federal, Newark	7 June 43	19 Sept 43	25 Oct 43	Stricken 1 Aug 73
DE182 *Gustafson*	Federal, Newark	5 July 43	3 Oct 43	1 Nov 43	To Netherlands 23 Oct 50
DE183 *Samuel S. Miles*	Federal, Newark	5 July 43	3 Oct 43	4 Nov 43	To France 12 Aug 50
DE184 *Wesson*	Federal, Newark	29 July 43	17 Oct 43	11 Nov 43	To Italy 10 Jan 51

Below: *Hemminger* (DE746). (Real Photos)

CANNON (DET) CLASS—*continued*

Ship	Builder	Laid Down	Launched	Commissioned	Fate
DE185 *Riddle*	Federal, Newark	29 July 43	17 Oct 43	17 Nov 43	To France 12 Aug 50
DE186 *Swearer*	Federal, Newark	12 Aug 43	31 Oct 43	24 Nov 43	To France Sept 1950
DE187 *Stern*	Federal, Newark	12 Aug 43	31 Oct 43	1 Dec 43	To Netherlands 3 May 51
DE188 *O'Neill*	Federal, Newark	26 Aug 43	14 Nov 43	6 Dec 43	To Netherlands 23 Oct 50
DE189 *Bronstein*	Federal, Newark	26 Aug 43	14 Nov 43	13 Dec 43	To Uruguay 3 May 52
DE190 *Baker* (ex-*Raby*)	Federal, Newark	9 Sept 43	28 Nov 43	23 Dec 43	To France 29 Mar 52
DE191 *Coffman*	Federal, Newark	9 Sept 43	28 Nov 43	27 Dec 43	Stricken 1 July 72
DE192 *Eisner*	Federal, Newark	23 Sept 43	12 Dec 43	1 Jan 44	To Netherlands 3 May 51
DE193 *Garfield Thomas* (ex-*William G. Thomas*)	Federal, Newark	23 Sept 43	12 Dec 43	24 Jan 44	To Greece 15 Jan 51
DE194 *Wingfield*	Federal, Newark	7 Oct 43	30 Dec 43	28 Jan 44	To France Sept 1950
DE195 *Thornhill*	Federal, Newark	7 Oct 43	30 Dec 43	1 Feb 44	To Italy 10 Jan 51
DE196 *Rinehart*	Federal, Newark	21 Oct 43	9 Jan 44	12 Feb 44	To Netherlands 1 June 50
DE197 *Roche*	Federal, Newark	21 Oct 43	9 Jan 44	21 Feb 44	Expended 11 Mar 46
DE739 *Bangust*	Western Pipe & Steel, S. Pedro	11 Feb 43	6 June 43	30 Oct 43	To Peru 26 Oct 51
DE740 *Waterman*	Western Pipe & Steel, S. Pedro	24 Feb 43	20 June 43	30 Nov 43	To Peru 26 Oct 51
DE741 *Weaver*	Western Pipe & Steel, S. Pedro	13 Mar 43	4 July 43	31 Dec 43	To Peru 26 Oct 51

Below: *Roberts* (DE749).

CANNON (DET) CLASS

Ship	Builder	Laid Down
DE742 *Hilbert*	Western Pipe & Steel, S. Pedro	23 Mar 43
DE743 *Lamons*	Western Pipe & Steel, S. Pedro	10 April 43
DE744 *Kyne*	Western Pipe & Steel, S. Pedro	16 April 43
DE745 *Snyder*	Western Pipe & Steel, S. Pedro	28 April 43
DE746 *Hemminger*	Western Pipe & Steel, S. Pedro	8 May 43
DE747 *Bright*	Western Pipe & Steel, S. Pedro	9 June 43
DE748 *Tills*	Western Pipe & Steel, S. Pedro	23 June 43
DE749 *Roberts*	Western Pipe & Steel, S. Pedro	7 July 43
DE750 *McClelland*	Western Pipe & Steel, S. Pedro	21 July 43
DE751 *Gaynier*	Western Pipe & Steel, S. Pedro	4 Aug 43
DE752 *Curtis W. Howard*	Western Pipe & Steel, S. Pedro	18 Aug 43
DE753 *John J. Van Buren*	Western Pipe & Steel, S. Pedro	31 Aug 43
DE763 *Cates*	Tampa Sbdg. Co.	1 Mar 43
DE764 *Gandy*	Tampa Sbdg.Co.	1 Mar 43
DE765 *Earl K. Olsen*	Tampa Sbdg. Co.	9 Mar 43
DE766 *Slater*	Tampa Sbdg. Co.	9 Mar 43
DE767 *Oswald*	Tampa Sbdg. Co.	1 April 43
DE768 *Ebert*	Tampa Sbdg. Co.	1 April 43
DE769 *Neal A. Scott*	Tampa Sbdg. Co.	1 June 43
DE770 *Muir*	Tampa Sbdg. Co.	1 June 43
DE771 *Sutton*	Tampa Sbdg. Co.	23 Aug 43
DE772 *Milton Lewis*	Tampa Sbdg. Co.	23 Aug 43
DE773 *George M. Campbell*	Tampa Sbdg. Co.	14 Oct 43
DE774 *Russell M. Cox*	Tampa Sbdg. Co.	14 Dec 43

Also cancelled: *DE114–128, DE754–762, DE775–788, DE801–904.*

Displacement: 1,250tons/1,270tonnes (standard); 1,600tons/1,625tonnes (full load).
Length: 306ft/93.27m (oa); 300ft/91.44m (wl).
Beam: 36ft 7in/11.15m.
Draught: 10ft 5in/3.2m (mean).
Machinery: 2-shaft General Motors diesels.
Performance: 6,000bhp; 21kts.

–*continued*

Launched	Commissioned	Fate
18 July 43	4 Feb 44	Stricken 1 Aug 72
1 Aug 43	29 Feb 44	Stricken 1 Aug 72
15 Aug 43	4 April 44	Sold for breaking up 1 Nov 73
29 Aug 43	5 May 44	Sold for breaking up Oct 1973
12 Sept 43	30 May 44	To Thailand July 1959
29 Sept 43	30 June 44	To France Nov 1950
3 Oct 43	8 Aug 44	Stricken 23 Sept 68
14 Nov 43	2 Sept 44	Stricken 23 Sept 68
28 Nov 43	19 Sept 44	Sold for breaking up Oct 1973
30 Jan 44	–	
1944	–	Cancelled 1 Sept 44
16 Jan 44	–	
10 Oct 43	15 Dec 43	To France Nov 1950
12 Dec 43	7 Feb 44	To Italy 10 Jan 50
13 Feb 44	10 April 44	Stricken 1 Aug 72
13 Feb 44	1 May 44	To Greece 15 Mar 51
25 April 44	12 June 44	Sold for breaking up Oct 1973
11 May 44	12 July 44	To Greece 15 Mar 51
4 June 44	31 July 44	Stricken June 1968
4 June 44	30 Aug 44	To S. Korea 1956
6 Aug 44	22 Dec 44	To S. Korea 1956
6 Aug 44		
1944		Cancelled 1 Sept 44
1944		

Bunkerage: 279tons/283tonnes.
Range: 11,500nm at 11kts.
Guns: three 3in (3×1); two 40mm (2×1); eight 20mm.
Torpedoes: three 21in (1×3).
Complement: 186.

EDSALL (FMR) CLASS

Ship	Builder	Laid Down	Launched	Commissioned	Fate
DE129 *Edsall*	Consolidated, Orange	2 July 42	1 Nov 42	10 April 43	Stricken 1 June 68
DE130 *Jacob Jones*	Consolidated, Orange	26 June 42	29 Nov 42	29 April 43	Stricken 2 Jan 71
DE131 *Hammann*	Consolidated, Orange	10 July 42	13 Dec 42	17 May 43	Stricken 1 Oct 72
DE132 *Robert E. Peary*	Consolidated, Orange	30 June 42	3 Jan 43	31 May 43	Scrapped 1967
DE133 *Pillsbury*	Consolidated, Orange	18 July 42	10 Jan 43	7 June 43	Stricken 1 July 65
DE134 *Pope*	Consolidated, Orange	14 July 42	12 Jan 43	25 June 43	Sold for breaking up Sept 1973
DE135 *Flaherty*	Consolidated, Orange	7 Nov 42	17 Jan 43	26 June 43	Stricken 1 April 65
DE136 *Frederick C. Davis*	Consolidated, Orange	9 Nov 42	24 Jan 43	14 July 43	Lost 24 April 45
DE137 *Herbert C. Jones*	Consolidated, Orange	30 Nov 42	19 Jan 43	21 July 43	Stricken 1 July 72
DE138 *Douglas L. Howard*	Consolidated, Orange	8 Dec 42	24 Jan 43	29 July 43	Stricken 1 Oct 72
DE139 *Farquhar*	Consolidated, Orange	14 Dec 42	13 Feb 43	5 Aug 43	Stricken 1 Oct 72
DE140 *J. R. Y. Blakely*	Consolidated, Orange	16 Dec 42	7 Mar 43	16 Aug 43	Stricken 2 Jan 71
DE141 *Hill*	Consolidated, Orange	21 Dec 42	28 Feb 43	16 Aug 43	Stricken 1965
DE142 *Fessenden*	Consolidated, Orange	4 Jan 43	9 Mar 43	25 Aug 43	Expended 20 Dec 67
DE143 *Fiske*	Consolidated, Orange	4 Jan 43	14 Mar 43	25 Aug 43	Lost 2 Aug 44
DE144 *Frost*	Consolidated, Orange	13 Jan 43	21 Mar 43	30 Aug 43	Stricken 1 April 65
DE145 *Huse*	Consolidated, Orange	11 Jan 43	23 Mar 43	30 Aug 43	Sold for breaking up 11 June 74
DE146 *Inch*	Consolidated, Orange	19 Jan 43	4 April 43	8 Sept 43	Stricken 1 Oct 72
DE147 *Blair*	Consolidated, Orange	19 Jan 43	6 April 43	13 Sept 43	Stricken 1 Dec 72
DE148 *Brough*	Consolidated, Orange	22 Jan 43	10 April 43	18 Sept 43	Stricken 1 Nov 65
DE149 *Chatelaine*	Consolidated, Orange	25 Jan 43	21 April 43	22 Sept 43	Stricken 1 Aug 73
DE150 *Neunzer*	Consolidated. Orange	29 Jan 43	27 April 43	27 Sept 43	Sold for breaking up Oct 1973
DE151 *Poole*	Consolidated, Orange	13 Feb 43	8 May 43	29 Sept 43	Stricken 2 Jan 71
DE152 *Peterson*	Consolidated, Orange	28 Feb 43	15 May 43	29 Sept 43	Stricken 2 Jan 71
DE238 *Stewart*	Brown Sbdg., Co., Houston	15 July 42	22 Nov 42	31 May 43	Stricken 1 Oct 72
DE239 *Sturtevant*	Brown Sbdg. Co., Houston	15 July 42	3 Dec 42	16 June 43	Stricken 1 Dec 72
DE240 *Moore*	Brown Sbdg. Co., Houston	20 July 42	21 Dec 42	1 July 43	Expended 22 April 74
DE241 *Keith*	Brown Sbdg. Co., Houston	4 Aug 42	21 Dec 42	19 July 43	Stricken 1 Nov 72

Above: *Camp* (DE251), the only long-hull FMR type to be re-armed with single 5-inch guns. May 1945. (USN)

EDSALL (FMR) CLASS—*continued*

Ship	Builder	Laid Down	Launched	Commissioned	Fate
DE242 *Tomich*	Brown Sbdg. Co., Houston	15 Feb 42	28 Dec 42	26 July 43	Stricken 1 Nov 72
DE243 *J. Richard Ward*	Brown Sbdg. Co., Houston	30 Sept 42	6 Jan 43	5 July 43	Stricken 2 Jan 71
DE244 *Otterstetter*	Brown Sbdg. Co., Houston	9 Nov 42	19 Jan 43	6 Aug 43	Stricken 1 Aug 74
DE245 *Sloat*	Brown Sbdg. Co., Houston	21 Nov 42	21 Jan 43	16 Aug 43	Stricken 2 Jan 71
DE246 *Snowden*	Brown Sbdg. Co., Houston	7 Dec 42	19 Feb 43	23 Aug 43	Stricken Sept 1968
DE247 *Stanton*	Brown Sbdg. Co., Houston	7 Dec 42	21 Feb 43	7 Aug 43	Stricken 2 Jan 71
DE248 *Swasey*	Brown Sbdg. Co., Houston	30 Dec 42	18 Mar 43	31 Aug 43	Stricken 1 Nov 72
DE249 *Marchand*	Brown Sbdg. Co., Houston	30 Dec 42	20 Mar 43	8 Sept 43	Stricken 2 Jan 71
DE250 *Hurst*	Brown Sbdg. Co., Houston	27 Jan 43	14 April 43	30 Aug 43	To Mexico 1 Oct 73
DE251 *Camp*	Brown Sbdg. Co., Houston	27 Jan 43	16 April 43	16 Sept 43	To S. Vietnam 20 July 70
DE252 *Howard D. Crow*	Brown Sbdg. Co., Houston	6 Feb 43	26 April 43	27 Sept 43	Stricken Jan 1965
DE253 *Pettit*	Brown Sbdg. Co., Houston	6 Feb 43	28 April 43	23 Sept 43	Expended 29 Sept 74
DE254 *Ricketts*	Brown Sbdg. Co., Houston	16 Mar 43	10 May 43	5 Oct 43	Stricken 1 Nov 72
DE255 *Sellstrom*	Brown Sbdg. Co., Houston	16 Mar 43	12 May 43	12 Oct 43	Stricken 1 Nov 65
DE316 *Harveston*	Consolidated, Orange	9 Mar 43	22 May 43	12 Oct 43	Stricken Jan 1966
DE317 *Joyce*	Consolidated, Orange	8 Mar 43	26 May 43	30 Sept 43	Stricken 1 Dec 72
DE318 *Kirkpatrick*	Consolidated, Orange	15 Mar 43	5 June 43	23 Oct 43	Sold for breaking up 1 Mar 75
DE319 *Leopold*	Consolidated, Orange	24 Mar 43	12 June 43	18 Oct 43	Lost 10 Mar 44
DE320 *Menges*	Consolidated, Orange	22 Mar 43	15 June 43	26 Oct 43	Stricken 2 Jan 71
DE321 *Mosley*	Consolidated, Orange	6 April 43	26 June 43	30 Oct 43	Sold for breaking up Sept 1973
DE322 *Newell*	Consolidated, Orange	5 April 43	29 June 43	30 Oct 43	Stricken 23 Sept 68
DE323 *Pride*	Consolidated, Orange	12 April 43	3 July 43	13 Nov 43	Stricken 2 Jan 71

EDSALL (FMR) CLASS

Ship	Builder	Laid Down
DE324 *Falgout*	Consolidated, Orange	26 May 43
DE325 *Lowe*	Consolidated, Orange	24 May 43
DE326 *Gary*	Consolidated, Orange	15 June 43
DE327 *Brister*	Consolidated, Orange	14 June 43
DE328 *Finch*	Consolidated, Orange	29 June 43
DE329 *Kretchmer*	Consolidated, Orange	28 June 43
DE330 *O'Reilly*	Consolidated, Orange	29 July 43
DE331 *Koiner*	Consolidated, Orange	26 July 43
DE332 *Price*	Consolidated, Orange	24 Aug 43
DE333 *Strickland*	Consolidated, Orange	23 Aug 43
DE334 *Forster*	Consolidated, Orange	31 Aug 43
DE335 *Daniel*	Consolidated, Orange	30 Aug 43
DE336 *Roy O. Hale*	Consolidated, Orange	13 Sept 43
DE337 *Dale W. Peterson*	Consolidated, Orange	25 Oct 43
DE338 *Martin H. Ray*	Consolidated, Orange	27 Oct 43
DE382 *Ramsden*	Consolidated, Orange	26 Mar 43
DE383 *Mills*	Consolidated, Orange	26 Mar 43
DE384 *Rhodes*	Consolidated, Orange	19 April 43
DE385 *Richey*	Consolidated, Orange	19 April 43
DE386 *Savage*	Consolidated, Orange	30 April 43
DE387 *Vance*	Consolidated, Orange	30 April 43
DE388 *Lansing*	Consolidated, Orange	15 May 43
DE389 *Durant*	Consolidated, Orange	15 May 43
DE390 *Calcaterra*	Consolidated, Orange	28 May 43
DE391 *Chambers*	Consolidated, Orange	28 May 43
DE392 *Merrill*	Consolidated, Orange	1 July 43
DE393 *Haverfield*	Consolidated, Orange	1 July 43
DE394 *Swenning*	Consolidated, Orange	17 July 43

-continued

Launched	Commissioned	Fate
24 July 43	15 Nov 43	Stricken 1 June 75
28 July 43	22 Nov 43	Sold for breaking up Sept 1969
21 Aug 43	27 Nov 43	To Tunisia 27 Oct 73
24 Aug 43	30 Nov 43	Stricken 23 Sept 68
28 Aug 43	13 Dec 43	Stricken 1 Feb 74
31 Aug 43	13 Dec 43	Stricken 30 Sept 73
2 Oct 43	28 Dec 43	Stricken 15 Jan 71
5 Oct 43	27 Dec 43	Sold for breaking up June 1969
30 Oct 43	12 Jan 44	Sold for breaking up 12 Mar 75
2 Nov 43	10 Jan 44	Stricken 1 Dec 72
13 Nov 43	25 Jan 44	To S. Vietnam 25 Sept 71
16 Nov 43	24 Jan 44	Stricken 15 Jan 71
20 Nov 43	3 Feb 44	Sold for breaking up 12 Mar 75
22 Dec 43	17 Feb 44	Stricken 2 Jan 71
29 Dec 43	28 Feb 44	Stricken 1 May 66
24 May 43	19 Oct 43	Stricken 1 Aug 74
26 May 43	12 Oct 43	Sold for breaking up 12 Mar 75
29 June 43	25 Oct 43	Sold for breaking up 12 Mar 75
30 June 43	30 Oct 43	Stricken 30 June 68
15 July 43	29 Oct 43	Stricken 1 June 75
16 July 43	1 Nov 43	Stricken 1 June 75
2 Aug 43	10 Nov 43	Stricken 1 Feb 74
3 Aug 43	16 Nov 43	Stricken 1 April 74
16 Aug 43	17 Nov 43	Stricken 2 July 73
17 Aug 43	22 Nov 43	Sold for breaking up 24 Sept 75
29 Aug 43	27 Nov 43	Stricken 2 April 71
30 Aug 43	29 Nov 43	Stricken 2 June 69
13 Sept 43	1 Dec 43	Stricken 1 July 72

EDSALL (FMR) CLASS—*continued*

Ship	Builder	Laid Down	Launched	Commissioned	Fate
DE395 *Willis*	Consolidated, Orange	17 July 43	14 Sept 43	10 Dec 43	Stricken 1 July 72
DE396 *Janssen*	Consolidated, Orange	4 Aug 43	4 Oct 43	18 Dec 43	Stricken 1 July 72
DE397 *Wilhoite*	Consolidated, Orange	4 Aug 43	5 Oct 43	16 Dec 43	Stricken 2 July 69
DE398 *Cockrill*	Consolidated, Orange	31 Aug 43	29 Oct 43	24 Dec 43	Stricken 1 Aug 73
DE399 *Stockdale*	Consolidated, Orange	31 Aug 43	30 Oct 43	31 Dec 43	Expended 23 May 74
DE400 *Hissem*	Consolidated, Orange	6 Oct 43	26 Dec 43	13 Jan 44	Stricken 1 June 75
DE401 *Holder*	Consolidated, Orange	6 Oct 43	27 Nov 43	18 Jan 44	Lost 11 April 44

Displacement: 1,253tons/1,273tonnes (standard); 1,602tons/1,627tonnes (full load).
Length: 306ft/93.27m (oa); 300ft/91.44m (wl).
Beam: 36ft 7in/11.15m.
Draught: 10ft 5in/3.2m (mean).
Machinery: 2-shaft Fairbanks Morse diesels.
Performance: 6,000bhp; 21kts.
Bunkerage: 320tons/325tonnes.
Range: 10,800nm at 12kts.
Guns: three 3in (3×1); two 40mm (2×1); ten 20mm.
Torpedoes: three 21in (1×3).
Complement: 186.

RUDDEROW (TEV) CLASS

Ship	Builder	Laid Down	Launched	Commissioned	Fate
DE224 *Rudderow*	Philadelphia NYd.	15 July 43	14 Oct 43	15 May 44	Stricken 1 Nov 69
DE225 *Day*	Philadelphia NYd.	15 July 43	14 Oct 43	10 June 44	Stricken June 1968
DE230 *Chaffee*	Charleston NYd.	26 Aug 43	27 Nov 43	9 May 44	Sold for breaking up June 1948
DE231 *Hodges*	Charleston NYd.	9 Sept 43	9 Dec 43	27 May 44	Stricken 1 Dec 72
DE579 *Riley*	Bethlehem, Hingham	9 Sept 43	29 Dec 43	13 Mar 44	To Taiwan 10 July 68
DE580 *Leslie L. B. Knox*	Bethlehem, Hingham	7 Nov 43	8 Jan 44	22 Mar 44	Stricken 15 Jan 72
DE581 *McNulty*	Bethlehem, Hingham	17 Nov 43	8 Jan 44	31 Mar 44	Stricken 11 Feb 72
DE582 *Metivier*	Bethlehem, Hingham	24 Nov 43	12 Jan 44	7 April 44	Sold for breaking up May 1969
DE583 *George A. Johnson*	Bethlehem, Hingham	24 Nov 43	12 Jan 44	15 April 44	Wrecked 12 Oct 66

Below: *Riley* (DE579), as completed. (USN)

RUDDEROW (TEV) CLASS

Ship	Builder	Laid Down	Launched	Commissioned	Fate
DE584 *Charles J. Kimmel*	Bethlehem, Hingham	1 Dec 43	15 Jan 44	20 April 44	Stricken June 1968
DE585 *Daniel A. Joy*	Bethlehem, Hingham	1 Dec 43	15 Jan 44	28 April 44	Stricken 15 May 65
DE586 *Lough*	Bethlehem, Hingham	8 Dec 43	22 Jan 44	2 May 44	Stricken 1 Nov 69
DE587 *Thomas F. Nickel*	Bethlehem, Hingham	15 Dec 43	22 Jan 44	9 June 44	Stricken 1 Dec 72
DE588 *Peiffer*	Bethlehem, Hingham	21 Dec.43	26 Jan 44	15 June 44	Stricken Jan 1966
DE589 *Tinsman*	Bethlehem, Hingham	21 Dec 43	29 Jan 44	26 June 44	Stricken 15 May 72
DE684 *De Long*	Bethlehem, Quincy	19 Oct 43	23 Nov 43	31 Dec 43	Expended 19 Feb 70
DE685 *Coates*	Bethlehem, Quincy	8 Nov 43	9 Dec 43	24 Jan 44	Stricken 30 Jan 70
DE686 *Eugene E. Elmore*	Bethlehem, Quincy	27 Nov 43	23 Dec 43	4 Feb 44	Sold for breaking up May 1969
DE706 *Holt*	Defoe, Bay City	28 Nov 43	15 Feb 44	9 June 44	To S. Korea 19 June 63
DE707 *Jobb*	Defoe, Bay City	20 Dec 43	4 Mar 44	4 July 44	Stricken 1 Nov 69
DE708 *Parle*	Defoe, Bay City	8 Jan 44	25 Mar 44	29 July 44	Stricken 1 July 70
DE709 *Bray*	Defoe, Bay City	27 Jan 44	15 April 44	4 Sept 44	Expended 26 Mar 63

DE226–229, DE232–237, DE281–283, DE590–606, DE674, DE721, DE722, DE687–692, DE710–720 all converted to APD before completion. Cancelled: *DE284–300, 607–632, DE645–664, 723–738, 905–1005.*

Displacement: 1,430tons/1,452tonnes (standard); 1,811tons/1,839tonnes (full load).
Length: 306ft/93.27m (oa); 300ft/91.44m (wl).
Beam: 37ft/11.28m.
Draught: 11ft 2in/3.4m (mean).
Machinery: two Foster-Wheeler (*DE579–589*), Babcock & Wilcox (*DE224, 225*) or Combustion Engineering boilers; 2-shaft G.E.C. geared turbines and electric drive.
Performance: 12,000shp; 23kts.
Bunkerage: 378tons/384tonnes.
Range: 6,000nm at 12kts.
Guns: two 5in (2×1); four 40mm (2×2); ten 20mm.
Torpedoes: three 21in (1×3).
Complement: 156.

Below: *T. F. Nickel* (DE587). (Real Photos)

JOHN C. BUTLER (WGT)

Ship	Builder	Laid Down
DE339 *John C. Butler*	Consolidated, Orange	5 Oct 43
DE340 *O'Flaherty*	Consolidated, Orange	4 Oct 43
DE341 *Raymond*	Consolidated, Orange	3 Nov 43
DE342 *Richard W. Suesens*	Consolidated, Orange	1 Nov 43
DE343 *Abercrombie*	Consolidated, Orange	8 Nov 43
DE344 *Oberrender*	Consolidated, Orange	8 Nov 43
DE345 *Robert Brazier*	Consolidated, Orange	16 Nov 43
DE346 *Edwin A. Howard*	Consolidated, Orange	15 Nov 43
DE347 *Jesse Rutherford*	Consolidated, Orange	22 Nov 43
DE348 *Key*	Consolidated, Orange	14 Dec 43
DE349 *Gentry*	Consolidated, Orange	13 Dec 43
DE350 *Traw*	Consolidated, Orange	19 Dec 43
DE351 *Maurice J. Manuel*	Consolidated, Orange	22 Dec 43
DE352 *Naifeh*	Consolidated, Orange	29 Dec 43
DE353 *Doyle C. Barnes*	Consolidated, Orange	11 Jan 44
DE354 *Kenneth M. Willett*	Consolidated, Orange	10 Jan 44
DE355 *Jaccard*	Consolidated, Orange	25 Jan 44
DE356 *Lloyd E. Acree*	Consolidated, Orange	24 Jan 44
DE357 *George E. Davis*	Consolidated, Orange	15 Feb 44
DE358 *Mack*	Consolidated, Orange	14 Feb 44
DE359 *Woodson*	Consolidated, Orange	7 Mar 44
DE360 *Johnnie Hutchins*	Consolidated, Orange	6 Mar 44
DE361 *Walton*	Consolidated, Orange	21 Mar 44
DE362 *Rolf*	Consolidated, Orange	20 Mar 44
DE363 *Pratt*	Consolidated, Orange	11 April 44
DE364 *Rombach*	Consolidated, Orange	10 April 44
DE365 *McGinty*	Consolidated, Orange	3 May 44
DE366 *Alvin C. Cockrell*	Consolidated, Orange	1 May 44

...ASS

Launched	Commissioned	Fate
11 Dec 43	31 Mar 44	Stricken 1 June 70
14 Dec 43	8 April 44	Sold for breaking up Nov 1973
8 Jan 44	15 April 44	Stricken 1 July 72
11 Jan 44	24 April 44	Stricken 15 Mar 72
14 Jan 44	1 May 44	Stricken May 1967
18 Jan 44	11 May 44	Lost 9 May 45
22 Jan 44	8 May 44	Expended Jan 1968
25 Jan 44	25 May 44	Stricken 1 Dec 72
29 Jan 44	31 May 44	Stricken 1 Jan 68
12 Feb 44	5 June 44	Stricken 1 Mar 72
15 Feb 44	14 June 44	Stricken 15 Jan 72
12 Feb 44	20 June 44	Expended Aug 1968
19 Feb 44	30 June 44	Stricken 1 May 66
29 Feb 44	4 July 44	Expended July 1966
4 Mar 44	13 July 44	Stricken 1 Dec 72
7 Mar 44	19 July 44	Stricken 1 July 72
18 Mar 44	26 July 44	Expended Nov 1967
21 Mar 44	1 Aug 44	Stricken 15 Jan 72
8 April 44	11 Aug 44	Stricken 1 Dec 72
11 April 44	16 Aug 44	Expended Jan 1966
29 April 44	24 Aug 44	Stricken 1 July 65
2 May 44	28 Aug 44	Stricken 1 July 72
20 May 44	4 Sept 44	Stricken Sept 1968
23 May 44	7 Sept 44	Sold for breaking up Oct 1973
1 June 44	Sept 1944	Stricken 15 Mar 72
6 June 44	20 Sept 44	Stricken 1 Mar 72
5 Aug 44	25 Sept 44	Stricken Sept 1968
8 Aug 44	7 Oct 44	Stricken Sept 1968

Above: *John C. Butler* (DE339). This class were completed with 5-inch guns. (USN)

JOHN C. BUTLER (WGT) CLASS

Ship	Builder	Laid Down	Launched	Commissioned	Fate
DE367 *French*	Consolidated, Orange	May 1944	17 June 44	9 Oct 44	Sold for breaking up Oct 1973
DE368 *Cecil J. Doyle*	Consolidated, Orange	12 May 44	1 July 44	16 Oct 44	Stricken 15 Mar 72
DE369 *Thaddeus Parker*	Consolidated Orange	23 May 44	26 Aug 44	25 Oct 44	Stricken 1 Mar 72
DE370 *John L. Williamson*	Consolidated, Orange	22 May 44	29 Aug 44	31 Oct 44	Stricken Sept 1968
DE371 *Presley*	Consolidated, Orange	6 June 44	19 Aug 44	7 Nov 44	Stricken Sept 1968
DE372 *Williams*	Consolidated, Orange	5 June 44	22 Aug 44	11 Nov 44	Sold for breaking up Oct 1973
DE373 *William C. Lawe*	Consolidated, Orange	–	–	–	Cancelled June 1944
DE374 *Lloyd Thomas*	Consolidated, Orange	–	–	–	Cancelled June 1944
DE375 *Keppler*	Consolidated, Orange	–	–	–	Cancelled June 1944
DE376 *Kleinsmith*	Consolidated Orange	–	–	–	Cancelled June 1944
DE377 *Henry W. Tucker*	Consolidated, Orange	–	–	–	Cancelled June 1944
DE378 *Weiss*	Consolidated, Orange	–	–	–	Cancelled June 1944
DE379 *Francovich*	Consolidated, Orange	–	–	–	Cancelled June 1944
DE402 *Richard S. Bull*	Brown Sbdg., Houston	18 Aug 43	16 Nov 43	26 Feb 44	Stricken 30 June 68
DE403 *Richard M. Rowell*	Brown Sbdg., Houston	18 Aug 43	17 Nov 43	9 Mar 44	Sold for breaking up May 1969
DE404 *Eversole*	Brown Sbdg., Houston	15 Sept 43	3 Dec 43	21 Mar 44	Lost 28 Oct 44
DE405 *Dennis*	Brown Sbdg., Houston	15 Sept 43	4 Dec 43	20 Mar 44	Stricken 1 Dec 72
DE406 *Edmonds*	Brown Sbdg., Houston	1 Nov 43	17 Dec 43	3 April 44	Sold for breaking up Oct 1973
DE407 *Shelton*	Brown Sbdg., Houston	1 Nov 43	18 Dec 43	4 April 44	Lost 3 Oct 44

JOHN C. BUTLER (WGT) CLASS—*continued*

Ship	Builder	Laid Down	Launched	Commissioned	Fate
DE408 *Straus*	Brown Sbdg., Houston	18 Nov 43	30 Dec 43	6 April 44	Expended May 1966
DE409 *La Prade*	Brown Sbdg., Houston	18 Nov 43	31 Dec 43	20 April 44	Stricken 15 Jan 72
DE410 *Jack Miller*	Brown Sbdg., Houston	29 Nov 43	10 Jan 44	13 April 44	Stricken 30 June 68
DE411 *Stafford*	Brown Sbdg., Houston	29 Nov 43	11 Jan 44	19 April 44	Stricken 15 Mar 72
DE412 *Walter C. Wann*	Brown Sbdg., Houston	6 Dec 43	19 Jan 44	2 May 44	Stricken 30 June 68
DE413 *Samuel B. Roberts*	Brown Sbdg., Houston	6 Dec 43	20 Jan 44	28 April 44	Lost 25 Oct 44
DE414 *Le Ray Wilson*	Brown Sbdg., Houston	20 Dec 43	28 Jan 44	10 May 44	Stricken 15 May 72
DE415 *Lawrence C. Taylor*	Brown Sbdg., Houston	20 Dec 43	29 Jan 44	13 May 44	Stricken 1 Dec 72
DE416 *Melvin R. Nawman*	Brown Sbdg., Houston	3 Jan 44	7 Feb 44	16 May 44	Stricken 1 July 72
DE417 *Oliver Mitchell*	Brown Sbdg., Houston	3 Jan 44	8 Feb 44	14 June 44	Stricken 15 Mar 72
DE418 *Tabberer*	Brown Sbdg., Houston	12 Jan 44	18 Feb 44	23 May 44	Stricken 1 July 72
DE419 *Robert F. Keller*	Brown Sbdg., Houston	12 Jan 44	19 Feb 44	17 June 44	Stricken 1 July 72
DE420 *Leland E. Thomas*	Brown Sbdg., Houston	21 Jan 44	28 Feb 44	19 June 44	Stricken 1 Dec 72
DE421 *Chester T. O'Brien*	Brown Sbdg., Houston	21 Jan 44	29 Feb 44	3 July 44	Stricken 1 July 72
DE422 *Douglas A. Munro*	Brown Sbdg., Houston	31 Jan 44	8 Mar 44	11 July 44	Expended Jan 1966
DE423 *Dufilho*	Brown Sbdg., Houston	31 Jan 44	9 Mar 44	21 July 44	Stricken 1 Dec 72
DE424 *Haas*	Brown Sbdg., Houston	23 Feb 44	20 Mar 44	2 Aug 44	Stricken July 1966
DE438 *Corbesier*	Federal Sbdg. Co.	4 Nov 43	13 Feb 44	31 Mar 44	Stricken 1 Dec 72
DE439 *Conklin*	Federal Sbdg. Co.	4 Nov 43	13 Feb 44	21 April 44	Stricken 1 Oct 70
DE440 *McCoy Reynolds*	Federal Sbdg. Co.	18 Nov 43	22 Feb 44	2 May 44	To Portugal 7 Feb 57
DE441 *William Seiverling*	Federal Sbdg. Co.	2 Dec 43	7 Mar 44	1 June 44	Stricken 1 Dec 72
DE442 *Ulvert M. Moore*	Federal Sbdg. Co.	2 Dec 43	7 Mar 44	18 July 44	Expended July 1966
DE443 *Kendal C. Campbell*	Federal Sbdg. Co.	16 Dec 43	19 Mar 44	31 July 44	Stricken 15 Jan 72
DE444 *Goss*	Federal Sbdg. Co.	16 Dec 43	19 Mar 44	26 Aug 44	Sold for breaking up Nov 1972
DE445 *Grady*	Federal Sbdg. Co.	3 Jan 44	2 April 44	11 Sept 44	Sold for breaking up May 1969
DE446 *Charles E. Brannon*	Federal Sbdg. Co.	13 Jan 44	23 April 44	1 Nov 44	Stricken Sept 1968
DE447 *Albert T. Harris*	Federal Sbdg. Co.	13 Jan 44	16 April 44	29 Nov 44	Stricken Sept 1968
DE448 *Cross*	Federal Sbdg. Co.	19 Mar 44	4 July 44	8 Jan 45	Stricken 1 July 66

JOHN C. BUTLER (WGT) C

Ship	Builder	Laid Down
DE449 *Hanna*	Federal Sbdg. Co.	22 Mar 44
DE450 *Joseph E. Connolly*	Federal Sbdg. Co.	6 April 44
DE451 *Woodrow R. Thompson*	Federal Sbdg. Co.	–
DE452 *Steinaker*	Federal Sbdg. Co.	–
DE508 *Gilligan* (ex-*Donaldson*)	Federal Sbdg. Co.	18 Nov 43
DE509 *Formoe*	Federal Sbdg. Co.	3 Jan 44
DE510 *Heyliger*	Federal Sbdg. Co.	27 April 44
DE531 *Edward H. Allen*	Boston NYd.	31 Aug 43
DE532 *Tweedy*	Boston NYd.	31 Aug 43
DE533 *Howard F. Clark*	Boston NYd.	8 Oct 43
DE534 *Silverstein*	Boston NYd.	8 Oct 43
DE535 *Lewis*	Boston NYd.	3 Nov 43
DE536 *Bivin*	Boston NYd.	3 Nov 43
DE537 *Rizzi*	Boston NYd.	3 Nov 43
DE538 *Osberg*	Boston NYd.	3 Nov 43
DE539 *Wagner*	Boston NYd.	8 Nov 43
DE540 *Vandivier*	Boston NYd.	8 Nov 43
DE541 *Sheehan*	Boston NYd.	8 Nov 43
DE542 *Oswald A. Powers*	Boston NYd.	18 Nov 43
DE543 *Groves*	Boston NYd.	9 Dec 43
DE544 *Alfred Wolf*	Boston NYd.	9 Dec 43
DE545 *Harold J. Ellison*	Boston NYd.	–
DE546 *Myles C. Fox*	Boston NYd.	–
DE547 *Charles R. Ware*	Boston NYd.	–
DE548 *Carpelotti*	Boston NYd.	–
DE549 *Eugene A. Greene*	Boston NYd.	–
DE550 *Gyatt*	Boston NYd.	–
DE551 *Benner*	Boston NYd.	–
DE552 *Kenneth D. Bailey*	Boston NYd.	–
DE553 *Dennis J. Buckley*	Boston NYd.	–
DE554 *Everett F. Larson*	Boston NYd.	–

*Suspended August 1946, resumed 1954. Also cancelled: *DE380–381, DE425–437, DE453–507, DE511–515, DE555–562*

Displacement: 1,430tons/1,452tonnes (standard); 1,811tons/1,839tonnes (full load).
Length: 306ft/93.27m (oa); 300ft/91.44m (wl).
Beam: 37ft/11.28m.
Draught: 11ft 2in/3.4m (mean).
Machinery: two Combustion Engineering or Babcock & Wilcox boilers; 2-shaft Westinghouse turbines with electric drive.
Performance: 12,000shp; 23kts.
Bunkerage: 347tons/352tonnes.
Range: 6,000nm at 12kts.
Guns: two 5in (2×1); four 40mm (2×2); ten 20mm.
Torpedoes: three 21in (1×3).
Complement: 156.

Design There had been pre-war suggestions of the

—continued

Launched	Commissioned	Fate
4 July 44	27 Jan 45	Stricken 1 Dec 72
6 Aug 44	28 Feb 45	Stricken 1 July 70
–	–	Cancelled June 1944
–	–	
22 Feb 44	12 May 44	Sold for breaking up Nov 1972
2 April 44	5 Oct 44	To Portugal 7 Feb 57
6 Aug 44	24 Mar 45	Stricken 1 May 66
7 Oct 43	16 Dec 43	Stricken 1 July 72
7 Oct 43	12 Feb 44	Expended 30 June 69
8 Nov 43	25 May 44	Stricken 15 May 72
8 Nov 43	14 July 44	Stricken 1 Dec 72
7 Dec 43	5 Sept 44	Expended Jan 1966
7 Dec 43	31 Oct 44	Stricken 30 June 68
7 Dec 43	26 June 45	Stricken 1 Aug 72
7 Dec 43	17 Dec 45	Stricken 1 Aug 72
27 Dec 43	31 Dec 55*	Sold for breaking up Aug 1977
27 Dec 43	1 Dec 55*	Stricken 1 Nov 74
–	–	Cancelled 7 Jan 46
17 Dec 43	–	Cancelled 7 Jan 46
1944	–	Cancelled 5 Sept 44
1944	–	Cancelled 5 Sept 44
–		
–		
–		
–		
–		Cancelled June 1944
–		
–		
–		
–		
–		

Above: *Raymond* (DE341). (Real Photos) **Below:** *Walton* (DE361). (Real Photos)

need for a destroyer-type ship for escort duties in an anti-submarine role, but these had come to nothing, partly because of a reluctance to build a second-rate ship and partly because it was felt in some quarters that an existing destroyer design could be built or modified more rapidly. The outbreak of war in 1939 triggered new appraisals of the escort-destroyer concept, but once again, despite much discussion, there was no agreement as to how the conflicting demands of cost, armament and construction speed could be reconciled. By 1941, however, British Atlantic experience had clearly demonstrated the need for large numbers of escort vessels and the subject was re-examined by the USN for their own purposes. Word of this then reached the British Admiralty who made it known that they would be interested in obtaining such vessels under Lend-Lease. Eventually a sketch design was prepared for a ship armed with two 5-inch DP guns, 280 feet long, capable of 24 knots and equipped with a triple bank of torpedo tubes for anti-raider use. This met with less than unanimous approval and in May 1941, the proposed fifty ships to be built as escorts, were cancelled. US enthusiasm for such a ship was luke-warm at best and throughout there was a preference for standard destroyers as being the real solution. There the matter might have rested but for the desperate British need for escort vessels. In June, the British Supply Mission to the USA requested 100 of the escort vessels, obviously unaware of their cancellation and the US views on the type. President Roosevelt approved the supply of 50 destroyer-escorts to Britain on 15 August 1941 and the design was modified to incorporate British ideas in bridge design and armament.

The major problem in the production of destroyer-escorts turned out to be the main machinery, for originally, a 12,000shp geared turbine plant was specificed. Turbine production was already over-loaded and in consequence, an alternative propulsion was examined which led, in fact, to the six-class sub-division of the DE programme, although all were originally intended to be identical. The obvious alternative was diesel power with electric drive, derived from submarine practice, and the design was revised to incorporate this. Unfortunately, the demands for diesel engines were very heavy, both from submarines and landing-craft and as a result, diesel electric-powered ships, received only half the designed number of diesels, having 6,000bhp for 21 knots. These were the *Ewarts*, short-hull class, which were not considered particularly successful. To increase the installed power to the original 12,000shp, turbo-electric drive was adopted for the *Buckley* and *Rudderow* classes, but the hull had to be lengthened to accommodate the more bulky power plant. The speed was raised thereby almost to the original 24 knots. This new 300-foot hull then became the standard for all DEs, although the *Cannon* class received the 6,000bhp diesel/electric drive in the long hull, and the *Edsall* class, a diesel power plant of the same output. Finally, the *John C. Butler* class received a steam turbine installation of 12,000shp.

Although designed originally with an armament of two 5-inch DP guns in mind, this outfit did not appear until the later ships. Instead, three single 3-inch/50 guns in open mountings were fitted, two forward, one aft. Bofors production was limited and DEs were not high on the priority list for this weapon and in consequence, received the quadruple 1.1-inch gun in lieu. The ASW outfit consisted of a 'hedgehog', two depth-charge rails and eight throwers. By 1942, the USN expressed concern about the weak armament of the DEs, which resulted in the *Rudderows* and *John C. Butlers* receiving two single 5-inch/38 guns in destroyer-type gun-houses, one forward, one aft. Torpedoes were retained in the long-hulled units except for those transferred to Great Britain.

Orders began to be placed from November 1941, initially with Naval yards, but most of the eventually huge DE programme was built in smaller or specially set up yards, not in the destroyer programme. By the spring of 1943, a total of 1,005 ships had been ordered, but because of later cancellations, only(!) 563 ships were actually completed.

Modifications Radar was added to all and many Atlantic units received HF/DF. 20mm outfits were increased to eight in the long-hulled units, nine in the short, with some carrying ten. Units operating in the Mediterranean received four single army-pattern 40mm guns in lieu of their torpedoes, but later two twin power-operated mountings were substituted. *DE448–450*, *DE510* and *DE537–538*, however, completed with one quadruple and three twin 40mm as well as ten single 20mm. *DE371* and *DE372* completed without torpedo tubes. In 1945, *DE217–219*, *678–680*, *696–698* and *700–701* were re-armed with two 5in; ten 40mm and no torpedoes. *Camp* was the only FRIR re-armed thus.

Nearly 100 units of the TE and WGT types were converted to Fast Transports (APD), equipped to carry four LCVP at davits and armed with a single 5-inch DP gun, three twin 40mm and six 20mm. Aft, a pair of kingposts (in TEV conversions) or Lattice Masts (in TE conversions) supported two 5-ton cargo booms to work deck loads carried on the quarter deck. Thirty-seven units of the TE type were converted after completion (*DE53/54, DE60, 62/63, 65/66, 68–70, DE154–156, DE158–161, DE205–209, DE211/212, DE215/216, DE576, DE637, DE675–677, DE693, DE694, DE789* and *DE792–794*) and the remainder while under construction (*DE668–DE673*). Five TE conversions (*DE214, DE665, DE666, DE790* and *DE791*) were cancelled. These ships formed the series *APD37–86*. *APD87–136* were TEV units, converted while under construction, ex-*DE226–229, DE232–237, DE281–283, DE590–606, DE674, DE721, DE722, DE687–692, DE710–DE720*.

Service Widely employed in the Atlantic and Pacific theatres with a few units going to the Mediterranean. In the Atlantic, their main tasks were ocean escort duties for convoys bound for Great Britain and also the US forces in North Africa. They were also employed as part of the escort to carrier-based hunter-killer groups, operating mainly in the central Atlantic, south and west of the Azores. In this role, the combination of carrier-borne ASW aircraft, effective ASW vessels and 'Ultra'-Intelligence, produced very successful results against German U-boat operations. Overall, DEs accounted for thirty German submarines (*U66, U85, U154, U172, U233, U248, U371, U488, U490, U505, U515, U518, U546, U548, U549, U550, U575, U603, U709, U801, U853, U856, U857, U866, U869, U879, U880, U1062, U1224* and *U1235*). Of these *U515* was, in fact, captured while *U1224* had been sold to Japan and was en route home as *Ro501*. Three were sunk by U-boat torpedoes in the Atlantic, *Leopold* by *U255* south of Iceland, *Fiske* by *U804* north of the Azores and *Frederick C. Davis* by *U546*. *Holder* was damaged beyond repair by German aircraft torpedoes off Algiers, and *Fechteler* was sunk by *U967* off Oran. *Rich* was mined off Normandy and *Donnell*, torpedoed by *U765* on 3 May 1944, was so badly damaged that she was not repaired, but finished up as a floating power-station at Cherbourg. *Menges*, torpedoes by *U371* on 3 May 1944, was repaired with the stern of *Holder*.

In the Pacific, DEs accounted for 29 Japanese submarines (*I5, I6, I10, I13, I16, I25, I32, I37, I41, I45, I48, I54, I177, I180, I362, I370, Ro39, Ro42, Ro47, Ro55, Ro104, Ro105, Ro106, Ro108, Ro109, Ro115* and *Ro116*). *England* sank six of these in twelve days in the Central Pacific in May 1944. *Shelton*, however, was torpedoed and sunk by *Ro41* off Morotai, *Eversole* by *I45* east of Leyte and *Underhill* by a human torpedo off Luzon.

Four DEs took part in the battle of Samar in October 1944, in a fleet action for which they were never designed. These were *Dennis, John C. Butler, Raymond* and *Samuel B. Roberts* which, with the destroyers *Hoel, Heermann* and *Johnston*, were screening Admiral Sprague's six escort carriers. In a valiant attack on the Japanese battleships and heavy cruisers, *Samuel B. Roberts, Raymond* and *Dennis* launched all their torpedoes but failed to hit. *Samuel B. Roberts* was destroyed by gunfire and *Dennis* badly damaged, but *Raymond* was untouched, despite making a gun attack on the Japanese heavy ships. *Hoel* and *Johnston* were also sunk, but between them the DDs and DEs restricted the powerful Japanese force to sinking only the carrier *Gambier Bay* with both *Fanshaw Bay* and *Kalinin Bay* damaged.

More than fifty Pacific Fleet DEs participated in the Okinawa assault where, like the destroyers, they came under heavy Kamikaze attack. Eleven were damaged to various degrees including *Riddle, Fieberling, John C. Butler, Manlove, Oberrender, Whitehurst, Foreman, Rall, Bowers, England* and *Wesson*, the last seven very badly of which *England* and *Oberrender* were beyond repair. One of the *APD* conversions, *Bates APD47*, was also damaged beyond repair by Kamikaze attack at Okinawa.

Below: *McCoy Reynolds* (DE440) in July 1944. (USN)

Yugoslavia

Yugoslavia rose from the ashes of the Austro-Hungarian Empire, destroyed by the First World War. The new state, officially the Kingdom of the Serbs, Croats and Slovenes, was proclaimed on 1 December 1918, prior to which date there had been a degree of chaos in the region, following the Armistice, when numerous 'sailor councils' and splinter factions had taken over many of the former Austro-Hungarian warships. Yugoslavia made demands for a large proportion of the former Empire's fleet, but the Allies decided otherwise, when in 1920, they allocated the new state one old coast-defence battleship, *Erzherzog Kronprinz Rudolf*, four small coastal torpedo-boats, twelve sea-going torpedo-boats and a miscellaneous collection of auxiliaries, monitors and launches. These were taken over in March 1921. An expansion plan envisaged in 1922 called for 24 destroyers, a like number of submarines and a large fleet of seaplanes. This was quite clearly unrealistic and nothing came of it. In fact the only addition since 1921 were six ex-German *M*-class minesweepers purchased in that year. The Navy fell into three distinct arms, the seagoing fleet, the riverine (monitor) command and naval aviation. As far as this volume is concerned, only the former will be considered. Lack of funds hindered any expansion ideas, as it did in many navies, but in 1926 the former German light cruiser *Niobe* was purchased, and in 1927 the first new construction was ordered, two MTBs from England, two submarines, also from England, and two more from France. Some of the older ex-Austrian torpedo-boats were then scrapped.

In January 1929, political changes resulted in the state becoming the Kingdom of Yugoslavia and the navy, the Royal Yugoslavian Navy. Expansion plans now began to come to fruition; a new large flotilla leader was ordered in Britain, MTBs in Germany, minelayers in home yards and a number of new auxiliaries obtained. Three more destroyers were added in the late 1930s, two built in home yards. Finally in 1939, a large destroyer was laid down at the Split shipyard and two Type IIB submarines ordered in Germany.

When Germany and Italy attacked Yugoslavia on 6 April 1941, there were avilable three destroyers and two submarines as the most effective units of the fleet, with a couple of MTBs. The remainder of the fleet was useful only for coastal defence and local patrol work. The main base was Kotor, close to the Albanian border, but Zara, an Italian enclave, was to the north of the coast and to prevent a bridgehead being established, four of the old torpedo-boats, six MTBs and some other craft were dispatched to Sibenik, fifty miles to the south of Zara, in preparation for an attack. Before this could be launched, the German Army invaded Yugoslavia through Croatia and this concentration of force was returned to Kotor. The situation deteriorated rapidly in the face of German and Italian land and air power and on 14 April, the government asked for an armistice. None of the destroyers and only a couple of MTBs and a submarine were able to escape to Allied bases, the rest of the fleet being sabotaged or captured by the Italians and subsequently used by them.

The few craft which had escaped to the Allies were used for local defence and patrol duties off Alexandria and in the Levant until shortage of spares and poor condition caused them to be paid off. Those destroyers taken over by the Axis forces had, on the other hand, a much more active career.

T1 CLASS

Ship	Builder	Laid Down	Launched	Commissioned	Fate
T1 (ex-*76T*)	Stabilimento, Trieste	24 June 13	15 Dec 13	20 July 14	Stricken 1959
T3 (ex-*78T*)	Stabilimento, Trieste	22 Oct 13	4 Mar 14	23 Aug 14	Captured April 1941

Displacement: 262tons/266tonnes (standard); 320tons/325tonnes (full load).
Length: 190ft 9in/58.2m (wl); 188ft/57.3m (pp).
Beam: 18ft 9in/5.7m.
Draught: 5ft 1in/1.5m (mean).
Machinery: two Yarrow boilers; 2-shaft Parsons turbines.
Performance: 5,000shp; 28kts.
Bunkerage: 24tons/24.3tonnes (oil)+18tons/18.2tonnes (coal).
Range: 980nm at 16kts.
Guns: two 66mm; two MG.
Torpedoes: four 18in (2×2).
Complement: 38.

Design Former Austro-Hungarian seagoing torpedo-boats which had seen service during the First World War, survivors of four which had been acquired in March 1921. The other two, *T2* (ex-*77T*) and *T4* (ex-*79T*) had been deleted by 1939, the latter having run aground and become a total loss on the Dalmatian coast, in 1932. By the outbreak of the Second World War, they were quite obsolete, but saw considerable service. A sister ship was the Romanian *Sborul* (q.v.).

Modifications Few if any in Yugoslav hands.

Service The rapid collapse of Yugoslavia prevented any real active service for these two ships and they fell into Italian hands in April 1941. *T1* was returned to Yugoslavia by Italy in December 1943 and thereafter served as *Golesnica* until scapped in 1959. Her sister *T3* was lost in German hands after the Italian capitulation (see Germany *TA48*).

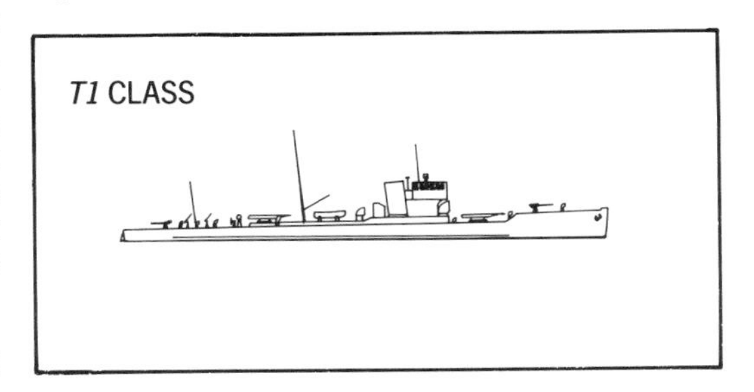
T1 CLASS

T5 CLASS

Ship	Builder	Laid Down	Launched	Commissioned	Fate
T5 (ex-*87F*)	Danubius, Porto Ré	5 Mar 14	20 Mar 15	25 Oct 15	Captured by Italy April 1941
T6 (ex-*93F*)	Danubius, Porto Ré	9 Jan 15	25 Nov 15	16 April 16	Captured by Italy April 1941
T7 (ex-*96F*)	Danubius, Porto Ré	24 Feb 15	7 July 16	23 Nov 16	Captured by Italy April 1941
T8 (ex-*97F*)	Danubius, Porto Ré	5 Mar 15	20 Aug 16	22 Dec 16	Captured by Italy April 1941

Displacement: 266tons/270tonnes (standard); 330tons/335tonnes (full load).
Length: 192ft 9in/58.8m (oa); 191ft 11in/58.5m (wl); 189ft 7in/57.8m (pp).
Beam: 19ft 2in/5.8m.
Draught: 5ft 1in/1.5m (mean).
Machinery: two Yarrow boilers; 2-shaft A.E.G. turbines.
Performance: 5,000shp; 28kts.
Bunkerage: 20tons/20.3tonnes (oil)+34tons/34.5tonnes (coal).
Range: 1,200nm at 16kts.
Guns: two 66mm; two MG.
Torpedoes: four 18in (2×2).
Complement: 25.

Design These four ships were also ex-Austro-Hungarian units, differing from the *T1* class mainly in that these boats had twin funnels. Their armament, speed and dimensions were identical with the Stabilimento boats of the *T1* type, and were thus quite obsolete. Two sister ships served in the Romanian Navy as *Naluca* and *Smeul*.

Modifications None in Yugoslav hands.

Service All four were captured at Kotor in April 1941 and incorporated into the Royal Italian Navy as their *T5–T8*. Only *T5* survived to be retroceded to Yugoslavia on 7 December 1943. Re-named *Cer*, she was eventually discarded in 1963.

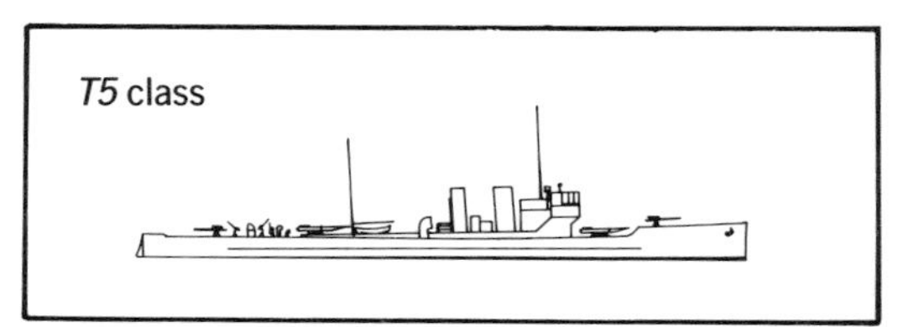

BEOGRAD CLASS

Ship	Builder	Laid Down	Launched	Commissioned	Fate
Beograd	At. & Ch. de la Loire (Nantes)	–	23 Dec 37	28 April 39	Captured 17 April 41
Ljubljana	Yarrow, Kraljevica	–	28 June 38	Dec 1939	Captured 17 April 41
Zagreb	At. & Ch. de la Loire (Split)	–	30 Mar 38	Aug 1939	Scuttled 17 April 41

Displacement: 1,210tons/1,229tonnes (standard); 1,655tons/1,681tonnes (full load).
Length: 321ft 6in/98m (oa).
Beam: 31ft/9.45m.
Draught: 10ft 5in/3.18m (mean).
Machinery: three Yarrow boilers; 2-shaft Parsons (*Beograd* Curtis) geared turbines.
Performance: 40,000shp; 38kts.
Bunkerage: 120tons/122tonnes.
Guns: four 4.7in (4×1); four 40mm (2×2); two MG.
Torpedoes: six 21.7in (2×3).
Mines: 30.
Complement: 145.

Design Built to a French design by At. & Ch. de la Loire, these destroyers were engined by Yarrow & Co. of Great Britain. In appearance, they resembled British destroyer layout rather than French, although the close spacing of the guns was common French practice. The main armament consisted of four 4.7-inch (120mm) 46cal Skoda QF guns in single shielded mountings. Two twin 40mm guns, sided on the after shelter deck, comprised the AA outfit and two triple banks of torpedo tubes completed the armament. The machinery installation, supplied by Yarrow, operated at 400psi and developed 44,000shp for a designed maximum speed of 38 knots, but *Beograd* is reported to have exceeded 39 knots on trials. The leading ship, *Beograd*, was laid down in France at Nantes, but the other pair were built in Yugoslavia, one by the Yarrow-managed yard at Kraljevica, the other at At. & Ch. de la Loire's yard at Split.

Modifications None in Yugoslav hands.

Service *Ljubliana* foundered off Sibenik in January 1940 and was in dockyard hands under repair at the Tivat Arsenal when war broke out. Captured by Italian forces on 17 April 1941, *Ljubljana* was repaired and commissioned in the Royal Italian Navy as *Lubiana* (q.v.). *Zagreb*, lying at Kotor, was blown up by two of her officers to prevent her capture. *Beograd* was damaged by near misses from dive-bombers off Sibenik when her starboard engine was put out of action, after which she limped to Kotor for repair. Here she was captured by the Italians, repaired and recommissioned as *Sebenico* (q.v.).

Below: *Beograd* in 1939. (Wright & Logan)

DUBROVNIK

Ship	Builder	Laid Down	Launched	Commissioned	Fate
Dubrovnik	A. Yarrow	10 June 30	12 Oct 31	May 1932	Captured 17 April 41

Displacement: 1,880tons/1,910tonnes (standard); 2,800tons/2,845tonnes (full load).
Length: 371ft 6in/113.2m (oa); 345ft/105.1m (pp).
Beam: 35ft/10.66m.
Draught: 10ft 7in/3.22m (mean).
Machinery: three Yarrow side-fired boilers; 2-shaft Parsons geared turbines.
Performance: 42,000shp; 37kts.
Bunkerage: 520tons/528tonnes.
Range: 6,600nm at 13kts.
Guns: four 5.5in (4×1); two 3.3in (1×2); six 40mm (2×2, 2×1).
Torpedoes: six 21in (2×3).
Mines: 40.
Complement: 200.

Design This large flotilla leader was ordered from Yarrow on 4 August 1929. Her layout followed contemporary British practice in general, but a much heavier gun calibre, 5.5-inch was specified. These guns, Skoda 14cm-pattern, were of Czech manufacture, having very long, distinctive barrels, 56 calibres in length. They were quick-firing in open shields, using separate ammunition with an 88lb shell. Two were forward, two aft, 'B' and 'X' guns superfiring. Electric ammunition hoists were fitted. As originally designed, the light armament was to consist of six Skoda 40mm AA guns, two twins between the funnels and two single on the main deck abreast the after control station. Six 21-inch torpedoes in two Brotherhoods triple mountings were carried on the centre-line. The ASW outfit comprised two chutes and two throwers with ten depth-charges carried. Also included in the original design was a platform for a seaplane, presumably on the lines of that fitted to Dutch destroyers, but this was cancelled before the ship was laid down. While under construction the seaplane equipment was supplanted by a twin 3.3-inch (8.35cm) Skoda L/35 mounting (and six hundred rounds of ammunition) on the centre-line between the torpedo tubes. Fire-control systems for the main armament were of Dutch origin and the communications system from Belgium, a mixture of equipment sources which would later cause operational problems. The main machinery developed 42,000shp with Yarrow side-fired boilers fitted with air pre-heaters, operating at 300psi. *Dubrovnik* ran her six-hour full-power trials on the Arran mile on 4 May 1932, reaching 37.2 knots with 48,500shp.

Modifications No significant alterations prior to April 1941, except that the Skoda 40mm may have been exchanged for Swedish 37mm Bofors guns.

Service Like all other Yugoslav warships, the speed of the Axis invasion prevented any operational employment and the ship was captured on 17 April 1940, then saw extensive service under first, the Italian flag as *Premuda*, then the Kriegsmarine ensign as *TA32*.

Above: *Dubrovnik*. Note twin 3-inch gun. (Yugoslav Navy) **Below:** *Dubrovnik*. (Yugoslav Navy)

SPLIT

Ship	Builder	Laid Down	Launched	Commissioned	Fate
Split	At. & Ch. de la Loire (Split)	July 1939	1940	4 July 58	?

Design A flotilla leader of enlarged *Dubrovnik* type designed by At. Ch. de la Loire. She was to be armed with five 5.5-inch guns, ten 40mm AA and six 21-inch torpedo tubes. Laid down in 1939, she had been launched by the outbreak of war, but was still incomplete when captured by Italy. Renamed *Spalato* by the Royal Italian Navy, she was never completed by them and was eventually captured by German forces on 8 September 1943. Scuttled on the German evacuation of Yugoslavia, *Split* was not finally completed until well after the war and then to a different design.

Select Bibliography

Anon. *Historia Naval Brasileira.* Ministério da Marinha, Rio de Janeiro, 1985
Anon. *I Caccia-torpediniere Italiani.* Uffico Storico della Marina, Rome, 1965
Anon. *Japanese Aircraft Carriers and Destroyers.* Macdonald, London, 1968
Bekker, Cajus. *Hitler's Naval War.* Macdonald & Jane, London, 1974
Bragadin, Marc'Antonio. *The Italian Navy in World War II.* Naval Institute Press, Annapolis, 1957
Campbell, John. *Naval Weapons of World War II.* Conway Maritime Press, London, 1985
Cioglia, S. 'Classe Soldati', in *Aviazione e Marina*
— 'I Caccia della Classe Freccia', in *Aviazione e Marina*
Colledge, J. J. *Ships of the Royal Navy*, vol. I. David & Charles, Newton Abbot, 1969
Divine, A. D. *Navies in Exile.* John Murray, London, 1944
Fraccaroli, Aldo. *Italian Warships of World War II.* Ian Allan, Shepperton, 1968
Friedman, Norman. *U.S. Destroyers.* Naval Institute Press, Annapolis, and Arms & Armour Press, London, 1982
— and Hodges, P. *Destroyer Weapons.* Conway Maritime Press, London, 1979
Gardiner, Robert (ed.). *Conway's All the World's Fighting Ships, 1906–1921.* Conway Maritime Press, London, 1985
— *Conway's All the World's Fighting Ships, 1922–1946.* Conway Maritime Press, London, 1980
— *Super Destroyers.* Warship Special No. 2. Conway Maritime Press, London, 1978
Gröner, E. *Die Deutschen Kriegsschiffe, 1815–1945.* J. F. Lehmanns Verlag, Munich, 1968
Guiglini, Jean. 'The 2,400-Tonners', in *Warship International*, February 1981
Güth, Rolf. *Zerstörer Z34.* Koehler Verlag, 1980
Harnack, W. *Die Deutschen Zerstörer von 1934 bis 1945.* Koehler Verlag, 1977
Jentschura, H., Jung, D., and Mickel, P. (trans. A. Preston and D. J. Brown). *Warships of the Imperial Japanese Navy, 1869–1945.* Arms & Armour Press, London, and Naval Institute Press, Annapolis, 1977
Kemp, Lieutenant-Commander P. K. *H.M. Destroyers.* Herbert Jenkins, London, 1956
Kühn, V. *Torpedoboote und Zerstörer im Einsatz, 1939–1945.* Motorbuch Verlag, 1974
Le Masson, H. M. *Histoire du Torpilleur en France.* Académie de Marine, Paris, 1963
— *French Warships of World War II.* Macdonald, London, 1969
Lenton, H. J. *German Warships of the Second World War.* Macdonald & Jane, London, 1975
— and Colledge, J. J. *Warships of World War II.* Ian Allan, Shepperton, 1964
March, Edgar. *British Destroyers.* Seeley Service, London, 1966
Meirat, Jean. '"Fantastic" was the Word', in *Warship International*, March 1978
Meister, J. *Soviet Warships of World War II.* Macdonald & Jane, London, 1977
Nani, Augusto. *I Caccia-torpedinieri Classe Navigatori.* Le Marine, Rome.
Preston, Antony. *Destroyers.* Paul Hamlyn, London, 1978
Raven, Alan, and Roberts, John. *Hunt Class Destroyers.* Man o'War No. 4. Arms & Armour Press, London, 1980
— *V and W Class Destroyers.* Man o'War No. 2. RSV Publications, New York, and Arms & Armour Press, London, 1979
— War Built Destroyers O to Z Classes. Ensign No. 6. Bivouac Books, London, and Sky Books Press, New York, 1976
Reilly, J. C. *United States Navy Destroyers of World War II.* Blandford Press, Poole, 1983
Rohwer, J., and Hümmelchen, G. Chronology of the War at Sea. 2 vols. Ian Allan, Shepperton, 1974
Roscoe, T. *United States Destroyer Operations in World War II.* Naval Institute Press, Annapolis, 1984
Roskill, S. W. *The War at Sea.* 4 vols. HMSO, London, 1954, 1956, 1960, 1961
Ruge, Friedrich. *The Soviets as Naval Opponents.* PSL, Cambridge, 1979
Silverstone, P. H. *U.S. Warships of World War II.* Ian Allan, Shepperton, 1966
Taylor, J. C. *German Warships of World War II.* Ian Allan, Shepperton, 1966
Thomer, Egbert. *Torpedoboote und Zerstörer.* Stalling Verlag, 1964
Watts, A. J. *Japanese Warships of World War II.* Ian Allan, Shepperton, 1967
Whitley, M. J. *Destroyer! German Destroyers in World War Two.* Arms & Armour Press, 1983; Naval Institute Press, 1984

Periodicals (various issues and editions):
Jane's Fighting Ships
Flottes de Combat
Warship International, Journal of the Warship records Society
Warship Supplement, Journal of the World Ship Society

Index of Ship Names